PSYCHOANALYSIS: OBSERVATION, THEORY, APPLICATION

PSYCHOANALYSIS:
OBSERVATION, THEORY,
APPLICATION

Selected Papers of Robert Waelder

Edited by

SAMUEL A. GUTTMAN, *M.D.*, *Ph.D.*

INTERNATIONAL UNIVERSITIES PRESS, INC.

New York

Library of Congress Cataloging in Publication Data

Waelder, Robert
    Psychoanalysis—observation, theory, and application.

    Bibliography: p.
    1. Psychoanalysis—Addresses, essays, lectures.
I. Title. [DNLM: 1. Psychoanalysis—Collected
works. WM460 W127p]
RC509.W3   616.8'917   74-6432
ISBN-0-8236-5250-5

Manufactured in the United States of America

CONTENTS

PART II

PREFACE

Many have said that no one understands the theories of Sigmund Freud and their analytic applications better than Robert Waelder. The undertaking of editing his writings, many of which are here translated for the first time, has been a considerable and rewarding task. As his literary executor I hope that I have done him justice in showing the amazing scope of his knowledge and interests. I myself learned a good deal in reading and rereading his papers, and hope that this collection of his work will broaden the reader's horizons, as it did mine.

The translations of all the papers that were originally written in German were completely revised. One of these is "The Principle of Multiple Function," which, I believe, is one of the classics of psychoanalysis, and will continue to gain in importance as our understanding of psychoanalysis becomes more sophisticated.

In selecting the papers included in this volume, nearly a hundred items were examined. All publications that had appeared as books (Waelder, 1939b, 1960a, 1966a, 1967a) were excluded, as were papers that had been incorporated in these books (e.g., Waelder, 1956). Other items that were omitted are reviews of outdated books (1928, 1929, 1932, 1934, 1939a); obituaries (1954d, 1960c); panel reports and discussion remarks (1930, 1935, 1940, 1948, 1949, 1950, 1954a, 1954b, 1954c, 1957, 1958, 1960, 1965b, 1965c, 1967c); plus several letters to editors, long papers, and comments in which Robert Waelder spoke as a concerned citizen on such diverse topics as: the loyalty oath (1954c), civil disobedience (1964), the New Left (1967-68), guaranteed annual income (1967c), and the new intellectuals (1968).

The final selections are introduced by Robert Waelder's 1956 Freud Anniversary Lecture, because in this lecture he spoke not only of Freud, but revealed a great deal about himself as well. This personal scientific document is followed by two main sections. The first contains contributions to psychoanalysis. The second is devoted to the application of the psychoanalytic viewpoint to history, law, politics, social work, and other fields.

It is my belief that Robert Waelder was a man ahead of his time, and that his astonishingly accurate predictions are only one of the unique features of this book. He had the unusual ability to cut through anything that was spurious, and his keen mind zeroed in on what was essential, true, and in need of clarification.

Although Robert Waelder had lived through many of the controversies that beset the history of psychoanalysis, he chose to be a scientific observer, both in his teaching and writing. This, perhaps, more than anything else is responsible for the objectivity and insight he showed in his many articles.

It is my firm belief that this book is a must, not only for students, but for those who have worked in and around the field of psychoanalysis for many years. Truly, Robert Waelder was "a man for all seasons," an astonishingly erudite man, an understanding person, and a devoted friend. This book is just a small tribute to a great mind.

Samuel A. Guttman, M.D., Ph.D.

Pennington, N.J.
April, 1975

ACKNOWLEDGMENTS

Editing this volume, which contains only a part of Waelder's work, would never have been possible without the editorial work, advice, and translations of Lottie M. Newman. Muriel M. Gardiner and the late Robert C. Bak also retranslated many papers. Helen Kolson was most diligent in sorting a mass of Robert Waelder's letters, manuscripts, and notes and assisted with some of the proofreading. Alice Guttman, who shared equally in the job of proofreading, also encouraged and helped in ways too numerous to mention. This work was lovingly done, an arduous task, accomplished between patients and meetings, and would not have been possible at all without the help of the aforementioned people. They have my deep appreciation.

My sincere thanks to the editors of the various journals and books who have made it possible to include much of this material.

Samuel A. Guttman, M.D., Ph.D.

Pennington, N.J.
April, 1975

Introduction

Sigmund Freud Centennial Lecture
(1956)

The 100th birthday of a great man is one of the external land-marks which we use from time to time as an opportunity to look back in order to gain whatever perspective is possible. Time is a strange critic. Things that have been written some time ago show varying degrees of obsolescence. Many are no longer read because they are like yesterday's newspaper; they are stale, like yesterday's bread. Some obsolesce in a month, a year, a gener-ation, while others have kept their freshness over hundreds and thousands of years. On this 100th anniversary of Freud's birth, about half a century has passed since his main works were written. Half a century is not very long, but it is something, particularly in a time of rapid change like ours, and I think one can say when one reads Freud's work today that, with very few exceptions, it is as fresh as if it had only just been written. The degree of obsolescence of Freud's work in fifty years has been extremely small. There may be two radically different reasons why older things hold little interest for us. One, as mentioned before, is that they are stale. But sometimes there is the opposite reason: that a work that once was accepted is now taken for granted. Schopenhauer once said that truth is but a brief holiday

This lecture was presented May 5, 1956, at the El Rodeo School in Beverly Hills, California. Dr. Ernst Lewy as President introduced Dr. Waelder in the name of the Los Angeles Institute for Psychoanalysis and the Los Angeles Psychoanalytic Society. Reprinted from *The Annual of Psychoanalysis*, 1:26-35, New York: Quadrangle/The New York Times Book Co., © 1973, The Chicago Institute for Psychoanalysis.

1

between two long and dreary seasons; during the first it was rejected as sophistry and during the second it is forgotten as commonplace. Freud's work, as far as I can see, is neither dated nor, indeed, yet commonplace; on the contrary, it is strangely alive.

Perhaps we may consider for a moment the essential ideas that Freud advanced in the last few years of the 19th century; he made many more contributions, but I want to point out the fundamental ones. There was, first of all, the idea of the so-called dynamic theory of human behavior, or, if you like, the idea that human behavior is ordinarily the outcome of conflicting inner tendencies. That thought is still very fresh. Even today, in books written by good authors, in the practices of our law courts, or in our political discussions, we more or less assume that a person, by and large, follows one goal at a time. The idea that in the ordinary course of events men are not single-minded, that what they do is the outcome of an inner strife, that their behavior does not prove that they had willed that all the time, but merely indicates that there was an edge—perhaps only a slight edge—for one group of motivations over another group of motivations, which often might have been shifted to an opposite behavior by a minor change in the weight of the inner vote: that is an idea which has not yet become common property.

The next great concept was that these inner conflicts are not always solved by a decision in favor of one or the other inner tendency, or by a compromise, but that we sometimes escape the necessity of deciding between alternatives by sweeping the disagreeable problem under the carpet, so to speak, by driving it out of our consciousness. We call that "repression." And as a result the motivating force has not become invalidated, but has become unconscious. This is the great concept of the power of unconscious motivation. And then comes the idea that neurosis is due to such inner conflict, which has not been solved but is merely evaded by driving it underground—a tremendous new concept. Before this, as much as psychiatry had looked out for the psychological reasons for mental disturbance, it had always sought them in external pressures.

Freud's new idea was that we become ill not from external pressures, great though they may be, but from not being at one with ourselves, i.e., from inner conflicts, and that the role of external frustrations is limited to that of a possible stimulus for arousing inner conflicts. We shall see that this idea, far from being stale, has not yet been generally accepted, even by psychoanalysts.

Finally, the next two concepts hold that there are two weak spots in the organization of the mind, two areas in which man may easily fail in the solution of his inner conflicts, and in which, therefore, repression and its pathological consequences may easily occur. The first of these weak spots in our mental organization has to do with a specific type of challenge, viz., with the sexual challenge. It is in dealing with our sexual drives that we may show ourselves inadequate, unable to adapt, unable to reconcile inner and outer conditions, and therefore much more likely than in other areas to escape the problem by repressing it. Our sexual drives are the troublemakers because they are less capable of adjustment then other tendencies.

Then too, there is a period of time in which we are particularly vulnerable, viz., childhood. It is a time of a temporary weakness in our mental organization, and conflicts occurring in this period are more likely to remain unsolved than the conflicts of a later, mature time. These last two concepts constitute the sexual and infantile genesis of the neuroses. There are many more ideas and theories in psychoanalysis, but the four propositions mentioned may be said to be the fundamental ones. If a holocaust should destroy all our libraries and all people with psychoanalytic learning, it is quite possible that from these few basic propositions psychoanalysis could, in good time, be reconstructed.

It is not easy for us to imagine how tremendously difficult it was for Freud to arrive at these propositions, which ran strongly against common sense and against deeply imbedded prejudices of the time. But it is necessary to remember that the time of Freud's youth and of the most creative period of his manhood was the Victorian age, in which the attitude of man toward his sexuality was one of denial. Sexuality was not talked about in civilized society, except at stag parties, and then with an air of lugubriousness. It was thought to belong to animal aspects of human nature, i.e., to a subhuman part of man which was not to be faced frankly and honestly. Of course, that does not mean that man in the Victorian age did not express his sexual urges, but in polite society they could not be faced. Perhaps not often in history has there been so great an alienation of man from his biological roots as in just this era.

Two examples may illustrate the Victorian attitude toward sexuality. The first occurred not so long ago. At the outbreak of the First World War in 1914, the British War Minister, Field Marshal Earl Kitchener, gave the order of the day to the British army, which every British soldier had to carry with him at all times. He said—I do not quote literally—"During your operations you will be exposed to some temptations of wine or women. You must resist both temptations absolutely and unconditionally. While you have to treat all women with perfect courtesy, you must absolutely avoid any intimacy." Thus, only a little more than forty years ago it was considered to be a practical policy to ask soldiers going into battle that they should live in complete abstinence. You see how much has changed since that day; not so much perhaps in the behavior of soldiers, as in the attitude toward it. Another example shows how impossible it was for Victorians to admit that the higher and the lower aspects of man could have any relation with each other. About half a century ago, William James suggested in his classical book on pragmatism that the ideas of philosophers may be conditioned or influenced by their temperament. That seems to us to be quite a rather innocuous idea, probably true, but nothing to get excited about. Yet James found himself constrained to apologize for suggesting that something as dignified and as high as a philosophical system could have anything to do with things as low as emotions or temperament, and, even as late as 1935, F. M. Cornford, the English classicist, philosopher, and poet, while quoting that passage from James, still felt that the idea that philosophical thought might be influenced by temperament had been advanced by a "breezy American." Such attitudes account for much of the opposition and disparagement that Freud found in his earlier years.

Whenever a man has conceived great new ideas, it is interesting to ask how these ideas grew in his mind, how he got them along his way. There is a positivistic myth of the scientist, according to which a scientist is a purely receptive person who has no preconceived, guiding ideas, who observes what comes along. But that is a myth. If we study the history of thought, we get an entirely different idea. We find that the nuclei of the mature thoughts of great scientific creators existed in their minds early, for reasons unknown, long before they made their first observations. And it looks as if they set out in the world to find the proof for these embryonic ideas. I cannot prove to you that this is true of Freud. But I can give you a little detail which might be suggestive. We have a letter that Freud wrote shortly after his seventeenth birthday; he has just passed the "Matura," the much-dreaded graduating exam in classics and in mathematics, with which a boy finished the gymnasium and qualified for entry in a university. The letter, written to a slightly older friend, is a report on what happened in the exam and how he did in it. It is a delightful letter, showing great sense of humor and remarkable maturity for a boy just past his seventeenth birthday. Let me quote a few sentences that seem to be characteristic of the man that Freud was to become. Freud's letter is an answer to a letter from the friend, and we can only surmise what the friend may have written. Says Freud:

> You brush aside too easily my worry for the future. You try to comfort me by suggesting that he who is afraid of mediocrity is thereby saved already. Saved from what, may I ask? Certainly not safe from being mediocre. What does it matter, after all, whether one is afraid of a thing or not? Is not all that matters whether what we feel is real or not? True enough that stronger minds have been afflicted with doubts in themselves, but does that prove that everybody who questions his worth is a strong mind? He may be a weakling in spirit, but an honest man; Honest through education, habit, or sheer self-torture. I do not want to persuade you to pitilessly analyze your feelings in moments of doubt, but if you do, you will find how little certainty you have in yourself. The magnificence of the world lies in this vastness of possibility, but unfortunately there is no solid ground for our knowledge of ourselves.[1]

[1] This quotation is from a letter Freud wrote to Emil Fluss dated Vienna, at night, June 16, 1873. The author's own translation differs somewhat from the one which appeared as Letter 1 in *Letters of Sigmund Freud*, edited by Ernst L. Freud (1960).

We can find in these few lines the germs of some of the ideas that Freud shaped in later years. There is, for instance, implied in Freud's words the possibility of a "pitiless analysis" of one's feelings. There is also implied the idea that a thing may not be all that it seems to be on the surface—that is, honesty may not always be the result of education but may have its root in self-torture. There is implied the idea that something valued very highly, like honesty, may have its basis in something valued very lowly, a neurotic habit. Here you see in a seventeen-year-old, who had hever seen a psychiatric patient and never knew that he ever would, an attitude of mind which made it possible for him to be the founder of the science of human personality.

The position of Freud, of course, has been unique in the field of psychoanalysis. Very nearly all that we have comes from Freud's own work. The contributions that we, the disciples of Freud, have made are relatively negligible. There are few examples in science in which a discipline has been so completely created and dominated by one man. The closest example that I know of would be the position which, for a much longer time, Euclid had in the history of geometry. Although his principles of geometry were written around 300 B.C., even up to the present time elementary geometry is taught in our schools according to textbooks only slightly different from Euclid's original book.

In the case of Freud this unique situation has given vent to a great deal of criticism. There are those analysts and near-analysts who say that we disciples of Freud are the members of a religious sect who swear to the words of the master, that we have closed our minds to scientific progress, and that they, unhampered by dogmatism, are now the only ones to uphold a progressive outlook. They are for advances in psychoanalysis; they emphasize new ideas, such as, e.g., the influence of culture on the neurosis of the individual, which Freud is said to have overlooked. They substitute for the libido theory the broader concepts of what they call "interpersonal relations." This widespread school of thought and its advocacy of progress against our own "reactionary orthodoxy" is well known. Are we Freudian analysts really opposed to new ideas? Are we people who wish to freeze the progress of scientific development in the molds of what one man has thought? I would not say that this is impossible; it takes all kinds of people to make a world, and devotees of conservation can be found everywhere. But, on the whole, if I look among the circle of men who I knew were close to Freud, I think I can honestly say that we had no greater desire than to see scientific progress, that we were looking out for new ideas and were not only ready to welcome them but eagerly desirous for them, hoping that perhaps it would be vouchsafed to any one of us to produce a new idea of importance that would carry our science forward.

But when we are confronted with the supposedly new ideas of the progressive analysts, we feel impelled to reject them. We do so because they are not new ideas, but merely a return to the old pre-Freudian concepts. As we have seen, one of the fundamental innovations of Freud's was the idea that an inner conflict rather than external frustration causes neurosis, and that sexuality and childhood have specific significance as the vulnerable areas of our development. If the new progressives come and tell us that the pressure of culture is responsible for neurosis, i.e., not inner conflict but outside pressure, they have returned to the pre-Freudian viewpoint. If they tell us that not sex but rather the more liberal and broader concept of interpersonal relationships and insecurities is the thing to look at, again they have thrown out of the window the Freudian theory that pathology comes about because of the human difficulty in adjusting to the exuberant growth of specifically sexual challenges; if they say that childhood has been overemphasized, they have thrown that aspect of Freud's theories out of the window too. In other words, they simply discard Freud's concepts wholly or partly. Let there be no doubt that I do not criticize them for so doing. It is their inalienable right to have their own ideas, and if they think that the Freudian concepts are wrong, it is indeed their duty to say so and to say it loudly and repeatedly. Science must be free, and we all, regardless of how strongly we may be convinced that we are right, may yet be wrong. But the question in our minds is why the critics who wholly or partially reject Freud's concepts and return to the pre-Freudian ideas, do not frankly say that this is what they are doing; why do they represent their views as a progress in, rather than a retreat from, psychoanalysis? Their intellectual ancestor, Alfred Adler, was clear about what he did. He held that psychoanalysis was mistaken, and he gave to his own system a different name. As to his present-day successors, we cannot help feeling that they are rejecting Freudian ideas while at the same time trying to retain the prestige value that has meanwhile come to be attached to the name of psychoanalysis. It is perhaps this element of disingenuousness which has aroused some emotionalism in our response.

I should like to give an example from the history of science to suggest that similar things have occurred before in comparable situations. Copernicus published his work on the heliocentric system in 1540. It was heatedly discussed for generations. It was not proved at that time; there were strong arguments against the idea that the fixed stars should have parallactic involvement, i.e., should give the appearance of rotary movement in a small yearly circle if the observing astronomer traveled around the sun. No such parallaxis was observed, though it does exist, because it exceeded the prevailing limits of observation. Those who opposed the Copernican system, however, must not be thought of as merely narrow-minded. When Kepler, in 1608 or 1609, found the three laws of planetary motion which were based on the heliocentric assumption, that was an important argument in favor of the heliocentric theory, though it was not yet real proof. Later again in 1670, or 130 years after Copernicus, Newton could show that Kepler's laws, which were based on the heliocentric hypothesis, could be explained by laws of gravitation that were equally suitable to explain the fall of bodies on the earth. It was then that the discussion came to an end and the heliocentric theory was generally accepted. But perhaps the case was not scientifically closed until the discovery of the parallaxis of the fixed stars. In that more than a century in which the struggle was on, there was at one point a compromise suggested between the heliocentric and the geocentric philosophy, which gained many adherents. It was proposed by Tycho Brahe. According to this compromise proposition, all planets, with the exception of the earth, circled around the sun, but the whole solar system circled around the earth. This system, which could be made mathematically consistent, was widely accepted in the first decades of the 17th century.

It seems to me that much of the present so-called progressive psychoanalysis is comparable to the system of Tycho Brahe, which compromised between the new ideas and the old habits of thought. The progressive analysts tell us that Freud was somewhat right about inner conflicts, but not quite right, because they are really more a matter of cultural pressures. He was right about the importance of childhood, but not quite right, because it is not really so much the childhood. He was somewhat right about the unconscious, but the unconscious is really not quite so unconscious after all. But perhaps the case is not yet scientifically closed, as it was with the discovery of the parallaxis of the fixed stars. The progressive school of thought must of course have the freedom to propagate its ideas, but we Freudian psychoanalysts may be forgiven if we are unwilling to accept concessions to popular prejudice as the manifestation of scientific progress.

That, of course, leaves us with another question, which I think is quite appropriate to consider on this anniversary: namely, in what direction can real progress be expected to come about? We cannot countenance the idea that no matter how great the achievements of Freud have been, his work should have been not only the beginning but also the end in the development of psychoanalysis. Where can further scientific development be expected? It seems to me that there is an immense difficulty in psychoanalysis regarding its further progress, and that is the tremendous difficulty of transmitting knowledge, insight, and experience from one person to the other, from teacher to pupil. There is a difficulty of language, of communication. It is already quite difficult even to explain the structure of a case to our colleagues. It works all right in a group of analysts who work together in close cooperation. But in meeting analysts from another circle, one has some difficulty in describing a particular psychic structure in a way that really communicates the idea that one wants to convey.

So formulated, it would seem that this difficulty in psychoanalysis is not unique. There has been a great deal of discussion and speculation about the question why the so-called scientific revolution of the 17th century had not already occurred in antiquity, in the Hellenistic age, which was already a sophisticated, secular civilization. Perhaps it can be considered most

concretely if we look at the history of Greek mathematics. The
Greeks had a splendid period of mathematical development
between approximately 400 and 200 B.C., in which a number of
outstanding men, two of whom are known to everybody, Euclid
and Archimedes, created among themselves practically the
whole of what we call today "elementary mathematics." Archimedes came within a hair's breadth of inventing the calculus
that Newton invented almost two thousand years later and
which was the prerequisite for the development of mechanics,
dynamics, or physics. Then the development of Greek mathematics came to a stop; for 400 years there is no important
mathematician, there is an isolated figure in the second century
A.D., and another isolated figure in the third century A.D., and
then it ends. One of the most likely causes is that the Greek
mathematics was geometric and not algebraic. That means that
there was no language or symbolic formulae through which they
could express their ideas in a way that would be understood by
everybody. They had to describe what they meant in plain
words of ordinary speech, and it is extremely difficult to understand a geometric proposition that is explained in common
language. Hence, dissemination of the theory was dependent on
mouth-to-mouth contact from teacher to pupil; it could hardly
be understood from mere reading. Such is the situation in
psychoanalysis today, where the continuation of psychoanalysis
is still dependent on person-to-person contact and preceptorial
tuition. It seems to me that the main bottleneck for the progress
of psychoanalysis today is the question of communication, the
possibility of transfer of ideas from one to the other.

Thus, if psychoanalysis has not progressed very much beyond
Freud, this is, in my opinion, not because Freud had finished his
work and left little to be done by his successors, nor is it due to a
lack of talent among Freud's followers. Rather, it seems to be
due to the fact that psychoanalysts have to devote most of their
lives to trying to rediscover for themselves what Freud already
knew. Science progresses best and most rapidly when every idea
is quickly disseminated and widely understood by a great
number of people. We have not reached that condition. Also,
there is in our field an immense waste: many of the most
experienced and able psychoanalysts carry ideas in their minds

which they have not completely been able to communicate to their students and which disappear from the earth when they die, as was apparently the case in other sciences at earlier stages, before more convenient and less subjective means of transmitting knowledge had been found. In fact, what many older psychoanalysts do at the present time is to instill, almost hectically, into a limited number of students as much as possible of the knowledge that they themselves have accumulated, lest it may disappear from the earth.

A very similar condition existed, to use an example closer at home, in the history of medicine before the laboratory, when experience at the sick bed was the only source of knowledge. There were, through the centuries, a number of apparently great diagnosticians, but they were individual men who had achieved in their own experience the ability to evaluate minute symptoms and from them form a diagnosis of illness. Little of their knowledge could be transferred to their students. So knowledge appears and disappears again in a tremendous waste of nature, while, of course, an electrocardiogram or a blood-pressure measurement can be transmitted to somebody else regardless of his talent or experience. I presume that if in psychoanalysis means are found to supplement clinical observation by other methods less dependent on individual intuition and experience, and if methods describing our results are found that are more precise and more easily disseminated, the progress of psychoanalysis will become very rapid.

I have so far spoken only about Freud's lifework, psychoanalysis, and have said nothing about Freud's person. I am probably influenced myself by Freud's own attitude in this matter, his own reluctance to have his person be considered a matter of public interest. Freud thought people should be interested in psychoanalysis, but he didn't like it if they became personally interested in him. He felt that as a person he was not important. I have no doubt that this was his opinion. The story of Freud's personal intolerance is a myth if I ever heard one. The Freud whom I knew was indifferent to things done or said against his person; his interest was in the field. This supposedly very intolerant man had once come to a break with one of his students, not on account of a scientific controversy, but on account of some action by the disciple which Freud thought was detrimental to the position of psychoanalysis, precarious as it already was. The same man some few years later wrote a pot-boiler biography of Freud that was quite critical of him. Later again, for reasons of his own, this man wished to return to the fold, and Freud received him without the slightest difficulty. He felt no resentment over any personal injury. The only thing of which the Freud that I knew was really intolerant was intellectual dishonesty; there he knew no compromise.

It is not easy to convey any picture of Freud's person, partly because it has been so much distorted by legend. It is difficult to convey an idea of his princely generosity, of the penetration and depths and relevance of his remarks to any major or minor problem, and of his mellowness. I should like to relate one personal experience of the last time that I saw him. It will be eighteen years ago, in three days (May 8, 1938). It was in Vienna, under the Nazi rule; my family and I had just received our passports and permit to leave and wanted to leave right away, as one was in jeopardy every moment. The Freuds still had to wait another four weeks for their passports. I went to say goodbye to Freud. Practically all Viennese analysts of my generation had a signed photo of Freud. Though I, on occasion, had asked for Freud's signature on an etching or a photo for somebody else, I was always inhibited in asking this favor for myself. Now was the last opportunity, and I pulled myself together. I owned no etching of his, and there was no possibility of getting one under the circumstances. I happened to have an unmounted photo that the late Paul Federn had once given to me, so I took it up and Anna Freud mounted it in an improvised fashion on a piece of cardboard, and I asked Freud to sign it. This is what he wrote under the picture: "Behalten Sie mich lang in guter Erinnerung," which in English would approximately mean, "Keep long a good memory of me." If Freud had said only "keep a good memory of me" without that word *long*, I think it would have been a superfluous appeal. There wasn't any chance that I would forget him, or cease loving him until my last day. But what I find so immensely touching is the qualifying word "long." By writing this word "long," he implied that he did not expect me to do that for the rest of my life but only for a long time. He took it for granted that the day might come in my lifetime in which I would either forget him or no longer think well of him. I don't know whether I can convey my own feelings, but what is so immensely touching is, now that we have made a full turn and are back to the passage in the letter of the seventeen-year-old, the quiet acceptance of the transcience of human loyalties and of all things human, an acceptance entirely without bitterness. The fact that he felt everything was temporary and transient did not mean for him it was any less valuable while it lasted. He wrote a fine little paper on this entitled "On Transcience" (1916). I understand that the feeling of awe before the infinite and the humble awareness of our own nothingness has been called by many people the essence of "religious experience." Freud in one passage said that his humbleness before the vastness of the world and the awareness of one's own insignificance is not a religious but a *par excellence* irreligious experience, because, as he used the word, religion is merely the wish-fulfilling escape from the facts. That is a question of semantics which I will not enter; but, however you call it, Freud had this sentiment in the greatest possible degree. In his relation with others there was therefore something which I might express best in the words of a poet. He had what W. H. Auden said about Shakespeare's Prospero: "The power to enchant that comes from disillusion."

Part I

Part I

CHAPTER 1

The Psychoses

Their Mechanisms and Accessibility
to Influence
(1924)

"In the narcissistic neuroses ... [our] technical methods
must ... be replaced by others; and we do not know yet
whether we shall succeed in finding a substitute."
                                        —Freud (1916-17, p. 423).

In the course of its investigations psychoanalysis has taught us
to recognize the laws which govern the instinctual life of man
and to bring this knowledge to bear upon other mental phenomena. It has thrown light upon the principal relations governing
the object libido, which is directed toward and dependent upon
the outside world, and has applied its discoveries to the cure of
the transference neuroses. While we do not expect to add
anything fundamentally new to the highly developed theory of
these mental strata, we keenly regret that our knowledge barely
extends beyond the frontier of narcissism and, above all, that our
means of influencing the mind do not yet extend to the
psychoses. We suspect that the very nature of this illness imposes
a limitation, if not on our understanding, at least on our power.
For the distinguishing mark of psychosis is that the existing
capacity for transference cannot overcome the narcissistic fixa-

This paper was read before the Vienna Psychoanalytic Society on March
12, 1924. It was first published as "Uber Mechanismen und Beeinflussungs-
möglichkeiten der Psychosen," in *Internationale Zeitschrift für Psychoanalyse*,
10:393-414, 1924. Reprinted from *International Journal of Psycho-Analysis*,
6:259-281, 1925. The present version was revised by Dr. Robert C. Bak.

tions which are recognizable in the symptoms. Since the transference alone furnishes the energy with which, together with the patient's conscious will to recover, we are able to master the fixations of neurosis, by our very definition there would seem to be no scope for an analogous mastering of psychosis.

In what follows, however, I hope to be able to refute this conclusion as premature, for it is based on a theoretical conception that is by no means unassailable. Apart from the difficulties inherent in this interesting problem, we also expect that any new knowledge of the operation of the ego instincts may from the practical point of view of its ultimate application to the treatment of mental illness throw open new realms of the mind to our influence.[1]

I shall first present a hypothesis concerning the conditioning factors by which a psychosis comes about or is avoided in those "borderline" characters in whom the phenomena of transition to a psychosis are so readily observed. These considerations should strengthen our hope of being able to cure certain of the psychoses, for we shall convince ourselves that in psychosis, just as in neurosis, the distinction between "normal" and pathological is by no means a basic distinction in the psychic realm.

At the outset of psychoanalytical research it was necessary for the investigator to overcome his narcissistic resistance to comparing his own mental reactions with those of psychoneurotics. Having advanced thus far, he came to recognize the truth of a certain principle and to rid himself of a misunderstanding which was always lying in wait for him. He realized that no mechanism has either an inherent incompatibility with reality or an intrinsic real value, but that it is only the quantity of libido, the material with which it is concerned, its relation to other mental phenomena occurring simultaneously, and the place it occupies in the whole psychic picture which does or does not confer a pathological character upon the final result. This rule necessitates a complete severance of two principles of classification of mental processes: that according to mechanisms and that according to value for reality. If these two principles are confounded, understanding of a given fact is invariably rendered more difficult;

---

[1] Moreover, we must not forget that the "organic" probably borders closely on the narcissistic.

whereas if they are sharply distinguished it often facilitates the solution of a problem.[2] The validity of this statement has been abundantly confirmed by the findings of analytic work; I propose to show that it also obtains in the case of psychosis.

By "illness" in the mental sense we understand not departure from a norm but incapacity to arrive at gratification of the desire for pleasure in any way that is actually possible. In analytic terminology we call this a turning away of the libido from real objects. Let us consider some of the principal things which may

[2] Here we touch on an important error in the psychology of "understanding" (Dilthey's and Jaspers' *Verstehungspsychologie*) which divides mental phenomena into those which are and those which are not "understandable." This comprehensibility depends on the person making the observations: it is not accurate to say that schizophrenic experience falls entirely within the category of the incomprehensible. There are many perfectly "healthy" persons of the schizoid type who can "understand" even schizophrenic processes. According to this psychology, the standard by which all phenomena are to be measured is the healthy man, with the exception of certain groups of schizoid types. This psychology assumes without further ado that this system of referring one phenomenon to another has a peculiar psychological significance, an assumption which underlies the old idea that mental disease is invariably conditioned by the occurrence of an organic process and represents a course of psychological events which differs *toto genere* from the normal. I am of course not disputing the fact that some process does take place, but, since Kretschmer's researches, we can scarcely doubt that even the different forms of "normality" are differentiated by organic processes. Ideler has already recognized that this idea, which has taken root among us since the days of the early psychiatrists, constitutes a reassurance for the observer, who is confounded by mental disturbances, for it is an idea which enables him to retain his narcissistic sense of superiority in spite of his powerlessness as a physician. Certainly, it is not inconceivable that this should represent the true state of affairs, but in any case it cannot be permissible to adopt without question the hypothesis of the psychological significance of a classification of this sort. To my mind this is the reason why the psychology of "understanding" has failed to perceive many connections, especially those that are most important from the therapeutic point of view. Obviously adaptation to reality has ultimately a biological meaning, for the existing social reality has a biological basis (Schilder). But this relation, which science cannot as yet adequately explore, is too complex to be made the criterion of what takes place in a given individual at the present moment. For social community, though its basis be biological, is simply a cross-section and a compromise of the biological tendencies of the individual or a product of the historical evolution of that cross-section, which for the individual is fortuitous. A community of persons at the same stage of civilization will more or less agree on a classification of food according to its nutritive properties and its pleasantness to the taste, but this could not serve as a method of classification in physiological chemistry, although it has of course ultimately been determined by biological and physiological evolution.

happen when such an abnormal application of libido takes place. In the course of its development, the libido may remain attached to a specially strong fixation point, so that, in spite of all the new influences which real experience brings, it either cannot be released, or it returns to that point in a short time at the slightest frustration (inhibition in development). There is another possibility: the libido may develop normally for the time being and later this development may be interrupted by a regression to past forms of gratification. A repression of this sort may be caused by actual forces which recall the libido (as in war neurosis, "insurance neurosis," Ganser's syndrome, and hysterical puerility), as well as by frustration from without or from within. In any given case of illness we shall probably always find both mechanisms at work. Again, the regression may either go back to the ego or to libidinal object fixations. The different lines that the process may follow in the latter case should be considered; if the libido recathects an abandoned point of fixation, the determining factor is the strength and the nature of the repression. If this is weak, the libido finds outlet in actions; this solution, which is seen in some perversions and various antisocial reactions, may be conceived of as based upon a disturbance in the development of the ego ideal or a later, regressive, psychotic libido impoverishment of that ideal. Where there are powerful forces of rejection at work, however, we have to distinguish between their motive and their aim. Apparently there are two principal types of repression corresponding with two principal types of ideal: the one which is moral in content: "I must not do or think this, for it is immoral; my father has forbidden it"; and the other which is narcissistic and which prompts something as follows: "This may not be, for it would humiliate me; it does not accord with my lofty and noble personality." The first form of repression leads by way of compromise formation into neurosis; the second seems to be the basis of a withdrawal of the libido into the ego by way of compensation (Tausk), that is to say the basis of psychosis.[3] This hypothesis agrees essentially with the earlier conception according to which psychosis results from

[3] The compensation which Tausk (1913) describes and which may be used as a most effective tool in the technique of analysis belongs *typically* only to purely narcissistic forms of repression; it *may* occur in other forms (the train of thought being: "I may allow myself something of this sort too") if the

fixation on the narcissistic level, for it is on these points of fixation that the structure of the ideal depends.

When regression has taken place, there may be a hypercathexis of the ego or, if this is avoided, there may be an attempt to direct the libido once more to objects. If this attempt is wholly successful, it is followed by a restoration of the former condition and the whole ego process is canceled; hence this case falls outside the scope of my discussion. If, however, the attempt fails altogether or in part, a fresh turning of the libido to the outside world can be accomplished only by a projection of part of the inner world onto the outside world. We can distinguish between two mechanisms: one mechanism ends with the libido regression leading back to the ego; this we may term a regressive psychosis. In the other mechanism there occurs, following upon the regression, a (not wholly successful) attempt at restitution; this form I shall call a restitutive psychosis. The clinical picture of the psychoses seems to be determined by these mechanisms. Thus, catatonia should be called a regressive and paranoia a restitutive psychosis. It is to be anticipated, and is in agreement with our experience in psychopathology, that in the regressive psychosis it is generally not the whole ego which is libidinally cathected, but varying parts of it to a variable degree. In an analogous manner, when restitution takes place, there is projection of different parts of the ego in a variety of ways.

The principle laid down at the beginning of this study leads us to expect that neither one of the two mechanisms possesses any particular reality value, and it would seem natural to connect any such value first with the ego's object and the ego's attitude to that object, and then with the particular mode of projection. Actually, we know that even a regressive hypercathexis of the ego, or of part of the ego, such as occurs in all of us every day transitorily and in some of us permanently in the formation of character, by no means necessarily strikes us as pathological. It is perhaps rather more difficult to realize this in the restitutive psychotic processes, because among these we must include partly unsuccessful attempts at directing the libido to the outside

---

necessary narcissistic elements are present. It is probably due to this compensation, together with the impoverishment of the superego, that in psychosis the subject is conscious of the normally unconscious complexes.

world. In this connection I wish at present to remark only that all our conscious thinking can be nothing but rationalization and our creative thinking is in addition the projection of libidinal processes. We have long taken for granted that the direction and the object choice of our thinking can be construed as rationalization and projection, but the same is true of the *content* of our thoughts, not merely when that content is conditioned by complexes which make it erroneous, but when our judgment is correct and our insight accurate. Psychoanalysis invariably shows that this content is to be regarded as the projection of inner experience.

In order to illustrate the nature and results of these mechanisms and to determine whether the different forms of the various reality values are subject to specific regularities, I turn to a clinical example.

By chance I came across a healthy man of the schizoid type who was free from serious pathological disabilities, and whom I shall call A.T. He was a young scientist, unusually able and original, whose mental constitution showed signs of narcissism and psychotic characteristics. His attitude toward those around him was marked by a condescending superiority, which had some actual basis in his intellectual gifts, and his inner adaptation to other people was minimal. He felt different from mankind in general; he was perfectly able to understand others intellectually, but their nature seemed to him alien. In his mind he was independent of the opinion of most people (he made an exception of a few persons whom he esteemed highly), and his chief problem in life was the fostering of his own self-respect, an attitude which determined most of his mental sensations. Like all psychotics, he exhibited a weakness of those repressions which are found in normal people and neurotics. Material which in them is deeply overlaid and can be brought to the surface only by long and laborious work came to light in T. in response to mere questioning; it was always conscious and carried with it no sense of guilt. To the narcissist the outside world means far too little for him to let its laws dominate his mind.

In his childhood T. had passed through a period of deep depression with thoughts of suicide—these apparently followed on conflicts in his home. In other respects, too, the boy's mental condition had probably sometimes caused uneasiness in those around him. After he had thrown off this phase during the years of puberty his choice of a profession and his interests, which were mathematical, declared themselves. The turn which his sublimations thus took was notably different from his earlier philological and literary bent. The only intimation there had been of this change was his interest in grammar and, while he was still a child, a considerable skill in chess which included the power of playing blindfold. His family insisted on his giving up chess. Immediately after he had taken up mathematics in the higher forms at school, there set in another persistent state of depression, the actual motivation of which was the difficulty of scientific work; this state gradually disappeared in his later years at college.

This libidinal development was intimately connected with his relations to his father. It was not actually proved, but it was very probable, that narcissistic identification with the father played a leading part in T.'s depression in childhood. Suicide represented a symbolic parricide. His later choice of interests denoted a repudiation of the identification with his father, who was of another turn of mind: the father's mode of thought and the mathematical bent which the son's mind took might be termed diametrically opposite. This form of mastery over the father had been heralded in childhood by his preoccupation with and skill in chess, and revealed the boy in contest with the father within him; at the same time it foreshadowed the future course of sublimation by which in time he was to gain the mastery over his father.

In the adult no symptoms of any importance could be observed, except certain phenomena which one would be inclined to call splits in consciousness; they appeared whenever his narcissism was wounded and symbolic castration took place (e.g., failure of a scientific experiment). He himself described these phenomena as follows: at such moments it was as if there were two different beings thinking within him, between whom he tried in vain and with a sense of anxiety to establish communication. These states lasted only a few minutes, but were very distressing. (I shall return to them in the therapeutic section of this paper.)

Otherwise, in his outward behavior he attained an adequate conscious adaptation to reality, going in fact further in some directions than most normal people. To an external force which was too strong for him he submitted without any sense of humiliation. His feelings for those close to him (transferences) were in themselves slight and analysis could put them out of action surprisingly quickly. Preserving an inner indifference, he accepted human beings as they are without difficulty, wherever it was not possible to bring his surroundings into line with his will by means of his narcissistic personality and his "somnambulistic assurance" (to use his own phrase).[4]

How nearly T.'s character and personality bordered on psychosis and what was the factor which just kept them clear of it may be illustrated by the following example. Once, when I was giving him some theoretical explanation of psychoanalysis and the nature of psychosis, I told him of a demented patient who demanded as a matter of course that his mother should have intercourse with him. I pointed out that the man's narcissism prevented his acknowledging the incest barrier, whereupon T. objected that he, too, never could understand the incest barrier and above all had never even felt it, and that, where brothers and sisters were concerned, he utterly refused to recognize the incest prohibition. The adaptation to reality which governed his conduct would accordingly seem to be simply due to the recognition of its outward necessity and not to the compelling effect of inner experience, so that even the moral content of his ideal was determined by narcissistic impulses, the will to live and to fulfill himself. For this reason he could think forbidden thoughts without any resistance or sense of guilt. But the fact that anything was condemned by people in general, even though in his own mind he did not share their feeling, was enough to determine his actual behavior. He would never have given utterance to a demand remotely resembling that of the demented patient I quoted. But where a sister was concerned he refused to recognize even this inhibition by reality. (True, he had no brothers or sisters.) Thus T. showed the germ of characteristic schizoid reactions; moreover, at times the schizoid

[4] On the effect of narcissistic personalities, see Freud (1914a).

blocking and flow of thought could be detected. It is the more remarkable that in spite of this he managed to keep his feet planted in reality and in his behavior never (except for one symptom) noticeably crossed the pathological borderline. Fortunately we need not explain this phenomenon by reference to insufficient regression of the libido, for the case is clear enough to give us a deeper insight. But, before we try to specify the factors which enabled T. to ward off psychosis, let us look at his intellectual constitution.

His field of work was mathematics; in this, as in other things, he was under the sway of a logical compulsion. He was able, when presented with difficult material, rapidly to separate out the premises and from them to conduct a subtle logical analysis. Consequently his mind was remarkably open to anything systematic and he accepted almost without resistance those parts of psychoanalytic theory which I tried to put before him as far as possible in a systematic structure. Here I may note that, in accordance with his whole mental attitude, he was not merely lacking in aesthetic and ethical resistances to analysis but soon turned these into objects of derision. Thus resistances to bringing to light unconscious attitudes in himself did not play any very large part in his analysis, for as a matter of fact they were seldom strongly repressed: usually he was quite conscious of his attitude. At the same time we must take into account the fact that scarcely at any point did the attempted analysis go very deep.

Although T. seemed ready to accept any train of reasoning to which there was no logical objection, he was inclined, on the other hand, to repudiate a conception or idea if it was not clearly and unambiguously formulated and carefully worked out, or if in any point it seemed to him still indefinite. His mode of apperception was apparently not instinctive but always by means of reason and logic. Even problems of everyday life he liked to think over in terms of mathematics.

In the science of his choice, a field which demands the application of logical faculties, he was distinguished by that capacity for a profound grasp of the problems which is often the result of creative work. It was scarcely surprising that his critical faculty (and also his power of self-criticism) were strongly developed. We may feel that it was no mere chance that a man of T.'s character chose this particular field of interest. But, before going further, let us consider the psychological mechanisms of mathematical work.

In the first place it strikes us that in the scientific mode of thought we can distinguish different forms, the extreme types of which might be called "narcissistic" and "object-libidinal" thinking. By this I do not simply mean the obvious difference in the interest of the thinker, though that does always play a part, the narcissist prizing more highly the knowledge itself and the investigator whose libido goes out to an external object setting greater value upon the application of knowledge in human civilization. It is not this difference of values and aims which I want to discuss, but the difference in the actual mode of thinking. If it is characteristic of the object-libidinal mode to consider the facts and the facts only, as Freud (1914a) puts it, it is the peculiarity of the narcissistic mode to consider concepts and nothing but concepts. The scientist whose method is the object-libidinal deduces from his observations hypotheses which remain uncertain until further knowledge is won and which, if circumstances require it, make use of concepts that are not altogether clearly defined. According to their practical utility he has no scruples to make use of complex conceptions, so long as the final and most simple cannot easily be arrived at. To him the value of his findings is always their relations to actuality. " . . . ideas [hypotheses] are not the foundation of science, upon which everything rests: that foundation is observation alone. They are not the bottom but the top of the whole structure, and they can be replaced and discarded without damaging it" (p. 77).

With the narcissistic scientist it is otherwise; he likes to see every theory fitted as soon as possible into a systematic structure. His aim is to deduce all his conclusions from a few clearly defined postulates which are independent of one another. He endeavors always to get down to elementary concepts which cannot be dissected further and to build up his theory from a synthesis of such concepts. He willingly abandons [5] the inter-

---

[5] A remark of T.'s is characteristic of this readiness to abandon the attempt. He said that he would feel a resistance to the scientific study of the problems of psychoanalysis because they were highly complex and could not be experimentally reduced to their elementary concepts.

pretation of phenomena which are too complex for such a synthesis. The narcissist regards a scientific theory as useful if, by means of it, a definite field of phenomena can be reduced to an arbitrary, well-defined conceptual system in such a way that all relations deducible from the system by formal logic, if they be translated by way of this theoretical scheme into terms of phenomena, find confirmation in them, that is to say in the facts.

It is not difficult to justify the use of the term "narcissistic" in this connection, especially as the word has already often been employed in this sense. If it is of the essence of narcissism "to create a world for oneself" (*sich seine Welt zu dichten*), to use the fine phrase of Strindberg's *Totentanz*, we may call a method narcissistic if it allows us to build mental constructions comparatively freely and arbitrarily.

The sciences may be arranged in a series according to the method principally employed in them. We see at once that at one end, the object-libidinal, we must surely place history, and at the other, the narcissistic, mathematics.

There can be no doubt that a capacity and inclination for work in these sciences, as for every form of creative work, are derived from object-libidinal sublimations. But at the same time we cannot fail to recognize the narcissistic character of this kind of activity, and thus we might speak of a "union of instincts,"[6] involving both narcissism and object libido, so that they cooperate toward the same end. At this point we are for the first time tempted to revert to a question which we left open; the gist of our survey is this: that the reason, and the only reason, why T. escaped the psychosis which his disposition would otherwise have produced was that his choice of a profession and the path taken by his sublimations did bind a great part of his narcissistic libido in a manner perfectly in accord with reality and thus rescued it from the formation of pathological psychotic symptoms. The existence of such sublimations which, if I may be allowed the expression, have a peculiar affinity to narcissism

[6] The concept of a "union of instincts" (*Triebverbindung*) has been evolved in connection with Freud "fusion of instincts" (*Triebmischung*) (1923b). The reason why I have used a different phrase is that in the case before us a further step is involved. The phrase "union of instincts" should be used whenever it is intended to signify that different instincts share in producing a phenomenological unity.

would accordingly render the subject immune from psychosis, for, to use a happy phrase of T. himself, they constitute a *channel* ready for the reception of the volume of libido which, in psychotic dispositions of this sort, is perpetually flowing back into the ego.[7] The fate of the libido thus regressing into the ego could at one period be directly observed; there was a time when T., as it were, froze in relation to the whole outside world, and he then even withdrew all the tender impulses which he had hitherto had in his married life and did not feel the need of a fresh cathexis. Sexual intercourse became a purely physical matter, his wife being less a person than a means to an end. But this withdrawal of object-libidinal instincts (love inhibited in its aim, as Freud calls it) was not at this time characterized by the formation of any pathological symptoms: there was simply an increased intellectual productivity. I think this hypothesis becomes the more probable when we consider the strikingly narcissistic mode of thought which T. made use of in his scientific work and which here again simply indicated an inferiority. If we try to fit the connection that I am here assuming into the theory of psychosis, we must recollect that as factors in the etiology of the psychoses we are familiar with the damming-up of the libido, its withdrawal into the ego, and in certain circumstances the attempt to direct it outward again toward objects. Accordingly, we should not expect mental disease when the libido in regression or restitution is flowing in the same channels as the sublimations; when this happens we should realize that it is a solution of the whole process, analogous to the mechanism but compatible with reality. From this point of view narcissism can no longer be regarded as the instinct which finds its satisfaction in the ego as in an object; on the contrary, we must go on to the idea that only certain and arbitrarily selected parts of the ego constitute the objects of the narcissistic instincts. It is not the withdrawal of the libido into the ego which is in itself responsible for the outbreak of psychosis, that is, the break with reality; only those parts of the ego which are involved in regression and restitution, or the relation of these parts to the outer world, are the factors which make the ultimate solution compatible or in-

[7] We now understand why schizophrenia so seldom develops in really schizoid persons of the markedly intellectual schizoid type.

compatible with reality. Thus, for instance, narcissism may be employed in a manner compatible with reality in the work of the mathematician, for whom it is permissible, nay obligatory, to construct a world logically out of his own mental creations. In any case narcissism is always so employed whenever a union of instincts, such as I have described, takes place between narcissism and a sublimation of object libido and diverts the main stream of narcissism from the possibilities of abnormal application, so that, a sufficient quantity having been absorbed and in spite of there still being the same excess in the totality of narcissistic libido, there is no noticeable development of morbid symptoms. Evidently this is the opinion of Stärcke (1921), who believes that psychosis is the result of purely "infantile" narcissism.

So far our discussion has led to the formulation of a hypothesis for which we should like to have further empirical confirmation.

I once had the opportunity of observing a highly gifted man whose mental constitution was closely akin to that of T. and who chose the same branch of scientific work but without success, whereupon he became the victim of pathological psychotic reactions. At a certain critical stage in his life he crossed the borderline which we draw between the normal and the pathological. T., on the other hand, always remained on the side of the normal. This difference in the tendency to break with reality is based on a second difference. Both men attempted to satisfy their narcissism in a culturally valuable fashion by uniting it with object libidinal sublimations; both turned to a narcissistic science, but, while T. attained success in this science, the other man could not point to any noteworthy original achievement. That is to say, the attempt in which the one succeeded came to grief in the other, either because the existing sublimations were not sufficiently strong or his interest was not deep enough, or for some reason or other he was distracted from his aim. In the case under discussion all these causes conspired together. Here we see two people of kindred psychotic disposition and similar intellectual endowment who tried to escape in the same way from the psychoses with which they were threatened. The one who succeeded in scientific achievement and was able to employ his narcissism in a manner compatible with reality remained firmly rooted in reality, while the other lapsed into psychosis.[8]

Accordingly, the result of this discussion which, in my view, does not amount to anything more than a plausible essay in psychoanalytical interpretation, would seem to justify the following statement: in the steady transition from the normal to the psychotic there are certain quite definite relations between the presence or absence of pathological psychotic symptoms and the intellectual constitution. These relations are wholly analogous to those with which we are familiar as existing between neurotic symptoms and sublimations in the transition from the normal to the neurotic. Thus, the man who is able to direct a greater part of his narcissistic libido to sexual sublimations displays less pathological phenomena and preserves a better adaptation to reality.

We see that these relations recall those laws upon which light has been thrown by the study of neuroses. In the treatment of the latter, it was an important discovery that certain libidinal tendencies incompatible with reality could be sublimated by changing their object. We can observe an analogous situation where the ego instincts are concerned. Narcissism is not in itself incompatible with reality; even where there is a marked preponderance of the narcissistic systems over the object instincts, together with a hypercathexis of the ego, we can conceive solutions by which a person attains a perfectly satisfactory attitude toward reality. One such solution may be observed when such a union of instincts with specific sublimations takes place.

Thus we are faced with the general task of studying the manifold relations of ego instincts and object instincts which, in the normal or the sick person, combine to produce a phenomenological unity, and also of studying the forms this combination may assume, and the conditions under which a solution and combination of these elements, a chemical reaction, as it were, takes place. But the law governing these transformations will be, here as elsewhere, the pleasure principle which in general determines the course of the libido.

[8] As the present paper is intended only to formulate a theory, from now on I shall not enter in any greater detail into the discussion of cases.

We also had a union of instincts in the clinical picture of the demented patient I mentioned earlier, whose narcissistic attitude caused him to persist in an infantile form of object love. Here narcissistic libido combined in an attempt at restitution with unsublimated object libido incompatible with social standards. A case of this sort always results in a pathological attitude, that is, one at variance with reality. Possibly there is also present here another, considerably more intimate, form of "union."

Accordingly, we may say in general that there is an affinity between the different possible methods of employing the libido with varying meaning for reality but by the same mechanisms; and further that a union of instincts with sublimation leads to a favorable issue, which in certain circumstances may be of positive value for cultural development. Sublimations of object libido as a whole may be conceived of as forming a series according to their greater or lesser affinity to narcissism. In sublimation itself we can clearly distinguish two mechanisms: an object-libidinal process, i.e., the change of the object of interest, and a simultaneous process of regression and restitution, the result of which conditions the capacity of the subject for sublimation. Here we have arrived by a different route at Freud's thought (1923b) that sublimation invariably takes place by way of the ego. We need plead no excuse for deferring the discussion of the pressing questions which now arise as to the nature of sublimation and the forms and conditions of projection.

We now understand that narcissism may manifest itself in very different forms, in ways valuable from the cultural point of view, in the detrimental form of psychosis, or even in phenomena essentially indifferent from the point of view of reality.[9] At once, however, we begin to wish to deduce from the insight we have won methods for the treatment of psychotic conditions. If it is true that the occurrence of the illness depends on the possibility of using the libido which is flowing back into the ego in regression or restitution by combining the instinct with the sublimations in a manner compatible with reality, and if this

[9] Cf. here the possibilities of repression of object instincts described by Freud (1910b).

union is, as it appears to be, related to object libidinal processes which are accessible to our methods, then we may hope to be able to find a way of curing a psychosis which has already broken out.

The task of our therapy[10] can be definitely stated, since we have committed ourselves to the opinion that, even in the psychoses, the fundamental principle of the independence of mechanism and reality value is not transgressed, and that, moreover, we are forced to the conclusion that object-libidinal processes (the other factor in the union of instincts), that is to say, processes in the higher mental strata, are responsible for this reality value.

The therapeutic task which now confronts us may be called the "sublimation of narcissism," but we must not be misled by the phrase into forgetting that the same word is applied to a similar but by no means identical process. In the sublimation of instincts directed toward outside objects the instinct is detached from its original object and turns to another, associatively connected with that object. A "sublimation of narcissism," on the other hand, presupposes this sublimation of "object instincts," in order that narcissistic libido may be freed from any existing attachments and, following the path of greater pleasure, ally itself with that sublimation. The way is a similar one to that along which Freud shows that the world has traveled from animism to science. If the animistic philosophy has its origin in the narcissistic projection of mental phenomena upon the outside world, in the scientific phase this narcissistic libido has been "sublimated." That is to say, it has effected a union of instincts with those object-libidinal sublimations which lead to scientific research and it becomes recognizable both in the narcissistic elements of every scientific work and in the actual striving after increasing mastery of the outside world.

In sublimation the object libido changes its aims; in the sublimation of narcissism it would seem that the objects within the subject's own ego have to be changed and probably at the same time the mode of union of narcissism with these objects.

---

[10] It is obvious that in the following therapeutic discussions I am for the moment confining myself to the less serious forms of schizophrenia, paranoia, and those phenomena which are on the borderline of neurosis.

In the psychoses of the schizophrenic type, because the patient's tendencies to observation are withdrawn from the outer world into the ego, his own pathological mental processes are experienced by him like processes outside himself; his delusional system is a theory which in itself is not open to any objection and is designed to account for what is to him a particular aspect of reality. If we succeed in actually reviving the full experience of other mental phenomena, the capacity to construct theories will be applied to them as well; some of the various possibilities are now compatible with reality.

Before entering upon the therapeutic discussion, let me relate what happened to the symptom in T. of which I have spoken. As mentioned, this symptom constantly made its appearance after disappointments in this scientific work. To connect it with feelings of inferiority and the castration complex was therefore natural, but this did not solve the problem of what the possible conditions would be under which, if our views are correct, the outbreak of a psychosis in this case would be conceivable. Obviously, this could be imagined only as based on lasting frustration in his scientific work, such as would rob of its value the attempt at restitution which was compatible with reality. And now we note that slight disappointments due to an occasional failure constitute slight frustrations of this sort, which are followed by a momentary regression into psychosis—a transitory regression, because a mistaken calculation can have no lasting importance as a frustration. On the patients's gaining complete insight into the mechanisms discussed in this paper and into their general connection, this symptom was first of all replaced for quite a short time by ordinary depersonalization states. Subsequently it vanished completely, and I see no possibility of its return, for its conditioning factors are now conscious and the disappointment, when it occurs, can at once be recognized as unimportant, seeing that communication has been established with the conscious capacity of judgment, which appreciates the insignificance of the occasion. Of course it is conceivable that regressions of this sort might take place after actual, grave frustrations in sublimation. But I do not see any basis for these in reality and I think that, even if this actually took place, the subject's self-knowledge would make it easy for the libido to take up a fresh position in reality. The possibility of a hysterical origin of the symptom must be considered but, taking into account the character of T., which was quite unlike the hysterical type, and remembering the result of the treatment, I think this possibility may be dismissed out of hand. Suggestion does not come into question and, that being so, has a hysterical symptom ever been known to dissolve in consequence of an insight into the psychogenesis of logic?

Before we begin to discuss the extension of analytic therapy to the psychoses we must consider again what has to be presupposed in general of the exercise of influence upon the mind as a whole. According to our dynamic view, mental life is determined by a system of forces. In order to intervene in this system we need a force to enable the (morbid or healthy) subject of our intervention to effect a libidinal cathexis of the therapist. The possibility of a transference seems therefore to be the prerequisite for any sort of influence on the mind.

This fact imposes upon us the duty of considering the dynamic relations, in order to be able to decide whether it is theoretically possible to conceive of anyone from the outside world exercising at will an influence upon a narcissistic neurosis, that is to say, upon an illness in which the decisive part is played by ego instincts which are not turned toward that world. Moreover, for the purpose of comparison we must reflect upon the nature of the effect produced by ordinary psychoanalytic therapy in neurosis.

The motives which create and maintain pathogenic symptoms in neuroses are unconscious; to these is opposed the conscious will of the ego, which draws upon reality and which is impotent because it does not know its adversary and can make its attack only upon the final manifestations of the unconscious instinctual forces. This is the reason why all efforts of will on the part of neurotic persons are so fruitless. Analytic treatment first of all brings knowledge of the cause of the illness, the genesis of the symptom, and all the forces which maintain it. To the determinants of the mental process a fresh factor is added, namely, the knowledge of mental laws, and this must alter the issue, just as an experiment is influenced by the mere presence of a measuring instrument. In our case the change will consist in an alliance being effected between the will of the conscious personality, which is almost always a will to recovery, and the unconscious motives in the neurosis. The enemy and his hiding place are recognized and it is possible to measure one's strength with them. If the conscious will is the stronger, it alone will suffice for mastery of the formerly unconscious will. This is the rare case, in which the patient's understanding of the genesis of his illness suffices to cure him. In all other cases we have one more powerful weapon in the transference; in his relation with the patient the physician takes on all those qualities to which enormous libido quantities have been fixated by pleasurable experiences in the past. These qualities form an associative bridge by which this same libido is transferred to the person of the physician in order that it may pass over from him to real objects. This whole mass of libido can now be used to reinforce the conscious will to get well. If the scale still turns in favor of the forces which impel the patient to neurosis, then even this method is useless and we must acknowledge that the libido fixations are too strong.

But there is one thing which we must not forget. Sick persons, as well as normal, find a constant support in daily experience. That is to say, these experiences are readily employed by the libidinal tendencies which are responsible for the symptoms as well as by the conscious will directed toward reality, and every pleasure is turned to account by the conscious will or the libidinal tendencies. And the self-knowledge attained through psychoanalysis can accomplish something even in cases in which the will to recovery, together with the libido massed in the transference, cannot master their enemy. For self-knowledge will bar the way against this reinforcement of the impulses of the id, against which the battle is being fought, whereas the will to recovery can feed upon reality after analysis as before it. Thus it may happen that, even in such difficult cases, with the passage of years the scales finally come down on the side of health. The situation is comparable to the position of two armies, encamped opposite one another and each receiving equal reinforcements from allies, so that the relative power of the two remains constant or even favors the army of the neurosis. But all changes must march through passes and along roads which the army of consciousness can control. If the general of this army knows the position of the enemy and if his intelligence service is sufficiently well organized to inform him in good time of the forces which are joining the adversary and the direction his march is taking, it will be possible to cut him off from all his reserve forces and gradually gain the upper hand. It is to this that we must trace the often long period of incubation in the therapeutic effects of psychoanalytic treatment: short periods of this sort are to be explained as manifestations of unresolved transference.

This exposition would not be complete without a reminder that bringing into consciousness the development of the libido presupposes in itself that the resistances have been overcome, which task again has to be accomplished by the transference. Thus even in those cases in which insight into the etiology of the illness induces the recovery of the patient the dynamic power which alone can give him this insight is furnished by the transference.

To these older technical methods must be added others developed by Ferenczi and Rank (1924). In their view, the main task of the treatment is that a repetitive enactment of a piece of experience in the transference should be effected, and that the analyst should then furnish a fresh solution of it. The physician is chiefly assisted in bringing the unconscious factors into consciousness by the infantile forms of gratification coming to be discounted because they arouse actual "pain." The common feature in all these forms of technique is that the transference is introduced in order directly to counteract an existing force (resistance to consciousness, tendency to regression, fixation of instinct, tendency to rejection on the part of the ideal).

It is *a priori* clear that a similar method is bound to fail in psychosis; for we speak of a psychosis only when the narcissistic binding of a symptom is so strong that it outweighs the possibility of effecting a transference. The conceptions which have emerged in the course of this investigation have shown us not only that it is, as is well known, impossible to overcome a powerful narcissistic binding, but have also led to the supposition that fortunately this is not necessary. The narcissistic libido has merely to change its points of attachment (its objects in the ego); the transference will serve only to bring about such changes in the object libido that the resulting products will have a tendency to attract narcissistic libido and to combine with narcissistic elements or with such elements as have free valencies in respect to narcissism, if I may be permitted the expression. But this narcissism will flow toward the point of greatest pleasure; the task of the transference is simply to foster object-libidinal positions, by means of which the narcissism is expelled from other combinations and its partner is repressed.

At this point we must not overlook the fact that the schizophrenic's capacity for love is often confined to the narcissistic type; the only form of transference which can then be effectively established is the narcissistic, the physician himself taking up to a large extent a schizoid attitude and acting the ego ideal of the patient, only with the trifling difference that he is also able to appreciate reality.

In practical psychoanalytic work, when we study the vicissitudes of the instincts, we need to direct more attention to the factors which condition the formation and the resolution of unions of instincts and to devote special care to the unions of narcissism and object libido. Experience only can give us deeper insight into the laws in question and devise our therapeutic technique accordingly.

The only feature which the therapy of the psychoses has in common with the customary treatment of the neuroses is the use made of consciousness; it seems as if in psychoses of the schizophrenic type insight into the mechanism has a markedly greater power of assisting recovery than in neurosis. All self-knowledge consists in the establishing of communication between different tendencies which hitherto were cut off from one another. Possibly this explains why it plays a greater part in a mental condition the principal phenomenon in which, side by side with the withdrawal of libido, is splitting.

In the case of T., the importance of self-knowledge, together with the establishment of communication and the recognition of the triviality of the occasion for regression (this regression being as it were based on a misunderstanding), is to be found in the narcissistic pleasure which he experienced in recognizing his impulses and mental mechanisms.

Accordingly, we shall try to give the patient insight into the conditions under which the symptom originated and understanding of those factors in himself which operate to produce pleasure; further, we shall endeavor to establish communication wherever blockages occur. But above all he must be brought to understand the kinship between his disposition to psychosis, and, in particular, to a given type of psychosis and must learn what a "psychosis" really is and that it does not imply any sort of value judgment.

In psychotic processes of the regressive type it is most important to create for the libido a fresh object within the ego. Freud (1932b) describes in detail the process of identification by which the ego presents itself to the id in the likeness of the love object, in order to be loved instead of this object. In an analogous way we have to induce another ego component, of which a cathexis can be effected without detriment, to offer itself as an object. If we cannot wrest a wild beast's prey from it by force, we can still get the better of it by craft, by throwing it something else to devour.

When we come upon a psychosis of the restitution type which is still in process of formation, our task must be to direct that restitution along paths compatible with reality. Similarly, cases of fully developed restitution psychosis really come to the same thing, for they, too, constantly require fresh nourishment; moreover, these forms also display the tendency readily to regress anew to the ego. To sum up the characteristic features of this therapeutic attempt, we may say that a given clinical picture has to be altered by means of an intervention into the healthy part of the personality which has not undergone narcissistic fixation; it therefore depends upon the existence of such a part. The intervention itself is directly concerned with the object libido; it is only secondarily and as a result of such intervention that the ego instincts can be influenced. Throughout the process use is made, as it were, of a potential energy. We proceed by a circuitous route, in which a considerably lesser degree of possibility of object cathexis is required than in the attempt to exercise a direct influence in overcoming the narcissism.

This therapeutic technique may further be expressed in purely phenomenological terms as follows: the whole body of capacities and interests may, as I have said above, be arranged in a series according to particular points of view. At one end are those which, when sufficiently developed, act as a protection, rendering the subject immune from the formation of psychoses. The prognosis for intervention in a psychosis depends upon whether there can be found in the remaining and still accessible part of the personality seeds of such capacities and interests capable of development. In the maturing of such seeds we may look for a complete reversal of the restitution psychosis, if in so doing we have succeeded in opening up a more pleasurable restitutive path.

Now we come to the dynamic question which lies at the root of this theoretical study: have we at our disposal, in the faint trace of object cathexes or in the narcissistic transference, the requisite force for an intervention of this sort? It would seem that this question must be answered in the affirmative. It is true that we cannot exercise control over directly narcissistic fixations, but on the circuitous route which we have chosen we are moving only in those strata which are still exposed to contact with the outside world, and we have selected as our "point of Archimedes" the remainder of the personality still preserved in health. Thus, whatever may be the difficulties with which this method of treating the psychoses may still be faced and wherever we may have to fix the limits of its applicability, at least we are not confronted with anything dynamically impossible. The cures which psychiatry has so far effected, no less than the spontaneous processes of recovery,[11] may be interpreted in accordance with the view advanced here.

[11] It will be recalled that in the paranoiac, Dr. Schreber, during the last part of his stay in an institution, his psychosis finally became reduced to a clearly defined delusional system, the rest of his personality being completely restored. I think it not impossible that this partial recovery was connected with the struggle for mental freedom (upon which he brought to bear his remarkably acute juristic intellect) which Dr. Schreber put up simultaneously with, and in consequence of, this improvement. I would suggest that the meaning of this connection is that this reversal of the morbid process became possibly only when the patient's narcissistic libido attached itself to this intellectual work and to the real goals which it set before him. Unfortunately in this case we do not know the causes for this change in the points of attachment of the subject's narcissism and its union with other instinctual tendencies. Strindberg acquired a postpsychotic personality to some extent compatible with real life and which enabled him to overcome his delusion when he found a path of restitution compatible with reality. In this

Bleuler defines schizophrenia as a contest with autism, obviously undertaken on behalf of object relations. Autism is what we have termed the form of narcissism incompatible with reality. To supplement this, and in part to carry it further, we may require in addition that the narcissism opposed to reality be changed into a form compatible with reality. I would point out here that this train of thought (upon which this paper is based) is closely connected with the theories formulated by Bleuler (1911a).

From the historical point of view the place of this investigation in the evolution of the psychoanalytic theory of the psychoses will be somewhat as follows: Freud and Abraham having postulated the withdrawal of the libido into the ego and having compared this with the narcissistic phase of libidinal organization, Freud went on to discover in the symptoms of insanity attempts at restitution. I am now suggesting the possibility that these processes may be resolved in ways either compatible or incompatible with reality, and am endeavoring to indicate the relations existing between these different ways. Our therapeutic efforts must take two directions: first, that of bringing into consciousness the libidinal processes; and, secondly, that of influencing the healthy parts of the personality.

Since I intend to reserve the account of clinical cases for a separate discussion, the technical side may be mentioned here only insofar as it can be immediately deduced from my theoretical postulates. At all events the treatment must begin with an

---

connection he writes: "I will not deny that the beginning was difficult and that the empty space which enclosed my personality clamored to be filled. The fact that I had severed my contact with other human beings seemed at first to diminish my strength; at the same time, however, my ego began as it were to coagulate and to solidify round an inner core, where all that I had ever experienced accumulated, was digested and absorbed as mental food. Meanwhile it became my habit to reproduce in literary form all that I saw and heard in the house, in the street or outside in the world of nature. Thus I related all my observations to my work of the moment, and in so doing I felt my power grow, and my solitary studies proved more valuable than those which I had pursued outside in social intercourse with my fellow creatures." In an analogous manner Gerard de Nerval freed himself from the acute phase of his psychosis, when he perceived the necessity for being able to master at will the sensations which he experienced as pleasurable. At the same time, having discovered that dreams must have a meaning, he devoted himself to their interpretation. His theories on the subject, however, were still strongly tinged with mysticism and so his recovery was only very incomplete.

extremely passive period which enables the analyst to find out what are the possibilities before him. In this phase the transference (which is preeminently a narcissistic one) will sustain the relation. Only after this period can he plan his intervention, and begin the endeavor to effect sublimations which have an affinity to narcissism. Generally speaking, we shall always advance hand in hand with narcissism, avoiding frustration in regard to the narcissistic ideal and steadily aiming at affording narcissistic gratification compatible with reality. Only a very wide experience will determine how far these methods enable us to influence cases of psychosis.

In my opinion, a communication which presents more problems than conclusions is justified by the hope that by summarizing the experience of different observers we may hasten the practical solution of the problems under discussion.

CHAPTER 2

Schizophrenic and Creative Thinking

(1926)

Up to the present time psychoanalysis has not been extensively applied to the psychology of thought. This is due to the nature of the psychoanalytic method, which was developed for the purpose of investigating unconscious content, that is, of examining the mode of function of mental strata which, phylogenetically older, underlie the layer of coordinated thought processes. The more archaic functions manifest themselves in dream processes and in schizophrenia. From this point of view psychoanalysis is not called upon to make any comment on the laws regulating thought, which is a matter for experimental research; the relation of the individual phenomena of thought to unconscious processes is, however, a subject which concerns it, as is also the expression of instinctual functioning through the creation of thought structures.

For the purposes of this brief study, the intention of which is mainly to point to certain problems, we shall adopt the familiar procedure of examining pathological manifestations. We do so, not because we share the general impression that there is only a quantitative difference between the normal and the pathological or that a pathological state merely magnifies what can be observed in normal life. On the contrary, we believe that,

First published as "Über schizophrenes und schöpferisches Denken," in *Internationale Zeitschrift für Psychoanalyse*, 12:298-308, 1926. Reprinted from *International Journal of Psycho-Analysis*, 7:366-376, 1926. The present version was revised by Dr. Robert C. Bak.

although they are often difficult to formulate, there are many important qualitative differences on both sides which are easily overlooked on account of the quite striking analogies. We start from pathological data because we hope in this way to elucidate some aspects of the problem, not because we hope to explain all its aspects.

Considering first of all schizophrenic forms of thought, we find that paranoid and hebephrenic forms, although not the only types, are nevertheless the most striking and the most fully described. To illustrate the paranoidal type we shall select the most thoroughly analyzed example of paranoia, viz., Freud's dissection of Schreber's delusional system (1911a).

The main element of Schreber's paranoid system was his belief that he had been turned into a woman who was to play an important part in the regulation of cosmic affairs, who would in fact be essential for the world's salvation. Unhampered by any considerations of general validity, we may proceed to study this very typical example apart from the other elements in the delusion.

The first point to be recognized concerning this pathological idea is the feminine attitude; regarded from the point of view of instinctual life, the fantasy is a homosexual one. As Freud has shown, this change of attitude had already been indicated in various ways before the outbreak of the actual psychosis. We can therefore regard a regression to homosexuality as the first phase in the formation of Schreber's delusional idea. At this stage there are obviously many avenues open: a regression of this type can be seen in the case of obvious perversions as well as in some neuroses, and to indicate how these paths diverge it is necessary to single out certain specific manifestations in the development of the delusion.

A second point in the formation of the paranoid idea is the manner in which this mode of instinctual functioning is experienced: it is not regarded as a process occurring within the individual's own personality, if we may use the term, but as a result of external influence. By displacement of the ego boundaries, to adopt the current phraseology, a variation in object cognition occurs: an internal manifestation is experienced as external. An analogous mechanism of projection is seen in the normal individual, where instinctual activity is often regarded as something foreign to the ego, as an influence to which one submits or which one rejects. Familiar expressions, e.g., "it came over me," "it carried me away," betray this attitude, and psychoanalysis has found an apt term for this in designating instinctual life as the id. The analogy is, however, too limited: the id of a normal person is more ego-alien or ego-dystonic than his conscious will, it is less a subject than an object. Notwithstanding this, a normal person always knows that he should not seek for "it" outside his own personality. The paranoiac does so.

So far we can recognize in the formation of the delusional thought system a regressive outbreak of passive homosexuality and the variation in object relations characteristic of schizophrenia. Taken by itself the first would run: "I become—instinctually—a woman"; the second is modified to: "I am changed—by external means—into a woman." To this formula is added a subjective interpretation which expands an isolated thought into a religious system: "this sexual change in me will bring about the world's salvation."

This third step discloses the paranoiac's desire to coordinate his experience with his image of the world. He cannot bear simply to accept the situation; he must immediately fashion some theory to explain it. His idea of world redemption and the part played by his change into a woman is a theory produced in order to coordinate and satisfactorily explain his new experience. This dovetailing of experience into a wide concatenation brings about the specific paranoid reaction. Borrowing an expression from Gestalt psychology, we may speak of structures being "seen into" the outer world (or of internal processes being experienced externally). We would suggest that any hypertrophy of this tendency should be called hypergnosis in contradistinction to agnosis or diminished perception of "shape."

Hypergnosis must be present to give the impression of a paranoid picture: in its absence the displacement of ego boundaries is suggestive merely of schizophrenia, never of paranoia. The significance of hypergnosis as a *differentia specifica* of paranoia can be illustrated by a case reported by Kronfeld: a catatonic patient told of the confused and chaotic impressions he had experienced in the catatonic state; he said that the chaos had been outside him and not inside him. In this case definite experiences and the perception of them existed outside the ego boundary, yet the third stage of delusional formation was absent, viz. the "seeing into." Had he been hypergnostic he would have coordinated the experiences projected into the outside world, either as well-regulated sensory perceptions (visual and auditory hallucinations) or as theoretical elaborations (a delusional system). Mere displacement of ego boundaries without hypergnosis brings about a schizophrenic but not a paranoid state.

So far we have distinguished in the development of a paranoid system the stages of experience, the process of projection and a hypergnostic coordination into an image of the world. Our presentation is incomplete insofar as it takes no account of paranoid systems dealing ostensibly with abstractions and not, as in Schreber's case, with his own person. Apart from paranoiacs with delusions of persecution, jealousy, or redemption, there are cases with inventive mania, cosmological theories, ideas of world reformation, physical discoveries, and many more. The connection between these forms and the forms previously described lies in the word "ostensibly." As a matter of fact, analysis shows that judgments on matters external to the ego represent in deeper layers judgments concerning personal experiences. Paranoid theories are not concerned immediately with the original material but with presentations which by a process of displacement are substituted for the original material. The idea can then be kept from consciousness, whereas in the simpler type first described, e.g., Schreber's case, the ego-dystonic content, e.g., fantasies of passive homosexual outrage, appear directly in consciousness. As an example of the second type let us analyze briefly a distorted idea from a confusional case.

A patient with mild schizophrenia is entirely absorbed with the subject of parental conflict. Hardly any other idea occurs to him except by way of his parents' attitude to it. The origin of this conflict was the son's rebellion against the strict religious and patriarchal views of his parents, particularly of his mother. His life is one constant repetition of situations of rupture and reconciliation with them. On occasions of rupture he is usually stuporous and ceases all activities, but after successful reconciliation his energies return, merely to prepare for the next catastrophe.

This patient has elaborated a philosophical system which absorbs most of his activity and which he regards as of the first importance. In such a highly educated person (a physician) his philosophical system must appear doubly trivial, barren, and crazy. His main idea runs that fundamentally there can be nothing but agreement between science and religion; this has always been apparent to him and he seems to have regarded the idea almost as a revelation.

From what source does he derive his evidence? He may at some time or other have heard of the scholastic theses on this subject; but how can this truth be accompanied with such intense conviction unless it is related to some equally profound experience? The experience, it seems, must be his perpetual bondage to his parents, above all to his mother. He feels in some dim way that love alone could control his peculiar and often extremely reprehensible conduct and has a foreboding that, unlike other men, his bondage will never yield to that degree of independence which is a prerequisite of tender feeling. And this experience of compulsive dependence which he does not admit—it is manifested by open revolt and by violent accusations against his parents, colored largely with guilt feelings—becomes apparent to him only in the distorted form of his main thesis. Religion represents the pious and strict mother, who implanted profound conscientious scruples in her son with regard to his adoption of the profession of medicine; he himself represents natural science. The unity of religion and science is for him no mere shibboleth; his is a lasting conviction, because it is based on experience—not of course an "experience" of the unity between science and religion but of the unity of the persons from which this allegory is built up.

Here, then, is an example of the instinctual language being translated into terms of cultural life: one of the factors in the process seems to be the wish to repudiate the facts of instinctual life, hence a kind of repression. The thought we have just analyzed is not actually paranoid in nature: the element of projection of the fundamental experience into the outer world is lacking. Had such an element been present the experience would not have been formulated as "my parents and myself constitute an indissoluble unity" but rather "external forces compel me to be one with my parents." The thought translation would then run somewhat as follows: "scientific principles are modified by external influences, perhaps by some apparatus, in such a way that they are at one with religion"; the thought would then be definitely paranoid. Although not paranoid in the strict sense of the term (the fundamental experience does not appear to be homosexual), this analyzed thought will serve to illustrate the processes of "translation."

We are now in a position to reduce the processes of delusion formation to their elements. Some definite experience is internally objectified and, owing to the individual's hypergnostic tendency, becomes the foundation of a system; either foundations are formed to support the experience, or the experience is converted into a generalization. In this way the experience itself may not be represented, its place being taken by translations, seemingly different in content, derived from any suitable spheres of ideation. In this instance the seemingly paranoid formation is merely a copy of the original one.

We may now attempt to differentiate between the mechanisms of obsessive thoughts and delusional thoughts. We cannot do so in terms of content, since typical delusional ideas, e.g., of redemption or persecution, can appear as true obsessive thoughts in cases of pure obsessional neurosis. The obsessive and the delusional form are distinguished phenomenologically by the existence of evidence of the experience. In the latter instance evidence is advanced and there exists a state of complete refractoriness to corrective modification; in the former the thought obtrudes itself in a compulsive way, but is discredited by the subject who exhibits ambivalence and doubt. We believe that underlying this difference there is another concerning the unequivocal nature of the experience. The other processes of paranoid thought formation are also observed in obsessional neuroses (with certain minor differences), but the underlying experience appears to be contradictory and in no sense unequivocal instinctually. In Schreber's case, had a complete breakthrough of homosexuality not occurred, had the opposing tendencies been strong enough to lead to open conflict, the experience would *ceteris paribus*—variation of experience of object and hypergnosis—have led to the presentation of the content of his delusion in the form of obsessive thoughts, fantasies of homosexual assault of an extremely compulsive nature, fantasies of redemption recurring persistently in spite of repudiation.

It would be quite wrong to attempt to explain the difference between obsession and delusion on the grounds of a stronger sense of reality testing. For in the presence of other characteristic factors, an unequivocal experience invariably routs the reality censor (one has only to think how frequently delusional thoughts persist in personalities otherwise completely intact). To put the matter more correctly, every delusional thought has passed the reality censor and is based on a true experience. The generalizations and theoretical superstructures are alone false. We must not of course ignore the fact that the degree of capacity for generalization and theoretical naivity is not much in excess of that displayed in daily life by most other people of the same cultural development.

The distinctions we have drawn between obsession and delusion enable us to explain why obsessional thoughts frequently acquire a delusional form, and why an obsessional neurosis may develop into paranoia. In all such cases an experience originally contradictory, associated with conflict, and represented in obsessive thoughts, is gradually divested of conflict and comes to be accepted *in toto* by the individual. We shall shortly have occasion to describe the transformations in the ego ideal which precede this change.

The conditions in delusional formation which we have so far described seem to be necessary ones but do not cover the whole ground. For when Schreber was looking for some construction by means of which he could coordinate his altered instinctual life into a cosmic scheme, there were undoubtedly numerous possibilities open to him. It still remains unexplained why his theoretical venture took the particular form of a delusion of redemption having a characteristic megalomaniac pattern. It is only by study of the alterations taking place in the ego ideal that we can get a more precise idea of the course of events.

That the homosexual tendencies forced their way into action

and consciousness implies a breakdown of the corresponding part of the ego ideal; the prohibition "I must not love men" must first of all be removed. Does this imply a breakdown in the ego ideal?

One gathers that the process is not one of demolition but rather of an internal shift. The original prohibition of homosexuality is not swept aside in the rush of the instinctual drive without substitution; in fact it secures a considerable amount of compensation. The moral component of the ego ideal certainly comes out of the conflict greatly weakened, but only after the narcissistic component became highly invested as a compensation. To Schreber himself the new demand of the ego ideal ran "I must be the Savior of Humanity"; so that he could afford to be easy over the breakdown of his ideal in another direction, viz., "Even if I have homosexual ideas, they do not signify the same for me as for others: in my case it is no mere instinctual gratification but a destiny which falls on me along with this my function of savior."

It is perfectly clear from a study of Schreber's ideas that this compensatory process played a decisive part in forming the content of his delusion. As Freud has shown, Schreber did not in the first instance explain his experience on the savior hypothesis but connected it with the much more direct assumption that he was molested sexually. This tendency did not, however, develop any further; it lacked the narcissistic compensation necessary for a breakdown of the moral ideal. Schreber's idea was that all attempts to change his sex for unnatural purposes (i.e., in order to satisfy some person's sexual desire) had completely miscarried, whereas his castration for purposes in keeping with natural law (i.e., as a method of world redemption) seemed to him a quite reasonable outcome of the conflict.

This compensation, which itself proves the existence of narcissistic fixations, alone enabled the instinctual drive to break through; moreover, this process in the ego ideal explains why among many possible theories this particular delusional idea arose in his mind. The ultimate form of the delusion must reproduce this process in the ego ideal; the new delusion must be made to tally with fresh demands on the part of the ideal. Hence we must amplify our original presentation of the origin of delusional thinking, in that the content of the idea is definitely decided by a rearrangement of the elements in the ego ideal permitting the fundamental experience to be worked out.

We have already exceeded the limits of a description of paranoid thought formation: the example we have given in illustration of "translation" of an instinctual situation and our investigation of obsessive thoughts have carried us beyond our original theme. They enable us, however, to arrive at a generalization which brings us to the real thesis of this paper. In my opinion this mechanism of paranoid thought formation can be regarded as a prototype of the mechanism of creative thinking and of normal thought processes generally.

I believe that it is in keeping with psychoanalytic experience to assume that nondelusional true creative thinking is also based on an experience. The inclination for some particular subject and fixation on these thoughts arise solely from the experience; contradiction in the experience gives rise to doubt concerning the thought formations, while what is unequivocal in the experience produces the evidence for the thought processes and the unalterable conviction regarding them.

We can also observe in nondelusional thought the second factor, viz., projection.[1] A certain degree of objectivation is present in all thought, although of course in normal cases it does not go beyond the boundaries of the ego. It is our belief that objectivation is not a result of thought operations but that objectivation of the experience is a prerequisite of the appearance of thought elaboration.

Hypergnosis invariably plays a part in the development of creative thinking: a hidden connection must be grasped. We might call this a developed perception of "shape." This can be correlated with the usual form of perception of "shape" by means of a simple observation. In the case of visual thinkers productive ideas are often perceived in optical "shape" forms, while analogous "shape" experiences are recorded by auditory and motor types.

The translation of experience into thought content must, in accordance with our theory, also occur in normal thinking. At

---

[1] Sandor Rado (1922) was the first to observe that creative thought owes its origin to a projection of self-perceptions.

any rate this certainly happens when the thoughts relate to matters other than the subject's own instinctual life.

Hence we must assume that certain displacements also occur normally within the ego ideal. The possibility of experience, its ultimate translation and transferred representation imply very slight retrogressions and compensatory formations in the ego ideal, although these are not so archaic in nature or so obvious as in the simple case of the Schreber delusion.

This outline must also serve as a basis for the normal processes of thought, insofar as these are concerned with completed thought presentations. We may assume that in such instances there is some variation in the intensity and perhaps in the content of the fundamental experience, that there are minor degrees of difference in objectivation, and that the process of hypergnosis is less marked.

We are now in a position to consider the difference between paranoid and true creative thinking, and this leads to the further question whether in the psychological mechanisms of thought formation it is possible to distinguish between true and false. The latter problem is beyond the scope of this discussion, since it takes us from the region of psychology to theories of cognition and cannot be clearly formulated without some such theoretical basis. As we are limited here to purely psychological considerations, we can only present certain common, possibly typical differences between paranoid and correct thinking, without of course claiming that these have universal application or are incapable of other interpretation.

In the first place, can it be said that a preference for one definite form of experience (the homosexual form) is typical of paranoid thinking only? This could be decided only after abundant analytic investigation of the processes of creative thinking. Again, may there not be some typical difference in the degree of projection which determines whether only relative objectivation of the experience takes place without overstepping ego boundaries or whether displacement into the outer world occurs? We may hazard the guess that projection of the latter sort is the basis of any weakening of the reality censorship. It disturbs the whole context of the experience, which then appears to the individual to be purely environmental and yet in opposition to external reality. A condition has arisen which we describe as a case of reality censorship, since the external world as experienced by the individual no longer coincides with the actual external reality. The basis for this profound variation of objective experience appears to be a regression to the early period of development in which numerous isolated ego instincts had not yet been unified by more developed ego instincts and when ego boundaries were correspondingly vague.

Our assumption that damaged reality testing is due to the injury of ego boundaries in the process of experiencing individual experience gains some support from an analogous process occurring in normal life. Whenever a minor injury of ego boundaries occurs in a normal person and makes him seek for the explanation of his fate outside his own person, a weakening of the reality-testing faculty occurs. Actual facts are reinterpreted and external reality is seen in a false light.

Moreover, typical differences between paranoid and normal thinking appear to relate to the functioning of the ego ideal. Disintegration of the ideal is never so extensive in the case of normal thinking, and above all compensation formation never involves the same primitive narcissistic stages as it does in paranoia.

We have so far dealt more with paranoid and creative thinking, approaching the latter problem by way of the former. We still have to consider two varieties of schizophrenic thinking, paranoid and heboid. We term "heboid" that form of disordered and confused thinking which flies from one idea to another. The pathological form of this is seen in the hebephrenic "flight of ideas," which is in curious contrast to the ordered thinking of paranoia. In my opinion, this manifestation can be best understood on the assumption that it consists of numerous fragments of paranoid formation, each one rapidly displacing the last, none of them being carried to a conclusion. We may take it that there is here a rapid change of significant experiences and that the source of this change is to be found in a kind of dissipation of libido. Heboid thinking is then to be regarded (with the differences noted above) as a pathological prototype of that variety of normal thought which is called inconsequent, never keeping to one subject for any length of time.

In sharp contrast to the schizophrenic types is a variety of thinking seen in a pathological form in amentia. In contrast to the types already described, the fragmented thought formations of such patients indicate a reduced appreciation of "shape," or, to keep to our terminology, a kind of hypergnosis. It is characterized by an incapacity to synthesize experience. This too has its counterpart in normal life.

Within the limits of this contribution we have not been able to deal with every form of pathological thinking nor to give a full description of the corresponding normal types. We have had to content ourselves with provisory formulations of a theory concerning the functional dependence of thought processes on instinctual life. The results of investigation of the processes of ordered thinking which have been reached by cognitive psychologists have not been referred to here. Doubtless there are many points of view common to both methods of approach which will have to be considered and given proper valuation in any future comprehensive theory of thought.

CHAPTER 3

Discussion on Lay Analysis

(1927)

Psychoanalysis originated and developed in answer to a medical problem; it was indeed the work of a physician who departed entirely from any analogous method in medicine. From this field of origin, however, psychoanalysis very soon definitely extended; it laid claim to deal with normal psychology and to develop methods of technique which applied to the healthy no less than to the sick. At the same time it has so far enlarged the conception of mental illness beyond the truly narrow clinical boundary that it practically includes almost everything that lives. We now speak of the "neurosis" of a person in the same matter-of-fact way that we speak of his "character," "personality" or "abilities." With this widening of its objects and its problems psychoanalysis has ceased to be, if indeed it ever was, a branch of medical science, and certainly cannot become a part of it as long as it persists in its wide-reaching claims. We must even refrain from including psychoanalysis in categories which, although outgrown, have become agreeable from habit.

At this juncture the *legitimate* cooperation of nonmedical, so-called "lay, " persons begins, whose interest in psychoanalysis has arisen on the basis of other scientific work outside that of medicine. A psychoanalytic movement which is to do justice to its problems in connection with human development cannot do without this cooperation; quite apart from the fertile connection

First published as "Diskussion der Laienanalyse," in *Internationale Zeitschrift für Psychoanalyse*, 13:298-299, 1927. Reprinted from *International Journal of Psycho-Analysis*, 8:275-277, 1927.

with other problems which it continually helps even the medical analyst to maintain, its function is to work toward the final synthesis of the psychoanalytic science of the mind with all the valuable findings of other psychological methods. By means of the infiltration of academic psychology with analysis (which has scarcely begun today) and even indirectly through its teachers who receive such training, we may expect that more extensive knowledge on the part of the public which is so desirable for the extension of analytic practice.

If, however, nonmedical workers are to be permitted to study analysis, then it follows from the nature of our science that practice on living subjects can no longer be denied them.

It must be admitted without hesitation that medical, and in particular psychiatric and neurological knowledge, is always an advantage and sometimes indispensable for the practice of analysis; a medical training will not be lacking to the ideal analyst. But other prerequisites are equally important for this ideal—conditions which in individual cases the physician can probably fulfill, just as a lay person may acquire medical knowledge, but which are nevertheless not in any way acquired through the medical training itself. For example, that training in methodical thinking which can be acquired only by the study of the exact sciences, or psychology or biology. Insofar as one observes tolerance toward medical men in respect to their lack of knowledge or efficiency in these branches, the same tolerance must be displayed in respect to the nonmedical qualification of those who fulfill other valuable conditions for analysis; the more so because the lack of medical training, which relates less to method than to facts, can be readily compensated for by a medical diagnosis and by constant consultation with a medical man versed in analysis.

So much with regard to the desirability of lay analysis from our analytic point of view. My view would be in favor of admission of it, even if all these arguments were invalid, and would be determined by an attitude of liberalism (not corresponding, it is true, to current tendencies), which sees in the daily-increasing system of professional specialization and tests of efficiency an expression of a petty, provincial state of mind and one of the most destructive influences of the present day, both culturally and economically. It is certainly not honorable to drag in the interests of third parties; the community does not protect its members from the manifold hygienic, material, social, and mental dangers of life, and it is not comprehensible why it should take up the task of protecting them from the possibility of even real quackery.

These observations aim at defining a practical and theoretical standpoint which need not necessarily coincide with the tactical one of policy. From the tactical standpoint one would be well advised not to make the position of the psychoanalytic physician more difficult in respect to the rest of the medical profession; to overcome this difficulty I believe that a medical diagnosis before the "lay" analysis must serve the purposes of diagnosis and exclusion of unsuitable cases, and thus, in addition to medical consultation during the analysis, will surely meet all objections.

CHAPTER 4

Review of S. Freud

*Inhibitions, Symptoms
and Anxiety (1926a)
(1928)*

This book not only discusses a series of the most important problems of psychoanalysis, but at the same time throws new light on nearly every question within the range of psychoanalytic investigation, even if only in passing. Its extraordinary richness of content presents the reviewer with a particular difficulty. Confronted with this wealth, he has hardly any other course open than to make a selection, in which naturally an element of subjective interest is bound to enter. Perhaps this danger will be most readily diminished, even if not avoided, by presenting the material along the lines of the leading problems of the work.

Freud begins with the question of the difference between inhibition and symptom. Clearly, both ideas have ground in common; there are inhibitions which are symptoms and symptoms which consist essentially of inhibitions; but they do not in general coincide. Now, what are inhibitions? Freud discusses the various kinds of inhibition, and on the basis of analytic experience distinguishes three mechanisms. In one group of cases an activity appears to be inhibited on account of the meaning which it takes on; when an activity becomes sexualized, i.e., takes on a sexual meaning for the person concerned, or when this

---

First published in *Internationale Zeitschrift für Psychoanalyse*, 14:416-423, 1928. Reprinted from *International Journal of Psycho-Analysis*, 10:103-111, 1929. Also in *Psychoanalytic Quarterly*, 36:1-11, 1967.

meaning, which may indeed be present in any case, becomes excessively pressing, the activity itself becomes subject to the defensive measures appropriate to its sexual significance.

In the second group it is not the meaning of the activity that is responsible for its inhibition; rather it is the possibility that the activity might result in successful achievements in reality. A person governed by the need for punishment must deny himself an action which the world or fate would reward with success. And finally the inhibition of an activity, apart from its meaning and its possible results, may be founded on a general impoverishment of the ego. An excessive absorption of energy at one particular point, e.g., as is the case in mourning, or an excesive expenditure of energy, e.g., in order to safeguard repressions or laboriously to maintain a labile equilibrium, render the ego weak and powerless for other tasks, and appear to leave it inhibited in relation to them.

Clearly, all these cases have an element in common: they relate to limitations of an ego function, which may thus be seen to constitute the essence of an inhibition; the first distinction between inhibition and symptom then becomes self-evident, for a symptom cannot be described as a process of the ego.

These introductory considerations lead us to the first fundamental problem of the book: to the question of the boundary between ego and id, of ascertaining the part which each system plays in every psychic act. The boundary in question is the boundary between instinctual and purposive processes, between being at the mercy of drives on the one hand and the choice of suitable means for particular purposes on the other; and this purposiveness need not even be objectively appropriate, but may have validity only in the psychic realm. It is the boundary between drivenness and control. This attempt at arriving at a distinction does not imply that one group of psychic phenomena is viewed as deriving from the id and another group as having been formed by the ego; the aim is rather to determine and specify the share of each in every phenomenon.

This is the point at which A. Adler came to grief. To him, all mental processes appeared to be explicable in terms of the ego alone; neurosis and character were merely purposive. But even a conception of a quite opposite nature, a possible demonological theory of mental life, as it were, does not meet the facts. Freud decisively rejects every attempt at a philosophical simplification of the problem in this or that direction; only exact empirical investigation which encompasses the structural details of every act can gradually bring us nearer its solution. The boundary between ego and id can be found only on the basis of abundant observations methodically interpreted.

It is not difficult to fit this problem into its place in the history of analytic science. The first feat of analysis was the discovery of the id. Ego psychology existed before the advent of psychoanalysis. The essentially new contribution made by analysis was the discovery of forces that affect the ego, limit it, and even determine it. The second of these modes of influence pointed the way to the next object of analytic inquiry, to analytic ego psychology which has investigated the share of the libido in building up the ego. And now we see the third task, that of dividing off empirically the spheres in which each of the two systems is active.

In this book Freud investigates three phenomena with regard to the share of the id and ego in each: anxiety, resistance, and— in less detail—regression. One may ask why these phenomena in particular are difficult to fit into place. The conditions are in each case very characteristic. If we consider anxiety as experience, then there can be no question that in regard to it we behave essentially passively; we are seized by anxiety, and therefore even the older theory postulated that the origin of anxiety has no connection whatsoever to the ego. On the other hand, anxiety also has a certain function which occasions a revision or amplification of the first, very simple statement about it. And again, resistance was originally ascribed only to the ego; here it was an observation, that of the repetition compulsion and the negative therapeutic reaction, which complicated the theory and made it necessary to recognize resistances of the id and of the ego ideal. Finally, with regard to regression, things are very similar to anxiety; the reversion of libido to old positions appears at first to be merely a legitimate reaction of the libido to privation; only closer observation reveals its function for the defensive tendencies of the ego. Alongside this group of problems a second one is developed in the course of the book; the results of the new investigation of anxiety supply the means for probing more deeply into the problem of the choice of neurosis.

The major part of the book is then devoted to the discussion of the problem of anxiety. Since its inception analysis attempted to explain the origin of anxiety and provided a theory that was founded on the simplest case open to observation. In the actual neuroses Freud was able to establish specific connection between the appearance of anxiety and disturbances of the normal course of the libido. This discovery led to the conclusion that in every case anxiety appears in the place of unsatisfied, undischarged libido, as a transformation product of libido, as it were—a conclusion that provided the starting point for a theory of anxiety.

In this book Freud now subjects the whole question to a renewed investigation with the help of the two carefully studied phobias of Little Hans and the Wolf-Man. The result of these considerations does not bear out the universal validity of the older conception. In both cases it is clear that anxiety did not arise as a direct result of repression, as a product of the transformation of the affects inhibited in their normal course by repression, but that it already preceded repression and in fact was the cause of repression. This anxiety, as far as its content is concerned, is in both cases castration anxiety. Little Hans had to fear the punishment of castration if he persisted in the further pursuit of his instinctual tendencies; his anxiety related to the real consequences of his action as threatened by the outer world. With the Russian it is a somewhat different matter; his instinctual tendencies were of a passive-homosexual nature and their fulfillment threatened the loss of his masculinity: castration anxiety as the external result of an instinctual gratification, or as an accompanying phenomenon belonging to the nature of the instinctual gratification itself; fear, that is to say, of the retribution of the outer world or of the instinctual claims dangerous to the integrity of the personality. The factor that both phobias have in common is that this anxiety appears on closer analysis to be the precondition and cause of repression, and not only its waste product. And this conclusion cannot be altered by the possibility that the anxiety might be increased by the process of repression.

Thus, the anxiety in the phobias is a reaction to a danger and a warning signal on the part of the ego, which makes it possible to ward off the instinctual danger. The earlier conception, which postulated an invariable relationship between anxiety and the damming up of the libido, still remains, but it is not yet clear how the two theories can be united in a single point of view. It is tempting to try and subsume the old conception under the new one by assuming that the damming up of libido is felt by the individual as a danger; but for the present we cannot get very far with this.

Freud comprehensively reviews everything that psychoanalytic investigations have been able to tell us about anxiety. The earliest theory explains the formation of anxiety in terms of the damming of libido. Next, anxiety is viewed as the reaction to danger, a conception not far removed from the everyday view of the subject; as a biological reaction, we may say, thus relieving psychology and putting the solution of the problem into the field of biology. But this still leaves unexplained the nature of the danger. Further, the work of psychoanalysis has shown us that anxiety affects are connected with a reproduction of the act of birth, an assumption on which Rank attempted to build a complete theory of neurosis and character. Anxiety also appears along with a reproduction of the reaction to danger, and the recent analysis of infantile phobias has led to the view that anxiety may originate in the ego as a provoked signal which is to interfere, by virtue of the pleasure principle, through the pain which it induces, with the course of the instinctual processes, and divert them away from a direction which might lead to an internal or external situation of danger. But these possibilities are not in any way to be considered as different forms of anxiety, in the sense that anxiety would have one origin in one case and a different one in another case. On the contrary, they are characteristics of anxiety which have a general validity, though at one time this and at another time that connection may be the more striking. We are now confronted with the task of working out a new point of view which will coordinate and include them all. This point of view is to be gained from a consideration and more precise conception of the idea of danger.

The observation of the first and simplest situations which may be considered as dangerous, say a small child being left alone, gives us a penetrating insight into the essence of danger; it is the condition of nongratification and with it the growth of tensions resulting from ungratified needs.

Danger appears to be—and this has a universal application —everything which allows the stimulus tensions to increase to such a degree that the psychic apparatus no longer feels able to cope with them. This view of the meaning of danger supplies a bridge to the first theory of anxiety, which represented anxiety as the immediate effect of an increase of stimulus tensions that had been denied appropriate discharge. The new, more thorough researches show how this effect may be forestalled by the ego and how the ego already reacts with anxiety to the possibility of such an increase in tension in the future—with an anxiety which through the mechanism of the pleasure principle henceforth influences the course of events and so prevents the actual occurrence of this possibility, thus acting as a warning signal. The first studies made during the earliest period dealt with the automatic appearance of anxiety; the present investigation shows how the ego can, as it were, discount the future situation by weakening it and through this capacity make effective action possible. We now also understand the Januslike quality of anxiety, which appears to flow like a torrent from the id and yet at the same time is the servant of the ego. In the immediate reaction to the increase of stimulus tension lies the share of the id; in the anticipation of the future and the reasonable action thereby made possible we have the share of the ego.

The relationship between anxiety as automatic phenomenon and anxiety as signal seems to be analogous to the relationship between the pleasure principle and the reality principle. Both can be reduced to the single conception of being the product of excessive stimulus tensions. It is essential to the reality principle that the ego should anticipate future pleasure-pain situations, thus enabling the mechanism of the pleasure principle to be set aside and the action influenced appropriately.

The phenomena of anxiety can now be differentiated according to two points of view. They may be considered according to their greater or smaller distance from the danger; the nearer the danger the more automatic the reaction, and the further from it the more active and impressive the role of the ego. Thus we may distinguish different kinds of anxiety according to their object, according to the content of the danger to which they react. If we succeed in correlating the particular forms of anxiety differentiated by their content with the particular types of neurosis, we would have gained a new vantage point for the problem of the choice of neurosis. At this point in our observations we are confronted with the subsidiary problem of applying our deeper insight into the essence of anxiety to the question of the choice of neurosis.

In the earlier psychoanalytic theory there were two concepts of which we could avail ourselves for this problem: the concept of fixation, the retention of old pleasure conditions or their regressive revival, and that of an internal divergence of development, of the unequal development of ego and libido.

Freud does not now reject these views, but complements them by adding a point of view which takes into account the fundamental importance of anxiety in setting in motion the process of neurotic repression. The essence of the neurotic now appears to be the retention or revival of past and obsolete conditions of anxiety. That the libido regressively cathects earlier positions is not yet enough to cause a neurosis; the conditions for a neurosis are present only when the ego scents in this cathexis a danger which, though almost entirely appropriate to the infantile attitude, is anachronistic in the case of the adult (i.e., when the ego has preserved its infantile condition of anxiety). It is easy to assume that various danger situations correspond to various stages of the development of the ego, and that the anxiety conditions may be retained as "petrifactions" of various stages of development; the question then arises whether these "anxiety fixations," if one may so call them, may be exclusively correlated to particular neuroses. Initially Freud distinguishes fear of loss of love, castration anxiety, and anxiety in face of the superego, and postulates the following relations: fear of loss of love is especially characteristic of women; it belongs to the genital phase and is characteristic of hysteria. Castration anxiety is typical of men; it belongs to the phallic phase and has an unmistakable relation to phobias. Finally, superego anxiety, essentially also man's affair, comes to the fore in the latency period and forms the center of the obsessional neurosis.

These considerations appear to open up a new approach to

the old and obstinate problem of choice of neurosis. But the correlation of forms of anxiety with stages of ego development and with types of neurosis does not yet exhaust all the possibilities contained in the new conceptions. We must still distinguish the various forms of defense and relate them to these correlations. The concepts of "defense" and "repression" have not yet been thoroughly differentiated. Freud proposes to reserve the old term "defense" for the more general idea; repression should refer only to a characteristic special case of defense. From the great number of other defense mechanisms, Freud singles out for detailed discussion two processes peculiar to the obsessional neurosis (undoing and isolation). On closer observation even regression no longer appears to be exclusively an automatism of the id, but reveals the participation of the defensive ego; so that this process too can be placed among the mechanisms of defense. The question now arises whether these forms of defense do not have a regular connection with particular disturbances, such as, for instance, might be presumed to exist between hysteria and repression. Our task, which arose from considering the nature of danger, has now been extended to the attempt to correlate specific phases of infantile development with specific danger situations, specific forms of anxiety, specific defense mechanisms, the peculiar nature of the counter-cathexis, and, finally, with a particular symptomatology, a type of neurosis. The problem of the choice of neurosis has thus been probed to a much greater depth; the missing links, so to speak, which were lacking between the first and last factors, have been supplied.

Yet, even the addition of these links into the chain of the genesis of neurosis cannot alter the fact that what is really specific in neurosis still eludes us. Neurosis is the automatization of anxiety reactions; but what is ultimately responsible for the fact that one group of people falls victim to this automatization, thus remaining in an important part of their being perpetually infantile, while the rest of mankind manages to escape it to a degree sufficient for practical purposes? What specifically causes the development of a neurosis?

Two attempts have been made to answer this question. One of them, Adler's, presupposes the inferiority of an organ; it is too simple to do justice to the phenomena; the other, Rank's, is so far removed from empirical experiences that it has little connection with real events. Psychoanalysis has no solution. Freud draws attention to three factors which tax man's mental life and thus represent potential dangers: a biological, a phylogenic, and a purely psychological one. We do not yet know what is specific in neurosis, we know only where it might be sought. The first has its roots in the long-drawn-out helplessness and dependence of the child; thence comes man's eternal need for love. To this must be added the peculiar and surprising fact of the twofold thrust of his developing sexuality; it twice imposes on human development a violent change of direction and thus contains possibilities of miscarrying. Finally, the purely psychological aspect of man's predisposition to neurosis must be sought in the differentiation of the mental apparatus, in the construction of institutions which represent the claims of the outer world, so that an external battlefield is extended to within man's mind. Each of these three factors makes extraordinary demands on man and hence points out the territory in which the characteristic causes of neurotic reaction must be sought.

Having discussed the problem of anxiety and applied the results gained to the choice of neurosis, Freud goes on to subject the phenomenon of resistance to a renewed investigation, with a view to correlating it with the structures of the mind. He distinguishes five forms of resistance. Two of them are directed against making the unconscious conscious (the repression resistance and the transference resistance) and proceed from the ego. A third one which also proceeds from the ego but works as a resistance against recovery is rooted in the secondary gain of the illness. The resistance stemming from the need for punishment, which likewise prevents recovery, is to be ascribed to the superego. Finally, the resistance due to the repetition compulsion must be described as an id resistance. Insight into the two last-named, discovered most recently, has greatly advanced analytic theory.

This reviewer is not entirely sure how the line is to be drawn between the transference resistance, which pertains to the ego, and the repetition-compulsion resistance, which must be ascribed to the id; both repeat instead of remembering. Perhaps the distinction between the two should be sought in a displacement of the accent; in the sense, say, that the transference resistance repeats in order not to have to remember (the main meaning: I will not remember), while the repetition-compulsion resistance rejects the memory in order that it may repeat (accent: I will repeat).

If we now cast a glance over Freud's revisions and corrections of the analytic concepts of anxiety and resistance, we realize that in both cases they take a different direction. With anxiety the earlier view, according to which the ego was, as it were, only the object, must be corrected in the sense that the ego is now seen to take a leading part. With resistance, on the contrary, the ego no longer appears to be the sole actor as in the earlier theoretic assumption. Both signify in the first place a complicating of analytic theory; yet there can be no doubt that only they complete the insights that can be gained from employing Freud's differentiation of the psychic apparatus introduced in *The Ego and the Id* (1923b).

A continuous transition now takes place between the functions of the ego and the id: on the one hand, a descent into the id by way of automatization, on the other hand, an ascent into the regions governed by the ego by way of *play*. The repetition compulsion can enter into the service of the ego. "The ego which experienced the trauma passively, now repeats it actively in a weakened version, in the hope of being able itself to direct its course. It is certain that children behave in this fashion towards every distressing impression they receive, by reproducing it in their play. In thus changing from passivity to activity they attempt to master their experiences psychically" (p. 167).

This book is almost too full of new problems and indications for new solutions; the lines cited point to the direction in which we can seek the solution of yet another question: how the process which is the opposite of automatization, the emergence of psychic phenomena into the ego and thus out of compulsion into freedom, takes place.

In this book Freud has opened new paths in every direction. Three questions, above all, appear to be of decisive importance for the problems which confront psychoanalysis. The first is the delineation of the contribution which each of the psychic structures makes to a particular psychic phenomenon. The second concerns the nature of the ego, which appears to have the capacity of anticipating the future and, by setting in motion a mechanism of the pleasure principle, forestalling and changing the course of events. This points the way to a causal explanation of the reasonable control exercised by the ego. Finally, the third issue concerns the question of the specific etiology of the various neuroses, a problem which can now be restated on a vastly extended basis: to the old concept of libido fixation are added the new ones of danger, its various contents, and different forms of reaction.

All who know psychoanalysis and work with its assumptions are conscious of the fact that what is essential to it is to be found not in a set of theoretical propositions stemming from a specific period of time, but in its method and its development. This development can perhaps be characterized by the statement that psychoanalysis continually divests our knowledge of the mind of its subjective features and distortions. Thus it indeed conforms to the development of scientific thought in general, which by an endlessly converging process overcomes its basic antinomy—that is to say, that its means of dealing with its subject are themselves part of this subject, and that therefore investigation of the mental is itself mental. The essence of psychoanalysis, as that of every science, lies in this method and in the inviolability of this law. The knowledge that psychoanalysis is an evolving science has once again been brought home to this reviewer by his study of *Inhibitions, Symptoms and Anxiety*.[1]

---

[1] This book was again reviewed in 1967 (see Ch. 19).

CHAPTER 5

The Principle of
Multiple Function

Observations on Overdetermination
(1930)

The immediate occasion of the following exposition is the new
concept of the theory of anxiety which Freud has given us in his
book *Inhibitions, Symptoms, and Anxiety* (1926a). In his earlier
concept, Freud assumed that anxiety erupted from the id as the
immediate result of the tensions of excessive, unsatisfied needs,
and that the ego was, as it were, a defenseless victim. The new
concept modifies this; Freud states that in a situation of danger,
of threat of future excessive, unsatisfied tension, the ego's
anticipation of this state may result in the experience of anxiety.
This anxiety is at the same time a signal which causes a readjustment of the organism for the purpose of avoiding the danger, for
example, by flight or by suitable defense measures, thus fulfilling
a biological function. This new concept naturally was not
intended to set aside or replace the earlier concept, nor did
Freud mean that anxiety might come about at one time in this
way and at the next time in the other way. Undoubtedly it
meant that in each concrete case both theories—anxiety sweeping over the ego, and anxiety formed as a danger signal by the

First published as "Das Prinzip der mehrfachen Funktion: Bemerkungen
zur Überdeterminierung," in *Internationale Zeitschrift für Psychoanalyse*,
16:286-300, 1930. It appeared in English in *Psychoanalytic Quarterly*,
5:45-62, 1936. The version published here is an entirely new translation
perpared by Dr. Muriel M. Gardiner.

ego—represent two sides of one actual phenomenon, described one time from the side of the id and the other time from the side of the ego. This twofold method of observation gives rise to the conjecture that this method might be applicable to all psychic phenomena, and that a twofold or perhaps, generally speaking, a manifold approach to each psychic act would be not only admissible but even required by psychoanalysis.

In the id, according to psychoanalysis, there is gathered together everything by which a person is driven, all inner tendencies which influence him, every *vis a tergo*. In the ego, on the other hand, reside all man's purposeful actions, his direction. When it is cold outdoors and I remember to take my gloves before leaving the house, this is a typical, everyday example of the way the ego works. In its division between a person's ego and id, psychoanalysis recognizes the two aspects of his being driven and his being directed. For the purpose of this discussion, I am deliberately ignoring the important question which of the two is primary and which is secondary. While for psychoanalysis it is important to know both phenomena, it is equally important to recognize that being driven is the primary one. In this study I shall leave aside the problems relating to this fact and take as my point of departure the statement that both phenomena, being driven and being directed, are dealt with in psychoanalysis, the former in the id and the latter in the ego. The id is, as it were, the continuation of that which the biologist knows as peripheral tendencies to regulate the living creature, and the ego represents the central control in the organism. The scheme of processes in the id would then be: instinct—instinctual expression; and in the ego: task—task solution, or attempt at solution. The ego is always faced with tasks and strives to find solutions for them. All human activity (activity not merely in the sense of motor action) has passed through the ego and is therefore an attempt to solve a task. Even in extreme cases of impulsive action, which at first glance appear to be guided purely by drives, the ego has played its part: the peremptory demand for satisfaction of the emerging drive was the task confronting the ego, the actions which followed were the means of solving this task.

If it is correct to call the scheme of processes in the ego attempts to solve a task, we must then ask: what are the tasks the ego must solve? Or rather: can we find meaningful groups and classify this great wealth of tasks with which the ego is actually confronted. Some of these tasks clearly come to the ego from without, or are caused by ego-alien forces, for example, the impulsive acts caused by drives. How many such possible tasks exist can be seen when one realizes how many alien forces the ego is faced with. First there is the id, the world of drives which approach the ego with their claims. There is the outer world, with its demands on the individual. Finally, there is, from a certain point of development on, in increasing measure, the superego with its commands and prohibitions. All make demands, and thereby present the ego with the task of finding ways and means of satisfying these demands—in other words, of attempting a solution. In what follows I shall discuss a fourth task, which the repetition compulsion presents to the ego. It is usual, in psychoanalysis, to consider the repetition compulsion as the deepest layer of the id. However, it seems to me useful to distinguish between the demands of those drives which require concrete satisfaction and the demands of the tendency to repeat and continue earlier experiences, even unpleasurable earlier experiences. It is perhaps better to say, I shall distinguish between these two sides of instinctive force, without intending thereby to examine the position of the repetition compulsion. If in this context I am granted the liberty of speaking of the repetition compulsion as of a separate force, we see that the ego is confronted with concrete tasks stemming from four different sides outside itself: the outer world, the repetition compulsion, the id, and the superego.

But this passive role does not exhaust the work of the ego. The ego does not simply accept orders and carry them out. Rather, it generates an activity of its own toward the outer world as well as toward the other forces in the individual himself. This activity of the ego is characterized by an attempt to assert itself, to succeed, and to assimilate in its organic development the outer world as well as the ego-alien forces in the individual. This activity of the ego was first observed when it was directed toward the outer world. But it seems that, from the beginning, the ego also makes efforts to bring its instinctive life under its central guidance. This follows from the fact that the ego experiences every excessive increase of drives, even those that do not carry with them any threatening consequences from without, as a danger, the danger that the ego's organization will be submerged, destroyed. The ego evidently takes an active stand toward its instinctive life; it has a tendency to master it, or rather to assimilate it into its organization. When Freud (1920a) introduced the concept of the repetition compulsion, he stressed the fact that the ego maintains a similar stand toward the repetition compulsion and uses the repetitions that are thrust upon it by this deepest psychic trend to master threatening experiences. In the actual occurrence of repetitions, it is not at all easy to determine to what extent the ego must submit to a force from "behind," and to what extent it uses this force as a means of control. These two sides of the actual repetition experience can be separated only in the abstract. That there is inherent in the ego a similar tendency toward the superego would be easy to illustrate through examples.

The function of the ego is, accordingly, not limited to attempts to solve tasks imposed from without, namely, by the repetition compulsion, the id, the superego, and the outer world. On the contrary, the ego itself confronts these four regions with its own concrete tasks: to subdue them, or rather, actively to assimilate them into its own organization. So there are eight tasks which the ego must attempt to solve; four of them imposed upon the ego, and the other four imposed by the ego itself. Or rather there are eight groups of tasks, since each task I have mentioned contains a whole group of problems. For example, in the task of satisfying drives imposed by the id, there are as many problems as there are drives demanding satisfaction.

Accordingly, the processes in the ego can be described as definite attempts at a solution; man's ego is characterized by a number of specific methods of solution.

So it would seem that there is a general principle which directs our psychic life, which we might call *the principle of multiple function*. According to this principle, every attempt to solve a task is necessarily, at the same time, an attempt to solve other tasks, even if incompletely. Every psychic act can and must be understood as an attempt to solve simultaneously all eight tasks, although the ego may at certain times succeed better in its attempted solution of one particular task than of another.

In considering this principle, we are at once struck by the fact that it is completely impossible for the attempted solution to be equally successful at one stroke in regard to all eight tasks, since these are inconsistent with each other. Above all, in the first group, the tasks imposed upon the ego contradict those tasks that the ego itself imposes. For example, gratification of drives contradicts the ego's mastering of drives; obeying the commands of the superego contradicts the ego's conquest of the superego through assimilation. Then there will usually be other antitheses among the ego's tasks, for example, between those imposed by the id and those imposed by the outer world or by the superego. Finally, even within a single group of tasks opposition is still possible, for instance, when opposing drives are seeking satisfaction, or opposing superego commands appear in a conflict of conscience, or antagonistic claims of the no less demanding outer world make themselves felt. The whole body of tasks, whose solution the ego is always attempting afresh, has three layers of contradictions; complete simultaneous solution of these eight tasks is impossible. From this follows the compromise character of every psychic act; psychoanalysis found this first in relation to the neurotic symptom, which is conceived of as a compromise between drive and defense against drive; but it would seem that the compromise character in this more general sense must hold true for every psychic act. This principle may even provide a possible gateway to the understanding of the eternal contradictions and dissatisfactions which, quite apart from neurosis, form the common lot of mankind.

As it is quite impossible for any one act to be equally successful in solving all tasks, and inevitable, according to the principle of multiple function, that the attempt should meet with greater success with one task than with another, we are able to understand the exceptional position of those psychic acts which achieve a relatively far-reaching solution. This is the case, first and foremost, in the sexual act when it combines complete physical, sensual satisfaction with happy feelings of love. Therein lies fulfillment of instinctual needs, of the most obscure repetition drive, satisfaction of the superego's demands, of the claims of reality, as well as the self-discovery and verification of one's ego in the face of all these realities. It would seem that the incomparable significance of the act of love in the household of the psyche is to be understood in the circumstance that it comes closest to being a complete and equable solution of the ego's contradictory tasks.

If, therefore, every psychic act is somehow, even though incompletely, an attempt to solve all the tasks which exist permanently in the ego, this is possible only because every psychic act has a multiple meaning. If, let us say, working on a machine, which is first of all an attempt to solve the task of adjusting to the outer world, is at the same time, even if only partially, an instinctual gratification, this is possible only because this work on the machine has another meaning as well. In other words: multiple meaning corresponds to multiple function.

Here we have met with one of the oldest, most familiar, and most fundamental concepts of psychoanalysis, overdetermination, a concept which appears to distinguish psychoanalysis most sharply from other schools of psychology. As a consequence of empirical impressions, overdetermination seemed at first to be something accidental, existing in greater or less diversity or perhaps at times not at all. When overdetermination was observed, the explanation seems to have been that one psychic tendency alone did not have the power to achieve a psychic effect, and that a combination of several such tendencies would be necessary to pass the threshold of psychic effectiveness. Clearly, this idea is analogous to some older concepts of earlier neurology. There is, without doubt, a logical difficulty inherent in this concept of overdetermination: a complete determination is possible; natural science knows the concept of necessary and sufficient causes; and as long as one remains on the ground of natural science it is not easy to understand in what way an occurrence can be determined more than sufficiently. In mathematics, the concept of overdetermination is actually nonsense. A triangle is adequately determined by three determining components. By four, it would be overdetermined, something altogether impossible. Furthermore, overdetermination encounters a practical difficulty in psychoanalysis: in the psychoanalytic method of interpretation the introduction of the concept of overdetermination offers neither a guideline nor a boundary for the required overinterpretations. Overdetermination is, as it were, open to infinity. No principle of psychoanalytic interpretation can give any guidelines as to how far overdetermination extends or when it should be considered exhausted.

The principle of multiple function may be able to resolve all these difficulties. It contains no logical problems, for it does not maintain that a psychic act is still further determined beyond its complete determination; it says only that such an act must have multiple meaning; that is, even if it is initiated as an attempt to solve one task, it must at the same time in one way or another be an attempt to solve the other concrete tasks. The entire phenomenon of the multiple function and the multiple meaning of every psychic act is then no longer analogous to older neurological conceptions pertaining to the summation of stimuli and threshold values; rather, it is, in accord with more recent assumptions of neurology and biology, to be understood as an expression of the total function of the organism. Since the organism always reacts in its entirety, and all these tasks are constantly alive within it, every attempt to solve a task must be codetermined, changed, set right, through the presence and effectiveness of the others, so that it will serve, even if incompletely, as an attempt to solve all these tasks, and thereby essentially maintain its multiple meaning. It is no longer an accident, which may be present or absent in a particular case; it is inherent in and follows from the structure of the psychic organism itself. Finally, it gives us certain guidelines for the psychoanalytic principles of interpretation. The multiple meaning of a psychic act is obviously exhausted when it has been interpreted as an attempt to solve all eight tasks, or, more correctly, the tasks of all eight groups. The multiple meaning has naturally not ceased to be infinite, but certain directions are traced out into this infinity. It is a matter of course that the principle of multiple function does not touch upon or go into the valence attributed to each of these meanings.

The principle of multiple function admits of a number of applications, a few of which will be sketched here. First of all, it gives us an understanding of the pansexuality with which psychoanalysis has been reproached, meaning the tendency of psychoanalysis to seek a sexual meaning in everything, even when a realistic interpretation provides a conclusive meaning. Since multiple function and therefore multiple meaning apply to every psychic act, and one of these functions and meanings concerns the gratification of instincts, and since man's instinctive life is never for a moment silenced or paralyzed, obviously every act of man, including all his purposeful actions directed toward reality, must also yield to overinterpretation in regard to its content of instinctual satisfaction. Furthermore, as is well known, it is a distinctive feature of psychoanalysis that it attributes a special role to this side of the meanings (instinctual gratification) and usually regards this as the motor power behind everything else. This second side of psychoanalysis, along with such matters as the question of origin, of what is primary, will not be considered here. The reason for why it is admissible and necessary to explain the sexual content of every phenomenon can be deduced from the principle of multiple function.

This principle also explains why sexuality is a modeling factor of character development. Character is largely determined by the specific methods of solving problems, and these methods are peculiar to the individual and remain relatively constant. According to the principle of multiple function, these methods of problem solving must also provide for the gratification of the individual's dominant drives. If the instinctual life is considered the earliest and dynamically most powerful part of the total personality, then obviously the dominant drives will play a decisive role in the individual's perferred methods of problem solving, that is, his instinctual life will be a guiding principle for his character development. This will be taken up briefly later, in connection with the problem of a psychoanalytic characterology.

An individual's particular conditions for love and for work are an expression of the principle of multiple function. These conditions mean that a person succeeds in loving or working— that is, in solving the tasks relating to love or work—only when certain other strong drives are satisfied at the same time. From this standpoint, we can also obtain simple descriptions of such processes as countercathexis, reaction formation, sublimation. Sublimations, for example, can be described as successful solutions of the task of adaptation to, or mastering of, the outer world, while at the same time, because of another inherent meaning, they represent the successful gratification of some stronger drives.

By means of this principle it is also easy to understand that the orgastic experience of a psychically rich, differentiated person can be of quite another quality and incomparably more intense than that of a more shallow, impoverished person. The person who has within him a rich, diversified system of tasks will in the experience of orgasm in a happy love relationship harmonize many significant meanings; the act can be a simultaneous solution to many different tasks. Altogether it would seem, seen from the standpoint of this principle, that psychoanalysis is a kind of polyphonic theory of psychic life, in which every act is a chord, either consonant or dissonant.[1]

The principle throws a certain light especially on the three problems of neurosis, character, and form. In psychoanalysis, neurosis was originally understood as a compromise between two trends. This would mean that neurosis is determined by at least two functions and meanings. Generalizing, one may say that neurosis, like all other psychic phenomena, is an attempt to solve simultaneously all the ego's various problems, and accordingly neurosis has an abundance of meanings. This corresponds to the current psychoanalytic concept of neurosis. A number of theories of neurosis have been formed, on a psychoanalytic basis, or partially deviating from this. The first and simplest is Adler's, which sees in neurosis the solution of only one of the eight tasks, namely, that of mastering the outer world.[2] As there are eight tasks, obviously eight such theories are possible, each of which reflects only one side of the neurosis. Somewhat richer are the

[1] Accordingly, this principle includes those phenomena which must be attributed to "the synthetic function of the ego." What impresses one as the special synthesizing function is that every act of the ego has, characteristically, a multiple function.

[2] This is of course not the only difference between psychoanalysis and individual psychology. For, quite aside from the fact that psychoanalysis takes account of multiple motivation, it does not find these meanings of equal importance, but considers instinctual life as primary, whereas individual psychology regards directedness as primary, and instinctual life as an expression of directedness. This question of ontological primacy has been, as mentioned earlier, disregarded in this paper. It forms the central point of Ch. 21.

theories which rest neurosis on two pillars, and see in it the simultaneous fulfillment of two tasks, for example, instinctual gratification and punishment. Simple reflection shows that twenty-eight such theories are possible, if one regards these aspects as equal in neurosis. The possibilities can be further enriched if one side is subordinated to the other "for the sake of" the other, for instance, punishment for the sake of instinctual satisfaction (this last formula, incidentally, corresponds to Alexander's [1929] theory). The opposite subordination is, of course, also conceivable. If one now proceeds to the possible theories of neurosis which see in neurosis the simultaneous solution of three or more tasks, and considers the possibilities of subordinating one to another, the result, as one can figure out in an idle hour, is that the number of possible theories of neurosis, based on psychoanalytic grounds, reaches into the tens of thousands. The value of these concepts, such as Alexander's especially, which certainly contains a very significant piece of reality, is thereby not even remotely questioned. And yet it is to be hoped that we will not be burdened with all these theories. The principle of multiple function includes them all, in principle, and leaves the distribution of valences and the various subordinations to individual research, or to the special theory of neurosis.

One can also make certain statements about the possibilities of a psychoanalytic theory of character. A person's character, as already mentioned, is determined by the specific methods of task solution in typical situations which an individual adheres to continuously, that is, by the nature of the attempts at solution chosen by him. Expressed in this way, it would seem for the moment as though the character had no immediate connection with instinctual life or with the superego, because these determine groups of tasks according to their content, but do not determine the specific methods of solution, which, in the face of these tasks, the ego chooses. In the face of every instinctual attitude, all possible attempts at solution, to help toward its gratification, would be conceivable, and accordingly all possible character types. This is, however, contrary to the experience of psychoanalysis, according to which certain instinctual constitutions are matched with certain character types, not without exception, but with undeniable frequency. At this point, the principle of multiple function steps in. In consequence of this principle, the specific methods of solution for the various tasks of the ego must always be so chosen that, no matter what the immediate goal of solution may be, they will at the same time bring instinctual gratification. That means, however, considering the dynamic power of human intellectual life, that the drives, from among all possible attempts at solution, play the decisive role, so that especially those attempts at solution will be preferred and maintained which, according to their content, at the same time also gratify the dominant drives.

This relationship between a preferred attempt at a solution of a task and instinctual life can be illustrated by two simple examples. The first is the relationship between oral instincts and identification, familiar to psychoanalysis primarily through Abraham's writings. Identification is an attempt to solve tasks in a certain problem situation. It can be designated a character trait, when an individual, in a certain combination of instincts, superego demands, and difficulties with the outer world, regularly finds his way out through identification, as his specific method of solution in a diversity of problem situations. Now we know that this tendency toward identification is developed particularly in the oral character, and we immediately understand this factual connection on the basis of what has already been said. Identification as a method of solution will be chosen, from among the various methods possible in the same situation of diverse tasks, by individuals with strong oral drives. This is because, along with everything else for which it is an attempt at solution, identification satisfies these oral drives, owing to its meaning of incorporation. In this case, then, the oral instinctual disposition operates selectively among the various methods of solution, in that those which gratify the oral wishes are always the ones realized. There appears to be a similar relationship between the instinctual disposition to passive homosexuality and paranoid projection as a method of solution. Every specific method of solving a conflict situation which a person experiences as coming from without, and in which he submits passively to these outer forces, is an attempt to solve certain tasks; it is a gratification of love and hate relationships and a defense reaction, and more besides. Furthermore, this attempt at solution (projection) is itself a satisfaction of passive-homosexual drives. Perhaps this explains why this mechanism (i.e., the attempt at solution) of paranoid projection occurs exclusively or at least primarily in the case of a passive-homosexual drive disposition; that is to say, perhaps the present purely empirical association between homosexuality and paranoia thus becomes understandable.[3]

Let us now, after these examples, return to psychoanalytic characterology. We have seen that the justification for setting up character types according to the dominance of drives—to speak, for example, of an anal, oral, or genital character—rests on the fact that the preferred methods of solving tasks, according to the principle of multiple function, must also satisfy the dominant drives, and that the individual with a markedly dominant drive tends to prefer one particular method of solution. It is necessary here to emphasize the word "tends," since, owing to the enormous complexity of the tasks operating each time in the ego, the connection naturally does not hold true without exception. With an oral character, we find of course other methods of solution besides identification; the connection between the dominant drive and preferred methods of solution is simply a matter of statistical frequency. The consequence, for a future psychoanalytic theory of character, is that it cannot be a linear theory but must be at least two-dimensional according to the dominant drive and specific methods of solution, between which there will exist certain statistical connections.

The above examples, in which an attempt at solution, in other words a certain element of form in psychic life, is connected with drive dominance, that is, with content, lead us finally to the third phenomenon which our principle opens up, the problem of form. Yet this problem is not easily accessible from the psychoanalytic approach, which deals specifically with the psychology of content. However, the principle of multiple function shows us that the forms of reactions in the ego can be in no way separated from content, for they must be so constituted that, due to their nature, they are at the same time an attempt to

---

[3] These remarks are valid for male paranoids, and should not be simply transferred to the apparently much more complicated conditions in the case of women.

solve the content problem, for instance, gratification of drives. Thus in one of the examples given, settling certain conflicts through their projection, the specific paranoid mechanism, is undoubtedly a matter of form in psychic life, and yet this form is not independent of content (in this example, instinctual life), because this form is chosen in the case of a certain configuration of drives which can be satisfied through it, through its meaning. So one may say that, according to the principle of multiple function, the content of psychic life—above all, of instinctual life—is important in the choice of forms of working out, forms of adjusting, forms of solution, in short, form itself. One sees what possibilities there are of treating form problems in psychoanalysis. It goes without saying that this by no means exhausts the problem of form in psychic life.

The principle of multiple function may have a part to play in social psychology as well. We draw upon this principle to study multiple functions of typical social phenomena, for example, a historical movement in the light of its economic side (adaptation to the outer world or mastery of the outer world), in regard to satisfaction of drives, of collective ideals, etc.

Finally, we may expect to see this principle at work in dream life. The dream is the area in which overdetermination was originally discovered. Moreover, the general character of the dream remains a reduction of psychic experience in regard to its content (relaxation of the superego, relaxation of the tasks of the ego), as well as in regard to its methods of working (substitution of working methods of the conscious, in the attempt to solve, by methods of the unconscious), and, finally, in a temporal sense (withdrawal of the present in favor of the past). Considering all these phenomena of reduction, or regression, which signify an alteration of tasks and a reversion in the specific methods of solution from the working method of the conscious to that of the unconscious, the phenomena of dreams can also be described by the principle of multiple function. Everything that occurs in a dream then also appears understandable in eightfold function, or in eight groups of meanings. The distinguishing characteristic of the dream rests only in the change, the displacement of the tasks, and the reversion in its methods of working.

Finally, we may ask: what are the various ways in which

development in psychic life takes place, or any change to which man is subject, and what kinds of change we can distinguish? As every psychic act is, at one and the same time, an attempt to solve various tasks, the psychic act necessarily changes when the tasks change. Development or change takes place on the basis of development or change in instinctual life, in the outer world, or in the superego. So the biologically determined development of instinctual life in puberty will present the ego with tasks other than those of prepuberty, and in this way alter all the processes in the ego, all attempts at solution. Changes in the outer world constantly present the individual with altered tasks. And, finally, we can also speak of a development of the superego. The core of this superego originates as an attempt to solve a situation of conflict, and, by gradually becoming more and more independent, the superego itself develops. All these possibilities concern cases in which a change comes about because the tasks change according to their content. They can be extended to include the possibility that those tasks actively initiated by the ego itself also develop as regards their content. Furthermore, the methods of solution develop in two ways: from the primitive-archaic to other methods, as, let us say, from the way of working of the unconscious to that of the conscious, or from the magical thinking and experiencing of a certain childlike stage to the thinking of an adult; and secondly, the development of the methods of solution peculiar to the individual, which constitutes character development or ego development in the narrower sense. Finally, as a further reason for development, there is the fact that every attempt at solution by the ego carries with it the seeds of its own destruction, for no sooner is it begun than it ceases to be a solution. For through every act the world and all its elements are altered; for example, among other changes, the outer world is generally altered, and something is changed in the drives through the gratification or frustration this act contains, etc. To give a rough example, someone who takes up a profession as an attempt to solve a combination of claims from the outer world, urgings of the instincts, demands of the superego, and pressures of the repetition compulsion, and also as an attempt to master all these forces, has, through this new excercise of his profession, created a new piece of reality. Now a new outer world exists, which presents its claims, and which the ego intends to master. The wishes pressing forward from the instincts must be to some extent changed or displaced in this new situation; certain demands of the superego may perhaps make way for others to appear, and so forth. In brief, through the attempt at solution itself, everything is altered, so that now new tasks confront the ego, and the attempt at solution in reality is such no longer. So, along with the development or change of content of the various task-directing forces, such as those of the instinctual life, and along with the development of the methods of solution, we may regard the characteristic inherent in every attempt at solution, after it has once been set in motion, to be such no longer, as a basis for psychic development.

We see, accordingly, that from psychoanalysis there emerges an aspect of the enormous multiplicity of motivations and meanings of psychic occurrences. Freud, who from the beginning, in contrast to the other psychological schools, almost all of which were oriented toward ego psychology, has founded his psychoanalytic outlook on the importance of the *vis a tergo* and the dependences of the ego, has nevertheless warned against exaggerating this point of view, and has also clearly rejected a demonological theory of psychic life (1916-17). Because of the multiplicity of these, it is perhaps fitting to be on one's guard against premature simplification.

The concepts id, ego, and superego are not used in this paper in the sense of completely distinct parts of the personality. One sees in applying the principle discussed here that these forces are rather to be understood as different sides which can be demonstrated in every psychic act of the well-developed human being. Each individual act or fantasy has its ego side, its id side, its superego side, and a side answerable to the repetition compulsion; according to this principle, an eightfold aspect can be demonstrated.

Finally, let us add a few observations of an anthropological nature. It seems to us as though these three elements of psychoanalysis, or from our standpoint phases of psychic life, would also correspond to stages of organic life. Instinctual pressure perhaps belongs to all organic life. The ego—or something morphologically comparable—comes into being when the organism develops a central control, which apparently occurs at the time of the separation of the individual from collective vegetation, that is, the individuation in the animal kingdom—perhaps, however, not until the central nervous system appears. The superego is the domain of the human being. It is the element by which man for a second time—that is, in addition to central control—goes beyond himself, taking himself as an object, whether acting in a punishing, aggressive way, or lovingly caring, or, finally, being disinterestedly objective, as in self-observation and the ability to depart from his own point of view. Here also belongs the ability to see a garden as a garden, regardless of the place from which one observes it at the moment. Here belongs the faculty of not only experiencing the world around one in its momentary relationship to one's drives and interests, but also of recognizing its existence apart from one's own ego, as something outliving the ego. In this sense, it is a function of the superego when a human being—the only living creature to do so—makes his testament. The proposition that it is the superego which distinguishes the nature of man from that of animals agrees with everything we know from animal psychology about the difference between man and animal (which cannot be discussed in detail here). There is always the possibility of surmounting the drives and interests hidden in a given situation, of going beyond them in one's thinking, experiencing and acting, that is, of placing oneself above them in the superego.

Then it would seem that Freud's determination of factors is of importance for all the steps of organic life: organic life in general, the central control of the organism after the individuation of organic life, and finally the ability of man to reach beyond himself. Perhaps, corresponding to the principle of multiple function in the psychology of man, there is a similar principle in the animal kingdom. Only, because in this case the tasks imposed are less rich, the principle functions with much less multiplicity.

CHAPTER 6

The Psychoanalytic Theory
of Play

(1932)

Children's play has been the subject of scientific discussion by
psychologists of various schools of thought. Child psychology, as
it is taught in our universities, has occupied itself with the
remarkable phenomenon that a considerable part of a growing
child's day is taken up with play and has undertaken to make
various contributions to the interpretation of this phenomenon.
It will now be our endeavor to see what psychoanalysis has to
contribute to the question of children's play.

Comparing the literature of academic psychology with the
more casual psychoanalytic publications dealing with this subject, it will immediately be noticed that each draws attention to
a different group of games. Academic psychology studies chiefly
what one might designate "official" games of children—games
which are typical and played by all children. In the psychoanalytic literature, on the contrary, interest is chiefly centered
on games of a different type—those of a more individual nature,
to which the child clings for a certain time only. Naturally, it
cannot be said that academic psychology is not interested in the

First published as "Die psychoanalytische Theorie des Spieles," *Zeitschrift
für psychoanalytische Pädagogik,* 6:184-194, 1932; reprinted in *Almanach
der Psychoanalyse,* 152-171, 1933. The paper was revised by the author for the
English translation, which was prepared by Sara A. Bonnett. Reprinted from
Psychoanalytic Quarterly, 2:208-224, 1933, with some reediting by Dr. Muriel
M. Gardiner.

individual games or that psychoanalysis is not concerned with the traditional, typical ones; but it is hardly possible to overlook the fact that the two place the stress differently.

The psychoanalytic theory of play is not able to supply a unitary explanation for the phenomenon called "play," by which all games and all manifestations arising from them can be interpreted. On the contrary, here, as is usually the case in psychoanalysis, a single phenomenon may have various meanings, may perform various functions and cannot be explained by a single general interpretation: in short, as we say in psychoanalysis, the phenomenon has a number of determinants. In the following discussion, we propose to study intensively those elements in the psychoanalytic play theory which are most characteristically psychoanalytic.

First of all, it may be stated of children's games that they elaborate material which has been experienced by the child. This material may then, in the child's playing, be expressed in various ways. The incident experienced in reality may be given a different arrangement in play, but at all events the material is gathered from experience. For example, we see the child playing mother with a doll, or playfully representing father and mother with another child, or teacher and pupil, or policeman and robber, or the like. The material which becomes elaborated is at times derived from an experience such as an observed situation involving mother and father, teacher and pupil, and so on. Hence, the pleasure principle is our first guide to the study of psychic phenomena. We consider a manifestation comprehensible when we see that it results in a gratification of a desire for pleasure. This is without doubt frequently the case in children's play. In the game with the doll, it is difficult not to recognize the nature of the gratification in the situation, namely, the child's wish to be a mother herself—a special case of a general principle found in many other games, the desire to be big and grown up. If the child, through experience, has once become acquainted with the happy situation of an automobile ride, or if his imagination has been stimulated by stories about it—if he then wishes to ride and realizes this wish in a game, we can immediately comprehend the meaning of the game. There is to be sure no explanation of why these particular wishes should find their materialization in a game; but the phenomenon is, at all events, aligned in the field of fantasy gratifications familiar to us from other sources, and its content, at least, is understandable.

These few examples indicate that in the playing of children, numerous gratifications of the desire for pleasure are demonstrable; that frequently, or perhaps even always, play deals with some portion of a pleasurable situation, or with some of the determinants of its realization; that, in fact, much of children's play is a manifestation of the pleasure principle.

Now, however, a difficulty arises. Though on the one hand, it is evident that the pleasure principle will explain many circumstances in children's play, yet, on the other hand, one cannot help realizing that the child, in playing, with extraordinary frequency reproduces or at least proceeds from situations which were in actual experience devoid of pleasure. As a simple illustration: a child was taken to a dentist who had previously inflicted great pain on the child. He therefore felt very apprehensive. According to the pleasure principle, we should offhand suppose that the highly disagreeable situation, once it was fortunately in the past, would have been set aside, and that the child would be only too glad to let the matter drop. The pleasure principle hardly prepares us to expect the return of this situation in play. Nevertheless, in reality, this often occurs. The child at home on the following day will play dentist, utilizing a doll or a conveniently available sister or brother. In this way, it is often precisely the highly unpleasurable situation which becomes material or, at any rate, a starting point for a subsequent game, which as a rule is played for a time and then gradually abandoned. Guided by the pleasure principle—which, for many other reasons, we confidently accept as the valid principle of psychic life—we arrive at a point which seems to contradict this principle, and we must ask how this can be.

A theory of Karl Bühler, referring not exactly to this situation, but to a similar one, may be applicable here. According to Bühler, play cannot be explained by the idea of pleasurable gratification. But play is pleasurable and consequently, according to Bühler's theory, is connected with a form of pleasure other than the pleasure of gratification. Bühler speaks of the "functional pleasure," i.e., of the pleasure experienced in pure performance without regard to the success of the activity. Gratification pleasure represents pleasure in the *success* of an action, while functional pleasure represents the joy in the activity itself. The most vivid example of functional pleasure is the playing of children. In play, we find joy in all the activities and functions involved in the development of the child. Play activities have for a time the teleological significance of an exercise preparatory for future functions, a belief formerly entertained by philosophers, for example, by Groos (1922);[1] but the functional pleasure represents the experimental evidence that such preparation does take place.

Within the confines of this paper, it is not possible to discuss this theory exhaustively, and only a few references to it can be made here. The fact that pleasure can be derived from performance, independently of its success, meets with no doubt. But in such pleasure two components are to be differentiated. One component may again be called gratification pleasure, if in the activity itself a decided gratification is embodied,[2] for example, in the activity of playing at being the parents, the gratification of being big and grown up oneself, and of being father or mother; a

---

[1] Without denying the teleological function of most games as preparation, there are indications that there are games in which a preparation cannot be discovered; moreover, there are some which distinctly make for unpreparedness. To these latter, for example, belongs the game of playing baby. It sometimes happens that a child, in about its third year, plays at being a baby again and acts out a playful helplessness and inability to speak. This game is certainly not a constant occurrence, but, on the other hand, it is not so infrequent that it can be overlooked. It makes its appearance occasionally after the birth of a younger sister or brother. In this case, the purport of the game is obviously a wish fulfillment. The child wants to participate again in the advantages which the newborn child enjoys either in reality or in his eyes. The game is sometimes associated with the onset of enuresis. Without going into the details of such a manifestation, it is at least an example of the fact that all games do not necessarily signify a preparation.

[2] The fatal equivocation inherent in the word "gratification" *(Befriedigung)* is inconvenient in this connection. On the one hand, it means "to attain peace" or "to come to rest," on the other, in a broader sense of every pleasurable realization—for example, in the expression "gratification in work." Psychoanalysis uses the word in the broader sense throughout. It has, however, nothing to do with the metapsychological question of whether gratification in the last analysis represents the equalizing of tension in the psychic system—as was formerly assumed—or whether it represents an excitation process, as has been supposed since the publication of Freud's paper "The Economic Principle in Masochism" (1924d).

second component independent of this might well represent the functional pleasure in its true sense. The existence of such a functional pleasure may be granted without reservation. There is no reason for doubting its existence, and it may play a role, particularly during the period of growth of the organism—that is to say, in childhood.

Although we grant the existence of this sort of pleasure, nevertheless functional pleasure does not seem to us sufficient to explain the above-mentioned games in which the material was a disagreeable experience; and specifically, it seems insufficient on the following grounds: functional pleasure is purely formal and, from its very definition, not dependent on the circumstances in which it was experienced. But the content of play is manifestly not a matter of indifference. Again and again one sees that the child suddenly but very definitely chooses a particular game which later on he will abandon. There is no justification for the assumption that the child's playing the game at this particular time is a coincidence and requires no further explanation. Why, to return to our illustration, on the day following the child's experience with the dentist, which threw him out of equilibrium, is the game of dentist played? Why does this game persist for, let us say, a fortnight, and why does it then cease completely?

If this game could be so completely explained by the idea of functional pleasure that there was nothing to be added, then one theme would be interchangeable with another, and the content of one game replaceable by another. If this were the case, the child in our illustration would be ready, instead of playing "dentist," to play any other game bearing some similarity to this game in respect of the function involved. But this interchangeability of content does not exist. Indeed, a particular game is given preference at a particular time. The content is not a matter of indifference and is not interchangeable. Therefore a theory of formal pleasure is not sufficient to give us a thorough understanding of phenomena which are also quite definite with respect to content.

The games of the type mentioned above have, in addition, a characteristic course which can likewise not be explained by the assumption of a functional pleasure. Thus, to go back to our illustration, the child plays at being a dentist repeatedly and very enthusiastically for several days; then the theme appears more and more rarely, is accompanied by less affect, and finally disappears; if it reappears occasionally, this has, generally speaking, certain definite precipitating causes. The course of the game's intensity and affective content produces the impression that here an affect is being discharged, or better, that an affective residue, left over from the experience itself, is gradually being assimilated.

This brings us to the Freudian theory of children's play and its principal function in the child's life. Before I present this theory, I must briefly digress into one chapter of relevant psychoanalytic theory: the repetition compulsion. In the life of human beings there are repetitions of many kinds. It happens quite often that an individual repeatedly does the same thing, or that, over and over again, he lives through the same experience. Not all repetitions occurring in human life but only a quite definite group of them can be regarded as manifestations of the repetition compulsion, according to the psychoanalytic meaning of the term. When a person creates the same situation over and over because he is seeking gratification which he never finds (the Don Juan type), the fact that he is "repeating" is obvious. Such a repetition is not to be explained by the repetition compulsion, however, but rather by the constant striving for a particular goal and by the frustration of each attempt to attain it. A different kind of repetition may be observed in the constantly renewed efforts toward accomplishment made by a severely inhibited individual. Here also the impression of repetition arises, yet this phenomenon is also explicable through its psychic setting, and the repetition compulsion need not be invoked as an explanation. Another type of repetition arises through mental rigidity and impoverishment—a type which appears, for example, in senile dementia. One could probably thus differentiate numerous other types of repetition in psychic life, of which each has its individual explanation but which nevertheless do not involve the specific repetition process which psychoanalysis regards as due to the "repetition compulsion."

By this repetition compulsion proper we understand the process described as follows: the individual has been through a specific experience, which was too difficult or too overwhelming for him to assimilate immediately. This unabsorbed, or incompletely absorbed experience weighs heavily upon his psychic organization and calls for a new effort at coping and for a reexperience. This experience has two aspects. Considered as a process of the id, that is, insofar as the individual is passive and lives in accordance with forces within himself, it is a compulsion which influences him and drives to reexperience. This process has an active side as well; considered as a process of the ego, it represents at the same time the ego's attempt to assimilate the experience more completely through renewing and thereby gaining the mastery over it. The repetition compulsion, therefore, is Janus-faced. In one way, it is a fate to which we are subjected, in another way, an active attempt to master this fate. The whole process is perhaps best compared—if the comparison is permissible—to the rumination of certain animals. The morsel is too large to be digested at one time and the undigested meal remains in the stomach. It must be chewed again if it is to be digested. This process, too, if one is willing to hazard carrying the comparison so far, has two sides: the pressure of the undigested meal is, so to speak, the passive, id component; and digestion by the act of chewing the cud, the ego component of the process. The point at which our analogy finally forsakes us is this: to chew the cud once or several times (in the organic example) is sufficient, while in the repetition compulsion a very frequently repeated chewing occurs, in one case more frequently, in another less frequently; and in some cases, as we shall see, assimilation is never really complete in spite of persistent rumination.

The two aspects of the repetition compulsion, its Janus face, may also be described in another way. During the repetition, the individual passes over from passivity to activity and in this manner psychically masters the impressions which were originally received in a merely passive way. Freud has repeatedly described this feature of the repetition compulsion. Thus he says (1926a, p. 167):

> The ego, which experienced the trauma passively, now repeats it actively in a weakened version, in the hope of

being able itself to direct its course. It is certain that children behave in this fashion towards every distressing impression they receive, by reproducing it in their play. In thus changing from passivity to activity they attempt to master their experiences psychically. [With more particular reference to children's play, the same idea is expressed in an even earlier paper, to which I shall return in the subsequent discussion.] It is clear that in their play children repeat everything that has made a great impression on them in real life, and that in doing so they abreact the strength of the impression and, as one might put it, make themselves master of the situation [1920a, p. 16]. In the case of children's play we seemed to see that children repeat unpleasurable experiences for the additional reason that they can master a powerful impression far more thoroughly by being active than they could by merely experiencing it passively. Each fresh repetition seems to strengthen the mastery they are in search of [1920a, p. 35]. Here the relation of activity to passivity is especially interesting. It can easily be observed that in every field of mental experience, not merely that of sexuality, when a child receives a passive impression it has a tendency to produce an active reaction. It tries to do itself what has just been done to it. This is part of the work imposed on it of mastering the external world and can even lead to its endeavouring to repeat an impression which it would have reason to avoid on account of its distressing content. Children's play, too, is made to serve this purpose of supplementing a passive experience with an active piece of behaviour and of thus, as it were, annulling it. When a doctor has opened a child's mouth, in spite of his resistance, to look down his throat, the same child, after the doctor has gone, will play at being the doctor himself, and will repeat the assault upon some small brother or sister who is as helpless in his hands as he was in the doctor's. Here we have an unmistakable revolt against passivity and a preference for the active role. This swing-over from passivity to activity does not take place with the same regularity or vigour in all children; in some it may not occur at all. A child's behaviour in this respect may enable us to draw conclusions as to the relative strength of the masculinity and femininity that it will exhibit in its sexuality [1931b, p. 236].

As I have said, the passages quoted explicitly refer to the theory of children's play, which we may now consider. We have up to now been formulating the psychological processes in those phenomena which psychoanalysis describes under the concept of repetition compulsion, and stating the remarkable double position that the repetition occupies between a pressure *a tergo* and an assimilative attempt on the part of the ego.

All of this is based on an assumption concerning the relationship of the psychic organism to the outer world. Psychoanalysis assumes that the psychic organism is able to ingest and assimilate the stimulations of the outer world in small doses only, if so quantitative a figure of speech may be used. If, in a given unit of time, the excitations of the outer world impinge upon the individual excessively, the ability to absorb them fails and the mechanism of the repetition compulsion comes into play. The stimuli not disposed of exert a pressure and must be dealt with repeatedly and, so to speak, belatedly, must be divided into small portions.

The repetition compulsion, then, purely empirically, is not a blind primal impulse which demands, "Repeat!" It is a pressure exerted by unfinished processes, and it is a constant striving to assimilate. The reality of its empirical existence is hardly open to dispute; proof for it is constantly found in everyday events.

After this digression into the theory of the repetition compulsion, we are prepared to discuss the psychoanalytic solution of the previously mentioned problems of children's play. In all the cases in which the child's play originates in disagreeable experiences, where the pleasure principle does not enable us to understand why the child does not leave them alone but continues to busy himself with them, the experiences which he elaborates into games are, at least at the moment, too difficult for the child to bear. The experience at the dentist's, in our illustration, was an onslaught of more events in a relatively brief interval of time than could be endured by the immature, untempered, extraordinarily plastic and responsive psychic organism of the child. The capacity for assimilation, naturally, very much depends on age. As one grows older, the ego becomes stronger, and consequently the capacity to endure difficulties grows; the difficult experiences of the past function as preparations for future tolerance (a sort of hardening). With the increasing rigidity of the personality, the protective crust against outer excitations becomes denser and less permeable (this becomes especially conspicuous in old age, but is already indicated in adult life) and with this diminishing plasticity the receptivity and readiness of the individual to react decline.

All these circumstances, along with many others, contribute toward the fact that, infinitely more often than an adult, a child is confronted with experiences which he cannot immediately assimilate. To the psychic organism just establishing its existence, for which everything is still novel—some things attractively pleasant, many things painful and menacing—excessive stimulation (trauma as it might be called in a certain sense) is plainly a normal experience, while in the life of the adult it surely constitutes the exception. This, probably, is one of the reasons why the abreaction of traumatic experiences by games plays so important a role precisely in childhood. That the child not only experiences trauma more frequently than the adult but also—just because all its strength is engaged in growth—the child is in an incomparably better position to surmount it, is fortunately true, but is extraneous to our discussion. The fact is not altered that traumatic stimulation in childhood is the general rule.

According to the conclusions arrived at by psychoanalysis, play may be a process like a repetition compulsion, by which excessive experiences are divided into small quantities, reattempted and assimilated in play. To return to the problem mentioned at the start—namely, why unpleasant experiences so often constitute the material of games, we may say that although these experiences are unpleasant, they were at the same time too difficult. Play may now be characterized as a method of constantly working over and, as it were, assimilating piecemeal an experience which was too large to be assimilated instantly at one swoop.

Bühler (1927) is quite aware that unpleasurable experiences are repeated in play but believes that this takes place only after the experiences have been freed of their painful quality. He says: "The fact that unpleasurable happenings find an echo in the play of children has markedly impressed Freud. The fact, as such, is completely and readily evident. Indeed, Groos observed it and aptly described it as follows: The pain in an experience must be overcome before the experience can be repeated and enjoyed in play. This is true for adults and children too. Let us suppose that the child was once bitten by a dog, or that it burnt its finger on a candle. Nothing in the world will induce the child to repeat this experience in reality or in play, until the situation is inwardly settled, and the child on a fresh occasion feels reassured and superior to the situation" (p. 189f.). The difference between Bühler's view and the psychoanalytic view is due to a question as to the facts. The contrary thesis of psychoanalysis would be accurately worded as follows: a painful experience is repeated in play not after it has been overcome and mastered, but before, while it is still unmastered; and it is eventually mastered because of the playful repetition itself.

Thereby, play becomes aligned with assimilative procedures which operate by repetition, as do others in the psychic life. Furthermore, according to psychoanalytic theory, play has in this way a teleological function as well. This function is not so much the preparation for future activities in adult life as it is the assimilation of the mass of excitations from the outer world, which affect the organism too severely or too suddenly to permit of their immediate disposal.

The assimilative process in play can take place in various ways, and probably various types could be differentiated. First of all, the simple fact that the child reproduces in playing a passively received experience, a transformation from passivity to activity, is significant. In one group of games, in addition, the child adopts another role than the one played in reality; if in real life, he was the sufferer or a frightened spectator, he becomes in play the active party, the rescuer or the *deus ex machina*. In this group, then, the turning from passivity to activity is emphasized by the choice of role; the illustration of the dentist is to the point here. In another group, the child changes the outcome of the situation experienced and furnishes it with a different solution. Presumably it is possible to differentiate other such types of assimilative processes.

As has been pointed out, still other assimilative processes or attempts, patterned on the mechanism of the repetition compulsion, play a significant role in adult life. The simplest example might be an adult who has been through some unusually difficult experience and who is constantly occupied in his thoughts with this experience, or who talks about it incessantly for a period of time—sometimes forever. This process, too, is under the sway of the repetition compulsion. The unassimilated invasion of reality into the psychic organism has the same disturbing effect as a foreign body. That which is not disposed of harasses the individual and demands that it be tackled again; the ego at the same time through once again dealing with the experience attempts to assimilate it. Here again we see the Janus face of the repetition compulsion turned both to the id and the ego.

Mourning also belongs to the assimilative processes in the category of repetition compulsions. The loss of a beloved person is a painful experience. At the moment of the loss there is pain but as yet no grief. We know from Freud (1917) that a gradual severing from the lost love object takes place, achieved, obviously, through the mechanism of reality testing, which informs us repeatedly that the loved object is no longer accessible. Mourning is the suffering entailed by this task of separation. This task, however, is accomplished under the sway of the repetition compulsion. The lost object constantly comes to mind, fresh accesses of ungratified affection are freshly painful. In this constantly repeated resurgence of the painful experience a gradual assimilation occurs simultaneously with the course of normal grief. The affect fades away little by little.

The dreams of war neurotics and traumatic neurotics present another example of such processes. The terrifying experience of being shelled, or of the other traumas from which traumatic neuroses result, returns repeatedly in dreams. From the standpoint of the pleasure principle this would be incomprehensible, nor can it be explained by the wish-fulfillment theory of dreams. The process is the same as in the previous examples; it is subject to the repetition compulsion: the trauma insists on returning because it has not been assimilated, and, at the same time, the ego strives to conquer the experience.

To a certain critic, the close similarity of children's play to the traumatic neuroses sounded dubious. The interpretation on one and the same principle of such severely pathological phenomena as the dreams of war neurotics and of a manifestation so delightful and vital as children's play appeared to carry this principle *ad absurdum*. We believe that this objection is unjustified; both instances have in common that they are dealing with an attempt to assimilate an overwhelming situation. On the other hand, the two cases differ inordinately in regard to the success of the processes. In one the attempt fails and, despite all repetitions, assimilation does not take place, while in the other a relatively satisfactory assimilation of the occurrence is attained.

With the recognition that play belongs to the group of gradually progressive assimilative processes which are spurred on by the repetition compulsion, play, at least in respect of this one determination—and in my opinion, its most crucial one—has been clearly classified; but not all the problems pertaining to it are solved. For there are other processes of this sort, as we have seen from a number of examples, and we must ask what distinguishes play from them. At first glance, one would be inclined to say that play has a blissful and unreal quality which distinguishes it from the others; and perhaps the *differentia specifica* of games may be defined on this basis. Play as a fundamental and successful phenomenon is encountered only in children, that is, during a period of growth, in which the traumas of life touch the ascending limb of the vitality curve. This is also the time of extraordinary plasticity of both somatic and psychic material. It is certainly not yet possible to see this relationship with the desired degree of clarity, but apparently it is not mere chance that the abreactions in play are correlated with the stage of greatest plasticity of the psyche and that, seemingly, they presuppose a psychic substance which has not yet been completely structuralized. When this plasticity has dwindled, and the possibilities have narrowed and made way for a well-formed reality, and when the diffuse amorphous psychic organism has become a structure, then, apparently, other less alluring procedures take the place of play.

Another specific characteristic of play, which even today may be stated somewhat accurately, is related to the quality of unreality. In children, the boundaries between reality and fantasy are still hazy; the two realms overlap occasionally. This crucial characteristic of the child's world, as is well known, did not always attract the attention even of observers schooled in analytic psychology, and it has not been made the subject of exhaustive psychological study. It is obviously this merging of reality and fantasy which makes possible the abreaction of an experience in play.

It remains for us to indicate how our knowledge may find practical application in education. If it is true that an abreaction to traumatic experiences occurs in play, the teacher is in a position to help the child obtain this kind of abreaction. When the child has had a very disagreeable experience, which is productive of shock or anxiety, it is possible for the teacher to play the experience with the child, and somewhat casually permit the game to end with an outcome different from the experience, or with the child in a different role, thus assisting the child to effect a comparatively speedy assimilation.

This discussion has not attempted an exhaustive treatment of the phenomenon of play, nor is it an exhaustive account of everything which psychoanalysis can contribute to the understanding of the subject. I have commented only on the one aspect of play in children which seems to psychoanalysis of most significance for its understanding. It contains in no way the assertion that every game, without exception, must be such an assimilation process, or that these determinants should be accepted as the final ones in the understanding of every single game.

A simple example of a game not in harmony with this interpretation is the playful reaching out for all objects, which puts in its appearance during the latter months of the first year. This behavior is perhaps the first which may be regarded as a manifestation of the instinct of mastery. At this particular time the child has reached an age when he is slowly becoming aware of the world, and when objects in the outer world lose the originally menacing character to which the primal predominantly negative reactions of the child bear witness, so that the child finds pleasure in gaining mastery over more and more objects. The pleasure he feels in this is perhaps remarkably similar to the one designated by the term "functional pleasure," but we must not ignore the specific quality of mastery.[3]

An additional function of play becomes evident if we consider that during play the child ventures to take over in a permissible way, roles which are ordinarily prohibited to him, and which later, once the superego has formed, are also forbidden by his own conscience. *Play is thus a leave of absence from reality, as well as from the superego.*[4] Thus, play also helps in assimilating the impositions of education, in a way other than the one described.

The striking parallels to the play of children appear to be, as previously mentioned, fantasy and daydream. The two cardinal functions which we believe can be found in play we also encounter in fantasies: instinctual gratification and assimilation of disagreeable experiences. To a large extent fantasies are manifestly wish fulfillments, be they successful love, wealth, satisfied amibition or power, or whatever a daydream can conjure up as having been realized. In certain fantasies, however, the other role is involved: in these, experiences of a painful and disagreeable nature are constantly revived and return; unassimilated material presses for renewed efforts, and only in this manner can it be assimilated, slowly and in small doses. To be sure, in the case of fantasy, the first meaning, that of wish fulfillment, is infinitely more frequent, so that one can seldom point out illustrations of the second function of fantasy; whereas, in the case of play, its significance as a frolicsome abreaction is undoubtedly just as important and as frequent as that of the

---

[3] In the empirical sense one can confidently speak of an instinct of mastery, but by this term we do not mean the ultimate in the realm of instinct. From the standpoint of the theory of instincts, the mastery instinct, like all others, is a blending of love and destruction, a destructive instinct which has been turned outward and rendered harmless through love.

[4] I wish to thank Ernst Kris for this formulation, which seems to me a felicitous one.

realized gratification of a wish. The difference seems to be based on a circumstance we have already discussed: the ubiquity of traumatic experiences during the tender years and their relative rarity in the life of the adult, hardened and protected by various kinds of armor.

Here the question may be raised as to the psychological difference between play and fantasy. Some of Freud's observations seem to answer this question. "Might we not say that every child at play behaves like a creative writer, in that he creates a world of his own, or, rather, re-arranges the things of his world in a new way which pleases him? It would be wrong to think he does not take that world seriously; on the contrary, he takes his play very seriously and expends large amounts of emotion on it. The opposite of play is not what is serious but what is real. In spite of all the emotion with which he cathects his world of play, the child distinguishes it quite well from reality; and he likes to link his imagined objects and situations to the tangible and visible things of the real world. This linking is all that differentiates the child's 'play' from 'phantasying'" (1908, p. 143f.). Freud's answer, then, is that a child's fantasies occupy themselves with a real object, while in the case of an adult, reality is severed from the world of fantasy. This pertains to that intermingling of reality and the fantasy world which is a familiar and characteristic feature of the infantile mind. *Fantasy woven about a real object is, however, nothing other than: play.*

To summarize, the psychoanalytic contributions to the problem of play may be indicated by the following phrases: instinct of mastery; wish fulfillment; assimilation of overpowering experiences according to the mechanism of the repetition compulsion; transformation from passivity to activity; leave of absence from reality and from the superego; fantasies about real objects.

If we compare these with the contributions which we owe to academic psychology, and which one can couch approximately in these phrases: phylogenetic echoing of serious affairs; atavism; mimicry; excess energy; preparation for future functions; functional pleasure—without in the least questioning the value of this point of view for a comprehensive theory of play, one can hardly avoid the impression that the psychoanalytic contributions are more valuable for an understanding of the individual child, his individual development, his difficulties and his attempts at their solution. They teach us to regard play as a sign of the child's psychological situation, and they can give us leads as to how to intervene properly in childhood conflicts.

CHAPTER 7

The Problem of Freedom in Psychoanalysis and the Problem of Reality Testing

(1934)

Allow me first of all to ask your indulgence if in the remarks which I am about to make I do no more than suggest some fresh formulations bearing on facts which as such will be familiar to every analyst. To begin with, I should like to say at once, for the benefit of those in whom the title of this paper may have inspired a certain misgiving, that I have no intention of entering into any metaphysical discussions or of debating the problem of free will, which for centuries has been the crux of philosophical systems; the problem to be investigated is the purely psychological one of freedom *from* something, for example, from affects or anxiety, or freedom *for* something, say freedom for coping with a task set before one. Anyone afflicted with an obsessional neurosis and acting under a compulsion is psychologically not free; if he is "freed" from his compulsion, he will have acquired a measure of freedom.

Rather than circumscribe my subject matter with elaborate definitions, I will try to take you at once to the heart of the

Based on a paper read before the Thirteenth International Psycho-Analytic Congress, Lucerne, August 28, 1934. First published as "Das Freiheitsproblem in der Psychoanalyse und das Problem der Realitätsprüfung," in *Imago*, 20:467-484, 1934. Reprinted from *International Journal of Psycho-Analysis*, 17:89-108, 1936.

matter with the help of some passages from Freud's writings, which will at the same time serve to show that this kind of problem has always occupied a focal position in psychoanalytic interest. Thus, for example, Freud (1916-17) says in reference to the development of the obsessional neurosis: "The whole position ends up in an ever-increasing degree of indecision, loss of energy and restriction of freedom" (p. 260). In another passage we read:

> Since the rules of analysis are diametrically opposed to the physician's making use of his personality in any such manner [as guide or prophet], it must be honestly confessed that here we have another limitation to the effectiveness of analysis; after all, analysis does not set out to make pathological reactions impossible, but to give the patient's ego *freedom* to decide one way or the other [1923b, p. 50]. [Or again:] It [the cultural superego], too, does not trouble itself enough about the facts of the mental constitution of human beings. It issues a command and does not ask whether it is possible for people to obey it. On the contrary, it assumes that a man's ego is psychologically capable of anything that is required of it, that his ego has unlimited mastery over his id. This is a mistake; and even in what are known as normal people the id cannot be controlled beyond certain limits [1930, p. 143].

Having delineated the theme of my paper, I now turn to consider the concept of freedom. In its most general sense, the essence of freedom can be said to reside in the fact that man is not tied down to his biological situation and his environment, to the *hic et nunc* of his actual existence, but is on occasion able to pass beyond the actualities of his perceptual world, to rise above himself, and to objectify his standpoint of the moment. Thus it has been given to man to concern himself with and apprehend things which lie beyond the range not merely of his immediate perceptual world but also of the paramount necessities of a given moment—as for instance you do, when you devote your attention to problems that certainly are not a matter of immediate vital importance. By virtue of this freedom, man is able to make himself the subject matter of his own reflections, to objectify himself, and to abstract himself from his own situation. The philosopher Georg Simmel (1922) has called this "the transcendence of life," in accordance with the literal sense of the word *transcendere:* to step over, to place oneself above and beyond. A concrete manifestation of this is seen when a man, by virtue of his separate individuality, makes a will, thereby showing that he is aware that his life is limited, and from an imaginary vantage point beyond his transitory biological existence, as it were, is making dispositions for a time when he will have ceased to exist.

An array of facts[1] point to the assumption that in this transcendence, this rising above oneself, lies the essential difference between man and beast, that here and here alone we find the dimension which is missing from the life of the animals.

These considerations, at first sight so far removed from practical interests, have been applied in the field of pathology to elucidate neurological disturbances. Head (1920), Goldstein and Gelb (1920) have traced a whole series of phenomena in the asymbolias, e.g., the so-called central aphasia, back to disturbances of just this dimension or stage in the development of

---

[1] These facts include in the first instance the investigations made into the language of animals, which have shown that their means of expression lacks a dimension, namely, the function of representation, this being reserved to human speech, and that animal language can only perform the tasks of expression and notification (K. Bühler, 1934). Further material is yielded by Wolfgang Köhler's observations (1929) on the difficulties encountered by the animals in tasks that involved imagining something (such as an implement) not added to the environment, but subtracted from the field of vision. Of the same order, finally, is the circumstance that animals are without culture in the human sense. (Thus men concern themselves with the psychology of apes, but not apes with that of men.) Furthermore, we can scarcely attribute to animals such affects as irony and humor, which presuppose a capacity to rise above oneself. How the arrangement of organic life in grades is to be reconciled with the idea of evolution, whether there is a kind of uninterrupted process of transition from the animal stage to the human, what the position is with domesticated animals, are all questions which we cannot here submit even to the most cursory examination. A particularly noteworthy attempt to outline the development from the animal stage to the human has been made by Bally (1933) who proposes the following sequence: biological retardation of development—prolonged care of the young—emancipation of functions from biological aims. While the conceptual framework of Bally's work does not completely coincide with the formulations attempted here, I believe that ultimately the two theories are identical or capable of being reduced to a common denominator.

human life; for example, an aphasic subject is unable to find a certain word when he is asked for it to describe an object or situation, but has no difficulty in making use of the same word when in a vital situation he needs it to express his state of mind; he is ready with words and gestures conveying threats and curses when he wants to threaten and curse, but remains silent and uncomprehending when one asks him for words and gestures conveying threats and curses.[2]

If now we translate this into the familiar idiom of our psychoanalytic terminology, we find that this rising above oneself, this self-scrutiny, self-appraisement, and self-elimination which bring with them the possession of a world transcending an environment bound to perception and the instincts, are a function of the superego, which we have long come to recognize as a differentiated grade in the ego. We know that in his superego man turns toward his own ego, sometimes attacking and punishing it, as in the phenomena of conscience, sometimes treating it kindly and comforting it, for instance, in humor, or again regarding it with emotional indifference, as when he observes himself and eliminates his personal standpoint. What is common to these modes of superego attitudes is self-observation, objectification of one's self, the attainment of a position above one's own ego.[3]

It appears that there are three aspects of the problem of freedom: the formal function of his superego lifts man above things; at the same time, owing to his perceptions and affects he stands in their very midst, absorbed by them; but besides this, he finds himself face to face with them. We can therefore speak of a threefold freedom: its most general form which constitutes the

[2] For the purposes of the conclusions to be drawn, it is not essential to accept the theories of Head and Goldstein in their entirety or to determine the extent of their sphere of application. It is quite enough that such disturbances exist: a circumstance taken into account by other theories as well.

[3] Although the term "superego" is not infrequently used as a synonym for "conscience," we should nevertheless remember that Freud (1914a) originally introduced the ego ideal in the context of discussing delusions of reference, that is, as a system of self-observation, and that even in his later presentation of the tripartite structure of the psychic personality he states the problem in the form of the question: "How can the ego take itself as object?" (1933b, p. 58). I therefore believe that I have not extended the psychoanalytic concept of the superego.

essence of man, and is founded in the existence of the superego; a second form of which we may say provisionally and without strict regard for accuracy that the more he is "in the thick of it," the more he is in the grip of instincts and affects, the less this freedom is his; and thirdly, freedom to assess objects and reality as they are. Commensurate with these three aspects of freedom, we find a threefold derangement of it: the failure of the superego's function, overabsorption in affects, loss of freedom in relation to objects. These three disturbances or limitations of freedom seem to be realized in the three great realms of psychopathology: neurosis, psychosis, and asymbolia. In asymbolia, the formal function of the superego is apparently injured or eliminated; in neurosis man is too greatly dominated and absorbed by his instincts and affects, i.e., by fixations and anxiety; in psychosis, freedom is lacking in relation to objects. We see that this threefold stratification in the problem of freedom and its disturbances coincides in the main—although not wholly—with the tripartite division of the personality with which analysis has made us familiar. On the basis of these formulations, we might add that asymbolia resides in the superego, neurosis in the id, and psychosis in the ego.

We will now proceed to consider the law which appears to hold in this sphere. Man is indeed able, in virtue of the formal function of his superego, to rise above himself, his impulses, and his past, but he can do so only under certain conditions. A comparison will perhaps help to illustrate my meaning. When Archimedes discovered the laws of leverage, he exclaimed: "Only give me a fixed point in space and I will lift the world from its axes!" We, too, need to have a fixed point if we are to lift the psychic structure from its axes, rise above our instinctual life and our past; a fixed point, however, located not in space, but in our mental life, in our instinctual life and past. Thus man is able, it is true, to rise above his instinctual life (to overcome his fixations, for instance), but only if he once more finds a fixed point in his instinctual life and secures a foothold in his instinctual needs—for example, when he once more finds instinctual satisfaction in the very act of rising above himself; and he is able to vault beyond his past as it persists in his present life—if that were not possible, there would be no psychoanalytic therapy—but he can do so only if he regains his foothold in a past which really lives on. Accordingly we may say that man is able, in virtue of the formal function of his superego, to rise above his id, his instinctual life, and the vicissitudes of his past, yet only if he finds again in the id the Archimedean point which he needs. We see that the two axioms "man is free" and "man is not free" are both equally true and equally false. We are entitled to say that he is free, since he is always potentially capable of placing himself above and beyond the bonds of his historical and biological past.[4] We are entitled to say that he is not free, since he can do this only if at the same time he is able to secure a foothold in that past, and only to the extent to which he does so.[5]

It seems theoretically important to distinguish between plasticity—in a biological sense—and transcendence, raising oneself above oneself. We talk of plasticity in referring to the adaptation of a living being to a changing environment, when its experiences have not left an imprint so deep that that fact acts as a fixation for the experiences immediately following, and when its impulses readily find another object in place of one which has failed them. The psychic plasticity of a human being is at its height in early childhood and suffers a sharp decline with age; but the formation of grades in the ego gives rise to a process which is something altogether different from the simple case in which the libido turns away from one object and is diverted to another; what happens is that an instinctual impulse is objectified, one rises above it—subject to the limitations imposed by the condition above discussed—and outgrows it, continuing the process at a higher level.

The former is a purely horizontal process, an impulse turns

---

[4] The further elaboration of these theories would require us to distinguish between rising above something in a purely intellectual and in an experimental way (e.g., self-observation and humor).

[5] I have elsewhere (1930) attempted, using a different terminology, to hint at a formula to cover this same state of affairs. The philosophical influences at work in those formulations are there discussed in detail. I owe much to them for the phraseology employed; the facts themselves belong to psychoanalysis and were drawn from its field of experience. In psychoanalysis, R. Sterba (1934) has been the first to adduce anthropological considerations following a suggestive passage from Herder. The present study has many points of contact with the lines of thought developed in that paper.

away from one object to another; the latter is, as it were,
vertical, no longer simply a libidinal process, but one which
passes through the superego.

L. von Krehl (1929) observes that a number of people will
scarcely trouble about a fishbone which is caught in their
mouth, whereas in many others the disturbing excitation evokes
reactions of defense which grow more and more in intensity until
finally the presence of the foreign body comes to dominate their
whole existence and all their psychic energies are concentrated
on its removal. There are people of great plasticity who pay little
heed to a disturbing excitation of this kind; but if the disturbing
excitation has released its reactions, if the plasticity of the
organism has been inadequate, the excitation can no longer be
mastered except in a second way; we are, of course, leaving out
of account the removal of the foreign body, which is out of the
question in the case of a psychic stimulus. If, then, plasticity has
proved inadequate and fixation has taken possession of an
individual, the only way which remains open is that of psychoanalysis.

But the distinction between plasticity and the attainment of a
higher position, which in its turn is founded in instinctual
satisfaction, is as a rule of as little practical significance as it is
important in theory. For the plasticity of instinctual life is also
the basis on which the "vertical" function develops; the greater
the plasticity of instinctual life, the more readily forthcoming
will be the instinctual satisfaction necessary to help one to rise
above one's fixations.

Our "law" also enables us to see in a particular light Freud's
momentous idea that there exists a hidden but close affinity
between the superego and the instincts, perhaps the most daring
thought in the whole field of psychoanalysis, and in any case the
farthest removed from popular ideas and expectations. This idea
coincides exactly with what our attempted formulation leads us
to anticipate; namely, that the attainment of a position above
oneself from which one considers, praises or punishes one's own
ego must in any case have secured a foothold in instinctual
life, and that it is only with the support of instincts that one can
put oneself above instincts.

This formulation also provides a good starting point for an

explanation why analysts in their therapeutic endeavors wish to effect changes in the id but will always address themselves to the ego.

From this point of view, man appears to be, as psychoanalysis also showed, a creature endowed with limited degrees of freedom; the limitations of freedom are the sites at which scientific psychology has established its colonies.[6] From here, a path opens out toward the differentiation of three fundamental types of pathological process. It is of little moment whether or not the types so discovered coincide completely with the empirical concepts of neurosis, psychosis, and asymbolia derived from clinical experience, as little as it is necessary for the chemical elements to appear in a pure form in nature. The three types which we have separated out do not provide us with a key to the understanding of these three groups of illnesses, if only because we know that every illness, whether we are dealing with neurosis, psychosis, or asymbolia, is a process which passes through a course of development, and in which we find attempts to ward off the pathological process, attempts at assimilation, restitution, adaptation, and so forth.

But I am inclined to think that along this path we may arrive at a means of setting up a system of coordinates in the realm of pathology, and that we do in fact find three distinct pathological processes corresponding to the three fundamental disorders at which we arrived, as it were, by way of deduction from the basic structure of the problem of freedom. Proceeding from the investigations of Head and Goldstein, we have already mentioned one of these fundamental disorders, namely, the cessation of human freedom in its most general form, the disturbance of the function of the superego, the maintenance of man's animal tie, as we might call it, to the conditions of his existence. We can now find a more exact formula for neurotic disorder, which in a provisional and incomplete statement we defined as an overly great absorption in affects. In the neuroses, the subject does indeed rise above himself, the neurotic has insight into his illness and is

---

[6] It cannot therefore be a coincidence that this scientific psychology originated as psychopathology, as the science of mental illness. We could in fact say that in the sphere of the central phenomena of personality there *could* only be a psychopathology.

able to take himself as the object of his reflections, but the Archimedean point never alters. His lack of freedom corresponds to the fixity of the props supporting his capacity for objectification. Lastly, we find the third form of disturbance, that affecting freedom in relation to objects, in the psychoses.

It has to be admitted that this last subject has not yet been as fully elucidated as would be desirable. The fact is that we understand the id and the superego better than we do the ego. From this third aspect of freedom and its disturbance a path leads us to the problem of the psychoses. The ego, or more correctly, its higher layers, issue from the two-sided situation between transcendence and absorption, between superego and id. I propose to select two examples from the higher functions of the ego which will demonstrate how far they really constitute the third coordinate: I refer to "intentional" activities and to causal thinking.

Man, as I have said, stands on the one hand above things, and on the other in their midst. It is in this double situation of being absorbed by and being above them that he comes to conceive objects "intentionally," as things that stand over against him; we regard this attitude as the third form of freedom. Now we know that a disturbance of volition is a characteristic of schizophrenia. A similar position obtains in relation to causal thinking, or, to put the matter in a more correct and generalized form, the "why" question. The existence of the superego gives us the category of possibility, enables us to conceive possibilities which are not realized. On the other hand, our perceptions and affective life keep us absorbed in reality. It is in this tension between reality and possibility that the question "why?" first originates.

On quite general principles we are entitled to distinguish two layers within that system which psychoanalysis has called the ego: those ego functions which we would assume to be present even in animals and which do not presuppose the existence of a superego, and those which are modified by the presence and existence of the superego and the capacity derived from it to occupy a position above oneself. I would suggest that the one should be called the "animal ego" and the other the "human ego." The animal ego comprises the central control of the organism, which we can assume with certainty comes into evidence very early in the animal kingdom, at the latest with the appearance of the central nervous system; we can then attribute to the human ego those higher functions which would not be conceivable without the formal function of the superego, for example, the "intentional" apprehending of objects or the "why" question, but also quite definitely the testing of reality.

The development of the higher layers of the ego (the "human ego") coincides with that of the superego, or of the formal function of the superego.

This may enable us to understand the reason why Freud (1921) at one time ascribed the function of reality testing to the superego and at another to the ego; our investigation suggests the provisional statement that reality testing is a function of the ego, but belongs to those of the ego's functions which have been modified by the existence of the superego.

In all these higher acts of the ego which we ascribe to the human ego, we are able to distinguish an id component and a superego component, as we tried to do when discussing "intentional" activities and the "why" question. Three simple illustrations may serve to clarify this statement.

The extent to which a man is approachable (in the everyday sense of the word, when we say that a man is or is not approachable) has an id and a superego aspect. The id aspect is represented by the amount of love which the individual in question entertains for his fellows and the way in which he deals with his aggression; the superego aspect is manifested in his readiness to abstract himself from his own standpoint and assume that of another, to put himself in the other man's shoes, as we are accustomed to say.

Similarly, we can distinguish these two components in the process of reality testing. The id component consists in a man having a sufficient quantity of free object libido and his ego not being poisoned by narcissism; for we have learned from Freud that whenever libido has been withdrawn into the ego to any considerable extent so as to upset the equilibrium maintained between narcissism and object libido, manifestations of megalomania, the sexual overestimation of one's own ego, make their appearance and reality testing breaks down; just as an immoderate overflowing of the whole of the libido onto an object jeopardizes reality testing, although in a different manner. But, besides this, the id component is dependent on the distribution of Eros and aggressiveness; if a complete severance has occurred between them so that all erotic strivings are concentrated on a single person or group of persons and all aggressive ones on the rest of mankind, reality testing will suffer, since it is possible to see clearly no longer where one feels only love or hate. The superego component in reality testing consists in man's distinguishing, by virtue of his capacity for self-observation, between inner and outer world, between reality and fantasy.[7] Thus disturbances in all these higher acts of the ego may issue from two directions, from the id as well as from the superego.[8]

As our third and last example we may refer to the fact of communication or confession; Reik's writings (1925) have long made us familiar with its superego aspect, the compulsion to confess under pressure of the sense of guilt; and a paper by Dorothy Burlingham (1934) revealed the id aspect in exhibitionism and attempts at seduction.

These provisional examples serve to demonstrate, if only incompletely, that the "human ego" resides in those layers of the ego which, supported by the id, develop in an individual who has a superego; disturbances in that sphere comprise the third category of psychopathology, that of the psychosis.

We could still add a number of equivalents to the formulations already attempted for the three principal types of pathological process which I have presented in terms of the three conceivable forms of disturbance of freedom. I will suggest only one: the category of the possible is absent in asymbolia, the neurotic is overabsorbed by reality—and here reality includes fantasy, psychic reality—and the psychotic fails to distinguish between reality and possibility.

I shall attempt to clarify the three principal types of pathological process by means of a schematic example. Proceeding from the supposition that someone has lost a loved object through

[7] I have discussed these questions in greater detail in Ch. 23.

[8] This can also be seen in the pathological field: psychotic manifestations can appear in neurological disturbances as well as following instinctual outbursts.

death, we can ask which reaction corresponds to the three types. The aphasia patient probably will no longer be able to utter or comprehend the name of the lost object; for him, the world extends no further than the horizon of his immediate perceptions, his mind no longer reaches beyond them; unless a place can be found for it here, a thing ceases to exist. He has lost the category of the possible, his existence is confined to his actual environment at a given moment and to what his vital needs turn his attention to.

The neurotic may react with a protracted period of mourning or will perhaps develop a symptom which will allow the dead to survive in a psychic reality expressive of his longing, or with feelings of guilt and so forth. The neurotic has at his disposal the category of the possible, but he is absorbed by a part of his affective life, by pain, longing, or a sense of guilt. Here we see that every gradation exists between neurotic and normal. In this theoretical sense, even normal reactions of mourning can be described as a minor neurosis.

Lastly, the psychotic will perhaps develop a delusion that the dead person is still alive or will hallucinate his presence. He also has at his disposal the category of the possible. He has not, as in asymbolia, reduced the world to the dimensions of his immediate surroundings and instinctual needs. The function of his superego is still maintained. Like the neurotic, he remains absorbed by affects, but he no longer distinguishes reality from possibility, he mistakes a part of the world of possibility for reality. Accordingly, his disorder is related to the higher functions of the ego.

This example, also shows us how fully we are entitled in all three cases to speak of a curtailment of freedom.[9] The aphasic subject's loss of freedom consists in his becoming enslaved to the things of his immediate surroundings and to current actualities, and in his no longer retaining that freedom to break away from his perceptions and the actual moment which is the most

---

[9] We also see where it is inadequate: what the asymbolic subject in our example fails to transcend (namely, the perceptual situation) is not the same thing as what absorbs the neurotic (namely, the affect). Whether this amounts simply to a flaw in the example itself or whether it betrays an as yet unresolved difficulty running through the whole argument must be left undecided.

universal feature distinguishing human beings. The neurotic in his mourning reaction or the torments of his longing and feelings of guilt enjoys this species of freedom, but he stands in the shadow of his affects and lacks the freedom to choose a point in the life of his emotions which could help him to rise above the remainder of his affects. The psychotic, lastly, also has not sacrificed the most universal form of human freedom, but he lacks freedom to apprehend things as they really are.[10]

From the considerations which I have so far allowed myself to submit to your judgment a further line of thought carries us on to the problem of ego expansion and ego restriction. Let us recall Freud's dictum: "Where id was, there ego shall be" (1933b). We conceive of this ego expansion as an increase in freedom, indeed in that form of freedom which we found to have been diminished in the neuroses: freedom from absorption in one's instincts and affects, freedom to choose the Archimedean point in order

---

[10] If a loose conjecture is allowed here, I would surmise that there also are three biological processes corresponding to these three principle types. Absorption in instincts and affects has a corollary in modifications in the chemical substances—a very early prediction of Freud's which recent work on hormones seems to corroborate; we know that the asymbolias arise from injury to the cerebral cortex, that is, from injuries to what are phylogenetically the most recent parts of the central nervous system. The correspondence between the more peripheral changes concerned in sexual chemistry and what I have described as absorption in affects is only too obvious; whereas we are, of course, still completely in the dark as to the biological process which corresponds to the psychoses. It would be much too crude and misleading to base an analogy on this—peripheral disturbances in sexual chemistry, central disturbances in the phylogenetically most recent parts of the central nervous system—and then to conclude that here we have before us disturbances of the phylogenetically older parts of the central nervous system. Besides many other factors, the problem is complicated by the law in virtue of which, in the higher animals, functions are transferred to the phylogenetically more recent parts of the central nervous system; even functions of a lowly order are, in the higher animals, regulated by higher organizations of the central nervous system. This law accords well with our psychological conceptions of a modification of the ego (the human ego) through the existence of the superego. We should certainly expect to find not a simple localized cleavage, but a severance between acts and modes of function. As, however, we already appear to have found analogies for at least two dimensions, it is perhaps not vain to hope that we shall one day discover them for the third; or more correctly, for the third and fourth, seeing that human and animal components of the ego may very well correspond to different forms of organization of the central nervous system.

to rise above oneself. The way in which this comes about and is constantly being realized in psychoanalytic therapy has, I believe, been delineated in the "law" that a man rises above his id if he finds the Archimedean point in his id. The problem of ego restriction which Anna Freud (1932) raised is also relevant here. Anna Freud described a variety of forms in which the child masters anxiety; one of them consists in withdrawing from the danger zone, in renouncing and abandoning activities which bring him into jeopardy. In that case freedom from anxiety is purchased at the expense of a restriction of the ego. A permanent curtailment of freedom has been effected, has become as it were—*sit venia verbo*—character.

Before the problem of ego strength and ego restriction can be scrutinized more thoroughly, we must distinguish between real strength of the ego and what we might describe as a pseudo-strength of the ego, which seen from the outside often presents a very similar appearance. An example of this pseudostrength of the ego would be when the fear of being considered a coward is stronger than the fear of danger. Some recent trends in education which aim at allowing the child a greater measure of freedom during the latency period lead, as Anna Freud has shown, to the child's withdrawing under the pressure of his anxiety from activities which bring him into danger, and consequently restrict his ego. In more antiquated forms of education which even now find favor in many circles, this way was closed to the child, since cowardice was utterly condemned and feared even more than danger. Under such conditions, the ego does not suffer a restriction; what remains is not a strong ego, although it may sometimes appear to resemble this; we would call it a pseudostrength of the ego.

As a second example of pseudostrength of the ego we can cite the partial persistence of infantile omnipotence fantasies, when the belief in omnipotence has found confirmation in reality for some reason or other at a time so early that thenceforward it remains within the general confines of reality, without overstepping the borderline of psychosis (see Nunberg, 1932).

Real ego strength, on the other hand, seems to consist in the capacity to rise constantly above one's instincts and affects and—this is the crux of the matter—to apply the Archimedean lever at any number of different points in one's own id.[11] This gives to the ego a measure of real freedom, all that man with the inherent limits upon his freedom is able to achieve. Here we again come upon a theme to which I have previously alluded, namely, that plasticity also forms the basis for the "vertical" process of raising oneself above an instinct with the help of an instinct. This suggests that the antithesis of a strong ego may be found in the adhesiveness of the libido.

I now propose to consider a few tentative applications of the point of view I have here presented.

Our attitude in social relationships differs from our educational-therapeutic attitude in that in the former we treat our fellowmen as if they were completely free; we make demands, appraise and condemn. As educators and therapists we treat the other party, or, more correctly, the object of our educational or therapeutic activity, as one who is not free; or, to be more precise, as though his freedom were limited in the several ways I have described. Why indeed this should be the case, why man's social relationships require him to treat others as though their conduct were entirely free—failing this, the social relation is disturbed—would need a separate investigation.

A further application takes us to the problem of predicting human action and human conduct. Fundamentally, it is possible to do this only if freedom is limited to a certain degree. Accordingly we can predict an individual's conduct most accurately when we are dealing with the most extreme form of limitation affecting freedom—in asymbolia. Goldstein states that he does not conclude his investigation of a patient until he is able to forecast with certainty his reactions to any given situation. The probable correctness of a prediction concerning

[11] When one rises above an impulse with the support of the *same* impulse, we call it "sublimation." The word describes the process and its result. This definition differs from the usual one (diversion of the impulse to other, more valuable aims) as a "vertical" description of the process, taking into account the structural stratification, as distinguished from a purely "horizontal" one. It seeks at the same time to do justice to Freud's dictum (1923b) that sublimation regularly takes place through the mediation of the ego and may help us to understand why a repressed impulse is not capable of being sublimated.

the future behavior of a psychotic is less certain, but predictions exist here as well: they go by the name of psychiatric prognoses, which we know to be subject to considerable uncertainties. Lastly, in the case of the neurotic, the probable correctness of a prediction will be further reduced. In fact, it is possible to make predictions only to the extent that limitations of freedom exist; but since these limitations are necessarily present in every human being—the differences between neurotic and normal are, as we see here, only a matter of degree—it is even possible to make predictions in the sphere of normal psychology. In brief, we may say that the greater the limitation of freedom, the more probably correct the prediction will be.

This last point is also relevant to the attempt to develop a scientific sociology which in the last resort must be based on psychology to be able to lay down general propositions concerning human conduct. In one direction, the task of sociology is facilitated by the existence of a field (in addition to the sphere of maximal limitations on freedom) in which it is possible to predict human behavior with a degree of probability approximating to certainty, at least in the sense of a statistical mean: namely, the field of individuoperipheral manifestations. We say of a process that it is individuoperipheral if it is unaccompanied by internal conflict, as in the case of the satisfaction of needs which are more or less common to all men and approved by the superego, and if the means employed in obtaining this satisfaction are known and legitimate. Thus we can predict that people will prefer a cheaper market if they can obtain the same commodities with the same psychic satisfaction at a smaller sacrifice. This is not a case of limitation upon freedom, but an individuoperipheral activity—no conflict arises. Such behavior can also be predicted. This fact is at the basis on the one hand of a large part of nonanalytic psychology, insofar as this has been stated in laws, and, on the other, of political economy as the only body of scientific laws within the domain of the social sciences.

After this brief survey of the field of applied psychology, I shall consider some aspects of freedom in the course of man's life, psychoanalytic therapy, and psychoanalytic education.

How then does freedom develop throughout the course of man's life span? Are we here dealing with a constant quantity or with a process of average regularity? It seems to me that two curves are here superimposed one upon the other. On the one hand, man only gradually awakens to the freedom which has been given him. The superego does not exist from the very first day, nor does the formal function of the superego appear in the reactions of the infant; even when that function becomes visible in behavior, it still has far to go before reaching its zenith. A variety of experiences has taught us that the child only very gradually comes to acquire a certain degree of relativism, that he finds it extremely difficult even during the latency period to eliminate his own standpoint and recognize its subjective nature, and that maturity is required in order to objectify permanently one's destiny and actual situation.[12] Finally, humor, the finest achievement of the superego, seems to be a prerogative of more advanced years (see Kris, 1934). Accordingly, we may speak of a development of the function of the superego, or of man's gradual awakening to the kind of freedom which we have described as its most general form.

But this rising curve has a counterpart in another, declining one. Every day of our experience leaves behind irrevocable traces which tend to limit our freedom. I refer in part to external matters—love, marriage, and a career create conditions which mark out a framework for later life—in part to internal matters, in the sense that the experience of each day turns some of the potentialities latent in the individual into reality, and thus causes a limitation of his possibilities; each day represents, as it were, a partial fixation involving a limitation of freedom in regard to his later life.

The superimposition of these two curves seems to determine the curve of human life, which coincides in its course with the biological one—again clearly not a coincidence—leading up-

---

[12] This does not imply that self-observation is in all its forms an ideal thing. Self-objectification has its pathological forms as well; for example, the obsessional type (in the sense of Freud's libidinal types) becomes, in the pathologically exaggerated form of obsessional neurosis, the spectator and reporter of his own experience. (Cf. in this connection Fenichel, 1931). Relevant to this phenomenon is the question of an intellectual and experimental rising above something; in addition, there is the fact that it is always only a part of experience which is so observed—the other part is repressed and shut out from the field of view accessible to self-observation.

ward, to begin with, until it reaches its culminating point, at which it remains for a time, and then finally declines. On the upward gradient, awakening to one's possibilities still outweighs the twofold limitation imposed on freedom by the increasing demands of external reality and by growing fixation. The horizontal section corresponds to the maximum individual freedom man is capable of attaining within the conditions prescribed for him by his constitution, his past history and his environment, and so far as circumstances or illness permit. The downward slope shows where man becomes more and more the petrified image of his past.

A further application, finally, brings us to the problem of psychoanalytic therapy. Various forms of therapeutic influence are known to medical science, such as eliminating the point at which the pathological process has set in (for instance, an operation for the removal of the diseased tissue), reinforcing the organism's powers of resistance, or the implantation of another biological process (e.g., transplantation). Psychoanalysis makes an appeal to man's freedom itself—to such freedom as is his, of course, and so far as it is his, to the limited but nonetheless existing degree of human freedom—and in this way it serves not only to overcome illness, but also to strengthen the ego and to augment freedom. Psychoanalytic therapy thus stands nearer to the therapeutic ideal than any other method of cure known to medicine. The distinction between the psychoanalytic and other psychotherapeutic procedures is found to be similar to that which in my earlier formulation I tried to draw between a real strength and a pseudostrength of the ego; these latter procedures do not extend human freedom, but interpolate a new determinism and create a fresh situation of absorption (e.g., by means of an unregulated transference to the physician). A satisfactory result may be obtained if the sole object has been the removal of a symptom; just as the teacher who wishes his pupil to be good at sports may feel satisfied if fear of being a coward restrains the boy from flight from the danger zone. But it is certainly not therapy in the strict sense of the term.[13]

Here we can also discern the limits of psychoanalytic therapy.

[13] We have thus reached by another route the same distinction between the psychoanalytic and other forms of therapy as Rado (1925).

All that we have long known empirically concerning these may be arrived at by way of deduction from our scheme; for example, the fact that the therapeutic prospects of analysis depend not so much on the severity of the neurosis as on a part of the personality having remained intact, and the extent of this. One point more than any deserves mention: the degree of freedom which an individual enjoys consists not in his being granted certain kinds of freedom and denied others, but in the circumstance that there is a contradistinction between absorption in the totality of one's affects and rising in a fundamental sense above everything. I have already said that the two axioms "man is free" and "man is not free" are equally true and equally false. Perhaps this also explains that psychoanalytic therapy can at one moment convey the impression that a man has completely changed and at another that he has at bottom remained the same. In this favorable instance of a successful therapeutic treatment, he has become a completely different man, for he has risen above his instincts, affects, habits, and morbid reactions. He has remained quite unchanged, for he has at the same time found once more a foothold in his psychic nature and in his past history.[14]

Proceeding from the ideas discussed an attempt could be made to outline the theoretical bases of psychoanalytical education. Every preanalytic pedagogy recognizes two ways of influencing the child. One of them is training, associating one kind of

[14] The American poet-philosopher George Santayana (1926) makes a sage in the underworld speak of a book entitled "The wheel of ignorance and the lamp of knowledge." The wheel of ignorance would have the world based on a number of principles, regarded numerically, like the spokes of a wheel; the correct view sees in these principles viewpoints which illuminate things first from one side and then from another, like a lamp swinging in space, shedding its cones of light upon things. "My benefactor has entitled his profound work The Wheel of Ignorance and the Lamp of Knowledge; because, he said, the Philosopher having distinguished four principles in the understanding of nature, the ignorant conceive these principles as if they were the four quadrants of a wheel, on any one of which in turn the revolving edifice of nature may be supported; whereas wisdom would rather have likened those principles to the four rays of a lamp suspended in the midst of the universe from the finger of Allah, and turning on its chain now to the right and now to the left; whereby its four rays, which are of divers colors, lend to all things first one hue and then another without confusing and displacing anything." This poetical comparison may serve as an illustration to show that we have not here set freedom and the lack of it side by side as materially distinct sectors.

conduct with pleasure and another with pain, the method of rewards and punishments; at bottom, it is the same method as is applied by the animal psychologist when in a maze experiment he trains the animal by means of electric shocks to follow a particular direction. The other method consists in holding up to the child an ideal, a hortative "shall." The first method estimates the freedom of its object as practically nonexistent, the second, as unlimited. The first method is animal and subhuman, the second divine and superhuman. Thus, nonanalytic psychology oscillates between a method proper to animals and another proper to God, but loses sight of one adapted to men. In contrast to these, psychoanalytical pedagogy represents a beginning of a human education. It regards its object as a creature endowed with a measure, albeit a limited measure, of freedom, takes into consideration the lack of freedom or the limitations on freedom present at the time, and tries to work with such freedom as is available and gradually to extend it.

CHAPTER 8

The Problem of the Genesis
of Psychic Conflict
in Earliest Infancy

Remarks on a Paper by Joan Riviere
(1936)

During the last few years several psychoanalytic writers in our literature have shown growing interest in the early phases of ego development, and pioneer work has been done in various quarters with the object of throwing light on this obscure subject. One such piece of work, which has been carried out with special thoroughness, stimulated the considerations I propose to put before you in this paper. Various writers have contributed to a growing body of observations and theories. I would mention especially the works of Melanie Klein, which are based on her experience of the analysis of children conducted by means of the play methods which she was the first to introduce; these theories are presented in her book *The Psychoanalysis of*

This paper was first published under the title "Zur Frage der Genese der psychischen Konflikte im frühen Kindersalter: Bemerkungen zur gleichnamigen Arbeit von Joan Riviere," in *Internationale Zeitschrift für Psychoanalyse*, 22:513-570, 1936. Reprinted from *International Journal of Psycho-Analysis*, 18:406-473, 1937.

The following paper embodies the conclusions of many discussions which have taken place on these problems among members of the Vienna Psychoanalytic Society. For some of these conclusions I alone am responsible; in other cases I have made use of ideas contributed by others.

Children (1932), but her writings on this subject go back to the year 1923. Ernest Jones (1927, 1929, 1932, 1935) has conducted a number of investigations from a similar standpoint; his writings deal principally with female sexual development, with problems concerning hate and the sense of guilt, and with the condition which he calls aphanisis. The material for these writings has been amassed during more than two decades. Joan Riviere has treated problems of the neuroses in the light of these theories in some papers and we are also indebted to her for an exposition of the whole subject that is remarkable for its lucidity (1936). Edward Glover (1956) has studied problems of ego development and choice of neurosis, the genesis of obsessional neurosis, and addiction to alcohol, and has considered the possible application of his conclusions to sociology. James Strachey (1934) has examined the therapeutic process from the angle of these theories. John Rickman (1936) and others have dealt with the upbringing of children.

A large number of other writings testifies to the fruitfulness of the views in question and their applicability in various fields.

The authors named are far from being in complete agreement; some of their hypotheses vary greatly. I will give a single example of this difference of opinion. Glover (1935) explains the phenomenon of *ambivalence* from the succession of great fluctuations of introjection and projection, the swing of the pendulum between the two being very wide during the first year of life while their subsequent alternation follows more rapidly on one another, with a lesser swing during the second year. That is to say, ambivalence is a very swift alternation between processes of introjection and projection with a comparatively small degree of intensity. Joan Riviere holds that the basis of ambivalence is the child's attempt to keep the image of the good object separate from that of the bad, for, if they were to merge, the good object itself would no longer be really good and the child would have no refuge, and no support for his reparation tendencies. This is an instance of two quite different theories appearing in this group of writings, and it may be asked whether there is any justification for presenting these theories together, even though they do not agree in all particulars, and making them a common starting point for our discussion.

I think that in spite of this and a number of other divergences all these theories have a common element, so that they may rightly be considered together. The following seem to me to be the point they have in common:

1. It is invariably assumed (*a*) that the experiences of the individual at a very early period of life, above all during the first year, are known to us or at least are discernible by means of analysis like the experiences at later periods; (*b*) that they can be described in terms of mental life; (*c*) that they are of great importance in the later development of neuroses and the formation of character; and (*d*) that throughout this early period fantasy is active, or at least that there is a kind of psychic life which approximates and is comparable to what we generally speak of as fantasy and that these psychic activities are consolidated and developed in a degree far beyond that which Freud and other writers are inclined to attribute to them at this age.

2. It is assumed that these processes during the infant's first year are determined on the instinctual side by oral-sadistic impulses and on the side of the ego by the process of introjection and projection.

In this respect these theories approximate closely to various psychoanalytic conclusions arrived at by Freud and to the views embodied in Abraham's writings, but in respect both of their generalizations and of the question of timing the writers whom I have in mind go beyond what is held by all analysts in this connection.

3. The instinctual side and the ego side of the experiences of early infancy are represented as being closely related. For instance, cannibalistic impulses are held to be the basis of mechanisms of introjection and anal excretion that of the mechanism of projection. From this point instinctual development and ego development continue to be closely related and are shown to be interwoven in a remarkable manner.

4. Further, in all the works mentioned the relation between fantasy and reality is conceived of in a somewhat different form from that commonly accepted in psychoanalysis. Although the fundamental principle of Freud's complementary series is consistently adhered to, much of what we have been accustomed to attribute to the interplay between the individual and his envir-

onment is explained as the product of an inner fantasy activity, which is evoked and intensified by external experiences but which would occur in essentially the same way even without such experiences. There are two possible views, one at either end of the scale, with regard to predisposition and environmental influences. According to the one, the living being is regarded as so much plastic material upon which the accidental happenings in his environment leave manifold imprints, while, according to the other, that being has already its definite form and its development is at most accelerated or retarded by the influence of environment. These are two extreme conceptions between which Freud always endeavored to hold a middle line. The authors I have quoted seem to incline more to the second possibility than do other analysts.

5. By devoting their attention to the experiences of early infancy and deriving from these initial processes the later phases in the evolution of the infantile psyche these writers place great weight on certain early processes, the existence of which they have inferred or conjectured. Other factors tend to be relegated to the background: among these I will mention especially the classical Oedipus situation and the closely allied castration complex on the instinctual side and, on the ego side, all those later, higher elaborations, attempts at solving conflicts, methods of defense against anxiety and unpleasure, and so forth, which certainly exercise a decisive influence upon the later fate of the neuroses and the formation of character.[1]

To all this it may be replied that the theories in question abandon none of the views with which we have long been familiar but merely add to them. I do not think, however, that it is possible simply to add to the body of our knowledge without altering it in some respect. It is never simply a question of displacement of accent: there are also displacements in the structure itself. When Freud added the infantile factors in the genesis of illness to those accidental factors with which the old psychiatry was familiar, or when to our knowledge of conscious

---

[1] Compare in this connection the study of these "higher" ego elaborations contained in Anna Freud's work *The Ego and the Mechanisms of Defense* (1936). By "higher" ego elaborations we must understand those which do not or at least do not necessarily occur in the first two years of life.

psychic processes he added the notion of those which are unconscious, it was not a question of a mere addition, which left unchanged all that had been before. We take a different view of the accidental causes of illness when we recognize their infantile antecedents.

The points listed above seem to me the common characteristics of the scientific writings we are considering, though they may differ from one another on this or that particular point. And because they have so much in common I think it is legitimate and imperative to study all these works together.

In this paper I propose to discuss a number of questions raised by these theories. I should like to say in advance that I have no controversial intention. Controversy would be particularly unprofitable since my standpoint in regard to them is that of an outsider and my only means of forming an opinion about the experience on which they are based is the study of the works published and the comparison of them with my own experience or that of other analysts. Moreover, I am not in a position to enter into controversy, for I do not know what point of view the authors in question adopt with regard to all the problems upon which I shall touch. Probably their standpoint would be similar in many instances to that which I shall advocate. In other instances this may not be so, but, since I do not know where there is a difference of opinion about the points I shall discuss, it is, if only for that reason, out of the question to discuss them in a controversial spirit, except in a few isolated cases. The purpose of this paper is much more modest. It is to enumerate and invite discussion of the questions which in my view have been rendered acute by the formulation of these theories and so to contribute something to future study or discussion of them.

It is doubtful whether an essay so circumscribed can really be called a scientific work at all. The purpose of scientific works is, first, to make public discoveries which the author has made or theories which he has evolved; secondly, to present conclusions arrived at by others; and, thirdly, to criticize and refute the views of other writers. I can lay claim to none of these three intentions. The attempt to envisage the problems raised by a particular theory and to make a kind of catalogue of questions for future discussion deserves the more modest title of an appendix to scientific work.

1. Sources of Our Knowledge of Processes Occurring during the First Year of Life

In every theory about the processes occurring early in life the principal question is that of the means of our knowledge: how do we know anything at all about psychic processes, how can we discover anything about them, how can we corroborate our conjectures? Of course this question always arises and applies to the experiences of any other period of life and we know that it is upon this that one of the arguments against psychoanalysis in general is based. Many of our opponents deny that we have any right to speak of unconscious processes. So the question as to the sources of our knowledge of the psychic processes might be formulated in the widest possible terms. But I think that there is no necessity to raise so comprehensive a problem here. For the purposes of this study we can be content with taking as our starting point the fact that we are all agreed as to the sources of our knowledge of psychic processes in later life. Insofar as this question has any bearing on our subject it will be discussed when we are considering the criteria of interpretation.

Accordingly we will confine ourselves to the only question which can still seem problematical to analysts, namely, what are the sources of our knowledge of psychic processes occurring at an age when the child as yet cannot speak and to which, as it seems, memory cannot go back in later years.

There are two principle methods of discovering the psychic processes of an individual whom we are studying. One is direct observation at the time when the processes are occurring, the other is analysis at a later period. If we use the second method we have, again, two means at our disposal: the memory of the analysand and reconstruction by analyst and patient. Direct observation, memory, and reconstruction[2] are the methods which have thrown light on infantile processes occurring at a

---

[2] The term *reconstruction* is not used here to denote simply that which is commonly understood by it in ordinary analytical phraseology. I mean by it any construction of the past which is not simply memory in the individual in question. We have the same sort of thing in judicial proceedings, when everything which is not admitted by the accused or vouched for by witnesses is called circumstantial evidence. The material for reconstruction varies. Sometimes different pieces of analytic material are used. This is what analysts generally mean when they use the term reconstruction. In other cases the past

somewhat later age, say, from the third to the fifth year of life. Let us now see what can be done by these methods when we come to the study of the first year.

In the first place, with regard to direct observation we may say that we have far more data at our disposal when the child is somewhat older. When we observe a three-year-old child, we can examine not only his behavior but also what he says. Moreover, the behavior of a three-year-old child is highly complex and consists not merely of expressional movements indicating instinctual impulses and the like, but of very complicated activities. In the case of children in their first year verbal communication is entirely lacking. We can observe only their behavior and this is confined to a very small number of manifestations, of the nature of expressional movements or—and this not directly after birth but somewhat later—declarations and demands. There are no complicated activities. So when we study the first year, we can directly observe only the child's behavior, and his modes of behavior are very limited. One would be inclined to suppose that from the observation of behavior we can infer only relatively few and simple psychic processes in the infantile organism and that other, more complicated processes either do not occur or, if they do occur, do not betray themselves in behavior and cannot be detected, at any rate by this kind of observation. I think it is, to say the least, an open question if the possibility exists of deducing with any sufficient degree of probability a large number of complicated psychic processes from the behavior of young infants, behavior with which we are very familiar, much of which has been examined and catalogued by academic as well as by analytic psychology.

---

is inferred from *repetition,* from *acting out* (in the transference) alone. If we wish to be exact we must discriminate between these cases. We have included the latter under the heading of reconstruction for the following reasons. If we describe something as a piece of repetitive acting, we have already formed a theory about it, for without a theory we could merely state that the patient was *behaving* in a particular way. The fact that this behavior is a repetition requires to be proved. Thus, acting out is not in itself evidence of the past experiences which we infer from it. If, from the acting out, i.e., from a certain type of behavior, we retrospectively construct past experiences, this amounts in my view to a kind of reconstruction.

Let us consider in particular the manifestations of oral-sadistic impulses. What they study of behavior teaches us in this respect is at most the nature of the affect and the goal and object of the instinct. For example, it may make it plain that the child is experiencing rage and manifesting a desire to bite, which is directed toward a particular object, or a desire to incorporate, which is sadistic in character. But apart from the simple inference as to his instinctual and affective situation we learn nothing: we have no evidence in his behavior of any fantasy. For instance, Melanie Klein speaks of the fantasy of the father's penis in the mother's body and of the tendency to destroy and incorporate the contents of that body. This is a fantasy which we know occurs from what the child tells us himself at a later period, probably when he is about three years old, but, so far as observation of behavior is concerned, I do not see how it can possibly prove that this fantasy exists during the child's first year, seeing that his behavior is confined to gestures.

A second point needs to be considered in this connection. Oral-sadistic manifestations do not occur with the same intensity in all children during their first year. There are children who, when they experience oral frustration, will cry for hours at a time, and burst into shrieks of rage, and at infant welfare clinics, where the feeding of the infants is strictly regulated, one comes across babies who scratch their faces with their nails till they bleed. But this is not true of all children. There are some who, when the initial difficulties have been overcome in the first four to eight weeks, never or very rarely scream, and in whom no paroxysms of rage in their very early days are observable (in their case the first manifestations of rage appear at the end of the first year) and who give the impression of a happy childhood with a strong positive libidinal attachment to those who look after them. It is true that we ascribe aggressive impulses to all children in whatever circumstances, and we have reason to do so.[3] But it seems to me a mistake to treat these facts as indicating

[3] The mere existence of aggressive impulses is clearly not a sufficient basis for Melanie Klein's theory. This is what she says on the point: "The idea of an infant of from six to twelve months trying to destroy its mother by every method at the disposal of its sadistic tendencies—with its teeth, nails and excreta and with the whole of its body, transformed in imagination into all

a mere difference in the intensity of the aggression and ignore them; there comes a point when quantity is transformed into quality. It may well be true that nobody, not even the richest person, can gratify all his material desires, but the recognition of this fact does not carry us much further when we come to the social problem, the difference between rich and poor. At all events a theory which assumes that in all children there is a great wealth of oral-sadistic impulses and fantasies in earliest infancy has to be squared with the fact that manifestations of oral sadism in the behavior of infants scarcely vary less[4] than does the degree of material prosperity enjoyed by different individuals in the present state of our civilization.

At the present moment I do not see how this phenomenon can be satisfactorily explained by a theory according to which fully developed oral sadism is universal in infants during their first year. We know that the very authors whom I have quoted expressly emphasize the fact that the oral-sadistic reactions of children are reactions to oral frustration, and further, as I need hardly mention, to peace or unrest in their environment, or to aggressiveness in those responsible for their upbringing, and so forth. It follows, too, that the strictness or laxity of a child's dietary regime has a considerable effect upon his aggressive impulses. We cannot help wondering whether all the children

---

kinds of dangerous weapons—presents a horrifying, not to say an unbelievable, picture to our minds. And it is difficult, as I know from my own experience, to bring oneself to recognize that such an abhorrent idea answers to the truth. But the abundance, force and multiplicity of the imaginary cruelties which accompany these cravings are displayed before our eyes in early analyses so clearly and forcibly that they leave no room for doubt" (1932, p. 187f.).

[4] In my view, if we leave out of account possible cases of a constitutional disposition to excessive aggression, we meet with violent manifestations of aggression in children only when there are exceptional conditions in their environment. For instance, they may be subjected to a strict regime with regard to their food (it does not take much to make a regime strict) or there may be an absence of calm in their surroundings; the people who bring them up may indulge their aggressive impulses or a child may suffer from some painful bodily illness or from a mother's ambivalence where there should be love, or his training in cleanliness may be premature and so forth. If there are no such injurious external influences, I think that early manifestations of aggression can largely be avoided or at least so limited that they do not pass beyond the line which separates the normal from the pathogenic.

whom these investigators studied happened to have been brought up in a particular way, for the methods of training infants vary according to their nationality, social position, etc. Is it not possible that the children in question had been subjected to a strict regime, applied or recommended by the exponents of the modern theories of child hygiene, who are concerned only with the infant's physical well-being? We are loath to entertain the idea that a generally applicable theory can have been partly determined by what is really a chance selection of material and we will dismiss this possibility. But an impression remains that the material provided by reality itself may have happened to be of a particular kind and this may have helped to disguise the difference of intensity in the maxima and minima of infantile aggression.

Let us now consider the other two ways in which we may learn something of the experiences of earliest infancy. First let us take memory. One source of our knowledge of such early processes is the memories which emerge in analysis when amnesia has been dispelled. Here I am using the word *memory* in its strict sense to denote the reappearance of a fragment of the past in the shape of the knowledge that such and such a thing did once happen and that the subject experienced it. There are other ways in which the past may return when it has persisted in the patient's mind, but, though these certainly belong to the mnemic function, I think they are better described by another name. Now we find ourselves confronted with a grave difficulty when we are dealing with the very earliest period of life, when the infant is as yet incapable of speech. Our impression is that the earliest recollections which human beings retain or which emerge in analysis go back to the second year. At any rate I know of no case in which it was possible to *prove* that an individual consciously remembered what happened in his first year, though I know of many instances of ostensible memories which were discovered to be fantasies produced at a later period. We must of course guard against being overhasty and giving to a negative pronouncement the value of a general law, and we shall bear in mind the objection that it does not follow that what has not yet been proved never can be proved. Since the difficulty of recovering memories becomes increasingly great and the number of those recovered more and more meager the further back we go in life, one may think that in principle there is no limit to the capacity for memory.

Thus we shall hesitate to conclude that there is an inherent impossibility about any particular phenomenon because, so far, we lack material to prove it. I think, however, that a certain theoretical consideration is in place here.

There is a good reason for expecting that it will be quite impossible to recover conscious memories (in the sense in which we have used the term) of the very earliest period of life. When we remember an occurrence and know that it took place in the past, we direct our thoughts to it as an object of experience and it is natural to suppose that only those experiences can be really remembered at a later date which, at the time when they occurred, were viewed by the subject at a certain distance with "intentional" reference to them as objects. At the moment when we had a particular experience we must, as it were, have stood at a distance from it, have objectified it, if we are to be able later to make it the object of conscious memory. No doubt everything which was not so experienced remains imprinted upon the psyche and continues to live and exert an influence, but in this case the mnemic function acts in a more primitive way: it cannot precisely be called memory. It helps to determine the subsequent life of the individual and the affect associated with it may be reproduced, or it may give rise to mental images, but it is not remembered. It seems that we have come back to the old distinction, long current in analysis, between acting and remembering.[5]

The power to objectify experience is apparently not present from the beginning: it is rather the result of development. We are probably right in assuming that children arrive at this stage at the end of their first or the beginning of their second year. We shall come back to this point later, when we discuss the problem of superego formation, and for the moment we will content

[5] This idea has been ably formulated by Max Scheler (1927), no doubt under the influence of psychoanalysis. He discriminates between tradition and memory and says that in the case of the former the past persists in the present, while, in the case of the latter, an experience is as it were thrown back by memory into the past to which it properly belongs.

ourselves with recognizing that the beginnings of the capacity
for speech (or, more correctly, of the representational function
of speech) probably indicate that the child has reached that stage
of experience which is a necessary condition of memory at a later
date.

We believe that everything which is experienced earlier
continues to exert an influence but that it cannot be the object of
conscious memory. Perhaps the very reason why impressions
received during this earliest period have such a particularly
strong effect is that they lose nothing of their force through being
remembered—they cannot be apprehended as having no present
existence or be thrown back into the past; we must, I think,
entirely agree with Joan Riviere when she says that the circumstance that a baby cannot express feelings in any way that we
can understand "may be one of the major causes of its special
sensitivity to these earliest experiences and their especially
significant after-effects." But this does not alter the fact that
these theoretical considerations serve to corroborate our view
that the lack of memories which can definitely be proved to go
back to the first year of life is not simply accidental but rather
inevitable and determined by the ego development of the child.
If this is so, however, we cannot hope to corroborate theories
about processes occurring in the first year of life by means of
memories produced by individuals.

It may be objected that these are theoretical assumptions
which themselves have not been proved and therefore cannot be
adduced in support of the assertion that there is a limit below
which memory, properly so-called, cannot reach; these considerations, however, are not the only ones to be taken into
account. There are others, commonly accepted by psychoanalysts, which bear them out. When we say that an ability to
stand at a certain distance from a particular experience and
transcend it potentially is a necessary condition of the capacity
subsequently to objectify it in memory, we are of course not
asserting that this capacity makes its appearance suddenly, when
the infant begins to speak, and exists from that moment in its
final and fully developed form. We are sure that it is slowly
evolved, like the faculty of speech itself. If, as we assume, the
complete absence of the capacity to objectify at the very

beginning of life constitutes a fundamental limitation for later memory, it cannot but be that the still imperfect development of this capacity at a later age is a quantitative if not an insuperable difficulty in the way of subsequent memory. Here we are once more on familiar ground. Freud (1931b) said of the preoedipal phase that all the experiences of that past era seem "so grey with age and shadowy" (p. 226), and other analysts have gone on to conjecture that human memory goes back to the time before the oedipal period only seldom and with difficulty. It is a fact that the vast majority of the memories of childhood belong to the period characterized by the castration and oedipus conflicts. There is a simple explanation of this phenomenon, on the lines of what has just been said. Speaking of the development from matriarchy to patriarchy, Freud (1909b) said that it signified a mental advance, for reliance was now placed on inference and thought, instead of on the testimony of the senses. Thus it was a step parallel to an advance in ego development, toward release from an immediate dependence on the instinctual needs of the moment and on the actual perceptual situation. We may suppose that the same applies to the advance from the pre-oedipal mother fixation to the patriarchy of the oedipus complex. The paucity of memories of the preoedipal period may thus be similarly explained by the imperfect development of the ego at that period, just as the complete absence of memories of the first year is explained by the nonexistence of the ego function in question.

It seems then that we have good grounds for believing that conscious memory of the very earliest period of life is fundamentally impossible and that the few examples which we should be inclined to regard as such memories really belong to a later period and have their source in what the individual has been told.

At this point it may be objected that it is no great loss if true memory is lacking: memories are not a pure source of knowledge and we know how frequently they are deceptive. This is quite true and nobody will imagine that every memory has the value of proved material. Analysts, of all people, are constantly occupied in discovering the elaborations and distortions which have taken place in people's memories. But this imperfection in the material does not prove that it is worthless, any more than the fact that spurious fabrications are made where excavations are being carried out proves that archaeology is of no value. Perception too is liable to error and yet science cannot do without it. We are tempted here to quote the anecdote of a man's remark about women, told by Freud (1926b) in connection with the question of medical training for psychoanalysts: speaking of women, a man once said, "After all, a woman is the best thing *of the kind* that we have."

Another objection might run thus: even if we have no memories going back to the first year, we have other nmemic products, for these experiences continue to exert a living influence and to be reproduced, whether in the reemergence of visual images or in that of affects in the transference situation in analysis. This cannot be disputed, but it really comes under our next heading: reconstruction from analytic data.

In this connection we can only make certain general statements, which are sure of general acceptance. Nobody doubts that in reconstruction the greatest caution must be exercised, especially when there is some discrepancy between the scope and the details of the processes reconstructed and the proved data at our disposal. A single instance from analytic writings will suffice. In "The History of an Infantile Neurosis" (1918) Freud discusses the question whether his reconstruction of the patient's observation of coitus in his second year corresponded to a reality. And yet this same experience was on the whole very probable, and certainly by far the majority of children have witnessed such a scene in very early infancy either in consequence of confined living quarters or through the carelessness of the parents. We know that Freud did not come to a definite conclusion and finally left it an open question whether what the child really witnessed was the sexual act performed by animals and not by his parents; since the Wolf-Man grew up in the country, he had ample opportunity of observing the latter.

We can hardly escape the impression that the attempt to get at experiences of the first year must encounter very considerable difficulties and that theories about a rich fantasy life in this period are harder to verify than statements about what occurred at a later age. It might be reported that, because of these difficulties, it is not fair to demand from those who have investigated this period of life proofs of the same degree of cogency as those which psychoanalysis has at its command where its conclusions about later periods are concerned. But we soon realize that this is no argument, for, to quote Freud again, "Ignorance is ignorance; no right to believe anything can be derived from it" (1927a, p. 32).

Of course we can try to find a substitute for material which is lacking and, arguing that the psychic processes in very early infancy must still bear a strong resemblance to biological processes, we may look for that substitute in biology.[6] But so far it has not been found there.

Naturally, nothing in what has been said constitutes an argument against the validity of the theories put forward by Melanie Klein or other analysts with regard to the earliest period of life; but I think it is now evident that these theories cannot be said to be so convincingly attested as the other components of psychoanalysis.

2. Criteria of Interpretation

When we study the writings I have quoted, we often come across certain phrases which occur in other analytic works as well. We read that "analysis showed" this or that, or that it led to such and such a conclusion, and so forth. Phrases of this sort are calculated to put an end to any further discussion. If we cannot agree with the author at this point, we must be on our guard lest we should be thought to be casting doubt on the material itself instead of questioning the soundness of his conclusions; and we shall be liable to come under suspicion of being prevented by something in ourselves from finding those conclusions as obvious as he does.

Of course, as I have already said, this phraseology is not peculiar to the writers in question but is to be met with in

---

[6] Of course, by *biology* we understand here not merely the science of physiology and kindred researches, but biology in its more recent and comprehensive aspect, the aim of which is to investigate the vital processes in general.

psychoanalytic works in general. It is impossible for an author in every instance to adduce the analytic material upon which his conclusions are based, consisting as it does of innumerable details. Nor is it necessary for him to do so, for, apart from a few writings addressed to nonanalytic readers, analytic works are written for analysts and it is presumed that every analytic reader will be able to supply from the experience which he himself has accumulated that which is not fully described or expressly stated.

But the case before us is clearly one in which the views of a number of analytic investigators do not seem to their colleagues in the same field to be fully established, and therefore we sometimes feel that we cannot be satisfied with the bare statement that the analysis showed this or that, but that we should like to know exactly what the facts were in every detail, and what conclusions were drawn from them, and precisely why these conclusions were drawn and not others. I do not think that it is enough to quote the obvious analogy between the hesitation felt by many analysts in accepting particular analytic theories and the doubts experienced by those outside analysis with reference to the conclusions of analysis in general. In particular, it seems to me unprofitable to deflect the discussion of an objective question to that of the possible emotional bias of the skeptic. For psychology is a two-edged weapon, as Freud (1931b) pointed out when he said that "The use of analysis as a weapon of controversy can clearly lead to no decision" (p. 230). Psychology has always a twofold application. Moreover, the general resistance to the conclusions of analysis which we all know to be the affective basis of its rejection by the world in general has never been used as an argument for their validity. On the contrary, it was not till after this seemed to have been abundantly proved that Freud asked himself the question why these conclusions had not long ago become common property, and still met with rejection even after his discoveries. The logical outcome of discrediting any doubts which may be expressed with regard to the findings of an analyst would be to assert that every analytic interpretation must be correct—a conclusion which can hardly be admitted.

In a word, the question of the criteria of interpretation,[7] which is of itself exceedingly interesting, becomes acute when we have interpretations which do not appear convincing to all analysts in the light of their own experience. So long as those engaged in analysis were to all intents and purposes in agreement, the discussion of the question of criteria could be deferred, but when wide divergences of opinion become apparent it is time to find a place for it on our program.

It is not my intention to enter here upon the whole problem of the criteria of interpretation; it would take us altogether too far outside the scope of this essay. We are confining ourselves to the points raised by certain controversial theories; there is thus no need to discuss issues the analysts themselves do not question.

Let us ask first what are our criteria in those fields of psychoanalysis in which there is no controversy.

Here it is advisable to distinguish between two types of interpretation. The first is that which relates to the present life of the analysand, the unconscious processes which are at work in him *hic et nunc,* and the second that which is arrived at by a reconstruction of the past. It is evident that the criteria of interpretation are not quite the same in the two cases.

In interpreting current unconscious processes, no matter whether they belong to the sphere of instinct or to that of ego elaboration, we look for some direct confirmation. The unconscious processes enter consciousness, sometimes immediately and sometimes only later, and the patient admits that they actually are taking place or have taken place in him. Generally such interpretations are followed by associations which indicate the operation of these unconscious processes in other connections. In some cases this does not happen, but the interpretation may all the same have been correct. If it was correct, it always makes it possible for us to understand and interpret the other type of reaction in the patient, namely, his resistance. What I said above applies to the interpretation of resistance as well: the patient becomes conscious of his resistance. Once the interpretation of it has been worked through, the way is clear for the other

---

[7] See Bernfeld (1932), Hartmann (1927), and Chapter 9 in this volume.

interpretations to enter consciousness or to be supplemented by fresh associations.[8]

The situation is more difficult in interpretations relating to the past. Here the patient's emerging memories often take the place of his conscious confirmation of our interpretation of his present experiences. And some of the memories which follow are analogous to the associations which, in the first case, indicate the operation of the instinctual impulses or methods of ego behavior in other connections. But these confirmations are not equally convincing. Memories are always open to the suspicion of error and of having been produced by the patient in order to please and so forth.[9]

There are various other possible ways of obtaining corroboration. In some cases a third party, possibly a relative of the patient, corroborates the fact that certain incidents happened which we have inferred in our interpretation. For technical reasons we usually refrain from using this method, but the fact remains that an interpretation can be, and in many cases has been, verified in this way. Or the patient's own store of memories furnishes corroboration of incidents which we have merely inferred to have happened.

But the final proof of the results arrived at by psychoanalytic interpretation lies outside analysis, in the direct observation of children. Of course, it is not possible to use this method to verify an interpretation in an individual case, for we cannot transport

[8] It is not necessary for the purpose of this study to discuss the technical problem of interpretation or certain grave pathological cases in which this formula does not apply exactly.

[9] It might be said that the same thing may happen when we are interpreting current processes: the patient's admission that he detects in himself certain impulses may be mistaken or prompted by a desire to please, etc.; that is to say, it may be the result of suggestion on the part of the analyst. If we are giving an account of the criteria of interpretation for the benefit of nonanalysts we should have to consider this objection fully, but for the purposes of this paper it may be disregarded; we know that suggestion has no place in analysis and that it would indicate a blatant lack of skill on the part of an analyst if he did not realize that certain associations were being produced from a desire to please and proceed to analyze the motive for them. It is evident that the possibilities of deception are greater in the case of the analysand's confirmation of interpretations relating to the past than in the case of that which relates to currently operative processes.

the patient back into his childhood and observe what he actually did. Certain fundamental facts, however, *can* be verified by direct observation of children, for instance, the existence of the oedipus conflict and the castration complex. These were originally arrived at by a process of interpretation in the analysis of adults: it was inferred that they had occurred in the patient's childhood. But the final proof lies in the fact that direct observation provides evidence of all these processes. The results of observation in this case are extraordinarily definite. We have only to allow children to express themselves fearlessly and we shall observe beyond any possibility of doubt all these tendencies and anxieties. It would probably be quite right to say that the evidence of these infantile processes could be presented in a sound film.[10]

It is true that this in itself is still no proof of the validity of interpretations relating to individual variations in individual cases. But this extra-analytic evidence does establish the following points: (1) that certain processes occur regularly and are never absent; (2) that individual variations exist and, moreover, that direct observation provides evidence that such variations later give rise to precisely those products which we discover in analyzing persons in whose infantile history, according to our interpretation, these variations played a part. Thus, for instance, the analysis of certain neurotic symptoms and character traits in female patients leads us to infer an elaboration of the castration complex. For example, a certain type of object relation may

[10] I must take leave to dispute one passage in Joan Riviere's paper. On p. 397 we read: "Even the most important part of the Oedipus complex, the gross sexual and aggressive impulses and phantasies, would hardly be regarded as proved or its existence as definitely established by extra-analytical observation alone." I think that the evidence is as convincing here as evidence can ever be when it relates to what goes on in the mind of another. If we fail to realize the large body of evidence for such psychoanalytic conclusions and are inclined to think that those conclusions are based solely on considerations of plausibility and on such experiences on the part of the analyst as bear them out, we shall very likely go on to suppose this kind of corroboration would suffice in the case of analytic propositions in general, and that anyone who required more in the way of proof would be making a demand with which psychoanalysis does not and need not comply. This is to fail to appreciate the great gulf between the more convincing evidence which is required and forthcoming for our psychoanalytic theory and the much more uncertain basis for hypotheses concerning processes occurring during the first year of life.

represent an active castration tendency which has its source in penis envy. The corroboration furnished by the direct observation of children is that we find that little girls who elaborate the fact of the difference between the sexes in this particular way go on to develop this particular type of object relation.

This brings us back to the observation of behavior as the final means of verifying analytic interpretation. It is evident that it is no small loss if we must do without corroboration through direct observation.

A more comprehensive view of the matter may throw light on all this. In the literature we often find statements suggesting that a theory must be correct because its various elements agree with one another and bear one another out.[11] Let us consider whether the consistency of all the various elements is really a criterion of the correctness of the whole system.

One thing, however, is certain: the lack of such inner

[11] It might be contended that Freud makes use of a similar argument to justify the technique of dream interpretation (1900, p. 527f.): "If we were in fact met by objections such as these, we might defend ourselves by appealing to the impression made by our interpretations, to the surprising connections with other elements of the dream which emerge in the course of our pursuing a single one of its ideas, and to the improbability that anything which gives such an exhaustive account of the dream could have been arrived at except by following up psychical connections which had already been laid down." But the "surprising connections with other elements of the dream" are not taken by Freud to constitute a proof: he merely cites it by way of illustration of the "impression" produced by our dream interpretations and he points out that often, when the analyst is pursuing one dream element, other elements are illuminated in a surprising way. When he speaks of the "improbability" that any explanation which so completely covers and elucidates a dream can be arrived at in any other way than by following up psychic connections previously established, he means that it is improbable that an explanation which comprises a large number of phenomena in a single whole can be based on chance. In a book entitled *Die Psychoanalyse Freuds: Verteidigung und kritische Bemerkungen,* Bleuler (1911b) endeavors to estimate this probability. But Freud does not regard this as the real proof of the validity of our technique of interpretation. And the next argument which Freud uses in the passage I have quoted—the identity of "the procedure by which we resolve hysterical symptoms; and there the correctness of our method is warranted by the coincident emergence and disappearance of the symptoms" (p. 528)—is again not accepted by him as a completely satisfactory proof. Freud seeks and finds such a proof only when he discusses the problem of free association. There are many other criteria of the validity of psychoanalytic dream interpretation. For instance, forgotten dream fragments frequently reemerge after one fragment has been interpreted; buried experiences of childhood are revealed as the

agreement, an inconsistency in the separate parts of a theory, is a strong argument against it. Either it is incorrect as a whole or parts of it need to be revised. Thus consistency is certainly a necessary condition for the correctness of a theory, but it is doubtful whether consistency alone suffices to prove it. To frame the question in this way is to answer it in the negative. Even quite erroneous theories often seem to provide the explanation of a whole series of phenomena. To give an extreme example: paranoiacs often feel that every detail in their daily life confirms their beliefs, and they argue that these beliefs alone contain the key to everything that they experience. Interpretations cannot be used to prove other interpretations; they must be corroborated, at least in some one point, *extrasystematically*, by something which is not itself interpretation.

This is very unsatisfactorily expressed because it leaves out of account the fact that the evidence upon which a system of interpretations can be based and which is not itself interpretation nevertheless does contain elements of interpretation. (For instance, our direct observation of children—like any other observation of children—naturally contains such elements.) But some interpretations approximate less closely and others more closely to that which is verifiable intersubjectively. We might arrange interpretations in gradation and say that all those of the nth grade must be corroborated by at least one interpretation of the grade $n - 1$, so that ultimately the proof lies in that which is intersubjectively verifiable. Such a theory of gradation is very likely correct, but for our present purpose we may content ourselves with observing that the agreement of all interpretations is not itself a sufficient basis for a theory but must be reinforced, at least in one point, extrasystematically by proven facts.

---

result of an interpretation; the inference drawn is confirmed by the patient's present state or by his direct assent; or an interpretation enables us rightly to diagnose physical or psychic processes active at the moment (e.g., pregnancy in a patient who had not yet realized her condition, or some symptom such as agoraphobia which has not yet been confided to the analyst) or to predict what will happen later (e.g., when a dream reveals that a negative transference is emerging or that the patient has an inclination, which will manifest itself only after some time, to give up analysis). Cf. in this connection Hartmann (1927).

This viewpoint seems to me to be applicable to the confirmation, through the direct observation of children, of infantile processes arrived at by interpretation in the analysis of
adults.

It is hardly necessary to mention that yet another criterion,
the criterion *ex juvantibus*, cannot legitimately be adduced
here. Indeed it seems to me to be a proof of the high level of all
psychoanalytic discussions that they consistently refrain from
using this argument. A cure can often be effected by more than
one method. The question is what is meant by cure. On this
point analysts have long taken up a very different position from
that adopted by clinical psychiatry and the other methods of
psychotherapy, whose practitioners speak of cure when certain
symptoms known to them have disappeared. But psychother-
apists as a rule do not and cannot know all the patient's
symptoms and they do not stop to consider the price paid for the
removal of a symptom. The same difficulties in regard to the
problems of cure occur in analysis, though in an infinitely more
subtle form. So it is a very good thing that we do not rely on this
argument.

In concluding this section I shall survey the methods of
verification that analysis can employ.

The fundamental difficulty is that human beings are not
suitable subjects for experimentation. By "experimentation" we
mean the deliberate variation of a single condition while all
others are kept constant. Moreover, experimentation presupposes that only a limited number of conditions exists and that
these can be varied or kept constant at will. Thus experiment in
the strict sense of the term can take place only in the sphere of
phenomena we can control, i.e., inanimate objects. Life eludes
experimentation in this strict sense; for life is a historic process. If
we vary one condition in two different individuals in different
ways, we still have no experiment in the exact sense of the term.
The second individual cannot be used as a "control" for the first,
for these two individuals are not identical in every other respect.
So we are not justified in immediately attributing the difference
of the results obtained in the two to the variation of a particular
condition. If, on the other hand, we vary a condition in two
successive experiments on the same individual, we cannot as a

rule draw any convincing conclusion, for, when the second experiment takes place, the individual is no longer in the same state as in the first, owing to the fact that he has already been subjected to it. For instance, if we want to know how a child reacts to tenderness or severity in his upbringing and try first the one and then the other, the child who has experienced severity is no longer the same as he was before that experience, and it has not been proved how he would have reacted to indulgence if his desires had not previously been thwarted. Thus the necessary conditions for experiment cannot be obtained in this way.

It is true that these conditions of (ideal) experiment are not strictly applicable even in the case of the natural sciences. Even in physics the number of conditioning factors, all but one of which should be kept constant, is not really limited but infinite, and some of these factors are not within our control. An experiment made in 1900 cannot, to be quite exact, be reproduced in 1936, for not all the previous conditions—for instance, the position of the Milky Way—can be exactly repeated. Strictly speaking, even an experiment in physics is a historical act in a process which cannot be reproduced. But experience has shown that we are allowed to neglect a sufficiently large number of parameters.

We must not overlook the possibility of obtaining proofs in psychology which are comparable to those obtained by experiment. Experimental biology testifies to such a possibility. The life of the lower animals is also a historical process, though of more limited dimensions than human life, and yet it can be made the subject of experiment.

Although the situation where human beings are concerned can never be exactly comparable to an experiment in physics, experiments or something comparable to them can be undertaken under the following conditions:

1. On the periphery of personality. Here experiments can really be made, either by taking two individuals and varying a particular condition in the case of one of them, or by varying the same condition in one and the same individual in two successive tests. For instance, an experiment with contrasting colors does not alter the behavior of the subject when he undergoes a second test. This is the rationale of a large part of academic psychology;

for analysis, concerned as it is with the central phenomena of personality, this case is of little interest.[12]

2. Quasi experiments conducted with a large number of persons. We have seen why we obtain no convincing proof if we vary a condition in the case of one experimental subject and keep it constant in the case of another. The difference in the other qualities of the two individuals is too great for us to be able to ascribe the difference in our results with any certainty to the variation of this single factor. The greater the number of persons experimented with, the more limited is this source of error. If we have a sufficiently large number, we may legitimately draw a general conclusion, for we may expect that the variations will be distributed equally on both sides and cancel one another out.

Under this heading we must place the conclusions arrived at as the result of attempts to exert a psychical influence on humans in accordance with some theoretical system (e.g., methods of education).

This kind of quasi experiment plays a significant role in analysis, when we draw conclusions from a large number of cases. Naturally it is not necessary for a condition to be varied *at will*. The observation of a large number of cases in which one factor varies *by chance* (for instance, the way the individual has been brought up) answers the same purpose. For example, when we observe how regularly an acute neurosis develops in men who underwent operation for phimosis between their third and seventh year and when we compare these statistics with the far smaller percentage of cases of acute neurosis in other men, we feel it legitimate to draw certain conclusions.

3. Experiments of nature. In many cases nature itself provides the conditions of experiment; we might say that every abnormality is an experiment of nature. This is why in psychoanalysis investigation of the pathological takes the place of experiment in the natural sciences.

A particularly impressive example of such an experiment of nature is that of uniovular twins, for we may assume that their

---

[12] Modes of behavior belonging to the periphery of the personality may in fact be defined as those in which a first experiment does not alter the behavior of the subject in a second experiment.

heredity is identical and that their differences are due to factors in their environment. Hartmann (1934-1935) showed that complementary anal character traits may occur in such twins, one being miserly and the other a spendthrift, thus demonstrating the unity of the anal character.

4. Experiments in cases in which the living object's freedom is somehow restricted (e.g., in hypnosis or in experiments with posthypnotic suggestion). Under this heading comes the experimental confirmation of dream symbolism, obtained by Schrötter (1911), Roffenstein (1923), Betlheim and Hartmann (1924). We have an example of this kind of experiment in analysis when we draw an inference as to the nature of the transference material from transference phenomena which appear regularly.

This is how we finally arrive at our evidence in analysis, if we have not already received satisfactory corroboration in the direct assent of the patient to our interpretation.

It is time to return to our subject. We have made a wide detour and seem to be a long way from it. But all our considerations converge upon a single point, namely, that in my opinion we do not yet have sufficient evidence for theories about processes during the first year of life.

All the fantasies which have been described as belonging to this early period have been abundantly proved to occur at a later age, in children of about three years old. I believe that we shall obtain evidence that they occur even during the course of the third year. It is, I think, no small merit in the writings which we are considering that they have drawn attention to these fantasies. Their existence is not in question, only their occurrence so early in life. We might be tempted to say that they could not have arisen as late as the third or fourth year but must date back to an earlier period. The obvious argument in support of this view is that these are oral fantasies and we are accustomed to describe the first year as the oral phase. I do not think, however, that this is a sound argument. First, as regards the ascription of oral fantasies to the oral phase, I would point out that orality does not come to an end when the libido takes up the anal position. Freud never intended to assert that a particular libidinal position excluded all others; he was merely describing a certain organization of the libido. Secondly, the classification of libidinal development in several phases was a tentative piece of work, a fine idea because it accounted for the phenomena in question at a single blow, but nevertheless it was a piece of pioneer work, and there are many points in connection with these phases of development which remain obscure for the very reasons I gave when I spoke of the obscurity of that "grey and shadowy" past. Now when it comes to deciding that fantasies which we encounter must have originated at an earlier period, which is as much as to say that it is an impossibility for them to have arisen at the present time, this argument seems to me no more convincing that it would be to insist that Shakespeare's *Hamlet* or *Lear* must have already existed in his mind in childhood. It is true that the germs of the dramas were there—fantasies to be subsequently elaborated, a particular bent of his genius and much else besides belonged to the poet's early childhood—but the finished product came into existence only when he reached maturity. Similarly the fantasies[13] belonging to the third year may have their antecedents in processes which occur at the very beginning of life and be woven of this early material, combined with the experiences subsequently acquired during the development of the instincts and the ego, and as a result of external happenings. But I see no grounds which compel us to conclude that the fantasies themselves belong to these early periods.

3. The Formation of the Superego

One of the controversial questions relates, as we know, to the so-called early superego. An account of the formation and subsequent development of the superego may be useful as a basis for the discussion of differences of opinion.

We know that in *The Ego and the Id* (1923b) Freud speaks of the formation of the superego at the time of the passing of the oedipus complex. It is founded on the child's identifications with

---

[13] The word "fantasy" is used here in the sense in which it is used in common parlance, whence psychoanalysis adopted it. Experiences which have not been dealt with by thought processes would be more correctly described as impulses, anxieties, etc.

the parents, which, unlike the so-called "identifications within the ego," are opposed to the rest of the ego. The oedipus conflict terminates in these identifications, which, in relation to the ego, embody the libidinal and aggressive tendencies of the object on the one hand and, on the other, the subject's own tendencies turned back upon the ego. All this is very familiar, as is Freud's explanation why the oedipus complex ends in this way. This naturally leads on to the differences between the masculine and the feminine superego. In boys the oedipus complex comes to an end more abruptly and more suddenly than in girls. In the latter it seems rather to die away gradually, the only causes for its destruction in girls being lack of fulfillment and fear of the loss of love, while in boys castration anxiety is another contributing factor. Much later in life men have, as it were, their revenge on the opposite sex. The end of the second sexual phase, the period of maturity, terminates abruptly for women, whereas in men there is a gradual process of decline. These differences in the passing of the oedipus complex and the formation of the superego have been adduced as the explanation of the differences in the superego in the two sexes; in men it retains traces of its origin in castration anxiety and in women of the fear of loss of love. Man's superego, it follows, is less dependent on other people's opinion, while woman's is more akin to social anxiety. The saying attributed to Martin Luther, "Here stand I, I cannot do otherwise" (the command of the superego which set him in open opposition to the forces of the community) is said to be characteristic of the male superego, while such an attitude is not easily conceivable in the case of women.[14]

This theory of the formation of the superego during the fifth year has met with a good deal of contradiction. It is contended that it really dates much further back and is established at a very early period. To assume that the superego originates when the child is four years old is said to be as mistaken as to suppose that sexuality begins at puberty.

The theory of superego formation, as I have outlined it, was never intended to suggest that we can perceive nothing compar-

[14] It is not to be supposed that this attitude is never met with in women, only that it is comparably rare and that women with a superego of this sort probably give us an impression of masculinity.

able to the processes of the superego before a child is four years old. What is meant is rather that at this age a psychic institution is formed which contains within itself a consistent code of laws and divides the world into good and bad, and that the behavior of the child from that time on is decisively different from what it was before. This difference in children's behavior in their fourth and in their sixth year is clearly noticeable in their upbringing. Anna Freud (1934) has described this change as follows (p. 187f.):

> The formation of the superego facilitates matters for those who are training and educating the child. Whereas up to this point they have carried on the struggle with a being absolutely opposed to them, they now have an ally in the enemy's camp. The educator of the older child can rely on this superego to support him, he knows that he and the superego will join forces against the child. Thus the child finds himself confronted by two authorities, the transformed part of his own personality and his love object who is still present in reality." [He becomes docile to a degree hitherto quite unknown.]

The change which takes place in the child at the end of the first sexual period is familiar to educators. The common practice of sending children to school from about the sixth year is certainly not accidental. It is determined not only by their intellectual development but by what Freud describes as the development of the superego, for they are now able to grasp the idea of duty. Probably it was for the same reason that in the Middle Ages children were removed from the sole care of women and entered their father's sphere of interest on reaching this age.

There can be no doubt that at about this time, revolutionary processes occur in the domain which we assign to the superego. But this does not mean and was never supposed to mean that even earlier, right back to the second year, there were no phenomena similar to the superego, such as, for instance, a sense of guilt. The existence of such phenomena is commonly admitted by psychoanalytic writers and has been discussed by them in the literature since Freud directed attention to the problems connected with the superego. It is true that it has been customary to speak of "prestages" of the superego (Fenichel, 1926). Let us for a moment disregard the question whether "prestages" is a suitable term for these phenomena. At all events we believe that a sense of guilt and remorse already manifest themselves at a much earlier age. Naturally in the case of a two-year-old child it is very difficult to distinguish between fear of an external object and a sense of guilt. Only too often we have the impression that no guilt is felt unless the external object whom the child fears knows of the transgression or—since to a child all adults are omniscient—is believed to know of it. It seems, then, that the guilty feelings lack one of the distinguishing marks of the superego, namely, its capacity to operate independently of the presence of a feared external object. Yet, in spite of this and even when we take into account everything which can possibly be a manifestation of anxiety,[15] there remains something that indicates the existence of an inner voice.

We know of two sources for these phenomena. One is the child's identification of himself with the people who bring him up and the other derives from the course taken in him by the conflict of ambivalence and from the limitations imposed on his aggression by the outside world. In the first case he identifies himself with adults, just as he does later at the passing of the

---

[15] There is another difficulty which must be mentioned in this connection. The writers whose works we are considering often speak of an "introjected object"; the fact that this object has not the characteristics of the real object but those with which the child's fantasy endows it is held to prove that it is not a real object but an internalized object. I would suggest that we should differentiate between two things: *an inner institution* and *an image of an external object*. Such an image may not coincide with the reality: the object may be distorted in fantasy by the addition of characteristics which have their source in the mind of the subject. But this is not the same thing as an introjected object. There is a difference between a patient's rejecting a certain mode of behavior at the bidding of an inner voice and refraining from it from fear of another person—however unreal this person may be and however little the characteristics with which he is endowed in the patient's imagination correspond to the reality. There are various criteria by which we may test this difference. I mention only one: the development of neurosis differs according to whether it is based on a true sense of guilt or on fear of an imaginary avenger; the methods adopted to deal with the pressure of an inner institution or the dread of a fantasied object are not the same. In the second case the patient often resorts to modes of defense designed to appease, deceive, or outwit the imaginary antagonist. Such attempts do not work so well with respect to a true inner institution.

oedipus complex; he makes their commands and prohibitions his own and we may say that they are introjected. This is a fact which can hardly be questioned. We notice that children toward the end of their second year will speak in a deep voice when quoting the commands of their elders. Melanie Klein gives a very good illustration of such behavior.

In considering the genesis of the phenomena of conscience from the conflict of ambivalence and the external restraints upon aggression we must distinguish between two things: the libidinal and the aggressive roots of these phenomena. In the one case it is the child's aggression which meets with an external check or is restrained by his own love tendency and recoils on himself. For instance, it has often been observed that a child who is prevented from hitting another child will hit himself. This turning back of the aggressive impulse upon the self may even give rise to behavior suggestive of a need for punishment.

If, however, an aggressive impulse has actually been carried out and the object has suffered an injury, the tendency to make reparation comes into play in consequence of the ambivalence in the object relation. The aggressive impulse has been satisfied and appeased by the act and its intensity diminishes: love once more makes itself heard and seeks to restore the object which has been injured. This is the account which Freud (1930) gives of the origin of remorse.[16]

Psychoanalytic writers commonly describe all these impulses as prestages of the superego. They closely resemble the superego proper. We can trace them as early as the second year. Why are they called prestages? Fenichel (1926) says on this point: "What characterizes all these 'pre-stages' is that they exist together in a loose and independent way, rather like the partial drives before their integration into a single sexual organization. They lack the essential characteristics of the superego—its unity, its sternness, its opposition to the ego, its unconsciousness, and its power, all of which are proper to it as the heir of the oedipus complex" (p. 110).

I believe that at the present time the majority of analysts hold similar views about these prestages and their difference from the

---

[16] Nunberg (1926) draws attention to the libidinal components in the sense of guilt.

later superego proper. We may wonder whether Fenichel's description is not somewhat too precise in this or that point, for instance, when he implies that these phases are never opposed to the ego or never unconscious, but on the whole the impression he conveys is that we are here dealing with relatively isolated phenomena, separate internalized commands and prohibitions which have not yet been welded into a unified code, single and relatively disconnected acts prompted by remorse and the need for punishment.

Questions of terminology ought not to be made a bone of contention but should be cleared out of the way by agreement on a definition. I think that there is no reason why these antecedent phases should not also be called the "superego," if anyone wishes so to call them. But, in order to do justice to the facts, we must then state that that which occurs in the fifth year of life is the decisive step taken in the development of the superego and may perhaps be termed its integration. There would be little difference in the result.

Let us now go back another step and ask whether at a still earlier period we can find anything which might be included in the concept of the superego. I think that we do find something of the sort at the end of the first or the beginning of the second year. I refer to the advance in the child's development when he reaches the point of being able to objectify his own self. This is a stage which I mentioned before when I discussed the theoretical question of an ultimate limit to memory. The child now begins to detach himself from the biological situation characterized by vital instinctual needs and from his perceptual environment and develops the capacity to adopt another, imaginary standpoint. When this advance is made, there opens up a wealth of undreamed-of possibilities in the shape of speech and culture. A number of experiments in animal psychology suggest that it is here that the real difference between human beings and animals lies. The newly acquired capacity manifests itself in many ways, e.g., in the ability to understand a hypothetical situation. Some experts in cerebral pathology hold that it is precisely this function which is impaired and partially lost in asymbolic disturbances.

There seem to be good reasons for assigning this function to the superego. The power to objectify the self and to achieve detachment from it and from the vital needs of the moment probably depends on that formation of different levels within the ego which is the most essential characteristic of the superego. We remember that Freud (1914a) introduced the concept of the superego in connection with ideas of reference, and again in the *New Introductory Lectures on Psychoanalysis* (1933b) raises the problem in connection with the question how the ego can take itself as an object. Moreover, it is certain that all the phenomena of the superego presuppose this function; whether we punish ourselves or comfort ourselves, there must be some stratification within the ego, an imaginary standpoint from which we confront the rest of our personality. This was my reason for endeavoring to show that the function in question is the essential characteristic of the superego and that what really distinguishes human beings from animals is the appearance of what in psychoanalytic terminology we call the superego function, to which I have given the name of the "formal superego function" (Ch. 7), I personally am solely responsible for this classification and terminology and I am not sure how many analysts would agree with me. I see no objection if anyone prefers to give some other name to this advance in ego development and to reserve the term "superego" for something much more concrete. Nevertheless I think we should still be justified in extending the concept of the superego to include the function of which I have been speaking. In that case the first traces of this development, which is completed only gradually, are (as we know from exact data as to mental development) found at the end of the first or beginning of the second year.

But what can be meant by speaking of a superego at a still earlier period, in the first months of life? We have no evidence that any function of self-objectivation, without which there can certainly be no superego phenomena, appears so early. All that we know of mental development contradicts such a notion.

Several authors refer to autosadistic tendencies or aggressive impulses violently assaulting the subject's own ego; they are said to derive from the introjection of an object which has become "bad" through the projection of the child's own aggressive impulses and they are sometimes spoken of as an early superego. We need not consider this theory of the origin of aggressive impulses against the self, nor need we discuss whether they are so powerful as some authors are inclined to believe. Let us be content to admit that such aggressive impulses do exist and to ask whether it is right to describe them as the superego.

Not every aggression against the self is an aggression on the part of the superego, any more than all self-love is the superego's love for the ego. Freud (1927b) says that in humor the superego treats the ego in an affectionate and comforting way, and we are familiar with the application of this idea: the ego's wooing of the superego for its love and the superego's affectionate tenderness toward the ego (see Jekels, 1952). But all self-love does not come under this heading; otherwise we should have to say that narcissism was a superego phenomenon and that every narcissistic impulse was a form of humor—which is certainly not to be recommended, however closely related humor may be to narcissism. It is the same with aggression against the self. We can maintain neither that every self-destructive tendency emanates from the superego nor that every autosadistic impulse testifies to its existence. To speak of the superego at a stage when id impulses alone are involved would be to extend the concept of the superego far beyond what is scientifically admissible. The logical conclusion of such an extension would be to describe the death instinct itself as a part of the superego.

It is of course a different matter to say, as Joan Riviere does, that "'archaic' feelings are a permanent element in the organization of the superego." There is no fundamental objection to this view. The autosadistic tendencies of an early period may contribute to the subsequent formation of the superego and lend to that institution something of their own aggressiveness, just as narcissism contributes to the positive relations of the superego to the ego, of which humor is an instance. But this belongs to the prehistory of the superego.

Now let us adopt the synthetic method and try to describe the development of the superego. We can distinguish six periods. The first is a period of latency, during which it may be said that, roughly speaking, nothing like the superego exists. This period covers the first year of life. Of course, the vicissitudes of the instincts during this period do exert an influence on the subsequent development of the superego. The second stage is characterized by the appearance of the formal superego function, which develops gradually till the individual reaches maturity.

During the third period the so-called prestages occur, the various isolated internalizations of external commands and prohibitions, by means of identification, and the earliest phenomena of remorse and the tendency to self-punishment. The next phase is that of superego formation—or, if we prefer the term, of the integration of the superego—which takes place with the passing of the oedipus complex. In this phase the prestages are welded together, as Fenichel says, just as the component instincts become welded into a homogeneous sexual organization. A powerful inner code is formed, in which the separate commands and prohibitions are combined and the world is divided into good and bad. From that time on, part of the child's psyche is the ally of those who educate him and is in harmony with the demands of the outside world.

There follows a long phase in which the superego, thus formed, has not yet become firmly established and is still in communication with external objects in the manner described by Anna Freud (1927). The process of superego formation can still easily be reversed, at least in part, and once again revert to a relationship to a new object, whereupon an internalization of the new object takes place. We say that the child or adolescent is not yet established in his character and we hesitate to allow him to get into bad company. This period of the superego's susceptibility to influence is a long one, probably lasting till the end of the twenties, though naturally the susceptibility diminishes as time goes on. The superego now enters upon its final phase and acquires that measure of stability which the individual in question has achieved. Of course, even then it is possible to influence it by mechanisms similar to those used during the earlier period. Illustrations of such influence can be found in women who are in love, in persons under hypnosis and in crowds. Apart from all this, a strictly conducted analysis may still modify the superego by analyzing its origins in the patient.

4. Fantasy and Reality

Another problem raised by the writings we are studying is that of fantasy and reality or, as we may say, of reality and psychic reality. I have no doubt that in principle all analysts are agreed that we have here a complementary series; the fewer the factors of the one group, the more factors of the other group are necessary for the occurrence of a particular phenomenon.

Here we must distinguish two problems, which are not identical: the biological and social factors in psychoanalysis and constitution and environment. In the former case we have to consider which phenomena are biologically determined and which are produced by social influences, in other words, what is the relative part played in each phenomena by biology and social environment. There is, for instance, the much-discussed question whether the concept of mental disease is biological or social, or again, whether the oedipus complex is a biological or a social phenomenon, whether puberty in civilized societies is an artificial product, and so forth. On the other hand, when we consider how much in neurosis is to be attributed to the patient's character or to other individual constitutional qualities and how much to environment, we are dealing with the second problem.

The question of fantasy and reality, as raised in the works of Melanie Klein and others, is clearly part of the first problem. So far, psychoanalysis has not formulated a detailed theory of the subject. This is an indication of Freud's unwillingness to generalize and his constant preference for the study of concrete individual questions. We can imagine two standpoints, one at either end of the pole. The one would tend to see psychic products as the precipitation of external influences. This might be called the sociological preoccupation. It is embodied in its most extreme form in the writings of W. Reich, who was formerly an analyst but finally disassociated himself altogether from psychoanalysis on this question as well as on a number of others. According to Reich, neurosis is a social phenomenon and, if social conditions are altered, there are good chances of its disappearing. We find a less extreme expression of the sociological bias in various psychoanalytic writings. Some analysts, for example, contend that anxiety always has its origin in an external threat, so that all anxiety is derived from objective anxiety. A similar, although modified, view is put forward by Fenichel, who follows Freud in describing a trauma as an excessive increase in need tensions, but goes on to imply that this traumatic situation arises either in consequence of some external barrier in the way of gratification or of the inadequacy of the apparatus by which gratification is sought. He is quite consistent in concluding that, if the apparatus for gratification remains intact, the strength of the instincts cannot produce anxiety. Although Fenichel is introducing the factor of physiological immaturity or of the individual's helplessness in the face of instinct by reason of his lack of an adequate executive apparatus, his view too may be regarded as a sociological preoccupation. The discussion of the death instinct is approached from the same angle by those authors who describe aggression exclusively as the reaction to external frustration.

The biological preoccupation attaches less importance to the factor of environment. According to this view, external experiences simply provide the material upon which the inner forces work.

If we wish to classify the writings of Melanie Klein and the other authors whom we are considering, we should say that their standpoint is diametrically opposed to the sociological view, that is to say, it is biological. But this is not quite correct, for we find, contrary to expectation, that the facts of psychic reality described by Melanie Klein are not of a biological nature or covered by biological laws. One could say that we are dealing with a kind of quasi biology which has no biology in it!

Although psychoanalysis has not yet formulated a generally valid theory of the mutual relation of biological and social factors, it may nevertheless be said that it has in the main held a middle course on the problem or, to put it another way, that its theory is dialectical. Historically, psychoanalysis at first chiefly devoted attention to the external causes of illness (for example, in the theory of traumas). Later Freud discovered that the fantasies of hysterics often did not correspond at all to the truth but were nonetheless pathogenic; they were a part of psychic reality.

Now let us try, while avoiding all generalization, to give a schematic outline of the view held by Freudian psychoanalysis on this subject. So many points remain obscure that our scheme can be only a framework, leaving room for many differences of opinion on details.

I have tried elsewhere (Ch. 5) to draw up a scheme of the

ways in which development or change in general takes place in psychic life. I took as my starting point the principle of multiple function, and I defined this to mean that every psychic act has a multiple function in that it must comply with the demands of the outside world, of instinct and of the superego and, further, with the will of the ego to emancipate itself from these alien institutions. If every psychic act represents a more or less successful attempt to perform several tasks (namely, those set for the ego by the id, the superego and reality[17] and those which it sets for itself), we see that psychic modification may take place either through a change in the nature of the tasks or in the methods adopted for their solution.

In the first place, the tasks themselves may be modified through the development of the instinctual life, a modification of the environment, or the development of the superego. In addition to these, what we have described as the ego's strivings to emancipate itself from the forces of the nonego is subject to development. Secondly, a development takes place in the ego's method of solving its tasks; the investigation of these methods is one of the subjects of ego psychology. Thirdly, there is another factor which really comes under the heading of modification of the tasks themselves. When a psychic act is performed in an attempt to deal with a situation involving multiple tasks, the act itself alters the situation. We do something and in so doing we change the outside world, with the result that the world thus modified sets us new tasks. Similarly, the instinctual situation changes when we gratify or refuse to gratify an instinct. I think this scheme will be generally acceptable because it is sufficiently broad.

Now what, in relation to this question, is the view of the authors whose works we are considering? When we read what James Strachey says about the alternation of the processes of

[17] It is somewhat inaccurate to speak of the tasks set by reality, unless we add an explanation of how real happenings become inner tasks. This takes place through all those tendencies in the subject which are directed toward the object world: the libidinal and aggressive id instincts; the impulse of self-preservation; anxiety and the effort of the ego to enlarge its boundaries; and the superego demands in reference to the subject's relation to the outside world.

projection and introjection in the familiar vicious circle, we have the impression that there must be a "rotation of fantasies."[18]

Speaking of the relation between reality and fantasy, Melanie Klein (1932, p. 302) states: "We know that the child's early phantasies and instinctual life on the one hand and the pressure of reality upon it on the other interact upon each other and that their combined action shapes the course of its mental development. In my judgment, reality and real objects affect its anxiety-situations from the very earliest stages of its existence, in the sense that it regards them as so many proofs or refutations of its anxiety-situations, which it has displaced into the outer world, and they thus help to guide the course of its instinctual life. And since, owing to the interaction of the mechanisms of projection and introjection, the external factors influence the formation of its super-ego and the growth of its object-relationship and its instincts, they will also assist in determining what the outcome of its sexual development will be."

According to this admirably clear statement, reality can have the effect of intensifying or lessening anxiety situations. Strachey is therefore applying this notion quite logically when he describes the process of cure as a gradual alleviation of the anxiety situation by means of the reality of the analyst. It appears that all that reality does is to increase or diminish the quantity of anxiety; if it has any further influence, it can be only insofar as development is determined by the intensity of anxiety, as is stated in the last sentence of the passage which I have quoted.

Here we have the difference in the evaluation of the reality factor. Those who hold that my earlier scheme was correct will hardly believe in a "rotation of fantasies" and will feel that Melanie Klein's description is not comprehensive enough. Real experiences, in our view, are sometimes more than mere proofs or refutations of anxiety.

We certainly notice a very marked difference when we compare my scheme with Joan Riviere's description of the genesis of a psychic conflict. She gives an account of a practically

---

[18] I am using a term coined by E. Bibring in a hitherto unpublished paper on technique.

automatic development of anxiety and of its elaboration by means of the processes of projection and introjection. Her estimate of the part played by reality is not a high one. She states indeed that the infant's aggression is the result of oral frustration, but it is assumed that that degree of frustration which is universally and inevitably experienced suffices in practice to produce the aggressive impulses under discussion. If such real experience as is common to every individual is enough to give rise to these phenomena, the latter cannot be said to depend upon the nature of the reality in individual cases. Reality moderates aggression or renders it more violent. Joan Riviere describes very impressively the favorable results which ensue from the presence of good objects, but she regards all this only as a matter of quantitative displacements within the process, though admittedly these have a powerful influence upon further development.

Of course, I do not imagine that what I have said is a refutation of Melanie Klein's view. My object has been not to refute it but to bring out the differences of opinion on this question. The fact that I believe my own view to be correct is, of course, no argument, nor is the fact that it agrees with the view of most analysts. There is one thing to be said, however, even though it is only an *argumentum ad hominem*: the scheme which I have outlined suggests itself naturally and we have a right to ask for exact proofs of any other theory, whether it differs from mine in its biological or its sociological preoccupation. But here we have come back to the questions discussed in the first sections of this paper and we ask: what are the final proofs upon which this kind of demarcation of fantasy from reality is based? A reference to the results of analysis is also clearly no argument, for the very point in dispute is whether these particular conclusions can legitimately be drawn from such results. On the other hand it would not be accurate to say that this point cannot be exactly proved: a proof which would be sufficient for all practical purposes could probably be obtained by some of the methods of verification discussed in my second section. Direct observation of a sufficiently large number of children would provide such proof.

In order to make it clear wherein the differences of opinion lie I would point out that I am *not* here arguing that more things are to be ascribed to the factor of reality than is suggested in Melanie Klein's writings. It is not a mere problem of addition, not simply a question of how many psychic processes have their origin in objective impressions. The point is rather that in our view reality enters into psychic development in quite another sense and that there is no such thing as a rotation of fantasies, but that the arc of life inevitably throws its curve through the outside world. This is what is indicated in my scheme.

Readers of the case histories communicated by the child analysts associated with Melanie Klein sometimes wish, when they read the various fantasies reported, that they knew more of the real incidents in the lives of these children. Acts of aggression directed against the contents of the mother's body occur, as we all know, for the most part when the mother is pregnant, or when the child has been told of the possibility that she is going to have a baby, or when he has some other occasion for thinking about the arrival of a brother or sister. Actions which represent something in the behavior of an infant are carried out by a child when the real situation provides him with a motive for playing the baby or some other motive for this sort of behavior. Whatever the content of these fantasies and however necessary it may be to study all the elements in them, they can never be wholly understood without a knowledge of the child's actual situation. So it is not enough to examine their content; they are never a mere continuation of old fantasies, woven, as it were, of themselves and detached from real life. We can judge exactly why the child produced this particular fantasy or game at this particular moment, and what he is trying to convey by it, only if we take into account at the same time the problems presented by reality.

Let us take a concrete example of what to us seems to be an underestimation of reality, which may perhaps be more exactly described as a *different* estimation from our own of that factor. We shall be leaving theory and launching straight into a problem of technique, but everything which we have already discussed from the purely theoretical standpoint must have its application to all the questions, small and great, which arise in our analytic work.

Melanie Klein and some other writers commonly represent

the relation of the patient to the analyst as transference pure and simple; the possibility that such a relation may be in part based on reality is not considered by them. This does not correspond to Freud's idea of the transference, according to which there are relations between patient and analyst which are based on the real situation, though of course also on the wishes and modes of reaction which the patient has developed in the past and brought with him to his analysis. Every relation contains elements which are of the nature of repetitions and other elements which have their basis in reality. The repetitive elements in an object relation are the more numerous in proportion as the inner urge to translate them into reality is strong and as the object permits of this, i.e., in proportion as no counteraction springing from the psychic structure of the object itself destroys the incipient repetition. When the element of reality is almost *nil* we speak of transference.[19]

There is no doubt that, for a number of reasons which I need not go into here, the analytic situation is especially favorable for the production of transference, so that its appearance in analysis is an invariable rule. It is determined above all by the behavior of the analyst as *receiver*, the extent to which he refrains from any counteraction which might nip the patient's incipient transference in the bud. But it would surely be an exaggeration to say that the patient's relation to him is exclusively transference, and this exaggerated notion is refuted, in my view, by the mere fact that very often patients pass extremely shrewd judgments upon the analyst. These judgments may contain elements of transference, but this is not necessarily the case. When they are not complimentary the analyst may be tempted to interpret them as transference, but he is not always right in so doing.

For instance, Melanie Klein always describes the anxiety felt by children in analysis as transference, but other child analysts are by no means convinced that the fear of the analyst which may be observed even during the first analytic session is really transference and not a fear which has its basis in the actual situation. There is good evidence that children have a number of reasons for being afraid of analysis. In the first place, a child,

[19] These conditions of transference have been formulated by Anna Freud (1926), but Freud's conception of the transference was always on these lines.

just like an adult at beginning of analysis, does not understand what analysis is about, but he very soon feels (feels immediately, when Melanie Klein's technique is employed) that in analysis his secret and hidden thoughts and all his misdemeanors are being made the subject of discussion. Children often believe that the adult wants to find out these things in order to punish them, or to tell their parents, who will punish them; if this does not happen, then they become afraid the grownup is going to seduce them. In his own conflicts between his instincts and the defense against instinct a child can imagine only that the adult who is concerning himself with them will take one side or the other in the conflict, and so he fears punishment or seduction. It is a long time before he grasps that the adult wishes to do neither the one nor the other but to help him by bringing his conflicts into consciousness and showing him how to overcome them.[20]

Hence it is quite possible that some of the anxiety manifested by children at the beginning, and not only at the beginning, of analysis may be based on a real situation; for the child has had experience of punishment and seduction but knows nothing of the help which the analyst is trying to give him.[21]

There is another possibility which we feel must be taken into consideration: the anxiety with which children react to a "deep" interpretation (and we know that in Melanie Klein's technique such interpretations are given very early, indeed practically at once) may well be a fear of seduction. I am far from asserting that this is so, but the fact that this possibility is not weighed,

[20] Cf. Jenny Waelder's account of this situation (1935).

[21] It may rightly be contended that this is not "real" anxiety, for there is in reality no reason for the child to fear either punishment or seduction by the analyst and the anxiety has been imported by him into the situation in consequence of other experiences. If we like, we can call this transference too, but it is certainly not what we generally understand by the term. When Melanie Klein interprets the child's earliest anxieties in analysis as transference, she means that aggressive fantasies have been transferred to the person of the analyst, together with the anxieties accompanying them. The expectations with which a child approaches a new situation, the reality of which is as yet unknown to him and cannot yet be understood by him, are derived from all his previous experience and clearly bear a much closer resemblance to "real" anxiety. We must not allow an error in the presentation of the subject or an inaccuracy in terminology to prevent our making it quite clear what we intend to convey.

proves, I think, that Melanie Klein and the child analysts who adopt her views attach less importance to reality than do others. If the child's anxiety is "real," we can well imagine that, when it is interpreted as transference, the effect would be to allay it. He would then certainly react in the ways described by Melanie Klein, and these reactions might well have a therapeutic effect. But—and this brings us back again to the problem of the criteria of interpretation—this does not prove that the interpretation given was correct.

In connection with the problem of transference love and the real relation to the analyst there has been criticism of Anna Freud's recommendation (1926) that when an analyst begins to analyze a child, he must be at pains to establish contact with him. It is well known that this is repudiated by the child analysts in Melanie Klein's circle. From their standpoint this refutation is logical, for, if every relation to the analyst is transference, and contact and transference are therefore identical, there is no need for the analyst to bring about the transference relation by artificial means; it will develop of itself, and all that he has to do is to interpret it. Indeed, we are told that the interpretation itself serves to establish analytic contact. But this idea differs from Freud's concept of the transference, which admits of a relation based on reality, the opportunity for this being the greater in proportion as the patient's hunger for repetition is less and as the analyst departs from the attitude of complete passivity which assists the repetition, for these are the factors by which transference is determined. Anna Freud tells us that the repetition compulsion and the analyst's passive response are conditions of adult analysis far more than of child analysis. The child has but little hunger for repetition, for he still possesses his libidinal objects in reality; while the degree of the analyst's passivity may vary in matters of technique, but can never, when he is analyzing children, be absolute.[22]

[22] However passively an adult may behave in his relation to a child, he is for the child always a person in authority and therefore exercises an educating influence, whether he will or no. Owing to the transference there is a similar situation in the analysis of adults, but there it can be resolved if the transference itself is analyzed, whereas in the case of a child, who is essentially a dependent and immature being, it is an unalterable reality.

Anna Freud's views on the part played by education in child analysis have

Even in the analysis of adults the establishment of contact between patient and analyst has always had a place, although a modest one. We try in the first analytic sessions to bring this contact about. It is true that this happens very quickly in the case of adults, and so there has not been much discussion of the subject.

5. Early Ego Development

We have a more difficult task before us in this section than in the previous ones. When we were discussing the development of the superego or the problem of fantasy and reality, we were able to outline our own view and to contrast one thesis with another. But in the case of the early development of the ego it can hardly be said that a theory exists and we must content ourselves with pointing out uncertainties and doubtful questions.

In studying the theories under discussion one obtains the impression that many writers assume an exact correspondence between phases of libidinal development and phases of ego development, so that Abraham's scheme of the former (1924) becomes a scheme of the latter (see, e.g., Glover, 1935). To us it seems problematical from the outset whether any such exact correspondence exists.

Let us take a single point. The process of introjection is said to be modeled on that of oral incorporation and the process of projection on that of anal expulsion. Oral incorporation and anal expulsion are ego functions connected with the preservation of life, but we generally consider them as *id tendencies*. Projection and introjection are *attempts of the ego to solve its conflicts*. It does not seem altogether justifiable to equate these two pairs of processes offhand.

Under the headings of introjection and projection we include various phenomena. Let us begin with projection. Some-

been much misunderstood. She never maintained that one should introduce an educational approach (as an extra-analytical measure) whether for technical or therapeutic reasons, i.e., as a thing one can do or leave undone at will. Her view was that an adult cannot avoid being in the position of an educator in relation to a child, for every situation in which adult and child are in contact is an educational situation; it therefore seems advisable to make the best practical use of what cannot be avoided.

times it is assumed that all perception is based on projection. This has not been established, but it is one of the contexts in which we use the term projection. Again, when an individual displaces into the outside world a stimulus which arises in his own mind, we call it projection; it was in this connection that Freud first introduced the concept of projection. Or, to take another example: by the age of seven months a child will touch his nose or his ear with his finger in imitation of an adult. This shows that at that age children already have some idea of the form of their own body and also of that of the other person. Pötzl explains this as projection of the idea of the body. Or here is another point: toward the end of their second year we notice that children, when accused of a fault, begin to reply that someone else did it; they will blame a doll, etc. This is the mechanism of shifting one's own guilt onto someone else, and this too is a form of projection. Again, at a later age, possibly at about four years, children will try to anticipate some attack which they fear by launching an attack themselves, a mechanism which Anna Freud (1936) describes as "identification with the aggressor," and this also is projection. Finally, we speak of projection in the case of the "influencing machine" of schizophrenics or when psychotics hear voices. Are all these phenomena which we call projection really the same thing? Do they really in origin and form represent a single process? It may be so, but in using the word projection, which refers to a formal characteristic in all these processes, there is a danger that we may overlook the fact that this question demands separate investigation.

I think that the position is much the same when we come to introjection. Here again we have an enormous number of manifestations, concerning which we are by no means certain that they are all identical in character; still less is it certain that, whenever this mechanism comes into play, a tendency to oral incorporation is at work. We will consider only three mechanisms of introjection, all of which are designed to protect the subject against his aggressive impulses.

One mechanism may be formulated as follows, "I hate not him but myself." The mental process here may also be described as identification, but it is really a mechanism for the avoidance of the dangerous situation brought about by aggression against the object. It does not seem to me proved that oral incorporation tendencies are necessarily at work here or are at least the prototype of this mechanism. The final product may nonetheless give the impression of identification.

This distinction between an oral manifestation and an attempt on the ego's part to solve a conflict (which, as we have seen, gives the impression of identification) comes out more clearly in the two other mechanisms. The one may be expressed by the formula, "Do not hurt me, for I am already hurting myself; you must not punish me, for I am already punishing myself." This is one of the methods by which the individual seeks to allay the anxiety aroused by a threat from someone else. It is a mechanism which plays an important role in the formation of the superego.

A similar mechanism is that of identification with an oppressor. It is a peculiarly oppressive situation to be the helpless victim of someone stronger than oneself. The situation is relieved if one identifies oneself with the oppressor, for then one leaves the ranks of those who are mastered and joins the masters and so can share in their triumph. This mechanism too has its place in the formation of the superego.

In both these cases the processes may be described as identification, but they seem to me to have almost no connection with oral incorporation. They are simply instances of the familiar attempt to solve a conflict by turning from a passive to an active role. Perhaps it may be said that not everything which looks like identification is necessarily oral incorporation. Although it is certain that there is a special proneness to identification where oral tendencies are concerned, it is in my view no less certain that everything described as identification cannot be equated with oral incorporation. This is only an example to illustrate the enormous multiplicity of these problems. It is doubtful whether the attempt to fit all these phenomena into the Procrustean bed of a single simple scheme is a profitable one.

Let us now consider the so-called psychotic modes of behavior belonging to early childhood. Glover (1934) speaks of the "psychic, frequently psychotic, reactions and mental systems characteristic of infancy and early childhood." We read too of "the small child passing through its schizophrenic and obsessional phases from the age of about one year onwards" (pp. 36, 40).

Other authors suggest that the psychotic modes of reaction may be observed in the infant's first year, from about the age of three months onward, and speak of paranoid anxieties and melancholic depression. Now, of course, they do not mean that there is a phase in the normal development of the small child which amounts to a psychosis, but they do mean that "the mental function of all children up to the age of three or thereabouts is psychotic *in pattern*—that is to say—the child's primitive instincts, his archaic anxieties and his bizarre reactions to reality, are the very warp and woof of any subsequent insanity." Attractive as this notion may be aesthetically, we feel doubtful about it on various grounds. Let us go back to the direct observation of children. It is difficult to discover as a regular phase in normal infants anything which we could call paranoid anxiety or melancholic depression. In very favorable surroundings (I have already shown what constitutes a favorable environment) infants often manifest no sign at all of anxiety, at least after the first weeks of life. The earliest form of anxiety seems to be that relating to the loss of the breast; even this is absent if the breast is regularly forthcoming. Only later, when they have learned to recognize familiar figures, do they display anxiety at the approach of strangers and, in many children, this is the only anxiety situation which occurs in the second half of their first year. And how is paranoid anxiety supposed to manifest itself in behavior? Again, direct observation of most infants reveals no trace of anything suggestive of melancholic depression.

The whole notion of relating a normal stage in ego development so closely to psychosis is a repugnant one.[23] We fear that those who hold this view misconceive the nature of psychosis and do not realize the great gulf which separates it from normal life at every stage. The very great difference between the still imperfect development of the function of reality testing and its

---

[23] Repugnant, but not, I think, because it would involve a fourth wound to human narcissism; no pronouncement about so early a stage affects us strongly.

disintegration is not to be underestimated. The difference is as great, or so it seems to be, as between an early stage of mental development and feeblemindedness. In normal development there is no phase comparable with feeblemindedness.

Altogether I think that we have here an overstraining of the concept of regression. It is as though every pathological phenomenon must have its prototype in a normal stage of individual development. Whether this is so may be a debatable point where the psychoses are concerned; that it is not a general phenomenon of psychopathology may be proved by an illustration from cerebral pathology. In optical agnosia patients lose the capacity to perceive forms and they make use of a roundabout method: they let their eyes or hands travel over the objects before them with an almost imperceptible movement and then rapidly draw their conclusions. But this capacity, acquired in their abnormal condition, has no place in normal development.

In psychosis the ego organizations break down and begin to function pathologically. Many psychotic phenomena may represent regression to earlier stages of the ego, others perhaps a reversion to more primitive modes of functioning of the system, modes which never had an independent place in its development. This too is a kind of regression, but it is not regression to an earlier stage. Others again may be new formations of reactions by the damaged organism (as in the instance of agnosia). Here everything that already exists is, of course, utilized. These are psychotic attempts at dealing with a situation; they have no prototype either in ontogenesis or in phylogenesis, nor can they be altogether explained as a reversion to primitive modes of functioning.

M. Katan (1934, 1936) has stated that mechanisms come into play in the psychoses which do not exist in normal development, and that projection and introjection in mental illness are by no means identical with these processes in normal persons and neurotics. For the psychotic is always making an attempt at recovery; in schizophrenic projection the outside world which has been lost is being reconstructed on the model of the ego, while in melancholic introjection the ego which has been destroyed is reconstructed on the model of its objects. Whether we share Katan's views that the mechanisms are actually different in psychotic illness is a separate question, but we do feel sure that psychosis and normal development are not so closely related as some writers appear to suppose.

The analytic study of the psychoses is in its infancy. We have not yet solved the riddle of exactly what constitutes psychosis. With the exception of the processes described by Katan, something similar to everything which has been observed in psychosis occurs in normal life and in neurosis. The characteristic feature of psychosis, the irremediable disturbance of the function of reality testing, is still an enigma. It seems likely that we shall shut the door on the true explanation of psychotic phenomena if we try to account for them by assigning them to phases of normal development.[24]

Rather than continuing the discussion of fundamental principles I shall present a concrete example which illustrates all the differences of opinion between the two schools of thought, as would each detail if we examined it more closely. Joan Riviere (1936) says that "the discharge of excreta would in phantasy be *felt* as a transference of the painful excretory substance on to or into the object.... The persecutors in a paranoia are feared like *revenants* who may appear from nowhere; and we know that they derive from faeces." The existence of anal persecution was discovered by Stärcke (1935) and van Ophuijsen (1927). The above passages suggest an explanation of it. During the analysis of a child Jenny Waelder (1936) gained some insight into anal persecution. A child in the latency period was afraid of persecution by an imaginary figure, and the name which he gave the latter sounded almost exactly like a vulgar term for excrement. His own excrement aroused in this child acute anxiety and so did the drain in the toilet, which he regarded as an uncanny place. One day he told the analyst something of the causes of his anxiety. He said that animals eat up their enemies, and then the enemies are very angry and come out of the animals' bodies again during evacuation; so one can't help fearing that then they would avenge themselves. Here we may have a clue to the strange fantasy of the anal persecutor: one has devoured one's enemies, and the feces are nothing but these same enemies

[24] On the other hand, various English authors hold that that by so doing we shall *open* the door to the true explanation of such phenomena.

reemerging after the "passage through the ego" (Federn, 1952; E. Weiss). The fantasy is quite like a fairy tale and recalls familiar themes. We remember how Little Red Riding Hood's grandmother, when devoured by the wolf, continued to live in his belly, although a little restricted in space. This fantasy is very like those reported by Melanie Klein, but there are differences. It is a fully worked-out fantasy, apparently belonging to a later stage of development, not simply the infantile displacement outward of excreta which are felt to be hostile because painful. The hated objects of the aggression were oedipal objects; the fact that the aggression took the form of the impulse to devour them and to expel them anally is, of course, a consequence of pregenital development. In other cases perhaps the hatred would not be directed against the oedipal object; nevertheless there is a fantasy—one that has the character of a fairy tale, belongs to a later stage, and is woven out of oral and anal themes which lie ready to hand; but it is not the simple process described by Joan Riviere. Another difference is that the fantasy related by Jenny Waelder's little patient does not represent a phase of normal development but is part of a pathological development. Thus, according to the one view, the infant, at a very early period, and as a regular and normal step in development, construes the daily process of defecation as anal persecution, while, according to the other, this is an unusual fantasy which occurs at a much later age and is not a part of normal development.

It may be said that here theory is opposed to theory and that one has the advantage of being "deeper."[25] But one theory has a sound basis; a child endowed with insight has himself supplied the answer to the riddle. The other theory depends on constructions in a past which is lost in obscurity.

6. An Example

I think that some of the points which I have made here may be illustrated by an example. It was communicated to me by an analyst who made these observations on her own children.

---

[25] In Section 7 I shall discuss the question of the deep unconscious.

A little girl of three years whose upbringing had presented no difficulty in her first year and little difficulty in her second and third years, suddenly began to show signs of trouble. She was heard one day saying to herself, "Mummy has smashed me up." At about the same time when the mother was drying her daughter after her bath, the little girl displayed great anxiety every time the mother approached her genitals with the towel.

Now let us pause for a moment. We might suppose that this was an instance of the processes described by Melanie Klein and that the child was suffering from a fear of retribution for aggressive acts directed against her mother's body or that she was projecting her own aggression onto her mother. But this supposition is not borne out. On the contrary, we have good reason for seeking the causes of these sudden troubles in the little girl's mind elsewhere—in the familiar difficulties of the castration complex and penis envy.

Some months before this episode, this child and a sister a year older than herself had seen a little boy naked when they were playing on the beach. Probably this was the first time that they had noticed the difference between the sexes. The elder sister, at that time three years and three months old, reacted immediately and very definitely; the younger at first showed no reaction. We are not here concerned with the reactions of the older child; I will merely say that for a long time she was occupied in working over this experience and several times discussed it with her mother in the presence of her younger sister. Thus we are inclined to suppose that the latter's reactions, as manifested in the incident I have described, were part of the castration complex and that her complaint that her mother had injured her was the familiar accusation, of which Freud has told us, that the mother was to blame for the little girl's lack of a penis. We shall soon see the further material by which this interpretation is borne out.

There is another argument against construing the child's behavior as a manifestation of oral-sadistic aggression and anxiety. Though her mother observed her carefully, the baby gave no sign during her first year of the presence in the oral phase of any considerable degree of aggression or anxiety of that kind. During her first three months she cried very little, nor did she ever really scream with rage. During her second month the summer holidays occurred and this made it possible for her mother to dispense with the by no means strict rules as to the times at which the child was fed and to suckle her whenever she demanded it. The effect of this was that, at the age of three months, the baby ceased to cry for food. It appears that her fear of being hungry and of her mother's breast being withheld had been so completely allayed that, from that time on, it was a matter of indifference to her when she was fed. She did not protest if this did not always happen at the usual time or if there was an interval of even ten hours between her feedings during the night. For months at a stretch, the child, who was physically healthy, was never heard to cry, much less to scream. At the same time she was by no means dull but gave the impression of an active, intelligent little mortal. It was much later, at the end of her first year, that she showed signs of aggressiveness and then in another direction. From this early infantile history it seems unlikely that violent oral-sadistic aggressive impulses and anxieties had developed at so young an age.

But the convincing proof of the nature of the difficulties which arose when the child was three lies, I think, in other incidents of this period and in her later development. It happened that, at about the same time that she made the remark I have recorded and displayed anxiety lest her mother should touch her genitals, the children's father went into the nursery and tried to shake hands with them. The younger of the two refused to give him her hand, saying, "I won't give you my hand, I will only give you my finger." When her father asked in amazement why she did so, she replied, using her own childish terms, that it was because he had a penis and "a little bag." (Her knowledge of the scrotum could only have been derived from the incident on the beach several months previously; it had never been mentioned in the conversations between her elder sister and the grownups.) It is true that she said this only once. Only a few hours later, when her father, hoping to elicit the same reply, again asked her to give him her hand, she refused, as she had done before, but gave as her reason, "because you've got an apron." The displacement had been made with extraordinary rapidity, within a few hours. (The fact that she had turned her father into a woman is another story.)

From that time on, certain difficulties arose which might

perhaps be called symptoms. At meals the child did not want to have her meat cut up and wished to take all her food only in large pieces, not divided up in any way, so that in fact it was impossible for her to eat them. For instance, she would not allow anyone to break off a piece of cake for her, and so forth. A dog which she knew was once brought to see her when it had just been shaved and the effect was to give her a shock. She became more and more preoccupied with the idea of "big and little" until she could think of nothing else. The rivalry in relation to her elder sister, which had long ago been allayed, broke out again. The younger child constantly thought about how much older her sister was and how soon she could catch her up. She fantasied that she was big and her sister little and invented a game in which she was the mother and her elder sister the baby. She took a great delight in this game. Anyone who entered the nursery was immediately scrutinized as to his or her height, and at night she would beg grownups to sit beside her cot, using the phrase that "big" X (man or woman, as the case might be) was to sit beside her. Spectacles worn by adults were for her an object of the liveliest interest, and at one time, whenever her father, who wore glasses, approached her, she immediately began to talk about them and to investigate them, refusing to talk about anything else. She also evolved a theory that she had once been big and had only just become little.

I believe that all this material goes to prove that everything I have related represented attempts on the child's part to work over her castration complex by methods familiar to us in our female patients and not a conflict springing from oral-sadistic aggression and anxiety. The desire to have food which is not cut up is perhaps reminiscent of the fantasies described by Melanie Klein, but the fact remains that this slight symptom appeared *at that particular moment* and that the child herself explained it in her remark to her father as clearly as we could possibly expect.

The little girl also developed a transitory symptom in the shape of a tic. On one occasion she took hold of her nose and asked if it was a big one. This gesture very soon became a tic: every minute she put her fingers to her nose. At this point her mother intervened with an interpretation and gave a suitable explanation that nothing had been taken away from the child; that all boys and men were from their birth like the little friend whom she had observed; that all girls and women, including her mother, were like herself; and that the one form was just as nice as the other and that some day she would have children. At first this interpretation had no effect, but its effect was instantaneous when it was repeated by the other child, the sister a year older then herself. The tic vanished the same day.

Finally the child developed a habit of blaming her mother for everything disagreeable which happened. If she dropped anything, it was her mother's fault, although the latter was often nowhere near: she should have looked after her better. The same explanation applies here—the child was reproaching her mother, who was really "to blame for everything," seeing that she had not borne the little girl as a boy. This state of affairs had persisted for some months, when the episode occurred for the sake of which I have chosen this example.

One night the mother was awakened by the child's crying and saying, "It blew on my tummy." As the child was partly uncovered, the mother at first thought that she felt cold. But the little girl went on to say that she had wanted to bite her genitals and that then it blew. So it was a question of a dream and of one which, in comparison with most of the dreams of children of this age, had been much distorted. The mother soothed the child for a moment and suggested that she should go to sleep and that they would talk about it in the morning.

The next morning the mother asked the child to tell her the dream again. She learned another detail: there was a man at the window whose face was smashed and he had a piece of bread in his hand. The man mustn't come into the room.

The mother asked about the astonishing dream element that the child had wanted to bite her own genitals. The little girl said (naturally using her childish words) "The genitals were big, the genitals were little." She then stood up, blew out her abdomen and said, "It blew like that."

Now let us pause again. Once more we are tempted to think of the fantasies described by Melanie Klein. The "biting" and the blowing-up of the child's own body naturally suggest aggression against the mother's body and anxiety about the integrity of her own. But investigation of these elements leads to another conclusion.

The mother's intimate knowledge of every detail in the

child's life enabled her to understand the situation immediately from the little girl's words and gestures. In the last few months she had manifested acute anxiety. In her nursery, as in that of many other children, there were toy balloons which could be blown up. Sometimes, if one blew too hard, a balloon burst. The child had displayed great anxiety when she had tried to blow one up herself and when her governess did so. Often the little girl would cry out that they ought not to do it, the balloon would burst. When she herself tried to blow it up she was awkward about it and held the mouthpiece, which was made of soft rubber, between her teeth instead of between her lips, so that she generally did not succeed. She had been told not to bite it and then it would go better. It must be noted that a balloon in a collapsed condition, the rubber bladder with a tube-shaped mouthpiece, really does look very much like a penis with the scrotum.

The mother's knowledge of this detail enabled her to understand a fragment of the dream. The dream thought obviously was that the child wanted to blow up her own genitals and make them big like those of the little boy and that she was seized with anxiety lest they should burst. This explained the other dream fragment: that it had "blown on my tummy." Thus the biting could hardly be described as aggression: it simply indicated what she did to her balloon.

The mother interpreted this fragment to the child, telling her that she had been afraid of her genitals bursting if they were blown up. The child replied, "But they have burst already," thus betraying the fantasy that her genitals had once been blown up, had burst and so had arrived at her present miserable condition. It was plain that in her fantasy her mother was to blame.

The detail of the man with the smashed face and a piece of bread in his hand, who was at the window and must not come into the room, was explained as follows. On their daily walks the children used to meet a cripple, who begged for bread. This experience supplies another proof of the possibility of being damaged: "He must not come into the room."

Upon the mother's interpretation the child's face lighted up, proving that her mother was right and that really a certain amount of material had been released. Remembering the psy-

choanalytic success of the elder sister, which I have already
recorded, and the generally recognized fact that children are
especially impressed by what other children tell them, the
mother repeated her interpretation and explanation in another
form. On the child's asking whether she also had dreams and
begging her to tell one, she recounted an imaginary dream of her
own. She said she had dreamed of a little girl who cried bitterly
because she was girl and who thought that her mother had once
blown her up and that then she had burst and now was smashed.
But a great crowd of children told her that she was not smashed
but just as nice-looking as boys were. The mother described the
conversation between the little girl and the other children, in
which the little girl was finally convinced, and how she was now
quite contented. The child followed this story with a delighted
smile, indicating a sense of relief.

This does not by any means exhaust the meanings of the
dream. On the previous day (not for the first time) the little girl
had heard it said that children were once inside their mother's
body. She had, of course, long known about pregnancy; some
time before, she had had a married nurse who became pregnant
and remained in service for a time. The children had known that
she was going to have a baby and, later on, she had brought it to
see them. Thus the dream was concerned with the dangers of
feminine existence: not only had her own originally male genital
burst, but if she ever had a baby, she would be in danger of the
same fate.

No doubt we could still learn much from the dream. For our
present purpose it has not been necessary to consider the
elements which relate to the oedipus complex.

In this example all the elements of the fantasies described by
Melanie Klein appear to be present: aggression against the
mother, oral-sadistic activity ("biting"), fear of injury to the
subject's own body, a swing-over to self-injury, the idea of injury
inflicted by the mother. And yet they could apparently all be
simply and satisfactorily accounted for by an explanation to
which the child herself directly assented and which is not what
we should expect from Melanie Klein's writings.

We might, of course, pursue the analysis further and possibly
come to the conclusion that the biting did indicate oral aggres-

sion. But, even if further psychoanalytic investigation revealed oral-sadistic anxieties, the impression persists that the child's conflict and the formation of her slight neurotic symptoms had their source in penis envy and the attempt to deal with it, and derived their force from that affect. Further investigation would hardly lead us to Melanie Klein's theory but simply to the recognition that pregenital (e.g., oral) impulses influence the child later when he experiences the well-known castration and oedipus conflicts. Such pregenital antecedents of these complexes have constantly been sought and described. For instance, no one has ever disputed the fact that a passive anal position of the libido, encouraged when a child is given enemas for constipation, has an effect later on the complexes in question. There can indeed be no doubt about the matter if we are considering influences of this kind which pregenital development may exercise on conflicts during the third and fourth years.

But, in my opinion, although the child's conflicts at this age *may* bear a specific pregenital impress, this is not invariably the case. The experiences connected with the castration complex, penis envy, and the oedipus complex seem in all circumstances (for reasons which we do not yet know) to have concealed within them elements of pathogenic conflict. On the other hand, the oral and anal phases can, I think, be passed through without such conflicts, and probably educational influences will suffice to keep them free from pathogenic elements, at least in children who are not too heavily handicapped constitutionally.

We are quite prepared for the objection that this material cannot legitimately be utilized, because the child has not been analyzed. Well, the word "analysis" is not a magic formula. We are in the habit of saying that certain material is not evidence because the individual in question has not been analyzed, by which we mean that we do not know enough about him and that the analyst's long and intimate study of the patient and their joint work under the conditions of the fundamental analytic rule would have enabled him to find out much more and by means of free association to accumulate far more material than would otherwise be possible. In the case before us the situation is different. Surely the analytic observation of the child from her earliest days by one who was at once her mother and analyst, together with her intimate knowledge of all the events in the child's life and the discussion, in complete accordance with analytic principles, of what was not yet understood, provides material equivalent to analysis by a strange analyst. Perhaps, indeed, the mother would know more than an analyst could easily discover. She was able to explain the dream because she knew every detail in the life of the child, whereas a strange analyst would have been in a much more difficult position. We cannot say for certain whether the child, who was at this time three and a half, would have told the latter about the balloon and her own fear of blowing it up and her awkwardness with the soft mouthpiece. But we may suppose that, if the analyst had been treating a still younger child, she would never have succeeded in getting this information.

It might be objected further that the mother was not a suitable person to observe her own child, even though she herself was an analyst. We all know many instances of the unreliability of what parents tell us about their children. This is an objection which cannot be simply dismissed, but we wonder why the mother, who was able calmly and without any internal conflict to note the child's aggression against her when it was prompted by resentment at having been born a girl or at having been made a girl by "bursting" and who recorded how the little girl turned from her under the influence of the oedipus complex, should shrink from understanding the aggression when it sprang from oral conflicts. To judge by our experience of adult analyses it is not the episodes connected with the very early days which rouse the strongest resistances; the happenings of the first year of life, quasi-biological processes, do not affect us so much as the bitter conflicts arising out of the oedipus and castration complexes.[26]

[26] I have already deprecated the polemical application of psychoanalysis and said that in my view it is unprofitable. Scientific discussion must be based on a comparison with reality. We have therefore no intention of trying to displace the discussion, for to do so does not elucidate any problems and it degrades analysis into a mere weapon of force, besides which it is never convincing even in its analytical aspect. So I have no polemical intention when I say that Melanie Klein's displacement of accent from the conflicts of the third and fourth year to problems of oral wishes, frustrations, aggression, and anxiety at an earlier age is a displacement from the line of greater to a line of lesser resistance.

7. The Importance of the "Deep" Unconscious

From time to time the writers of the works which we are discussing attack some statement by the opposite side on the ground that it applies only to consciousness or to the mental strata nearest to consciousness, while in the unconscious, the depths of the psyche, it is otherwise. No one can take exception to a reminder of this sort; we are all endeavoring to learn more about these deeper strata and until they have been investigated as thoroughly as possible no analysis can be said to have been completed. But the remarks which I have in mind seem to imply something more than the mere reminder that certain statements are true of the higher strata only. The implication is that what goes on there is of little or no concern to analysts and indeed does not really occur at all. There seems to be some idea that only the unconscious "really" exists at all. Anyone who studies the more superficial strata of psychic life is, we may suppose, very likely himself a superficial sort of person.[27]

I could give many instances of this. Let us consider the point in the light of a technical example.

Anna Freud (1926) demonstrated that in child analysis it is necessary to impart to the child some insight into his illness or at least something equivalent to such insight. The position of a child who comes to be analyzed is different from that of an adult, who knows that he is ill and generally comes on his own initiative to receive relief. When children are brought to be analyzed it is always because their parents decide that it is the right thing for them. Often a child's symptoms are such that his parents suffer more on account of them than he does himself. He is not, as it were, a system complete in itself. In an adult the illness and insight into the illness, or the illness and the desire to get well, are all comprised in the individual himself, but in a child the various aspects of the case are represented by several people. The child is ill and it is the parents who possess the insight into his illness and have the desire for his recovery.

The analysts of Melanie Klein's persuasion have raised a number of objections to the attempt to give children this insight.

[27] We see how easily we may be led astray into taking the pictorial terms of psychoanalytic topography too literally.

They say that it is contrary to analytic principles, that it is a form of education, substituted quite unjustifiably for analysis, and that we cannot possibly be sure that by exerting this kind of educational influence (however it may answer its purpose) we are not making regular analysis impossible. Nor does the adult's will to recover achieve much, for it exists "only" in his consciousness. If we analyze it, we shall discover it in various neurotic wishes, such as the wish to gratify infantile impulses or to keep them under and strengthen the ego's defenses or possibly to get rid of them by some magical means, as Nunberg (1925) has shown. To give a child insight into his illness is to evoke, instead of to analyze, anxiety.

This criticism almost suggests that Anna Freud's views are a complete novelty where psychoanalytic technique is concerned, a kind of incursion of education into analysis. But this is not so. In reality her ideas on child analysis are the application to children of psychoanalytic knowledge, long familiar and generally accepted, which has not before been called in question.

Nobody doubts the conclusions of analysis with regard to the will to recover, which are embodied in Nunberg's paper. It is true that all these neurotic wishes can and must be brought to light in the analysis of the wish to get well. But this does not mean that there is no such thing as a wish to get well and Nunberg never drew any such conclusion. In adult patients there is a conflict. One part of the personality, namely, the conscious personality, desires to get well while another part clings to the neurosis. The fact that neurotic tendencies come into play even in the will to recover does not really alter the situation in the conflict. And we utilize this conflict in the analysis, for we enter into an alliance with the healthy part of the personality to fight against the neurosis. Elsewhere (Ch. 7) I have said that we need a "fixed point of Archimedes" in order to lift the neurosis off its axes.

We know that it is especially difficult to cure an adult patient who lacks insight into his own illness, has no will to recover, and is not in conflict because the ego fully sides with the illness. If a pervert is content with his perversion and does not want to get rid of it, analytic treatment will be unavailing unless it can somehow succeed in setting him at odds with his abnormality. It has therefore often been said that in order to be analyzed the patient must suffer. Where insight into his illness and the will to recover are lacking in an adult neurotic, it has always been the practice of analysis to convey such insight to him artificially and to make him discontented with his symptoms. The great difficulty in analyzing character neurosis, in which the symptoms form an integral part of the ego structure, is this lack of insight.

In analyzing adults we naturally try to kindle this insight as far as possible by purely analytic methods: we show the patients their true condition. Sometimes this is enough. If so, it is because there is after all in the patient's mind a certain inner discord. But it is not enough in every case. At times the analyst exercises an influence which we need not hesitate to call educational. For instance, he points out to the patient what may be the consequences of his symptoms in real life or what an unfavorable view is taken of them by other people, notably by the analyst himself.

This is a commonplace of adult analysis and has been the subject of a great deal of discussion, sometimes in connection with the treatment of cases in which the ego sides with the illness or forms part of its structure (e.g., in perversion and character neurosis) and sometimes in connection with the analysis of persons who are very largely normal.

Applying this familiar analytic principle to the analysis of children Anna Freud has pointed out that what we encounter only occasionally in adults is a regular feature of child analysis and that therefore with child patients we must regularly use the method which is only occasionally necessary in the case of adults.

The line of criticism to which I have made reference in this section seems to imply that any process which takes place only in the conscious personality is as good as nonexistent. In adult patients the will to recover exists for the most part only in consciousness, in the higher strata of the ego. It is therefore assumed that it may almost be said not to exist at all, since it is only the unconscious side of the human mind which is credited with the power to exert a "real" influence, the degree of "reality" varying directly with the depth of unconsciousness involved. But this is a view which one is tempted to describe as the creation of a mythology of the unconscious.

We wonder what meaning interpretations of the unconscious could possibly have, were there not some conflict in the mind of man, a disharmony between the will of the ego in its higher strata and that which is imposed on it by the id, the superego, and its own lower strata. Surely the aim of interpretation is always to enable the higher strata of the ego to find a different resolution of its instinctual conflicts by making the unconscious conscious. But for an inner disharmony in the human psyche interpretation could not possibly have any effect (see Ch. 21).

Jones has contributed to psychoanalytic theory one of its most important concepts, the term for which has become so much a part of ordinary speech that those who use it hardly realize that it is a psychoanalytic concept at all. I refer to *rationalization.* It is true that, when we expose something as a rationalization, we reveal unconscious motives of a different kind from those which are manifest. Yet it is not only these other motives which "really" exist. The mere fact that rationalization takes place shows that there is a second trend in the psychic life. This trend, like the will to recover, may be feeble; in the past it has been so feeble that it could not hold its own against instinct. Nevertheless, it has been strong enough to prevent the latter from advancing directly to its goal.

In the creation of a mythology of the unconscious we have the antithesis to the preanalytic thesis. According to preanalytic and nonanalytic psychology the only psychic system is that of consciousness. Those who hold the antithetical view maintain that the only thing that really exists, or at any rate is worth the analyst's investigation, is the deep unconscious. There is probably a greater measure of truth in the antithesis than in the thesis, but it is not true either.

We can see how it is that many analysts have concentrated exclusively on penetrating to the "depths," investigating the unconscious life of fantasy and revealing the contents of very early stages of mental development. This endeavor to explore the unconscious is justifiable and necessary, so long as the unconscious is not held to be the sole object of research, for this is to neglect other psychic strata, the whole complicated network of ego elaborations (with the exception of the very earliest, or what are supposed to be the very earliest, defense mechanisms).[28] But this brings us to the subject of the next section.

---

[28] Edward Glover (1937) says that there are three main therapeutic

8. The Relation of the "Deep" Unconscious to the Psychic Strata Nearer to Consciousness

My readers will be aware that, while the writers whose papers are the subject of this discussion have been endeavoring to enlarge our knowledge of unconscious fantasy life, other analysts have devoted more and more attention to the study of the ego, though their interest in the deep unconscious has not flagged. Freud laid the foundation for this extension of psychoanalytic interest in two works (1923b, 1926a). In *The Ego and the Id* he formulated one of the most revolutionary thoughts in psychoanalytic theory, namely, that the pair of opposites, ego and id, is not identical with the pair, conscious and unconscious, and that a part of the ego itself is unconscious. In *Inhibitions, Symptoms and Anxiety* he repudiated a demonological theory of mental life, according to which our life is the passive instrument of obscure forces within us, a theory which seems to have arisen as a kind of antithesis to Adler's theory of the omnipotence of the ego. Freud recommended that in every analytic investigation the part played by both the ego element and the id element in a given phenomenon should invariably be examined. In the same work he generalized the concept of defense, subsuming under it, as specific forms of defense, repression and other mechanisms (isolation and undoing were described in this book for the first time), and so the various forms of defense became a subject for further inquiry. These suggestions have borne fruit in more fields than one. It may be that the idea of the analysis of resistance and of character has been somewhat one-sidedly pursued; it has been discussed repeatedly of late years. But, apart from this, a large number of writings testify to the growing interest in ego psychology. The most recent important conclusions on the subject are to be found in the work by Anna Freud (1936), to which I have referred more than once.

We have been long familiar with the fact that neurosis is a

---

approaches in analysis: (1) the analysis of mental mechanisms; (2) the analysis of affects; (3) the analysis of instinct. The mechanisms named by him are faulty repression, displacement, reaction formation, projection and introjection. There are doubtless, he says, others to be considered *but we know little about them.*

process comparable to the processes of organic disease. A conflict may, for instance, give rise to anxiety. To defend itself against this the ego has recourse to defense mechanisms, and these in their turn produce undesirable results. Joan Riviere described extraordinarily complicated processes which she assumes to take place during the first year of life. Ultimately it always comes to this: the individual attempts to solve the conflicts in ways that prove useless and lead to fresh conflicts. The ego engages in a process of elaboration, the products of which in their turn evoke defensive measures on its part. When we consider the multiplicity of changes which take place in the instinctual life and in the external world, we realize that here is indeed a complicated process and that our knowledge of its various phases is still far from exact. What we encounter as neurosis in an adult or an older child is the provisional end product of such a process, in the course of which the pathogenic conflict has been many times overlaid by later ego elaborations. In analysis this process has to be reversed.[29] The idea that analysis must proceed from stratum to stratum, penetrating gradually from the most recent to those furthest back, is an established principle of analysis. But sometimes it has been wrongly taken to mean that the material which emerges in analysis always belongs to one particular stratum— obviously a misconception. What is really meant is that the neurosis (or the character which we are analyzing) undergoes metamorphosis, as a result of analysis, into successively older forms, the whole process of its development being recapitulated in the reverse direction. Now, since the neurosis itself represents a very late phase in the process, all the ego elaborations must be analytically studied and resolved, and this means that the neurosis gradually resumes its earlier guises, until finally we reach the old pathogenic conflict. It follows that analysis has to deal with the whole course of the neurotic process, immensely long though it be, and with all the ego's modes of elaboration in their higher and very highest forms. This is really simply a consequence of the fact that neurosis is not a linear phenomenon but a developmental process.

But this touches on the relation of the deeper strata of the

[29] In this and what follows I am making use of Anna Freud's account of the matter. A similar account is given by E. Bibring (1937).

unconscious to the ego and the strata nearer to the ego. The study of these higher strata is an indispensable part of analysis. The analysts whose work we have been considering sometimes try to make immediate contact with a lower stratum. Perhaps this is more evident in the analysis of children than in that of adults. We know that Melanie Klein holds that one can make direct contact with a child's unconscious, that so-called "deep interpretations" can be given at once, and that it is actually through these that the child establishes a relation with the analyst. But other analysts would from their point of view regard an attempt of this sort as a leap.

It is certainly possible to contend that a child lives more closely to the unconscious contents of the id than an adult, though even here there is much that is highly problematical. At all events we may reasonably expect that in children the neurotic process will be in an earlier stage than in adults. That is one reason why we feel more hopeful in analyzing children. But even in a child a process of modification has already taken place; the rapidity with which such modifications take place is often very great. And therefore many analysts are inclined to think that, even in analyzing children, it is not wise to take leaps and that, in their case too, all the complicated ego modifications must be brought to light and studied as extensively as possible.

In Melanie Klein's writings *some* modes of ego modification are discussed in great detail, notably those of introjection and projection. But there are others which need to be studied as well, "higher" and more complicated methods adopted by the psyche in response to the instincts, anxieties, and affects.

Further, attention has often been drawn to the fact that that which is arrived at by a leap, even though true, has not the value of reality to the subject. We know from the analysis of adults that there are shadows of the past, which have become shadowy as the result of later elaboration by the ego. If they are exhibited to the patient, he may perhaps understand them intellectually but he does not experience them affectively. Only when the process of elaboration has been resolved do they regain their vividness.

So far, we have considered the objections to the overleaping of the higher strata of the ego from the point of view of therapeutic technique. But I think that, without a most exact study of the higher ego processes, the *correctness* of the conclusions drawn in this way about the deeper unconscious is questionable. We have an enormous variety of phenomena in the final products—the whole multiplicity of life. On the other hand, we have a relatively small number of unconscious themes. Thus, a great multiplicity of elements is brought into conjunction with a comparatively small quantity. The gap between the two is filled precisely by the ego's manifold attempts at solving its conflicts. In order to discover the unconscious motives we must subject the finished products to a very exact and minute phenomenological examination. This involves the exact study of those aspects of a given phenomenon which we conceive of as representing the methods by which, at this particular moment, the ego is seeking to solve its difficulties. Comparatively small differences in the phenomenology of a manifestation may lead one to look in quite a different direction for the original conflict. We can think of instances of how slight differences in the description of a present-day situation may lead to other unconscious themes if we make a direct attempt to reach and effect contact with the unconscious without examining the whole process in detail.[30]

The conclusion seems to be that it is essential in analysis to go beyond such processes as introjection and projection or displacement and repression and to study all the methods of modification which the ego has in its arsenal and the number of which multiplies rapidly as the individual grows older. The thorough examination of the deeper strata of the unconscious remains, as

---

[30] E. Bibring speaks of "singling out" a patient's present patterns of behavior and arriving, by way of a large number of intermediate patterns, at the original infantile pattern. The present pattern embodies the instinctual impulses and anxieties now operative, as well as the ego's present methods of elaboration (some of which are stereotyped responses to impulses and anxieties which have ceased to exist). Only by means of the most careful phenomenology and by taking into consideration all the ego mechanisms now operative can the present pattern of behavior be properly isolated out. If this is done imperfectly—possibly through neglect of the exact study of the higher ego elaborations—or if all the earlier patterns are not equally clearly isolated, there is a danger that we shall never arrive at a correct knowledge of the infantile material. The consequences of such inexact interpretation have been indicated by Edward Glover (1931).

it has always been, one of the desiderata of analysis, whether in the treatment of individual patients or in analytic theory in general. But without the study of the ego, including those strata in it which are conscious or near to consciousness, our therapeutic technique is suspect and the unconscious fantasies whose existence we infer in this way labor under one more uncertainty.

Summary

In what has been said I have purposely avoided entering into controversy about any particular points in the theories under consideration and have contented myself with suggesting a number of problems which radiate from these theories and the study of which we hope may lead to a deeper discussion of the subject. I should like, however, to mention certain general impressions—which are, of course, subject to revision.

Melanie Klein and her colleagues have described a number of fantasies (in particular, oral fantasies) which we meet with in the analyses of adults and of older children. In doing so they have followed out a line of thought which has always been included in the sphere of analysis and which was embodied especially in Abraham's writings. We welcome the addition to our knowledge which this line of investigation promises. And we should express our gratitude to Melanie Klein for grasping and working out one of the difficult thoughts outlined by Freud in *The Ego and the Id,* which has now become the common property of analysis—the fact, namely, that the aggression of the superego is not merely acquired from the object but also represents the subject's own aggressiveness turned in upon himself.

But what follows gives us pause. We hesitate to believe that the only effect of reality is to confirm or to refute irrational anxieties; that the fantasies of mankind follow a predestined course, are merely rendered more or less intense by the action of reality, and are always to some extent operative; that violent manifestations of aggressiveness during the first year of life are universal; that in infancy there are mechanisms at work resembling those of psychosis, so that psychotic illness in later life can be explained as the effect of modes of reaction which are part of normal development; that the fantasies in question date from a very early period (we should be inclined to place them later, in the third or fourth year of life, though we should admit that they are determined by fixations in the first two years); in fact, we doubt whether we have sufficient clues to enable us to infer the experiences of earliest infancy with that degree of certainty which we commonly look for or whether we can claim any degree of scientific accuracy for detailed conclusions about them. Finally, we cannot but feel that an excursion has been made into the shadowy past, while much that could be more satisfactorily proved and that is indispensable for analysis has been left unregarded.

Anyone who is interested in the elucidation of these problems is bound to test all the points here enumerated upon the largest possible body of material. The constant reiteration of assertion and counterassertion, based on alleged individual experience, is not likely to be very fruitful.

Psychoanalysis has a dialectical structure. The poles of its dialectic are fantasy and reality, biology and social environment, constitution and experience, unconscious and conscious, transference and real relationships, the id and the ego. The works which I have discussed in this paper incline very markedly to the one extreme, while the majority of analysts, following in the footsteps of Freud, hold a middle course.

CHAPTER 9

Criteria of Interpretation

(1939)

In a detective story by G. K. Chesterton, the amateur detective Father Brown and his friend Flambeau, a former master thief turned staunch defender of justice, happen upon a lonely castle in Scotland whose misanthropic owner has just died. A superficial search of the castle discloses several strange things that arouse their suspicion: unset diamonds strewn all over; quantities of snuff lying about loosely and not stored in boxes; candles, but no candle holders; and masses of tiny wheels and pieces of metal, seemingly having been pried out of clocks and watches. "Who would make a story out of these?" asks Flambeau. "That's easy," says Father Brown.

The deceased Lord was an admirer of the *ancien regime* in France. Therefore he loved candles. The little pieces of metal came from a workshop which the Lord had built in imitation of Louis XVI's hobby of metal working. The snuff was to revive a custom prevalent at that time, and the diamonds were to be used for a replica of Marie Antoinette's collarpiece.

One would ask in astonishment whether he really believed this solved the puzzle. "Of course, not," replied the priest-detective. "I merely wanted to show that these diverse and curious things could be pieced together." And he might continue: the deceased Lord may have been a criminal, leading a

This paper was presented at the 15th Congress of the International Psycho-Analytical Association, Paris, August 1939. It was first published as "Kriterien der Deutung," in *Internationale Zeitschrift für Psychoanalyse*, 24:136-145, 1939. The English translation by Lottie M. Newman is here published for the first time.

double life. He used the snuff to numb his victims; the candles, on his nightly raids; and the diamonds and pieces of metal to cut plate glass.

Again we would ask whether he would really maintain this hypothesis. And Father Brown would again deny it and continue: perhaps in the hope of inducing the deceased Lord to make a major investment, a gang of crooks had persuaded him that a cache of diamonds was hidden on his property. They delivered some of them to him, claiming they had been found on his grounds; the metal wheels and pieces were to be used for diamond cutting and polishing; the candles were needed in the exploration of caves; and the snuff, the only luxury of the Scottish shepherds, had been prepared as payment for their help.

Father Brown merely wanted to demonstrate that one could find several theories to tie the given elements into a story. The true solution at which they finally arrive was different. The misanthropic Lord, distrustful of everyone, had hired as a servant an idiot whose honesty had impressed him. He promised this servant that after his death all the gold in the castle would belong to the servant. The idiot had stuck to those words quite literally. He took the golden snuff boxes and left the snuff; he removed the golden candle holders, but not the candles; he took the golden diamond settings and left the diamonds behind; and he carefully removed the inner clockwork of the watches to acquire only the golden cases.

This short, somewhat fantastic story demonstrates that a hypothesis designed to explain a series of empirical facts may indeed account for all of them and yet be far from being the correct interpretation. Using this example, we can ask: if one of Father Brown's earlier, more playful attempts at interpretation had been correct, how could this be proven? Assuming his hypothesis about the gang of crooks searching the Lord's property for diamonds had been correct, corroborating evidence could have been obtained by questioning the shepherds; furthermore, some correspondence about the project would have been found, or bills for items delivered to the castle. Or, there might be some clues that such documentary evidence had been destroyed. These considerations point to the factors from which criteria of interpretation can be derived. An interpretation must provide an explanation for all known facts, but this is not enough. All the conclusions which can be derived from such an interpretation about the previously unknown circumstances must be borne out by facts. An interpretation must go beyond the observable facts on which it is based; it must contain, so to say, more substance than that from which it is derived.

With this we have found the criterion of interpretation: all inferences that can by sheer reasoning be drawn from an interpretation must be confirmed by empirical facts. In this way interpretation facilitates the discovery of new facts. Of course, we shall regard something as confirmed only when other explanations of the facts derived from an interpretation and subsequently corroborated by empirical evidence can for all practical purposes be ruled out.

The criteria of psychoanalytic interpretation, it seems to me, must be the same criteria of interpretation used in other sciences or everyday life. The principles of drawing conclusions and proving them are the same in psychoanalysis as in all other fields—be that history, linguistics, or criminology. An interpretation is securely established not only when it has fully taken account of all the facts it was called on to explain, but also when all the conclusions that can be derived from it have been empirically confirmed and no other plausible explanation can be found. The more closely an interpretation approximates this ideal confirmation the more plausible it seems.

Furthermore, I do not believe there exists a fundamental difference between psychoanalytic interpretation and the theories of the exact natural sciences. In the natural sciences, too, a hypothesis advanced to explain a series of observed phenomena is corroborated only when the theoretical conclusions derived from it by pure logic find confirmation in the empirical world.

A classical example of this type would be Newton's theory of gravity which received spectacular confirmation when the previously unknown planet Neptune could be observed at the exact location where calculations based on the gravity theory had required it to be. Physicists say that in developing a theory, a system of facts is coordinated with a system of concepts in such a way that all the conclusions required by logic in the conceptual system correspond to consequences required by nature in the factual system. A similar process can be applied to all interpretations—even to psychoanalytic interpretations, although this may require a qualification. Psychoanalysis deals with unique individual phenomena that are not accessible to experiments in the strict sense of that term; therefore, the same degree of certainty cannot be achieved and one must be satisfied with plausibility and, having taken all precautionary measures, one can be satisfied with this.

In order for an analytic interpretation to meet these requirements, it is first of all necessary that no single detail, however minute, remain unexplained. This applies not only to symptoms but also to general attitudes and reactions. This requirement will of course not be fulfilled by every single interpretation, but it should have been met by the total system of interpretations at the end of a completed analysis.

Psychoanalytic interpretations, whether they refer to a single occurrence or a comprehensive reconstruction, receive confirmation through the immediate accession of new material. Since every analyst is familiar with this type of confirmation, I shall cite only two brief illustrations.

The life story of a man was decisively influenced by the fact that an older sister who had died early was mourned by the family as a prodigy. Very early he had formed the hypothesis that her outstanding qualities had been due to their mother's nursing her, whereas when it was his turn his mother lacked sufficient milk and so had to turn him over to a wet nurse. His further life was taken up by a constant acting out, in part to obtain the wished-for oral satisfaction from women, and in part to revenge himself for the damage that supposedly had been inflicted on him. This man had a dream in which he found himself together with a child whom he cared for with extraordinary kindness. Knowing this man's problem and also many other details which I shall omit here, the analyst without asking for associations ventured an interpretation: You want to show your mother how she should have treated you. Even while this interpretation was being given and elaborated, the patient indicated that he had more to say and as soon as the analyst had finished, the patient continued: "Yes, I still wanted to tell you that I had the feeling my mother was watching me."

The second example is also taken from the analysis of this

man. This same man who lived in constant fear of women and the castration threat emanating from them was suddenly free of anxiety on a day when events in the external world really threatened him as well as all others in his surroundings. Further discussion revealed that he could part with his neurotic anxiety because his anxiety objects, the women he feared, were far too preoccupied with the common real danger to inflict harm on him. (The reasons why he was less sensitive to existing real danger are not relevant here.) A special aspect of this man's anxiety related to the fact that in his innumerable affairs with women, he never had dared to look at the female genital. Linking several elements of the situation, the analyst suggested: "I believe that now you would dare look at a woman's genital." "That's exactly what I did yesterday," the analysand, somewhat taken aback, replied.

These two examples will suffice to remind analysts of these everyday analytic experiences.

I shall now discuss a number of precautionary measures which if adhered to will increase the chances of interpretations being correct. This does not mean, of course, that from a therapeutic point of view it is always indicated to proceed in the way I shall describe, because the therapeutic success usually, but not necessarily always or entirely, coincides with the correctness of interpretations. To facilitate my discussion of the precautionary measures, I shall use the model of a different, well-known procedure of intrepretation and arbitrary select criminology.

1. The correctness of interpretations evidently requires that all facts be carefully registered, that the field of observation be sufficiently broad, and that the description of the phenomena be as exact as possible. In a criminal investigation, the detective will examine every speck of dust, every crumb and every little splinter on the scene of the crime and its surroundings. In analysis, even if one aims only at a correct interpretation of a symptom, the analyst does not confine himself to a study of the symptom; rather he studies a person's entire psychic life in the hope of learning all the details. We do this because we want to study not only the neurosis but the entire psychic life; but we would have to do this even if we were interested only in a symptom. For the same reason all manifestations must be

described as carefully as possible because minor differences in the phenomenology of a process may require entirely different interpretations.

Exact registration of facts also implies that we do not take anything for granted but regard everything as problematical. Similarly, a good detective will be struck by a variety of things that a less experienced or a less able person will not pay much attention to. This means that he sees a problem in why this thing is precisely on this spot and the like. In analysis this would be analogous to our asking whether a particular form of behavior, a specific reaction to a stimulus, is really the only possible way in which human nature can respond to the given circumstances. If this is not the case, then that specific reaction or behavior becomes a problem that needs to be investigated.

2. A second principle is that an investigation not be prematurely given a definite direction. Criminologists are familiar with this, too. If early in the game a detective decided on a theory and then single-mindedly follows only this theory, he is apt to pay no attention to clues that would lead in a different direction. Actually, the danger is even greater because in the meantime the clues that might have led to the discovery of the crime are wiped out. The analogous principle in analysis would then read: the analyst should avoid making interpretations of current behavior in terms that include the presumptive infantile conflict before he has sufficient knowledge about its essential facts. In the psychoanalytic situation, too, there is an analogy to the danger of real clues being wiped out while one pursues wrong clues. The analysand may register the subtle suggestion implicit in the analyst's suggestion; the patient's resistance may be only too ready to comply with it on the basis of an unverbalized agreement: I accept the thought hidden in the analyst's interpretation and he will not touch upon my secret.

The analyst observes a specific type of behavior. He makes the analysand aware of it, describes it, and interprets some of its constituent elements. All of it taken together seems to point to a specific infantile conflict. In most instances, however, a number of possibilities exist and very minute differences in the interpretation of current behavior may lead to very different infantile themes. If one raises an arrow in New York, it makes very little difference whether it points to Japan or nearby China, but the difference at the end point is considerable.

An example which was previously discussed in a case seminar in Vienna may serve to illustrate matters. A patient's stereotyped complaint that she cannot accomplish something, that she is incapable of doing it, may point equally to the female castration complex and to experiences relating to the struggle over giving up masturbation. In such cases the analyst is in danger of prematurely focusing on one of the two possibilities; in consequence, the specific infantile complex he suspects will be carried over into his interpretation in the form of background music, as it were; and the analysis will prematurely be given a definitive direction—with all the dangers this implies for the correctness of interpretations.

One might object here that psychoanalytic interpretation must in any case reach beyond the known facts. However, the question is: does one bring the assumed infantile conflict into the analysis on the basis of supporting material or without direct material?

This leads to another problem: the degree to which certain fantasies may be stimulated in an analysand. We have all heard the argument frequently voiced by people who are unfamiliar with analysis that a patient's experiences in analysis are "imported." This is of course not possible in a correctly conducted analysis because a patient's motives for accepting an interpretation are themselves subjected to analysis. But is is also here that human beings can avail themselves of an incredibly rich fund of possible fantasies and therefore yield easily to a suggestion. The analyst having gotten on a wrong track will surely find the patient's resistance to be his most important ally.

I present another example to illustrate these points. A beautiful woman has physically as well as in her entire life assumed the posture of a statue. The theme of resting like a statue plays an important role in her fantasies. In the analytic hours she frequently lies with hands locked behind her back on the couch. This statuesque posture could be explained in a variety of possible ways. For example, the stiffness might suggest defense against affects, which would be in accord with the patient's total behavior (and which, if formulated precisely, would turn out to be correct). One might also suspect that one has to do with a masochistically provoking gesture in the sense of "the attacker can now do with me what he wishes." One might consider that in the attempt to cope with the castration complex, the whole body was turned into a penis. Many other possibilities might suggest themselves and for each one would find some material on which to base an interpretation. However, prolonged analysis disclosed a much simpler origin of this patient's posture which she had first assumed in order to ward off the temptation to masturbate when she was lying down to sleep.

Incidentally, analysis has available a method whereby it can do justice to the many different possibilities that always exist and thereby give each a chance, as it were: occasionally one should also offer interpretations that one does not regard as correct in order to study their effects.

3. Criminology and analysis have a further principle in common. In the process of investigation one must consistently give consideration to the fact that the object of investigation is being changed by the act of being investigated. The detective must bear in mind that the scene of the crime may have been altered by the team examining the scene, e.g., which fingerprints have been left by them. And the investigating prosecutor must be clear about what he knows and what he merely suspects and consider how a man's subsequent depositions will change after he has been informed that he stands accused of having committed a specific crime.

In analysis, therefore, we must constantly pay attention to the analysand's reactions to interpretations and this is probably the most important task after we have given an interpretation. Freud (1937b) put together the various points of view that are relevant to this undertaking. We know that a patient's yes as well as no, the acceptance or rejection of an interpretation, can be a reality-based intellectual agreement or disagreement, but it need not be and in fact only rarely is based exclusively on reality reasons. In most instances an accepting as well as a rejecting reaction derives primarily from emotional sources. But this also implies that a patient's yes or no must, like everything else, be subjected to examination. A rejection may be a manifestation of the resistance or of the negative transference, or an invitation to a pleasure-yielding battle, and many other things as well. Agreement may also be a manifestation of the resistance, in line with the formula described above where a patient adopts a less dangerous path in order to make sure that the greater danger remains hidden. Or agreement may derive directly from instinctual sources, as is the case, e.g., in oral-passive persons who live in expectation of receiving a momentous gift which they hope will materialize by their compliance.

In view of these many possibilities—and there are always others—it is mandatory that the reaction to each interpretation be analyzed. We would have to do this in any event because analysis aims at bringing to light whatever is hidden. But more immediately relevant to the topic of this essay: this rule also provides the tool by means of which we can guard against errors in interpretation and correct such errors as may have been made.

The previously cited paper by Freud (1937b) contains another important thought. Freud states that the delusions of psychotics contain a historical truth that must be deciphered correctly. What we grant the psychotic must also be permitted to the nonpsychotic analysand: his rejection of an interpretation may in some sense contain a truth. In earlier times we used to express this thought by saying: the patient is always right. The area where the patient is right in saying no to an interpretation has also been specified in Freud's paper: a patient's no indicates as a rule that the interpretation is incomplete. Thus, a patient's rejection of an interpretation should always be taken as a sign that it required supplementation, i.e., as a clue indicating that the entire phenomenon has not yet been grasped. On the other hand, this cannot be expected to occur as long as an analysis is still in progress.

4. Finally, as a last requirement, I wish to state that all our interpretations must be capable of synthetically being reconstructed again, whether these interpretations deal with minor everyday events or are comprehensive constructions of symptom and character formation. Again criminology provides us with a model. When the investigator believes he has found the explanation of a crime, he attempts to reconstruct the manner in which it came about. Frequently, he does so not just by pure reasoning

but also by recourse to experimentation. Starting with existing clues, the detective proceeds backward to the commission of the crime. In reconstructing it, he takes the opposite course: he retraces the steps as they actually were taken and which left behind the only clues that he found. Likewise, the analyst must be able to retrace all the steps that induced him to make a specific interpretation, whether this related to details of the patient's behavior or the entire development of the patient's neurosis. In this process of reconstruction, each element must be plausible, i.e., it must be confirmed by empirical experience.

This might be regarded as circular reasoning. On the one hand, the analyst employs certain rules to make interpretations; on the other, he employs interpretations to establish new rules. But this reasoning only appears to be circular. We always interpret by employing known principles and rules which then lead us to new, previously unknown propositions. Moreover, our trust in the analytic method is founded not only on psychoanalytic interpretation, it rests, in part at least, on direct observation, e.g., the observation of children.

If, then, we proceeded by giving equal attention to all phenomena; if we considered everything a problem that was not unequivocally determined by an external event; if our interpretations explain all manifestations; if all the conclusions that can be derived from the interpretations have found empirical confirmation; if all other possible interpretations of the observed phenomena have been examined and discarded; if all interpretations can synthetically be reconstructed again; if all the individual elements are in good agreement with other experiences, especially those obtained by direct observation; if in our analytic work we have taken the precaution to formulate interpretations of current material in such a way that they do not prematurely implicate a specific infantile conflict as long as the latter is not yet clearly indicated in the material; if, finally, in each case we subjected the patient's reaction to our interpretations to analysis—if we adhered to these principles, we may attribute a sufficient measure of probability to our interpretations.

To some it may seem that the analyst has been assigned too much of a task. But this is in principle true of the criminologist as well. What differs is the material with which the analyst works. The experienced analyst considers all the points outlined above in his preconscious mind. The criteria of interpretation must be sharply focused on only when they constitute the topic under discussion. In practice, the analyst's method of working is still best described with the words that Freud's teacher, Charcot, used to characterize his own method of working, which was also characteristic of Freud both in the actual conduct of analyses and in the field of applied analysis: *to look at things long enough until they themselves appear to tell you what they are.*

CHAPTER 10

Present Trends in Psychoanalytic Theory and Practice

(1944)

The variety of schools of thought and of unsettled controversies, even over fundamental issues, which exists in psychoanalysis—unlike the conditions in the natural sciences but similar to those prevailing in the social sciences—seems to be largely due to two factors: Psychoanalysis does not deal with an emotionally more or less indifferent subject matter (as do the natural sciences) but with the core of the personality; it "stirs too deeply the soul's unconscious springs" (Byron). Furthermore, unlike the state of affairs in the natural sciences, experimental control in psychoanalysis is very difficult to achieve, and is outright impossible for the interpretation of the individual case.

The earliest deviations from the Freudian theory were the teachings of C. G. Jung and Alfred Adler. Jung attempted to explain mental disorders, especially those of a more advanced age, in terms of regressions to a collective unconscious: men shrink back from their tasks of life, and the symbols of the collective unconscious, their racial heritage, emerge. Adler explained neurosis and character patterns as devices in the struggle for existence, i.e., as we may say today, in terms of the ego mechanisms of dealing with external danger. Thus both

Read as part of a symposium on this subject at the Detroit meeting of the American Psychoanalytic Association, May, 1943. Reprinted from *Bulletin of the Menninger Clinic*, 8:9-13, 1944. Also in *The Yearbook of Psychoanalysis*, 1:84-89. New York: International Universities Press, 1945.

Jung and Adler did away with the sexual aspect of neurosis and put less emphasis on the individual's past than did Freud. However, neither of them introduced an entirely new idea; each selected one concept of Freud's and made it the cornerstone of his "new" theory. A collective unconscious was assumed in psychoanalysis in the concept of symbolism; dream elements, for the understanding of which the dreamer's life and associations furnished no clue, were considered to be symbols, common to mankind, or to the race—residuals of experiences of a prehistoric past. In a similar way, the intentional aspect of neurotic symptoms in the service of ego purposes was known to psychoanalysis before Adler. Freud (1905) described it at some length in the case history of Dora. Incidentally, this concept was not even original with Freud but was widely accepted in pre-Freudian thinking.

Another system was then inaugurated by Otto Rank. Rank, too, concentrated on one motif of psychoanalysis, the concept of transference, and made it the basis of a new theory and technique. Treatment, with him, was no longer meant to make conscious the unconscious; it was merely to be a training in relationship. The patient should learn relationship with another person and in this way discover his own "self" in its uniqueness. Even this therapeutic application—transference as a school of relationship—was not an entirely new concept; but that which, in psychoanalysis, was a mere accessory, became for Rank the Alpha and Omega of treatment.[1]

In order to appreciate the trends of the last twenty years in psychoanalytic theory and practice it may not be superfluous to recall the state of knowledge that prevailed among psychoanalysts in the early 1920s. Most analysts at the time had assimilated the concepts of the oedipus complex and the pregenital stages of the libido, the concepts of fixation and regression, and those of resistance and transference. Fundamental as these concepts were, and I suggest still are, they did not always seem sufficient for the understanding of the problems of neuroses or for their successful treatment. Guided by these ideas alone, analysts were sometimes inclined to make "short-circuit interpretations," i.e.,

[1] These remarks do not apply to Rank's latest ideas which seem to differ too widely from psychoanalytic concepts to be dealt with in this paper.

to jump directly from the surface phenomena to deep interpretations in terms of unconscious drives or of an infantile situation.

Dissatisfaction with this state of knowledge and therapeutic frustration were the driving forces that led psychoanalysts to search for new answers. They searched mainly in three directions, and with time three schools of thought became more and more discernible. I shall discuss each of these briefly.

1. Some analysts thought that in order to get more complete insight and better therapeutic results one had only to penetrate deeper along the road into the unconscious and into the past. There was a kind of tacit assumption that the more remote from consciousness an impulse was, and the earlier an event or a fantasy had occurred, the greater was its pathogenic value.

The guide along this road was Karl Abraham. His theory of the "part objects," his attempts at subdividing the oral and anal stages and at finding the precise fixation points for every mental disorder were examples of a still cautious application of the idea. Others—mostly analysts trained or influenced by Abraham— went further. The most elaborate product of this line of approach is probably to be found in the writings of the British "school" of psychoanalysis as represented by Melanie Klein, Ernest Jones, and others. These authors speak of an exuberant oral sadism in the first few months of life, and of an early application of the mechanism of introjection and projection which are looked upon as the basic ego mechanisms. They describe very early stages of projection of boundless aggression to the outside world, comparable to paranoid conditions, and of introjection of fantastically evil objects, comparable to melancholic depressions. Mental disorders appear as the products of a fantastic struggle of good and bad internalized objects, and of their introjection and projection; and therapy consists of the breaking of a vicious circle through the introjection of a good object (analyst).

From this point of view, Freudian interpretations in terms of the emotional conflicts of later childhood, such as, for example, castration fear or penis envy, appear not as entirely wrong, but as superficial, not penetrating to the powerful fantasies of a deeper unconscious.

Freud had suggested that an adult neurosis was built over the scars of a childhood neurosis, mainly of the years from three to six; we may say that the British school suggests that such childhood neurosis was built over a "prehistoric," quasi-psychotic condition of the first year of life.

2. Entirely different from this approach, another school of psychiatric thought is inclined to believe that psychoanalysis has devoted too much interest to the unconscious fantasies and to childhood while not studying carefully enough the patients' current lives, their rivalries, their insecurity, their cultural restrictions. This school of thought, of which Karen Horney is a representative, views man as living in an intensely hostile world, impeded or even disarmed in his self-defense by his own cravings for dependence, and developing neurotic symptoms as a means of protection. As was the case with Adler, the interest of this school of thought is mainly devoted to the methods utilized by the ego to deal with external challenges. However, this second attempt at explaining neurosis exclusively through ego psychology has assimilated much more psychoanalytic data than did the first one of Adler.

3. A third line of approach may be called more specifically Freudian. Some authors point out that psychoanalysts, for a long time occupied with the task of describing the newly discovered instinctual phenomena, worked with only a few conceptions about the ego (among them, e.g., repression). They believe that the psychology of the instinctual drives has to be supplemented by a psychology of the ego, i.e., of the integrative function. But they differ from Adler and Horney insofar as they propose to study the ego not merely in its relation to the outer world but equally in its relation to the inner world of instinctual drives, and to study in particular the interrelation between these two kinds of integrative efforts. Their favorite subject is therefore the study of the methods of dealing with external stimuli (instinctual goals, dangers) and with internal stimuli (instinctual drives, anxieties, guilt feelings).

A representative exponent of this approach is Anna Freud who, in her study of defense mechanisms, advances the proposition that man uses similar techniques in dealing with objects, with anxieties, and with instinctual drives, and that every individual has but a limited repertoire of such mechanisms.

This increased attention to and interest in ego psychology is not meant to eliminate the concept of the instinctual drives, nor to make deeper unconscious strata, the sexual drives, or childhood experiences appear any less important. Rather it aims at a microscopic analysis of phenomena in terms of their instinct and ego components. It aims at eliminating the short-circuit interpretations in favor of an inching downward and backward from a broad basis of character study with a view to thus arriving at more exact reconstructions of unconscious fantasies and of the whole process of the neurotic career. Interpretations made from this viewpoint compare with psychoanalytic reconstructions made in the early phases of the history of psychoanalysis as highly documented historical investigations compare with a brilliant vision of the past. The ultimate technical ideal of this ego psychology is actually to transform the neurosis into its earlier stages, and finally into the precipitating conflicts—to roll the process of neurosis back along the road of its development.

Let us now try to survey the various schools of thought in a more systematic way. The controversies in psychoanalysis seem to be centered around a few dichotomies: (1) conscious vs. unconscious; (2) biological vs. sociological; (3) current vs. past; (4) sexual impulses vs. nonsexual impulses (i.e., self-preservation and aggression).

The Freudian position as regards these dichotomies is somewhat as follows:

The neurotic conflict is considered to be at least partly unconscious, both descriptively and dynamically. The contents of the unconscious are thought to be similar to conscious contents; they have at times been, or may occasionally still be, conscious.

The question as to the degree to which phenomena vary with cultural conditions is open to research and I know of no preference, in Freudian thought, for one or the other possibility—unless it be the insistence that culture itself is liable to analysis in terms of human psychology and external nature.

As to the third dichotomy, Freud considered current pressures and infantile carry-overs as forming a supplementary series. Among the various ways in which the past reaches out into the present, special importance is attributed to the persistence of unsettled problems of the past, especially those of childhood. The unsettled problems of our childhood have sensitized the individual, as it were, for later stimuli of a similar nature just as a photographic film, which has been sensitized by previous exposure, has its threshold for later exposures lowered.

While thus approaching the pathogenic importance of infantile experience, the Freudian school does not hold that an experience is the more significant the younger the individual is. Rather the individual is considered to be most vulnerable in those special periods of life in which there is the greatest discrepancy between the severity of the problems presented and his ability to meet them, i.e., in childhood in the time of the full prime of infantile sexuality (from about three to six), again in adolescence, and finally in the years around the climacteric.

Finally, in the Freudian line of thought it is held that a conflict over a sexual drive is involved in every disorder even though other conflicts also participate. But it is the interference of the sexual conflict element which is considered to be most responsible for making the conflict pathological. The cause for this strange recurrence of the sexual motives in maladjustments may be found in the rebellious nature of the sexual drives. Self-assertive and aggressive impulses seem to be more apt to adjust themselves to adverse conditions while sexual drives tend to recur and only rarely resign.

One can try to allocate within this frame of reference the places of the various other schools. The British school emphasizes the importance of an unconscious that is conceived as being much more remote from consciousness and more different from it in its contents. Almost exclusive interest is devoted to the historic past, in particular to the first two years of life. Aggression bears the brunt of responsibility for disease and sex has been detoxified to become the desire for the incorporation of good objects. "Culturalists," for example Horney, seem by unconscious to mean something much nearer to consciousness than the unconscious of the Freudian conceptions; explanations are sought to a large extent in current problems, and hostility and dependence rather than sex appear as the troublemakers. Ferenczi, in his later ideas, agreed with most of the Freudian concepts, but he believed again in the sexual trauma as the basis of neurosis and thus put more emphasis on a later childhood period. He abided by the idea of the sexual aspect of neurosis, but he considered it as introduced by the selfish adult seducer rather than as being genuine in childhood. His ideas "desexualize" psychoanalysis to some extent by assuming that the child desires only a sexual tenderness and that the sensual component of infantile sexuality is an artifact, introduced by the adult.

Various other theories which time does not permit me to discuss seem to be characterized mainly by a specific distribution of emphasis within the above-mentioned dichotomies.

CHAPTER 11

The Structure of
Paranoid Ideas

A Critical Survey of Various Theories
(1951)

Many psychoanalysts will agree that the structure and formation of paranoid ideas have not yet been fully understood.
Psychoanalysis came into being through the study of classical
neurosis, and we are still more familiar with this than with any
other subject. In other areas of psychopathology our knowledge
is more fragmentary and we cannot yet tell the whole story.

Paranoid ideas present a major challenge to psychological
theory. This is not due to the fact that paranoiacs adhere to
erroneous concepts about many things. We all entertain erroneous concepts about many things. Our misconceptions may
partly be due to intellectual factors, i.e., to our ignorance, to the
fact that we can approach the new and unfamiliar only in terms
of the old and familiar, and to insufficient power of abstraction,
of emancipating ourselves from previous impressions; and partly
to emotional factors, to what William James called *the will to
believe.*[1]

But most people, i.e., those who are not paranoid, can

Part of this paper was presented to the Philadelphia Psychoanalytic Society
on December 16, 1948. Reprinted from *International Journal of Psycho-
Analysis,* 32:167-177, 1951.

[1] I have discussed these factors on another occasion (Ch. 27).

modify their beliefs under the impact of experience. As a rule, we do not part with our beliefs immediately when experience testifies against them, but we yield to repeated evidence.

Paranoid ideas, however, cannot be corrected by experience. Kraepelin (1901-1905) has therefore defined delusions as "erroneous judgments not subject to correction by experience."

This is a challenge to our theory because it seems to contradict a law of psychology, both human and animal, namely, that one learns through experience. Why, or under what conditions, are misconceptions of reality not subject to the corrective influence of experience? Under what conditions are people unable to learn?[2] A theory of delusions will have to account for their inaccessibility to influence. No theory that fails in this point could be held satisfactory.

Survey of Various Psychoanalytic Concepts

Narcissism and the Maldistribution of Libido

The first attempt to explain delusions was made by Karl Abraham (1927) in a paper written under the influence of Freud and in Freud's paper on narcissism (1914a). As is generally known, Freud and Abraham suggested explaining delusions of grandeur by a withdrawal of libido from the object world and its concentration on the ego. Libido has thus become narcissistic; since the sexual object is always overvalued, the ego, now the exclusive object of the libido, is overestimated and magnified.

---

[2] The problem of paranoia is of great interest from the point of view of applied psychoanalysis, too. Many systems of thought which have profoundly influenced the course of history have been more or less akin to paranoid systems. One may even say that history is, to a large extent, the outcome of two forces, viz., on the one hand the process of learning from experience, the struggle for a better adjustment to, or a better mastery of, reality, both natural and man-made, and on the other hand the ever-continuing rise of paranoid structures. The struggle between democracy and totalitarianism is, to some extent, a struggle between "ordinary" people, with all their ignorance and unwisdom, who are capable of learning through experience if given time, and paranoiacs or people infected by paranoid ideas. It is a fight in which all the initial advantages are with the paranoiacs, but which they are bound to lose, because of their lack of elasticity, unless they can turn initial advantages into complete victory.

This is an explanation in terms of libidinal cathexes. It is an attempt to explain megalomania by reducing it to a familiar condition, viz., to the overvaluation of an object in the state of infatuation.

It suggests that any concentration of libido is detrimental to the sense of reality, and that a more equal distribution of cathexes may be the best condition for a balanced judgment of reality. Since the concept of a destructive instinct has been added to our instinct theory, this early hypothesis can be generalized. We may say that not only the concentration of erotic drives upon one object, be it an outside object or our own ego, but also any concentration of destructive forces upon others or upon ourselves is bound to distort or to destroy the sense of reality. The attitude which groups with strong cohesion show toward outsiders offers an example of the former, the self-debasement of the melancholic of the latter.

Thus, the concentration of both erotic and aggressive drives upon an object is detrimental to the sense of reality, and the most favorable condition for a balanced judgment seems to be a wide and not too unequal distribution of libido and destruction. The fact that, as a rule, obsessional neurotics with their proverbial ambivalence seem to retain, even in conditions of grave illness, their ability of judging reality fairly correctly dovetails well with these generalizations.

The hypothesis should also supply us with an explanation of the fact that delusions are inaccessible to influence. If the megalomaniac's libido is concentrated on his ego, and if he therefore overvalues himself grossly, corrective experience cannot reach him because he has no free libido to take it in and weigh it properly. In this way, the hypothesis makes judgment, and even perception, a function of cathexis.

This, however, meets with some difficulties. First, there is a theoretical difficulty; how does the idea that judgment is a function of libidinal cathexis fit in with the anaclitic type of object choice? If the libido follows the self-preservative instincts, i.e., if we love what is useful to us, there must be a perception of facts and an appreciation of their utility before there is any libidinal cathexis.

There are clinical difficulties, too. We know of cases of

circumscribed paranoid systems in persons who have not withdrawn their libido from outside objects; they may have strong,
sometimes warm, object relationships and they often succeed in
defending and protecting these relationships against the threatening intrusion of their paranoid ideas. It would be difficult to
explain, in such cases, the breakdown of reality testing as a
consequence of a libidinal retreat which has not taken place on
any large scale. One may point out that object libido was withdrawn in a certain area and that this limited withdrawal has
undone the reality testing, but it would be very difficult to work
this idea out in concrete terms.[3]

Furthermore, it seems questionable whether the delusion of a
man who claims to be Jesus Christ is really of the same quality as
the overvaluation shown, e.g., by a mother for her child.
Mothers or lovers can be conspicuously blind to the flaws of their
beloved, though these may be patent to everybody else. But they
do not go as far as paranoiacs; there is a vast difference between
their affectionate misjudgments, however stubbornly defended,
and those of real paranoia. It seems more correct to say that the
misjudgments due to love and hatred are still on the fringe of
"normality," while paranoid ideas have crossed that line.

Projection

According to another hypothesis, delusions are a product of
projection. An inner process which has become subject to this
mechanism is perceived as coming from outside.

The hypothesis may go a long way toward an understanding
of paranoid ideas,[4] but the concept of projection needs further
clarification. Is projection meant to be an elementary mechan-

---

[3] The fact that patients suffering from paranoia have sometimes preserved
good object relationships seems to me to invalidate those theories which
consider the complete loss of object cathexis a prerequisite of *all* delusion
formation.

[4] Projection is a convenient concept of psychoanalytic explanation and one
may wonder whether it has not often been applied to situations in which a
more detailed examination may have led to a different evaluation.

For instance: I observed a middle-aged man who had ideas of reference. It
was not a case of paranoia but an obsessional neurosis with paranoid
tendencies. His paranoid constructions might easily have been interpreted as
projections—this, indeed, was occasionally suggested by the patient on the

ism, one of the fundamental and irreducible responses to challenge, or is it a complex mechanism?

First, we should distinguish between two cases of projection which seem to require independent consideration, viz., the projection of a superego voice and the projection of an instinctual drive. A girl who believes that people call her names, accuse her of being a prostitute, etc., has projected a critical voice of her superego. A person who attributes his own aggressive designs or temptations to others projects an id impulse.

The first case is easily comprehensible. The superego is the result of the internalization of external commands and prohibi-

---

basis of his reading knowledge. But closer examination seemed to favor another view. The patient lived in perpetual expectation of attack or insult and his attention was pitched high to detect microscopic signs of hostility or disparagement in others. The sooner he noticed approaching danger, the better would he be able to prepare himself. In the lingo of his analysis we called it his "radar." In the background of this patient's history was a vulgar father, who indulged in incessant verbal abuse and occasional serious physical threats. The patient's passive homosexual trends which were amply manifested would increase the danger; he knew that, if attacked, he would be strongly tempted to surrender and had therefore all the more reason to safeguard himself against attack.

The same person showed another mechanism in a paranoid idea which occurred in the transference. Once during an hour he thought that I suspected him of theft. The examination of the circumstances showed convincingly that in the immediately preceding moment he had expected blame in a matter in which he was far from guiltless. The sudden idea that he was to be accused of a theft of which he was obviously innocent was not a projection of an impulse but an attempt at rapidly changing the scene of action, away from his actual guilt and from the danger of being called to task for it, to another subject in which he would feel on safe ground. It was as if he would say: I have no more done what you blame me for than I have stolen your money.

A young man with slight paranoid ideas attributes to his partner the criticism which he keenly feels of himself. This seems to be a case of projection of the superego. But closer examination suggested that there was a more complicated process at work. He is a dreamer who easily forgets about reality and becomes absorbed in his fantasies; he tries to get and to keep up contact with others but loses it constantly. Whenever he loses contact, he is afraid that he might suddenly be attacked and thus be taken off guard. In his attempts to establish contact, which does not come to him naturally, he tries to identify himself with others and to find out and produce in himself "how they feel." Trying to get inside another person in his effort to establish contact, he must attribute his own ideas about himself to the "host" and see himself with his own eyes from within the host's body. The process is similar to the identifications in adolescence which Anna Freud (1936) described as attempted restitutions for the loss of objects.

tions. Once the voice of the superego has been projected, an earlier condition has been restored. Projection of the superego is a regressive process.

No such explanation, however, applies to the second case, viz., the projection of instinctual drives. How does it happen that one can experience one's own instinctual urge as belonging to another person?

Freud suggested in different contexts two different answers to this question; they may be called *the biological and the psychological concepts of projection.* According to the former (1920a), projection is an attempt to treat an inner stimulus as though it came from outside in order to apply to it the defenses which have proved useful in dealing with external stimuli.

According to this concept, projection is an elementary response to painful stimuli. But this assumption is not free of difficulties. We may wonder, first of all, why projection thus conceived is more readily applicable to some stimuli (such as instinctual drives) rather than to others (such as pain). Furthermore, a mechanism as elementary as this must be expected to manifest itself very early in life, as one of the most primitive responses. This conclusion has indeed been drawn by Melanie Klein (1948) and her collaborators, but it seems to me that conclusive evidence for these early manifestations is still wanting.

Finally, the hypothesis does not seem to explain why the result of the mechanism should not be subject to corrective experience. Assuming that we try to treat inner stimuli as though they were outside, why is it that cumulative experience of outside events which are not in accordance with our projections does not gradually unteach us such deceptions?

A "psychological" concept of projection was introduced by Freud (1922) in his discussion of "projected jealousy":

> The jealousy of the second layer, *projected* jealousy, is derived in both men and women either from their own actual unfaithfulness in real life or from impulses towards it which have succumbed to repression. It is a matter of everyday experience that fidelity, especially that degree of it required in marriage, is only maintained

in the face of continual temptations. Anyone who denies these temptations in himself will nevertheless feel their pressure so strongly that he will be glad enough to make use of an unconscious mechanism to alleviate his situation. He can obtain this alleviation—and, indeed, acquittal by his conscience—if he projects his own impulses to faithlessness on to the partner to whom he owes faith. This strong motive can then make use of the perceptual material which betrays unconscious impulses of the same kind in the partner, and the subject can justify himself with the reflection that the other is probably not much better than he is himself [p. 224].

This idea gives a different picture of projection. An urge—of infidelity—is denied; it keeps up its pressure and causes an uneasy conscience. In order to free himself from a sore conscience, the person seizes upon observations which betray similar temptations in his partner, and attributes his infidelity to her. In this context, projection, far from being an elementary response, appears as a highly complex mechanism; its ingredients are the denial of one's own urges, the desire to shift the blame, and the exaggeration of traits actually observed.

A *syntactic* characteristic of the projection mechanism calls for our attention. The outcome of projection has the form of an assertion or assumes this form whenever verbalized: "They have aggressive designs against me," "He wants to seduce me." This is not true of other defense mechanisms such as, e.g., repression, reaction formation, undoing. Defense mechanisms applied against instincts may make the individual unaware of his strivings, or cut them off from access to the motor system, change their aim or object, or lead to various forms of counter-cathexis. But a statement, a claim, is an unusual outcome. There seems to be one other defense mechanism only for which this holds true, viz., denial. This fact seems to suggest, in accordance with Freud's above-quoted analysis of projection, that projection is a form of denial, i.e., denial with a specific countercathexis. It is denial to say to a fact: it is not true. We may disclaim it with or without adding our own version of what we claim to be the truth. We call it projection if we fortify the denial of our own impulses—or guilt—by blaming somebody else. A two-year-old child may disclaim responsibility for having wet the bed; if he claims that the dog or the teddy bear is the sinner, he has made a projection. In fact, he has merely strengthened his denial (I have not done it) by a particular form of countercathexis (he has done it).

The Break with Reality

Another approach was outlined by Freud in his paper on neurosis and psychosis (1924c). The paper deals with psychosis as a disease, not with delusions as symptoms, but its concepts are applicable to the latter, too. Psychosis, Freud suggests, is the outcome of a conflict between the ego and the outside world. While in psychoneurosis the ego sides with reality and turns against the id, the ego in psychosis allows itself to be swept away by the id and is thus separated from reality. Emancipated from reality, the ego creates for itself a new world which is set up in accordance with the desires of the id. Freud raises the question of what mechanisms the ego uses in untying itself from reality and suggests that this mechanism, like repression, consists of a withdrawal of libidinal cathexis.

Denial and Fantasy

Later contributions, however, suggest that the mechanism in question is *denial*.

Anna Freud (1936) discusses the role of denial (of a frustrating reality) in childhood as a means of avoiding anxiety, and adds this about psychosis: "In certain acute psychotic confusional states the patient's ego behaves toward reality in precisely this way. Under the influence of a shock, such as the sudden loss of a love object, it denies the facts and substitutes for the unbearable reality some agreeable delusion." (p. 80).

Freud, too, had used the concept of denial to explain an acute hallucinatory condition. He used the example of a woman who, in an acute state of confusion after the loss of her child, carried a piece of wood along, claiming that her child was alive and that the fetish in her hands was her child. Freud pointed out that the fact that the patient hangs on to her fantasy child and does not permit it to be separated from her for a moment proves that a continuous effort of denial must be extended to ward off the realization of the truth which is constantly knocking at the door.

However, the idea of denial, without its name and in a different frame of reference, had been used by Freud much earlier (1911a) in his formula for the four types of paranoia: delusions of persecution, delusional jealousy, erotomania, megalomania. All these formulae begin in this way: "I do not love him"; this is followed by contradicting claims which support the denial (such as, e.g., "I hate him"; or "I love her"), i.e., various types of countercathexis. In these earlier considerations, denial was assumed to be applied not to a frustrating reality but to an instinctual drive.

Restitution

Delusions have also been explained as attempted restitutions (Freud, 1924c). The patient who has lost the world through withdrawal of his libido tries to rebuild it. "The delusion formation, which we take to be the pathological product, is in reality an attempt at recovery, a process of reconstruction" (Freud, 1911a, p. 71). This conception is of great, perhaps crucial importance for an understanding of psychosis. Yet it is questionable how much it can help us to understand the content of a particular paranoid idea.[5] And in which way restitution is connected with the paranoid mechanism remains unexplained —unless we assume that restitution operates through projection.

The Historical Truth

In one of his last papers (1937b) Freud introduced a further idea about delusions. Delusions may contain an element of truth, albeit distorted, and it may be due to this content of truth that people stubbornly adhere to their delusions and cannot be dissuaded from them. The old analytic rule of thumb that the patient is always right, in a sense, and that it is up to the analyst to discover in what sense he is right, may thus apply to paranoia as well.[6]

---

[5] The above survey of psychoanalytic concepts was written, for the most part, in 1948; important ideas on this subject by M. Katan which appeared subsequently (1949, 1950a, 1950b) have not been included in this review.

[6] We may remember that Helene Deutsch (1922) had shown that the stories of pathological liars contain an element of truth.

Freud did not arrive at this idea under the impact of clinical observation, but it suggested itself to him in the course of his historical and prehistorical studies (1939). The simplest example is Freud's interpretation of the myth of the chosen people.

The belief of the Hebrews that they were the chosen people may be called a kind of collective delusion. It is important to realize that it is not simply a case of parochial arrogance and provincialism such as is indeed common to most, perhaps all, civilized people. It is more specific than this; the Hebrews did not merely claim to be equipped with more excellent qualities than other nations. They claimed that God had actually chosen them from among all the nations, this child among all His children, to be His people, and had entered into an alliance with them.

Freud, in his reconstruction of early Hebrew history (1939), suggested an explanation for this secular delusion, namely, that it is a poetic elaboration of the historical truth. The Hebrews were indeed chosen, according to Freud, not by God but by an Egyptian lord and follower of Akhnaten who had condescended from his rank and had chosen, arbitrarily, the Hebrew people to be the worshippers of his God, Aten, after the Aten cult had been swept away by reaction in Egypt. The Hebrews, according to this reconstruction, had actually gone through the experience of being chosen by a mighty man and rescued from Egyptian servitude—an experience which was bound to make an indelible impression upon a humble and as yet unhistoric tribe. It was due to the lasting impact of a real experience early in the history of their nationhood that the Hebrews clung so stubbornly to their idea of divine selection, regardless of all their subsequent misfortunes.

Another example is furnished by Freud's idea about monotheism and the Christian doctrine of the sacrificial death of the son of God. The historical truth of the powerful primeval father who was killed by his rebellious sons constantly pressed to return to consciousness. Throughout the ages of polytheism people have repeatedly come close to the monotheistic conception—a symbolic expression of the historical truth, in Freud's hypothesis—until eventually the breakthrough was completed and monotheism was established. The redemption of mankind through the sacrifice of Jesus represents, according to Freud, the breakthrough of another part of the historical truth, i.e., of the crime of parricide which the sons time and again had committed in primeval ages, which was repeated in historical times—e.g., in the murder of Moses—and is repeated, on a psychological level, in the childhood of each generation. The son of God took the guilt of all upon himself and atoned for the deed with his life.

Once Freud had arrived at his hypothesis in the course of nonclinical pursuits, he searched in his memories of earlier clinical experience for material to which it might apply. The following two cases, observed by Freud at a much earlier time, were now reconsidered in the light of the new concepts.[7]

There was a case of a woman with delusional jealousy. Without basis in reality, she suspected her husband of illicit relationships with a number of elderly women, who, in fact, were most unlikely to attract the man's attention. Analytic material suggested that these women resembled a nursemaid of her childhood. Furthermore, analytic material has led to the suspicion that the patient's father had once had a sexual relationship with this nursemaid. Looked at in retrospect from the point of view of the new hypothesis, this material permits the following interpretation: the patient's pathological jealousy was the consequence of a breakthrough of the real experience of her father's affair with the nursemaid. This intensely felt content of truth makes the delusional idea inaccessible to influence.

The other case was one of inventor's delusion. Each time the patient worked at a new "invention" he expected enthusiastic welcome for his contribution; each time there was disillusion and resentment. There seemed to have been a childhood situation in which the boy, after discovering masturbation, hastened to communicate his find, in expectation of praise. His claim, as an adult, "I have made a discovery (or an invention)" would in this way have a nucleus of truth.

An Idea of Tausk's

Another hypothesis about the paranoid mechanism was intimated in a posthumously published article by Tausk (1934). Tausk relates a piece of psychopathology of everyday life.

[7] Oral communication.

Time and place are Central Europe before World War I. In
order to evaluate the story it is necessary to remember that the
Norwegian playwright Hendryk Ibsen enjoyed a tremendous
popularity on the continent. His works and personality were
discussed everywhere and landmarks of his career, e.g., the fact
that he had once been a pharmacist, were matters of common
knowledge.

Tausk reports a scene which occurred during a conversation
on dramatic literature with a certain Mr. B., a writer and
admirer of the Norwegian poet. It happened in the studio of a
mutual friend. The place was filled with many objects of art;
among them was a bust of Ibsen. Everything in the studio had
long been familiar to Mr. B.

Mr. B. suddenly stopped before Ibsen's bust with an expression of bewilderment and asked: "Who is this man? I seem to
know him."

Tausk knew Mr. B.'s personal circumstances. Mr. B. had
recently been involved in a love affair with the wife of a
pharmacist and the irate husband had threatened to beat him
up. Mr. B. had used the threat to terminate a relationship of
which he had already grown tired. It was an unsavory affair.
Tausk made a kind of short-cut interpretation and merely said:
This is the pharmacist, and Mr. B. who realized at once what it
was all about, did not look too happy.

The implications of Tausk's remark are obvious. Ibsen was a
pharmacist, as was the man to whom Mr. B. owed an embarrassing experience. He did not want to know Ibsen any longer as
the poet might remind him of the pharmacist of his private life.
In order to eliminate the offensive pharmacist he tries to
eliminate whatever may remind him of him. Then follows the
return of the repressed; the statue of Ibsen forces itself on his
attention. But owing to the withdrawal of libido, the returning
object has changed its character; instead of being familiar it
appears strange. In Tausk's own words:

> Why did B. have to halt precisely before Ibsen's bust,
> since there was nothing unusual about it to attract his
> attention? Now, actually, there was something unusual
> about the bust; it had *become strange* to him, and there-
> fore could not but attract his attention in this studio, in

which every object had long been familiar to him. The repressed Ibsen returned in this form—as a messenger from the repressed pharmacist. An aspect of the paranoid mechanism is clearly revealed here. Persons from whom the paranoiac has withdrawn his libido reappear to him as *strangers* [p. 140f.].

It must be emphasized, for better or worse, that Tausk deduced this idea about the paranoid mechanism from the discussion of a case which had nothing to do with paranoia.

Possibilities of an Integrated Theory

The wealth of constructive ideas in this area is impressive. Surveying the field, we see, on the one hand, concepts about a break with, or a withdrawal from, or a denial of, reality; on the other hand, concepts of restitution, of the return of the repressed (Tausk), and of a historical truth that forces itself into recognition.

Could it be that all these concepts describe various aspects of the total picture, that the clue which permits the jigsaw to be put together is the mechanism of *denial*, and that paranoid ideas are as much the *results of unsuccessful denial* as psychoneurotic symptoms have long been known to be the results of unsuccessful repression (or of a limited number of other defense mechanisms, e.g., isolation)?

The mechanism involved in the motion away from reality seems to be denial. As far as the hypothesis of historical truth is concerned, it is quite likely, and is actually assumed by Freud, that the facts which force themselves upon the patient are facts which he had denied when they occurred. At least one, possibly two, of Freud's examples fit in with this assumption. The woman with delusional jealousy may well have tried to deny her father's relation with the nursemaid. The killing of the primeval father, or the repetition of the crime in the murder of Moses, was probably denied by the perpetrators.[8]

What was denied in the above-mentioned examples was a

[8]It seems to me that there is inherent in Freud's thinking the assumption that reality, or truth, however forcefully denied, has a tendency to come back

real occurrence—the murder of the primeval father or the father's relationship with the nursemaid. Denial is usually looked upon as a mechanism to deal with external facts, with danger, anxiety, grief or guilt, but not with instincts. Yet the existence of projection—which appeared as a form of denial with a particular countercathexis—suggests that denial may also be a method of dealing with instinctual drives.

A unified theory may be contemplated approximately along these lines: something is denied—we leave it open whether it is a frustrating event or an instinctual drive. Fantasies are used to support the denial—countercathexis. (This covers the hypothesis of denial of reality and its substitution by fantasy.) The results do not constitute paranoid delusions, though on occasions they may approximate to them when great intensities are involved.[9]

---

and to present its bill, and that there will be no peace until it has been recognized. The indestructible power of truth (*magna est veritas praevalebit*) is an analogy and counterpart of the indestructible power of the instincts (*naturam expellas furca, tamen usque recurret*). These two assumptions are complementary in Freud's philosophy.

The dynamic behind the instinct is obviously their driving power, and one may ask what dynamic force is responsible for the demands for recognition of reality. This force seems to be *fear*, i.e., fear of being defenseless vis-à-vis dangers if we do not watch and recognize reality.

This may be illustrated by an example taken from the analysis of the young dreamer with the labile contacts (cf. footnote 4). He used to complain about "shock feelings" which he experienced in his body. It turned out that they occurred when he had withdrawn from contact with people into his fantasies and became suddenly aware of his loss of contact. That made him feel panicky because he was defenselessly exposed to surprise attack and could be "caught with his pants down." He had to reestablish contact with the utmost speed. It was as if a troop of soldiers, camping in enemy territory, should discover that the sentries had fallen asleep.

In countless instances, the return of reality merely leads to a recognition of the facts as they are, and no pathology occurs. But if powerful resistances are at work, the truth may appear in distorted form. In Freud's words: "In the mechanism of a delusion we stress as a rule only two factors: the turning away from the real world and its motive forces on the one hand, and the influence exercised by wish-fulfilment upon the content of the delusion on the other. But may it not be that the dynamic process is rather that the turning away from reality is exploited by the upward drive of the repressed in order to force its content into consciousness, while the *resistances* stirred up by this process and the trend to *wish-fulfilment share the responsibility for the distortion* and displacement *of what is recollected?* This is after all the familiar mechanism of dreams, which intuition has equated with madness from time immemorial" (1937b, p. 267).

[9] The existence of neurotic strata in psychosis has been emphasized by M. Katan (1949, 1950a, 1950b).

Then, there may be a return of the disclaimed in distorted form. (This covers the theory of restitution, the theory of historical truth, and whatever may be useful in Tausk's concept.) The return of the disclaimed must have the form of a claim. The knowledge of its essential truth makes it inaccessible to influence. This would be the paranoid product proper. The returning material may, or may not, unite with the countercathexis which served to uphold the denial, to form a symptom held from two sides (compromise formation).

Projection is denial with a special countercathexis. Since the mechanism consists in disclaiming, the countercathexis has the form of a claim.

But there is one more connection to be considered. Not only has the countercathexis the same formal structure which the defensive operation had. The return of the warded-off material, too, is bound to have the same formal characteristics. This relation, which may be of general significance, may be called the *isomorphism* of symptom and defense mechanism. If the defense was denial, the return of the disclaimed has the form of a claim.

The Delusion of Persecution

The hypothesis may be tested by applying it to the delusion of persecution. The point of departure is, as in psychoneurosis, a pathogenic conflict, i.e., a conflict which the ego was unable to settle to its satisfaction. In this case, it was a conflict over a homosexual temptation. The defense mechanism is denial.[10] The fact that one loves a person of the same sex can be denied in different ways. One may say: "No, it is not true, I do not love him"; or one may say, "No, it is not true, I am not a homosexual." Both ways of denying are used; they have different consequences.

Countercathexis is applied to keep the defense effective. The countercathexis for the first form of denial may be: "Rather, I don't care for him"; or: "Rather, I hate him." The countercathexis for the second form of denial may be: "Rather, he is a

---

[10] This does not exclude the possibility that other mechanisms are used, too; it merely suggests that it is denial that starts the development along the dangerous road.

homosexual." In this way, we already have the outline for a possible paranoid system. But there is as yet no real paranoia; the warding off of an urge by denying its existence and clinging to contradicting claims may sometimes look similar too, without really being, paranoia.

But there may be a return of the denied. This possibility seems to apply only to the first of the two forms of denial discussed. The homosexual object, love for whom had been denied, may return. At this point, Tausk's suggestion can prove useful. The beloved returns from the shadow world with changed appearances; from a familiar and beloved object he has turned into a stranger. Strangeness, in the unconscious, is close to hostility. All these elements merge in the final paranoid system. Just as the hysterical symptom may be a compromise between the need for gratification and the need for punishment—a frontier station under joint occupation (Freud, 1924c), so may the idea of persecution be an expression both of the fantasies which were substituted for reality and of the warded-off drives, the object of which has returned with changed features.

Diagram

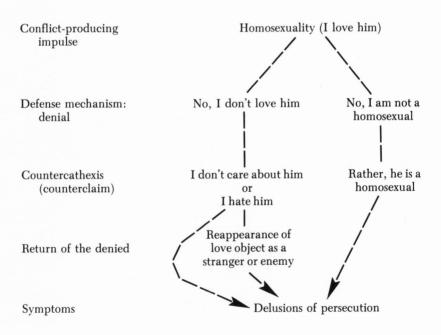

The Denial of Instinctual Drives

The suggested explanation of ideas of persecution depends on the assumption that the instinctual drives can be denied and that this process is characteristically different from repression and has different consequences.

This assumption has been challenged; it has been argued[11] that, in fact, denial of instinctual drives is but another name for their repression and must consist, like the latter, in a withdrawal of preconscious cathexis.

When we speak of "repression," we almost always think of unsuccessful repression. Yet unsuccessful repression is merely the result of an effort that aimed at more and failed; there are probably many cases of successful repression for each case of an unsuccessful one, but they escape our attention precisely because they were successful. In Freud's words (1926a, p. 94f.):

> If the ego, by making use of the signal of unpleasure, attains its object of completely suppressing the instinctual impulse, we learn nothing of how this has happened. We can only find out about it from those cases in which repression must be described as having to a greater or less extent failed.

The difference between denial of an instinctual drive and its (unsuccessful) repression lies, first of all, in the *intent*. The child did not start out to banish the instinctual representation from consciousness; he tried to *conquer* the instinct. The withdrawal of preconscious cathexis is merely what happens if the endeavor that had aimed at a higher objective fails. In the denial of an instinct, however, no such attempt at conquering it has been made. It is as if the ego felt powerless to do anything against the instinct and merely disclaims its existence. Thus, unsuccessful repression is a monument of a struggle in which the ego had turned against the instinct. It was in vain, but *in magnis voluisse sat est*. Where great things are at stake, it is enough to have honestly striven—enough, at least, to be protected against psychosis.

Furthermore, the instinct remains closer to consciousness in

[11] Private discussions.

denial than in repression. The "psychological concept" of projection is an example to show how the denied instinct remains in
the limelight; he who projected his aggressiveness onto others has
his mind occupied with aggressiveness, albeit somebody else's.

Denial is betrayed by its countercathexis, i.e., by the noisy
counterclaims.

Applications

The hypothesis discussed may help to explain the difference
between psychotic and normal projection. It is generally known
that projection, the mechanism *par excellence* of psychotic
delusions, is quite common among neurotic and normal people.
Yet no clear criterion of what makes projection a psychotic
mechanism has been suggested. According to the hypothesis
brought forward here, projection—the denial of one's own
drives fortified by blaming somebody else—is not psychotic.
When it appears as a "psychotic projection" it is actually more
than projection; it is the forcible, disguised, return of the person,
love for whom the patient had denied (and, perhaps, projected).
This person may, or may not, be the same person who was used
for projections, and this fact may obscure the difference between
simple projection, which is subject to correction by repeated
experience, and the distorted return of an object which is not.[12]

The hypothesis may also throw some light upon the relation
between paranoia and querulosity. These two syndromes seemed
always to be closely related, but their kinship was sensed rather
than clearly understood. From the point of view of the proposed
hypothesis, the paranoia began with the denial of an instinctual
urge. The querulous person, on the other hand, publicly denies
his guilt, proclaims his innocence or his grievances, and goes to
great lengths in his efforts to persuade others into accepting his
claims. Both have therefore a basic attitude in common.

Paranoia and the Methods of Adaptation

One of the fundamental concepts of psychoanalysis tells us
that the instinctual drives of every individual must come into
conflict with reality, i.e., with the laws of nature, the aspirations

[12] It is characteristic that projection of one's own aggressive designs, a most
common phenomenon, never seems to lead to psychosis.

of his fellowmen, and the institutional setup. The process of adjustment can be alloplastic or autoplastic, and is in fact always a mixture of both in varying proportions. In the alloplastic type of adjustment the individual changes the conditions in the world around him to such a degree that he can satisfy his instinctual drives as they are; in the autoplastic type, he cuts down and alters his instincts until they can be satisfied in the reality as it is. Both methods are "normal" if they are successful, i.e., if the individual actually succeeds in changing either reality or instincts so that the two can meet. Under such conditions, alloplasticism leads to the active, aggressive, autoplasticism to the passive, submissive, form of normality. Both methods may have pathological consequences if they are not successful. If the individual cannot change reality sufficiently to suit his needs, the result of the alloplastic approach may be psychopathy or delinquency. If he cannot permanently silence or remold his rebellious instincts, the result of autoplasticism may be psychoneurosis.

But there is a third possibility besides alloplasticism and autoplasticism; in this case no attempt is made to change either reality or instinct—it is as though the ego did not feel equal to either endeavor. Instead, the individual persuades himself that there is no real conflict and denies either the unpleasant facts in the outside world or the operation of his instincts. Whoever applies this method with success becomes a dreamer; perhaps, if favored by talent, a poet or artist. But if the denial is unsuccessful and if the individual has not been called back to reality by this very failure, the possibility of psychosis emerges. Just as alloplasticism is not as such psychopathic, nor autoplasticism as such neurotic, but each a necessary, though not sufficient, condition for the development of one or the other, so is "escapism" not as such psychotic, but may become so if the method fails.

The denial of external reality and the denial of instincts require separate consideration. The latter seems to be more dangerous than the former. The return of a denied instinct against resistances strong enough to forestall an undistorted breakthrough may take the form of a violent, delusional assertion.

Every child uses, at times, all the methods of solution in his conflicts with reality. If one method does not work, another one is resorted to. What prepares the ground for pathological development is probably a quantitative factor and, even more than that, a kind of inflexibility which makes it impossible to shift from one method to another.

Generalizations

If the hypothesis should prove correct, some simplifications of our formulations would become possible. Neurotic symptoms are known to follow this pattern: conflict between instinctual drive and ego—repression (or one of the other mechanisms operative in neurosis) and countercathexis—return of the repressed—compromise formation. Delusion formation would follow the same pattern, with denial taking the place of repression: conflict between id and ego—denial and counter-cathexis—return of the denied—compromises. The original defense mechanism would determine the form in which the warded-off material returns (isomorphism). It may be that further generalizations are possible and that *all* pathological processes, neurotic, psychotic, psychopathic, have the same basic structure, i.e., conflict—defense and countercathexis—return of the warded-off. The difference between pathological productions would be determined by the nature of the conflict, by the choice of defense mechanisms, the choice of counter-cathexes (though this choice is limited by the nature of the defense mechanism), and by the conditions under which the warded-off returns (though its form is determined by the defense mechanism).

In this way, the defense mechanism is largely responsible for the form of pathology and the old problem of the choice of neurosis can for the most part be reduced to the problem of the choice of defense mechanism.

Concerning an Alphabet of Defense Mechanisms

By defense mechanisms, in this connection, I mean *elementary defenses*. The defense mechanisms which are described in our literature are on a variety of levels. Some may indeed be regarded as elementary responses, others are certainly highly complex composites. Some merely indicate what happens to the instinctual representation, and to the access to the motor system. Others imply a special form of countercathexis (e.g., reaction formation). In others, like regression and sublimation, changes in the aim or the object of the instinct are implied.

A list of known defense mechanisms reads sometimes as if a list of chemical substances should go like this: hydrogen, salt, chlorophyll. It is one of the tasks of our ego psychology to develop an alphabet of defense mechanisms, *a catalogue of elementary responses.*

It may be that the elementary mechanisms of dealing with *instinctual drives* can be arranged in a sequence, according to the greater or lesser *degree of change* they impose upon the instinct. At the head of the list is, of course, successful repression, which, for all we know, has put an end to manifestations of the instinct. It is followed by mechanisms which succeed in changing the aim or the object of the instinct such as, among others, regression or displacement. Then there follows unsuccessful repression in which the unconscious cathexis seems to remain unchanged but preconscious cathexis has been withdrawn. Then there is isolation in which not even unawareness has been fully achieved. Finally, in denial—or its most common specimen projection—the ego has not even tried to fight the instinct.

Summary

1. Various attempts at explaining psychoanalytically the formation of paranoid ideas are reviewed. With one exception they do not seem to explain satisfactorily the distinctive characteristic of paranoid ideas, viz., their inaccessibility to influence. The exception is provided by Freud's late hypothesis that the adherence to a delusional idea is due to its intrinsic, though distorted, content of truth.

2. There are three possible solutions to the conflicts between individual instinctual equipment and reality: an equilibrium can be established by changing reality (alloplasticism) or by changing the instinct (autoplasticism) or by changing neither but denying one or the other. These methods lead, wherever success-

ful, to various types of normality, i.e., a dominating type, a submissive type, and a type with a rich fantasy life. When unsuccessful, they provide the breeding ground for psychopathy, psychoneurosis, and paranoia.

3. Furthermore, it is suggested that if warded-off instinctual drives make their comeback, the return has the same form as the defense mechanism had; they return, as it were, through the same door through which they were ousted (isomorphism). If the defense mechanism had the form of denial, the return must have the form of an assertion. One type of paranoid ideas at least, the delusion of persecution, may be the result of an (incomplete) return of a denied instinct.

CHAPTER 12

The Function and the Pitfalls
of Psychoanalytic Societies

(1955)

I should like to use this occasion for a fresh consideration of the functions of psychoanalytic organizations and of the dangers which they engender. Let us recall, first of all, what the original function of psychoanalytic societies was when they came into existence almost half a century ago. At first, Freud presented his results and his concepts to neurological, psychiatric, and general medical groups, in the expectation that they would be received and discussed on their merits, like other contributions. When he found that the response to his work was highly emotional and without much regard for logic and good taste, he withdrew from active participation in these societies, and once a number of students had gathered around him, the first informal psychoanalytic group was set up to discuss psychoanalytic data and concepts among themselves rather than bringing them before a psychiatric or a neurological forum.

Psychoanalysis was a controversial matter and a psychoanalytic group became the gathering place for those who held certain views in common and who wanted to go on working from that basis rather than discussing the validity of their views

Presidential address, delivered at the annual dinner of the Philadelphia Association for Psychoanalysis, June 26, 1954. Reprinted from the *Bulletin of the Philadelphia Association for Psychoanalysis*, 5:1-8, 1955. Also as "Psychoanalytische Gesellschaften: ihre Aufgaben und Gefahren," *Psyche*, 10:677-687, 1956.

with outsiders who challenged their fundamental assumptions. Thus, a psychoanalytic group was characterized not only by a common field of inquiry—as is the case with psychiatric or psychological societies—but also a common approach and some common assumptions. Every trained psychiatrist may, of course, belong to a psychiatric organization, regardless of his scientific views. But the psychoanalytic group as it emerged in those days was something like a party within psychiatry. Many people have expressed criticism that, in a field of scientific endeavor, people should organize on the basis of opinion rather than merely on the basis of common interest and training and that they should exclude from their councils others who disagreed with them on fundamentals. This was indeed the situation; I do not think there is any reason to apologize for it.

The new doctrine was not fully proved and is not fully proved today. All of us here believe, e.g., that there is an unconscious mental life, that it holds the key for an understanding of psychoneurosis, and that the early childhood years have great importance for the shaping of neurosis and character. But these theses have not yet been proved and demonstrated beyond the possibility of any reasonable doubt, such as, e.g., it has been established that one cannot drive one's car without fuel.

The fundamental assumptions of psychoanalysis can still be questioned by sane individuals and this incompleteness of proof offers, of course, a convenient opening for emotional resistances. I do not mean that our basic assumptions are incapable of proof; they can, and eventually no doubt will, be conclusively proved. They might, e.g., be proved by a research program that would observe daily and record in minute detail and with adequate controls the lives of a considerable number of individuals from childhood to maturity and into old age. But that would be a tremendously expensive program of research and it would probably take more than a century or closer to two centuries before the results would be conclusive.

But Freud felt satisfied with the soundness of a few basic assumptions and was eager to explore the new world to which he had found an access. He had to choose between staying within the traditional psychiatric groups where every discussion would unavoidably have been stalled at the point of some fundamental questions—such as: is there an unconscious? have dreams a meaning or are they meaningless like jumbled type? is there sexuality in childhood?—or to join together with students who were equally satisfied with the soundness of these few assumptions and go on from there. As you know, Freud chose the latter and I do not think that much progress could have been made otherwise.

As mentioned, this procedure has been criticized as being a form of religious or semireligious seclusiveness, and there are even psychoanalysts who have felt embarrassed by the idea that they should have united with others on the basis of doctrines rather than merely on the basis of common scientific interests.

I remember some situations which show the uneasiness of some psychoanalysts. Twenty years ago, in a committee meeting at the International Congress in Lucerne, the question came up whether we had any moral right to drop a member if his views were drastically opposed to fundamentals of psychoanalysis. A prominent analyst maintained that we, as a scientific group, could not exclude anybody on account of his views. I asked: "What about Adler?" and he replied: "Adler was not excluded for his opinions. It was a different question. It was a question of practice." I did not inquire at that time what that meant, but many years later another prominent psychoanalyst who had been in the foreground of the fight against Karen Horney in the New York Psychoanalytic Society told me that he had not taken his stand against Dr. Horney on the ground of the opinions propagated in her books; he would have been unalterably opposed to any such thing. He had fought Dr. Horney exclusively on questions of teaching.

You see from these examples that some analysts find it distasteful that a psychoanalytic group should require from its members the acceptance of certain propositions, because they feel that that would interfere with the freedom of thought which we all agree is fundamental for science. This, I submit, is a misunderstanding both of the concept of freedom of thought and of the structure of a psychoanalytic society. No doubt, every member of a psychiatric or psychological organization may hold or reject any psychiatric or psychological theory without having his membership status questioned. But if in a psychoanalytic group a member should arrive at the conclusion that the concept of an unconscious mental life is a fallacy, I would listen to his arguments and respect his opinion, but I would feel that he should take his place in some other organization rather than this one. And if his arguments should convince me, I, in turn, would feel compelled to resign from the psychoanalytic movement.

Comparable situations have existed in other, even the most exact, sciences in certain stages of their development. Even the paradigm of exactitude, mathematics, provides us with an example. When calculus and the theory of differential equations were developed in the 18th century, their conceptual foundations were still shaky and vague. The great mathematician d'Alembert is reported to have said with reference to this: "Just let us go ahead—faith will eventually follow." In fact, it took another century until the conceptual basis of calculus was carefully worked out.

There is an example of this kind, though of very short duration, in physics. Rutherford made, in 1918, the momentous discovery of the split of the nitrogen nucleus which became the starting point of nuclear physics. His experiments were made by observing the fluorescence caused by charged particles hitting a zinc sulfide screen. It was a very subjective method of observation. The fluorescence phenomena in question were extremely weak. Observers had to stay for some time in a completely dark room until their eyes had accommodated; even then countings by different people varied greatly. It was in essence a matter of subjective interpretation—of the ability of some people to *see* it—as psychoanalysis is still today.

I was told in the middle '20s that in the Physical Institute in Cambridge, which pioneered in this research, only about half of the students who were put to that kind of work could go on with it while the others had to be dropped because they did not get right results—i.e., results which the leading physicists in Cambridge were convinced were right. This is not too different from the situation which we have in psychoanalysis. We say that students who get results comparable to our own—who can "see" what we think should be seen—are analyzing correctly and others who cannot reproduce our results are incapable because of lack of psychological understanding or because of resistance. The restriction of membership in a psychoanalytic group to those who we think can "see" the minute phenomena of psychic life is no more "unscientific" than was the screening of students in the Cambridge physical laboratory.

But in physics the period in which one had to rely on subjective methods was short; objective methods—the Geiger counter, the cloud chamber—took over soon and ended the period of dependence on the visual accuracy of the observer. Nevertheless, the example shows that similar problems can exist even in the most exact sciences. We shall probably have to wait a long time until in psychoanalysis, too, methods not open to any doubt will be developed.

Thus, psychoanalytic groups were in those days groups of people who shared some fundamental assumptions which were not held by others and who joined together to give each other support in a threefold sense: intellectual support by mutual stimulation; economic support, which was vitally important for people who were looked at askance by their professional colleagues; and moral support, which made it easier to stand alone against a world.

Such was the situation half a century ago. But many people argue that those days—the heroic age of psychoanalysis, so to say—are past; that psychoanalysis is generally recognized and respected except for a few islands of opposition for which psychoanalysts may have to blame their own anachronistic seclusiveness; and that we now can, and should, operate in the same way as other scientific and professional organizations. What remains for a psychoanalytic society would be a function similar to that of other scientific and professional groups, viz., to meet at certain intervals in order to hear a scientific paper— often more in order to meet one's colleagues than in expectation of enlightenment; and to protect the interests of the profession in something like a trade-union way. In addition to this, there may still be the distinctive characteristic that most psychoanalytic groups operate training institutes, which most other professional organizations do not.

With regard to the latter point, we have two philosophies in American psychoanalysis today. According to one, institutes should be independent of societies and should be part of the departments of psychiatry in the universities. In that case the function of a psychoanalytic society would indeed be limited to the hearing and discussing of scientific papers and to the protection of the professional interests of the members.

According to the other philosophy, societies have to run institutes and this may even become their major function. In this case, the society appears to be necessary to provide the legal framework for the operation of an institute. It may lead in practice to a situation in which, while the society owns the institute in law, the institute owns the society in fact; societies may then become annexes to training institutes.

In considering this situation, we should ask ourselves, first, whether it is really true that psychoanalysis has been widely recognized and that the days of struggle are over. Of course, this is a very general question, and it is therefore difficult to answer.

It seems that there is a measure of recognition in psychiatry. Not that the psychoanalytic approach has been generally accepted in psychiatry; but psychoanalysis has gained something of the respect with which we look at individuals and institutions who have proven themselves by surviving into old age. The very fact that a person has survived is a kind of justification; life and death appear as the verdict of destiny. In a case like this, there is even a good empirical argument in favor of the criterion of survival, for psychoanalysis could survive only if patients came to be analyzed so that the survival of psychoanalysis suggests that psychoanalysis had something to offer to the patients.

As far as medicine in general is concerned, I cannot see that psychoanalysis is taken too seriously; for the most part, it has not entered clinical thinking at all.

In education, the field in which we may expect psychoanalysis to yield its socially most important applications, the reaction to psychoanalysis is divided. The conservative wing ignores or rejects psychoanalysis while the liberal wing seems to accept it—or, at least, often uses a psychoanalytic vocabulary. But upon closer examination one can see that the liberal educators have merely adopted those aspects of psychoanalysis that seem to support their own philosophy while omitting other, equally important, aspects.

In the social sciences, on which psychoanalysis should have a great bearing, the general attitude—with some notable exceptions—seems to be one of disparagement.

In the 20-odd scientific or scholarly periodicals which I receive regularly, a large percentage of reviews of psychoanalytic literature, and of references to psychoanalysis in general, is still contemptuous and unfair.

In literature and the arts, finally, we see that misunderstood versions of psychoanalysis are enthusiastically accepted and propagated by some while others disparage what they know, or think they know, of psychoanalysis. Once again there are notable exceptions.

Most public reactions, including those of educated people, to psychoanalysis, both positive and negative reactions, are still based on a misconception of the term "repression." Most people think that repression means restraint and inhibition and they therefore misinterpret the proposition that psychoneurosis comes from (unsuccessful) repression and think that psychoanalysis suggests that neurosis, or indeed other undesirable things, comes from restraint and inhibition.

Thus, as far as I can see, whatever real recognition of psychoanalysis there is is in the last resort due to the patients, i.e., to the fact that they have been coming in increasing numbers and that psychoanalysis has therefore been able to maintain itself and to expand.

Closely connected with the question of recognition is the question whether resistance to psychoanalysis has disappeared as has been claimed in some quarters. If my memory serves me such a claim was once made by a prominent psychoanalyst at a psychoanalytic convention. My impression is that what has happened is rather that resistance has changed its form. Outright rejection is rarer than it used to be. Instead there is a measure of acceptance of this or that psychoanalytic thesis, usually coupled with a strong rejection of other parts of psychoanalysis. After all, resistance is far from having disappeared among psychoanalysts and I have only to remind you that Freud in one of his late papers (1937a) in a somewhat puzzled way asked by what means many practicing psychoanalysts manage to keep psychoanalytic insight apart from their own personality and prevent it from having any impact on them.

Freud's great achievement, it seems to me, was to have cleared a part of the jungle of the id, and made it habitable for civilization. But his clearings are comparable to the cities which the Mayas built in the middle of the tropical jungle: incessant labor is necessary to defend them against the exuberant growth of jungle life which threatens to swallow them up again. It is incumbent upon us, Freud's successors, at least to preserve and, if possible, to enlarge his conquests.

So it seems that the original function of a psychoanalytic society as a group of people having a common approach which is threatened by enmity from without and by resistance from within, and who have joined together to support each other on a road so uncertain and so full of pitfalls, is still basically valid.

In particular, I should like to call your attention to four points in which it seems to me that psychoanalytic societies are a necessity for psychoanalysis.

The first point has to do with the fact that the analysis of an individual requires, to a large extent, productive, or creative, thinking. True, psychoanalytic theory and the accumulated experience of psychoanalysts over more than half a century, published in the literature or handed down through tradition, provide us with innumerable clues and guideposts. But invaluable though they are, the analyst is still, particularly in his day-to-day work, like a navigator in an uncharted sea—equipped, to be sure, with a knowledge of the stars and a compass and with experience in seamanship. The analytic work has more similarity with, e.g., the work of an epidemiologist who studies the outbreak and spread of an epidemic, trying to discover a pattern; or with the work of an anthropologist who sets out to study a new culture, than with the work of a practitioner of standardized skills.

Because of this, one is, in psychoanalysis, less immune to failure with a particular case than one is in those disciplines in which the practitioner has merely to fit a new case into one of his classifications and then to apply the standardized treatment. There is no analyst, no matter how skillful and experienced, of whom we can be sure that he will be successful in solving every case, just as no research scientist can be expected to be successful with every problem which presents itself to him. That makes it all the more necessary for analysts to pool their resources and to support each other in the problems which they meet, each in his own practice.

The second point is closely related to the first. It was made by Gitelson (1952). He pointed out that every analyst has necessarily only a limited vision. There is no analyst who can see everything. For one, his vision may be limited by his personality. There are, e.g., analysts who understand very well hysterical personalities, others who understand obsessional types, others who have a sense for the paranoid, or the delinquent. Very few will be equally sensitive to all manifestations of the human mind. But limitation of vision is not only due to crude differences in personality; it is also due to the limitations of our individual experience, in life and in work, to religious or antireligious, national, political, or cultural bias, and of course to our resistances. It would be illusory to expect that these limitations of vision could all be corrected by the prospective analyst's own analysis, regardless how thorough. Since we are all partially blind, the best we can do is to support each other so that the vision of one may make up for the myopia of the other, and vice versa.

The third point: psychoanalysis is an occupation in which practitioners work alone with nobody observing them and without any controls. If a surgeon operates on a patient, the result is known immediately among many people in the hospital. What happens in a psychoanalytic situation remains between analyst and patient and reaches out from this closed situation only in instances of extreme emergency. In this way the analyst works without checks other than those imposed by his sense of responsibility. There is always a danger of deterioration in the work of people who do not have the benefit of comparison with the work of others and who are in no way supervised. I do not think of deterioration in the crude meaning, of a blurring of the sense of responsibility—such instances, happily, are very rare—but in a more subtle sense. An analyst knows what he has seen in a patient, but he cannot know what he has not seen but might have seen, and he may get an exaggerated idea of the completeness of his observations and the adequacy of his interpretations. Once more I know of no better corrective than the cooperation in a group to provide opportunities of comparison and a measure of social control.

Finally, as my fourth point, I should like to call your attention to another danger of the analytic situation. Patients in positive transference tend to overestimate their analysts; analysts are taught to discard such judgments and to take them not as sound reflections of a mature judgment but rather as the consequences of a situation in which the patient has been made to regress. No doubt all pschoanalysts withstand the danger of flattery for some time; but if flattery continues as a daily fare year in year out, there is a danger that some people may eventually be persuaded to accept part of it as a reality. It is a great danger to be trapped in self-overvaluation and complacency

> for as you know securitie
> is mortal's chiefest enemie.

For all these shortcomings of the isolated psychoanalyst an active, living psychoanalytic community is not a completely adequate, but the only existing, corrective that we know.

After having talked so much about the need for psychoanalytic societies, I should like to say a few words about their dangers, too. They do not seem to me to be too different from the pitfalls of every institutional setup. There is in every institution a tendency toward formalization, codification, and bureaucratization. Then, there is a trend, described by a sociologist, Professor Michels of Turin, in one of his "laws" of social organization, for the organization to develop a life of its own. The law roughly states that whenever there is an organization devoted to a particular goal, it will invariably serve, in addition to this goal and sometimes even instead of it, its own maintenance and its own expansion of power. The Churches, e.g., were founded to serve religion; few people will question that they have developed their own institutional interests which are not always identical with the interests of the religion. In extreme cases the interests of the organization may well supplant the idea for the service of which the organization had originally been set up.

Hence, in our psychoanalytic organizations, too, policies are proposed, or adopted, in defense of some assumed interest of the association and we attack or defend them on this ground, but often forget to ask how these policies appear from the point of view of the interests of psychoanalysis. We should not be surprised that this trend exists, but we should be aware of it. It is in some degree unavoidable in any case of institutionalization and codification. The means are always in the habit of devouring the ends. We cannot entirely avoid it but may keep the process within manageable limits. Let us always remember that a psychoanalytic organization is here for psychoanalysis and not the other way around, that our basic purpose is to advance the understanding of human nature and human behavior and to serve the interest of the patients. Any interests of the organizations themselves should be countenanced only in as much as they can stand the test of whether or not they serve these basic goals.

CHAPTER 13

Introduction to the Discussion
on Problems of Transference

(1956)

Transference may be said to be an attempt of the patient to revive and reenact, in the analytic situation and in relation to the analyst, situations and fantasies of his childhood (Nunberg, 1951). Hence, transference is a *regressive* process.

Transference develops in consequence of the conditions of the analytic experiment, viz., of the analytic situation and the analytic technique. Among these one may mention:

(1) the fact that the patient suffers and comes to the analyst in expectation of help—a fact that puts him in the position of a child turning to an adult;

(2) the unilateral exposure, by the patient, of the most intimate aspects of his life—putting him in the position of the child that is nude in the presence of adults;

(3) the analytic rule of free association, requiring the patient to give up, as far as possible, goal-directed behavior and defenses against the rise of impulses—a rule which changes the balance between id and ego and thereby favors (temporary) regressions;

(4) the reassurance, explicit or implied, offered by the analyst, against the anxiety provoked by the rise of unconscious

---

This is the Chairman's introduction to the panel discussion held at the 19th Congress of the International Psycho-Analytical Association, Geneva, July 1955. Reprinted from *International Journal of Psycho-Analysis*, 37:367-368, 1956.

material, thus putting the patient in the position of a protected child; and

(5) the passivity of the analyst, i.e., the fact that the analyst does not respond to the patient's attitudes on the level of reality and does not play out his own personality so that the patient's fantasies are not stopped prematurely by counteractions from the outside world.

As the full development of transference is the consequence of the analytic situation and analytic technique, changes of this situation or technique can considerably alter the transference phenomena. Among the means of influencing it are the confrontation of the patient's fantasies with reality, and analytic interpretations.

This, as I understand it, is the subject of our discussion. How far should the regressive process of transference be encouraged or permitted to go on; and at what point and by what means is interference indicated?

There has been an ambivalent attitude toward the phenomena of transference from the very beginning. Perhaps it has something to do with the historical development of Freud's thought. When Freud embarked on an exploratory therapy of the neuroses, he used at first hypnosis for the exploration of the origin of the illness, later the method of free association, which required the patient's collaboration. It came as an unexpected complication that at certain times the patients, instead of loyally cooperating in the endeavor to unravel the Gordian knot of their neurosis, got involved with the person of the analyst on an infantile level. Thus, transference appeared as a resistance to the task of analysis.[1] It highlights the genius and the resourcefulness of Freud that he not only realized that this was unavoidable but that he could turn liability into asset, an obstacle to the progress of treatment into a vehicle of treatment. He understood that this emotional involvement was in itself a communication, or could be treated as such, since the patient in the transference demonstrated his basic infantile fantasies, though by repetitive action rather than by detached narrative. From this origin, transference carries its double aspect; it is partly viewed as resistance

---

[1] It is well known that it was this personal involvement which had discouraged Breuer from following up his original observation.

against analysis conceived as an intellectual process; and partly as a vehicle (or indeed the main vehicle) of analysis conceived as an emotional process.

Both aspects, however, have one thing in common; they both see the purpose of analysis in the uncovering of the cathected unconscious fantasies, in order to be able to disengage the forces interlocked in conflict, and to enable the patient to fight the conflict out on a realistic level.

But there is a third approach to the problem of transference which does not look upon it as an obstacle to, or a means of, uncovering the unconscious. Transference has also been looked upon as the condition under which it is eminently possible to bring direct influence to bear on the patient. Such direct influence either can take the form of new identifications in the superego or in the ego, or may consist of repeating old experiences (e.g., anxieties) under new circumstances and with different results, thus amounting to a retraining or corrective experience. It may well be said that such manipulations are non-analytic and therefore outside the scope of our consideration of the role of transference in analytic technique. This is a matter of semantics; transference has been used as an entry wedge for direct influence in treatments to which, on the whole, we would not deny the classification of having been analytic. Aichhorn (1936), for example, has made out a strong case in favor of the manipulative use of positive transference to encourage new identifications in the superego, in the case of delinquents, i.e., of people who seem to be in need of education in addition to analysis. But even in classical neurosis, Freud had used positive transference as a means of overcoming resistances—which is also a form of direct influence; and while this way of dealing with resistances seems, on the whole, obsolete, it can, perhaps, not be altogether outlawed.

However that may be, the three approaches discussed— transference as an obstacle to the treatment, transference as a vehicle (or as the most important vehicle) of the treatment, and transference as the opportunity of direct influence, through identification or retraining, seem to be the three guideposts, or coordinates, of the problem of transference in psychoanalytic technique. Perhaps all three points of view have their justification and their proper area of application in specific cases and situations. Let us hope that today's discussion will clarify issues and help toward the formation of dynamic criteria for each— under what conditions there is any real need for education or reeducation in addition to pure analysis; and what depth of regression is indicated with different patients before interference through confrontation and interpretation.

CHAPTER 14

Neurotic Ego Distortion

Opening Remarks to the
Panel Discussion
(1958)

Most of the interest of psychoanalysts has in recent years been devoted to the application of psychoanalysis beyond the area of psychoneurosis, and most of the discussions in our international or regional meetings have dealt with one aspect or another of what our late friend Ernst Kris termed the "widening scope of psychoanalysis." Our home base is, of course, the field in which and for which psychoanalysis first came into being and with which we are still most familiar, viz., the psychoneuroses.

Of the psychoneuroses we know, first of all, that they are illnesses, both from a subjective and and objective point of view; subjectively, because those afflicted with neurosis suffer, and objectively, because psychoneurosis interferes with mental functioning, and hence diminishes an individual's survival chances, a fact which is easily overlooked in soft times when even the handicapped person can prosper, but becomes apparent in times of great stress. Secondly, we understand the psychodynamics of the neuroses; we know that they are due to inner conflicts which have not been solved in favor of one or the other of the contending forces or through a compromise, but have been swept under the carpet, as it were, through repression (or

---

Presented at the 20th Congress of the International Psycho-Analytical Association, Paris, July-August 1957. Reprinted from the *International Journal of Psycho-Analysis,* 39:243-244, 1958.

processes involving repression) and to a return of the repressed in distorted form. Finally, we know that the psychoanalytic treatment which consists of undoing repressions and returning the repressed to consciousness, i.e., the restoration of interrupted internal communications, is in otherwise reasonably well-adjusted people with a fair frustration tolerance not only one therapy among many but *the* causal therapy of neuroses.

But when we leave the field of psychoneurosis and deal with other psychiatric conditions, such as delinquencies, psychopathies, and the so-called character neuroses and behavior disorders, not to mention the psychoses, things are no longer so clear. In some instances, i.e., in some forms of delinquency, it is no longer certain whether these conditions should properly be called illnesses, as they may not cause suffering and may actually have a positive survival value—at least as far as individual physical survival as different from the survival of love objects (persons or ideas) is concerned.

Then, the psychodynamics of these various conditions do not seem to be fully understood; more likely than not, these conditions are not merely due to the simple processes of repression and the return of the repressed, like the neuroses. Finally, it is by no means clear that psychoanalysis—the restoration of interrupted internal communications—is the causal treatment for all these conditions, or indeed in many cases an effective treatment at all.

An episode which took place more than thirty years ago may show at least one side of Freud's feeling toward "the widening scope." As is generally known, Freud had ceased early in 1924 to attend the meetings of the Vienna Psychoanalytic Association, because of his health; in 1926 smaller meetings at irregular intervals were revived in the waiting room of his office and continued until 1931. The subject of one of the earliest of these sessions was character, with the late Dr. Schilder making the opening presentation; he developed a multidimensional system of characterology. As was customary on these occasions, Freud opened the discussion, and in the course of his comments said that he felt like the skipper of a barge who had always hugged the coast and who now learned that others, more adventurous, had set out for the open sea. He wished them well but could no longer participate in their endeavor: "But I am an old hand in the coastal run and I will remain faithful to my blue inlets. . . ."

We are here today to discuss one of these areas newly explored by psychoanalysts, viz., the so-called neurotic ego distortions. The concept of ego distortions was introduced by Freud in a few lines in his paper, "Neurosis and Psychosis" (1924a):

> The thesis that neuroses and psychoses originate in the ego's conflicts with its various ruling agencies—that is, therefore, that they reflect a failure in the functioning of the ego, which is at pains to reconcile all the various demands made on it—this thesis needs to be supplemented in one further point. One would like to know in what circumstances and by what means the ego can succeed in emerging from such conflicts, which are certainly always present, without falling ill. This is a new field of research, in which no doubt the most varied factors will come up for examination. Two of them, however, can be stressed at once. In the first place, the outcome of all such situations will undoubtedly depend on economic considerations—on the relative magnitudes of the trends which are struggling with one another. In the second place, it will be possible for the ego to avoid a rupture in any direction by deforming itself, by submitting to encroachments on its own unity and even perhaps by effecting a cleavage or division of itself [p. 152f.].

Hence, we have to do with the struggle against a neurosis—or, for that matter, a psychosis—with attempts to canalize the neurosis (or psychosis) in a more or less acceptable form, to entrust it with functions for the preservation of the individual—as is the case in secondary gains—in short, with attempts to fight it off and to assimilate what cannot be fought off. One part of this struggle belongs to the original pathogenetic conflict, another to the secondary defense against the symptom; it is not always easy to distinguish clearly between the two. In the end, both sides, the ego and the neurosis or the drives behind the neurosis, have made concessions; in some instances, e.g., in mildly obsessional characters, we may feel that the ego got away with relatively few concessions, while in other instances the ego seems to have paid a heavy price. These latter cases, presumably, are the ego distortions in a narrower sense. But as often happens in a deal, one may not know who paid the heavier price until the end of the story has been told.

One of Freud's oldest illustrations of psychic events was taken from government. In this picture, the unsuccessful repression underlying neurosis is compared to a state of affairs in which a revolutionary party has been outlawed without having been destroyed, has gone underground and causes serious disturbances in the body politic. Ego distortions may then be compared with the disturbances caused by a pseudosolution in which representatives of a revolutionary party have been invited to enter the government *without* any genuine compromise having been reached; for had there been a genuine compromise, accepted by both sides, it would no longer be a neurotic—or psychotic—ego distortion but a more or less viable settlement of an inner conflict.

CHAPTER 15

Psychoanalysis, Scientific
Method, and Philosophy

(1962)

A symposium on this subject was held at New York University
under the chairmanship of Sidney Hook, on March 28-29, 1958,
and the proceedings are now available in book form (1959).
Most of the participants in the Symposium were philosophers,
while a few came from psychology, sociology, and other disciplines. Psychoanalysis was represented by Heinz Hartmann,
Lawrence Kubie, Abram Kardiner, and Jacob Arlow.

The Symposium was opened with a paper by Hartmann on
"Psychoanalysis As a Scientific Theory" in which the subject was
treated in general terms and special attention was given to
metapsychology. Hartmann's paper deserves careful discussion
by psychoanalysts, but most of the participants in the Symposium could neither know nor appreciate the nature of the
experience upon which his remarks were based.

Kubie enumerated the difficulties which stand in the way of
exact formulations in psychoanalysis; these range from exclusive
dependence on auditory data to the questionable justification for
inevitable quantitative pictures of mental life, or to the difficulty
of measuring these alleged quantities. Against these liabilities
Kubie placed the assets of the analytic situation and of the rule of
free associations.

Arlow, whose contribution came later in the proceedings,

This book review essay is reprinted from the *Journal of the American
Psychoanalytic Association*, 10:617-637, 1962.

had by that time discovered that familiarity with the elements of the psychoanalytic method could not be taken for granted; his approach was therefore simpler and more didactic. He tried to show that psychoanalysis is "not an esoteric cult" but that "psychoanalytic therapy is a meticulously painstaking investigation into human mental processes."

Kardiner developed his thesis, already presented by him on other occasions, that the social scientists "exclude man from their operational frame of reference" while the Freudians "go about complacently with the conviction that they do not need concern themselves with the cultural environment, or settling for the lip service that, of course, the environment must be taken into account, when the fact is that there is no technique for so doing." From him we also hear that Anna Freud "rediscovered the adaptive devices described by her father in 1900, but which since that time had enjoyed a position that was extraterritorial to the theory." Freud, so Kardiner thinks, "grappled with [the] problem—bequeathed to him by Adler—for many years and did not succeed," viz., the problem of developing a theory including both the environment and the "human unit." Freud did not succeed because "he could not tear himself away from the triumphs of the libido theory. He therefore left a libido psychology and an ego psychology. This is an incredibly confusing situation."

Thus, Freudian psychology is in a kind of solipsistic prison from which Kardiner has shown the way out. A sociologist, Ernest van den Haag, elegantly discharged the task of putting things straight again.[1] His paper is a model of lucid analysis.

---

[1] Kardiner's paper contains more misunderstandings of Freud's position than are dealt with by van den Haag. Kardiner writes: "Psychoanalysis is responsible for the fiction, promulgated largely by Freud, that culture is predominantly restrictive; the reverse is true. It is predominantly directive." Freud never suggested that culture is "predominantly restrictive"; it is difficult to think of a proposition more alien to the feeling of a man who, as Victor von Weizsaecker (1957) puts it, was "so firmly rooted in the soil of high intellectual culture and civil order" (p. 65). It is true that in Freud's writings the restrictive aspect of culture is more amply discussed than the "directive" aspect; but that is due to the fact that Freud's writings deal mostly with *psychopathology*, i.e., with maladjustments rather than with successful adjustments. Whenever Freud speaks of the situation as a whole, his words leave no room for Kardiner's interpretation, as when he says about the "process of evolution of culture": "We owe to that process the best of what we

In the further proceedings, Morris Lazerowitz attempted a kind of pathoanalysis of two philosophers, Spinoza and Bradley, trying to infer from their philosophical theories the unconscious processes in the minds of their founders. Such attempts are, of course, necessarily conjectural. In this case, they brought forth the most vigorous protests from most of Lazerowitz's colleagues, and a defense from some. Various views, mostly antagonistic to psychoanalysis—some violently so[2]—were voiced in the discussion. Near the end, John Hospers replied to some of the most glaring misunderstandings of psychoanalysis.

This Symposium offers us an opportunity to discuss some of the problems at stake: What are the essentials of psychoanalysis as distinguished from minor points of little relevance? Are psychoanalytic interpretations and theories unproved speculations? Are psychoanalytic concepts based on circular reasoning?

---

have become, as well as a good part of what we suffer from" (1933a, p. 214).

In another passage Kardiner states: "... the latency period was looked upon as a recapitulation of the ice age. Nowadays, one does not regard underwriting Lamarck as an excusable or amusing foible." Freud never suggested that the latency period is "a recapitulation of the ice age"—whatever that may mean. What he did suggest was that the bichronical onset of sexuality and the long delay of sexual maturation which it implied—an exclusive trait of the human species—*might* have developed during the glacial period. It is true that Freud saw such possible development in Lamarckian terms, i.e., through acquired characteristics being transmitted by inheritance, but this point is not important because the hypothesis can just as well be expressed in terms of mutations and natural selection.

In general, the fact that Freud believed in the inheritance of acquired characteristics (as did everybody else in the second half of the 19th century, *including Charles Darwin*), a fact at present often mentioned as an argument against Freud and against psychoanalysis, is not relevant for an evaluation of psychoanalysis because no important psychoanalytic theory or hypothesis depends on this assumption.

It is also interesting to note that Kardiner, like many others, takes extremely dichotomous positions in the psychological and the evolutionist aspects of the ancient nature-nurture controversy. In psychology, he attacks Freud for allegedly having attributed to the environment a merely inhibiting instead of a directive role; in the theory of evolution, on the other hand, he attacks Freud for having attributed to the environment a directive role instead of the merely elective one that 20th-century geneticists are allowing for.

[2] Two samples may show the tone: (1) "... philosophy transcends [psychoanalysis] as the ocean transcends a dishpan" (Donald C. Williams). (2) "... Freudian doctrine ... provides a language to say silly things in an impressive way" (Charles Frankel).

The Essentials of Psychoanalysis

It is well known that Newton casually allowed God a hand in the solar system to repair certain irregularities that he thought cumulative. Among people who know little else about Newton, this is, indeed, altogether too well known, considering what a trivial point it was, and how irrelevant for the structure of physics.—CHARLES COULSTON GILLISPIE [1960, p. 145].

In speaking of psychoanalysis or Freudian doctrine, one can distinguish between different parts which have different degrees of relevance. First, there are the data of observation. The psychoanalyst learns many facts about his patient which other people, as a rule, will not get to know. Among them are facts of unconscious life which people are not eager to relate to others, not even to psychological interviewers, or about which they do not care to tell the truth, or the whole truth, or of which they do not usually think but which will occur to them and which they will relate in the psychoanalytic interview because of its peculair climate mixed of relaxation and discipline, of intimacy and personal aloofness. To this, one must add the things which are not conscious or preconscious but can send derivatives into consciousness under the conditions of the psychoanalytic situation. The psychoanalyst learns not only about all such data but also about the configurations in which they appear. All these form what may be called the *level of observation.*

These data are then made the subject of interpretation regarding their interconnections and their relationships with other behavior or conscious content. This is the *level of clinical interpretation.*

From groups of data and their interpretations, generalizations have been made, leading to statements regarding a particular type such as, e.g., a sex, an age group, a psychopathological symptom, a mental or emotional disease, a character type, the impact of a particular family constellation, or of any particular experience, and the like. This is the *level of clinical generalizations.*

The clinical interpretations permit the formulation of certain theoretical concepts which are either implicit in the interpretations or to which the interpretations may lead, such as repression, defense, return of the repressed, regression. This is the *level of clinical theory*.

Beyond the clinical concepts there is, without sharp boundaries, a more abstract kind of concept such as cathexis, psychic energy, Eros, death instinct. Here we reach the *level of metapsychology*.

Finally, Freud, like other thinkers, had his own philosophy, his way of looking at the world, and he was more articulate than many in expressing it. His philosophy was, in the main, the philosophy of positivism, and a faith in the possibility of human betterment through reason—a faith which in his later life, in consequence of his psychoanalytic experience, became greatly qualified though not altogether abandoned. This may be called the *level of Freud's philosophy*.

These levels are not of equal importance for psychoanalysis. The first two, the data of observation and the clinical interpretations, are entirely indispensable, not only for the practice of psychoanalysis but for any degree of understanding of it. Clinical generalizations follow at close range. Clinical theory is necessary too, though perhaps not to the same degree. A person may understand a situation, symptom, or dream with little knowledge of clinical theory, and while this would certainly not be enough for a practicing analyst, one would still have to recognize that such a person has a considerable measure of understanding of psychoanalysis.

Metapsychology, however, is far less necessary, and some of the best analysts I have known knew next to nothing about it. These are the kinds of hypotheses about which Freud (1914a) said that they are "not the bottom but the top of the whole structure [of science], and they can be replaced and discarded without damaging it" (p. 77).

Freud's philosophy is largely a matter of his time and has little bearing on psychoanalysis. Interpretations and theories can be accepted by men who hold entirely different philosophies; at most, they might request an occasional change in the choice of words.

I do not see what difference it makes for the understanding

or the skill of a psychoanalyst whether he is an atheist like Freud and believes that the reality which is accessible to our senses is the only reality that exists, or at least the only reality that matters for us, or believes that beyond the world with which we are in contact through our senses there are other realities which may yet be important for our destiny. Neither position can be proved; which one we hold is largely a matter of temperament. The first position is taken by those who feel that one should not believe what one cannot prove and should be resigned to living with ignorance; the latter position is preferred by those who feel that a decision about absolute values is implicit in the conduct of our lives, that anything absolute points toward transcending realities, and that we may as well recognize in thinking what we cannot help taking for granted in our actions. In Kantian language, the first group follows the counsel of pure, the second that of practical, reason.

Similarly, I do not see why it should make much difference whether or not a psychoanalyst believes in progress—its possibility or its inevitability—through reason. Those who do will still have to acknowledge the fact that the enlargement of consciousness through psychoanalysis is not therapeutically effective in all pathological conditions, and in certain instances may even be harmful, and those who do not believe in it will have to acknowledge that enlargement of consciousness *is* the royal road of treatment in the classical psychoneuroses.

The degree to which these various layers in psychoanalytic writings are known to the outside world are in inverse ratio to their relevance for psychoanalysis. Outsiders often know something about Freud's philosophical writings—his ideas about religion, about the scientific view of the world, or about civilization and morality in general. This is due to the fact that Freud's philosophical writings deal with matters that are familiar to the general reader and do not require for their understanding any experience to which the outsider is not privy.

Next, the outsider will often know something about the speculative concepts on the fringes of psychoanalytic theory—about Eros and Thanatos, about psychic energies, about the difference between free and bound energy. These concepts, different from Freud's philosophical thought, do refer to psycho-

analytic experience and derive from it their claims for acceptance; they can therefore not be properly judged without a
knowledge of this basis. But it is possible to take them as merely
referring to common experience, and in this sense they can be
discussed, albeit inadequately, without special psychoanalytic
knowledge.

There is much less general knowledge of clinical theory.
Some of its terms—like instinct, repression, defense, sublimation—are generally known but almost always misunderstood.[3]

Finally, the outsider knows next to nothing about psychoanalytic interpretations as they are actually given by competent
analysts, or has a completely distorted picture of them. And he
has no knowledge whatsoever of the psychoanalytic data; as a
rule, he does not quite believe that the psychoanalysts have a
substantial body of data of their own. He suspects that psychoanalytic interpretations and theories are based on nothing more
than the kind of facts that are available to everybody.

Understandably enough, the critic of psychoanalysis is
inclined to discuss those matters with which he has a measure of
acquaintance, such as Freud's philosophy or the more abstract
concepts of theory, and to shun the discussion of observations in
analysis and their interpretation. I would recommend to psychoanalysts who enter into a discussion of psychoanalysis with
outsiders that they should urge the discussion to *concentrate on
psychoanalytic data and their interpretation* rather than on
theoretical matters: a simple neurotic symptom, e.g., its interpretation, the facts which have led to this interpretation, and the
consequences of communicating it to a patient.[4] The critic

---

[3] For a list of the most common misunderstandings of psychoanalytic
concepts, see Waelder (1960a, p. 252ff.).

[4] I must confess, however, that my own experience in this matter is not too
encouraging. I once tried to present such an example in great detail—a
neurotic symptom in a three-year-old child which was treated *in statu
nascendi* by the analyst mother; every step was reported and the rationale of
every interpretation was discussed in the light of possible alternate interpretations (Ch. 8). Although this piece was published in German in 1936, and in
English in 1937, and countless articles about the arbitrariness of psychoanalytic interpretations have been written in the meantime, not a single
author, to my knowledge, has taken the pains to deal with this presentation
and to do what one should expect in science: either to show the flaws in the
argument or else to accept its conclusions.

should be asked to state where, in his view, the conclusions of the psychoanalyst are unwarranted, and what alternative explanations he could suggest. Such discussion could be fruitful. The opponent of psychoanalysis will probably steer away as soon as possible from the data with which he is not familiar and return to generalities about which it is easier to sermonize. The psychoanalyst cannot prevent this from happening, but he can make it somewhat less easy for his opponent.

The Ugly Duckling

Perhaps there is always a danger that it will impoverish inquiry to elevate the logic of existing science into precepts of method.—CHARLES COULSTON GILLISPIE [1960, p. 218].

There was much discussion whether psychoanalysis could be called "scientific" or whether it was a candidate for future scientific status with something like a learner's permit—a "protoscience"—or whether it was "more like phrenology, chiropractic or Christian Science" (Sidney Hook). Several speakers felt that psychoanalytic theories were sufficiently ambiguous so that any kind of experience could be taken as confirming them and that psychoanalysts had not supplied adequate evidence for their theories wherever they are unambiguous. The first kind of criticism will be taken up later in these pages.

The evidence that psychoanalysts are asked to supply should consist of experiments or adequate statistics, undertaken on the material of sense perceptions; no allowance is being made for the kind of reasoning that we all apply in historical matters, or for the data of introspection or empathy. The condemnation of psychoanalysis for the failure to apply such evidence ranged from the fairly urbane indictment by Ernest Nagel that the "verdict" is "not proven," to considerably less urbane statements like that by Michael Scriven: "As a set of hypotheses [psychoanalysis] was a great achievement fifty years ago; as no more than a set of hypotheses it is a great disgrace today." This contributor seemed to advocate legal or other action against the practice of psychoanalysis; after pointing out that "experimental design in this area is difficult" but "far from...impossible" he stated that "we have the resources, the need and the absolute moral obligation to execute such experiments before encouraging *or condoning* the further practice of psychoanalysis" (italics mine).

Against verbal assault of this kind, the defenders of psychoanalysis took two positions: they either tried to point out that evidence of the kind requested by the critics did, in fact, exist, but was very complex and therefore difficult to present to the public in full; or they argued that psychoanalysis was still a young science; when given more time, such evidence would eventually be forthcoming.

Before entering into consideration of this issue, a digression on exactitude in science may be permitted.[5] The so-called exact sciences, particularly physics and chemistry, have been able to make quantitative predictions of a high degree of accuracy, and this intellectual achievement—apart from any question of practical application—has rightly been the marvel of the modern world. It means no diminution for the genius of the great men who built the edifice of the exact sciences to reflect on the conditions which have made this exactness possible. It seems to me that there are four conditions prerequisite for such exactness:

1. In order to be able to provide exact proof, the events which we study must be contemporary; they must happen right here and now, and they must be repeated over and over again, either spontaneously like the movements of the stars, or they must be capable of being repeated at will. Whenever the object of our study lies in the past—of the universe as in cosmology, of the earth as in geology, of animal life as in paleontology, of human events as in archaeology and history, of an individual life as in the rules of evidence in a case of law—the direct evidence cannot be supplied. All that we have is some form of indirect, or circumstantial, evidence.

In the natural sciences, the theory of evolution through natural selection is a case in point. It is generally looked upon as a scientific theory, and as one of the major scientific achievements of modern time. Yet, direct evidence can be said to exist

[5] The following argument is substantially the same that I presented at the Panel on "Validation of Psychoanalytic Theory" (see Brosin, 1955, p. 493).

only for very small evolutionary changes due to the differential survival of micromutations; e.g., the change from a strain of rabbits that is almost always killed by myxomatosis to a strain that is fairly resistant to it; or the daily changes of microorganisms in response to the introduction of antibiotics. But there is, of course, no such evidence for macromutations and megamutations with which the theory of evolution stands and falls.

Charles Singer, the great historian of science, once commented on this situation: "Evolution is perhaps unique among major scientific theories in that the appeal for its acceptance is not that there is any evidence for it but that any other proposed interpretation of the data is wholly incredible" (1941, p. 487).

But is evolution really unique in this respect? On what else do we base our belief that there lived, in the late 15th and early 16th centuries, a seafarer named Christopher Columbus who wanted to find a Western sea route to the Indies, was commissioned for his journey by Ferdinand of Aragon and Isabella of Castile, and discovered America in the process? All this rests on reports of various kinds, and reports can be mistaken or mendacious; no reproduction of the events is possible. But we accept these reports as true in their main outline—after having subjected them to exacting criticism according to what the historians call the "historic method"—because it is enormously unlikely that so many reports from different and apparently independent sources should fit so well together unless they all derived from the same real events; in short, we accept the story of Columbus "because any other proposed interpretation of the data is wholly incredible." The same is true when the criminal investigator tries to reconstruct a crime on the basis of confessions, testimony of witnesses, or circumstantial evidence, or a combination of them; we are satisfied that this reconstruction is correct when any alternate interpretation is utterly incredible.

This consideration is also the basis for the deciphering of a script—or indeed for the very assumption that certain frequently recurrent designs on stone, or clay, or parchment are characters of a script and not, e.g., mere decorations—for the deciphering of an enemy code, or the reconstruction of an ancient, forgotten language. These are all historical interpretations because what is reconstructed is the meaning of a sign for those who put it there,

or how an ancient people spoke. There is no complete evidence
that this was so; we cannot conjure it up and listen. It might all
be a delusion, a vast edifice of interlocking errors—except for the
fact that *the reconstructions fit an enormous mass of data from
many sources* and that the probability of this all being a matter
of coincidence is so infinitesimal as to be negligible.

This was the consideration on which Bleuler, nearly half a
century ago, based his defense of psychoanalysis, and it is not
without interest to note that not one speaker in this Symposium
referred to Bleuler's book (1911b). It was also in view of this
consideration that Alfred Stanton said that the psychoanalytic
method is closer to the deciphering of hieroglyphs than to
laboratory investigations (see Brosin, 1955).

To sum it up: what Singer considered a unique feature of the
theory of evolution—viz., that the appeal for its acceptance rests
on the fact that any other explanation of the data is wholly
incredible—is true of all *historical statements*, and the theory of
evolution falls into this category because it is an attempt to
reconstruct the past of living organisms, hence a historical
theory.

Yet, we cannot do without statements about the past; it is
unimaginable what our lives would be like if we no longer
considered any statements about the past as trustworthy. Our
lives would become wholly unlivable, and I have tried on
another occasion (1960) to show that all statements in the exact
sciences depend at some point on the possibility of making
accurate assumptions about the past.

2. In order to be able to make exact statements about
cause-effect relationships, it is necessary that the variables of a
subject be *loosely coupled* (Weaver, 1955), so that it is possible to
study the effect of a single variable alone, or at least to study not
more than two or three variables at a time. Where the variables
are very closely coupled, so that whenever one variable changes,
a host of others change simultaneously, conclusive evidence as to
cause and effect is very difficult to come by, as is the case in all
biological sciences.

3. Then there is a special case of this factor which deserves
special attention. It must be possible to assume that the subject
matter under study does not significantly change during the

investigation, i.e., that nature is holding still long enough for the examination to be finished. If this is not the case, we are faced with a new unknown in our material.

This condition is not always met in the study of living organisms; e.g., a virus may change its virulence quickly. In our own field, the living patient before us is changing constantly. The psychoneuroses seem to have changed since the early days of psychoanalysis, with simple and rather transparent cases of *grande hystérie* retreating from sophisticated urban quarters and being reported from backwaters only; and, in general, with repression, the simple form of defense, giving way to more complicated mechanisms.

This point is of particular importance whenever "evidence" would require very time-consuming research. Not only may programs of this kind be impractical, they may be theoretically unsound because we have no right to assume that the world does not evolve in the meantime.

4. Finally, very exact answers to questions can often be given if the subjects with which we deal are very small in relation to ourselves and to all things that matter to us. In that case, what we care about practically is not what happens to these small individual units but merely what happens to large aggregates of them. In this case, probability considerations may give us all the information we need.

All these conditions prevail in physics and chemistry, and they contribute to making these disciplines as admirably exact as they are. They do not exist in many other disciplines, particularly not in the biological and social sciences. The physicist deals only with contemporary, reproducible events. There are questions which can be asked about the past of a physical system— e.g., the past of the surface of the earth—but the disciplines that ask such questions are no longer called physics. The physicist keeps his record of exactitude clean simply by relegating such questions to other disciplines.

The coupling of variables in the subject matter of physics is happily loose. And the possibility of historical change can be neglected in inanimate nature; the laws of gravitation and the gravitational constant are apparently the same today as they were at the time of Ptolemy. If inanimate things should change their characteristics at all, there is every reason to assume that the change is too slow to be noticeable in historical time. As has already been pointed out, this assumption cannot be made for living matter.

Finally, those events in which we have a practical stake involve large agglomerations of particles, and statistical treatment is therefore adequate for our needs. In the latter respect, the exactitude of physics as compared with that of other disciplines rests again not on the actual power of foresight but on the nature of the questions asked. Physics shows up so much better than, say, medicine, because simpler questions are presented to it.

Let us consider a person who has survived a heart attack. Worried relatives ask the physician how long the patient can be expected to live. The physician will often reply that he cannot tell, that the patient's life expectancy is shorter than that of unafflicted persons of the same age, but that this is a statistical, or probability, statement which allows no simple conclusions for an individual case; this particular patient may die soon or may live for another twenty years or even more. Thereupon, the patient's relatives may leave the doctor's office, thinking that medicine is not yet an "exact science"; in fact, the doctor may have said that much apologetically himself.

Yet the doctor has actually predicted as much as the physicist if we compare, as we must, individual units with individual units, and populations with populations. Had the physicist been asked what will happen to an individual electron within a small period of time—e.g., whether it will go to a higher or lower energy level within the atom, capturing or emitting a ray—he could not have answered. If the electron could feel and think, it might be disappointed by the physicist's failure to answer what it wished to know; perhaps it would not think much of physics as a science. And if, on the other hand, we do not ask about individual human beings and their prognosis but ask merely about the destiny of large populations—as is actually the case, e.g., in epidemiology or insurance medicine—the answers that can be given are often quite exact.

It is, of course, different with the matters with which psychoanalysis deals. Our subject matter lies partly in the past—the life history of a person. Even when we deal with "contemporary" events, it is often a matter of dealing with the recent past—e.g., an anxiety attack just before the hour, a dream of last night, a family quarrel over the weekend—and in this sense historical. All variables are closely interrelated; we have no chance of observing the change of one without the simultaneous change of many others. Our subject is changing while we are working with him, is maturing or declining, and is assimilating experience in the process of living. We are definitely interested in an individual and his destiny and not content with statistical answers. For all these reasons, the prospects of exactness are not too good.

In their efforts to justify psychoanalysis in terms of the standards of the "exact sciences," psychoanalysts often make claims for the possibility of prediction in psychoanalysis which do not seem well founded to me. For example, Arlow gave as an instance of prediction: his experience with a patient whose meticulously detailed answers to questions in the initial interview permitted him to predict that certain other characteristics, such as monetary acquisitiveness and a particular emphasis on cleanliness, would also be present. This is certainly true, but it is not the kind of prediction that those who consider prediction the touchstone of science have in mind. For what Arlow has done was to infer from the observation of certain symptoms of the obsessive-compulsive character the existence of other traits of this type. It is the same as if a doctor made a diagnosis on the basis of some symptoms and now felt certain that other, as yet unobserved, symptoms of the disease would be there, too. *Ex ungue leonem*—you can tell the lion from the claw; if the hunter in the jungle sees a lion's paw through the foliage, he can "predict" that the lion's body will be there, too. But what we mean by prediction in science is more than that: it is not only that certain features always occur together, so that from the existence of some we can infer the existence of others, but that we are able to foresee *future changes* of the situation; or, in medical language, that we have prognosis and not merely diagnosis.

The power of prediction, in this sense, is actually not very great in psychoanalysis and is not likely ever to become very great, for reasons which were pointed out by Freud (1920b, p. 167):[6] our ignorance of the quantitative factor which makes it impossible to predict the outcome in the case of conflict.

I suggested on an earlier occasion (1936) that behavior can be predicted in either of the following extreme conditions: if it is wholly or predominantly determined by unconscious drives and primitive mechanisms, with little or no influence from reality factors (e.g., the possibility of predicting that a paranoiac who has been hospitalized will soon include the hospital staff in his paranoid system); or, on the contrary, if behavior is wholly or predominantly determined by the requirements of the situation with little or no influence from other sources (e.g., the possibility of predicting that a man will endorse his paycheck before, or when, presenting it to his bank for deposit). In both cases, there has been a diminution in the number of effective variables. Without such diminution, it is alleged, prediction is not feasible. This formulation is equivalent to the implications of Freud's above-mentioned views.

I have discussed at some length the advantages that are enjoyed by physics and chemistry. But not all the advantages are on one side, nor all the disadvantages on the other. There is another aspect of the matter, which has not yet been touched upon. The kind of evidence that I have so far considered and that psychoanalysis has been asked by its critics to supply is exclusively outside evidence, i.e., evidence of the kind required for statements about atoms and molecules and physical matters in general. It overlooks the fact that we have one source of knowledge about psychic events that is completely lacking in matters of the physical world, viz., *introspection* and its equivalent in the observation of other human beings, which, for the purposes of this discussion, I propose to call *empathy*.[7]

It is very difficult, perhaps impossible, to prove by mere

[6] See also Anna Freud (1958) and my discussion of her paper (1958; see also Ch. 17).

[7] I am, of course, aware of the fact that there are various theories about the nature and origin of our knowledge about the inner life of another person; it would lead far afield to try to discuss the merits of these various theories at this point, and I am using the term *empathy* merely to indicate the insight into the "thou," without prejudice with regard to any theory of how it is brought about.

outside evidence even so simple a statement as this: John is deeply in love with Mary. It is desperately difficult to find clear criteria to distinguish deep love from more shallow relationships, or from make-believe, or self-deception. But is it really necessary? Are introspection and empathy not sources of information too, *not infallible*, to be sure, *but not negligible* either? And if the very tight coupling of many variables and the fact that we are vitally interested not only in the statistical behavior of large aggregates but in the behavior of individual entities—if these conditions are disadvantages in our discipline as compared with physics and chemistry, one must hold against them the great advantage, not enjoyed by the latter sciences, that we know much about our subject through introspection and empathy, a source not open to the physicist or the chemist.

The story of the ugly duckling is well known. Other ducks called him ugly and looked down on him until it turned out that he was not a misfit of a duckling but a specimen of another, beautiful kind of bird, a swan. Psychoanalysis, largely, though by no means entirely, a matter of introspection and empathy, is treated as though it were a purely physicalistic discipline, and scolded and berated for its deficiencies as such. It is time to understand that the ugly duckling is not a duckling at all.

The interpretations offered by the psychoanalyst to his patient point out inner connections that can be fully experienced. Of course, any individual interpretation that is suggested in the course of an analysis may or may not be correct; the patient may or may not accept it, and his acceptance or rejection may be caused by realistic estimates or by emotional prejudices. But as analysis proceeds, mistaken interpretations will gradually wither away, inaccurate or incomplete interpretations will gradually be amended or completed, and emotional prejudices of the patient will gradually be overcome. In a successful analysis, the patient eventually becomes aware of the previously unconscious elements in his neurosis: he can fully feel and experience how his neurotic symptoms grew out of the conflicts of which he is now conscious; and he can fully feel and experience how facing up to these conflicts dispels the symptoms and, as Freud put it, "transforms neurotic suffering into everyday misery"; and how flinching will bring the symptoms back again.

There are patients who, at a late stage of their analysis or after its termination, can virtually make and unmake their previous symptoms at will.

These conditions are obviously difficult to envisage for those who have never experienced them, either in themselves or in the close observation of others; hence the clamor for a proof that would be convincing for *them*, too, without experience of this kind.

The speakers in the Symposium, as laymen in general, talked of "cure" of a neurosis in the sense in which an attack of common cold is cured: all symptoms of the disease disappear. There are cures of this kind in psychoanalysis, particularly in the case of those who can work out a completely satisfactory solution of their conflicts. But in many instances, "cure" is not a completely stable equilibrium; it needs eternal vigilance, like freedom. The new equilibrium is more like that of a high Gothic structure, needing constant repair, than like that of a Roman basilica. The symptoms will recur or threaten to recur, but the patient has learned to deal with them through self-analysis.

A person of great intelligence and sound judgment, with little formal schooling, who had undergone analytic treatment for a psychoneurosis (anxiety hysteria) wrote about eight months after termination of his analysis: "It is not easy adjusting to independence . . . . However, with a great deal of effort, I have been able to arrive at a degree of self-honesty that eliminates the anxiety I occasionally feel threatened by." This is a beautiful account of the situation; symptoms threaten again, but this graduate of analysis is able each time to solve them by self-analysis, so that the threatening symptoms are dissipated again.

Whenever a psychoanalyst is satisfied that he has untied the Gordian knot of a neurosis and has correctly understood its dynamics and its psychogenesis, his confidence is based on two kinds of data, one of outside observation of events, the other of the patient's self-observation. The first is the experience, repeated countless times during the working-through period of the analysis and again countless times during the person's later life, that this particular interpretation, or set of interpretations, and no other, can dispel the symptoms when they reappear, that they alone are the key that opens the lock; because particularly in the more serious neurosis of long standing, successful analytic therapy often does not bring about an ideal "cure" in the sense of our utopian desires, a traceless disappearance of disturbances without any price to be paid for it, but rather the ability to conquer them and to maintain a good, though contrived rather than stable, balance by vigilance and effort.

Then, as is well described in the above-quoted words of a former patient, there is an inner experience; what had been unconscious can now be consciously felt. To be sure, it is not always immediately available but can be felt if a real effort is made.

It is interesting and noteworthy that the only *practitioner* of an exact science who participated in this Symposium, the physicist Percy W. Bridgman, was also the only one among the nonanalytic speakers who had a clear realization of the role of inner experience in psychoanalysis. ". . . some of the features," he said in a very brief but meaty comment, "which distinguish psychoanalysis from other disciplines can be explained by the prominent role that introspection plays. This role is fundamental, because without the introspectional report that the analyst is able to draw from the patient some of the basic concepts of the analyst are merely verbal constructs. . . ."

It has been my experience of several decades that the kind of opposition to psychoanalysis which was voiced in this Symposium comes more often from the philosophers of science than from scientists who have themselves done research work in one of the exact sciences. In part, this is due to the fact that the scientists, as a rule, are more aware of the uncertainties in their own field than are outsiders. But it is also comforting to see that practicing scientists often have the imagination to realize, from a great distance, the nature of the problems in another field.

Heads I Win, Tails You Lose

Several speakers in this Symposium contended that psychoanalytic theory is so vague and ambiguous that whatever the facts may be, the psychoanalyst can always, by some twist, claim them as a corroboration of his theory.

These ideas about psychoanalysis seem to be based partly on the concept of overcompensation, or reaction formation, and partly on the concept of resistance. Since it is possible, according to psychoanalytic theory, that a reaction formation against an instinctual drive has taken place—e.g., solicitude for every living creature as a reaction formation against cruelty—the analyst can now, so our critics think, attribute both aggressiveness and kindness to the aggressive drives, the former as a direct expression, the latter as an overcompensation, and claim that his theory of aggressive drives is corroborated if he meets with savagery or if he meets with kindness—in fact by any kind of behavior.

Since the idea of compensation is not limited to psychoanalysis, this argument is rather widely applicable. There is, for example, the theory of immunity, according to which an organism that has gone through an infectious disease thereby often acquires immunity against it. Applying the argument of our critics, we might say that this is circular reasoning, too; for if a person falls ill, one can attribute it to invasion by a parasitic organism, and if he does not fall ill, one can attribute it to immunity acquired in consequence of such an invasion. If this is not the same argument, I wish to be shown the difference. The critic, in both instances, attacks a grotesque distortion of what the theory in question actually says.

In quite the same way, these critics seem to think, the psychoanalyst evaluates the response of his patient to his interpretations. If the patient accepts the interpretations offered by his analyst, the analyst will consider them thereby proved; if the patient rejects them, the analyst will take this as resistance and will in turn claim that the resistance proves his interpretations to be correct. Life is thus very simple for an analyst; his ground rules are: heads I win, tails you lose.

The argument probably stems from Freud's statement that there is no "No" in the unconscious; it is, of course, spurious. It is not true that in psychoanalysis, both acceptance and rejection of an interpretation are taken as corroborations. On the contrary, *neither* the acceptance *nor* the rejection of an interpretation by the patient indicates that the interpretation is or is not correct. Freud expressed himself on this point without any ambiguity, and since the myth of self-serving circular reasoning has a tenacious life, a full quotation of Freud's statement (1937b) on this point may be made.[8]

> A plain 'Yes' from a patient is by no means unambiguous. It can indeed signify that he recognizes the correctness of the construction that has been presented to him; but it can also be meaningless, or can even deserve to be described as 'hypocritical', since it may be convenient for his resistance to make use of an assent in such circumstances in order to prolong the concealment of a truth that has not been discovered. The 'Yes' has no value unless it is followed by indirect confirmations, unless the patient, immediately after his 'yes,' produces new memories which complete and extend the construction. Only in such an event do we consider that the 'Yes' has dealt completely with the subject under discussion.
>
> A 'No' from a person in analysis is quite as ambiguous as a 'Yes', and is indeed of even less value. In some rare cases it turns out to be the expression of a legitimate dissent. Far more frequently it expresses a resistance which may have been evoked by the subject-matter of the construction that has been put forward but which may just as easily have arisen from some other factor in the complex analytic situation. Thus, a patient's 'No' is no evidence of the correctness of a construction, though it is perfectly compatible with it [p. 262f.].

Sidney Hook contributed a new ornament to the old argument. His point of departure was the proposition that in empirical science as different from dogmatic revelation, it must be possible to state, for every hypothesis, what kind of observations would, if they were made, disprove the hypothesis.

This proposition is, of course, unchallengeable. For instance, we believe that procreation in mammals depends on the fertilization of the egg by the sperm; but a clearly established case of

---

[8] The quoted statement deals with constructions, i.e., historical interpretations with a considerable element of conjectural restoration of lacunae of memory; but the words apply just as well to all kinds of interpretation.

parthenogenesis would show that the sperm is not an absolutely necessary condition and the statement would have to be discarded or qualified. Since every empirical theory is based on a set of observations (A), the observation of (non-A) would disprove the theory. It does not matter how unlikely (non-A) may be; all that matters is that it is *thinkable*; if no set of observations is thinkable that would disprove a proposition, what we have is not a scientific theory but a prejudice or a paranoid system.

By this test, psychoanalytic theories can easily qualify as empirical theories. In any *individual* analysis, the hypotheses which are formed in earlier stages of the analysis are often disproved and almost always modified in the further courses of events as more and more facts become known. *General* theories that have been distilled from countless theories about individual cases could all be disproved by the appearance of appropriate material; e.g., the theory that repression, or an equivalent mechanism, is a *conditio sine qua non* of psychoneurosis would be disproved by presenting a case of hysteria, phobia, or obsessional neurosis in which, as far as can be determined, all inner conflicts have never ceased to be fully accessible to consciousness and no repression of any part or aspect of them can be detected.

The new version of the old argument is Sidney Hook's attempt, "unsuccessfully" pursued for thirty years, to test the empirical basis of psychoanalysis in the case of the theory of the oedipus complex. Suspecting all along that it was really a case of *a priori* dogmatism, Hook asked a number of psychoanalysts "to describe what kind of evidence they were prepared to accept which would lead them to declare in any specific case that a child did not have an oedipus complex." Unfortunately, the way the question was put did not make it sufficiently clear what Hook was after and so it led to nothing.

What Hook had in mind with his question was to determine whether a basic psychoanalytic theory was based on empirical data or was a dogma (or, perhaps, to show it up as a dogma); and since he obviously believes that there is a psychoanalytic theory according to which all children have an oedipus complex, he asked his question as quoted. But this is quite an inaccurate account of the psychoanalytic position. What psychoanalytic theory actually claims is that, in a developmental scheme, the oedipus complex belongs to the highest and latest stage of childhood sexuality. Developmental schemes are *ideal types* of development (*Idealtypen*—Max Weber); i.e., it is not implied that all individuals must go through all stages. Thus there may be individuals who do not reach the highest stage of development, i.e., individuals whose development is abortive. That, in turn, implies, not that there is no individual that has not reached the oedipus complex, but rather that any such individual will be severely retarded in other characteristics of his development as well, sexual, social, and intellectual.

The prospect of arriving at mutual understanding in such a conversation is at best not too promising; there is always a difficulty of communication between philosophers interested in the *logical* structure of a theory and scholars or clinicians interested in *facts* and probable facts. When the philosopher asks: are conditions thinkable that would disprove your theories? the clinician is likely to hear: is there any reasonable chance that such conditions will be encountered?

To this difficulty was now added a further source of misunderstanding, because, as Hook's question was worded, it was not clear that the issue at stake was the logical structure of psychoanalytic theory—whether empirically based or dogmatically revealed—rather than the material correctness of the theory of the oedipus complex or the range of the oedipus complex—whether or not well proved, whether or not ubiquitous.

If anybody wishes to examine the empirical character of psychoanalytic theory in this area, he may choose to examine the theory regarding the developmental implications of the oedipus complex; in this case he may ask psychoanalysts the following question: is it *thinkable* to you that a person could be found who had not gone through an oedipus complex in his childhood and had *yet* grown into a fairly normal adult, sexually, socially, and intellectually? Put this way, the interviewed psychoanalyst would probably reply that he did not care risking a penny on that chance, but that it was, of course, capable of being imagined.

Absence of any oedipus complex in childhood would mean

one of these things: either (a) genital sensations and fantasies were entirely absent; or (b) if present, they were completely objectless, autoerotic; or (c) if attached to objects, they were never directed to parents or other persons who took care of the child but were directed exclusively to the child's contemporaries (or, it may be mentioned for the sake of completeness of alternatives, to children still younger). These are the three logical possibilities of a child's not having an oedipus complex. As evidence that this was the case, I am prepared to accept the say-so of a competent child analyst (I can supply a list of persons acceptable to me)[9] who has had the child under constant analytic observation and who reports that no signs of **genital** impulses or fantasies directed toward those taking care of the child could be detected. I would, of course, attach less weight to the report that something has not been found than to reports that it has been; the fact that no organic cause of a pathological condition can be detected in extensive clinical and laboratory investigations is significant but not *conclusive* proof that such organic causes do not exist. One would therefore have to have the report on more than one case before wondering too much about it.

Two Gems

What has been reported so far is not entirely new in the history of the academic reactions to psychoanalysis. But some views were put forth in the Symposium that were new to me.

In the past, psychoanalytic ideas have been denounced as untrue or unproved; they have even been called a clear case of

---

[9] We cannot, of course, accept as expert testimony statements made by persons who have no training in the field, who do not know the techniques of how to get children to express themselves, and do not know how to be alert to signs and how to evaluate them; just as cardiologists will not accept as valid diagnosis the statements about a patient's condition made by his medically untrained friends on the basis of casual observation in social situations. It would not seem necessary to emphasize the obvious were it not for the fact that one of the members of this Symposium boldly declared "that an unprejudiced observation of the behavior of children who are not judged idiotic ... will show that the oedipal phase is far from being universal."

a paranoid system. But in all such criticism, the existence of a psychoanalytic theory, however unfounded, erroneous, or abstruse, was nevertheless recognized. However, in the present Symposium, one speaker declared that there was no content at all in psychoanalytic theory but that its statements were meaningless verbiage, a mere matter of linguistic redundancy. It was Donald C. Williams who made this discovery:

> The fault [of psychoanalysis] is not that its terms are metaphorical, nor that they are abstract, nor that their objects are unobservable, nor even that, like "phlogiston," they happen to have no object—all these may be healthy traits of live science and philosophy. The fault is that they are *not intended to stand for any actual entities at all*, but for such powers, potentialities, principles, virtues, essences, or entelechies as William James called "contentless entities" and as Comte relegated to the "metaphysical" stage of thought. . . . The psychoanalytic explanation either of behavior or of consciousness by impulses, repressions, traumas, complexes, compulsions, ids, libidos, and "the play of mental forces," rather than by imaginable neural or spiritual realities, is like the apocryphal Scholastic's *explanation of a clock's behavior by an essence of horadicity* rather than by wheels and springs. Since the sole real content of this sort of theoretic conception is exhausted in the evidence that provoked its formulation, it "explains" the behavioral or conscious events only, at best, by summarizing them . . . [italics mine].

Critical examination of the content and the implications of scientific concepts is an important thing and the investigation of linguistic pitfalls is a part of it. If Williams had aimed his criticism at some concepts of ego psychology—those of ego functions—he may have scored a point because these concepts of functions are at least potentially teleological, like homeostasis. If one were to take them as explanatory rather than descriptive and were, for example, to think that creativity can be *explained* by attributing it to the ego, or that delusions can be *explained* as being due to the breakdown of the function of reality testing, he would do something analogous to Aristotle's explanation of maturation of animal and plant as the realization of an inherent form, or entelechy, and would thus take a tautological formulation for an explanation (Waelder, 1960a, p. 171). But neither Freud nor any of his major disciples has, to my knowledge, ever been guilty of such a practice.[10]

But Williams does not just aim at the pitfalls of teleological concepts in ego psychology. He seems to think that all psychoanalytic concepts, such as libido and repression, have no content and are purely scholastic, and he includes in his condemnation even an old medical term (trauma) and an old psychiatric term (compulsion), apparently assuming that they are psychoanalytic inventions. Thus, the interpretation of a slip as expression of an inner tendency that interfered with the conscious intent, or the interpretation of a neurotic symptom as the outcome of a dilemma, are, for Williams, not the suggestion, correct or incorrect, of *real* connections, but have merely "explained the behavioral or conscious events by summarizing them...."

Since the school of logical positivism—the so-called Vienna Circle—has long specialized in debunking scientific theories as tautological, it is interesting to note that the representative of this school of thought in the Symposium, Philipp Frank, originally a physicist, felt that he could give psychoanalysis a clean bill of health on this account. While he did not attempt to pass judgment on the substantive correctness of psychoanalytic theories—an attitude of restraint not universal at this meeting—he emphasized that he saw no reason why they should not be recognized as examples of legitimate scientific conceptualization.

Any attempt to deal with all the misunderstandings and distortions of psychoanalysis shown by some of the speakers at this Symposium would need a volume in itself. But one more example may be permitted.

---

[10] Tautological statements of this kind can, however, occasionally be found in the psychoanalytic literature when ego functions are discussed. We read in a recent article on scientific creativity: "Decompensation occurred when the ego was unable to subject id impulses to binding by higher ego systems" (Giovacchini, 1960, p. 425). Since compensation, in the sense in which the word is here used, would presumably have to be defined as the "binding of id impulses by higher ego systems," or in similar terms, it is difficult to see how the statement could be anything but tautological.

Ernest Nagel pointed out that psychoanalysis sees all behavior as motivated, and since not all behavior is consciously motivated, the theory introduces unconscious motives: "these unconscious motives, wishes, drives, urges and intentions must be regarded as 'psychic' or 'mental processes.' " On the other hand, Nagel points out, these unconscious mental processes are really different from conscious motives; e.g., unconscious wishes may be directed toward a dead person while conscious wishes are not. Here Nagel finds a contradiction in the theory; on the one hand, unconscious wishes are believed to be psychic forces, hence like conscious ones; on the other hand, they are not like them because they may desire what we consciously do not: ". . . there is an important failure of analogy between conscious motives and unconscious mental processes, so that it is only by a radical shift in the customary meanings of such words as 'motive' and 'wish' that Freudian theory can be said to offer an explanation of human conduct in terms of motivations and wish-fulfillments." In short, since psychoanalysis claims that one can unconsciously wish things that a sane mind recognizes as impossible of fulfillment, it follows, according to Nagel, that Freud's unconscious is not a psychic thing at all.

The problem that proved so disturbing to Nagel seems easy enough to solve. The unconscious as seen by Freud is a psychic phenomenon; true, our concept of what is psychic does stem from our conscious experience, but it need not simply be identical with it; *not every characteristic of adult conscious* life need necessarily enter into our concept of what is "psychic." Some of these characteristics may be considered to be accidental rather than essential, and the high degree of integration and reality adjustment of our adult thinking is one of those accidentals. The definition which I have suggested (1960a, p. 75) might take care of this "difficulty": "Freud's basic discovery was that of an effective unconscious psychic life, the contents of which are not fundamentally different from those of consciousness, though closer to the infantile than the adult mind"—*not fundamentally different*, but not necessarily identical.

By his difficulty of accepting the unconscious as something psychic because it does not show *all* the characteristics of the conscious mind of an adult at its most highly integrated, Nagel has deprived himself of the possibility of understanding the fundamental point of psychoanalytic therapy, namely, the fact that psychoanalytic therapy is based on this very difference between the conscious and the unconscious mind—the contents of the former being in contact with each other, including the perceptions of the outside world, while the contents of the latter are isolated. Repression, which makes psychic content unconscious, thereby also protects it from the wear and tear of life, and the forces of adjustment begin to work again as soon as repression has been lifted and the unconscious content has entered consciousness.

To me, experiences such as these highlight the greatness of Freud. For, if it is so immeasurably difficult for men of wide learning to understand Freud's ideas sixty years after he presented them to the world, how difficult must it have been to conceive them for the first time?[11]

---

[11] Some of the ideas expressed here are taken further in Ch. 40.

CHAPTER 16

Selection Criteria for the Training of Psychoanalytic Students

(1962)

The selection of candidates is perhaps the most important question in psychoanalytic education; at least, it is the one that is least subject to future correction. A training analysis that did not yield as much as it should may be, and often is, supplemented by a later postgraduate analysis. The curriculum can be altered in the light of experience, and many a certified analyst will still avail himself of the opportunity of improved offerings. New supervision may be sought, often from analysts from another institute. The selection of candidates is the only thing in psychoanalytic education that is not subject to later improvement once the candidate has been graduated, and if the ratio of graduates who are not sufficiently qualified rises above a certain level of tolerance, effective limits are set to the further development of psychoanalysis and even to the intact preservation of past achievements. Things are not made easier by the fact that there are no objective criteria of selection, and that decisions have to be made on the basis of impressions, evaluated in the light of an

Read at the 22nd International Psycho-Analytical Congress, Edinburgh, July-August 1961. Reprinted from the *International Journal of Psycho-Analysis*, 43:283-286, 1962.

experience which is necessarily small even with the most experienced psychoanalytic instructors.

There is a large measure of agreement with regard to the qualities that are desirable in a future analyst. But this concensus is not as helpful as might at first be thought, because the list of requirements is so large that there is not much chance of finding any actual applicants who answer to all the specifications. I sometimes am reminded of the Greek sculptor of whom the legend says that he chose a number of models for the statue of a goddess, taking from one model the torso, from another the face, from a third the legs, etc., in this way to achieve for every part the perfection to which he aspired. There is perhaps no individual endowed with all the qualities we should like to see in the men and women in whose hands the future of psychoanalysis will lie. What is thus necessary is not 'only a grasp of what qualities are desirable, but also a list of *priorities* among them which tells us what is more, what less, important and what we may have to do without in one direction in order to secure something in another.

Opinion in these matters cannot but be subjective, because it is based on experience that is necessarily incomplete. It is therefore with all due qualification and with diffidence that I shall now add my own estimates to those that have been proposed by others in this meeting or in the literature.

With emphasis on this precaution, it seems to me that one characteristic that has often been mentioned as a prerequisite should not be given too much weight, while two other qualities, not always emphasized, appear to me to be of great importance.

I would put *less* stock than many in what is often called empathy or *psychological intuition* as I understand these terms. If all that is meant is that a candidate should be in good contact with human beings, and with his patients in particular, and should not be blind to the manifestations of the mind, then these requirements are indeed essential. There are people who are blind to psychic things in the same sense in which many people are at least partially color-blind, and they are no better material for the profession of psychoanalyst than a color-blind person is for becoming a painter, an art critic, or a juror at exhibitions of paintings.

But often, it seems, those who look for empathy in an applicant mean more than merely contact with human beings and an ability to see things with the benefit of instruction; they mean a particularly high ability to see, to sense, or to guess, on the basis of infinitesimal clues, what is going on in another person—a kind of immediate insight into the unconscious of others. Such ability is very rare; but I have known a very few people who would know more about a patient after one orienting interview than would others after a year of analysis.

Such talent is immensely important for a practitioner of *psychotherapy*, particularly of short-term psychotherapy, and for the leader of a clinic who has to decide about the disposition of cases after a few interviews. It has also some importance for the early spotting of dangers, e.g., a danger of psychosis or of suicide, although there should be signs of such possibilities which are accessible to the conscientious observer not endowed with the genius of intuition. But it is certainly of less importance for the *psychoanalyst*, who will see his cases for a longer time. There is a point at which the conscientious and experienced psychoanalyst who follows the productions of his patient attentively and weighs them carefully will draw even with his psychologically more highly endowed colleague who had an enormous head start through insights effortlessly won at an early time. Once this initial advantage of the highly intuitive analyst is gone, the odds may even favor the painstaking work with details over the intuition, inasmuch as those heavily endowed with the latter are often impatient with the work on minutiae. Also, intuition, while always impressive, is not always correct, and those favored by the gods with this gift are sometimes slow in revising their early visions when necessary.

Among the requirements for the psychoanalytic profession I should put special emphasis on a *wide interest* in, and a broad knowledge of, all things human. This requirement, it seems to me, follows from the fact that psychoanalysis is not the whole of our knowledge of human affairs. Psychoanalysis supplements, modifies, refines, and deepens the psychology of common sense by adding its findings about an unconscious psychic life. It adds facts and insight that are not available to conscious psychology or to commonsense psychology, but it does not displace them. In my youth it was often said that psychoanalysis added the microscopic view to the macroscopic analysis of clinical psychiatry. The implication of this statement was, of course, that the psychoanalyst should be familiar with clinical psychiatry first. This is true as far as it goes, but the relationship in question has wider scope than the old saying indicated. There is a vast body of knowledge in man's experience with human affairs, containing both conscious psychology and such glimpses of the unconscious as men have occasionally had. Psychoanalysis crowns the edifice, makes highly important alterations, and, in some instances, insists on changes in the foundation; but it does not replace it. These circumstances are manifested in the fact that a great part of the time in analytic treatment, perhaps most of it, must be dedicated to a kind of prepsychoanalytic analysis of things, an attempt to get at the core of events or attitudes in terms as yet nonanalytic; it is only after this has been done accurately with every situation that a further reduction to the still simpler psychoanalytic categories can safely be undertaken.

There is no specific place where this kind of knowledge, condensed and ready for use, can be found, no particular academic courses and textbooks. It is also much too vast to be embraced by any one person. Some of it can be found in the past experience of the race which we call history—political, economic, cultural history. Some can be found in philosophy and in the products of literary imagination, some in the accumulation of life experience of individuals. There is also the behavior of animals with their enormous variety of forms and behavior patterns. The psychoanalyst should have a broad basis in knowledge of this kind, and a broad interest in it that impels him to widen and deepen it constantly.

Another point has to do with a personality characteristic: I do not think that psychoanalysis is the best occupation for those whose personality is *lacking in depth,* even though they may be highly intelligent in many ways, may be decent and reliable people. The quality of depth is probably largely a creative response to suffering endured, in personal experience or through identification.

To sum it up, I would consider a person a good candidate who is free from the extreme forms of abnormality—i.e., is neither psychotic nor an addict nor a delinquent; who has interest in, and good contact with, human beings; is of very good intelligence; has depth in his personality and has a long-standing interest in, and hence a sizable body of knowledge of, the manifestations of things human. This catalogue may, perhaps, remind us of the famous line by Terence, *nil humani a me alienum puto*, I count nothing human to be alien to me. If, in addition to all this, our candidate has still a spark of creativity, he has the makings of a great analyst.

While the requirements for candidates in psychoanalysis have been under constant discussion, less attention has been paid to the question of *how* the institute can secure the information relevant for the decision in the individual case. A great deal of this information will, of course, come from the interviewers of the admissions committees, from the reports of those who have known the applicant and have seen him at work, and later, once the applicant has become a student, from the evaluations of classroom teachers and clinical supervisors. All this information is indispensable, but it is necessarily incomplete: all that these informants know about the applicant and student is only such aspects as appear to the nonanalytic observer; they know about his behavior and his achievements, about the external aspects of his personality. But there are features which, though perhaps not conspicuous in behavior at the present time, may still have a great impact on a person's performance in the future, and of which only the analytic observer is likely to know. Hence, for a complete picture, the training analyst may be called upon to supply, if not detailed information, at least his evaluation.

But that creates a new problem. The analyst is pledged to secrecy, and this obligation does not merely follow from the condition of privileged communication which is part of the practice of the healing arts; it is also, and specifically, part of the analytic contract in which the patient has obliged himself to observe, as best he can, the psychoanalytic rule. To convey analytic information to third persons, particularly to persons who owe allegiance not to the patient but to an institution, and who have to decide on the satisfaction or frustration of the patient's aspirations introduces a novel element into the analytic situation.

It would bring the analyst into a situation similar to that of a private doctor who reports on his patient to an insurance company on the basis of a waiver of professional secrecy which the patient had to sign together with his application for life insurance; or of a company physician with whom executive employees have to undergo periodical examinations. There is many a man in his forties who trembles at the thought that the next examination may show an elevated blood pressure, not only for the common reason that it would spell the beginning of the end of the illusion of immortality, but also because such result may have an immediate grave consequence: it may mean that the company will no longer consider this man for further promotion, and that he has thus reached the dead end of his career. The physician is legally protected in both cases, as the patient, in the first example, has empowered the physician in his waiver to open his files to the insurance company and, in the second case, has agreed to consult the company doctor. The patient had, of course, to do these things if he wanted to buy life insurance and wanted to stay employed with the company.

It may well be argued that the psychoanalyst owes allegiance not only to his individual patients but also to psychoanalysis, and that the upholding of proper professional standards means the protection of future patients; and that the analysand will appreciate the necessity of the procedure and will accept it. Both are true, but it does not answer the question what such double allegiance will do to the analysis, and whether a full acceptance of these ground rules by the analysand is not the symptom of an attitude that is likely to disappear once it has been analyzed. The attitude of acceptance implies a complete identification with the standards of psychoanalysis in general, and the interpretation of these standards in his particular case by his analyst—an identification so complete that the candidate would no longer wish to be accredited as a psychoanalyst unless he was considered suitable by his analyst. It would require an attitude on the part of the analysand somewhat reminiscent of Jesus' prayer on the Mount of Olives: "Not my will but Thine be done. . . ."

A normal person must be willing to subordinate himself to another person on functional grounds—to a teacher in matters pertaining to instruction, to a superior in matters regarding his work, to a guide in mountain climbing, or to a doctor in matters pertaining to his health. But in all these cases the subordination is not total; he retains the right to withhold from his functional relationship the intimate levels of his person and life. Or, conversely, a normal human being should be able to open his innermost sanctum to a psychoanalyst—but then he has the right to expect that the therapist will be his agent only and will use all information received only for the patient's benefit and not toward third persons at all except in the patient's own interest and, save for children and other persons not responsible, only with the patient's uncoerced consent.

It is altogether too much to ask that an adult who is neither psychotic nor otherwise incompetent should submit to another person in the functional sense without the right of keeping his innermost self out of it, and should open his most personal secrets to someone who owes allegiance not only to him.

In 1951 (Ch. 28) I suggested that we must distinguish between authoritarianism, e.g., the traditional monarchic absolutism of an earlier age, and modern totalitarianism, which is based on an enthusiastic and terroristic mass movement. Both require the unconditional obedience of all people to their laws and commands; but while the pressure of monarchic absolutism ends here, and the subjects of an authoritarian government can live quiet lives without interference as long as they do not disregard the laws or defy the government, the totalitarians demand, in addition, the acceptance, by the people, of their creed without mental reservation, i.e., the perpetual convincing display of enthusiastic approval. Totalitarianism, in short, claims both physical and spiritual authority, and is absolute State and compulsory Church at once, while the claims of authoritarianism are limited to the first, "secular," part.

The coercive power of the totalitarian state which includes torture and execution is, of course of an entirely different order of magnitude from the power of a psychoanalytic institute, which, at most, can drop a student from the training program— a step that wounds his pride but does not interfere with his career in psychiatry or with his livelihood. But any combination of power, however small, over a person's physical condition with spiritual authority is necessarily a demoralizing influence. The result of the cooperation of moral influence with physical pressure—a kind of pincer movement—is either the virtually complete submission to authority or a violent and ultimately ineffective attempt at freeing oneself through rebellion, and either of these reactions seems to me highly undesirable.

What, then, are we to do, if training analysts do not convey any information about their trainees to the institutes, and how can we prevent candidates with disabling characteristics not readily visible to the outside observer from being accredited as psychoanalysts? I know of no satisfactory solution of this problem. If the candidate's disabilities—those of which he has always been aware or those of which he has become aware, or which he has come to appreciate in his analysis—are of a kind that he himself must consider as disabling, the situation is relatively easy. He will probably himself not consider application[1] until there is a substantial improvement in his condition; and if he does consider it, the analyst may call his attention to these symptoms and to the necessity of having them conquered first, without thereby stepping beyond the role of healer. The intervention in such a case will not appear as arbitrary oppression but rather as the stating of facts and of the limits which they impose on all of us.

But what if there are traits which appear as disabilities to the analyst but not to the analysand? I have no satisfactory answer to this question. On the whole, I would rather see an occasional ill-suited candidate being graduated from an institute than see the basic climate of psychoanalysis changed for all—the climate in which the analyst is analyst only and does not at the same time have to play an important role in the patient's professional environment.

But, one may further ask, what about the extreme case in which there are disabilities which, while escaping the attention of teachers, colleagues, supervisors, are so serious that one cannot be sanguine about the possibility of this person's accreditation? I have no general answer to the question. But there is probably no area in human affairs in which all possible contingencies can be adequately covered in advance by laws and regulations.

---

[1] I am speaking here in terms of the rules that prevail, *inter alia*, in my institute according to which one can apply for admission as a student only after a period of personal analysis.

CHAPTER 17

Psychic Determinism and
the Possibility of Predictions

(1963)

Provisional Survey of the Field

The problem of determinism has not been systematically discussed in psychoanalysis. There are occasional references to it in psychoanalytic literature, which as a rule emphasize that determinism is part and parcel of the scientific approach and therefore a basic assumption of psychoanalysis as a scientific psychology.

Freud referred several times to the subject. In some instances, it was to justify the rule of free association; it would follow from the principle of determinism that nothing enters the mind haphazardly, without a cause. In other instances, it was to justify his interest in every detail of psychic life, no matter how trivial, and his readiness to take it as an expression of a psychic trend. "Psycho-analysts," says Freud, "are marked by a particularly strict belief in the determination of mental life. For them there is nothing trivial, nothing arbitrary or haphazard. They expect in every case to find sufficient motives" (1910a, p. 38). He speaks of "the strictness with which mental processes are determined" (p. 29), and of "a strict and universal application of determinism to mental life" (p. 52), or of "a strong belief in the strict determination of mental events" (1923a, p. 238).

Reprinted from the *Psychoanalytic Quarterly*, 32:15-42, 1963. Also as "Über psychischen Determinismus und die Möglichkeit der Voraussage im Seelenleben," *Psyche*, 20:5-28, 1966.

However, there is some question as to what Freud means by events being "determined": whether the word is to indicate that one can always find conditions which are both necessary and sufficient for the particular event to materialize, or merely whether one can find necessary conditions. The presence of a bacterial invader is a necessary condition of clinical tuberculosis but not a sufficient one; the state of the host organism is also relevant. If, then, we say that tuberculosis is not a matter of chance but that it is determined, we may mean either that we know the conditions necessary and sufficient for the outbreak of the disease, or, in somewhat less precise speech, we may merely mean to say that there is no tuberculosis without the presence of *tubercle bacilli;* the latter might easily have been said at the time when the role of microorganisms in contagious diseases had to be defended against a still doubting world.

As we shall see later in more detail, Freud seems to speak of determination more in the latter sense as appears, for example, in (1901): "Certain shortcomings in our psychical functioning . . . and certain seemingly unintentional performances prove . . . to have valid motives and to be determined by motives unknown to consciousness" (p. 239). To be determined is here equated with "having valid motives."

There is also another fact to suggest that Freud's determinism differed from what philosophers mean by this word. He introduced the concept of "overdetermination," which is not compatible with the traditional concepts of determinacy: "Indeed, they [psychoanalysts] are prepared to find *several* causes for one and the same mental occurrence, whereas what seems to be our innate craving for causality declares itself satisfied with a *single* psychical cause" (1910a, p. 38).

The idea that nothing happens without adequate cause implies that a cause either is or is not adequate; if the cause is adequate, the addition of any further "causes" (namely, of factors that work in the same direction) would alter the result; if it is not adequate, the result could not be expected. Complete determination leaves no room for overdetermination but merely for necessary and sufficient conditions. If overdetermination is possible or even required, one must wonder whether the determinants have the stringency of the classical concept of determinism, or whether they are not simply determining tendencies or trends—concepts that leave some leeway. Freud's views on this subject will be considered later more fully, in connection with his statements about predictions.

Most other psychoanalytic authors uphold determinism and see in it one of the fundamental propositions or axioms of psychoanalysis. This position is clearly stated by Brenner (1955):

> The sense of this principle [of psychic determinism] is that in the mind as in physical nature about us nothing happens by chance or in a random way. Each psychic event is determined by the ones that preceded it. Events in our mental lives that may seem to be random and unrelated to what went on before are only apparently so. In fact, mental phenomena are no more capable of such a lack of causal connection with what preceded them than are physical ones. Discontinuity in this sense does not exist in mental life [p. 12].

Here determinism is conceived as complete. This view is probably shared by most psychoanalysts, at least as long as they speak about the problem *in abstracto*. As a dissenting voice, we may quote the views of Marjorie Brierley (1947):

> Arguments about free-will versus determinism usually derive from abstract conceptions which express antithetic human wishes and are not based on evidence from psychological facts. The real situation appears somewhat paradoxical. The validity of psychological determinism is seldom questioned by psycho-analysts, because clinical evidence re-proves from hour to hour that we are what **we have become as a result of our past history, and that what we are now becoming is shaping our future. But, equally, there can be no question that living is creative and that, within limits variously circumscribed for different people, the ego appears to have some possibilities of** choice. Every decision is a fresh decision, which may represent a new beginning, a re-adaptation, not necessarily always predictable in advance, although explicable after the event. It would seem that the ego is fulfilling its

proper functions when it tries to take the most reasonable decision on the evidence before it, as if it were a responsible free agent. But the sounder the internal and external reality-sense of the ego, the better will it recognize the limiting conditions of its own choices and the more likely will it be to arrive at integrative, practicable decisions. In relation to the total personality, the adequately realistic ego might well say with St. Paul: 'I live, yet not I' [pp. 288ff.].

Brenner's psychic determinism is analogous to the view of the determinateness of inanimate nature that makes it possible for Laplace's cosmic spirit, who has complete knowledge about the state of the universe at a particular moment, to foresee its state at any future time. Brierley, on the other hand, sees the situation either in terms of incomplete determinateness and restricted freedom, or else sees it as a paradox, a genuine antinomy in which two opposing statements appear to be equally true. This position is taken by many philosophers and historians, for example, by E. H. Carr (1961), who states that "all human actions are both free and determined, according to the point of view from which one considers them" (p. 89)—whatever that may mean. The great physicist Niels Bohr, father of the quantum theory of the atom, has suggested that his "principle of complementarity," according to which the same phenomena have to be described in two mutually exclusive models, may be a universal principle rather than merely a principle of atomic physics. He would consider the issue at stake as another example of this universal phenomenon and would have us look upon determinism and freedom as both true, each in its own frame of reference. This view is apparently in line with the following statement attributed to Bohr: "There are the trivial truths and the great truths. The opposite of a trivial truth is plainly false. The opposite of a great truth is also true" (Becker, 1957).

Determinism and Responsibility

The question of determinism appears frequently in psychoanalytic literature in connection with the problem of criminal responsibility, as it presents itself in forensic psychiatry, or with the question of moral responsibility for one's actions in everyday life. Many psychoanalysts have taken a stand for a strict determinism and against a punitive attitude in matters involving crime (though not necessarily in matters involving their everyday lives). The ancient practice, common to all known societies, was punishment for offenses. In more modern times this has been modified in some societies by making allowances for a plea of "not guilty by reason of insanity" which is often believed to imply the prescientific notion of a free will which might have been impaired by a "disease of the mind" (to use the expression from the M'Naghten rule). The following statement by Ernest Jones (1928) represents this line of thought:

> On the assumption that mental states and impulses of a certain kind are caused only by 'disease' or 'sin', two equally vague conceptions in this context, doctors are asked to discriminate nicely between the two, and they naturally tend to flounder badly in the process. The underlying theory appears to be that the law permits some modes of conduct to be caused . . . by disease but not others. The latter are said to be the product of free will, which is omnipotent enough to create the first link in a chain of thought or conduct. By accepting a particularly arbitrary distinction between mental health and disease,[1] doctors pass beyond the facts of their own science, and by accepting the legal view of free will they abandon the only fundamental canon of science [p. 65].

Similar views have often been voiced by psychiatrists and by social scientists. They form the rationale for widespread current demands for a medical rather than a legal approach to the problem of crime and for the substitution of medical treatment for the time-honored administration of justice.

Yet, the quoted statement shows misunderstandings of the present situation and its rationale. By punishing misconduct, the law does not assume that "free will" is "omnipotent enough to create the first link in a chain of . . . conduct"; all it assumes is

[1] Jones refers to the M'Naghten rule formulated by the Law Lords of England in 1843. Its provisions are cited in Ch. 29.

that normal people are likely to react adaptively to punishment while at least certain psychotics are not. The M'Naghten rule to which the next sentence refers is not "a particularly arbitrary distinction between mental health and disease" as an apparently ineradicable myth has it. The purpose of the M'Naghten rule was never to define mental disease; nothing could have been farther from the mind of the Law Lords who formulated it.

The Law Lords did not intend to define mental illness, for though this may be difficult for moderns to believe, they had no intention of recommending that all the mentally ill be exempt from punishment. They would have felt that such a step would dangerously weaken the deterrent power of the law and emasculate it. What they tried to do therefore was not to define insanity but merely to say which persons among the insane could be exempted from punishment without threatening a general breakdown of deterrence. Pessimists with regard to unchecked human proclivities, they felt such exemptions ought to be very few in number.

Most of us do not share the intensity of their concern about weakening the deterrent power of the law, and we feel that the exemptions can safely be made much wider. But wherever the borderline lies, the distinction between the two kinds of conduct to which Jones refers cannot be so easily dismissed. We all make this distinction in our daily lives. Rules have been set up everywhere: for our children to go to school, for the teachers to instruct them, for everybody to be at his station in life and to attend to his responsibilities. There are rewards for those who properly discharge them and penalties for those who neglect them. To mete out reward and punishment has been an automatic reaction long before it became a rational, goal-directed policy; it is a natural response to like those who do what pleases us and to feel aggressive toward those who thwart our purposes.

But if we learn, for example, that a truant child suffers from an obsessional neurosis which makes it all but impossible for him to come in contact with the school bench, we will take a different view. Even apart from any question of moral accountability we will wonder whether reward and punishment—at least in such limited doses as we are prepared to apply, that is, excluding barbarous punishment—can achieve anything under these circumstances. We may find it more promising to try to understand the child's neurosis and to influence the child more indirectly, on the basis of such understanding.[2] Indeed forensic psychiatry can easily be formulated without the use of words such as free will, which Jones finds offensive, and which, in any case, are loaded with ambiguities. It can be formulated merely in terms of adaptive and nonadaptive response to punishment.

For example, the discrimination between the professional operator of illegal distilleries and gambling houses who has calculated his risks, on the one hand, and the paranoiac who firmly believes himself the victim of an organized, vicious manhunt, on the other, are neither arbitrary nor irrelevant. One difference, important for any attempt at influencing social behavior, is that the former is likely to be influenced by the rising costs of his activities while the latter is not. Of course, between the clear cases at both ends of the spectrum there is an intermediary or twilight zone in which matters are less clear. But this complication, common to all human affairs, does not make such differentiation necessarily impossible. The word "sin" does not appeal to modern secular thought, and other words may have to be substituted to indicate the important realities in question. But at stake fundamentally is the difference between action that can and action that cannot be easily controlled by reward and punishment, and this distinction is neither arbitrary nor useless.[3]

Moral judgments and moral appeals are a constant feature of everyday life. We unceasingly evaluate the conduct of persons, including ourselves sometimes, in relation to moral standards and allocate praise or blame accordingly. If all behavior is strictly and completely determined by factors that do not include something like a free-acting personality—for the inclusion of this

---

[2] It must also be mentioned that there is a limit to the degree to which we can substitute psychiatric rational planning for natural response while yet retaining ordinary social relations; the former could never become the guide for *all* our behavior. Above all, the treatment of others, not as free agents but as puppets, regulated by forces beyond their control and capable of being manipulated, to some degree at least, on this basis, does not go together with love and respect between equals.

[3] See the discussion of this subject in Ch. 29.

factor brings in an element of freedom through the backdoor—it is difficult to see why some should be praised and others blamed. Indeed it has often been argued of criminals that they are the product of their environment, particularly of adverse conditions in childhood, and that therefore they are not to be blamed for what they have become.

If the various influences that we believe have shaped human life are considered only as *pressures*—which implies the existence of a system on which pressure is being brought to bear, hence a system exercising a measure of choice—then moral evaluations are possible to the degree that resistance to such pressures appears possible for the individual in question. But if these influences are seen as *causes*, there seems to be no room for praise or condemnation.

Yet, psychoanalysts like other people continue to bestow praise and blame and to treat in their daily lives all but the sick as responsible individuals, capable within limits of exercising choice and accountable for it. I have seen prominent psychoanalysts react rather sharply when, in a discussion of someone's misconduct, dynamic and genetic interpretations of his behavior were suggested, with possibly exonerating implications. Some psychoanalysts have clearly expressed verbally what others apparently have only tacitly implied; namely, that they distinguish between the analytic situation and ordinary life; they are willing to suspend moral judgment, to a degree, if a man declares himself sick and asks for treatment and then to treat his every act as conditioned and to search for these conditions. But the confession of illness and the acceptance of treatment is a prerequisite for such an attitude, and unless a person seeks treatment, they will judge him as a morally responsible agent and will condemn him accordingly.

There are good reasons for this. The application for treatment implies a measure of alienation from one's own behavior, a willingness to consider it as at least possibly wrong, and is to this extent a form, however embryonic, of condemnation. Hence, it is the first step toward transforming delinquency into neurosis, and neurosis need not be morally condemned. By taking on the critical role himself, a person makes it possible for the analyst to drop his own criticism and to withdraw into neutrality.

The Difficulties of Complete Determinism
and Complete Indeterminism

It appears to be equally impossible to develop a consistent world picture based either on complete determinism or on complete indeterminism; both assumptions lead to untenable, or at least unimaginable, consequences.

If there were no regularities of behavior at all and everything happened entirely at random, and if no probability patterns could be distilled from the chaos of events, no rational action would be possible; for rational action implies the possibility of anticipating, to some degree, the consequences of one's action, and this in turn implies the existence of regularities. Were there no such regularities, we could not drive our car with any expectation that other drivers would, on the whole, keep to their side of the road. We could not expect the school bus to collect our children in the morning or, if it did, we should have little reason to expect them to be delivered at school, or that they would receive instruction in school rather than be subjected to some other treatment. There would be no point in our accepting money for our goods or services, since there would be no assurance that others would accept this money in return for their goods and services. A man would have no right to anticipate that his secretary would show up in his office or, if she did, that she would attend to the correspondence rather than engage (for example) in carpet weaving. Returning home, he would not know whether his wife was still the person he had known or whether she had been transformed in the meantime into a Madame Bovary, a Medea, or a Saint Wilgefort.

Whatever such an indeterminate world was like, it would be completely different from anything we know. Rational action would not exist. Perhaps a life of sorts might still exist for moments, as occasional flare-ups of chance, but probably not in anything like the richly woven patterns of plant, animal and human life on earth.

The difficulties encountered in trying to imagine a fully deterministic universe are of a different nature. We can deal with any particular sector of experience and study the course of events with a view to discovering their regularities. As a guide for research, this approach has been enormously fruitful. We may enlarge the area of our study, take in more and more phenomena, study ever larger aggregates, and still be on safe ground. But once we try to include ourselves in the subject and to see ourselves as part of the predetermined stream, we are faced with difficulties probably insurmountable. Even if we should succeed in including ourselves, conceived as fully determined entities, in the picture of a deterministic cosmos, we should still not have included as equally determined the fact of our having included ourselves and of having conceived ourselves as determined. And if our mind should succeed in taking the further step to include this judgment in the picture and to see it as fully determined and part of the stream of universal determinateness, we should should still have reserved a part of ourselves that remained outside and, in this sense, "free." No matter how hard we may try, it is impossible for the human mind to think consistently of a deterministic universe with oneself in it; one can include part of oneself into the maelstrom of determinism, but another part, a nucleus of selfhood as it were, invariably remains outside.

There is an old saying to the effect that nature will always return even though one may have chased her away with a hayfork: *naturam expellas furca, tamen usque recurret.* Psychoanalytic experience has amply corroborated this ancient wisdom. But it seems also true that a concept of freedom, however limited, cannot be completely ousted from the consciousness of man; it turns up in our deterministic efforts themselves, guiding, so we feel, these very efforts.

The difficulties of a consistent determinism were eloquently described by a distinguished contemporary philosopher, Sir Isaiah Berlin (1954):

> I do not wish here to say that determinism is necessarily false, only that we neither speak nor think as if it could be true, and that it is difficult, and perhaps impossible, to conceive what our picture of the world would be if we seriously believed it; so that to speak . . . as if one might accept the deterministic hypothesis and yet continue to think and speak much as we do at present, is to breed

intellectual confusion. If the belief in freedom—which rests on the assumption that human beings do occasionally choose and that their choices are not wholly accounted for by the kind of causal explanations which are accepted in, say physics or biology—if this is a necessary illusion, it is so deep and so pervasive that it is not felt as such. No doubt we can try to convince ourselves that we are systematically deluded. But unless we attempt to think out the implications of this personally, and alter our modes of thought and speech ... accordingly, this hypothesis remains hollow; that is, we find it impossible even to entertain it seriously, if our behavior is to be taken as evidence of what we can and what we cannot bring ourselves to believe or suppose not merely in theory, but in practice. My submission is that to make a **serious attempt to adapt our thoughts and words to the** hypothesis of determinism is scarcely feasible, as things are now and have been within recorded history. The changes involved are too radical; our moral categories are, in the end, not much more flexible than our physical ones; we cannot begin to think out, in real terms, to which behavior and speech would correspond, what the universe of the genuine determinist would be like, any more than we can think out, with the minimum of indispensable concrete detail (i.e., begin to imagine) what it would be like to be in a timeless world, or one with a seventeen-dimensional space. Let those who doubt this try for themselves; the symbols with which we think will hardly lend themselves to the experiment; they, in their turn, are too deeply involved in our normal view of the world ... to be capable of so violent a break [p. 33ff.].

If the world were organized in complete determinism, as this concept is defined by Brenner, the next moment would be fully determined by the present one and so on until the end of the world. The whole future of our lives and of those who follow us, of the whole human species, would be a foregone conclusion, down to the last detail, and everything that makes the essence of our lives, our problems, our strivings, our efforts, and our doubts would be, in its entirety, an endless chain of illusions. In the denouement of Schiller's Don Carlos, the ninety-year-old Inquisitor General says to King Philip II, with regard to the liberal heretic, Posa, who had for a moment won the heart of the lonely monarch:

> *Sein Leben*
> *Lag angefangen und beschlossen in*
> *Der Santa Casa heiligen Registern ...*
> [His entire life, begun and consummated,
> Was kept on file in the Sacred Office ...]

In a fully deterministic cosmos, these words would have universal significance. Our lives and those of our children and their children down to the remotest posterity would be on file, begun and consummated, with all the most minute details, and would have been from the beginning of time; all generations of men would merely play parts that had been assigned to them, as it were, long before the most primitive forms of life even came into being. This, to me, is hard to imagine.

The data of our experience suggest something different from either complete determinism or complete "randomization." They suggest that human behavior is indeed organized in regular sequences, or in several types of sequences which occur with different frequencies, but that in either case we have to do with probabilities—very high probabilities in some instances—rather than with inescapable necessities. This would mean that enough regularity exists in life to make rational action possible but not enough to make the future a foregone conclusion.[4]

[4] It might be worth noting that the early Greeks held a view of destiny according to which there was a framework of inescapable necessity but within which there was considerable latitude. There was Fate, from which neither gods nor men could escape. Once a man's day of doom had arrived, no god could help him any longer, and any Olympic protector he may have had withdrew so as not to be polluted by the contact with the doomed mortal. But long before that, a man might bring about his own undoing, beyond necessity. Mortals blame all their ills on us, says Zeus, but they suffer *beyond necessity* through their own foolishness. (The Odyssey, I, 13ff.). See the discussion of this subject by Onians (1951, p. 390ff.).

Predictions in Psychoanalysis

The question of determinism is closely linked to that of predictions. If everything is completely determined, it must be possible, at least in principle, to make predictions.

Determinism was defined as the doctrine according to which "each psychic event is determined by the ones that preceded it" (Brenner, 1955). If t is the time at a particular moment and $t + \Delta t$ the time at the subsequent moment, the thesis reads: the condition of the universe at the time $t + \Delta t$ is determined by its condition at the time t. This statement is logically equivalent to the statement: the condition at the time t determines that at the time $t + \Delta t$, just as the sentence "John loves Mary" is equivalent to the sentence "Mary is loved by John."

Many critical observers have marveled at the ability of the human mind to harbor contradictory, mutually exclusive, assumptions. Alexis de Tocqueville saw in it an effort "to reconcile contrary principles and to purchase peace at the expense of logic." Sir Richard Livingstone spoke of the ease with which "that capricious vessel, the human mind, holds at the same time two contradictory doctrines." We psychoanalysts, as students of pathology and as therapists, are more occupied with the cases in which contradictory strivings actually come into conflict with each other, than with those in which they peacefully coexist. Nevertheless, Freud was well aware of the fact that the latter are quite common; he pointed out, for instance, that the two sides of bisexuality, the heterosexual and the homosexual libidinal impulses, which are at times in severe conflict, can exist side by side in many cases without interfering with each other, and he concluded from this that there is something like a tendency to inner conflict as an entity of its own, and that it is this tendency which makes coexistence of different trends impossible. As is well known, Freud (1937a) attributed this tendency to free aggressiveness.

It is like an example of such tolerance for contradictions that many analysts who would insist on the complete determinateness of all things psychic are, at the same time, unfavorably disposed to the request for predictions, although the possibility of predicting is only the reverse side of the coin of determinism.

However, perhaps one should not be too critical of such contradictions because logically equivalent statements may yet emphasize different aspects of reality and so be psychologically different. In a somber mood over the premature death of Sandor Ferenczi, Freud (1933c) told the story of the Sultan who had two seers cast his horoscope. "I hail your good fortune, master," said the first; "you will see all your relatives die before you." This seer was executed. "I hail your good fortune, master," said the second; "you will outlive all your relatives." This seer was richly rewarded. The messages were the same, but the emphasis was different and, we may add, the first did and the second did not permit his own death wishes to seep through.

The fact that determinism implies in principle the possibility of predicting does not, however, mean that if events are determined, one can actually make predictions and even less that one can predict those things one would most like to know. The *existence of regularities* in the events is only one of the necessary conditions of predicting. Another one is *awareness* of these regularities; the fact that yellow fever was transmitted by mosquito bites did not enable us to predict that there would be no transmission in mosquito-free places, so long as this condition of transmission was unknown. A third condition of predicting is *information* about *all* relevant *parameters*. Even after the condition for the transmission of yellow fever is understood, one can make no predictions about transmission in given situations if one does not know whether mosquitos are, in fact, present.

If any one of these conditions is lacking, i.e., either if there is no regularity of any kind in the events themselves, or if their pattern has not been understood, or if we do not know or do not know sufficiently the present condition of the system, no predictions are possible except for those that can be made on the basis of probability considerations for aggregates of randomized elements, such as that in roulette every number will, in the long run, appear approximately as often as any other.

The third prerequisite of predictions, viz., information about the relevant parameters, may be lacking for two different reasons. It may be that we must have not yet measured them, or that we cannot measure them with the means at our disposal or with the means that we can imagine ourselves as developing, or that the measurement would not be a practical proposition because of its costs in terms of material and time. In all these cases we deal with what Kant called "possible experience"; no known law of nature excludes in any one of the above-mentioned cases the possibility that ways for such measurement may yet be found, even though they may be impracticable on anything beyond a simple scale.

But there are also cases in which accurate measurement of all relevant parameters is not only practically but also *theoretically impossible*, because it would run counter to what we believe are inherent and therefore unalterable limits of observation, as in the case of the impossibility of measuring both the location and the impulse of an electron with an accuracy greater than that indicated by the Heisenberg uncertainty principle.

In view of these conditions of predictability, there is clearly no basis whatever for expecting predictions under conditions in which one or the other prerequisite is lacking. Nobody can expect predictions when relevant parameters are unknown. The physicist predicts what will happen in an artificial setup of his own construction—e.g., in an electronic tube—the parameters of which are known to him. But he will not predict what will happen inside a volcano where conditions are only incompletely known—whether or not it will erupt within a certain period of time.

Similarly, it makes no sense to expect a psychoanalyst to predict a particular person's future behavior which depends, in part, on future events in this person's environment and the kind of stress or opportunity that he will meet, as well as on future developments in his bodily organism (as illnesses); these are all factors which may be determined in their own way, but which the analyst has no way of knowing. As the physicist predicts not what happens in empirical systems but rather what happens under specific conditions, so the analyst can reasonably be asked to predict only a person's future behavior not as it will actually materialize under unknown conditions but as it will be *under specific conditions*. Thus, we cannot expect him to say what the future destiny of the analysand will be, but he may be asked to predict how this analysand would stand up to a particular stress, for example, to a traumatic experience of the kind that had started him on his neurosis or had kept it going during the years, the reaction to which had been analyzed and worked through with the patient. Can this be predicted?

The answer probably would have to be that the analyst cannot predict it with exactitude, but that he is not entirely up in the air, either. When he considers an analysis as successfully concluded, the analyst deems it likely that the neurotic reactions have been sufficiently understood and worked through, so that either they will not reappear or that the patient will be able to deal with them unaided. He will also judge, in some cases, that the patient will be able to deal with ordinary pressures without renewed breakdown; in others, that he will be able to deal with such mild pressures only as he may meet in a favorable environment; and in a few cases, perhaps he will be confident that the patient can meet whatever comes. Such expectations often prove correct; sometimes, the prediction may turn out to have been inaccurate or even altogether wrong. The predictions may have been wrong for better or worse; discharged patients may later turn out less stable than the analyst had anticipated, or more so than he had dared to hope.

All in all, it may be said that predictions of this kind, made by a competent analyst, are neither without merit nor without fault. In any case, they are merely probabilistic; they predict a probable, not a certain development. In this way, they do not support the idea of complete determinateness, although, to be sure, neither do they contradict it.

While this may be a fair example of the possibilities and limits of analytic predictions about the further development of persons intensively studied under analysis, psychoanalytic psychology should also permit some predictions of human behavior in general.

There is, for instance, a large body of psychoanalytic experience about regressions of ego (and superego) development and of object relations of which a few examples may be mentioned. Under the impact of rejection, children will give up such acquisitions, with the most recent, as yet inadequately stabilized, accomplishments to go first. Children separated from their mothers, for example, may regress in their bowel habits or again suck their thumbs. Such regressions take place not only in macrodevelopment, in the large curves of life development, but also as microregressions, in the day's activities; as if a child already fairly weaned from thumb sucking takes the thumb in the mouth again when a more grown-up wish has been frustrated. Anna Freud (1963) described regressions in children from already achieved levels of integration and a return to primary process functioning under the influence of various factors such as fatigue or stress; a well-structured pattern of play disintegrates into a free-for-all.

Libidinal development proceeds from a purely self-centered state toward a state in which the object, while conceived as such, is valued only as a means for the child's own satisfactions, as deliverer of food, warmth, or comfort, so that the interest in, and affection for, the object is entirely dependent on satisfaction received, hence, necessarily unstable. From there, development may proceed toward a final state in which affections for other persons are increasingly independent of favors received and increasingly stable. In great frustration and danger, as in severe physical illness, regression takes place and persons return to the "need-fulfilling state" (Anna Freud, 1952). A woman who had survived a period of imprisonment in a Nazi concentration camp told me that people often expressed to her their sympathetic understanding for what they thought must have been her desperate longing for her children, about whose destiny she knew nothing. "The people do not understand," she said. "In order to feel any longing, one must have a full stomach."

Given this and similar kinds of experience, can we make predictions and say, for example, that under the impact of rejection a child will give up his latest ego or superego accomplishments, or that in great frustration and danger, child and adult will be reduced to concern for the self only? Such predictions can be made, but as probabilities rather than as inescapable necessities. As a rule, events will proceed this way; in some cases, however, the response may be progressive rather than regressive. In the ultimate degradation and despair of the Nazi concentration camp most people seem to have been reduced to the bare struggle for survival; a few, however, became what another age would have called saints—devoid of any concern for the self, utterly devoted to the service of others. The prediction of regression is valid in the great majority of cases but is not universally valid.

It may be countered at this point that psychoanalytic experience does not lead to the formulation of a law according to which certain frustrations must lead to regressions. Rather, it suggests that frustrations lead to a variety of responses according to variations of persons and circumstances, with regression the most frequent result, and that further research will enable us to find the additional conditions which determine that the outcome is regression in one case and, perhaps, progression in another.[5]

We know of conditions that favor one or the other of these developments and much more about it may be learned in the future. But will it ever be possible to find for each possible outcome the conditions that are necessary and sufficient to bring it about? Only in this case could one predict without qualification the response of a particular person to an emergency. For the time being, in any case, we can predict only developments of greater or lesser probability.

In a paper published in 1936, I suggested that predictions can be made in two marginal cases: either if "behavior is guided exclusively by the mature ego" or, on the contrary, if "steering by the mature ego is practically completely excluded and behavior is exclusively directed by biological forces (instinctual drives) and the primitive attempts at solution, made by the immature ego," i.e., "if the wealth of determinants of human behavior is diminished," *so oder so.*

An example of the first kind would be the high probability of the prediction that, short of major events like the death of a close person, illness, or interruption of traffic, the average bread-

[5] Even in our present state of knowledge we have some idea about this. In the 1930s when German writers were under great pressure to conform to Nazi ideology, Freud (1935) wrote to Thomas Mann in a letter of congratulation on his sixtieth birthday that, as a psychoanalyst who did not believe in the omnipotence of thoughts, he would refrain from expressing any wishes, but that he could express his conviction that Mann would never do anything mean in life. We feel that something we call character, which can make people impervious to the lures of gain, can also prevent them from regressing under pressure from their moral standards—at least as long as pressures do not exceed certain limits. The reaction to extreme pressure may be different, as the history of torture reveals.

winner will appear in his office or workshop on ordinary
working days at approximately the same time.

As an example of the second kind, we may predict fairly well
certain reactions in mental disease; e.g., what will happen if one
tries to dissuade a paranoid friend from his delusion by commis-
sioning a detective agency to investigate the alleged persecutions
to which he believes himself to be subjected. When the agency's
report has been submitted with the conclusion that no traces of
the alleged conspiracy and persecutions could be found, perhaps
even with the evidence of a friendly attitude on the part of the
neighbors, the paranoiac will not give it credence except,
perhaps, for a little while. Soon he will not only have found
reasons for maintaining his original convictions in the face of
adverse evidence, but he will have worked out a system of
hypotheses, accepted by him as factual, which will explain to his
satisfaction why the agency report contained the allegedly
erroneous conclusions.

Anna Freud suggested to me that predictions are possible not
only in the two extreme cases but also in the many instances in
between in which the two ingredients, primitive inner forces and
the sense of reality, are mixed in a characteristic and stable
proportion; such mixtures would form the essence of what is
called character.

What all these cases—reality-determined behavior, behavior
oblivious of reality, or a particular combination of objective and
subjective elements characteristic for an individual—have in
common is a *diminution of the number of relevant parameters*
on which human behavior depends. Predicting, then, would be
inauspicious as long as all the many factors which determine
human behavior are operative, but it would become increasingly
possible as the number of these variables diminishes.

Freud on Predictions

In Ibsen's *A Doll's House*, the heroine, Nora, leaves her home
and her family when her dream of complete mutual dedication
in marriage explodes in her face. The appeal to consider her

children does not move her; in her present condition, she says, she could not be of much use to them anyhow. One theatrical producer protested to Ibsen that this ending would not go down well with the public and he requested that Ibsen alter it. Under his prodding, Ibsen wrote an alternate ending in which Nora faints upon the mentioning of her children; presumably, she will stay for that reason. Aesthetically, the two versions will appeal to different persons; in actual life, either of them would be psychologically understandable. Either one could be explained and considered as "determined" after the event, but neither can be anticipated with certainty.

Freud (1920b) described these conditions in the following passage in which he also suggested the reasons for our limited powers of prediction:

So long as we trace the development from its final outcome backwards, the chain of events appears continuous, and we feel we have gained an insight which is completely satisfactory or even exhaustive. But if we proceed the reverse way, if we start from the premises inferred from the analysis and try to follow these up to the final result, then we no longer get the impression of an inevitable sequence of events which could not have been otherwise determined. We notice at once that there might have been another result, and that we might have been just as well able to understand and explain the latter. The synthesis is thus not so satisfactory as the analysis; in other words, from a knowledge of the premises we could not have foretold the nature of the result.

It is very easy to account for this disturbing state of affairs. Even supposing that we have a complete knowledge of the etiological factors that decide a given result, nevertheless what we know about them is only their quality, and not their relative strength. Some of them are suppressed by others because they are too weak, and they therefore do not affect the final result. But we never know beforehand which of the determining factors will prove the weaker or the stronger. We only say at the end that those which have succeeded must have been the stronger. Hence the chain of causation can always be recognized with certainty if we follow the line of analysis, whereas to predict along the line of synthesis is impossible' [p. 167ff.].

Freud made the same point in a small meeting at which I happened to be present and about which I reported on another occasion (1958). He told about the following experience: A few months before the break, C. G. Jung came to visit him. At the dinner table, Jung reported a dream of the preceding night. He had fought against a medieval knight in armor whose shield carried the Swiss arms. Jung immediately added his interpretation of the dream that the Swiss knight meant the Swiss nobleman, Rudolph von Habsburg, ancestor of the Austrian dynasty, hence the Austrian, Freud. Dream and interpretation were received with the slight amusement that is usual in such circumstances. It was a few months later that Jung turned against Freud in a hostile manner.

Would it have been possible, Freud asked, to anticipate at the time of the dream that Jung would soon carry out in fact what he had just dreamed about? Freud answered the question in the negative. It could not have been foreseen because one did not know the strength of the intrapsychic forces. Hostile tendencies toward father figures are common, perhaps universal, phenomena among men. In most instances, they merely find expression in dreams, in an occasional minor breakthrough in the psychopathology of everyday life, or in an occasional act of discourtesy. Sometimes, they are expressed in neurotic symptoms. Whether they will lead to more serious action depends on the relative strength of these tendencies and of the restraining tendencies which comes from positive affections, fear, or guilt.

It seems to me that the above-quoted lines of Freud contain the essentials for a clarification of the problem of determinism, not only in individual life to which they refer but also of determinism in history and the question of historical inevitability.

Freud's explanation, it should be noted first of all, does not exclude the possibility of predictions altogether; in all cases in which there is no conflict or in which one side of the dilemma is clearly stronger than the other, one can predict with fair accuracy.[6] It was predictable that Lear would not humiliate himself before Goneril and Regan; that once disaster had closed in on him, Macbeth would meet his fate with desperate courage; that Othello would react very strongly to the mere idea of his wife's infidelity. The leader of world Communism, it can be safely predicted, will never become a Trappist monk. These things would be too much "out of character."

It is only where human action is the outcome of a close contest of inner forces that different outcomes appear possible and predictions become tenuous. The situation is comparable to that in a national election in which a small fraction of the electorate can swing the result either way; the result is then at the mercy of "chance," of accidental factors, and is not predictable.

Freud's remarks may also explain the bewildering feature that has bedeviled human speculation since earliest times, namely, that human actions appear to be both determined and free, a paradox which had led authors of such vastly different intellectual background and experience as Niels Bohr or E. H. Carr, and many others with them, to view determinism and freedom as equally true, depending on the perspective. Things always appear fully determined in retrospect; the various forces involved have participated in the outcome according to their respective strength, and this strength is visible in retrospect. Before the event, however, when these quantities were as yet not fixed, or incompletely known, the outcome appeared as not determined, hence as "free."

---

[6] My earlier attempt, discussed above, to deal with the question of predictive ability follows from the Freudian explanation and is, in fact, a special case of it. If a person is moved exclusively by the id and primitive mechanisms, or exclusively by ego purposes and the reality principle, one or the other side in the struggle between primitive forces and higher forms of integration is powerless; hence *a fortiori* the relative strength is known, i.e., the strength of one side is practically zero.

The same reasoning applies to the "amendment" advanced by Anna Freud in the above-mentioned discussion: when there is a known stable ratio between the two kinds of forces, the relative quantitative strength is once again known, hence predictions are possible. On the other hand, see also Anna Freud (1958) on the limitations of prediction.

The question further arises whether our ignorance of the quantitative factor merely indicates a *lack of information* on our part *or* an *indeterminateness* in the things themselves. If the former is the case and we have to do with lack of information only, we should have to ask further whether the missing information might still be supplied by appropriate research from which we could learn how to measure these forces, or whether the uncertainty is inherent in the situation itself so that any measurement would necessarily be inadequate. To sum up: Are we ignorant of the quantitative strength of the forces involved because (1) we have as yet devised no ways of measuring them; or (2) because no sufficiently exact measurement is possible under any circumstances; or (3) because their relative strength changes constantly in a random manner, like the motion of particles in the Brownian movement?

In the first case, the obstacle would merely lie in the limitations of our present knowledge and skills; in the second, in the conditions of measurement; in the third, it would lie in nature itself.

The first possibility would clearly be the most harmless as it would be only the kind of impediment that is likely to be eliminated or at least progressively diminished with the progress of science. There is no reason to assume, however, that the obstacle to accurate measurement is more fundamental than that and not entirely remediable; it seems to rest in the second and third points.

As far as the problem of measurement is concerned, there is no indication whatever that psychic quantities like cathexes could be measured in the way physical quantities like space, time, and weight are measured, by coordinating them to standard units (as, for example, stretches of time are to periodical movements such as the rotation of the earth or the swing of a pendulum).[7] The only way in which any approach to the question of measuring psychic quantities seems at all auspicious

---

[7] It may be interesting to remember that such a system of measurement was once considered by Schilder (1924). He thought that one could search for pharmacological equivalents of psychic phenomena, i.e., the amount of a particular drug that would produce the respective phenomena. Any attempt to carry this appealing idea into practice would lead to great, probably insurmountable, difficulties.

is on a comparative basis, i.e., not in the manner of physics but in the manner of economics. In economics one "measures" the strength of human wants in terms of the price that people are willing to pay for their satisfactions, i.e., in terms of the things people are willing to do without in order to secure them. One thus arrives at an order of urgency of different wants, and this order is revealed by actual behavior. Similarly, we psychoanalysts could perhaps "measure" the strength of drives relative to each other. It is not unthinkable that we might in this way arrive at a relative quantification, somewhat comparable to demand and supply curves in mathematical economics. But it would still be actual behavior that served as criterion; i.e., a tendency is proved to have been the stronger one by virtue of the fact that it has actually prevailed. If relative strength of cathexes is thus inferred from actual behavior, one cannot predict behavior if this prediction requires the previous knowledge of these cathexes. We cannot predict the outcome through measurement of the strength of the forces involved if we need that very result to make the measurement.

But perhaps, it may be argued, one will find ways of measuring the strength of the forces by something short of their actual clash in real life, perhaps by a kind of sampling comparable to that applied with considerable success in public opinion polls. But no such sampling appears to be possible in matters of the mind; I can conceive of no test that would measure the relative strength of a person's love for another—say, for his wife or his children—and his egotism under extreme circumstances, in a "moment of truth," so that one could predict whether in such an emergency he would save himself or the other. There are instances in which one side is conspicuously stronger than the other, and in such cases the outcome may not be in much doubt. But in many cases the two forces are not so vastly different in strength for the outcome to be a foregone conclusion and, if this is so, no test that lacks the seriousness of a life-and-death matter can show which side would prevail in an actual showdown. Only the real situation itself and not a miniature replication of it would reveal "the truth" of the matter. This kind of test is, of course, impermissible on moral grounds; but even if it were not, it would not answer our question because it would prove nothing for the next occasion. An experience in earnest would have so profound an impact upon a person that it would change the constellation of inner forces. What was true this time need not be true on another occasion, with a person changed by the very experience. That is the story of Joseph Conrad's *Lord Jim*. He once failed in a critical life situation and behaved as a coward. This memory weighed heavily upon him throughout his later life; faced with a second trial, he met it like a hero.

But our ignorance of the quantitative conditions may be even more fundamental than such irremediable obstacles to accurate measurement and may lie in the facts themselves. There may be a constant change in the relative strength of forces in an irregular fashion, comparable to the situation in very close elections in which a last-minute shift of small groups of voters or a last-minute change in voter turnout may swing the election either way.

We may then sum up the situation as follows: that there are only limited possibilities for accurate predictions, and that this state of affairs is due not just to the "youth" of our science or to our alleged failure to adhere to rigid standards of investigation and verification, but to factors which appear to be inherent in the subject and which therefore are, on the whole, unalterable.

Yet, while this is so, there seems to be no point in proclaiming a doctrine of complete, universal determinism. Claims of total determinateness can be made good only by the actual delivery of predictions. Claims that go beyond the possibility of substantiating them are, at best, working hypotheses; at worst, they are like checks without coverage. Sooner or later, they will cause trouble; they interfere with the precise formulation of the data of experience which is a prerequisite of fruitful theory formulation.

CHAPTER 18

Historical Fiction

(1963)

Erich Fromm, author of the book, *Sigmund Freud's Mission*
(1959), was originally a social philosopher and critic of the social
scene. He came from the small but highly influential circle of the
Institute of Social Research in Frankfort, Germany, a scientific-
political hybrid of left-Socialist—not Communist—orientation.
He was in early contact with psychoanalysis, and has combined,
in his literary work and in his therapy, his social views and his
selections from, and modifications of, psychoanalytic ideas. He
was professor of psychoanalysis at the University of Mexico. He is
professor of psychology at Michigan State University and a
member of the Washington Psychoanalytic Society.

Fromm has been an articulate critic of Western society.
Though not an orthodox Marxist, he belongs to the Messianic
tradition of social thought, of which Marxism is itself the most
successful manifestation, i.e., he has a picture of a perfect society
of complete harmony ("the sane society") and he believes that its
establishment is a proposition of practical politics. Fromm is also
an articulate advocate of certain measures in American foreign
policy. He believes in principle in the merits of unilateral
disarmament but recognizes its impracticability and advocates,
as a matter of practical policy, gradated steps of reduction of
armaments which he expects will be reciprocated in kind by our
adversary. He is interested in Zen Buddhism. As regards psycho-

This book review essay is reprinted from the *Journal of the American
Psychoanalytic Association*, 11:628-651, 1963. Also in Italian in *Psiche*
(Rome), 2:53-72, 1965.

analysis, he has been sharply critical of Freudian, or "classical," psychoanalysis and has been one of the founders of what is often referred to as the "neo-Freudian" school, a school of thought of which Harry Stack Sullivan and Karen Horney have been noted representatives. He has also shown sympathetic interest in the relationship therapies developed by Rank and, in his latest period, by Ferenczi. All these interests appear to have a common denominator: the advocacy of universal brotherly love. Fromm is fundamentally an evangelist.

The book contains, first, a kind of character and pathographical sketch of Freud as Fromm sees him. Freud is described as having been socially conditioned by the Enlightenment, the climate of a "decaying" Austria-Hungary,[1] the capitalist ideology, and his Jewishness. In its more individual aspects, Freud's personality is seen as lacking "emotional warmth, closeness, love and ... enjoyment of life," but as equipped with a passion for truth and with great courage. Fromm's "analytic" considerations lead him to the conclusion that Freud was an oral-receptive person with a passive attachment to his mother, dependent and very insecure.

From this portrait of Freud, Fromm proceeds to what seems to be his main contention: Freud was not merely a scientist concerned with finding the truth; there are elements in psychoanalysis, Fromm contends, which do not go with the picture of science, viz., the talk of a "psychoanalytic movement," the concern about the preservation of a pure and unadulterated doctrine, the setting up of a "secret committee" to watch over its integrity, the alleged persecution of disciples who did not toe the line. Such features, Fromm maintains, belong to a political or religious movement. They reveal, according to Fromm, that Freud, though consciously seeing himself only as a scientist, was actually motivated by the ambition to reform the world by bringing the emotions under the control of Reason: "Neither Freud nor his followers admitted to others or to themselves that

[1] The power of the Austro-Hungarian monarchy was declining as the multinational state defended itself with difficulty against the rising tide of nationalism. There was much pessimism and resignation with regard to the long-term future. But, on the other hand, there was economic progress and a splendid intellectual and cultural life, with a broad basis in an educated and culturally alert middle class.

they aimed at more than scientific and therapeutic achievements. They repressed their ambition to conquer the world with
a messianic ideal of salvation" (p. 109).

Not only did they entertain such ambitions, but they apparently succeeded in founding a Church—replete not only with
priests but with a laity: "Psychoanalysis became a surrogate for
religion for the urban middle and upper-middle classes, which
did not want to make a more radical and comprehensive effort.
Here, in the Movement, they found everything—a dogma, a
ritual, a leader, a hierarchy, the feeling of possessing the truth,
of being superior to the uninitiated; yet without great effort,
without deeper comprehension of the problems of human existence, without insight into and criticism of their own society and
its crippling effects on man, without having to change one's
character in those aspects which matter, namely to get rid of
one's greed, anger and folly" (p. 112).[2]

Freud's reformist ardor did not go "to the roots" of things:
"he was not questioning the basic picture of man, but, as all
liberal reformers, trying to mitigate man's burden within the
very framework of the traditional picture of man" (p. 100). He
could not transcend the notion of man current in his society:
"Freud was . . . the psychologist of nineteenth-century society,
who showed that the assumptions about man underlying the
economic system were even more right than the economists
could have imagined. His concept of the Homo sexualis was a
deepened and enlarged version of the economist's concept of
Homo economicus" (p. 100).[3]

Yet, even so, Freud deserves honor for "his gifts, his honesty,

[2] One can see how one can get rid, to a large degree, of one's greed and
anger or, at least, control them, but how can we humans get rid of folly? In
order to do this, one would first have to know what folly is and how to
distinguish it from prudence, and in many cases one knows it, if at all, only
with the benefit of hindsight. Even then, our view often continues to change
as the perspective of time lengthens and the story unfolds further. A passage
like this illustrates the humorless claim to be in the possession of Truth and the
judgmental stance which permeate Fromm's writings.

[3] Fromm's view of economic theory is as prejudiced as his view of Freudian
thought. The charge that "the economists" of the 19th century pictured man
as exclusively motivated by greed has been made countless times, but that does
not make it any more true.

For one, "economic man" has never been more than a *model*, i.e., one of his courage and the tragic character of his life"; the last sentence of the book calls him a "truly great man," although little, if anything, in the preceding text had prepared the reader for such final evaluation.

Everybody who has ever studied myth formation and propaganda knows that it is incomparably more difficult to combat distortion, however great, than complete falsehood; for the former contains elements of truth, however warped, and therefore cannot be dismissed in its entirety. The nucleus of truth must be separated from the layers of misunderstanding and

---

those simplified assumptions about reality which underlie generalizing theories, in physics as well as in economics and political science. Their value lies in the understanding of the significance of one important aspect of reality, and in the approximation to the data of observation, which they provide.

The laws of classical mechanics were derived on the assumption of bodies moving in a vacuum, without friction, which was an unrealistic assumption under terrestrial conditions. The classical theory of electrolytes (Arrhenius) was based on the assumption that electric forces between the wandering ions can be ignored. Of course, this assumption was unrealistic; but weak electrolytes in which the concentration of ions is small, and the distance between them correspondingly great, approximate this marginal condition sufficiently to make the theory sufficiently accurate for them. One has to begin somewhere and can take care of the other factors later.

By overlooking certain aspects of reality, the model, or "ideal type," as it is often called in the social sciences (a term coined by Max Weber), has the effect of exaggerating other aspects, and may thereby assume the character of a caricature. Yet, the only people who have ever taken "economic man" literally, as a true and accurate picture of man's totality, have been those in Fromm's ideological camp; *there* it is widely believed that "the bourgeois," or "the capitalists," are merely personifications of monetary greed.

But whatever the role of the model may have been in the first half of the 19th century, economic theory underwent considerable refinement during Freud's lifetime, i.e., during the later 19th and earlier 20th centuries—a development in which Vienna, home of the theory of marginal utility, with Lausanne and Cambridge as centers of economic thought, played a prominent role. The theory was no longer based on the model of "economic man"—nor indeed, on any assumption about human motivation—but merely on the assumption that in the area relevant for economics, men act *rationally*, i.e., make considered choices between alternatives according to their preferences. The case of a man choosing more leisure in preference to more income; or of a man choosing voluntary service in preference to remunerative employment, cases which would have been outside the model of economic man, are fully covered by the later, more refined, version of the theory which, in psychoanalytic language, merely postulates that all action, or at least all action relevant for economics, takes place under the direction of the preconscious ego.

distortion—a process which requires detailed knowledge and painstaking labor. The casual reader cannot evaluate such subtleties and is left with the impression that there is some truth in the matter: *semper aliquid haeret.*

Let us consider the basic contention that Freud and his disciples were actually founder and apostles of a quasi-political or quasi-religious reform movement. It can be seen immediately that the ambition which Fromm attributes to Freud, and a political rather than scientific orientation, is true of Fromm himself and the Frankfort group from which he comes; they are primarily social reformers. But is it as true of Freud and his disciples?

It is true that Freud and his disciples gradually came to think that the value of psychoanalysis transcended that of a therapy of the neuroses. We felt—I beg permission to include myself in this group—that the discovery of the unconscious not only offered the key to psychopathology but also opened a new dimension in the understanding of all things human; and that the enlargement of consciousness not only offered a therapy of the neuroses but might in the long run turn out to be a step in human progress.[4]

Furthermore, we felt that this discovery was threatened with submergence again in an ocean of misunderstandings and distortions—like a tract of land that had been cleared in the midst of the jungle and needed constant effort to keep the jungle from moving in again. We *did* have a sense of mission: first, to see to it that psychoanalytic insight did not disappear; and then to do what we could to enlarge it.

Fromm contends that "Neither Freud nor his followers admitted to others or to themselves that they aimed at more than scientific and therapeutic achievements" (p. 109). This is completely untrue. These hopes and expectations, such as they were, were a conscious part of our lives. They were also often discussed in publications. In a little book Ferenczi and Rank (1924) offered their estimate of the future of psychoanalysis in all its aspects,

---

[4] I believe that this expectation was quite realistic as far as ego development is concerned, but perhaps not enough thought was given to the fact that higher ego development does not necessarily mean more humane aspirations, and that without the latter, the former is not an unmixed blessing. See Waelder (1939b) and (1960a, p. 250f.).

and ended with this statement: "The most important advance in psychoanalysis consists finally in a great increase of consciousness, or expressed according to our metapsychology, in raising the instinctive unconscious mental content to the level of preconscious thinking. This, however, from our point of view, means such an important step in the development of mankind that it may actually be regarded as a biological advance, and indeed as one which for the first time takes place under a kind of self-control" (p. 67f.). This is a rather far-reaching expectation. An extensive discussion of the cultural impact of psychoanalysis, with somewhat less enthusiastic expectations, can be found in Chapter 21 of this volume. Other aspects of the same matter were discussed by Alexander (1925). The most beautiful formulation of these humanizing potentialities of psychoanalysis came from the writer Thomas Mann. While some analysts would find such perspectives inspiring, others found them too "metaphysical."

But all this does not add up to a political or religious movement, or to an ambition "to conquer the world with a Messianic ideal of salvation" (p. 109). Freud was far too skeptical—or should I say: too civilized?—a mind to put much faith in salvation of mankind by any means, at any time. *He belonged in the humanistic, not the Messianic, stream* of European thought.

Fromm's chief arguments to demonstrate the political or religious character of the psychoanalytic movement are like this: "Is there any other case of a therapy or of a scientific theory transforming itself into a movement, centrally directed by a secret committee, with purges of deviant members, with local organizations in an international superorganization? No therapy in the field of medicine was ever transformed into such a movement. As far as psychoanalysis as a theory is concerned, the nearest comparison would be Darwinism; ... yet there is no Darwinian 'movement,' no directorium which leads that movement, *no purges which decide who has the right to call himself a Darwinist* and who has lost such a privilege" (p. 82; italics mine).

These or similar arguments have been voiced time and again, and it may be appropriate to take them up at some length.

A movement need not be political or religious; we often

speak of movements when a doctrine is advocated by some and rejected by others. It is true that there are no movements in physics or physiology today; but this is simply due to the fact that there is current agreement on fundamentals in these disciplines. In earlier times, these sciences were also subject to controversies on fundamental points; and there we may speak of movements in these disciplines, too. In the 17th century when the geocentric and heliocentric systems faced each other, one may speak of a "Copernican movement." There was a movement for vaccination in the 19th century. There is talk today of the movement of logical Positivism, or for the unity of science, etc.

As far as the "committee" is concerned, one cannot play Hamlet without the prince. Psychoanalysis was, and still is, surrounded by a sea of misunderstanding;[5] it was highly problematic whether it could be kept from being submerged by them. Under such circumstances it does seem odd to me that a few disciples, well versed in psychoanalysis, should make it their business to say, if need be, in Freud's words: "All this nonsense has nothing to do with psychoanalysis" (quoted by Fromm, p. 91). In itself such a situation has nothing to do with dogmatism; the unadulterated preservation of an idea is a prerequisite of its rational discussion and evaluation.

As far as the main piece of Fromm's argument is concerned, the claim for authority of accreditation in psychoanalysis, it should be clear that the claim to be a Darwinian is no analogy to the claim of being a psychoanalyst. The proper analogy to a Darwinian would be a *Freudian;* it has never occurred to Freud or the rest of us to try to lay down any laws as to who may, or who may not, call himself a Freudian. But to call oneself a *psychoanalyst* implies that one presents oneself to the public as a competent practitioner of an investigative method and a thera-

---

[5] Fromm's book itself provides many examples of such misunderstandings. Above all, Fromm shares the two most common of them, viz., the misunderstanding of the meaning of "sexual" in psychoanalysis, and the misunderstanding of repression. When Fromm speaks of Freud's concern with the sexual, he takes it in the pre-Freudian sense, as referring to bedroom stories. If he is aware of the fact that is means sensuality in a wider sense, this awareness is not brought out in the book. And, more often than not, he confuses repression with frustration (e.g., p. 113).

peutic technique *invented by Sigmund Freud,* and it is not outlandish for the man who invented and named a thing to request the right to inspect the products offered by others under this name, and to judge whether they are correctly so labeled.

What is persistently overlooked in the discussion of this issue is the fact that psychoanalysis was not a word of the common language which Freud had found and tried to usurp; that, of course, would have been presumptuous. But psychoanalysis is an *artificial name* which was coined by Sigmund Freud to label the therapeutic technique which he himself had developed, just as penicillin is an artificial word coined by Sir Alexander Fleming to name the drug he developed. And just as nobody questions the moral right of the discoverer of a drug to protest when the name of his drug is used for the sale of another product, I fail to see how one can question the right of Freud, or of the legitimate executors of his intellectual estate, to protest if the word psychoanalysis is used for procedures which, whatever their merits, have little or nothing to do with the psychoanalysis invented by Sigmund Freud.

Medicine as well as other professions have accrediting boards and similar certifying agencies, with the corresponding restrictions in the use of designations implying special competence. It is true that in the great majority of cases the test of competence does not imply the acceptance of a particular doctrine, but, once again, this is due only to the agreement on fundamentals now prevailing in the physical sciences and medicine, and was not always so. In the rare cases in which some assumptions are not universally accepted, the test of qualification *does* imply the acceptance of a position not universally endorsed.

The science of genetics is based on the assumption that the genes are the atoms of inheritance; this proposition is very widely, but not yet universally, accepted. A man who does not accept it cannot be called a geneticist, although he may, of course, be called a biologist or a student of inheritance. Psychoanalysis is based on the proposition that there is an effective psychic unconscious which is withheld from consciousness by repression. Psychoanalysis is a method designed to facilitate the rise of the unconscious into consciousness and a procedure to treat emotional illness by making its unconscious aspects conscious. A person who does not believe in the existence of unconscious processes; or, although believing in their existence, does not believe that their unconsciousness is due to repression; or, although believing this, does not think that certain emotional illnesses are advantageously treated by bringing this unconscious to consciousness—cannot be called a psychoanalyst. He may, of course, be a psychiatrist, a psychotherapist, a psychologist, a behavioral scientist, etc.

The real question is not why we try to set up standards and criteria but rather why those who reject the basic propositions on which psychoanalysis rests insist on calling themselves psychoanalysts and their various treatment methods psychoanalysis.

To sum up the argument: Fromm's picture of Freudian psychoanalysis as a quasi-political or quasi-religious movement seems to me to be quite out of focus. But it appears as distorted in an even more fundamental sense, inasmuch as it sees Freud as exclusively *practically* oriented, toward what psychoanalysis can *do* in the world, and entirely overlooks the fact that the practical did not hold first place in Freud's mind.

The whole idea of Freud as a would-be world reformer was at all arguable only *after* it became apparent that psychoanalysis could have consequences and applications beyond the treatment room, i.e., after Freud was well along in his fifties. But that could not have been anticipated in the beginning. What role should Freud's alleged ambition of world reform have played earlier, e.g., in Freud's most productive years in his early forties? What role could it have played when he suggested to Dr. Breuer that they follow up together the clues in the case of Anna O. and urge hysterical patients in hypnosis to remember the forgotten beginnings of their symptoms, and how could he have fathomed that this work could lead to a reform of the world? How could he have expected it when he grasped the fact that dreams had a meaning and devoted some years to dream studies? Later, up to the end of his life, he was often occupied with problems that had no conceivable application to a program of changing reality. I believe that *Totem and Taboo* (1913) was among the works he liked best; the later continuation of it, *Moses and Monotheism* (1939), was also close to his heart. Whether or not posterity will agree with his selections, their perusal makes it obvious that considerations of practical effects did not determine his preferences.

The simple fact is that Freud's outlook was very close to that of most, perhaps all, pure scientists, somewhat like what Henri Poincaré once expressed in these words: "I do not say science is useful because it helps us to build machines; I say machines are useful because as they work for us they will some day leave us more time for scientific research." In a quite similar way, Freud thought that it was fortunate that psychoanalysis had a therapeutic value because that alone made it possible for people to offer themselves for psychoanalytic research. Ernest Renan once said that the only thing that really mattered was the emancipation and progress of the human mind; Freud's feelings were not very different. Freud, it must not be forgotten, came from a Mediterranean, not a Calvinist, tradition, and contemplation, in the Mediterranean tradition, does not carry the stigma of sin.

His mind was, in fact, forever on a quest for new knowledge and new understanding in all things human. I remember his developing ideas on the most varied subjects, quite remote from any thought of practical—therapeutic, political, ideological— application. This is one aspect of Freud which has entirely escaped Fromm, perhaps because it is alien to the latter's own bent of mind.

Before leaving the subject of the alleged quasi-religious character of the psychoanalytic movement, an amusing detail in Fromm's argument may be reported. In order to demonstrate "how far the symbiotic, quasi-religious attachment to Freud went," Fromm quotes the following statement by Sachs: "I had found the one thing worth while for me to live for: many years later I discovered that it was also the only thing I could live by." And Fromm comments as follows: "We can easily imagine somebody saying that he lives by the Bible, the Bhagavad-Gita, or by the philosophy of Spinoza or Kant—but to live by a book on the interpretation of dreams makes sense only if we assume that the author has become a Moses and the science a new religion" (p. 67).

Here Fromm steps into a trap of his own making. What Sachs meant was, of course, that after many years he found out that psychoanalysis—viz., the practice of psychoanalysis—was *the only way he could make a living;* he was not a physician and when he joined the circle around Freud, nobody had as yet thought of lay analysis.

Another charge that has been levied against Freud and that seems to fit well with Fromm's basic contention is that of Freud's alleged authoritarianism. Freud, it is said, was intolerant of opposition, "expecting others to follow him, wait on him, to sacrifice their independence and intellectual freedom to him."

This picture of Freud has so often been drawn, and has been so widely disseminated, that it seems fitting that one of those who knew Freud sufficiently well to have an informed opinion in this matter should try to set the record straight. Not that I believe that truth will prevail if given a chance; but it may at least be rescued from being wiped off the map entirely.

If I were a lawyer and had to conduct the defense of Freud in a trial like that of Socrates, I would strongly advise my client against correcting this distortion of his personality, and for pleading guilty on this count. Juries do not like it if a defendant who is accused on many counts does not accept any guilt whatever; they do not like to believe that widespread accusations can be entirely without foundation; and in any case, they prefer their defendants humble. It is better to plead guilty on some minor count.

But I am not a lawyer, and I am not trying to plead a case, but to state a fact to the best of my knowledge. Be it therefore said that there is no truth whatever in the legend of Freud's authoritarianism, and that it was very easy to contradict him as long as contradiction did not involve personal attack.

For a psychoanalyst who knows that repressive processes are not always complete and that fragments of the repressed truth can often be detected in odd places, it is not surprising that the truth in this matter can even be detected in Fromm's book if one only scans it carefully enough. In his discussion of Freud's "rigid authoritarianism" Fromm calls Freud "intolerant of other opinions or revisions of his own theories." Fromm continues: "It is hard to ignore the bulk of evidence which supports this view . . . . Even Sachs, in his frankly idolizing biography of Freud, admits this: 'I knew it was always extremely difficult for him to assimilate the opinions of others after he had evolved his own in a long and laborious process. . . . If my opinion was opposed to his, I said so frankly. He always gave me full scope to expound my views, and listened willingly to my arguments, but *was hardly ever moved by them*" (p. 62; italics by Fromm).

I wonder how many of those who have read this passage in Fromm's book have noticed that the quotation from Sachs does not bear out Fromm's contention. The story was *supposed* to show that Freud was *authoritarian*, that he was "intolerant of other opinions"; what the story *actually* tells us is something quite different, namely, that Freud was *tolerant* of his disciple's opinions but *did not surrender his own views to him*. There is not the slightest hint that Freud attempted to impose his views on Sachs, or even to influence him in any way whatsoever. To call Freud authoritarian *because he did not follow the lead of others* reminds me of the words of the emperor Tiberius to his stepdaughter: *si non dominaris te iniuriam accipere existimas.*[6]

This is, in fact, the *whole* reality behind the charge of Freud's authoritarianism. Freud was what is now called an inner-directed person, whose course in life comes from inner impulsion rather than being merely a reflection of shifting outside pressures. Such a person has won his opinions himself, laboriously; hence they are not easily surrendered under the influence of others. But there is all the difference in the world between an inner-directed person who concedes the same right to others, and a tyrant.

These facts appear clearly in the correspondence between Freud and Rank at the critical time following Rank's publication of his *Trauma of Birth* (1924).[7] In these letters, we see Rank urgently pleading with Freud for the acceptance of his ideas. Freud does not see eye to eye with Rank in this matter and would let the matter rest there; one can agree to disagree. He actually pleads with the younger man, who has been something like an adopted son to him, to continue their relationship without Rank's pressing him any further on this issue. Freud writes:

My observation has, as yet, not permitted me to make a decision, but up to now has furnished nothing that would correspond to your interpretation....Your ex-

[6] If you do not dominate, you consider yourself injured.

[7] The correspondence, or as much of it as we know, can be found in Taft (1958).

periences are different; do they therefore cancel mine? We both know that experiences permit of many explanations, hence we have to wait for further experiences.

After all, the right to have an opinion of one's own prevails for me, too. I have endeavored to respect it with each of my friends and adherents,[8] as long as we could preserve a common ground. . . . I was not and I am not in agreement with Ferenczi's statements on homosexuality and with many points of his active therapy. In my opinion he puts a *too great store on complete agreement with me;* I do not. Suppose you had told me one day that you could not believe in the primordial horde and the primordial father, or thought the separation into Ego and Id to be inexpedient, do you really believe that I would not have invited you for meals or would have excluded you from my circle? It is true, you were always very reserved in taking a critical stand, *probably too much so.* And now you are shattered and offended that I refuse your *Trauma of Birth,* though you have my admission that it is never easy for me to follow a new train of thought that somehow does not go my way or to which my way has not yet led me [Taft, p. 106f.; italics mine].

If this is tyranny, it is tyranny of a very special kind.

But Rank cannot let go. One is reminded of a feature of adolescence to which Anna Freud once called attention: adolescents who complain bitterly that their parents do not recognize them as adults are quite often not content to live their own lives and let their parents go on living theirs, as adult sons and daughters would do. They are often bent on reeducating their parents, and the resistance with which *these* attempts meet in the older generation registers with them as oppression. Their mind has not yet been really emancipated from the childhood setting of a family ruled by the parents, and they visualize their own emancipation as adults not as the abolition of the whole pattern but merely as a change of place within the pattern; for

[8] A somewhat awkward rendering of what in German was obviously *Anhänger.* A better English translation would be: follower.

them, adulthood means that the role of parents has fallen to them, while the parents will be reduced to children. There are analogies to this in some of the former colonial, now independent, countries. The correspondence between Freud and Rank shows that this was the case with Rank in the disagreements following the appearance of his *Trauma of Birth*.

There is an item in this correspondence which may show those whose mind has not been closed that there is not only no basis for the allegation of authoritarianism, but that there is actually strong evidence for a unique absence in Freud of that tacit play of authority and superiority which is a universal undercurrent in the relation between different generations. Freud had told Rank of a dream of his, and Rank wrote him the same day, suggesting an interpretation of the dream:

"Dear Professor, This evening an interpretation of the witty dream you told me today has occurred to me, which is apt to be withheld from you and which, I hope, will amuse you" (Taft, p. 78).

So Rank puts himself without invitation in the position of psychoanalyzing his teacher, and we may wonder what the tyrant's answer will be. Here it is:

It is a long time since you have tried to interpret one of my dreams in such a powerful analytical way. Since then much has changed. You have grown enormously and you know so much about me...I cannot confirm everything you write...but I do not need to contradict you anywhere.

[Freud then continues by giving his associations and concludes with his interpretation: the dream, he thinks, indicates his fear lest a young man like Rank might supersede him:] The super-ego merely says to this process: "All right you old jester and boaster. This is not true at all!...you (the dreamer) are not David, you are the boasting giant Goliath, whom another one, the young David will slay." And now everything falls into place around this point that you (Rank) are the dreaded David who with his *Trauma of Birth* succeeds in depreciating my work. . . . Thus I can continue your interpretation [p. 78f.].

Where is there on record a man, sixty-seven years of age, in the evening of a life of great labor and productivity, who will accept an uninvited and apparently embarrassing interpretation of his unconscious from a young man, his disciple, not only with good grace but as a matter of course and with scientific objectivity, will applaud the young man for his insights and will freely discuss with him his own jealousies and fears?

The same picture emerges from the correspondence which Ludwig Binswanger (1956) has published. The whole lifelong relationship between these two men belies the myth of Freud's authoritarianism. Binswanger started his professional life as a disciple of Freud's but in middle life became increasingly involved with the philosophy of existentialism, until he became, and still is, the leader of the existentialist movement[9] in psychiatry. Freud, to be sure, did not follow Binswanger along this road, but Binswanger, different from Rank, did not press him to do so and did not attack Freud personally. Their relationship remained cordial to the end.

There is a moving letter, published by Binswanger, which shows that Freud, far from trying to force the younger man into the fold, expressed his gratitude to him for not having allowed their intellectual disagreement to interfere with their personal relationship:

Quite different from so many others [Freud writes], you have not allowed your intellectual development, which has more and more removed you from my sphere of influence, to interfere with our personal relations, and *you do not know how much one is touched by such delicacy* [p. 103].[10]

[9] The word comes naturally—I do not think it means that Binswanger is actually leading a political movement.

[10] Jones repeatedly pointed out that the stories of Freud's authoritarianism were myths. Fromm dismisses Jones's testimony in this matter contemptuously: "Jones is of a psychological naïveté in these assertions which ill fit a psychoanalyst. He simply overlooks the fact that Freud was intolerant to those who questioned or criticized him in the least. To people who idolized him and

That this man, of all men, should be called authoritarian, demonstrates how baseless the common belief is that widely accepted views must have some element of factual, as different from mere symbolic, truth. It was possible thirty years ago to convince the majority of a nation as highly educated as the Germans that the Jews were responsible for all their misfortunes and frustrations. It is possible to convince vast masses in Latin America, Asia, and Africa today that the United States is responsible for their poverty. So it is also possible to persuade people that Sigmund Freud was "authoritarian" and "not a man who loves."

All this, of course, is not to gainsay the fact that there may have been people who *felt* Freud to be oppressive. Perhaps Rank was one of them. He received a great deal from Freud, who provided for his higher education, started him on his career, first in applied psychoanalysis and later in analytic practice, and gave him the impetus for his creative work—perhaps more than a man can accept from another man—and it would be understandable if Rank, oppressed by this abundance, attributed to Freud's person what was inherent rather in the situation.

Enough, I believe, has been said about this subject, and it

---

never disagreed, he was kind and tolerant; just because, as I have emphasized before, Freud was so dependent on unconditional affirmation and agreement by others, he was a loving father to submissive sons, and a stern, authoritarian one to those who dared to disagree" (p. 66).

When Fromm published these lines (1959), Binswanger's report of his lifelong relationship with Freud, which survived their scientific disagreement entirely unscathed, had already been available since 1956. Since this report completely contradicts Fromm's contention that "Freud was intolerant to those who questioned or criticized him in the least," and completely corroborates Jones's testimony, which Fromm calls naïve and ill-fitting for a psychoanalyst, it is deplorable that Fromm did not mention, and deal with, the testimony adverse to his thesis.

We cannot be completely certain that Fromm knew Binswanger's book. True, he quotes from a letter published therein (p. 29) but since he does *not* give the origin of this quotation—as he otherwise always does—we do not have complete evidence that he was familiar with the book.

It may finally be mentioned that Jones was anything but a yes-man, as he is pictured by Fromm. Scientifically, he largely shared the views of Melanie Klein, and he favored her school of thought, which was certainly not in conformity with Freud's thinking. In other matters, Jones was a rather willful man, and this trait manifested itself, respect and admiration notwithstanding, in his relation to Freud, too.

might well be closed were it nor for the fact that Fromm's "most drastic example" of Freud's authoritarianism and intolerance, viz., his relation to Ferenczi, should not remain uncontested, because of the importance of this episode for a history of psychoanalysis. For years, Ferenczi had been experimenting with psychoanalytic therapeutic technique, hoping thereby to achieve what can, if at all, only be expected from deeper insight into the pathological process. The total yield of various such attempts had not been great. But toward the end of his life, Ferenczi presented the proposition that it was necessary to "spoil" the patients, i.e., to treat them tenderly like small children in distress. They had fallen sick, he argued, because of a lack of love in their childhood, and this was true not only of some but of all patients. The child had been holding out its hand for love—nonsexual love—and the adult, instead of giving it, had satisfied his own sexual urges at the expense of the child. In this way, Ferenczi returned to the pre-Freudian concept of a fundamentally asexual childhood, and to Freud's early trauma theory of the neuroses. The whole development of theoretical thought and therapeutic technique which followed Freud's realization of the fact that the stories told by patients of their sexual seduction by parents were usually untrue, the discovery of childhood sexuality and its vicissitudes, was thereby discarded.

There was nothing new about any of these ideas. To treat one's patients with tender kindness is probably the oldest psychotherapeutic device, used instinctively by every good nurse, indeed by every normal mother. Ferenczi went to considerable length in this matter; a middle-aged man may have been encouraged to sit on his lap, call him grandfather and talk to him in baby language.

But showing one's patients more than friendly interest and the serious desire to help were not considered advisable in psychoanalysis, for the simple reason that psychoanalysis is exploratory psychotherapy, and that the display of love, or any other emotional attitude toward the patient on the part of the analyst beyond what is required by civilized standards and professional obligation, will of necessity influence what kind of material will appear and offer itself for exploration. To love and to spoil one's patients may make them feel better just as the administration of an analgesic will improve the well-being of people in physical distress; but it interferes with diagnostic studies. Twenty years before Ferenczi made his suggestions, Freud had considered this possibility and dismissed it for these reasons (1912, p. 115).

But Fromm does not understand the problem for which these considerations attempt to give an answer; as usual, he castigates what he does not understand: "Freud's reaction to Ferenczi's idea that the patient needed love as a condition for his cure" is for him "one of the most drastic examples" of the dogmatism of "'official' psychoanalytic thought" (p. 107). But the issue at stake is not whether a patient "needs" love or, for that matter, drugs or electroshock, but whether these administrations are compatible with the conduct of a psychoanalysis.

There was nothing new in the theoretical position either; it was a revival of the pre-Freudian concept of an asexual childhood and of Freud's own early trauma theory.

For many of us young men who had admired and loved Ferenczi, the final phase in his development was bewildering and distressing. It was distressing to see the man to whom we had looked up as a leader in what appeared to us a less than admirable light; and when we learned, only a few months later, that Ferenczi was dying from pernicious anemia, then an incurable disease, the sorrow over his premature demise was at the same time mixed with a sense of relief at the realization that the strange occurrences of the last few months had obviously to be written off as the consequence of a severe organic disease, and therefore would not detract from the picture of the wise and inspiring leader which we had acquired earlier.

Ferenczi visited Freud in the summer of 1932 on his way to the Psychoanalytic Congress in Wiesbaden, and it was on this occasion that Freud's famous intolerance was so "drastically" displayed. Fromm has his information from Mrs. de Forest, a student of Ferenczi's, who told him what Ferenczi had told her more than twenty years previously about his visit with Freud. A court of law would not accept this kind of hearsay in evidence, and a trained historian would treat it with great caution. But let us assume that it gives a complete and accurate picture of the events. It would then indicate that Freud warned Ferenczi against dangers in his new technique, that he urged Ferenczi not to publish the paper, and that he terminated the conversation abruptly. That is all. That Freud did not try to prevent the publication is borne out by the fact that the paper was actually published by the *Zeitschrift*, in which Freud, as *Herausgeber*, held the power of decision. Nor did he try to interfere with the presentation of the paper at the Wiesbaden Congress. Who would accuse the chief of a university department or a hospital of intolerance merely because he advised his assistant against the publication of a paper which he considered embarrassing to the institution?

In order to put things into proper perspective, it is also necessary to add that repeated later references to Ferenczi's latest position, both in Freud's writings and in his conversation, while clearly stating his disagreement, were always cordial and gave warm recognition to Ferenczi's contributions and personality.

I have discussed some parts of Fromm's book at considerable length. It would fill as much space again merely to list all the various inaccuracies and arbitrary interpretations that can be found in this brief volume. I should only like to mention two examples to show the kind of reasoning through which Fromm arrives at his conclusions.

Fromm refers to the scene in which Freud, at the age of seven, was reprimanded by his father for having urinated in the parental bedroom in his parents' presence, and reports the father's remark, "That boy will never amount to anything." He thereupon quotes Freud: "This must have been a terrible affront to my ambition, for allusions to this scene occur again and again in my dreams and are constantly coupled with enumerations of my accomplishments and successes, as if I wanted to say: 'You see I have amounted to something after all'" (p. 56).

On this Fromm comments as follows: "This explanation given by Freud that the father's remark was the *cause* of his ambition is an error which one can find frequently in orthodox analytic interpretations" (p. 56). It is impossible to see where Fromm could have got the idea that Freud suggested this "explanation." Freud neither said nor implied that he considered his father's remark to be the cause of his ambition; on the contrary, by calling this remark "a terrible affront to my ambition" he made it clear that he thought that his ambition *predated* his father's remark; for how could there be an affront to something not yet in existence? In this case Fromm demolishes the proverbial bogeyman of his own making.

Furthermore, Fromm quotes from a letter that Freud wrote to his friend, Fliess, in January, 1900: "The new century—*the most interesting thing about which for us is, I dare say, that it contains the date of our death—.*" For Fromm, this proves that Freud was egocentric and could not love: "Here again we find the same egocentric concern with his own death and none of the feeling of universality and solidarity" (p. 37).

There is no reason why awareness of the finiteness of human existence—*memento mori*—should indicate egocentricity and inability to love, unless it is assumed that love means total abandonment of all self-concern, all the time, which would be a completely unrealistic expectation.

A selection of Freud's letters ranging from 1873 to 1939 that was recently published (E. Freud, 1960) will give the unprejudiced a picture of Freud as he really was—of the breadth of his culture, his enthusiasm, the depth of his humanity, the originality of his thinking and, as the years rolled on, his mellowness. Since Freud is persistently pictured by Fromm as "lacking in emotional warmth" and "egocentric," I should like to quote a few lines from Freud's correspondence. In all the world's literature I know of no more moving expression of sympathy to a bereft one than the words which Freud wrote to Binswanger upon the death of the latter's son:

Although we know that after such a loss the acute state of mourning will subside, we also know we shall remain inconsolable and will never find a substitute. No matter what may fill the gap, even if it be filled completely, it nevertheless remains something else. And actually this is how it should be. It is the only way of perpetuating that love which we do not want to relinquish [E. Freud, p. 386].

Gravely distorted though Fromm's picture of Freud is, it is still possible, as in a caricature, to recognize the sitter. The same can hardly be said of the picture of Freud and psychoanalysis found in a book, *The Freudian Ethic* (1959), by Richard LaPiere, a professor of sociology at Stanford University.

LaPiere's first thesis is that something is very wrong with contemporary America, that the nation is in a serious moral predicament. What has made this country and has made it strong was the "Protestant Ethic," in the sense of Max Weber's famous essay: initiative, devotion to hard work, self-reliance, a strong sense of responsibility. LaPiere sees these virtues disappearing; he sees a new generation of Americans, wont to rely on others and to have things done for them.

LaPiere is, of course, not the first to feel this country has gone soft. Many others have sounded the clarion call. Whether or not their diagnosis is correct is very difficult to judge. In a very large country and in a free and hence very diversified society, it is possible to give numerous examples that seem to bear out the thesis; it is equally possible to give numerous examples that seem to contradict it. It is one of the most difficult things to judge the moral fibre of a large nation; individual data can often be interpreted in different ways, the range of individual attitudes is enormous, and attitudes are not stable but depend to a great extent on external circumstances, such as the nature, clarity, and degree of the challenge and the quality of leadership. When the Oxford students, in 1935, swore that they would never, under any circumstances, fight for king and country, many people took it as a sign of the decay of British morale. It was disastrous that the leaders of Germany shared this interpretation. Yet, only five years later, these same youths manned the fighter planes of the R.A.F. and thwarted Hitler's ambitions at the price of their physical extinction—the modern parallel to the 300 of Thermopylae.

Happily, it is not the task of this review to evaluate the soundness of LaPiere's diagnosis of the nation's morale. But it can be said *prima facie* that the complaint about the loss of ancestral virtues is neither new nor specifically American, that it predates by far the "Protestant Ethic," and that the warning has been heard since the early days of recorded history. Most self-respecting Roman writers were what Horace called *laudatores temporis acti*. Horace himself was no mean representative of the species; he wrote: "The age of the parents, worse than that of the grandparents, bore us who are more worthless than they were and who are about to bring forth an offspring even more corrupt."

These lines were written at the time of Augustus—ever since considered the golden age of Rome. Lest anyone think that, since Rome did eventually fall, Horace's diagnosis may have been a remarkable example of acumen and foresight, let us remember that at the time of Horace the Roman Empire had still five centuries to go in the West and fifteen in the East. Moreover, we can go further back to, say, Homer, and listen to old Nestor saying that the heroes of the Trojan war could not stand comparison with the heroes of his youth (*Iliad*, 1:260f).

So common is the view of progressive degeneration that various thinkers have seen in it a general characteristic of advancing civilization (i.e., advancing in the sense of increasing control by man over his environment): in this view, civilization brings about its own undoing through its very consummation, by means of the ease and security of life which it achieves. The young no longer go through the hardships and are no longer confronted with the challenges deemed necessary to develop the qualities of toughness and endurance which brought the civilization into being in the first place, and which are needed to maintain it. This is one of the basic points of the many cyclic theories of history which proclaim an intrinsic necessity of the rise and fall of civilizations. In essence, it is the philosophy behind the old saying that it takes three generations from shirt sleeves to shirt sleeves.

It is a fundamental element, e.g., in the theory of history of the great medieval Moslem historian, Ibn Khaldun (1332-1406) who thought that "Bedouins are more disposed to courage than sedentary people" because "the reliance of sedentary people upon laws destroys their fortitude and power of resistance" (Muqaddimah, 2:5/6). But, unlike LaPiere and other contemporary writers who think along similar lines and seek the cause for the loss of "fortitude" in modern welfare measures, Ibn Khaldun saw clearly that *civilization as such*, i.e., the *existence of a legal order* as such, offers protection to the weaker ones and thereby diminishes the pressures under which the sterner habits of self-preservation develop.

Consequently, for the classical philosophers of a cyclic theory of history like Ibn Khaldun, the disaster of civilizations has the quality of a Greek tragedy; it is the inescapable consequence of characteristics which are only the reverse side of the very virtues of civilization. But this is not the case in LaPiere's picture. For him, America's real or alleged moral disease is due not to forces intrinsic in progress but rather to an extraneous factor, an invasion by a germ of spiritual decay. The decline of America's moral stamina is due to what LaPiere calls the "Freudian ethic," viz., an ethic of universal irresponsibility alleged to have been taught by Sigmund Freud. Here is what LaPiere thinks of psychoanalysis:

"The psychoanalyst...strives to relieve the patient of all responsibility for his difficulties and to shift it to society in the person of the patient's mother, father, sibling, husband, wife, son, or daughter, or all of these together" (p. 69). To this shifting of the blame he attributes what therapeutic relief there may be in psychoanalysis.

"Freudian doctrine" is, in LaPiere's view, "a doctrine of social irresponsibility and personal despair" (p. 53). What the author calls "Freudian ethic" is defined in the words: "absence of strong social motivations (the inescapable urges of the libido are, of course, antisocial drives), lack of constraining or inhibiting social principles, lack of supernaturalistic or other fixed faiths (except, of course, the Freudian version of the self), lack of set goals, lack of any rigorous system of personal-social values and sentiments, and complete absence of any sense of obligation toward others" (p. 64).

The new ethic, according to LaPiere, demands that man be taken care of by society: "This new ethic presupposes that man is by inherent nature weak, uncertain, and incapable of self-reliance and that he must, therefore, be provided by society with the security that is his greatest need.[11] Since the most outstanding and most popular proponent of this view of man has been Sigmund Freud, the newly emerging ethic has been designated by his name" (p. 285). It is also antagonistic to society: "Freud, like his patients, believed that they were victims of social circumstances; and, like them, he was in all respects antagonistic toward society" (p. 53).

LaPiere's picture of contemporary history finally assumes

[11] At this point one wonders whether LaPiere did not get his picture of Freud confused with his picture of Franklin Roosevelt.

apocalyptic dimensions; once again, there is a doctrine of history as the battlefield of the forces of light and darkness, the struggle between Ormuzd and Ahriman, incarnated respectively in the "Protestant Ethic" and the "Freudian Ethic." The formal setting is the same as in previous devil theories of history, but the actors have changed; the evil is no longer represented by the Jews, Jesuits, Freemasons or capitalists, but by the ethic of irresponsibility said to have been proposed by, of all people, Sigmund Freud.

Those with even the most modest knowledge of psychoanalysis may wonder how anybody could get this impression of psychoanalysis. It is conceivable that because Freud deals in his works with many aspects of human behavior, including those we consider evil, and does so, as a rule, without emphasizing his condemnation of the latter and without moral exhortations, some may have formed the idea that he approved of them. However, Freud's apparent detachment is due, first, to the simple fact that he was engaged in scientific work, and felt—correctly, I submit—that moral exhortations and condemnations have no place in a scientific treatise; in his own words: "For the purpose of an investigation...one may perhaps be allowed to wear a mask of assumed detachment" (1933a, p. 213). Besides, he took it for granted that he addressed an audience of responsible people, and was allergic to the self-righteousness and hypocrisy of most of this kind of preaching. He subscribed, as he wrote to J. J. Putnam, to "Th. Vischer's excellent maxim: '*Das Moralische versteht sich immer von selbst*'" (E. Freud, p. 308).[12]

But Freud's allegiance to the principles of civilized morality is immanent in every page he ever wrote; when the context requires it, he may become quite articulate, e.g., when he says this about the educability of man:

Probably a certain percentage of mankind (owing to a pathological disposition or an excess of instinctual strength) will always remain asocial; but if it were feasible merely to reduce the majority that is hostile towards civilization to-day into a minority, a great deal would

---

[12] The above quotation from Th. Vischer is rendered there as follows: "What is moral is self-evident." Actually, the meaning of the phrase is not merely cognitive but rather like this: Morality must be taken for granted.

have been accomplished—perhaps all that *can* be accomplished [1927a, p. 9].

How can anybody think that the man who wrote these lines preached a "doctrine of social irresponsibility and personal despair," of a "complete absence of any sense of obligation toward others?"

Freud's sense of personal responsibility did, in fact, go beyond the Protestant Ethic; let us look at what Freud said about moral responsibility *for one's dreams:*

> *Obviously one must hold oneself responsible for the evil impulses of one's dreams. What else is one to do with them?* Unless the content of the dream (rightly understood) is inspired by alien spirits, it is a *part of my own being.* If I seek to classify the impulses that are present in me according to social standards into good and bad, I must assume responsibility for both sorts; and if, in defence, I say that what is unknown, unconscious and repressed in me is not my 'ego,' *then I shall not be basing my position upon psycho-analysis,* I shall not have accepted its conclusions—and I shall perhaps be taught better by the criticisms of my fellow-men, by the disturbances in my actions and the confusion of my feelings. I shall perhaps learn that what I am disavowing not only 'is' in me but 'acts' out of me as well [1925a, p. 133; italics mine].

It is difficult to conceive of a clearer or more complete refutation of the views which LaPiere attributes to Freud. According to Freud, one is morally responsible even for mere wishes *expressed only in dreams,* and those who think otherwise have not based their position upon psychoanalysis; that one could doubt responsibility for one's actions had obviously not occurred to Freud.[13] *This* is the Freudian ethic, viz., the ethic of Sigmund Freud.

---

[13] Behind this discussion is the ancient question of determinism and its relation to responsibility—an age-old problem of philosophical speculation. I have discussed the position in this question which is implicit in classical psychoanalysis in Ch. 17.

It is worth noting that in this matter of responsibility for one's dreams, the ethic of Sigmund Freud goes beyond the view of St. Augustine. This Church father and moralist, who was also a man of great psychological insight, speaks of our "recapturing the peace of conscience" if, after having succumbed to sinful urges in a dream, we discover upon awakening, much to our relief, that we had not actually carried out *quod tamen in nobis quoquo modo factum esse doleamus*—what we yet deplore as something that had *somehow happened in us* (*Confessiones*, 10:30). Augustine's expression—"something that had somehow happened in us"—is much weaker than Freud's straightforward statement: "it is a part of my own being."

There is a humorous Latin expression used to characterize false etymologies: *lucus a non lucendo*, it is called a meadow (*lucus*) because it does not shine (*non lucet*). "Freudian ethic," apparently, is such a *lucus a non lucendo;* it is called Freudian ethic because it has no similarity with the ethic of Freud.

All this is not to say that the trends which LaPiere describes do not exist in the world of today. There is a tendency to favor the weak—the less gifted at the expense of the gifted, the lazy at the expense of the industrious, the wasters at the expense of the thrifty, and the irresponsible at the expense of the responsible. In criminology there is a tendency to exonerate the lawbreaker under all circumstances and to blame his behavior on "society," i.e., on the rest of the citizens who did not break the laws. Many a psychiatrist is opposed to both punishment and deterrence in dealing with the lawbreaker and would allow only for rehabilitation, preferably through psychiatric treatment. This would, in effect, amount to providing at public cost what other, inoffensive, members of the community can only have at considerable sacrifice to themselves.[14] Or, many child psychiatrists claim that all mental and emotional illnesses of children are due to culpable acts of commission or omission on the part of the parents, according to the saying: there are no problem children, only problem parents.

It is all part of a tendency to take all pressure off the weak

---

[14] Some years ago, I heard of a child in a "progressive" school who, when asked what happened in his school to a child who had been "bad," replied: "He gets to sit on the teacher's lap."

and inferior and thereby, in effect, lay ever greater burdens on the shoulders of the gifted and responsible, on the theory that the former are weak and therefore in need of support, while the latter are strong and therefore capable of carrying, and duty-bound to carry, the load of humanity. This tendency is far less outspoken on the domestic scene than it is on the international one, among the so-called underdeveloped nations.

This emotional climate is probably a reaction to the conditions that prevailed at earlier times. Then the strong had the world at their feet and the weak were left to get along as best they could or to perish; and the lawbreaker found no mercy. But the laudable compassion for the weak and the humble has now often gone to the opposite extreme. "Human beings," as Sir Richard Livingstone (1959) put it, "rarely walk in the center of the road; they reel drunkenly from the ditch on one side to the ditch on the other."

What else may have contributed to this modern trend is a question worthy of the best efforts of serious social scientists. M. Polanyi (1960) speaks of "moral passions overreaching themselves" (p. 1). Perhaps, one of their roots are the teachings of Scripture, taken literally, not moderated by Church and tradition, and deprived through secularization of any supranatural meaning.

Be this as it may, the process has little to do with psychoanalysis. The movement was well under way before Freud was born. J. L. Talmon, the prominent historian of ideas, places the birth of the idea that "frustration is the source of all evil" in the middle of the 18th century. He has devoted himself to the study of the history and the consequences of this belief; so far, two sizable volumes have appeared without his having reached the year of Sigmund Freud's birth.

Freudian thought itself offers no comfort to this philosophy. It considers it a half-truth which, for itself alone, is misleading. It maintains that frustration can do much harm to an immature organism if it overtaxes its carrying capacity at the time, and so may lead to lasting regressions or to an irrevocable withering of the drive; or if it comes as sudden shock, leading to traumatic neurosis. On the other hand, it also maintains that without frustration there is no development of frustration tolerance just as organisms reared under sterile conditions acquire no immunity. Hence, the psychoanalytic advice to education is not to try to protect the child against frustration but rather to time and dose it correctly, i.e., as I formulated it on another occasion, "to find for each situation the proper balance between satisfaction and frustration, in the light of the general principle that we have to search for the optimal mixture between two equally important but partly conflicting ingredients of healthy development, viz., love and discipline" (1960a, p. 254).

The idea that psychoanalysis is destructive of moral values is, of course, an old one. It is based on the most universal and most stubborn of all misunderstandings of psychoanalysis, viz., the misunderstanding of the concept of repression. The repression of an impulse means that the impulse has become unconscious without thereby losing its power to influence psychic activities; undoing repression means to bring the impulse back to consciousness where its further destiny is decided by a contest of strength between the impulse and other tendencies which are active in the person. Elementary though this is for psychoanalysts, it is little understood outside the psychoanalytic group. There, it is widely believed that repression refers to the obstacles, external or moral, that stand in the way of gratification of an impulse, and that the undoing of repression therefore means the removal of these obstacles and, consequently, the free expression of impulses in action. All this has been explained in psychoanalytic writings innumerable times, but the message does not carry.

There is also the ambiguity of the word "understanding." Psychoanalysis suggests that we should try to understand human affairs and their conditioning before passing judgment on them and before responding to them. But "to understand" means in this context strictly: to grasp the nature, significance, and causes of something; it does not imply what many people seem to take for granted: to exonerate, to condone, and to sympathize with it. Our valuation of human conduct, and our way of dealing with it, will not remain unaffected by such a serious effort at understanding it, but the change does not necessarily, nor even most frequently, go in the direction that is indicated by the popular saying: *tout comprendre c'est tout pardonner.*[15]

Despite its dissociation from facts—or, perhaps, because of it—LaPiere's doctrine has some of the ingredients of mass appeal. The drawing in stark contrasts of black and white, the view of human events as a struggle between light and darkness, with the former represented by ancestral virtues and the latter by an intruding alien creed; and the picture of the antagonist as at once immeasurably dangerous and yet basically insignificant and easily reduced to impotence once it has been recognized—all this is what people like to believe. So we read in a recent article about the alleged aimlessness of American life by Vice-Admiral Hyman G. Rickover, the prominent naval engineer and strategist, in a magazine of mass circulation, the *Saturday Evening Post:* "The so-called 'Freudian ethic' has led us astray by encouraging us to blame our personal inadequacies on 'society.'" So-called by whom? I have not met this expression except in LaPiere's book—Admiral Rickover seems to have taken his clue from LaPiere.

If we look at both books together, it appears that they attack Freud and psychoanalysis from opposite sides, with opposite arguments. Fromm criticizes Freud because, as he sees it, the latter was deeply rooted in 19th-century bourgeois culture—which to Fromm is something evil and contemptible—and because his psychology appears to Fromm to be an apology of this culture. LaPiere condemns Freud because, as he sees it, Freud has undermined this very culture which he finds very valuable. Fromm sees in Freud an inhibited Victorian, a Puritan, incapable of enjoying himself; LaPiere sees him as subversive of the "Protestant Ethic" and as the sponsor of irresponsible self-seeking and hedonism. Fromm thinks that psychoanalysis was eagerly embraced by people who did not want to make the serious effort of "criticism of their own society and its crippling effects upon man." LaPiere thinks that psychoanalysis preaches the doctrine that "society" is responsible for all frustrations.

[15] There is a widespread view that, in a criminal trial, the psychiatric expert will always tend to exonerate the defendant and so support the efforts of the counsel for the defense. The actual impact of psychoanalytic consideration of questions of criminal responsibility is discussed in Ch. 29.

The two books are therefore likely to find their major resonance in different quarters: Fromm's ideas will delight what Rose Macaulay called the not-so-very intelligentsia; LaPiere's ideas will appeal to people with a fundamentalist bent of mind.

But that does not mean that there could not appear, one of these days, another book that combines the arguments of Fromm with the arguments of LaPiere, without any awareness of the fact that they contradict each other. If such a book should appear, this much is predictable: it will be respectfully reviewed by papers and intellectual magazines and quoted by representative men in all walks of life.

CHAPTER 19

Inhibitions, Symptoms, and Anxiety: Forty Years Later

(1967)

The Equality of Ego and Id and the Beginnings of Psychoanalytic Ego Psychology

In the life of individuals as well as of groups or nations, events, onesidedly conceived even while they occur, immediately become subject to a process of editing and distorting in order to make them better conform to one's expectations and preferences. Thus, man's consciousness of the past is largely a collection of myths, with a nucleus of truth embedded in a cake of fantasy.

The history of psychoanalysis as it is widely seen today is no exception to this rule: the way things are now supposed to have been must appear distorted to those who have lived through parts of it. Of course, those of us who are survivors of an earlier period must be aware of the fact that our memory is not immune to the universal tendency of mythmaking and of seeing the past in the light of what has materialized later, and colored our wishes; we must beware of this temptation while giving our testimony.

It is now widely believed that in Freud's lifetime psychoanalysis was for all practical purposes a drive psychology, a psychology of the id, and that balance was restored later, in the

---

Reprinted from the *Psychoanalytic Quarterly*, 36:11-36, 1967. In the original publication, the author reprinted his earlier review of Freud's book. This part is omitted here because it appears in full in Ch. 4 of this volume.

1940s and 1950s, through the development of the new ego psychology. This, to my mind, is a myth; as myths do, it contains an element of truth under a thick crust of error. Its main disadvantage is that it blocks understanding of what actually happened, and so blocks the view to the underlying problems which, however unrecognized, are still with us.

As far as acknowledging ego and id as equal partners in psychic life in general and in the etiology of the neuroses in particular is concerned, it seems to me that we must distinguish between the level of clinical discourse, i.e., of conceptualization for practical purposes, and the level of ultimate, general theory. On the practical, clinical level, the recognition of this equality is a great deal older; on the theoretical level, the problem is as open today as it ever was.

On the clinical level, Lou Andreas-Salomé noted in her diary on April 6, 1913 that in a number of points—including, for instance, the view of neurosis as a disturbance of both "ego instinct" and "sexual instinct"—the "ego factor" has become "more equal" to the sexual factor (Leavy, 1964, p. 131f.) The development which then began continued and reached in *Inhibitions, Symptoms and Anxiety* the point of full consummation and clear formulation:

Just as the ego controls the path to action in regard to the external world, so it controls access to consciousness. In repression it exercises its power in both directions, acting in the one manner upon the instinctual impulse itself and in the other upon the [psychical] representative of that impulse. At this point it is relevant to ask how I can reconcile this acknowledgement of the might of the ego with the description of its position which I gave in *The Ego and the Id*. In that book I drew a picture of its dependent relationship to the id and to the superego and revealed how powerless and apprehensive it was in regard to both and with what an effort it maintained its show of superiority over them. This view has been widely echoed in psycho-analytic literature. Many writers have laid much stress on the weakness of the ego in relation to the id and of our rational elements in the

face of the daemonic forces within us; and they display
a strong tendency to make what I have said into a cor-
ner-stone of a psycho-analytic *Weltanschauung.* Yet
surely the psycho-analyst, with his knowledge of the
way in which repression works, should, of all people, be
restrained from adopting such an extreme and one-sided
view [p. 95].

These words are followed by the famous warning against the
fabrication of *Weltanschauungen,* described as protections
against anxiety without any cognitive value: "The benighted
traveller may sing aloud in the dark to decry his own fears; but,
for all that, he does not see an inch farther beyond his nose."
Thus, the ego was well recognized in the mid-20s as an equal
partner in the adventure of life—on the clinical level of discourse
at any rate. Whether it can be recognized as an equally
fundamental element in a general theory of the mind, however,
is a different question because the "ego" is a concept of a
different kind from, say, "instinct," "drive," or "id." A drive is a
force like, say, gravity; it pushes things in a particular direction
with a certain intensity. It is what the medieval philosophers
called a *vis a tergo,* a force pushing from behind. But the ego can
be so described only on the lowest level of its activities, viz., that
of reflex action; in its higher operations it is a *problem-solving
agent* and thus a *teleological* concept. It explains psychic
activities in terms of the purposes they serve. It is a close relative
of Aristotle's *entelechy,* the preexisting form which guides the
development of plant or animal according to nature; or a relative of the medieval physician's *vis medicatrix naturae,* the
healing power of nature.

In the first case, we try to explain behavior in terms of
necessary and sufficient conditions (the tire became flat *because*
it ran over a nail; the cells became necrotic *because* of anoxia,
etc.). In the second case, events are explained in terms of their
ends (we have our children vaccinated *in order to* secure them
against certain infectious diseases, etc.).

Seneca saw the difference between the Romans and the
Etruscans in that the former thought causally, the latter teleologically: *Nos putamus quia nubes collisae sunt fulmina emitti;*

ipsi existimant nubes collidi ut fulmina emittant. (We believe that lightning is emitted because clouds have collided; they think that clouds collide in order to emit lightning.)

That the ego is, in fact, largely a teleological concept may be seen from Freud's extensive definition in his last comprehensive treatise on psychoanalysis, "An Outline of Psychoanalysis," written thirteen years after *Inhibitions, Symptoms and Anxiety.*

Here are the principal characteristics of the ego. In consequence of the pre-established connection between sense perception and muscular action, the ego has voluntary movement at its command. It has the task of self-preservation. As regards *external* events, it performs that task by becoming aware of stimuli, by storing up experiences about them (in the memory), by avoiding excessively strong stimuli (through flight), by dealing with moderate stimuli (through adaptation) and finally by learning to bring about expedient changes in the external world to its own advantage (through activity). As regards *internal* events, in relation to the id, it performs that task, by gaining control over the demands of the instincts, by deciding whether they are to be allowed satisfaction, by postponing that satisfaction to times and circumstances favorable in the external world or by suppressing their excitations entirely. It is guided in its activity by consideration of the tensions produced by stimuli, whether these tensions are present in it or introduced into it. The raising of these tensions is in general felt as *unpleasure,* and their lowering as *pleasure.* It is probable, however, that what is felt as pleasure or unpleasure is not the *absolute* height of this tension but something in the rhythm of the changes in them. The ego strives after pleasure and seeks to avoid unpleasure. An increase in unpleasure that is expected and foreseen is met by a *signal of anxiety;* the occasion of such an increase, whether it threatens from without or within, is known as a *danger.* From time to time the ego gives up its connection with the external world and withdraws

into the state of sleep, in which it makes far-reaching
changes in its organization. It is to be inferred from the
state of sleep that this organization consists in a particular distribution of mental energy [1940, p. 145f.].

The goal-directed expressions abound in this text: "The ego
has...*at its command*...it has the *task* of...it *performs* that
task...by gaining *control*...by *deciding*...by *postponing*...it
is guided by *consideration*...." Causal explanations in terms of
tensions and pressures still turn up but they appear to be subordinated to the ego rather than determining it: ("The ego is
guided in its activity by *consideration* of the tensions produced
by stimuli. . . ."); energetic considerations appear in the description of sleep ("this organization consists in a particular distribution of mental energy") but this new distribution does not
appear to be the cause of sleep but rather the consequence or the
implication of an act of the ego ("the ego gives up the connection
with the external world and withdraws into a state of sleep...").
Only in the middle part of the quotation, dealing with pleasure
and unpleasure as functions of tension, is the treatment causal
(or mechanistic, if one prefers).

Teleological concepts may be quite illuminating on the
clinical level, but the question is whether they are satisfactory as
ultimate, irreducible constructs.

It is quite permissible for a physician at the sickbed to say
that his patient has a strong "will to live," has great recuperative
powers, and to base his prognosis on impressions such as these.
But "will to live" or "recuperative power" are not accepted in
physiology as ultimate, irreducible categories; they are to be
reduced to physiochemical processes.

In the decades preceding the First World War, the teleological approach was widely practiced in the historical disciplines
(or *Geisteswissenschaften* in the German style) but was thoroughly discredited in the sciences of nature. Characteristic for
the view of the time is the following passage from the Presidential Address of Dr. William H. Welch before the Congress of
American Physicians and Surgeons (1897): "The teleological
concept of a useful purpose in no case affords an explanation of
the mechanism of an adaptive process."

This was certainly Freud's view in earlier times. He always

tried to find explanations in terms of forces, tensions, conditioning by past experience, and the like. It is characteristic that in earlier times he speaks less of the "ego" than of *"ego instincts"* —a term suggestive of forces, vectors. Basically, it has probably always remained his view though, as the above-quoted passage from "An Outline of Psychoanalysis" shows, he grew progressively more tolerant of teleological concepts in later years.

Freud's approach has been severely criticized by Alfred Adler who claimed, in the trail of the ideas of Dilthey, Windelband, and Rickert, then dominant in German academic circles, that psychic life cannot be "explained" in terms of general laws but can only be "understood" in terms of purposes.

In the beginning of the century, the climate of opinion began to change and tolerance toward teleological conceptualization began to grow in some quarters. One of the first symptoms of the change was the appearance of the school of *Denkpsychologie* in Germany early in the century (Külpe, Ach, Bühler, Selz). The earlier school of association psychology (Wundt) had treated individual ideas as the atoms of mental life and saw them connected by laws of association which determined their sequence. The new school saw the process of thinking determined not by mechanical links between its elements but by its aim; it dealt with goal-directed behavior, and Selz's monumental work on the processes of organized thought was a study of problem solving.

Strange as it may sound, American behaviorism is also a symptom of growing permissiveness toward teleological concepts, though this fact is characteristically hidden behind a deliberately materialistic, technological language. "Behavior" is not really a mechanistic concept; an observer unaware of purposes and unsuspecting of their existence would only notice changes in the spatial distribution of matter. To speak of flight or fight or mating behavior means seeing one set of such changes of matter as meaningfully integrated by an implicit purpose.

Freud remained faithful to the imperative of analyzing—or trying to analyze—goal-directed behavior in terms of conditioning by antecedents; he tried to find the "mechanism" of which Welch spoke. *Inhibitions, Symptoms and Anxiety* offers a clear example of this tendency. After having stated that the ego gives an *Angstsignal,* an anxiety signal, which brings about the adaptive response, he searched for its mechanism and found it in the following process: the ego *anticipates* future events and samples the unpleasure of a future catastrophe in small doses—the anxiety signal—which then, through the pleasure-pain principle, sets the avoidance reaction into motion; this would be the "mechanism" of the adaptive response.

The question is open, of course, whether the process is thereby effectively reduced to mechanical terms because the implicit ability of the ego to anticipate still contains the whole secret: how does the ego do the anticipating? The same difficulty appears in the physiology of the reaction to danger: one has understood much about the chain from the pituitary gland to the adrenal gland and the release of hormones which put various organs into a condition of readiness, but it remains unexplained how the pituitary recognizes danger in the first place.

Be that as it may—the tendency toward finding the mechanism of a meaningful process, toward understanding "how it works," is unmistakable, in both cases.

Once again, the question before us is: is a phenomenon sufficiently explained by showing that it serves a purpose? Is, for instance, the appearance of milk in the young mother's breast after delivery satisfactorily explained by the fact that it serves the needs of the infant? Is the appearance of sublimations in a situation of instinctual frustration sufficiently explained by attributing it to an "ego function"? Perhaps necessity is the mother of invention, but does it not have a father, too?

Hume said that explanation is a place where the mind comes to rest. Does our mind come to rest when we learn that what happened has served a purpose?

It all depends on what kinds of insight we are after. If science is viewed in the way the ancients saw it, viz., as a contemplative understanding of the cosmos and as part of wisdom, then our understanding of phenomena in terms of their purposes, i.e., as part of a design, may be quite satisfactory; learning how well the female body prepares for the business of motherhood may give us a glimpse into an intricate design of nature—of "that unconscious omniscience which we call nature" (Lorenz, 1952, p. 126)—and so fill us with awe or with confidence.

But post-Galilean science does not approach nature in a spirit of contemplation and with a readiness to admire and to worship but rather as a conquering master; it wants to manipulate nature or at least to predict it; and explanations in terms of purpose have little predictive value. They would have predictive value if all organisms were always able to realize their purposes; in that case, knowledge of purpose would mean knowledge of behavior. But things are not that way; sometimes we can realize our purposes, sometimes we cannot. The female body produces milk when it needs it for the sustenance of its offspring, but in countless other instances we lack similar abilities. For a man trapped by, say, wild animals it would be very useful to have wings grow out instantaneously from his body so that he could take off in the air; but that does not happen.[1] If it did, there would undoubtedly be some who would "explain" it in terms of an ego function. These explanations bring to mind the remark of Mephistopheles about teleological explanations in his interview with the freshman student:

> *Encheiresis naturae* the chemists baptize it,
> Mock themselves and do not realize it.
> [Goethe, *Faust*].

Explanations in terms of purpose have predictive value only if we know the conditions under which the organism can fulfill this purpose and, in the case of alternate roads to fulfillment, the conditions under which one road is taken rather than another. But if we know these conditions—for instance, if we know what kind of inherited neurological patterns and/or what kind of postnatal experiences bring about a particular kind of ego—the whole concept of purpose becomes dispensable because

---

[1] In recent times, teleological explanations have come back under the cover of Darwinian evolution which is an attempt to explain mechanistically the appearance of functional design. It is not directly argued that something exists because it fulfills a function, but it is said that what exists is the result of selective survival of random mutations, i.e., among countless structures emerging haphazardly, only those which fulfilled a function have survived; in effect it amounts to the same. The difficulty with this kind of explanation is the same as with direct teleological explanations, viz., that adaptive changes are taking place in some cases—as, for instance, the development of resistant strains among microorganisms long exposed to antimicrobial drugs—but do not take place in others.

we can then directly correlate the resulting action with the determining conditions.

Thus, if we are content to contemplate, to admire or to worship, teleological explanations are quite satisfactory and the mind comes to rest; but if we want to influence the course of events, we must search for the "mechanism" which can give us an entry wedge for our intervention.

This was essentially the issue behind the 19th-century dispute between mechanists and vitalists. The problem is probably ultimately insoluble. On the one hand it is probably true that life, and particularly the higher forms of life, cannot be *completely* explained in terms of laws similar to those of classical physics; that there is an area of creative innovation and that life will therefore never be completely predictable. But it is also true that patterns applying to these very processes can still be found, though they do not exhaust them; hence, as long as our attitude to nature is active and interventionist rather than passive and contemplative, we must continuously seek for new regularities which permit predictions. The universal lawfulness of nature in the sense of Laplace may not be our metaphysical position; it must still remain our practical guide as researchers.

"O Lord," said St. Augustine, "give me chastity but do not give it to me as yet"; we may say in a similar vein that we will acknowledge the limits of our power *but not yet.*

Thus Freud's hesitation to admit the "ego" as an equal to the drives, not only on the level of clinical theory but also as one of the fundamental facts of nature, reflects his reluctance to accept teleological explanations as the last word; it reflects the ethos of modern science. It can be criticized *on that level* by those who are either prepared to challenge the whole modern approach to nature—the exclusive alloplastic orientation, the constant striving for domination—or are willing to resign themselves to definite limits of predictability and accessibility to influence in matters of life; but within the orientation of modern science, Freud's hesitation is justified.

So much about the equality of id and ego. A word may also be said about their delineation.

The model of the psychic personality as currently used seems to me to be more schematic than the model which emerges from the pages of Freud. We are wont to think of ego and id as separate agencies or structures, clearly differentiated from one another. With Freud, the boundaries appear to be more fluid— "the ego is not sharply separated from the id; its lower portion merges into it" (1923b, p. 24)—and there is a constant traffic or migration back and forth. In the words of my old review, there is "on the one hand a descent into the id by way of automatization, on the other hand, an ascent into the regions governed by the ego by way of *play* . . . the emergence of psychic phenomena into the ego and thus out of compulsion into freedom." Ego becomes id, id may become ego. This double process of freezing what had been liquid and of liquifying what had been frozen is an aspect in which Freud's vision seems to me to be truer to life than the currently more common form of the model.

Anxiety

The main point of the work was, of course, the revision of the theory of anxiety. An American edition has even changed the title into *The Problem of Anxiety* in order to make it conform to this fact.

The revision is widely known yet often misunderstood. Kardiner, Karush, and Ovesey (1959), for instance, state that the book "re-established the common-sense position that anxiety was a reaction to danger." What is a common-sense position is that *Realangst*, or realistic fear, is a reaction to danger; but that was never questioned. In his *Introductory Lectures* (1916-17), Freud spoke of "the fact . . . that realistic anxiety in the face of a danger seems to be a manifestation of the self-preservative instinct—which, after all, can scarcely be disputed" (p. 430). There was never any question that the concern of a man who undergoes a biopsy of a suspicious growth, or who travels a road made hazardous by guerilla attacks, is a reaction to danger, at least as long as it seems to be in reasonable proportion to the actual risks and does not become the source of secret pleasure.

The revision of the theory of anxiety did not deal with realistic fear at all but only with neurotic anxiety, i.e., with anxiety in situations in which average people can either detect no danger at all or no danger great enough to justify the intensity of the worry. The person who is afraid of dogs, the adult woman who is afraid to walk down Park Avenue or Regent Street in broad daylight, during the hours of heavy traffic, or the healthy young man who lives in constant terror lest he may come down with, or may already suffer from, a fatal disease, are cases in point; we then speak of neurotic anxiety because of its intensity, its refractoriness to ordinary explanations of fact and probability, and its omnipresence.

It was with reference to neurotic anxiety only that the famous shift of view has taken place. In the case of the agoraphobic woman, for instance, who is likely to harbor rape fantasies, one would have assumed, according to the older theory, that her frustrated sexual desires had been transformed into anxiety, while the new viewpoint holds that she is *afraid* of her sexual desires and that this fear, always present, becomes greatly intensified in situations of opportunity and, hence, of temptation. In short, neurotic anxiety, i.e., anxiety without, or without sufficient, danger, is now seen as basically similar to realistic fear, i.e., as a reaction to danger, albeit an *inner* one.

It is not too much to say that this revision has greatly altered and enriched psychoanalytic treatment; of all the later additions to the original theory conceived at the turn of the century—additions which include narcissism, repetition compulsion, an instinct of aggression, and unconscious guilt feelings—it is perhaps the most important one. For while hitherto the analyst's intention was exclusively geared to the vicissitudes of the libido, the analyst was now alerted to look for the specific dangers and pitfalls between which the ship of life, propelled by the drives, is steering its course. It is only after this innovation that a complete theory of the personality becomes possible.

The new view has been universally accepted among analysts and has long become an integral part both of theory and practice of psychoanalysis. We find it difficult to imagine that it could ever have been different.

But there is more to Freud's discussion of the problem of anxiety than just this. Freud did not mean to discard altogether the old view of anxiety as a transformation product of dammed-up libido; he considered it as valid for what he called *Aktual-*

neurose, i.e., neurosis due exclusively to current sexual practices involving the building up of tension without adequate discharge, and remediable through a change in the current mode of life. Freud maintained that this type of neurosis of which he had seen many examples in his earlier professional life did, in fact, exist. Few of his disciples followed him on this point; most of them held that the cases diagnosed as *Aktualneurose* in the early days would reveal themselves as genuine psychoneuroses if looked at with the more experienced diagnostic eye of a later day. Whether this is so or whether the late Victorian age did in fact produce a type of neurotic reaction which tended to disappear together with the more severe restrictions of adult sexuality, seems to me to be an open question.

In any case, Freud continued to believe that high sexual excitement with subsequent frustration can by itself alone produce anxiety, and that a general theory of anxiety must find a place for this phenomenon as much as for the phenomena of neurotic anxiety as a reaction to inner danger, or of realistic anxiety as a reaction to external danger.

We know the solution which Freud attempted in this book. Anxiety, he suggested, breaks out both as a reaction to a trauma (defined as a rapid accumulation of need tensions) *and* as a reaction to danger, i.e., to the anticipation of a future trauma; in one case, the organism is flooded by high-level tensions, in the other case such a catastrophe is only anticipated: the former would be the case of anxiety in *Aktualneurose*, or anxiety due to dammed-up libido, the latter would be the case of realistic anxiety or of neurotic anxiety as reactions to dangers. We see also why this attempt at a unified theory has been unsatisfactory: in the case of trauma, the "need tensions" by which the organism is flooded need not be sexual tensions; they may be situations involving, for instance, the threat of death. But the older theory of anxiety as a transformation product of dammed-up libido required that what had been dammed up were not need tensions in general but quite specifically *sexual* tensions.

Most psychoanalysts have disregarded this part of Freud's deliberations. They do not believe in the existence of *Aktualneurose* and they do not believe that anxiety is caused by high-level sexual tension without discharge; all anxiety, in their eyes, is a reaction to danger,[2] and the problem with which Freud struggled is to them an artificial problem, created by a faulty theory.

But whether or not *Aktualneurose* exists, it seems to me that there are *phenomenological* characteristics of neurotic anxiety —a kind of frustraneous excitement—which remind us of some sexual manifestations so that the possibility of relationship between anxiety and sexuality should not be so easily dismissed.

The most suggestive result along this line of inquiry, following soon after the publication of *Inhibitions, Symptoms and Anxiety*, was the discovery of the *sexualization of anxiety*, first published by René Laforgue (1930) and developed independently at the same time in Anna Freud's Seminar on Child Analysis in Vienna: anxiety—or, perhaps, we should better say: fear— develops as a reaction to danger, but it is seized by sexual drives and made a source of pleasure—of a masochistic sensation or, in what we may call "flirting with danger," of play of alternately mastering it and surrendering to it, the former with narcissistic, the latter with masochistic gratifications, and the former necessary to prevent the situation from getting out of hand, as masochistic lust, as a rule, is predicated upon the existence of limits beyond which things cannot go. The practical importance of these contributions need not be emphasized.[3]

Thus, the development of an integrated theory of anxiety is still a task before us. It seems to me that it might proceed approximately along the following lines.

There was an earlier attempt by Freud, a decade before *Inhibitions, Symptoms and Anxiety*, in which some important points were made; but Freud did not follow them up. This is the passage (part of which was quoted before):

I have said that there is something that does not tally with the relation (so thoroughly recognized apart from

---

[2] It is particularly interesting to note that Leo Rangell (1955), one of the very few analysts who actually believes in the existence of *Aktualneurose*, thinks that the anxiety in these cases is nevertheless not a direct product of accumulation of tension but has to be seen as a reaction to danger, too, viz., "the danger that (a) the helpless state will get worse, and/or (b) it will continue and never stop" (p. 397).

[3] For further clinical material on this subject, see Feldman (1951).

this) between anxiety and libido: the fact, namely, that realistic anxiety in face of a danger seems to be a manifestation of the self-preservative instinct—which, after all, can scarcely be disputed. How would it be, though, if what was responsible for the affect of anxiety was not the egoistic ego-instincts but the ego-libido? After all, the state of anxiety is in every instance inexpedient, and its inexpedience becomes obvious if it reaches a fairly high pitch. In such cases it interferes with action, whether flight or defence, which alone is expedient and alone serves the cause of self-preservation. If, therefore, we attribute the affective portion of realistic anxiety to ego-libido and the accompanying action to the self-preservative instinct, we shall have got rid of the theoretical difficulty. After all, you do not seriously believe that one runs away because one feels anxiety? No. One feels anxiety and one runs away for a common motive, which is roused by the perception of danger. People who have been through a great mortal danger tell us that they were not at all afraid but merely acted—for instance, that they aimed their rifle at the wild beast—and that is unquestionably what was most expedient [1916-17, p. 430].

The first important point in this passage is that men may act appropriately in danger *without experiencing any sensation of anxiety at all;* in fact, Freud even stated here that he considered anxiety as always inexpedient, and that he did not look upon it as the motor force of action. But whether or not one will get as far as the latter conclusion suggests, it seems to be well enough established that a sensation of anxiety is not needed as a goad to action in situations of great and immediate danger. But if this is so, if fear (or anxiety) is not an indispensable element in the sequence "perception of danger—adaptive reaction," the idea of an "anxiety signal" is in need of revision. What is obviously biologically necessary is a *danger signal* that sets in motion certain responses but that danger signal need not consist of the sensation of fear.

The existence of a warning system is obviously vital for any organism which is exposed to other than merely typical situations, i.e., that has an individual destiny, and a species not equipped with such a system would probably not survive. Hence, the very survival of a species might suggest that danger signals are operative.

If, however, the danger signal need not consist of the sensation of fear or anxiety, which would set the pleasure principle into motion, of what, then, does it consist? We have in the meantime learned a great deal about the physiology of the reactions of the organism to danger: it may well be that this process is physiological and that the sensation of fear or anxiety is merely the psychic representation of this process, or the organism's awareness of it, which may be a biological luxury, at least in the case of *imminent* danger.

If this is so, the next step would be to ask under what conditions the sensation of fear or anxiety appears, i.e., under what conditions the process rises to consciousness. Since the adaptive reaction without the experience of fear seems to be limited to cases in which *immediate action is both indicated and possible*— as, for instance, in Freud's example: shooting— the answer to this question seems to be that the sensation of fear appears when immediate action is either not called for (as in the case of more remote dangers) or impossible (as in the case of an individual trapped) or prevented by inner inhibitions (as in the case of ambivalence regarding the response, or of hesitation). In short, the *sensation* of fear seems to be predicated upon an *obstacle to motor activity*. In this sense, Federn's view of anxiety (1952) as inhibited flight seems to me to have captured an important aspect of the problem.

Second, we may have to distinguish between dangers to life and limb, i.e., to physical existence, on the one hand, and dangers to the level of narcissistic gratification on the other—to distinguish between dangers to the *existence* of the ego and dangers to its *libidinal satiation*. The danger of losing love has both implications at an early age; later, it belongs only to the second category. So does, at any time, the danger of castration.

Fear of dangers to the libidinal satiation of the ego, to its narcissistic level, i.e., fear of libidinal dangers, seems to take on some of the characteristics of sexuality; where the dangers are sexual in nature, the fear assumes the quality of sexual excitation. In such cases, the reaction to danger seems less realistic, less adaptive, than in the reaction to dangers to pure existence not involving sexual implications; this would be in accordance with the fundamental psychoanalytic principle that it is the sexual drives which disturb the business of adaptation.

Finally, there is the possibility of sexualization of the fear itself. The warning signal has then been turned into a source of sexual enjoyment or has become an object of sexual play, and its original adaptive function has been totally subverted.

We would thus have to make these distinctions: the simple case of a *danger signal* unaccompanied by sensations of fear and releasing the impulses toward appropriate action; the appearance of a sensation of fear where immediate motor activity is obstructed by external or internal obstacles, i.e., *consciousness as a consequence of motor inhibition*, with a biological function in the case of remote dangers; the enlargement of the concept of danger from the threat to existence to the threat of *libidinal* frustration, a consequence, probably, of the greater abundance in the higher forms of life and the more developed cultures of men; and the actual *sexualization* of fear itself. While the first layer appears as an inescapable necessity of survival, the second and third fulfill biological functions under certain circumstances but can also be inexpedient or pathological; the fourth and last is purely pathological or, at the very least, a *liason dangeréuse*.[4]

Defense Mechanisms

In another area, that of defense mechanisms, Freud's seminal ideas have led to a rich harvest which was brought in mainly by Anna Freud (1936). The ground for a psychoanalysis of defense mechanisms, and of psychoanalytic ego psychology in general, was laid by the realization that not only instinctual drives but also parts of the ego and superego are unconscious. It had at first been assumed that only drives were unconscious and that they were so because they conflict with the ideas and aspirations of the conscious personality. Since psychoanalysis is the psychology of the unconscious, it appeared that its concern was with the

[4] Allusion to the 18th-century novel under this title, by Choderlos de Laclos.

otherwise neglected or denied instinctual drives. This did not mean that there was no need for a psychology of the ego but merely that psychoanalysis, as a psychology of the unconscious, was not concerned with it; it was the business of what was then called academic psychology, i.e., conscious psychology. It was first in *The Ego and the Id* that Freud stated clearly that parts of the ego were unconscious, too,[5] and that they were so because of their connection with repressed drives, through something like "guilt by association." One cannot securely repress an idea and yet be aware of having repressed it because this awareness would set the mind on search and so keep the repression insecure. In *The Ego and the Id* Freud made the point particularly with reference to that "differentiating grade within the ego" which he had first called ego ideal and which he now called superego; *Inhibitions, Symptoms and Anxiety* applied it to ego activities in the narrower sense of the word.

While this development led to the conclusion that the ego was not the exclusive domain of the conscious psychologist but, in some aspects, an object of legitimate concern for the psychoanalyst as student of the unconscious, another innovation, made more specifically in *Inhibitions, Symptoms and Anxiety*, pointed the way toward the study of the defense mechanisms. *Abwehr* (defense) was Freud's first term for what he later called repression; and the later word, more plastic as a description of the process and more appealing to the imagination, made the earlier term dispensable; it disappeared from the literature. Freud now suggested that repression, while probably the most important of the "processes that have the same purpose—namely, the protection of the ego against instinctual demands" (1926a, p. 164)—

---

[5] Against this it may be held that Freud referred to defense as unconscious in one of his earliest papers: "symptoms arose through the psychical mechanism of (unconscious) defence—that is, in an attempt to repress an incompatible idea which had come into distressing opposition to the patient's ego" (1896, p. 162).

But the unconsciousness of defense was then neither explained nor elaborated and applied in theory and technique and Freud referred more than twenty-five years later to unconscious guilt feelings as a "new discovery" (1923b, p. 27). Thus, while the passage proves that the idea was present, or germinating, in Freud's mind, it can hardly be maintained that it was already part of psychoanalysis as a common and communicable body of knowledge or theory.

was not the only one; there were others such as isolation, undoing, reaction formation, or regression. Freud therefore proposed to reactivate the discarded term, to call it back to active duty, as it were, but as a generic term covering all these techniques, with repression being but one member of the class.

These two innovations—the (partial) unconsciousness of the ego and the existence of a variety of responses to instinctual challenges—together opened the way to the psychoanalysis of the defense mechanisms which Anna Freud pursued with so much success.

The defense mechanisms have become very popular, not only in psychoanalysis and psychiatry but also in allied professions such as social work and education. We can often hear that a person's "defenses" have been elucidated in a brief contact, in fact, in a few interviews.

Walter Rathenau said once that popularity is usually based on misunderstanding; the popularity of the defense mechanisms seems to be based on *two*. First, "defense" is widely believed to refer to the ways in which people protect themselves against pain and frustration in social relations[6] and to the stratagems and ruses which they apply in the struggle for existence and the jockeying for position—in short, the devices described and studied by Alfred Adler and his (conscious or unconscious) followers. The second assumption is that by focusing on these defenses, attention is deflected from the manifestations of sexuality which psychoanalysts had so long emphasized.

But both these assumptions rest on misunderstanding. The defense mechanisms of Freud or Anna Freud are not stratagems in the competitive struggle of the market place; they are responses to inner dangers. And since these inner dangers stem from the demands of instinctual drives, the occupation with them cannot detract attention from the instinctual drives against which these mechanisms defend, and cannot play down the importance of instinctual drives for human pathology and human destiny.

[6] See, for instance, the following statement by Kardiner (1959): "his daughter Anna rediscovered the *adaptive* devices described by her father in 1900, but which since that time had enjoyed a position exterritorial to the theory. *They were now called mechanisms of defense*" (p. 87, my italics).

Pasteur and Koch found microbial carriers of disease and so became the founders of the science of bacteriology. It was at first believed that contact with these microorganisms was not only a necessary but a sufficient condition of disease, that prophylaxis lay in avoiding such contact, and that therapy would be found in the destruction of these microorganisms. It was learned later that clinical disease depended not only on the presence of the respective bacteria or viruses but also on the condition of the host organism and that the control of microbial disease involved complex questions of balance; these experiences gave rise to the science of immunology. But this development did not mean that one could now forget about the invading microorganisms; it merely meant that those working with infectious diseases and concerned about their control had to study and to consider *both* the invaders and the responses of the host.

Anna Freud's work dealt with defense *mechanisms*, i.e., with the stereotyped, or automatic, responses of the ego. They represent a kind of fixation of the ego, analogous to the fixations of the libido. They are standardized, repetitive, and thus in some degree predictable. Moreover, as Anna Freud could show, each individual uses only a limited number of defense mechanisms and behaves in accordance with these patterns in dealing with his affects too. It is for these reasons that defense mechanisms are characteristic for an individual—as characteristic as his libidinal fixations and sexual fantasies.

The psychoanalysis of an individual is then no longer merely the study of the vicissitudes of his drives, supplemented by a study of the dangers to which he is particularly geared, but also the study of his specific responses to dangers.

This brought a new attitude to resistances in analysis. Resistance, as the name suggests, had hitherto been looked upon only as an obstacle, as that which interferes with the progress of analysis, and, hence, as something which has to be removed or conquered.

This statement is in need of some qualifications, though. First, it was well recognized that resistances are necessary and that results achieved without encountering sizable resistances, with patients always gladly cooperating, will turn out to be ephemeral; they are, as Freud was to formulate later, "written

on water" (1937a, p. 241). It was therefore said that "the overcoming of these resistances is the essential function of analysis" (1916-17, p. 291).

It was also known that resistances could lead to valuable information as Freud said close to the passage just quoted:

Resistances of this kind should not be one-sidedly condemned. They include so much of the most important material from the patient's past and bring it back in so convincing a fashion that they become some of the best supports of the analysis if a skilful technique knows how to give them the right turn [1916-17, p. 291].

Thus, the information which Freud at this point credited resistance with bringing to light is material from the patient's past, not the working of the ego; as far as the latter is concerned, Freud says a few sentences later:

... that what is being mobilized for fighting against the alterations we are striving for are character-traits, attitudes of the ego. In this connection we discover that these character-traits were formed in relation to the determinants of the neurosis and in reaction against its demands, and we come upon traits which cannot normally emerge, or not to the same extent, and which may be described as latent.... We are aware that these resistances are bound to come to light; in fact we are dissatisfied if we cannot provoke them clearly enough and are unable *to demonstrate them to the patient* [p. 291; my italics].

Hence, the manifestation of the "character-traits" is necessary not in order to be able to study their mechanism and to follow its pattern throughout the patient's life but in order to demonstrate them to the patient with a view to his overcoming them.

Finally, the means of overcoming resistances had changed in the course of time, from the *authoritarian* approach of hypnosis in the cathartic era over the *democratic* approach of gentle persuasion through the use of positive transference to the *indirect* approach of analyzing the motives or the historical prototypes of the resistance. But with all that, the goal had remained the same, viz., to overcome them.

With Anna Freud's innovation, however, it appears that resistances—or, more specifically, resistances of repression— were important communications about the standard operating procedures of the ego.

This outlook added a new dimension to analytic work. It also meant that the analyst has to take "his stand at a point equidistant from the id, the ego and the superego" (A. Freud, 1936), a principle which gave to the old principle of analytic neutrality a new and deeper meaning.

Together, these changes amounted to an enrichment and refinement of analytic technique as great as the consideration of specific dangers had been.

A decade later, Freud summed up the whole development as follows:

> ... the patient repeats these modes of reaction during the work of analysis as well ... he produces them before our eyes, as it were. In fact, it is only in this way that we get to know them. This does not mean that they make analysis impossible. On the contrary, they constitute half of our analytic task. The other half, the one which was first tackled by analysis in its early days, is the uncovering of what is hidden in the id. During the treatment *our therapeutic work is constantly swinging backwards and forwards like a pendulum between a piece of id-analysis and a piece of ego-analysis* [1937a, p. 238; my italics].

There still remains the task of drafting a systematic theory of defenses—a comprehensive map of the defense mechanisms, their typical chronology, their dependence on inherited reaction patterns and postnatal experience. The following may perhaps be suggested as preliminary considerations.

There is, first, the strong impression that defense mechanisms show different degrees of complexity, from the apparent simplicity of repression to the intricate complexity of a mechanism such as, for instance, "altruistic surrender." That suggests that some of the defense mechanisms may be composites, built out of more elementary building stones.

Second, repression does not seem to be just one mechanism among many, on an equal footing with the others, but seems to have a particularly important position inasmuch as repression—or something similar to it—accompanies all other defense mechanisms. It is the omnipresent mainstay of the show while the others are accidental, appearing in some cases and lacking in others. It is not for nothing that it has exclusively occupied the analyst's attention for so long. Thus, for instance, reaction formation is actually repression of certain drives *plus* emphasis on the opposite of the repressed drives as a means of counter-cathexis; altruistic surrender is repression of certain drives *plus* identification with a person who can indulge with impunity in the satisfaction of the desires one has ostracized in oneself or whom one has actively maneuvered into this role—an instinctual gratification through identification, freed from guilt feelings because of personal abdication.

It thus appears that defensive mechanisms can be mapped according to *three coordinates.* There is, first, one aspect that is never missing: an operation which *evicts* the representatives of the dangerous drive *from consciousness*—either radically as in repression or only partially as in isolation. They can be compared with different methods of censorship—one taking the entire issue of a periodical out of circulation, the other merely cutting out some passages or words from an offending article. Some analysts including myself think that there is an even less radical way of eliminating from consciousness, viz., the articulate denial.

These are ways of blotting out awareness—more or less radical, more or less effective.

Then, two other aspects have to be considered: the *channeling* of the warded-off drive into some kind of substitute gratification—as the new aim in the case of displacement, or the identification with those to whom everything is permitted (one might say: *quod non licet bovi licet Jovi*)—and a particular kind of *countercathexis* such as the overcultivation of the opposite in reaction formation or a magical ritual in undoing.

These appear to be the three aspects of defense mechanisms and the latter can be defined by indicating, (a) the particular way or degree of ouster from consciousness; (b) the type of countercathexis; and (c) the kind—if any—of rechanneling of forces.

Summary

This, then, is the rough balance sheet. Equality of id and ego have long become part and parcel of psychoanalytic thought and psychoanalysts try to distinguish between drive and ego aspect in various psychic activities, without much thought that it could be otherwise. All the time, however, whether teleological concepts are *ultimately* satisfactory remains in doubt as it always has been and, I am afraid, is likely to remain.

Id and ego are handled today in a more schematic fashion than Freud had intended them to be. The revision of the theory of (neurotic) anxiety and the realization of a variety of defense mechanisms have borne rich fruit and have changed the outlook and practice of psychoanalysis. The attempt to construct a unified theory of anxiety, encompassing both anxiety as a consequence of dammed-up libido and anxiety as a signal in danger situations, has not been successful, and most analysts do not feel a need for such a unified theory in the first place because they do not believe in the existence of the first type of anxiety. However, there seem to be relations between anxiety, or at least its more pathological manifestations, and sexuality, and the theory should give an account of these relations; the concept of sexualized anxiety, developed later, is an important contribution in this direction but does not, in my opinion, exhaust the subject of the relations between anxiety and sexuality.

On a number of other points, Freud's ideas have been quietly accepted and become noncontroversial parts of the clinical theory of psychoanalysis. I would mention in this group the theory of inhibitions as due either to a sexualization of an ego function or to a need for self-punishment or to a general impoverishment through absorption by an inner process. There are also points in which Freud's suggestions have as yet not been given sufficient thought; I would mention among them the role of countercathexis in pain, both physical and mental.

CHAPTER 20

Trauma and the Variety of
Extraordinary Challenges

(1967)

Some of the concepts that Freud used in organizing his clinical observations were his own inventions, such as, for instance, repression. In other instances, he adopted already existing concepts of science or of daily language as, for example, instinct. In the latter cases, the borrowed concepts tended to assume new shades of meaning under the impact of the psychoanalytic material.

Trauma belonged to the second class; it was taken from medicine. There it meant "bodily injury"; transferred to psychic life, it meant "emotional shock." This is the sense in which the term is used in Freud's early writings.

The Breakdown of the Stimulus Barrier

In *Beyond the Pleasure Principle* (1920a), Freud developed a more specific, sharply delineated concept of trauma.

It is probably not accidental that this short work was written soon after World War I. In the later war years, Europe was full of shell-shocked soldiers; one could see them shaking in the streets. Some of them had merely been exposed to the "ordinary"

Reprinted from *Psychic Trauma*, ed. S. S. Furst. New York: Basic Books, 1967, pp. 221-234. © Psychoanalytic Research and Development Fund.

361

experience of trench warfare; others had been subjected to more particular experiences of concentrated shock, such as, for example, being suddenly covered by a load of earth in an explosion—they had barely escaped being buried alive.

Freud examined this kind of experience and suggested that it consisted in a *breakdown of the stimulus barrier* (or protective shield): "We describe as traumatic any excitations from outside which are powerful enough to break through the protective shield" (p. 29).

Implied in this idea are the following assumptions:

1. That the organism is equipped with a kind of apparatus that deals with the tensions resulting from the onslaught of the outside world, with a view to eliminating or reducing them. It may do so either by appropriate changes in itself that make it possible to live with the external condition without unbearable suffering (*autoplastic* adjustment) or by bringing about appropriate changes in the outside world so as to eliminate or substantially reduce the source of the tension (*alloplastic* adjustment). In practice, "dealing with" or "assimilating" the stressor stimulus will mostly include both methods; one part will be dealt with alloplastically, another part autoplastically. The organism tries to eliminate as much outside disturbance as possible, and to accept and learn to live with the remainder.

2. There is the further implication that in carrying out this business of assimilation, the organism has a certain *capacity;* just as, for instance, a filter can handle so many cubic feet of water per minute and would not function if fed beyond the saturation point, so can the organism "digest" only a certain amount of stimuli in a given time.

3. In order to assure that the assimilating apparatus is not overburdened, a "stimulus barrier" cuts down on the amount of stimuli that can pass into the system in a unit of time. In this way, the stimulus barrier acts like a regulator of influx.

4. If, however, the influx is particularly high, it may overtax the capacity of the stimulus barrier; the dams may break, so to say, and the organism is suddenly confronted with a tidal wave of stimuli that it is incapable of handling through the ordinary process of autoplastic and/or alloplastic adjustment.

The immediate result of such a catastrophe is something like a breakdown of the functioning of the organism. The traumatized organism may not function at all, as is the case with an individual "under shock."

This condition has been aptly described by Greenacre (1967):

> . . . I would wish to point out that the severest traumatic stimulations of all, which are so great as to be overwhelming, tend to be *disorganizing* in their effect on the other activities of the individual. They may result either in states of aimless frenzied overactivity, sometimes culminating in tantrums or rage or, if the stimulus is acute and focused as well as sudden, it may produce a shocklike stunned reaction, presenting various degrees of unresponse, inactivity, or torpor [p. 140].

After the immediate shock has tapered off, the organism seems for a considerable time tied or bound to the traumatic experience, returning to it and reliving it. Thus men who suffer from traumatic neuroses may reexperience their trauma in fantasy or in dreams.

This long—sometimes indefinite—repetition at times seems to us like a broken record; something has happened that makes it impossible for the organism to proceed to new experience; it can keep turning indefinitely in the same groove, as it were.

Sometimes, however, one gets the impression that there is also a more cheerful aspect to these repetitions: namely, that the individual is not only forced to move in the same magic circle without being able to get out of it, but that he also actively tries to gain control or mastery of the situation that he had been unable to master at the time the event had occurred—much like a ruminant that digests afterward what it could not digest at first.

In a case analyzed by Dr. Jenny Waelder Hall many years ago, the patient, a boy of six or seven years, was often allowed to accompany his father on his frequent walks in the woods. One day, the father was attacked by a stag, gored in his thigh, and thrown to the ground, bleeding profusely. He was able to extricate himself from the situation by holding the animal by the antler with one hand and opening a pocketknife with the help of his teeth and then cutting the animal's throat. The child was meanwhile crying in helpless panic.

After the event, the little boy reenacted the scene for many weeks in his play. However, the story became more and more distorted as time went on. While in reality the child had been a passive onlooker gripped by terror, he assumed an active role in the later fantasy play; finally, the little boy became the hero who had killed the stag and rescued the desperate father.

Thus, in Freud's words, "the ego, which experienced the trauma passively, now repeats it actively in a weakened version, in the hope of being able itself to direct its course" (1926a, p. 167).

With this idea of the trauma as an "undigested" or "unmastered" experience and its repetitive reexperience, partly due to the buoyancy of the undigested material and partly to the attempt of the organism—the ego, in theoretical parlance—to win mastery inch by inch, Freud subsumed under one heading phenomena as different as the traumatic neurosis and the play of children.

Around the end of the first year of life, children find pleasure in peekaboo and other games in which an object disappears and reappears. Freud suggested that these games are stimulated by the regular experience that the mother, now clearly distinguished as an individual in the outside world and as the source of pleasure and security, frequently disappears from the field—a fact that is bound to cause distress to the child. Comfort is gradually won from the experience that the vanished apparition regularly returns, although indications of serious concern on this score can be observed in older children too. The games of the disappearance-reappearance type are, according to Freud, repetitions of the "trauma" in a weakened symbolic version in which the child assumes an active role instead of the passivity that is his lot in reality; he can *make* the object go and come again; he is, in fantasy, master of the situation.

The intensity of shock experienced by a soldier who is suddenly buried under a truckload of earth is perhaps of a different magnitude than that experienced by a child who finds his mother absent in a moment of need, although the latter may at times reach similar heights; but *in principle* the mechanism is seen in similar terms: a challenge too great for immediate assimilation is followed by the disturbance of proper functioning, a kind of obsession with the experience and a subsequent attempt at assimilating it through repetitive play, turning passivity into activity.

There is of course the further difference that in the case of the child the subsequent repetitions are successful in helping him to accept reality, while the similar procedure is far less successful in the case of the adult traumatic neurotic. In the first case, the challenge, at the appropriate time and in appropriate doses, is milder in degree and even necessary to stimulate normal growth because the child is destined to emancipate himself gradually from care. The challenge in the second case is extraordinary, not required for a biologically destined development since it is not part of man's destiny to learn to dig himself out from under an avalanche or landslide; there is no normal growth helping to overcome it, and the results are likely to be disruptive. Notwithstanding this difference of circumstance and the resulting difference in prognosis, the impact of the challenge and the response of the organism to it seem to follow the same basic pattern.

The whole process may be compared with certain biological processes, for instance, the outbreak of infectious disease. Invading microorganisms stimulate the host organism into developing various methods of defense, such as the production of antigens that can neutralize toxins molecule by molecule or the production of immunologically active cells that hunt invaders down. An organism *without immunological defenses* falls prey to the invaders, as is demonstrated by the disastrous consequences of introducing certain microorganisms into populations that have never had contact with them. The obvious psychological analogy is the defenselessness of the child in the face of major challenges.

Organisms that have acquired immunity can fight the infection off without, or with but minimal, clinical manifestations of disease. But an invasion so *massive* as to overpower the immune bodies of the organism will also lead to clinical illness.

Exaggerated Defense

The word "trauma" is also used in a somewhat different sense.

The following simple example is taken from a case analyzed some years ago by Dr. Margaret Temeles and supervised by this author. A man in his early forties had been impotent throughout his life except for one brief episode in which he claims to have consummated a relationship. At other times, and at the time of observation, he showed interest in women and flirted with them but was careful to keep the relationship within these limits so as not to meet failure. Isolated attempts at intercourse with a prostitute were unsuccessful.

This patient had the following experience at the age of about four. He was climbing in bed over his mother's body, apparently playfully excited; at this point, the mother's common-law husband (the real father was out of the picture through abandonment and divorce) came with a pair of scissors and went through the motion of cutting the little boy's penis off—facetiously and playfully, we may assume. For the child, of course, the matter is serious; at the very least, he cannot be sure where play ends and reality begins. Particularly in its early beginnings, phallic growth may wither under the impact of an experience such as this, just as buds are killed by a frost.

Without claiming that this experience was the sole cause of this man's severe and lasting inhibition, it is plausible to assume that it played an important part in its etiology. We will not hesitate to call such an experience "traumatic."

Yet there are significant differences between the consequences of this experience and those of the type illustrated by the case of the boy seeing his father attacked by an animal.

For one, in cases of this kind there is no evidence of a paralysis of functioning that characterizes experiences of the first-mentioned type, of the "states of aimless frenzied over-activity," or of "unresponse, inactivity" described by Greenacre. If such states exist at all, they are of very short duration.

Then the subsequent development does not show the repetition in dreams and in play. The little boy did not repeat the critical episode with his toys, giving it a different slant and changing his role from helpless victim to triumphant hero.

What happened was rather different; it was actually an act of immediate *autoplastic adjustment*. The child withdrew from the activities that had brought him into this perilous situation. What makes the result pathological is merely the fact that this adjustment went *far beyond the necessities of the situation*, i.e., not only far beyond what we know would have been necessary (because we know that the stepfather would not actually have cut the boy's penis off) but also far beyond what would have to appear necessary to a child who takes the threat at its face value. For it would have been quite sufficient for the child to desist from playing sexually with his mother. But the patient did much more; he not only gave up the oedipal play but withdrew from all phallic activities so completely that they could not be effectively recathected even under the impact of puberty. It is a case of *exaggerated adjustment*, one that pays an inappropriate price in terms of functioning, not only handicapping but actually surrendering a vital function for good. In this lies its pathological character.

One must ask, of course, why this particular child reacted so strongly to a challenge which, however severe, would probably have been less damaging to many others and might have been defied by some. This kind of question may make us consider the condition of the child at the time of the threat, his previous history as well as genetic factors. But this question lies outside the issues with which we are concerned here.

But it is of immediate interest for us to ask the question: What accounts for the difference between the *reactions* to this trauma and the *reactions* to the trauma of the earlier example?

The answer does not seem to be too difficult. The child who witnessed his father attacked by an animal and who was certainly frightened as to what would happen to him did not have to relate this event to any action of his; there was nothing he could desist from doing and thereby avert the danger.

The threat in the second case is clearly related to the child's own activities. The child was threatened with castration *because* he had engaged in sexually exciting play with his mother; if he desisted from so doing and—as was unfortunately the case with the patient in question—from all similar activities with any object at any time, he could save himself from danger. He had a chance of rescuing himself through autoplastic adjustment, but overdid it thousandfold, to his permanent damage. The first child had no such option; he could only suffer what came and could not forestall it by any kind of adjustment, at any kind of price. Hence the derangement of the organism in the first case; nothing was left except the attempt to work things over later, piecemeal, with the help of appropriate distortion and myth formation. Hopefully, one may grow stronger for the next time.

We thus see that the term "trauma" has been used not only for the onslaught of stimuli that leads to a break in the functioning of the organism, afterward to be repaired piecemeal as far as possible, but also to threats so severe that the individual panics and makes greater sacrifices than necessary to avoid the danger, thereby severely impairing the adequate function of the organism. The use of "trauma" in this second sense seems to me to be too firmly entrenched to be dislodged by critical efforts.

There are biological analogies to phenomena of this kind, too. Examples include the so-called General Adaptation Syndrome, which is seen as the consequence of defense overdone, and hayfever, which, according to Sir Macfarlane Burnet (1962), is "one of the human ills which can be traced to [the] unfortunate inability of some people to decide which antigens are worth reacting to and which are not" (p. 141).

Sensitization and the Building Up of Tolerance

Sometimes the stimulus is of a kind that all, or almost all, people will consider "traumatic." Our two examples are of this class; so are such events as the loss of a parent.

But in other instances, the stimulus is of a moderate or even trivial kind that most people will take in their stride or perhaps not even notice. An officer who had repeatedly been decorated for bravery in action fainted when a doctor approached him with a hypodermic needle. In such cases a stimulus may have assumed extraordinary significance on account of its *symbolic meaning* for the individual; in the present case, the implicit meaning was probably a homosexual threat, stirring up the patient's latent homosexuality. This suggests that the individual had been alerted or sensitized to dangers of this kind to such a degree that he will respond to the mildest hint as though it were the real thing. Such a condition may be due either to a latent inner instinctual danger that is activated by the trivial stimulus or to previous experiences that have increased the sensitivity of the organism to stimuli of a particular kind; and the former is likely to be due, in large part, to the latter—that is, the patient's passive homosexuality has probably been cultivated by previous experience.

Thus we may see little boys at a certain time react very strongly to the kind of veiled, perhaps teasing, castration threats that are a trivial event in childhood and that they may have disregarded not too long before. We may then, perhaps, ascribe the intensified reaction to the intervening experience of the observation of a little girl; a previously unimpressive threat becomes serious through the experience that creatures without a penis actually exist. In such a case, the observation of the difference in sex has not in itself been traumatic; it has alerted the individual and made him more receptive to a future threat which, however mild in itself, may set off a panic reaction; or a previously received and at first neglected threat may assume serious proportion in retrospect.

Previous experience, however, cannot only make a person more sensitive to subsequent stimuli; it may also make him less so. There is the possibility of *building up tolerance.* Soldiers can be hardened in training and by battle experience; while certain physiological expressions of anxiety were considered normal in what was once called a soldier's "baptism of fire," the seasoned soldier may take similar situations in his stride.

This raises the question: *Under what conditions* will extraordinary stimuli build up tolerance for future onslaught of this kind, and under what conditions will they lower it; under what conditions will one be toughened, and under what conditions sensitized? We do not yet have a complete answer, but this much can probably be said: *tolerance is built up by a gradual increase of the stimulation in small doses,* either short of producing a full traumatic reaction or with ample allowance for subsequent assimilation, while *sensitizing* is likely to take place whenever the first stimulus was not fully assimilated.

These phenomena too have their biological parallels, so psychological patterns can be seen as special cases of general biological regularities; an organism can build up tolerance to poisons or to pain, while sensitization is known to occur, for instance, in the reaction to foreign proteins.

Trauma and Stress

It has been suggested that the concept of trauma be enlarged so as to include stress, the corrosive influence of prolonged tension of lower intensity; that allowance should be made for a special category, "stress trauma" (Kris, 1956).

We may ask: what does psychological stress consist of? We speak, for instance, of the stress of high executive office; what, in psychological terms, do we mean?

The executive constantly has to make decisions the results of which he will be *responsible* for; that is, unfavorable consequences of these decisions will be brought home to him personally. That may mean danger of life or limb; the law of Hammurabi punished a physician with the loss of an organ or limb if a patient had lost his during treatment. Or, in milder conditions, he may suffer in his position, prestige, or possessions; at the least, he will be blamed for the consequences or he may be tormented by his conscience. Sometimes the decision may be clear-cut, with all the advantages on one side and none on the other; in such cases, responsibility is easy to bear. But often enough there will be assets and liabilities on both sides, and the decisionmaker cannot escape anxiety. Sometimes, the decision will be what is called "difficult," i.e., assets and liabilities are more or less evenly distributed, with no clear preponderance of either side; in such cases, the decisionmaker will have to bear grave anxiety.

Hence, there is tension and no way to avoid it; there is no possibility of complete discharge or even of sizable relief. A permanent state of tension ensues.[1]

The same is implied in other situations that we call stressful.

---

[1] Samuel Corson, a researcher in the physiology of stress in animals, calls stressful those situations in which an animal is confronted with a task it cannot solve. That implies approximately the same concept.

It was a great stress for soldiers in the trenches to be exposed to prolonged bombardment; they were naturally afraid but they could not escape the situation; they could neither withdraw into a safe area nor attack and so at least discharge tension in activity and hope that after a short period of heightened danger survivors would find rest and safety.

Thus psychological stress seems to be a condition of permanent exposure to danger without the possibility of escape.[2] For practical purposes, we may speak of medium- or low-level tension; for high-level tension is likely to be traumatic rather than merely stressful; the level of tension must, of course, be evaluated in terms of the existing tolerance.

Open Problems

All things discussed are contributions to a theory of responses to external stimuli and, thus, contributions to a general theory of adaptation; they are not the theory itself.

What is still needed is a general map of responses to tension as a function of circumstances—that is, as a function of four groups of variables: the nature of the challenge, quantitative factors, the availability of paths of discharge, and the present condition and previous history of the organism.

1. *The nature of the challenge.* It seems to me relevant whether the challenge is presented by a frustration or by a threat. In the case of frustration, it is important to know if it stems from physical pain or whether it involves an object-libidinal desire, a narcissistic need, or an aggressive impulse. In the case of a threat, we want to know if it carries a danger to life and limb, or whether it involves one of the aforementioned privations.

---

[2] I owe the consideration of the availability or nonavailability of an outlet to the late Dr. Paul Federn. He distinguished between fear and anxiety, and defined fear as the reaction to danger, anxiety as inhibited flight. I do not accept this theory in its entirety because I do not consider it useful to treat words of everyday language, such as "fear" or "anxiety," which are overloaded with ambiguities, as though they were clearly defined and properly delineated scientific concepts; and because I am inclined to think that more goes into what we conventionally mean by anxiety than merely inhibited flight. But the *availability or nonavailability of exit,* i.e., of a possibility of reducing tension, is a highly important aspect of the matter.

2. *Quantitative factors.* To this group belongs the absolute intensity of the stimulus, i.e., the degree of tension, and also the speed of accumulation or, in more general terms, the rhythm of rise and fall.

3. *The availability of outlets.* Here must be considered whether outlets are available at all and, if they are, what their costs would be in terms of other frustrations or dangers.

4. *The condition of the challenged organism.* This refers to the tolerance of the organism at the time of the experience—its tolerance to stimuli in general and to the specific stimulus in particular. This tolerance can be studied as a function of constitutional factors and of the previous history of the organism right up to the impact.

The three types of extraordinary challenges discussed in these pages—the two kinds of traumatic experiences, and psychic stress—seem to be well understood. The first kind of trauma is due to a sudden accumulation of tension as a result of frustration or danger, for which there is no possible outlet. The second kind of trauma, consisting of severe threats, leaves as only outlets the surrender of an instinctual position or a radical restriction of the ego. Stress is lasting medium- or low-level tension without the possibility of escape.

These hypotheses are building stones for a future general theory that will encompass them as special cases—a map of responses to external stimuli as a function of the four groups of variables.

Part II

Part II

CHAPTER 21

The Influence of Psychoanalysis
on the Outlook on Life
of Modern Man

(*1929*)

What has been and is the effect of psychoanalysis on the perspectives on life of modern man? I am thinking primarily of those people who have been most directly exposed to its influence either because in their own life they once passed through, so to say, the focus of the psychoanalytic beam, or because they live in close proximity to it. But we must also consider the effects on those who are somewhat removed from the center of psychoanalytic activities and to whom only broken rays filter down.

Before embarking on the main topic, however, we must attend to some preliminary considerations. Psychoanalysis is a science; how can a science have any effect on the attitude to life and life style of man? Science is, after all, only a map, according to Walter Rathenau's beautiful simile. It shows us the location of mountains and valleys, of jungles and centers of civilization, but it cannot point the way to where we should travel.

Although science and knowledge are not capable of setting

First published as "Die Psychoanalyse im Lebensgefühl des modernen Menschen." *Almanach der Psychoanalyse*, 47-62, 1929. The English translation by Lottie M. Newman is here published for the first time.

Translator's note. The term *Lebensgefühl* contained in the original title of this paper has been variously translated as "outlook" or "perspectives on life," as "attitudes to" or "feelings about life." Literally, it means life-feeling.

our goals, they nevertheless can influence our travel plan through life. To begin with, we may use science as a means to our ends, the choice of which is surely influenced by the availability of new and convenient means. The map can show us areas which we did not know existed; and psychological exploration can show us a previously unknown domain of new possibilities of living. We shall decide differently once we have learned of its existence. Furthermore, we realize that knowledge of any kind can exert an influence on our value systems. It does so when insight reveals the existence of an inner previously unnoticed contradiction that requires resolution and a decision one way or the other. This consideration is especially important in regard to the influence of psychoanalysis, as we shall see further on.

We should not forget that in addition to the influences exerted by psychoanalytic psychology as a science, psychoanalysis is also a therapy in which psychoanalytic knowledge is applied directly in the service of health. We know that psychoanalytic therapy aims not at a mere removal of symptoms but at a more profound reorganization of the personality, and this reorganization influences and shapes a person's entire attitude to life. Therapeutic analysis thus has several different effects, first of all on those who having submitted to it then transmit some of the changes brought about in themselves to others in their immediate environment.

Finally, we must not overlook the fact that psychoanalysis was created by one man and that his beliefs and Weltanschauung are clearly imprinted on his work. No doubt, it is possible and even desirable to distinguish between the objective content of a scientific theory and the subjective part, which is an expression of the personality of its creator and may tell us something about him. Such a distinction is of course a requirement of scientific critique. In the actual life experience of people, however, the personal, the unique, the individual elements are transmitted simultaneously together with the objective ones, so that all those who have been exposed to the effects of psychoanalysis must in some way have experienced and worked over some elements rooted in the personality of its founder.

We can thus say that psychoanalysis has by these various

routes contributed to the formation of modern man's attitude to life. In what follows I shall make no attempt to distinguish between the various routes by which psychoanalysis actually exerts its influences, but confine myself to tracing its, so to say, legitimate effects and exclude from my discussion those that may have arisen from misunderstandings.

Surveying the enormous variety of trends that have shaped our current intellectual outlook on life, we can trace one trend to three sources: Dostoyevsky, Nietzsche, and Freud. They have one element in common—the psychological approach, the attempt to follow out the "know thyself" of the Greeks even into the layers of mental life that are sequestered from consciousness and to give man who has learned so much about his external world some insight into his own inner life. What distinguishes Freud from his artistic predecessors, Dostoyevsky and Nietzsche, is to be found not so much in the content of the knowledge but in the attempt to arrive at this knowledge for the first time by means of a scientific method. Thus, what had previously been the sole and uncontested domain of intuition has, without entirely eliminating the latter, been more and more restricted and freed of its inherent sources of error. Among the three discoverers and explorers of the unconscious mental life Freud's unique position rests on the fact that he converted intuitive surmise into knowledge, experiences into insight, and artistic hunches into science.

Psychoanalysis focuses a microscope on the innermost life of man, inducing him to contemplate and perceive it, whereas previously for the longest time man had been concerned almost exclusively with the outer world and even in the psychological sciences concentrated predominantly on the external appearance of things. This turning back to the own ego, though aiming at insight into it, is not an end in itself. The partial diversion of interest in the tasks posed by the external world and the preoccupation with one's own inner life should be no more than a passing phase during which one's submersion in the unconscious, rather than becoming a lasting state, should merely provide a person with new energies to turn back once more to the tasks of life. Insight for the sake of action is the program of practical analysis.

With these considerations we touch upon one of those issues

which Nietzsche and analysis see as a central problem of life, namely, the relationship between insight and will, between psychologizing contemplation and action. During the first quarter of this century many writers have been preoccupied with various ramifications of this question: Does insight paralyze immediate action? Does introspection break the purposiveness of our will power? Does consciousness portend disaster (Seidel, 1910)? The great variety of ways in which writers have dealt with this theme merely demonstrates the degree to which psychoanalysis has agitated our current thinking and made such questions vital issues.

Here I shall single out for consideration only how one great writer has dealt with this problem, which in fact is one of the mainsprings of his creativity. The works of Thomas Mann are on one level of their manifold meanings pervaded by the antithesis of knowledge and will. The capacity to act is represented as the essence of morality, the dependence of which on insight or its independence from insight invariably constitutes the key problem. In "Death in Venice" Mann portrays a protagonist, Gustav von Aschenbach, who has repudiated the deadly and demeaning influence of insight, who has devoted his life to the fulfillment of an earnestly conceived Prussian ideal of duty, and who heroically has resolved to leave be the entire dark world of his own unconscious psychology—the Acheron (river of the underworld). In "Death in Venice," Mann formulated his viewpoint in words which he himself (1926) has characterized as strongly anti-analytic:

> But it seems that a noble and active mind blunts itself against nothing so quickly as the sharp and bitter irritant of knowledge. And certain it is that the youth's constancy of purpose, no matter how painfully conscientious, was shallow beside the mature resolution of the master of his craft, who made a right-about-face, turned his back on the realm of knowledge, and passed it by with averted face, lest it lame his will or power of action, paralyse his feelings or his passions, deprive any of these of their conviction or utility.

In this way we are introduced to the aristocratic and mature figure of Aschenbach, who condemns all forms of "indecent" self-absorption and dissection and who by sheer self-abnegation has devoted his life to fulfilling his dutiful tasks, an achievement for which he must struggle and sacrifice day after day. But the Acheron is merely denied and not conquered. The forces of the unconscious which persisted and grew in secret suddenly demonstrate their existence, and now we witness a series of events which inexorably lead to Aschenbach's doom. It is the inevitability of his fate that moves us so deeply. The whole magnificent edifice of this man's life is suddenly swept aside by chaotic forces and all that remains of his courageous morality is dignity in death. In this story the artist depicts the problem, but he does not resolve it. We are confronted with an antipsychological ideal, apparently the artist's own, an ideal of duty and accomplishment, but he himself shows us that this ideal is beset by the danger of that which has been repudiated, not recognized, and therefore not settled, seeking revenge.

Here I may point to the fact that psychoanalysis has extraordinarily deepened a problem that basically is an old one. The question whether life requires some inner dishonesty, some deliberate overlooking of certain things has after all been an age-old theme in literature. Only a few decades before "Death in Venice" Ibsen dealt with the problem of a lie maintained throughout life in *The Wild Duck*. But what an enormous difference in the perspectives of Ibsen and Mann! Both pose essentially the same question, but in one case it is external matters that are passed over and refused recognition, whereas in the other the problem is reduced to its essential core—the repudiation of inner forces and the dishonesty with regard to internal life. These two works, which deal with the identical problem on such different levels, are separated by the thoughts of Nietzsche and Freud.

Thomas Mann has dealt with this problem over and over again; in fact, the major part of his lifework could be described from this viewpoint. From among the many works which thematically belong in this category, I shall refer only to the solution attempted in *The Magic Mountain*. One of the meanings of the magic mountain is, after all, introspection, preoccupation with one's own inner world, rather than an active attempt to change the external world. The magic mountain is the domain of "indecent" psychology. And in contrast to the flatlands where man continuously labors with his tasks, the magic mountain appears in two different lights: it is dangerous; man can perish in it; but at the same time it is magnificent and opens up vistas into previously unknown worlds—indeed, the prospect of a new mankind seems to be concealed in it. The two great series of related endeavors are, in one domain, effectiveness with regard to the tasks of life, morality, health, life; whereas in the other, psychology, insight, knowledge, moral jeopardy, illness, and death are equated. Mann sees the final solution in the following formula: Life can be approached in two ways. One is the road of life itself (the immediate direct route); the other, the road of death (the detour via turning away from the external world to a submersion in the internal one—that is to say, the detour via the magic mountain) is the dangerous but inspired route.

From these artistic elaborations of the problem I turn back to a more sober consideration of it, although the meaning of psychoanalysis can be formulated in the words of the artist. Psychoanalysis seeks a type of man who finds it increasingly difficult to make his way in the flatlands but who will find his way back to the flatlands via a detour over the magic mountain; psychoanalysis points to the road of death, a road that is dangerous but inspiring. At the same time psychoanalysis removes the danger because, unlike the solitary protagonists of the novel, a person in analysis is not alone when he passes through a phase of introspection and is threatened with losing his bearings. He must embark on this only under the guidance of an expert— and this is one of the reasons (not the only one) why self-analysis will always remain an impossible undertaking.

This impressive example has demonstrated how the existence of psychoanalysis has influenced the attitude to life's problems in literature. I shall now attempt to examine this influence more systematically.

How does analysis basically view man's life? Analysis shows us that the roots of our destiny are to be found in us, in our own nature, to a disproportionately larger extent than we ourselves were inclined to believe. It further shows us that even those events which seemed to originate entirely in the external world have indeed been sought out and selected by our unconscious. If we add one word to the popular proverb "Everyone is master of his own destiny" and say: "In everyone is the master of his own destiny," we have characterized the analytic conception rather accurately. The proverb in its commonly known form is certainly not correct since our conscious will power is capable of influencing our destiny only to a very limited degree. But within us are active forces that can shape our fate. It is these forces which for the first time became conscious in Dostoyevsky, Nietzsche, and Freud and which Freud was able to explore by developing a systematic method capable of scientifically exploiting his own experiences. From his insight derives the program of psychoanalysis: to get to know the demon (the primitive and powerful instinctual forces) and its nature so that it can gradually be conquered; or, if we prove to be too weak for its mastery, at least to outwit it, to make compromises with it, as it were.

I shall proceed with my presentation of the effects of this analytic program in terms of two objections, probably the most important ones, which have been raised against analytic therapy. Both of them are aimed at conscious awareness: one concerns achievements; the other, experience. Insight paralyzes the will to act, says the first one; it destroys immediate experience, says the other. I propose not only to counter these objections but actually to demonstrate that analysis can contribute to the enrichment of opportunities in both directions.

The first objection maintains that insight leads to an affliction of the will, always has harmful effects on values, and is not confined to the therapeutically desirable goals which aim at analyzing pathological phenomena. Insight is always destructive even if the demon in us creates something good and valuable. Our antagonist may even point to certain analytic findings according to which the genetic roots not only of the pathological but also of the healthy trends, even of creativity, reach into the infantile instinctual drives. For this reason all uncovering of historical connections and all psychologizing penetration are to be feared.

In order to gain clarity about these interrelations, we must ask how and under what conditions insight and self-knowledge can overturn existing systems of values and have a demoralizing effect on them. I referred to this possibility at the beginning of this essay and attempted to formulate an answer. I said that this will happen whenever an inner contradiction in a person's value system can be uncovered. An example will illustrate these circumstances.

Let us assume that a person has a Weltanschauung, according to which health is the highest of all possible values. And now, for whatever reason, this person begins to realize that under certain circumstances health is in conflict with other values, that under certain circumstances the supremacy of the health ideal can be maintained only by denying other values. If as a result of this insight this person revises his Weltanschauung, the only reason for this is that precisely those other ideals that at one time or other can come in conflict with the health ideal have always been high on this person's scale of values. If this had not been the case or no longer is the case—if, for example, these other moral precepts had not been always held in high esteem—there would be no way in which insight into the contradiction between the high order of health values and other, also highly esteemed ideals could possibly change anything in the previously existing scale of values. It follows that insight can lead to a change in the scale of values only when these values have been in hidden contradiction to each other and when the newly acquired insight uncovers this contradiction and brings it fully into consciousness. This is true with regard to all other ways in which insight can influence a person's Weltanschauung. A Weltanschauung that is free of inherent contradictions, that is devoid of any hidden splits, cannot be affected by insight and conscious awareness— and therefore also not by psychoanalytic insight and awareness.

If as a result of a personal analysis we realize that our aims and endeavors, all that which we value most highly, invariably also satisfy our instinctual drives—that this unconscious connection may indeed be the most powerful motive and driving force—this insight can devalue our aims and endeavors only if we deem any kind of drive gratification as altogether reprehensible. But in that case our Weltanschauung has always suffered from inherent contradictions; we valued something in one sense and rejected it in another sense. And this inherent contradiction—this lie existing throughout life, as we can surely say—has prevented a genuine unification of the personality. It is

of course possible that our first confrontation with the existence
of such meaningful connections between our highest ideals and
the lowest forces may initially have a devaluing effect. But this
will happen only at the very first encounter, because then
experience will teach us over and over again that such connections are universal; and with this awareness, the powerful
will to live, which in the final analysis can never dispense with
its positive values, will find new ways of resolving the now
uncovered contradictions. It will not let its highest ideals be
devalued; it will only give up the demand that those highest aims
must have no unconscious connections with what is held in the
lowest esteem. Such a person will remove from his Weltanschauung the demand that his most lofty ideals in life must be severed
from all vital concerns and, so to say, hover in empty space.

Thus we can assert that insight as such is not capable of
destroying values; but it may appear to be doing that when it has
uncovered a previously concealed inherent contradiction in a
value system; when this value system has been erected on the
often surprisingly resistant, but by no means reliable basis of a
vital untruth. Yet, even in this case, the conflict is usually solved
differently. Devaluation occurs only as a reaction to the initial
and most superficial contact with dawning awareness; deeper
knowledge leads only to the renunciation of untenable demands
and merely frees our highest values from any untruth without in
the least shaking them.

When we encounter a case of broken will power that seeks to
present itself as the victim of insight, we can assume that the true
relationship between cause and effect is the reverse: it is not
knowledge that bent will power; rather, an unsound will power
uses insight for purposes of self-justification; such damaged will
power can be restored to health only (if at all) via the route of
genuine and deeper self-knowledge.

Briefly, then, we can say that the effect of knowledge is not
devaluation but is resolution of contradictions and thus unification. Precisely the same is true with regard to the effect of
psychoanalytic self-knowledge: it does not demolish a person's
most significant and meaningful aims, but it does remove
inherent contradictions in these aims and the paralysis of those
forces that were devoted to the maintenance of opposing aims.

At this point we can formulate our reply to the first objection: analysis does not weaken the will; rather, by resolving inner contradictions in its aims, it liberates it. The outcome of a personal analysis is not the distorted caricature of a rationalizing man that psychology likes to substitute for a man's neurosis, rather is it a personality that has become unified.

But if unconscious inner conflicts no longer require any expenditure of energy, it becomes possible to employ the liberated energies in external pursuits. If a person in accord with the precepts of our Western civilization believes that the solution of external tasks is the decisive requirement of life, he would have to favor the road into the unconscious because it is not only the mainspring of neurosis but it is also the great reservoir of all vital forces.

The second objection asserted that insight leads to the destruction of immediate experience. This argument is completely analogous to the first one; it merely repeats the same points it had made with regard to action now on the level of experience. And for precisely the same reasons, the very opposite is true.

Let us start out by examining this objection naïvely and without the benefit of theoretical tools. We are then astonished that this objection is raised only against analysis but not against innumerable other, comparable matters. Nobody believes that a musician who has mastered the laws of harmony and counterpoint will as a result be disturbed in his capacity of musical experience. We would not assume that a physician's capacity for erotic pleasure is in the least diminished by his detailed knowledge of the anatomy and physiology of the sexual organs. Empirical knowledge unequivocally speaks against such hypotheses.

To begin with, we should not equate "conscious" and "capable of becoming conscious." Knowledge of psychological connections does not mean its omnipresence in consciousness, any more than it means that the physician's anatomical knowledge constantly occupies the center of his attention.

But in all other respects the problem resolves itself in exactly the same way as the first one. An inhibition of and a depreciation in the capacity for immediate experience may arise when a person for the first time gains some superficial insight, but these will recede as the mature person can tolerate genuine knowledge. The immature boy may react to being given information about anatomical details with repudiation and disgust; the physician who has become intimately acquainted with the human body will no longer be disturbed in his capacity to experience because he long ago severed any connection the latter may have had with ethereal illusions. For the same reason analysis does not disturb a person's capacity for immediate experience when it provides insight into the psychological connections in which an experience is embedded; rather it increases a person's measure of tolerance of all things human and thereby also frees his experiential capacity from the dangers which otherwise might threaten it precisely because of these connections.

The knowledge that manure has been used does not disturb our enjoyment of fragrant flowers or tasty food. But if it should do so—then there is an urgent need for analysis, which will not banish all fragrance and tastiness but merely help establish that tolerance that will permit the full experience of these qualities.

Insight without increased tolerance would disturb the capacity to experience; insight with tolerance, which is after all the product of genuine insight, not only maintains the knowledge that such connections are universally valid, it even removes the dangers that otherwise threaten it by incidental bits of knowledge acquired piecemeal. So we can say again that a little analysis alienates experience, but a complete analysis will not only restore a person's capacity to experience but actually strengthen it and put it on a more solid foundation.

Knowledge of psychological connections may even become the basis on which an entirely new, genuine, and very deep form of experience may arise. Let me illustrate this with an example taken from a different field of human endeavor. Let us assume that a person has acquired thorough schooling in social and economic theory. He is well aware of his own social position and the role he plays in the economic life of his country. He has a clear picture of his own functions as well as those of others. The knowledge available to such a person will enable him not only to have a better understanding of his professional activities and the details of everyday events, but actually to have different, richer, and more intensive experiences than are open to others. In the same way knowledge of the manifold psychological connections within us and between people, of the routes by which one person's unconscious leads to that of another—such knowledge will gradually be transformed into powerful experiences pervading the whole personality. In this way a very minor occurrence, a most negligible detail can become significant, just as for an artistically trained eye every single detail of a painting has a significance that is not even noticed by others. Such a person may develop an extraordinary experiential sensitivity, a readiness to experience the world symbolically which permits words to become reality: "Everything transient is but a simile."

Max Weber spoke of science creating a disenchanted world; but knowledge can also create renewed enchantment. An understanding of the physical laws governing the functioning of a machine will interfere with the impression of seeing something magical, an impression which a small child or a primitive man will receive; yet the significance of this understanding in a person's direct experience will at the same time set into motion a new enchantment with reality that will finally be more complete and more magnificent than that which it destroyed.

This enrichment may yield not only an intellectual but also a wholly experiential understanding of all things human; such understanding, concentrated in a feeling of unity and meaningfulness of the world, can be called a religious experience in the purest sense of the word. This may succeed in freeing us from one of the most common afflictions of our time—it may conquer the alienation of civilized man. And this is one of the very few ways by which this conquest can come about by means other than impulsive or delusional ones.

Summarizing our arguments countering the two main objections of others, we can characterize the analytic perspective on life in both directions: unification of the personality, as seen from the aspect of action; and leading to full experience as seen from the experiential aspect. What both trends have in common is the resolution of internal contradictions and the transposition of knowledge to life.

With this, one of Nietzsche's ideals for the future seems to gain a more specific and circumscribed content. By means of the transformations that psychoanalysis aims at and under favorable conditions actually achieves, it may indeed be possible to take a first step in the direction of that development of which the prophetic philosophers are fantasying. We can now formulate in scientific terms what must occur to bring man to the point where *he lives* rather than "is being lived." The knowledge that our destiny is being forged within us to an extent that far exceeds conscious awareness can be used to provide the means and forces to forge it ourselves. We know that the center of the personality, the ego, is subject to the influences of other psychic forces. The power of the ego can therefore be augmented by loosening the ego's dependence on these forces. Such a development is the first goal that the analytic technique achieves and is at the same time the first step that is taken under the control of consciousness (Ferenczi and Rank, 1924).

If we now attempt to define the position of psychoanalysis in the history of thought, we no longer hesitate in saying: it is rationalism and belongs with Socrates, Voltaire, and the encyclopedists. Yet, a decisive factor separates psychoanalysis from its historical neighbors. Voltaire's rationalism was flawed by what he had to eliminate. He had to discard the inherent truths of myths and mysticism because these truths had not yet been cast in scientifically useful terms—a step that would have required an understanding of mythical thinking and the formulation of a new scientific language. He also had to sacrifice all the opportunities for direct experience which mysticism contains, without being able to offer a substitute for those vital values. *Psychoanalysis is that rationalism which for the first time attempted to rescue and make accessible to its scrutiny the truths and ethical values inherent in irrationality.* I believe it is not necessary to illustrate the many instances in which psychoanalysis correctly grasped the essential ideas of prescientific thoughts and presented them in scientific language. It should suffice if, for example, we point to the demonological conception of illness, which, freed of its scientifically useless trappings, psychoanalysis incorporated into the body of scientific knowledge. In the same way psychoanalysis endeavors to approach the experiential potentialities of a mythical Weltanschauung and to incorporate it into its own rational one.

I have described a movement that was begun by Dostoyevsky and Nietzsche and put on a scientific foundation by Freud—i.e., a movement initiated by the chance appearance of several leading personalities. We are justified in asking why such a movement should occur in our time which in so many respects can be characterized by precisely the opposite intellectual trends. Alexander (1925) has offered an explanation of why the onset of the psychological period occurred in our days. With the intensification of civilization man's life has become increasingly difficult; adaptation to the environment imposes continuously greater tasks upon the individual. Tradition-bound eras made it easier for the individual to learn to fulfill its demands. If reality becomes more complex, more variegated, and more contradictory, then in the same measure the possible conflicts confronting a person on his way to adapt to reality are increased, as is the danger of being wrecked by them.

Freud described two methods by which a person may approach his environment. One is autoplastically, i.e., the person changes himself to adapt to a given environment. The other is alloplastically, i.e., the person attempts to change the environment in conformance with his own needs. Many forms of biological development could be described as autoplastic solutions; the entire course of human cultural development, however, is a magnificent example of continuous and successful alloplastic solutions. The psychic development of man, it seems to me, has not kept in step with the cultural development. Once the cultural phenomena have been created, they no longer obey the will of their creator; they lead an independent life of their own; and with this has grown in the creators a tension that is no longer tolerable. Thus it becomes a biological necessity to let the pendulum swing back from a long period of exclusively alloplastic endeavors to a phase of autoplastic solutions. This is necessary to ease the tension, to enable man once more to find within himself the strength to live with his creations rather than be oppressed by them. The modern psychological movement is one such attempt: through internal changes it seeks to bring man to the point where he is no longer at the mercy of his creations. The autoplastic, psychological period, of which the psychoanalytic movement is the most essential and decisive part, may then lead to a type of man who, freed of conflicts, can take all its achievements for granted and who can then dispense with the psychology to which he owes them.

CHAPTER 22

Sexual Symbolism in
Primitive Society

(1929)

One tenet of psychoanalytic theory, i.e., sexual symbolism, has encountered special difficulties in being accepted. It maintains that all manifestations of the unconscious, in particular the language of the dream, are dominated by a symbolism the translation of which regularly leads into the sphere of sexuality. No doubt, for those who are unfamiliar with psychoanalytic observations, it is very difficult to believe that the unconscious mind regards every straight object as a penis and every concave one as a vagina. For this reason confirmation from sources other than the psychoanalytic situation proper was especially welcome.

Such evidence has been furnished by experimental means (Schrötter, 1911; Roffenstein, 1923; Betlheim and Hartmann, 1924). Schrötter and Roffenstein investigated symbol formation in experimentally induced dreams. They asked experimental subjects whom they had hypnotized to dream about a specific sexual event, which in the subsequent dreams was in fact represented by the symbols that are well known in analysis. For example, a young girl was given the posthypnotic suggestion to dream of fellatio; in the dream she ate bananas. Betlheim and Hartmann worked with a woman suffering from Korsakoff

First published as "Sexualsymbolik bei Naturvölkern." *Psychoanalytische Bewegung*, 1:73-75, 1929. The English translation by Lottie M. Newman is here published for the first time.

psychosis, i.e., a patient with an organically determined memory deficit. They told her simple stories which had a sexual content and which they asked her to reproduce after a certain lapse of time. In these stories the sexual elements had dropped out and been replaced by related symbols.

If it is true that the unconscious mind relates all objects and phenomena to something sexual, we would expect to find similar manifestations in the thinking of primitive men. While the processes operative in the unconscious are not universally parallel to the thought processes of primitive man, this assumption is, though by no means a rule, nevertheless a fruitful working hypothesis.

The work of Father Winthuis (1928), a Catholic missionary and ethnologist, contains relevant and important material. Winthuis lived for many years with the natives of the German colony of New Guinea. Having gained their trust, he succeeded in learning much about their peculiar way of thinking and experiencing, intimate details that are usually concealed from whites. I cannot judge whether some of the hypotheses advanced by Winthuis might have to be modified in the light of ethnological critique; I simply accept them as the basis for my discussion. In any event, Winthuis was hardly at all influenced by psychoanalysis; although his work contains an occasional reference to an analytic publication, the whole tone of his book clearly demonstrates that psychoanalytic theories are foreign to him.

Winthuis shows that the language of the Gunantuna of New Pommerania contains words with a double meaning, an ordinary verbal one and the other with a pictorial meaning. Surprisingly and unexpectedly, yet so similar to unconscious operations, the pictorial language has primarily sexual connotations. Thus, the word for "eye" is also the picture for the vagina; the word "nose" is the picture for penis. Winthuis relates that he once used this word in a lecture whereupon everyone began to laugh. "The people explained to me that I should not ever use this word in an address, but we must also note that they have no other word for nose."

Likewise, the word for "mouth" corresponds to the pictorial word for vagina; "tongue" to penis. The word "open" becomes in the conception of the Gunantuna *vagina aperta;* the words "pole" and "lance" are linked with the erect penis.

Similar rules apply to gestures and their interpretation. It is noteworthy, however, that this second, sexual connotation of words and gestures is not an unconscious meaning which is interpreted in the same way as we would interpret neurotic symptoms in terms of their unconscious meaning. On the contrary, the two meanings are fully equivalent in the unconsciousness of these people. That much equivalence exists can be attributed to a specific characteristic of primitive thought processes. It was first described by Levy-Bruhl who emphasized the identificatory quality of primitive thought which equates the representation of something with the thing itself. The dancer who in a ceremony represents God does not merely represent him, as we would say; he is God. In the same sense, pole or lance *is* the penis; the eye *is* the vagina.

Winthuis describes a ceremonial dance of Gunantuna women who draw several horizontal lines from the ear to the eye in their faces. Since the eye is the vagina and a line is the phallus, the whole drawing is a conscious invitation to cohabit. If any man comes in contact with a woman thus decorated, e.g., if he touches her basket or the color with which she painted herself, he is obliged to have intercourse with her because, as Winthuis points out, "This line in the woman's face does not merely *signify* the male organ, it *is* the organ of the man with whom the woman comes in contact, and for this reason he must cohabit with her."

These findings converge at several points: the primitive's mind makes equations that correspond to the way the unconscious mind operates, as disclosed by psychoanalysis; furthermore, as far as their content is concerned, these equations invariably lead into the sexual sphere, again in agreement with the psychoanalytic postulates concerning the content of the unconscious.

Winthuis presents a great deal more material relating to content. Speaking of primitive art, he assures us that a simple straight or oval line "is all that is needed to tell every primitive what the artist wishes to signify.... These examples should suffice to indicate that in primitive thinking whatever is straight is the phallus and everything round or curved signifies the vagina.....Everyone familiar with the pictorial language knows that everything reminiscent of sex, no matter how remotely, even if there is only the most minute indication of linear or round shape, the primitive man will relate it to sex. Hence, in his thinking, nose, tongue, speer, arrow, lance, arm, leg, pole, feather, tail, and the like all signify phallus, whereas head, eye, mouth, disc, ear, hole all stand for female."

According to Winthuis's testimony, therefore, the sexual symbolism which psychoanalysis postulates is operative in the unconscious of civilized man has an evolutionary parallel in the *consciousness* of primitive man. Moreover, the identificatory quality of primitive thinking, again analogous to the processes that psychoanalysis found at work in the unconscious, leads to a direct equation rather than a symbolization.

Since this communication deals only with sexual symbolism, I shall not go into the rest of the material presented by Winthuis or discuss his comprehensive theory of primitive culture. In conclusion, I merely wish to state that his ethnological material brings new evidence confirming the psychoanalytic theory of symbolization. Moreover, the assumption of an analogy between primitive thinking and unconscious functioning proved to be a useful working hypothesis.

CHAPTER 23

The Etiology and Course
of Mass Psychoses

(1934)

War and Mass Psychosis

The problem of mass psychosis has been subjected to intensive investigation by many renowned scholars. My approach is guided not so much by theoretical aims but by a practical consideration. Mass psychosis is a phenomenon which contributes to the initiation of wars or to the development and maintenance of passionately militaristic attitudes in a population. This essay therefore does not deal comprehensively with all mass psychosis phenomena, nor will it present a comprehensive psychology of war or of people ready to engage in wars. A leader of a country may decide on war on the basis of a great number of motives, and the population may follow him on that path for an equal number of reasons. Mass psychosis constitutes only one element of these motives, but it probably is the most dangerous one. If we believe the historians who assure us that Julius Caesar embarked on the Gallic venture because he was fully convinced

First published as "L'étiologie et l'évolution des psychoses collectives, suivie par quelques remarques concernant la situation historique actuelle," tr. M. Bonaparte. In: L'ésprit, l'ethique et la guerre. Paris: Institut International de Cooperation Intellectuelle (Société des Nations), 3(66):85-150, 1934. Also as "Ätiologie und Verlauf der Massenpsychosen: Mit einem soziologischen Anhang über die geschichtliche Situation der Gegenwart," Imago, 21:67-91, 1935. The English translation by Lottie M. Newman is published here for the first time. The Appendix on the Historical Situation of the Present has not been included.

that ancient civilization could be rescued only by putting a complete halt to the ongoing great migration of people; that having subdued this province the Roman Empire would have an eminently defensible outpost; and that his soldiers would follow him either because of the iron Roman discipline or because of their personal devotion to him—then mass psychosis apparently had no share in the outbreak of the Gallic War, and Caesar embarked on it for rational motives.

But in other wars, this may not be the case, and the dangers inherent in the group of motives of the mass psychosis justify all efforts to elucidate this phenomenon in the hope that such knowledge will also contribute to preventive measures. In this area of applied social psychology we may find what has been true in medicine: one does not discover the simple and effective measures which would once and for all do away with undesirable phenomena, e.g., not the great sterilizer that some pioneers in chemotherapy may have envisaged, but one does find new weapons in the struggle against evil and these make that struggle more effective than it has been.

The Concept of Mass Psychosis

The concept of mass psychosis itself presents a peculiar difficulty. The two parts comprising this term contradict and actually exclude each other. In most psychotic conditions the person has quit the community of man and no longer or only partially participates in its perceptions, experiences, and thoughts. A person is psychotic when the others, the healthy people, are no longer able to engage him in lively mutual contact, which otherwise occurs in the community of man. The phenomenon of the psychotic's contact disturbance defines the concept of mental illness to such an extent that in doubtful cases in which the psychiatrist wavers between the diagnosis of genuine psychosis and neurosis, he will use the uncanny feeling which he himself experiences in contact with such patients as the criterion for his decision. If mental illness is thus characterized by disturbances in the relationship with other people and by isolation from society, how can a mass be psychotic? Each individual who is in the grip of the so-called mass psychosis does not lose contact with the others and remains in the social group; indeed, by virtue of the intoxicating mood prevalent in such masses he may in fact be bound to the community by even stronger ties. We see that we can speak of mass psychosis only in an imprecise meaning of the term. The people who share in the mass psychosis are not psychotic in the psychiatric sense. Every one of them is psychically normal—to the extent that one can speak of psychic normality in a large number of people. As individuals they are accessible and capable of entering into relationships with others and behave like other healthy people —except within the system governed by the mass psychosis. In regard to the ideas comprising the mass psychosis, however, they are as little influenced by logical considerations and as incapable of being corrected as are the delusions of psychotics. In contrast to the latter, however, mass psychosis is a transient and time-limited phenomenon. As a rule, it does not persist throughout a person's entire life. Moreover, the fact that a person once believed in the delusional ideas of a mass psychosis does not permit one to make a prognosis of his future personal development, whereas every genuine, i.e., individual psychosis is indeed prognostic of this person's further development. Not only are the people in the grip of a mass psychosis healthy individuals in the clinical-psychiatric sense—we even maintain, paradoxically, that only the healthy are receptive to mass psychosis because they are the people who easily gain contact with others; they represent the social type and do not tend to isolate and sequester themselves. In contrast, the truly mentally ill who, isolated from the world, live in their own narcissistic sphere can hardly be seized by a mass psychosis. They have their own private delusional world and will only very rarely relinquish it in order to participate in the commonly shared delusional world that social men in groups erect.

It is of course true that a mass also contains a small number of people at the border of psychosis, who are not wholly mentally ill and who escape into the mass psychosis as a last means of preventing the complete submergence into their individual psychosis.

The Induction of Psychosis

Psychiatry has long been familiar with the phenomenon of the so-called induced psychosis. Let us assume that in an isolated village a messiah or prophet of a better world appears. His notions of how the world could be saved are delusional, as are his claims that he or a group of people is being systematically persecuted. Even though this man is clearly mentally ill, it frequently happens that the entire village will be infected by his delusional beliefs. For some time they will really believe in his paranoid delusions, even though every one of the villagers is healthy. If the paranoiac is removed from their midst, their normal mental state will soon reestablish itself. It is an interesting psychological phenomenon that mentally ill personalities, especially when they are strong, which usually is the case, can often exert a powerful influence on healthy people. The explanation can be sought in the fact that the narcissistic person who isolated from others indulges in love of himself has a peculiarly intense fascination for others. The ordinary man who is constantly dependent on the love and esteem of his fellowman suspects in this self-contained narcissism the long-lost paradise of his own childhood when he was not yet subject to the dire necessities of life. In this way the person who no longer loves anything but himself becomes the love object of others, and the person who recognizes no one but himself as the judge of his actions easily becomes the judge of the action of others.

The Requirements of De-Inhibition

The most important phenomenon of a mass psychosis that occasionally may have its share in the outbreak of a war or may facilitate the conduct and exacerbation of a war is the de-inhibition of the instinctual life, that is to say, primarily of the aggressive instincts. On the basis of analytic investigations of individual people, psychoanalysis postulated that aggressive strivings, impulses to destroy and kill, are an inherent part of human nature, having their counterpart in what generally is referred to as Eros or love, those drives that strive for the preservation of life and the creation of more highly organized formations.[1] The philosophical tenets of Empedocles who maintained that the world is moved by love and hatred, by attraction and repulsion, were revived by psychoanalysis on the basis of compelling empirical observations. The aggressive drives of man normally do not exist in isolation and do not result in the real destruction of the external world. This is due to Eros which is capable of entering into admixtures with the aggressive drives, thus rendering the forms in which the latter manifests itself less dangerous. The highest degree of inactivating the harmful effect of the aggressive instinct, of neutralizing it, is found in the true love between man and woman. With the aggressive element being confined entirely to the task of taking hold of the partner, it is so densely enveloped by erotic actions that it no longer manifests itself as aggression.

The various constituents of the aggressive drives are usually inhibited and the fact that such an inhibition comes about can largely be attributed to education. In its pure and naked form the aggressive instinct manifests itself only in certain borderline states of human existence, e.g., in criminality and more frequently in some mental illnesses which in their attacks of raving frenzy impress the observer as pure destructiveness.

In a mass psychosis a part of this aggressive instinct is liberated in a great number of people, who are neither psychotic nor criminal but normal and ethical beings, and turned against an enemy. Since the inhibition of the aggressive instincts is the product of centuries of cultural development and probably its most enduring achievement, we are confronted by the problem how such a de-inhibition can come about. How is it possible that the conscience of man acquired in thousands of generations and reerected by each individual in his own childhood can permit this to happen? Essentially, it is the result of the concurrent action of two mechanisms, one of which is a necessary ingredient of every group situation, while the other one is created by a specific idea.

In every group situation we find that the conscience of each individual is diminished and replaced by the voice of the leader.

[1] For a detailed discussion of the concept of an "instinct of Agression," see Waelder (1956) and (1960a, pp. 131-153).

Psychoanalysis speaks of a tripartite division of the personality: id, ego, and superego. The id is the instinctual which is rooted in the biological in the sense that every human psyche is housed in a body. The angels who according to scholastic philosophy have no body also do not have an instinctual life. The ego is the organizing part, the psychic structure which comes into being under the influence of the external world. Among the functions of the ego are perception and testing of the external world, the ability to act not on the impulse of the moment but in terms of the anticipated consequences, in brief, thinking in general. The superego again encompasses impulses which seemingly act on the ego from outside, as do the id impulses, but their nature is moral rather than instinctual. Its focal point is the conscience with all the demands we impose on ourselves. Beyond that, it is that agency by means of which man puts himself above his experiences and observes and criticizes himself.

In 1921 Freud formulated a theory of group behavior which since then has proved its value in many practical problems. He demonstrated that group phenomena could not be studied without taking into consideration that each group has a leader. This leader may be a contemporary person in flesh and blood, or it may be a historical person, or the image of a Godlike being, or in its most sublime form simply an idea. What then is the relationship between the group members and the leader and among the leaders themselves? The simple answer to this question is capable of explaining most group phenomena. Each member of the group puts the leader in place of his own superego; the position of the individual's conscience which commands us and decides whether our actions are good or evil is now taken up by a person in the external world who sits in judgment over us. Members of a group project their conscience onto a person in the outside world, a process that should not surprise us when we consider that the individual conscience is derived from persons in the external world. In our childhood it was first of all father and mother who judged our actions and the originally external voices of these persons became our inner voice only by means of introjection. Thus the relationship between an individual group member and its leader consists in the abrogation of part of his superego and endowing the leader with its force. The relations among the members to each other rest on the basis of this shared process which occurred in each of them: they now identify with each other, as people in general tend to do on the basis of having something in common. The relations of group members to a leader resemble a situation which occurs only between two people: the relation between hypnotic subject and hypnotist. The hypnotic subject too relegates a good part of his inner voice to the hypnotist. The extent to which this comparison elucidates the decisive relationship can be seen in those phenomena in which mass situations and hypnosis blend: confronted with mass hypnosis we no longer know whether to classify it as belonging to the hypnotic or the group manifestations.

Returning to our original question concerning the de-inhibition of the aggressive instinct, we can say that man relinquishes a part of his otherwise vigilant conscience and in its stead gives the leader full authority to wield moral power over him. It is no longer the individual's conscience that decides what is permitted and prohibited; the leader sets up the norms of behavior. If the leader permits aggression, perhaps even demands it, the individual can in good conscience pursue instinctual actions. In this way an instinctual action which otherwise would have been forbidden by the inner moral powers becomes, as it were, "pleasing to God."

This general mechanism operative in masses is usually augmented by an additional factor: people are offered some ideal. Quite likely, one would not yet succeed if one directly invited a particular instinctual action, e.g., to kill the enemy. People require, in addition, some ideal in order to perceive an action as moral and no longer as driven by instincts. One does not tell them to give free rein to their unbounded aggression against an enemy; rather they are asked to act in the service of a lofty ideal. In the course of history this ideal had many names: God, country, faith, future generations, etc. In any event, whenever aggression has been set loose, it was for the greater glory of a highly valued ideal. With his conscience thus quieted, man can satisfy the instincts that otherwise are laboriously held in check and simultaneously enjoy the pleasures that come with the fulfillment of an ideal.

Having demonstrated the importance of the aggressive instincts in the phenomena to be investigated, I turn to a discussion of their fate in the development of civilization.

Degrees of Domestication

In the course of man's development, which is called the development of culture and civilization, the instincts of man have been curtailed. In the sphere of the sexual instincts, man's sexual development has been retarded to an extraordinary degree, i.e., compared to that of his closest relatives in the animal world and to what we may surmise was true of aboriginal primitive man. Moreover, man's sexual drives have been forced to take ever wider detours on their way to reaching their aims; to be content with substitute gratifications that are increasingly far removed from the original aims. Even the attachment of substitute aims does not fully satisfy man; there always remains some restlessness which forever drives him on.

In the sphere of the aggressive instincts, this cultural development has brought about a progressive inhibition and curtailment of the destructive forces inherent in man. That part of aggression which was checked by the opposition of external forces is turned inward where in the form of punitive aggression directed against the self it becomes the motor of the powers of conscience.[2] Freud described this process as the distinguishing characteristic of civilization. He assumes that each generation must perform this task anew, forced to do so by *ananke*, the drive pressures of reality. But in the course of centuries this process repeated ever anew finally left some organic traces and thus became part of man's inheritance. He compares this process with the domestication of animals; we know that it is possible to effect some organic changes in them, e.g., that the central nervous system of the domestic dog differs markedly from that of the same species living in the wilderness.

The degree of domestication achieved differs in different men, different peoples, and different cultures. On the other hand, the clash of peoples and groups who have reached diver-

[2] In other writings the author alternately uses the words "domestication" and "internalization" (1935) and "detoxification" (1960a).

gent degrees of domestication appears to be one of the most significant driving forces in history. There is little certainty about the outcome, though it seems that in the long run the biologically stronger, less domesticated group is often victorious. Psychoanalysis has made us familiar with the hygienic danger inherent in the process of domestication; namely, it can reach a point at which the cruelty and strictness of the individual's conscience threaten his health. This happens when too much aggression has been turned inward as a result of which the overly strict conscience paralyzes man's capacity to act. The pathological border state of this phenomenon of an overgrown conscience is known to us from studies of melancholia.

Throughout the centuries the desirability of attaining the highest degree of possible domestication of the instincts has never been questioned. This is especially true in the Christian epoch of the Western world. Most of its traditional ideals, such as regard for humanity, consideration of others, justice, fair play, are ideals that require a maximal degree of instinct domestication, and primarily of aggression. This value has not been questioned throughout time and in many parts of the world is not yet questioned even today. Yet, here and there a different *Weltanschauung* has made its appearance—one that views this high level of domestication in a less favorable light. This *Weltanschauung* inclines to regard the above-mentioned ideals as products of degeneration, as protecting the weak at the cost of the strong, as apt to weaken the biological forces of the animal *homo sapiens*. This side would proclaim unbroken vitality and the might of the victor as its valued ideals.

Comparing these two *Weltanschauungen* with each other, we must acknowledge that each serves a particular value. There is no doubt that the restriction of the instincts serves man's social life—indeed, in view of the tremendous population increase social life would not be possible at all and soon lead to catastrophes without the most stringent curtailment of instincts. On the other hand, it is equally true that in this process the biological forces of man are weakened and even lost. Thus from the standpoint of preservation of live, domestication is a high value; from the standpoint of preservation of vital forces, it is a product of degeneration. Here we are up against an antinomy of human existence, and it may not be superfluous to point out that Freud has long been fully cognizant of it: a quarter of a century ago he formulated the goal of education as adaptative to reality with the utmost preservation of the original instinctual forces. This double goal does justice to the recognition that adaptation to reality jeopardizes the strength of the instincts and that their preservation endangers adaptation to reality.

The Impairment of Reality Testing

There is a point at which the processes occurring in mass psychosis do resemble those in true clinical psychoses. The factor responsible for this is the impairment and partial failure of reality testing, i.e., the capacity to test thoughts with regard to their reality content and to let facts correct them. Even the mental illness in which various complex delusional systems develop, i.e., paranoia, is not simply characterized by the patient's belief in wrong propositions. Rather, these wrong propositions are not accessible to correction by facts. This incorrigibility distinguishes a delusion from mere error.

The fact that in mass psychosis reality testing is impaired can be demonstrated by many empirical examples of such movements, e.g., the witch hunts of the early modern era; or the children's crusade in which the responsible persons apparently never entertained the thought that these children were bound to perish; and there are many other examples in more recent times. In the mass psychosis I have in mind, i.e., war, there frequently develops an image of the enemy that is delusional and for a period of time remains incorrigible. It is really the disturbance of reality testing that is responsible for the similarity between the real mental illness and the mass psychosis and that justifies the latter's name. The partial impairment of reality testing is essentially caused by two psychological factors:

The Situation of the Leader

As previously noted, the most important characteristic of group situations consists of the individual's putting a leader in the place of his own superego and in transferring a major part of his superego onto a person in the external world. One result of this is the previously mentioned de-inhibition of the instinctual life; but there are other consequences as well. The superego consists of more than a person's conscience, which is one but not the superego's only function. To the superego belong not only the functions of self-critique but also those that regard the self in a loving way; e.g., humor or (with a small admixture of aggression) self-irony. That is to say, the superego encompasses all those functions by which man puts himself above himself and objectifies or eliminates his own standpoint. We may attribute to the superego what the philosophers have called the transcendence of human life beyond its purely biological situation. To the superego, therefore, belongs self-observation. Thus, from the standpoint of his superego, man regards his own person not only critically and punitively but also lovingly and consolingly and at times even with neutral emotions. In evaluating the inner processes, however, the superego function of self-observation also contributes to the distinction between inner and outer world, between fantasy and reality, which in the mentality of primitive peoples and in the magical-mythical thinking of early childhood frequently blend with each other. If self-observation teaches me that a fantasy belongs to me, I shall be inclined to distinguish it from external happenings. The intactness of the superego is therefore necessary for the correct functioning of reality testing.

I shall cite one example to illustrate how the mythical-magical mode of thinking and the attendant sense of oneness with the cosmos are gradually given up with the growth of the superego. The oldest Egyptian Books of the Dead make man's continued life after death contingent upon the fate of his portrait and the care which his statue receives. This is a wholly magical conception which ascribes to the image, the psychic product, the power of influencing the course of events. In the later editions of the Egyptian Book of the Dead this magical theory is replaced by an ethical one: the fate of the deceased apparently depends upon the judgment pronounced by the Judge of the Dead upon the deceased person's merits and failures. With this the world of magic has been overcome; but the growth of the superego, the increasing pressure of conscience, which is apparent in this example, has accomplished an additional task: increased self-observation defined the borderline between ego and nonego and raised reality testing from the realm of mythical dreaming.

If the superego function is a prerequisite for the correct functioning of reality testing, then every change in superego functioning will have its corresponding repercussions on reality testing. In the group situation, a part of the superego is, as it were, put out of action. The individual has abrogated it to an external power. As a consequence, reality testing is open to disturbances in those areas in which the superego function has been eliminated or in which a part of the superego has been projected.

Eros and Aggression in Cohesive Groups

The second important factor is the distribution of Eros and aggression in cohesive groups. In normal circumstances the two basic drives are distributed diffusely. Every man has relations to a large number of other men; each such relation to a particular person is partly friendly and partly hostile—with the possible exception of the relationship to one's most intimate family. The "other" person may appear in the role of a life companion insofar as he is in the same profession; or perhaps as friend insofar as he is of the same faith; or as enemy insofar as he is a competitor in life's struggles. Every single individual belongs to various communities or groups which are not organized solely on the basis of one principle—friends, political, national, religious, professional, artistic, etc. The other person may belong to one such group and therefore be a friend, but not belong to another and therefore be an enemy. In psychological terms, we can say that every person's relation to another person—again with the exception of the immediate family—is a more or less ambivalent one in which Eros and aggression each have a share.

But the situation changes when a particular group develops strong ties and especially intense communalities. Then all the love is reserved for the members of the group, while those who do not belong to it are rejected, even hated as strangers and barbarians. In this case there is a total split between Eros and aggression, with each being directed to different persons.

Such splits of Eros and aggression are known to occur in

psychopathological conditions, especially paranoia. We know that various admixtures of libido and aggression are characteristic of specific types of illness and beyond that of those types in the area of normality which can be defined in analogy to different types in pathology. In hysteria—the least severe neurosis and that closest to health—the erotic and aggressive impulses are always satisfied in the same act. The same is true of the hysterical character and of those normal individuals who, without really being ill, resort to hysterical mechanisms. An example would be a mother who takes very good care of her children but at the same time tortures them precisely with her solicitude. In obsessive-compulsive neurotics, erotic and aggressive impulses alternate, one appearing after the other in a never-ending succession of ambivalence conflicts. This is also true, though to a lesser extent, for the type of healthy person that is related to the obsessional neurotic. Whenever an obsessional neurotic has shown another person some love, we may confidently expect that he will soon show some aggressive impulses and that a hostile act will soon be followed by a show of friendliness. In pathological cases anger and feelings of guilt alternate.

Here libido and aggression are no longer fused in one act, as they are in hysteria, which for this reason is closest to health. For a person is completely healthy only when his aggressive tendencies are so fully cloaked in love that they no longer appear as aggression. In obsessional neurotics libido and aggression are split, each alternating with the other, though both are still directed to the same object.

A different way of solving the ambivalence is seen in paranoia: there a total split of erotic and aggressive impulses occurs with a large number of people becoming enemies, i.e., persecutors. As the paranoid process progresses, the number of enemies tends to become ever greater; the system of persecution, of which the patient feels he is the victim, becomes ever more threatening. But alongside of this system most paranoiacs maintain to the very end a small group of people whom they do not regard as persecutors and who are outside of the delusional system. These are the patient's closest friends or family members, the few people who retain his love despite the hate-orgy of the pathological process. Thus, all love remains with a small circle of people, while all hatred is directed to the enemies in the outside world. We are familiar with the strange cases in which the paranoid process leads to a peculiar way out. The tendency to complete the delusional system, to include in it as much as possible, and to fill in all the gaps comes into conflict with the tendency to preserve a group of people outside of the system. In this case it sometimes happens that the closest friends are also included in the delusional system, but in a way that permits the patient to maintain his feelings of love and communion with them: they are included in the system not as persecutors but as the persecuted who, like the patient himself, and for the same reasons are being victimized and conspired against by the evil outside world.

This third form of dealing with the ambivalence— splitting it—closely resembles the distribution of libido and aggression in strongly cohesive groups. Here, too, all love is reserved for the members of the group, and all hatred directed to the outsiders. It surely is not a coincidence that this split is encountered in a psychosis of delusional persecution. Such a total split of the two basic human tendencies, with the friendly impulses directed to one group and the hostile ones toward all others, facilitates the breakdown of reality testing. One no longer can see clearly where one only loves or only hates. In reality light and shadow, though to varying degrees, are allotted to all objects.

The Etiology of the Mass Psychosis

The causes leading to the outbreak of those mass psychoses which I am discussing here are manifold, though an increase of aggression plays a special role.[3] Such an increase of aggression in a large number of people may be caused by various factors —first among them by dire need. Most people react to the frustration of wishes with aggression, a fact that can be observed in the simplest and most complex circumstances. The first aggressive reactions are seen in the young child whose wishes are

---

[3] In other papers on war and peace (1938, 1939b) the author discusses similar problems. There he adds and elaborates on anxiety as a motive for attack.

denied. If such a denial of human wishes occurs on a large scale—i.e., in times of need—one must expect an intensification of the aggressive drives.

We encounter another motive when a powerful aggressive pressure turned inward, e.g., intense pangs of conscience, becomes so strong that a turning of the aggression outward greatly relieves the individual. This process can be observed in pathological as well as nonpathological cases. It may even happen that a person commits a crime because of the pressures of his conscience.

A large number of causes probably will be found in the education of children. Education can surely avail itself of many different means by which it can mitigate, though not entirely curb, the expression of aggression in the child. If one attempts to deny the child only what is absolutely necessary in order to make him a civilized member of the human community; if one endeavors to compensate for such refusals by offering different forms of gratification and regularly treats the child with friendliness; if the adults and society are themselves aware of their own aggressive impulses, which frequently tend to be unconsciously acted out on the child, and control them; if the child is led to adapt to reality with patience and forbearance—then the aggression of the child can be restricted to that modest measure which finds useful employment in the struggles of life. Then none of the excesses will arise that threaten society or, if turned inward, jeopardize the individual's health. But this as a rule is not how adults behave toward children. Moreover, some forms of education as they are practiced in certain countries or by different social classes have the effect of quantitatively increasing aggression. The history of nations cannot be written without taking into consideration the methods used to educate children and how these are employed from generation to generation.

The Course of Mass Psychoses

A mass psychosis in which the aggressive impulses are all at once discharged toward the outside can run its course in two basic ways. It can occur either before the violent act has been committed, i.e., before the aggression has wrought real destruction, or it can occur after the evil has been realized. The aggression may be inhibited in its expression before the evil act is carried out. This may be done by an external power deploying superior forces to prevent an attack by the charging crowd. We know that in such cases when aggression is blocked on the outside, it turns back inside of the people themselves and changes to pangs of conscience and depression. But then the destructive urges have run their course.

If, on the other hand, a violent act has been carried out, then the gratification of the aggressive impulses may be followed by the appearance of Eros. It is a generally valid rule that a drive that has been gratified loses its intensity; when thirst has been stilled, there is no more thirst. If aggression is satisfied, it abates and libido can again rise up. As a result friendly impulses will predominate and express themselves in remorse and tendencies to make amends.

This process has its parallel in the development of the first moral manifestations in the child. They come about in different ways. In part they derive from introjections of parental demands and prohibitions which the child makes his own; he tells himself what he has been told by the adults. This path is of little interest in the context of this study. Of greater relevance is the fact that the phenomena of conscience in early childhood also derive from the vicissitudes of the aggressive impulses and their conflicts with love. If a child is inhibited in expressing his aggression against an external object, e.g., a sibling, either by an external power that prevents the expression of aggression—in either case the hostility ambivalence to the object to whom the child directs not only the hostile thought but also tender feelings so that his own love prevents the expression of aggression—in either case the hostiligy reverts to the person of the child himself. He may then beat himself if he had wanted to beat the other person. We thus witness the appearance of the self-punishing tendencies, of moral aggression directed against the self. But if the aggression has not been blocked before carrying out the destructive act, then the very satisfaction of the aggression shifts the balance between friendly and hostile impulses toward a renewed predominance of Eros which finds expression in a rising sense of remorse, in attempts to repair the damage, in a feeling of guilt and obligation to the person one has harmed.[4] Both components, the aggression against the self and the feelings of guilt and obligation toward another, the self-punishment and the remorse, are contained in moral phenomena as the aggressive and erotic constituent parts.

Whether aggression reverts upon the self before a violent act is carried out depends, of course, either on a strong external force preventing the realization of hostilities and, so to say, locking a person with his aggressions in prison, or on the strength of a person's own libidinal strivings that suffice to hinder the aggressive attack. Otherwise, there remains the question how many really destructive acts must be carried out before the aggression finds satisfaction and Eros can again have its say. That depends, of course, on the relative strength of the aggressive and erotic urges.

These are the few facts that can be stated with regard to the role and course of aggression in great mass movements. The practical implications are clear, though by no means comforting. No one can predict the degree of aggression that must be satisfied before the libidinal strivings can reassert their relative dominance. That this nevertheless does occur, history teaches us. Whenever aggressive and less "domesticated" people won a victory over more highly civilized cultures, they wound up assimilating the culture of the conquered people—which is to say that after the event they finally became "domesticated."[5]

[4] These considerations follow Nunberg (1926) who was the first to describe the share of libido and aggression in phenomena of conscience.

[5] *Editor's note:* In the appendix contained in the original paper the author traces the social and especially economic factors that lead to progressive urbanization, which in view of its inherent economic instability also has psychological repercussions. For a full elaboration of these thoughts, see Waelder (1967a).

The ideas discussed in this chapter were also used by the author in several other papers (1936, 1938), and a book (1939b) written during the same period of time, and in an address to the Royal Institute of International Affairs (1935). (The unpublished manuscript was made available by Mr. Duncan Hall.) In this address the author discusses the motives of war as deriving from id, ego, and superego sources. He singles out the role of aggression in communal life, much as he does in the present chapter, but then proceeds to a discussion of the implications, which we add here as an appendix.

APPENDIX

THE PSYCHOLOGICAL ASPECTS OF
INTERNATIONAL AFFAIRS

(1935)

In view of these considerations, what has psychology to say
concerning the problems of prevention of war and the organization of international peace? The possibility of permanent
peace seems to pose a psychological problem, for it involves
action by human beings who have varying degrees of control
over their instinctual motives. All attempts aimed at securing
permanent peace by means of juridical and technical measures
alone are, to my mind, utopian; for the question under what
conditions these institutions will become practically effective
depends on how man carries them out. This does not mean that
psychology may be used as evidence to prove that permanent
peace is altogether a utopia. For it can be shown that under
certain psychological conditions the manifold motives of war, as
outlined above, break down altogether. The instinctual impulses
which urge man to war can be suppressed or controlled or
satisfied in different ways. The gradual domestication of the
aggressive instinct seems to be a cultural fate; its *complete*
success is, of course, questionable and lies in a distant future. As
far as the claims of the superego are concerned, war is not an
inevitable demand of the superego; it may make other, peaceful
claims. The primitive responses of the immature ego recede as
the ego grows in maturity. And the rational motives for war play
a lesser part when the human ego is mature and is capable of
finding solutions of its tasks by other means. Finally, the more
mature man's ego is, the less statesmen are compelled to take into
consideration the reactions of the masses. Hence, it is not

From an address to the Royal Institute of International Affairs, Chatham
House, London, 1935.

admissible to regard psychology as pointing to the impossibility of permanent peace.

Several years ago, with the creation of an international peace organization, a new practical method was adopted to do away with war as an instrument of politics. One of contemporary man's most pressing problems is whether this medium is adequate for the fulfillment of the hopes placed in it. What are the chances that the existence of this organization and its operations can influence the action of man to prevent war?

Perhaps the name, League of Nations, is partly responsible for the disappointment, felt in certain quarters, in the efficiency of the League. This name, League of Nations, misleads the ordinary man into believing that a supernational being exists which will act independently of the states which constitute the League. This personification can be attributed to the magic, mythical thinking which lives on in civilized man of our mechanized time, and induces him to accept a symbol as a reality. We are not so far removed from those primitive beings who burn their enemy in effigy and who refrain from pronouncing a name in the fear of conjuring up the feared object. In the model of the mental personality, this magic thinking belongs to the primitive levels of the ego; it is largely responsible for the many disappointments and unjustified reproaches against Geneva.

When we examine the possible efficacy of the Geneva Covenant, we must first ask what the power of this international organization is. Its efficiency clearly rests on this power.

The first point to be considered is that the Geneva organization does not have at its disposal a military power of its own, and that any attempt to give it such power seems at present to be utopian. For the application of force the League remains dependent on the goodwill of its members to supply it with suitable means, and consequently is dependent on the uncertainties of political constellations. The fact that it lacks material power is in itself no death warrant of an institution; history provides us with an impressive example of a purely spiritual power which in spite of originally slender material resources acted at times as arbiter of the fate of nations: namely, the medieval papacy.

What does such spiritual power consist of? It can exist only when the recognition of an authority is rooted in the superego of every individual, so that it would be a sin against their consciences if they did not yeild to that guiding force. The institution of the papacy was powerful because at the time of its apex the superego of Western humanity was Christian and Catholic, and conscience prohibited the Christian ruler from using his full power against the pope. When he did so, his subjects, as a rule, revolted against him at the command of their consciences. As these conditions changed, the power of the papacy declined.

A spiritual power can therefore be unbounded, but only when its authority is implanted in the superegos of all the people. It is based in a superego appeal. When such spiritual power is once established, every single individual or every single nation that dares a revolt against this authority runs the risk of being overwhelmed by the others who remain loyal to this authority.

Were the idea of the League of Nations rooted in the superegos of all people, as in the case of the Roman papacy at the time of Innocent III, then the power of the League, even without material sanctions, would be no less absolute.

Although the ideology of the League of Nations is rooted in the conscience of many people and in the governing ranks of some nations, it has not become part and parcel of the general consciousness. Indeed, for some nations it is an object of scorn and contempt.

This in turn brings me back to the idea of "domestication" and the different degrees of domestication among the nations, i.e., the different degrees of their cultural pacification. With what physicists call a first approximation, we may say that the ideology of the League of Nations exerts a greater spiritual power over the more highly domesticated nations than over nations of a lesser degree of domestication.

When nations are warlike and peaceful in different degrees, an organization such as the League exercises its authority only over the more peaceful nations and is effective only in conflicts between them. But is the League also capable of determining the actions of less peaceful nations? Certainly, the League does not influence the conscience of those nations and their leaders, but it can help to prevent war in another way—by creating fear. Juridically speaking, the Covenant has made provision for such cases, but the question I am asking is: under what psychological conditions will the stipulations of the Covenant become effective and, therefore, how great is the danger in which the aggressor places himself? The answer is that in the first instance the execution of the clauses of the Covenant is for all signatory powers a treaty obligation. Thus a superego motive is at work; there is a moral obligation to take the necessary measures against the aggressor. How far this motive is effective is a separate question. One would certainly hesitate to overestimate it. Another motive for nations supporting the treaty may be the wish to safeguard their own future security through the establishment of a precedent. This is an ego motive. The willingness of a nation to fulfill its obligations may sometimes also be influenced by immediate interests or by pressure which is brought by other nations. These are ego motives, too. But since they depend on the political constellation, they may work either for or against the Covenant.

But there is one factor which will help the Covenant in a crucial case quite apart from all these considerations. If the League of Nations calls on its members to penalize a Covenant breaker possibly in the extreme form of military sanctions, this summons becomes an appeal to lay aside inhibitions of instincts in the service of an ideal. In such a case, the power of the League is based not only on the superego appeal, but also on the mightier appeal to cast off inhibitions in the service of peace, to fight for the greater glory of peace. We have seen how extraordinarily effective such a challenge becomes. This is the situation which an aggressor must fear. In this roundabout way, the League can help to prevent war even by those nations on which its ideal exercises no authority.

I have presented only a few fragments of what empirical psychology can contribute to the great problems of international relations. Psychology does not supply us with a magic key to these things which are so near to us. But, with the increase of knowledge in all other branches of investigation, the possibility of man's influencing the course of events has increased. We can therefore hope that a further investigation of psychological problems will contribute its share in helping man to control events. One of our present tasks is to develop a social technique derived from the social sciences in order to guide our actions according to science and not merely according to intuition. If I may be allowed to borrow a statement from General Smuts, one of the urgent problems of today is to bridge the gulf between the high development of the natural sciences and the relatively meager development of social sciences.

CHAPTER 24

Democracy and the
Scientific Spirit

(*1940*)

Whenever the great issue of democracy is presented in these days, we have in mind not so much the legal conception of representative government, but rather a way of life which we consider characteristic for our civilization. This civilization, usually called the Western civilization—a Mediterranean-Atlantic civilization, based on the traditions of Athens and Rome, Christianity and humanitarianism—is characterized by its conviction of the essential dignity of the individual soul. Its ideal is to insure a fuller life for all individuals and give the greatest possible encouragement to the intrinsic potentialities of human nature, so far as this is compatible with the equal opportunity of others. Democracy is only the legal form for this ideal of mutual respect and cooperation.

The ideal of democracy has not essentially changed since the time of Pericles. In our times, Professor Merriam has put some basic assumptions of democracy somewhat in these terms: the essential dignity of man and the cultivation of personality, primarily on a fraternal rather than a differential basis; a constant trend in human affairs toward the perfectability of mankind; confidence in the possibility of conscious social change, accomplished normally by consent rather than violence.

The concept of democracy, therefore, demands that what is best for the common good, and for the good of the greatest

Reprinted from the *American Journal of Orthopsychiatry*, 10:451-457, 1940.

possible number of individuals, should be accomplished by mutual consent rather than be imposed by some paternal agency. What the common good is, and what is good for the individual, may of course be a matter of considerable controversy; something more is involved than material welfare and the absence of pain and frustration, though those aims play a role in the conception. There is also a broader idea of a fuller life with all its spiritual implications. It may be extremely difficult to define what this richer life is. In practice, however, there will hardly be much disagreement as to what we really mean by it.

Thus, democracy is not the conception of a community in which the will of the people is carried out regardless of its merits. Any conception according to which the desires of the people should always be carried out, whatever their character, is a deviation from the ideal of democracy; I should like to term it the *nihilistic* conception of democracy. In the *idealistic* conception, it is the good that should be carried out, but by mutual consent rather than by coercion.

The ideal of democracy requires, therefore, a spirit of cooperation and reason. Essentially, it visualizes a type of man who has made his own the postulate of cooperation and respect for his fellowman; who has learned to control impulses that are opposed to this; who serves this ideal with strong reason.

This ideal is, in the last resort, the same that Freud has set up for psychoanalysis: where there was id, there ego shall be. Where there was a reign of instinctual drives, anxieties, and primitive mechanisms for dealing with these forces, there should reign a strong ego, capable of facing and controlling these mental forces, and of ruling and settling the conflicts under the guidance of a civilized superego. In the words quoted above, Freud has perhaps offered the most precise formulation of the intrinsic ideal of Western civilization. He adds: "it is a work of culture—not unlike the draining of the Zuider Zee" (1933b, p. 80).

It is not accidental, therefore, that the most vigorous anti-democratic movement of these days presents to the masses an ideal which is very nearly the opposite to Freud's formula. Their program as applied to the multitude is: where ego was, there id shall be.

The idea of a community of men, recognizing one another's rights, and settling their affairs by effectively controlling their emotions, passions, hatred, selfishness, anxieties, cowardice, and other human weaknesses is, of course, only a lofty ideal like the polestar which helps the mariner steer his course, though he does not hope ever to reach it. The practice of democracy has always fallen short of this ideal; democracy has worked—so far as it has worked—under particular conditions. It was successful either because conditions were so simple that all members of the community could get a broad view of and understand the common issues; or because in some cases external security and internal abundance were so great that the community was not really put to the test; or because an élite, inspired by allegiance to the community, virile and not too selfish, was in firm control by virtue of its prestige. Whatever these practical compromises may have been, the shadow of the ideal itself fell across them and transformed somewhat their imperfections.

We are all aware that in the present day the democratic ideal is once again challenged. The very choice of the topic for this assembly is but one of the innumerable tokens that things can no longer be taken for granted. The dangers are not merely dangers for representative government; the question is not whether representative government may, perhaps, give way once again to another form of government, monarchical or aristocratic, which also claims to be devoted to the ideals of Western civilization and merely to serve them by other means. Something far more fundamental than representative government is at stake. The threat of today is a wholesale threat to the very essence of this civilization and to the bulk of its traditions.

In earlier times when Western civilization faced mortal danger, it was not primarily due to attack from the barbarians outside. Rome had time and again disposed of the barbarians to whom she finally succumbed; there was no external reason that would necessarily have made them so much more dangerous a few centuries later than they were at first. The chief danger then, as now and always, is the *danger of internal disintegration*. So far as we may judge from the experiences of the past, there are three main factors which may cause such internal disintegration.

To begin with, there is something in civilization that defeats its own ends. Civilization, i.e., the building of the *civitas*, the place in which men live sheltered from the dangers of primitive life—means increasing security, wealth, and luxury; division of labor and increasing importance of intellectual activities. But these very achievements of civilization make the human race *softer*, and alienate people from the basic facts of human life on earth. The more security surrounds people, the less hardened they become, and the more liable, therefore, to fail in the hour of trial—yet it is the inexorable law of life that that hour cannot be spared them.

The second factor is closely related to the first. It is *the growth of the mob*, mostly in and around big cities. It was the fear of Thomas Jefferson, who foresaw the end of democracy in the growth of great cities.

By the mob, we mean not merely the transitory mass formations of people without strong convictions who easily fall victim to slogans and demagoguery; we mean as well the attitude of the spoiled child of our wealthy civilization who no longer thinks of the community as something which may legitimately ask for sacrifices, but rather as something which must provide him continuously with gratifications of his desires. The slogan of Rome's metropolitan mob "bread and circuses" is the classical expression of mob psychology for all times. In 1930 Ortéga y Gasset described it for our time in his book *The Revolt of the Masses*. Aristotle thought that every democracy was doomed to degenerate with time into mob rule and then fall down: he even preferred to use the word democracy for the latter alone, and the word *polity* for what I have termed the ideal conception of democracy.

The third disintegrating factor is the *retreat of religion*. If religion does not hold people in awe, because of fear of punishment in this life or an afterlife, if its teachings do not show them values above those of immediate indulgence, they may become altogether lacking in ideals. Then there are no values to inspire them to the sacrifices which the community may demand, and give them strong moral support in hours of tribulation.

There is not, in my mind, any intrinsic necessity whereby

such inspiration and moral support can be provided only by religion. It can equally be provided by secularized conscience, by man's devotion to an ideal, independent of any superhuman power believed to have set them up and to punish their violation. And there are men who, without believing in supernatural forces, show the same uncompromising devotion to their ideals, and derive as much moral support from them, as religious believers have ever done; but their number is few. As a matter of fact, secularized conscience has not succeeded thus far in building up, in any large number of individuals, anything comparable to religious belief as regards the compelling power of principles and the courage which real devotion can give. It may, perhaps, in the future. Viewed from this angle, the present crisis of our civilization in general, and of democracy in particular, may partly be due to a transitory period in which religion has lost its power, and secularized conscience has not yet been firmly established. Without any genuine belief in ideals, bereft of the hold that religious convictions have offered, people may fall victims to the pseudocreeds offered at every corner.

These disintegrating factors suggest the study of the possibilities of combating them by educational means. The problem is: how can children grow up in the comparative security of the modern world, and yet be firmly equipped with the virility fostered by more primitive conditions? It is the problem of diminishing pain and suffering without simultaneously attenuating the very capacity to withstand pain and suffering; or how the ideals of communal life can be inculcated in men's hearts without their being backed up by the authority of a supernatural being.

This is an educational problem, and so a problem for science. We have suddenly reached the center of our topic "Democracy and the Scientific Spirit." But we should approach this topic in more general terms. What can science, and the scientific spirit, contribute to democracy?

What is the scientific spirit? It should indicate, it seems to me, the appreciation of, and devotion to, the truth as such. The scientific spirit considers it valuable to find out the truth about human life and society and the world, animate and inanimate, around us, independently of whether this truth serves any immediate needs, whether or not it is pleasant. The approach to the world with a view to understanding it and the application of certain procedures that seem best fitted to this end—that is the scientific spirit. It is an attempt to transcend the subjectivity of our wishes, prejudices, habits of thinking, and the accidents of our time and place, in order to reach the truth of things. Is this scientific spirit of any help toward the achievement of the ideals of democracy? This is our problem.

Some may argue that truth as such does not show any values. Science can show us how things are, but it cannot suggest what we should aim at. It cannot show us what is right or wrong. It can put a map into our hands, but no map can tell us where we should travel. Precisely for this reason disappointment in science is growing in many circles. Those who are disappointed probably expected something other than science can give. They expected something to fill the vacuum which the abandonment of religion has left.

Science can reveal no values. The discoveries of the natural sciences can equally be used for the benefit of man or for his destruction. Technical inventions may be a means of promoting public welfare; or, according to another school of contemporary thought, they may be the means by which a new élite of masters may hold a subject population in terror and submission. It depends only on into whose hands the machines are given. Machines themselves have no spiritual discrimination—and when one sees engineers and technicians handling political problems, one is sometimes left wondering whether the machines have not somehow transferred some of their spiritual indifference to their devotees.

Thus we seem to be told that science is value blind, so to speak, and that Socrates and Plato were wrong in their idea that virtue is teachable. Once again, the sophists are acclaimed who told us that man is the measure of everything.

This modern relativism has its followers mostly among historians and philosophers. Psychiatrists are less likely to adhere to it, being brought by their work into intimate contact with the consequences of certain attitudes which can hardly be desired by the individual himself, and thus find it far more difficult to regard as equally worthy all the different sets of value which are logically possible.

Perhaps I may be allowed to use an example from the field in which I am particularly interested. Psychoanalysis has developed a form of treatment which combats neurotic symptoms, the outcome of emotional forces, by interpretations, i.e., by increasing insight. In psychoanalysis, thought and behavior are thoroughly investigated with a view to crystallizing recurrent patterns, finding out the common denominators of the various kinds of behavior, and discovering the devious ways by which they have come about. Unconscious factors must be brought to consciousness. There is no direct emotional influence involved. How can such a rational enterprise have a chance to overcome maladjustments which have their roots in instincts and emotions?

We see nevertheless that in many cases this approach in a scientific spirit has a therapeutic effect; it changes, however slowly, symptoms and mental habits. To be sure, it is not so in all cases. A man may have a certain way of dealing with children from which he gains secret sadistic pleasure of which he is unaware. If he becomes conscious of this pleasure, it is logically possible, of course, that he will continue to behave as he has done before. It is even possible he may welcome the discovery as an additional element of pleasure. But the average man will not respond in that way; rather, he will feel ashamed and this feeling will detract from the pleasure which so far he has secretly enjoyed. Such diminution of pleasure, brought about by casting light upon the unconscious motives, will begin a change in his mental habit.

The increased knowledge, therefore, has an influence upon the behavior and character, because there is something in the man which rejects sadistic indulgence. He could enjoy it before because it was carefully hidden from himself. It was withdrawn from the integration of the ego, isolated, so to speak, in a watertight compartment. Knowledge can work therapeutically by ending this isolation and bringing these things face to face.

But knowledge clearly could have little effect unless certain forces in the individual which condemn some of the desires, anxieties, or mechanisms are brought to light; they are moral forces—courage, the sense of love being more worthy than hatred, of health being better than disease, cooperation than destruction. And if such forces do exist, knowledge and the scientific spirit, when applied to the individual, can bring about considerable change.

The same applies to social situations. The scientific spirit cannot influence those who are wholeheartedly fighting for aims opposed to the democratic ideals. But in the case of most civilized men there is a certain amount of devotion to the fraternal approach to human affairs and to the concept of justice. In them an attitude which is obnoxious to the ideal can be unaffected only because it is not recognized as such, or because it is withheld from any communication with the ideal by a sort of prohibition of thought. Science and the scientific spirit are the only means of overcoming such conditions.

Thus, Socrates and Plato were not so wrong after all. One cannot demonstrate values by knowledge, but these values are, to some extent at least, already implanted in the hearts of many people. It is possible to show them the contradictions in their minds by scientific means, thus leading them on to make their own final integration.

Let us come back to the conception of democracy formulated by Professor Merriam. Some points, such as the idea of the essential dignity of man and the fraternal approach, are of a *moral* character. They require a domestication of human aggressiveness and a sense of justice. They require, furthermore, that this sense shall be incorporated in man's mind and not be dependent on external authority. In more scientific terms, they require the development of the superego in a specific direction, and its *real* internalization. Further requirements are the ability to control impulses and emotions; and reason, which is able to find out what best serves these goals. In psychoanalytic terms, a certain degree of ego development is needed.

The scientific spirit cannot contribute to the first part—building up and internalizing of social conscience—but it can contribute greatly to the second, the ego development. It may reveal our inconsistencies and thus help to bring about the integration of the mind under the guidance of the superego.

Let us finally consider what the chances of truth are in its eternal struggle against fallacy, lie, and delusion. Everyday experience provides us over and over again with numerous examples of how truth is defeated in this struggle. We may see, in individual life, how powerless reason is against emotions, and how easily it is distorted in order to comply with their demands. And we see in communal life, in human history, the frailty of reason as compared with the other forces at work. There is an almost overwhelming record of victories achieved by the tempest of emotions over the fragile house of reason and truth.

Yet, this is not the whole story. Delusions rule the day, but they change after a short period. There is hardly anyone today who believes in the fallacies that made history yesterday; there will hardly be anyone tomorrow who will believe in today's fallacies. Powerful fallacies are versatile and changeable, but truth, by its very nature, remains always the same. Its voice, however weak, is yet a source of continuous admonition. We may escape the facts by a thousand means, but they will not cease to remind us of their existence.

In a sense, man's way through the ages is a process of adaptation to reality by a biological entity rooted in the animal world but equipped with the potentiality of rising above it. The reality to which adjustment must be made changes and becomes more complicated by virtue of everything man himself has created in his efforts toward adjustment. This adaptation to conditions of reality is carried out by an almost infinite variety of means, some of which we term maladjustments. But whatever we do, reality does not cease to exist and its voice, though low, remains persistent.

Thus truth, however expelled, cannot be entirely destroyed. Freud spoke of the invincible power of truth when he referred to the fact that what he had arrived at as a result of a bold reconstruction of old history had never ceased to be an element of an undercurrent tradition. He even thought, in his last theory, that delusions of psychotics contain an element of truth, though distorted—that a real experience of the past, denied at the time it happened, has, under certain circumstances, broken through in distorted form. According to this idea, it is, paradoxically enough, just because of the hidden content of truth that people stick to such delusions and cannot be dissuaded from them.

It seems to be the fate of truth to lose all battles but the last one. Its force is insignificant in a short period of time, yet seems strong enough in the very long run. This may seem to convey little comfort to us who are not disinterested observers of this world, located on a far distant planet, but who live on it in a limited space of time. But it is not the function of science to provide us with comfort, and he who is after this commodity had better turn to religious and philosophical systems.

The relation between truths and fallacies which rule the day may be indicated by what one of the present dictators said about another subject, which, however, is not without relation to our question. Mussolini once said that all the democratic talk can no more harm his granite state than drifting sand dunes can harm the rocks. Had he all the implications of his picture in mind? For in the long run, in geological epochs, there are no rocks that can withstand the continuous gnawing of shifting sand dunes. *Magna est veritas et praevalebit.*

CHAPTER 25

The Scientific Approach
to Casework

With Special Emphasis on Psychoanalysis

(1941)

The last two centuries have witnessed tremendous triumphs in
the development of the natural sciences—physics, chemistry,
and biology—and their application to technology and medicine.
There has been no comparable development in the science of
man or in the technique of influencing human affairs to keep
pace with the rapid progress in the understanding and the
command of external nature. Many of the problems of our time
have their roots in this fact. A world that has become rich in
gadgets is not very much better equipped with adequate methods of social engineering than was the simple world of our
forefathers.

Many efforts are now under way to increase scientific insight
into man's mind and society and to develop methods of deliberately influencing them. Social work is one of these efforts. In
some instances, as in casework, one approaches individual cases;
in others one aims at a scientific technique of social planning.

Social casework, with its attempt at remedying unsettled
conditions of individuals, to some extent takes the place occupied

Reprinted from *The Family*, 22:179-185, 1941. This paper also appeared
in *Personality in Nature, Society and Culture*, ed. C. Kluckhohn & H. A.
Murray. New York: Knopf, 1948, pp. 531-539; and in *Principles and
Techniques in Social Casework*, ed. C. Casius. New York: Family Service
Association.

centuries ago by the priest. The priest, to be sure, did not offer any financial support, but he acted as adviser to his clients in difficult life situations, offered comfort to the suffering, moral support to the wavering, and relief from guilt to all.

The theoretical background for his social and therapeutic activity was not in doubt; it was the dogmatic philosophy of the Church. According to this philosophy, the soul was immortal and earthly life but a period of trial and preparation. To expect happiness on earth was as futile as it was pretentious. Suffering had its rightful place in this necessarily imperfect world of creation. Happiness, derived from the fulfillment of earthly appetites, was as deceptive as it was transient, and no happiness counted in the long run other than that which came from peace of mind and the hope of divine grace.

In two points, no doubt, the priest was in a position superior to that of his present-day successors: he was accredited with supernatural authority and he had the power of absolution. He could therefore relieve his clients from guilt feelings far more effectively than any present psychotherapist can.

The Protestant minister takes his place midway between the priest of the Roman Church and the modern caseworker. He no longer claims divine authority. In the Protestant conception the individual conscience is autonomous and the minister merely tries to help the individual find his own way to his God.

One step further in the development of individualism leads to the conceptions of modern casework and modern psychotherapy in which, without supernatural implications, people can be helped to work out their own destiny.

Within the methods of present-day psychotherapy we find the same difference between guidance and autonomy of the individual that prevails between the Catholic and the Protestant approach and between the latter and secular psychotherapy. This is the difference between nonanalytic psychotherapies and psychoanalysis.

The nonanalytic psychotherapies offer encouragement and moral support, persuasion and suggestion, training and advice, comfort and reassurance; they educate and reeducate, and give some sort of guidance. The psychoanalytic therapy, on the other hand, works with interpretations. It tries to bring to consciousness all the forces operative in the individual, thus affording the integrative efforts of the ego a chance of working out a solution. Thus, in the nonanalytic methods of psychotherapy, leadership is still offered; whereas, in the psychoanalytic method, such leadership has been reduced to the possible minimum—it is merely help in the process of gaining insight into oneself, without any active interference with the final solution.

We may say that the roles of Catholic priest, Protestant minister, nonanalytic therapist, and analytic therapist present a series in which the degree of autonomy of the individual increases while the amount of external guidance decreases. After this glance at the place of casework in the realm of time, let us now face the problem of its methodological place in the realm of contemporary science.

The social world has a highly complicated structure. Man, with his own complicated mental life, faces other human beings, the conditions of physical nature, and the culture in which he lives. Out of this structure, social casework singles out a particular problem presented by a particular individual in his environment. Society, with its political, economic, cultural conditions, forms the background of the picture. Society is beyond the reach of casework and has to be accepted as it is. The variables of casework are merely the individual himself and the conditions of his personal environment. The social conditions, many of which are bound to put strain on the individual, are mere constants in the problem. This is different from other attempts at influencing human affairs; in social planning, for example, the institutions of the culture are the variables of the problem.

Thus, though the whole of the social sciences will have some bearing on the problems of social casework, two chapters of knowledge are of particular importance—the psychology of the individual and social conditions as they present themselves in his everyday life.

There are two problems. One is diagnostic and one is therapeutic; one asks for the facts and the other for the possibilities of change and the ways of influence.

Diagnostic Problems

First, there is the familiar distinction between external and internal pressures. To what extent do external and internal pressures share in the responsibility for a particular state of unsettlement?

Whenever, in human affairs, we try to determine what share various factors have in bringing about a certain result, we meet with a difficulty: we cannot make an experiment. The natural scientist goes into his laboratory, isolates the various factors, and can thus determine their respective roles in causation. But we cannot make such an experiment with man. Sometimes a quasi experiment will be made in thinking; we may ask ourselves how other people respond to the same pressures, and how the same individual responded to challenges of a different nature but of equal severity. This may help both to prevent us from giving too much weight to the external conditions and to convince the client that internal difficulties contribute to a problem which he himself so often feels to be of a purely external character.

Psychoanalysts, in general, will be inclined to believe that only very seldom does external pressure bear the full responsibility for a serious unsettlement of life or of a lasting condition of unhappiness. For example, economic frustrations, even of a severe variety, are accepted far more graciously when they are a common destiny than when they befall just "me." Does this not indicate that it is not so much the economic frustration itself to which we react as the fact that we feel discriminated against? Is it not the injustice of fate, the lack of love to which we feel subjected, which upsets us rather than the actual want?

Moreover, psychoanalysts had the opportunity of observing time and again that people who were near the breaking point under a particular strain knew how to cope successfully with other no less difficult situations which did not touch their own internal problems, their own psychological weaknesses. And if inner difficulties have been removed, the external situation, though unchanged, often proves to be no longer unbearable.

Within the environmental conditions, however, only one group is sociological. To it belong such factors as possibilities of employment, financial responsibilities, and the like. Other environmental factors are psychological; they consist of the attitudes of people in his environment toward the client, and of the character or neuroses of the persons near to him—his parents, marital partner, children, or employer.

However, in distinguishing between the psychology of the environment as an external factor and the psychology of the client as an internal one, a complication is brought about by the psychological interplay between a person and his environment. Man has an almost uncanny ability of getting into contact with those who are the nearest complement of himself. The sadist will sense the masochist at a distance; he who desires being supported will instinctively, as it were, spot those who are desirous to support others; and he who is out to deceive others will be attracted by those who are willing to be deceived. Furthermore, though people do not consciously understand the unconscious tendencies of others, they frequently behave as if they had understood them. The neurotic reactions of various members of a family, for example, often form some sort of a dialogue between their unconscious fantasies. This factor must be considered when we try to change the environment, as when we place a child in a foster home. The child cannot help but try to establish with the new objects the same relationship he had with the old ones, and the change will be successful only if these new objects are so different from the old ones that they do not lend themselves to an attempt at transferring the old relationship, or if they are wise enough to refuse to cooperate in the game.

This last point leads us to the psychology of the individual himself. Of course, the whole of psychiatric and psychoanalytic knowledge can be brought to bear on the diagnostic and the therapeutic problems. Three aspects, however, seem to me to deserve our special attention. These are the role of internal conflicts, the infantile roots, and the sexual aspect.

Among the internal pressures, inner conflicts between various tendencies in our mind are especially important in neurotic maladjustments. If a country is in danger from without, internal disunion or cooperation of some citizens with the enemy will increase the danger. This is not to say that internal union is in itself a guarantee that the enemy outside will be successfully dealt with; but internal disunion will no doubt considerably diminish whatever chances of survival or victory may exist.

Likewise, the individual is tremendously hampered in his attempts at coping with his external situation if he is divided in himself. A person looking for employment will be far less efficient in dealing with his difficult task if there is something in himself that desires to be dependent on others; he has to fight an internal enemy together with the external one.

Human life is full of internal conflicts and even among the normal some of these conflicts never get settled. Unsettled conflicts between instinctual desires and fears are the core of neurotic difficulties. Usually there is one main conflict characteristic for an individual which permeates his life. If we succeed in spotting this main conflict, we have made an important step toward understanding him.

The second important aspect of the individual is his life history. Psychoanalysis maintains that neurotic difficulties have their background in the life history of the individual, especially in his childhood. This theory has been challenged in many quarters. Neurotic difficulties, it is claimed, can be adequately explained as reactions to the strain of current reality. What can it avail us, we are asked, to go back to the past, as this would merely push back the problem but not solve it?

Experience shows that every neurotic individual fails only in dealing with specific challenges to which he is allergic and deals adequately with other situations that other people are not able to handle. Some neurotics fail in every competitive situation, others in the relation to their superiors, but each group may prove equal to situations that the other cannot stand. Everyone responds neurotically to situations that touch a sensitive spot in his personality, usually situations similar to those he was unable to solve in his childhood. A man who has once broken his leg is likely to break it in the same place when he falls again.

The ego of an adult person is, to a considerable extent, capable of facing facts, bearing frustrations, and dealing with difficulties. For the most part, it will fail only whenever a weak spot has been left from unsolved conflicts of the past. It is not surprising that the child failed to solve the problem. His ego was weak, he had little knowledge of reality, was hardly able to influence events, and his capacity of enduring pain was small; he was likely to fail in a difficult situation. Every neurotic maladjustment is, therefore, to some extent a carry-over from the past.

Furthermore, the sexual aspect of neuroses must be kept in mind. Psychoanalytic experience has shown that in every problem that leads to neurosis a conflict over a sexual desire is involved. The term sexual, of course, does not merely refer to impulses related to propagation; it is meant in the broader sense of desires for pleasure that go hand in hand with some sort of physical excitement.

Passivity and the desire to be supported, which so often form a stumbling block in the way of treatment, have usually a libidinal nucleus. They have frequently been described as a shrinking back from responsibilities, or as a desire for protection and for a sheltered existence, as a child-adult relationship. Such descriptions are correct but incomplete. There is also an instinctual, libidinal desire of a passive or feminine or masochistic character and it is precisely this instinctual basis that makes it so difficult to modify such attitudes.

We can find such libidinal implications in all neurotic symptoms and neurotic habits. In recent years observation, especially of children, has shown that even anxiety, when it proves irritating, does so because of a sexual contribution. Fear as an expectation of an anticipated evil is one thing, but it has nothing to do with sexual tendencies and in itself alone usually proves bearable though disagreeable. But anxiety with continuous excitement is another thing; it is mostly not merely the expectation of an evil but some sort of indulgence in fear or flirtation with the danger. Fear is then sexualized, as it were; a secret pleasure is attached to it and it then becomes exciting, irritating, and unbearable. Incidentally, this is one more example of how external problems are aggravated by internal conflict.

But how can we explain that just sex, in the broader sense of the term, is the main troublemaker of life? The answer seems to be this: the nonsexual tendencies of man are easily adjustable but the libidinal impulses are very difficult to adjust. There is a certain element of insatiability in them; however often rejected, they always tend to come back. Neuroses are maladjustments; thus, the ill-adjustable parts of our makeup bear the brunt of responsibility for them.

An attempt at understanding as much as possible of the

psychological problems of a neurotic individual on the basis of
the material available from short-term observation may therefore be centered around the following questions: What are the
main internal conflicts of the person? What were his childhood
problems and what was his infantile neurosis? How is the present
difficulty related to these? In what libidinal pleasures does he
indulge in his neurotic habits?

The Therapeutic Problem

The accessibility to influence of the environmental factors
such as destitution or unemployment will be judged according to
the knowledge of the social conditions and of the remedies
available; no specific criteria for this can be suggested. But we
can give some criteria for the possibilities of changing the
psychological condition of the individual. What are the possibilities and the limits for such a short-term psychotherapy as
social casework can offer?

There are, first of all, the limitations presented by the nature
of the mental or psychological disfunctioning. Psychoses for the
most part present an almost absolute limit; feeblemindedness
leaves room merely for restricted possibilities of training; the
possibility of psychotherapeutically influencing delinquency,
drug addiction, or other psychopathies is still largely a field of
experimentation. For neurotic maladjustments, however, a few
general criteria can be worked out.

One is, of course, the severity of the disturbance and the
length of its duration; another one is the client's age. The older
he is the less are we entitled to expect profound changes because
of the increasing petrification of the neurotic patterns, the
diminishing elasticity of the personality, and the ever increasing
amount of lasting residuals of his own neurotic activities with
which the person is surrounded and which he cannot undo.

In addition to these well-known factors three criteria for the
chances of psychotherapy may be considered: the degree to
which the present disturbances seem to have their root in the
infantile rather than in the current conditions; the period of life
as being one of relative strength or relative weakness of the ego
in comparison with the instincts; and the potentiality or carrying
capacity of the healthy parts of the personality.

1. There is an infantile background for every psychological disturbance or maladjustment. Nevertheless, the share that the carry-overs of the past and the challenges of the present have in building up or keeping alive the psychological disturbance may vary considerably. An old wound may still be bleeding or else be cicatrized, as it were. In the first instance, no psychotherapeutic influence is likely to help unless it succeeds in revealing and working out the infantile problem. Unless this is done every treatment of a particular difficulty, though temporarily successful, would still leave the breeding place of such difficulties in operation. In the second instance, however, the old problems, though not really settled, may yet not create difficulties out of their own initiative. Once the current problem has been solved, the neurosis may be in abeyance again for a long time.

Whether a particular neurotic difficulty belongs to the first or to the second category may be judged from the following considerations: Has it persisted for most of the life or did it intrude only recently after a long period of comparative health? Have the symptoms themselves to a marked degree an infantile character inconsistent with an adult mind?

2. Another criterion refers to the particular period of life in which the maladjustment makes its appearance. There are periods of life in which normally the instincts are stronger than the ego and others in which the ego has a chance to prevail. That is to say, the curves that show the development of instinctual strength and the development of the strength of the ego from the cradle to the grave are not parallel. The instincts climb to a first peak in childhood, approximately at the age from three to six, the time of the prime of infantile sex. After this, in the period of latency, which is approximately the time of elementary education, they somewhat quiet down. In adolescence there is a sudden influx from biological sources and the instincts reach a new and probably all-time high, and when adolescence is over they tend to settle down to the level of the mature age. Once more, they increase markedly in the male, in the years before the climacteric, as if the anticipation of forthcoming decline would stimulate a new but last climax. They then definitely sink down in old age.

The curve of the ego development, on the other hand, in sharp contrast to the irregular curve of instinctual development, has a simpler shape. There is a gradual and rather regular increase of the strength of the ego up to the time of maturity; it then remains on the level thus achieved for most of the life and may, but need not, decline a little in old age.

Thus, there are three periods in life in which the strength of the instincts is superior to that of the ego and the ego has a hard job in dealing with them and in keeping balance. These are the height of infantile sex from about three to six, adolescence, and the years preceding the climacteric. They are the periods of unsettlement in mental life and most productive of neuroses. There are three other periods of comparative strength of the ego—latency, maturity, and old age—which, therefore, offer best chances for settled psychological conditions. They are also the periods in which psychotherapeutic influence has more chance to succeed than in the periods of turmoil. Psychotherapy can find as its ally in the ascending part of the curve of life the increasing possibilities of substitute gratifications which the expansion of life offers, and in the declining part the older person's increased capacity for resignation.

3. Finally, there is the criterion of the potentiality of the healthy parts of the personality. We may distinguish between the disease on one side and the other aspects of the personality that are not afflicted on the other. In some instances, the borderline is distinct: a few symptoms are insulated, as it were, within an otherwise normal personality. In other instances the neurosis seems to have permeated almost everything. We may say that the person either may have a disease or may be diseased.

The chance of psychotherapy is dependent on the capacities of the healthy parts of the personality. When Archimedes discovered the principle of the lever, he is said to have exclaimed: "Give me a solid point in the universe and I shall move the earth out of its joints."

In combating neurotic symptoms or behavior patterns we need some solid ground within the mind of the individual, something that can be used as an ally, and this can be offered only by the healthy parts of the personality. The carrying capacity of the unafflicted parts of the personality may be judged from the following: the strength of character as revealed by the ability to stand pain and frustration, to take blows, and, above all, by the morale[1] that has been shown in emergencies; the record of past achievements; the ability to sublimate, that is, the capacity of finding substitute gratifications in socially evaluated activities; intellect and talents on which such ability to sublimate partly depends; the strength of conscience; in a man, the degree of his masculinity as against feminine tendencies and, in a woman, the degree to which feminine attitudes prevail in her relationship to men and children.

These three criteria may be used, in addition to those of diagnosis and age, to get some fair estimate of the chances of psychotherapeutic influence, especially of short-term psychotherapy as an internal treatment of emotional needs in casework is bound to be.

Finally, one point which has no counterpart in mechanical engineering may be considered when we deal with human affairs and try to do some human engineering—what seems to be the most intelligent solution of a problem is hardly ever the wisest one. There is all the difference in the world between intelligence and wisdom. The seemingly most intelligent solution would be the best one only if man were a totally rational being. Wisdom will take into account his fallability, and the less perfect solution may easily be the more valuable one.

Another consideration is the time that must be allowed for the assimilation of stimuli, both external and internal. It takes time until unpleasant realities can be faced, transitions of attitudes can be worked out, and adjustments can be made.

The problem of casework is always that of some personal or environmental unsettlement; its aim a new settlement. We cannot forget, however, that such settlement can seldom be more than relative and will hardly long endure. This is due not only to the gravity of situations and to the limited devices of help available but to a considerable degree also to the character of our present-day life. Highly institutionalized cultures like the medieval Christian culture confronted the individual with conditions which he could scarcely hope to change. Most people had no reasonable chance of changing their place of living, their kind

---

[1] Strength of the ego, in an individual, is what morale is in a nation.

of work, their living conditions. Many desires met with insurmountable institutional barriers. The individual had to yield or else to break. In our modern society, however, limitations are far less stringent and considerable changes of life conditions are possible. Such a state of affairs keeps appetites and aspirations alive and thus intensifies inner conflicts. In a sense, it is with a great amount of personal unsettlement and neurosis that our culture pays the price for the possibility of constant change which it cherishes.

CHAPTER 26

Psychoanalytic Orientation
in Family Casework

(1943)

The extent to which psychotherapeutic activities, the direct treatment of emotional needs, can be integrated into the whole of social casework is controversial. It can be and has been argued that casework should be limited to the social services defined by the function of the agencies, and that psychotherapy proper should be left to the psychiatrist. But there are millions of neurotics in our society, and only a small fraction of them is able to secure individual psychiatric treatment. There are few facilities for the treatment of neurotics in outpatient departments. In times of old these masses turned to priests and there found some form of relief. The decline of religious faith during the last decades has left a vacuum; in our day many neurotics turn to social agencies for help, or are transferred to them by psychiatrists. Because of this actual need for some form of help or relief, constant pressure is brought to bear on social agencies to deal with such cases.

There is the practical problem of how a limited number of caseworkers can best be trained to carry out such treatment under the supervision of a psychoanalyst. The following presentation will merely try to outline the possibilities of short-term psychotherapy based on psychoanalysis.

Psychoanalysis is a *theory*, a *method* of obtaining and evaluating data, and a *therapy* of maladjustments. The basic

Reprinted from *American Journal of Orthopsychiatry*, 13:1-7, 1943.

conceptions of its theory as applied to psychopathology are: the inner conflict, wholly or partly unconscious, as the basis of psychoneurosis; the sexual implication; the infantile background.

In the psychoanalytic method the analysand is encouraged to express in words every idea or trend that enters his mind, without rejecting any as ineligible for verbal expression. Unconscious trends are thus afforded a chance to rise to the threshold of consciousness where they meet with the responses of the ego. The analyst has an opportunity of observing desires, anxieties, and ego operations.

The psychoanalytic therapy is based on the idea that unconscious tendencies have a greater emotional power than do conscious ones. Once all the elements of the inner struggle, the nature of the desires, the objects of the fears, and the methods applied by the ego have become fully conscious, the ego of a mature person has a chance to work out a more adequate solution. In the ideal type of psychoanalysis the therapeutic influence is limited to the effort of making conscious the unconscious, leaving the educational part of treatment—finding of new solutions, the task of integration—to the patient's mature personality.

The applicability of such a therapy is predicated on the integrity of the superego and the ego. The superego must be basically intact; certain types of delinquency—the nonneurotic types—are thus excluded. The ego must be basically intact, capable of appreciating reality, and capable of enduring a certain amount of frustration. This consideration excludes psychoses and mental deficiency, calling for a minimum of intelligence and maturity. Psychoanalysis also meets with great difficulties in those periods of life in which the ego is disproportionately weak as compared with the strength of the instincts, as in early childhood, in adolescence, and in the years preceding the climacteric.[1]

---

[1] In early childhood, this difficulty is more than compensated for by the greater plasticity of the individual, by the fact that the neurotic process is still in its early stages, and by the buoyancy of biological growth. Even so, the factor of ego weakness makes it indispensable to add educational influence to the procedure of psychoanalysis proper.

Since psychoanalysis calls for a certain amount of collaboration, its method is all but inapplicable in cases where people do not struggle with symptoms because they derive too much pleasure from them, as in some perversions and some forms of psychopathy. Often enough, analysis must wait until reality has administered to these individuals blows heavy enough to cause a feeling of suffering and a desire to change.

In addition to the possibilities that the ego may permanently or temporarily be too weak to deal with the conflicts, or may not be at all cooperative, it also happens that certain instinctual drives opposed to adjustment are, for constitutional or developmental reasons, too strong for the ego to cope with. Deep-rooted biological femininity in men or masculinity in women seems to set limits for analytic therapy.

Finally, there is an age limit for the workability of analysis. The older the person, the less flexible he becomes, and the residuals of his pathological decisions in the past surround and condition his life to an ever-increasing degree.

In comparing the therapeutic approach of analysis with other methods of psychotherapy, one may try to describe the working of these psychotherapeutic methods in terms of psychoanalytic theory. Two groups of psychotherapeutic activity seem to call for special attention.

One group of psychotherapies, religious and secular, offers encouragement, assurance, alleviation of anxiety, relief from guilt, consolation, moral support, and various kinds of suggestion. In all these instances the therapist takes sides in the patient's inner conflicts. He uses the power which the patient's helplessness and hope have bestowed on him and throws his influence into the scales in favor of one side or the other. By trying to diminish guilt and anxiety, he may favor a greater degree of instinctual expression or he may side with the superego, as the priest often does, and favor instinctual renunciation.

Another group of psychotherapeutic methods does not aim at influencing the patient, but rather at changing his life conditions and environment so they may better fit his needs. Instead of helping the patient make his own adjustment, as psychoanalysis attempts, or trying to influence him to a particular adjustment, as with the above-mentioned method of psychotherapy, an effort is made to adjust reality to the patient with a view to eliminating the motives of his ailment.

Somewhat similar to this is the therapeutic exploitation of the satisfactions the patient may derive from the therapeutic contact; not the patient, but the balance sheet of his satisfactions and frustrations has been changed.

Casework is an attempt to remedy unsettled conditions of individuals. The problems presented are manifold: sociological, medical, psychological. The psychoanalytic orientation can obviously apply only to one aspect of casework activities.

It can be argued that a psychological problem is involved in almost every case. Even in cases of merely external difficulties it can be said that other individuals have coped with similar conditions without help; the inability of our client to do so may be called *his* psychological problem. This may be so; in practice, however, we speak of a psychological problem only in those instances in which the average individual may himself be legitimately expected to find an answer to the challenges of his situation.

What are the chances of success for short-term psychotherapy based on psychoanalytic principles, and the criteria for the selection of cases? In the main, the contraindications and limitations are similar to those of analysis proper—the degree of integrity of the superego and the ego, and a certain cooperativeness of the latter. However, there is one more contraindication for short-term psychotherapy such as casework can offer. While it may influence neurotic tendencies of behavior, it has little chance of influencing outspoken clinical symptoms which should be left to psychiatric treatment, e.g., it may influence an obsessional trait of behavior, but it will hardly succeed in remedying an obsessional ritual.

On the other hand, short-term psychotherapy may well approach a group of cases which the analyst will view unfavorably. As casework does not aim to far-reaching psychological rehabilitation of a person, but rather at the solution of a current problem, and as its method is supportive and educational rather than analytic, it need not be deterred by such factors as old age or bisexuality. If an individual is neither psychotic nor mentally deficient and the core of the personality is intact, if he has some insight and some desire to straighten out his problems, and if his difficulties are not clinical symptoms deeply rooted in the unconscious, he can profit from short-term psychotherapy guided by psychoanalytic principles.

Data for such psychotherapy cannot possibly be gained by the method of free association. The application of this method might start processes which could not be controlled within the casework contact. Instead, the data will consist in what can be obtained in a limited number of interviews.

The psychoanalytically trained caseworker should be able to obtain, with occasional advice from an analytic consultant, the same approximate conception of the structure of the case that a psychoanalyst would be able to obtain in the same amount of time. The art of interviewing, of asking the psychologically relevant questions, and correctly evaluating the material presented seems to me to be the main task in the psychoanalytic training of caseworkers.

This material, at best, should enable the observer to judge the basic problems of the client, the main conflicts which permeate his life, his recurrent behavior patterns—in short, to reach some understanding of what may be called the structure of the case. The goal is to find some approximation to the basic formula of the career, i.e., the main conflicts and favorite methods of solving them, and of meeting external and internal challenges. It is found that one person is ruled by constant rivalry with competitors; another is a perfectionist; one lives in expectation of miracles; another is testing out whether he is the beloved child of higher powers; another derives sexual pleasure from a continuous state of uncertainty and tension; one withdraws from any test in which he fears he might be defeated; and still another uses other people's resources, literally and figuratively, while husbanding his own, etc.

Ideas about possible infantile psychogenesis are usually not very important for this kind of therapy, especially because there is no chance to prove or disprove their validity.

The *method* applied in the evaluation of data is to search for common denominators in various symptoms and types of behavior, both in important life decisions and in trifles.

Sources from which conclusions may be drawn are, first of

all, current psychological problem, case history, pathological productions of the past, and all recurrent behavior patterns. Clinical symptoms which cannot be treated in the casework contact, but need separate psychiatric attention, must be considered insofar as they contribute to the material necessary for an understanding of the main conflicts. Other important data are: what people expect from life and how they expect to get it (by hard work, through miracles, as gifts, their rightful due, etc.); their motives, conscious and unconscious, in asking for casework help, and the kind of help at which they unconsciously aim (financial or moral support, encouragement to carry out what they secretly wish without daring to accept responsibility for it, etc.); content of daydreams; relation between fantasy and reality; emotional reactions to experience in life and in the casework contact, i.e., the emotional reactions they have and those they might be expected to have but which are conspicuously absent.

Finally, it must be remembered that the interviews form a continuity, and the behavior of the day may be an answer to what occurred, or what the client felt had occurred, in a previous meeting. All these data may then be brought into line and integrated into a tentative conception of the client's personality which may serve as a working hypothesis for further procedure, subject to constant modification in the course of events.

Short-term psychotherapy which casework can offer should *not* be a kind of short analysis, no digest or condensation of it. It is basically nonanalytic psychotherapy guided by psychological insight into the structure of the case. This does not exclude the occasional suggestion of interpretation, i.e., an interpretation of the main conflict, not of an isolated tendency. On the whole, however, treatment will consist either in an attempt at directly influencing the current conflicts, or adjusting the external environment with a view to alleviating the conflicts.[2]

Psychoanalysis carried out by a psychoanalytically trained person will differ in many ways from psychotherapy applied by

[2] The criterion mentioned earlier in this paper of ego integrity and cooperativeness applies, of course, only to such therapy as aims at changing the client himself.

others. More staff work will precede the treatment approach in any given situation. The trained worker will not immediately ask himself what to do but try first to understand as much as possible and plan on the basis of such understanding.[3] He will always proceed with great caution, aware of the fact that he is working in twilight and does not know the whole situation. He will keep in mind that the client is bound to react to the therapeutic approach according to the pattern of his neurosis, and he will try to forestall such misunderstandings. He will proceed by a method of trial and error, constantly watching the client's reactions to understand them and modify his procedure according to insight thus gained.

With these qualifications, adjustment to reality and direct interference in favor of one or the other side in the client's conflicts are the main tools in the treatment of emotional needs. It may at times be possible to eliminate a traumatic influence, expecially with children or youth, by changing the environment, or finding an occupation in which a person can satisfy his unconscious desires without conflict.

In the attempt to bring an inner conflict to a solution by taking sides, one will meet with the alternative of aiming either at more instinctual expression, or at more renunciation and sublimation. Practically, the problem is less important than it seems. If a person could really be helped by encouraging him to express his desires, one may wonder why he did not choose this way himself. In many instances, encouragement of instinctual expression may, after a period of temporary relief, lead only to intensified conflict. There are, however, cases in which people expect just such encouragement. They have in fact already decided what they really want—permission from authority. If this is so, it may have therapeutic effect to grant this permission, but the same effect can be achieved by interpreting their unconscious wish to be permitted to do as they really wish.

An important element of treatment will be an educational influence aimed at strengthening the ego and helping the client overcome instinctual tendencies, anxieties or, above all, comfortable ways of dodging issues. Education is age-old, yet

[3] The analytically trained caseworker will show such caution in all instances, not merely in cases of a direct treatment of emotional needs.

psychoanalytically minded people will differ somewhat from others in their educational approach. The psychoanalytic educator keeps in mind the stratification of human personality—the situation of an ego which struggles against other forces. Education is traditionally either strict or lenient. If strict, it has the implication of harshness. If loving, it complies with indulgences. Its love is usually spoiling while its strictness frustrates the desire for love. Mild education, as a rule, cannot carry on forever with its compliance and often turns suddenly into strictness, which is then all the more shocking after previous leniency. The educational influence exercised in casework faces the same problems.

The psychoanalytically trained educator will try to avoid both pitfalls. It is not merely a question of finding the middle road between extremes; rather, it is the question of an attitude outside of these alternatives. He will offer love, yet insist on the demands of reality; he will show himself tolerant of weaknesses without faltering in his opposition to these weaknesses. He will offer help in the fight against them, always admitting that it is a hard struggle, and show every sympathy to the person in this struggle. His love will not connive at overindulgence, but his insistence on the reality principle will never be aggressive. He will encourage his client to make serious efforts to get over his difficulty, while promising his moral support if the effort should fail. Figuratively speaking, he will love the person's mature ego without encouraging his immature tendencies; he will always imply collaboration between the educator and the client, an alliance between them against the weaknesses in the client.

His attempt at strengthening the ego will proceed according to a principle applied in teaching; the teacher must not ask too much of his pupils, or they will fail and be discouraged; nor must he ask too little, or they will make no progress. The ego should at all times be burdened to its full carrying capacity, without being overburdened.

To sum up, a psychoanalytic orientation in casework is not a diluted analysis; it is a method of its own. It is psychotherapy which can derive from psychoanalysis refinements in the interview technique, methods of evaluating material, insight into personality problems, and a better possibility of planning nonanalytic treatment on the basis of such insight.

CHAPTER 27

Notes on Prejudice

(1949)

The word "prejudice" is not a scientific term. It is a word of everyday usage. The words of our daily language are rarely clear, precise, symbols of things or ideas. More often than not, they are used in more than one sense. They do not merely serve a representational function; as a rule, they also serve as expressions of emotions and carry directive implications, meant to stimulate a certain behavior in others. They are therefore rarely suitable for scientific use. Whenever words are bodily lifted from everyday language into scientific use, without distillation and purification, misunderstandings are likely to follow.

This holds true of the word prejudice, too. In conversational language it is used mostly in the sense of prejudice for or against something or somebody—usually against. We say a person is prejudiced against Jews or Negroes, e.g., and mean that he harbors antagonistic feelings toward them.

But not every kind of antagonistic feeling toward an individual or a group will be classified as a prejudice. A person who denounces a prejudice against, say, racial or religious "minorities" may himself feel antagonistic against certain groups, e.g., against industrialists, but he would probably be surprised at the suggestion that his antagonism could be called a prejudice. His feelings toward these groups, he is likely to insist, are provoked either by the blameworthy behavior of these groups or by the detrimental role which they are willy-nilly bound to play, and

First published in *Vassar Alumni Magazine*, 34:2-5, 23-24, 1949. Also in *Bulletin of the Philadelphia Association for Psychoanalysis*, 4:71-81, 1954.

are therefore no prejudice. Prejudice, thus, is unprovoked, or unjustified, antagonism.

But this raises the question: when is antagonism justified? There is apparently no concensus on this point. A person who eats various meats but refuses to eat lamb may be called prejudiced to this point. The Chinese who eat dogmeat may look upon our resistance to doing so as a prejudice. A cannibal may conceivably think that civilized man's abstention from human flesh is a prejudice—tasty and becoming as it appears to him.

In the absence of generally accepted standards, prejudice, in this sense, becomes a relative term. It depends on the values we cherish and on our judgment of a person or group with reference to these values, whether we will consider antagonism toward them as justified or as a prejudice. What is healthy feeling to one man may be a prejudice in the eyes of another. Prejudice may thus become a disparaging term of reference for the likes and dislikes of others—a kind of name-calling for the other person's preferences. The denunciation of prejudice may even become a weapon of prejudice—just as the warning against propaganda, so popular in the 1930's, served a particular brand of propaganda, or as the campaign against lobbyists is a weapon in the hand of certain lobbies.

But so subjective a concept is hardly commendable for scientific use. We should open the problem on a broader basis and study the conditions of antagonism in general.

However, the word prejudice has a sounder meaning, too. It means preconceived opinion—*prejudicium*. It is the case of the judge who enters the courtroom for the trial with the verdict ready in his pocket.

These two meanings, unprovoked antagonism and preconceived opinion, do usually but not always coincide. People who have disdain for Negroes and consider them as a kind of ape-men have both antagonism and preconceived ideas. But there are cases of antagonism without preconceived ideas (such as physical aversion against a person or a group without any rationalizations) or of preconceived ideas without antagonism (such as the widespread American belief that all issues can be settled to mutual satisfaction by letting the people get together and talk things over).

In the following, I shall first discuss some of the conditions of antagonism against groups, and then some types of preconceived ideas.

Antagonism Against Groups

Three Contributions to Group Antagonism from Normal Psychology

There seem to be three causes for group hostility which one might call normal: the primeval reaction to strangers, competition, and the reaction to cultural difference.

When infants reach an age in which they can distinguish between different persons (sometimes around the middle of the first year) they often show anxiety when approached by strangers. This response, under "normal," i.e., favorable conditions, will gradually be overcome through the accumulation of favorable experience and through adaptations. Under extreme conditions such as were experienced by children in concentration camps, the reaction may persist.

The fear reaction to the new and strange should be considered as biologically normal, i.e., as a warning signal in potential danger. Repeated favorable experience will allay suspicions. But in the world at large, outside the family shelter, experience will be favorable over a large scale and a prolonged period of time only if either love for one's fellowman, or identification with him, or moral restraint, have become so general as to do away with any actual danger. Short of this, a negative reaction to the stranger may still be considered as biologically useful.

This is the least dangerous of all the factors that contribute to group hostility, and there is a relatively simple answer to it whenever the expectation of danger from the stranger is unwarranted, viz., to get people to meet and to know each other.

Competition

Another source of antagonism is competition. It should be understood not merely in the narrow sense of rivalry in the pursuit of economic gain (though this is part of it) but in the larger sense of competition for any goal that we cannot all equally attain. There is always *at least one* goal which by its very nature is in short supply, i.e., the desire for differential status. Competition between individuals as well as between groups is a motive for antagonistic impulses, particularly if the competitor threatens to be successful.

Competition is a more potent factor in antagonism than the first one, and less easily accessible to influence. One is correct in judging the existence of competitors as diminishing one's chances of achieving one's ends, and only positive attachment to one's competitor, or identification with him or accepted moral principles, can successfully counteract the hostility which is aroused by a competitive setting. Education can do a great deal to make people accept others. Even without conscious and wise educational efforts, growing up among siblings and playmates is usually a school in which some of this acceptance has been learned by most people. Hence, competition is usually bridled and qualified by some of the counterforces mentioned. Competition alone will only rarely bring forth the more aggressive and more vicious forms of group antagonism.

Envy

A similar motive is envy. Competition is the attitude toward those who are in the race with us while envy is a possible reaction to those who have already won. Envy is probably the basis for the antagonism toward the rich. Most of us who are not rich feel that it is not fair that others should have a greater share of the desirable things in life. The feeling is like this: are we not all equally the children of God? Are we not all born equal?[1]

David Hume has pointed out that envy seems to appear only when the distance between ourselves and those really or allegedly more fortunate is small enough so that we compare ourselves with them. One envies one's contemporaries, hardly one's elders. People in a displaced persons camp may envy those among them who have a permit to enter the country of their

[1] There seems but little doubt that this feeling and its counterpart, a sense of guilt among many in economically privileged positions, is at the bottom of the socialist, or "liberal," sentiment of our time, and that theories of "surplus value" and the like are elaborations and rationalizations of a strong sentiment—*derivazioni* in Pareto's language.

preference; but they hardly envy the American soldiers around them with whom they do not compare themselves. There was little, if any, envy of the rich in the feudal era. Class hatred is thus a consequence of diminishing class distance.

Cultural Differences

Finally, there is the cultural diversity between men. Those who worshiped the Christian God turned against pagans or Jews, Moors or heretics. We are all inclined to turn against those whose sexual mores are markedly different from ours and who practice what seems immoral or repellant to us. The English-speaking nations have put the greatest value on the organization of political and social life along the principle of voluntary cooperation, compromise, and peaceful settlement of differences. Thus, they are tempted to look down at the bitter and sometimes bloody political strife among, say, Italians and consider them as politically immature or emotionally unstable. Italians, on the other hand, have put great emphasis on the aesthetic values in life, not just in the sense of "art appreciation" during a visit to a Museum, but in their daily surroundings and pursuits. They look down at their Anglo-Saxon visitors who, more often than not, seem to notice little of the aesthetic order of things around them.

There has been much condemnation of such attitudes as intolerant. Anthropologists have coined the word "ethnocentrism" and admonish us to conquer this vice and to become tolerant toward all manifestations of humankind. But to what degree is this really possible? True, a culture like ours whose supreme value is freedom and tolerance offers a far wider latitude than a culture in which other values are paramount, but there is a limit for tolerance in a free culture, too.

Freud (1921) wrote these prophetic words about tolerance:

Fundamentally indeed every religion is . . . a religion of love for all those whom it embraces; while cruelty and **intolerance towards those who do not belong to it are** natural to every religion. However difficult we may find it personally, we ought not to reproach believers too severely on this account; people who are unbelieving or indifferent are much better off psychologically in this matter. If to-day that intolerance no longer shows itself so violent and cruel as in former centuries, we can scarcely conclude that there has been a softening in human manners. The cause is rather to be found in the undeniable weakening of religious feelings and the libidinal ties which depend upon them. If another group tie takes the place of the religious one—and the socialistic tie seems to be succeeding in doing to—then there will be the same intolerance towards outsiders as in the age of the Wars of Religion; and if differences between scientific opinions could ever attain a similar significance for groups, the same result would again be repeated with this new motivation [p. 98f.].

When Is Tolerance Possible?

We may, indeed, ask for the conditions which make tolerance possible. It seems to me that it can occur only under one of three conditions. We can be tolerant if the difference of opinion or attitude does not extend to fundamental values. People who are Deists, i.e., who are religious to the extent that they believe in the Creator and His law, can be tolerant with regard to denominational differences which mean nothing to them. The Puritans of early day could not afford to feel this tolerance since, for them, the difference between true religion (in their view) and error was essential; as essential as the difference between going into the eternal kingdom or into eternal hellfire. An agnostic can easily afford to be tolerant toward religious and irreligious attitudes alike which mean little to him. But even anthropologists become intolerant when *their* basic values are at stake; they have not sufferance for ethnocentrism.

Furthermore, we may be tolerant even though an issue may touch our fundamental values if, though believing in them, we do so with something less than full conviction. Finally, and this seems like an extreme development of the second case, we can be tolerant if we do not really feel allegiance to anything or anybody and are cynical about all values.

But short of these cases, tolerance towards difference is not possible. If we hold any fundamental values dear, we will not countenance what would spell their undoing.

While thus antagonism is readily understood where fundamental values differ, it is more surprising to find dislike in instances of small difference such as, e.g., the dislike between Spaniards and Portuguese, or the traditional mutual dislike between the Americans and the British. The latter has almost vanished in recent decades under the impact of historical necessity which has forced the reluctant relatives together.

Freud called this the "narcissism of small differences." The fact that someone is close enough to us so that we feel called upon to compare ourselves with him, and is yet different, is conceived like a latent criticism of ourselves, an implied attack against the way we are, and an implicit invitation to mend our ways; and we resent it.

We should not leave the subject of cultural difference without mentioning the contempt which civilized man feels for the descendant of "primitive" cultures. This is an important element in anti-Negro sentiment. The African Negro was backward in comparison with the white man with regard to certain aspects of culture, i.e., with regard to science, technology, and efficiency of political organization. Had it not been for these differences, the white man could not have succeeded in making a slave out of the Negro. And it so happens that the white man is particularly proud of his achievements in these—rational—aspects of culture. There is contempt and condescension toward the primitive, or toward his descendants, feelings which may well go with the kind of affection adults may feel for children. But the latter can occur only as long as the descendant of the primitive culture behaves like a child, "knows his place." If he demands social equality, the reaction of the white man may be quite violent.

Psychotic Contributions to Group Antagonism

There is also the possibility of hostility such as is found in psychosis, particularly in paranoid psychosis. About paranoia a few words will be said later. At this point suffice it to say that it is a system of delusional ideas, inaccessible to influence. A typical, though not the only, form of it is the delusion of persecution. The paranoiac believes himself to be subject to persecution from outside, from a person, or a group, or from supernatural sources. In many instances, he credits his alleged persecutors with tremendous power and with unlimited evil designs; they become for him a Satan, Evil incarnate. The paranoid ideas usually develop into an elaborate system of inner consistency. Concern about the supposed activities of the evil forces can become a preoccupation of the afflicted mind, to the exclusion of all other life interests.

Ideas which closely resemble paranoid systems play an important role in collective hatreds. It must be emphasized, however, that this does not mean that people who share such collective sentiments are suffering from paranoia *as individuals.* Their ideas would indicate paranoia if they were their individual creation rather than a participation in a collective belief. Participation in what is often called group psychosis does not imply individual psychosis.

An example of the devil theory at work is the fury against "witches" and "sorcerers" which swept over Europe particularly from the late 16th until the early 18th century. Another example can be found in what is probably the deepest layer in anti-semitism.

The Christian era resented the Jew not merely as the stranger, or the competitor, or the person who had not seen the light of the true religion and worshiped the wrong way. There was all this, but there was more. The Jew was also the personi-fication of Evil in a metaphysical sense; he belonged to the people who had killed the Redeemer. It was probably the decisive factor in developing antisemitism from one example of dislike among many others, to the most lasting and most ferocious hatred in European history that Paul, in his efforts to have the new doctrine accepted by the Greeks, tried to weaken its ties to Judaism and presented the Jews, rather than the Romans, as responsible for the crucifixion. The Jew became then the murderer of God.[2]

[2] Cp. Sholem Asch (1945). This is, however, only a rough approximation to the Christian attitude towards the Jews; this attitude is really more subtle. Loewenstein (1947) has called attention to the ambivalence which is inherent in it. The Jews, on the one hand, are the chosen people from whom the Savior came and among whom he lived his earthly existence. On the other hand, the Jews have rejected him. They were therefore held in contempt and considered to be without human dignity, yet preserved for the Day of Judgment when they, too, would recognize Christ as the Redeemer. Loewenstein sees in this

To this Freud (1939) added another, more profound, interpretation. In Christianity, through the martyrdom of God's son atoning for the sins of man, something like an awareness, however disguised, of the primeval sin of parricide (the murder of the primeval father), which had been reactivated in each generation in the child's death wishes against his father and in the adult's quarreling with God (as revealed by the Prophets), and a readiness to atone for it had broken through. By their unwillingness to recognize Christ as the Redeemer the Jews did not join in the common admission of guilt and remained the unrepenting sinners.

The modern age is not given to supernaturalism and receives its inspiration from the progress of science and technology. Hence, delusions of paranoiacs have changed their topics. The paranoid schizophrenic who believed himself influenced by the mystic emanation from the picture of a Saint, so common half a century ago, has become rare indeed, at least in our parts of the world; instead, paranoid schizophrenics today feel themselves influenced and manipulated by radiation emanating from powerful wireless senders or cyclotrons. In systems of mass belief, too, secular concepts have replaced supernatural ones. A typical example of such a modern version is what Shils (1949) calls "the conspirational theory of society according to which ... every decision is made by a small group of men, always behind the scenes, who act with complete rationality, complete consistency, perfect foresight, and total malevolence."

In the 18th and 19th centuries, such a role was attributed to the Catholic Church or, more specifically, to the Jesuit order by some and to the Freemasonry by others. In our days, a great many people believe that our destinies are shaped in this way by the capitalists—"Wall Street." The Nazis thought that they had found in "World Jewry" the clue to an understanding of what made the non-Nazi world tick. As they saw it, the Jews were the evil force of history; incapable of producing culture themselves, they were bent on poisoning and destroying the culture of the

mixed reaction the basis for the modern secularized ambivalence toward the Jews, the strange blend of contempt and secret admiration. Evidence of the latter is, for instance, the anti-semite's fantastic overvaluation of the Jewish influence in the world.

Gentile nations. The old religious concept of Judas and the killers of Christ had returned in a materialistic edition. Thus, antisemitism stands out as a link between a supernaturalistic past and a materialistic present.

And yet the groups singled out for a "conspirational theory of society" hardly ever have had anything like the power with which they were credited. They were, in most cases, not united among themselves except, perhaps, when under attack. They acted no more rationally than other people; like others, they were swayed by emotions. They were no more consistent, either; as with others, their actions were the outcome of conflicting forces among them and within their minds. They were not endowed with any unusual power of foresight and were as open to benevolent considerations as are other people. Only those who have accepted a paranoid theory of events can act with what appears to others, not engulfed in their way of thinking, as complete malevolence.

Implication for Politics

We have not yet fully understood the causes or conditions for the formation of paranoid ideas in individuals; many very important contributions toward the solution of this problem have been made, but there is as yet no complete solution.[3] In addition to this problem of how an individual becomes a paranoid, there is still another problem involved. As has been mentioned before, collective ideas frequently appear paranoid without the individual members of such groups being paranoid in a clinical sense. Does this mean that the leaders of such a group are real paranoiacs while the flock permitted itself to be indoctrinated? Or, do such groups selectively attract individuals with *latent* paranoid trends? Is membership in such a group a comparatively harmless way of expressing such paranoid tendencies, a kind of self-cure, as it were? Or is there something in group organization, or in a particular type of group organization (e.g., in groups with very strong cohesion among their members and hostility toward outsiders, or in those with deep devotion to a leader) that favors manifestations outwardly similar to individual paranoia—manifestations likely to disappear once an indi-

---

[3] A critical survey of existing theories can be found in Ch. 11.

vidual has been taken out of his group? These are questions which one can readily see are implicit in many political issues of our time, yet questions for which we have no definite answer (see also Ch. 23).

However, it seems likely that all these factors cooperate. The leaders of certain groups are not infrequently true paranoiacs. Persons with latent paranoid ideas are attracted into their entourage. The average person feels the appeal of strong convictions (anyone, they instinctively feel, who believes so strongly in his case must be right) and join in with the movement if the leaders or any part of the ideology appeal to their emotions or to their interest. And the setting of a closely knitted group seems indeed to be unfavorable to the exercise of the critical faculty. We call "superego" that part of our mind that steps back and takes ourselves as object of observation, criticism, or approval. Conscience is its most conspicuous, but not its only, function. In many groups, the superego has largely been surrendered into the leader's keeping. Since on it depends whatever ability we have to transcend ourselves and our situation, members of such groups are even less able than others to emancipate themselves from any prejudice.

The paranoid concept of a group which necessarily and by its very existence incarnates the principle of Evil leads to the most dangerous and most vicious form of antagonism. A stranger I may fear and suspect; a competitor I may wish to hold down or to burden with heavy odds; with people whose way of life is utterly different from mine and who hold dear what I condemn and condemn what I hold dear I may wish to have no dealings. But Satan trying to bring all of us in his evil grip must be destroyed at all costs.[4]

Preconceived Ideas

Intellectual Factors in Prejudice: The Individual and the Group Average, or the Individual and Marginal Cases

One of the more simple forms of prejudice (in the sense of

[4] In addition to the "normal" and "paranoid" factors discussed, the mechanisms of psychoneurosis can also contribute to antagonisms against groups. They have not been discussed in this paper. More study seems to be required before their social significance can be determined.

preconceived ideas) is due to lack of differentiation between the
characteristics of an individual and the statistical average of the
group to which he belongs. A group may show a trait more often
or in greater intensity than the rest of the population. But that
does not mean that we can expect to find it in every member of
this group. The average height of American draftees is higher
than that of British draftees, but it does not follow that every
American youth is taller than any of his British contemporaries.
But this is what the prejudiced person expects. In other instances, every member of a group is even believed to show the
characteristics of a few marginal specimens of this group.

This often leads to discrimination against whole groups (e.g.,
in the reluctance to employ Negroes for more skilled jobs on
account of a lower average achievement of Negroes). In other
instances, it leads to preferential treatment; there were times in
this country when, for instance, artists or architects from Europe
enjoyed the advantages of a favorable prejudice.

The treatment thus accorded to individuals is undoubtedly
unjust in terms of the principle that every individual should be
treated according to his merits; but antiprejudice crusaders often
overlook the fact that under certain circumstances it may be a
rational policy, defensible in terms of expediency.

Suppose an automobile manufacturer has brought a new
model on the market and it turns out that 5 percent of the cars
have a mechanical defect. The prejudiced person will think that
the particular car that is offered to him has this defect—which
will most probably be wrong. But if we lack the skill or opportunity to find out which is which, or if we do not care to make
the effort, we may refrain from buying any car of this series.

This is the rationale behind regulations excluding meat
imports, from areas in which there is an endemic cattle disease,
not because all cattle of this region is believed to be diseased but
because some of it is.

*Intellectual Factors in Prejudice: Judging the New in Terms of
the Old*

It is inherent in the way our mind works to approach the new
phenomenon in terms of the old, already known. Only gradually, through new experience, will we learn that a phenomenon

differs from what we expected it to be. Generations of physicians may meet a set of symptoms known to be indicative of a certain disease, and make the specific diagnosis. But some day, a more farsighted medical mind may see slight variations in the symptoms and may find that they indicate a different organic process. It is the creative mind which can more easily emancipate itself from the learned combinations and configurations. But nobody can do entirely without them, or else we would have to approach every new situation in life without the guidance and the benefit of the accumulated experience of the past.

Human intellect operates most ideally if we approach each new situation in terms of expectations derived from the amassed and organized experience of the past, while keeping our mind open to the possibility that the situation may differ from any previously incurred, and stay ready to emancipate ourselves from our expectations. But even the greatest of human intellects have operated in this ideal way only on a few rare occasions in their careers. Short of it, too little rooting in acquired knowledge makes for aimless drift or skepticism; too little ability to emancipate oneself from it makes for prejudice.

In the latter part of the 19th century, the development of psychiatry was greatly handicapped by a bias for the neuroanatomical approach, in accordance with the slogan of the time: mental disorders are brain disorders. Studies of relationship between psychopathology and life history were ridiculed, while researchers were busy trying to find anatomical pathology among psychiatric cases. Since the anatomical and physiological approach in terms of localized machine defects had proved tremendously successful in 19th century medicine, the psychiatric field was approached in the same way.

Little Hans, the boy whose childhood neurosis and analytic treatment Freud (1909a) has described, sees his infant sister being bathed, and comments: "But the widdler is still quite small." He would have been correct in observing that there was no widdler; but he approaches the new situation in terms of his familiar experience. Not finding what he expected he does not infer that the sister does not have the organ in question but rather that it is still small and will grow.

This is, however, not only an example of assimilating new

experience by organizing it within the categories of experience already acquired. It is also motivated by his *wish* that it be so—by his will to believe since recognition of the fact of penislessness would mean that the organ which is his cherished possession cannot be taken for granted.

This leads us over to the next case.

Emotional Factors in Prejudice: The Will to Believe

William James coined this term for the influence which our emotions wield over our judgment. Most of us are inclined to believe only the good of those whom we love, and only evil of those whom we hate. So strong is this influence on our thinking that intense and unqualified feelings of love or hatred almost invariably impair our powers of judgment. Short of emotional detachment, the attitude most conducive to a balanced judgment of things is therefore an ambivalence of feelings, a mixture between love and hostility.

This is the reason why obsessive-compulsives, a type of psychoneurotics who are ambivalent toward practically everything, with love and hostility in equal doses directed toward every object and each getting the edge over the other alternatively for brief moments, are usually capable of keeping a sound judgment of facts. Although profoundly sick, they rarely lose the ability to judge facts. Hysterics, on the other hand, who are swept by strong emotions of love, while less profoundly afflicted, can be trusted far less in their evaluations of reality.

The lover does not see his beloved the way others do. Mothers are most reluctant to believe some of the less flattering truths about their children. Relatives or friends of psychotics refuse to believe in the seriousness of the patient's condition. Scientists are often much quicker to see facts which seem to fit in with their cherished theories than to see those which do not, etc.

Psychotic Elements in Prejudice: Paranoid Thinking

But there is another form of misjudging reality which is different. It is paranoid thinking. Kraepelin (1901-1905) defined paranoid ideas as "erroneous judgments not subject to correction by experience." He who holds a paranoid idea cannot be dissuaded from it. Errors due to the will to believe are difficult, sometimes very difficult, to correct; but they do yield to repeated experience. But paranoid ideas never yield to any experience or argument; they supply the great exception from the rule that man, like animal, can learn from experience. They are inaccessible to corrective experience because that experience itself is interpreted within the framework of the paranoid idea. If a paranoiac believes himself persecuted by his supposed enemies, any evidence to show that they harbor no hostile design, or have taken no hostile steps, would in itself be considered as engineered, or at least as influenced, by the supposed enemies to serve their plans. Archimedes is credited with having said after the discovery of the principle of the lever: "Give me a solid point in the Universe and I will raise the earth out of its joints." For the paranoiac there is no point outside of his system and no amount of evidence, however conclusive for the rest of us, can undermine his convictions. The paranoid ideas present the extreme example of prejudice that completely defies all attempts at correcting it.

CHAPTER 28

Authoritarianism and Totalitarianism

Psychological Comments on a Problem of Power

(1951)

The authoritarian form of government—some people call it despotism—is old, much older than any constitutional government. Our century has witnessed the appearance, or rather the reappearance, of a form of authoritarianism which differs from the traditional variety. It is sometimes called revolutionary dictatorship, sometimes totalitarianism.

Constant de Rebècque (1813) made what was perhaps the first extensive study of this subject. He developed a theory of "usurption" and distinguished it sharply from hereditary monarchy. His theory was, of course, derived from the historical examples of Cromwell and, particularly, Bonaparte whose regime Constant had bitterly opposed. Many of his reflections on "usurption" apply to modern totalitarianism; e.g., his remark that usurption is often a mixture of "the anarchy of Poland and the despotism of Constantinople" reads like a poignant commentary on the court of Adolf Hitler as described by Hermann Rauschning (1940) and H. R. Trevor-Roper (1957)

I should like to take as point of departure Constant's obser-

First published in *Psychoanalysis and Culture*, ed. G. B. Wilbur & W. Muensterberger. New York: International Universities Press, 1951, pp. 185-195. Also as "Grundzüge des Totalitarismus," *Psyche*, 21:853-868, 1967.

vation that "usurption" deprived people of the "right of silence," which was still theirs under despotism. The subjects of despotism were not permitted to voice opposition to their sovereigns but, as a rule, were not required to express their approval either. At times, they were even discouraged from doing so; it is presumptuous for children in a patriarchal setup to venture any opinion, favorable or unfavorable, on their father's decisions. But revolutionary dictatorship expects the citizens to voice their enthusiastic consent and nobody can hope to be left alone by claiming political ignorance or lack of political interest.

An example may illustrate this point. Austrian democracy was superseded by the authoritarian system of the Dollfuss-Schuschnigg regime (1934). The Social Democratic opposition was outlawed, the (Social Democratic) city administration of Vienna forcibly removed from office and replaced by government appointees, and an armed rebellion of Social Democratic paramilitary formations was put down. One of my neighbors in Vienna had been active in the Social Democratic party; like others in the same position, he was arrested the moment the rebellion began. After about two weeks, he was brought before a ranking police officer. There was no legal charge against him as he had spent the days of the rebellion in prison. "What should we do with you?" said the officer; "can you give us guarantees as to your future behavior?" "Well," replied my neighbor, "I am willing to sign a declaration to the extent that I will observe the laws in existence." "That's enough," said the police officer with apparent relief. My neighbor worded it himself and was released; he remained unmolested until the end of the regime.

It should be noted that he had made no effort to hide his disapproval of the course of events. His declaration was worded carefully to make it plain that he submitted to force. The agents of the authoritarian regime asked no more. By accepting his declaration, they implicitly accepted the autonomy of his conscience. What he had to do was frustrating but neither humiliating nor demoralizing. Such a procedure is unthinkable in a totalitarian system where mental reservations are not respected; he who is not a full-hearted supporter is treated as an enemy.

The Hitler salute was an example of the totalitarian insistence on public manifestations of approval. Germans were expected to greet each other with an expression of enthusiastic belief in Hitler. Nonconformists were thus constantly confronted with the alternative of exposing themselves to danger or professing belief in what they despised; the latter is humiliating and demoralizing. There is only one comfortable way out of the impass: if the nonconformist can persuade himself that the system is right after all and becomes a conformist, not merely outwardly but in his convictions.

A Definition of Totalitarianism

An attempt to define totalitarianism might start with the consideration of those characteristics of Western political systems from which totalitarianism clearly differs.

Power is in the Western systems severely restricted by law and custom and by the device of having it widely distributed. It is limited, first of all, with regard to the permissible means of coercion; the more cruel ones cannot be used. Torture, e.g., cannot be applied whatever the stakes may be.[1] Power is further limited with regard to the time that it may be held by an individual. Officers are elected for definite terms and are automatically retired unless reelected. In some instances reelection is restricted by law or custom. Furthermore, there are the various divisions of power like, in this country, the division between federal and state government. Government itself is divided between the legislative, executive, and juridical branches which set limits to each other's power.

We have separated political and economic power, too. Those who make or administer our laws or sit in judgment over us are not the same people on whom, as our employers, customers or clients, we depend for our livelihood. There have been instances in which, in fact though not in theory, economic power tended to incorporate political power ("company towns") or, more

---

[1] It might be countered that there have been cases, albeit rare, of torture in Western countries, too. This is true, but there is a difference between a state of affairs in which a certain behavior is institutionalized and one in which it is outlawed but occurs occasionally in violation of the law. It is the same difference as between a lawless jungle and a civilized society with a certain incidence of crime.

recently, cases in which political power tended to incorporate economic power. But such fusions, impressive though they occasionally have been, have always fallen far short of a complete political-economic power monopoly and opposition has not been slow in organizing itself against such power combines.

Last but not least there is the division between temporal and spiritual power. Temporal power can command obedience of our actions, spiritual power claims authority over our minds. The separation between the two is based on the Christian differentiation between body and soul. "Render unto Caesar the things that are Caesar's and unto God the things that are God's."

In psychoanalytic terms, a person holds spiritual power over people if deference to his moral (or religious) authority is required by their superego. The holder of spiritual power can influence the superego of his spiritual wards.

The body politic in Western culture has no spiritual authority. The government may lay down the law that prevents me from buying alcoholic beverages and can punish me for violating it. But the government does not request that I believe in teetotalism. The law protects me as long as I refrain from overt unlawful action.[2]

The separation between temporal power over the body and spiritual power over the mind is a product of Western Christendom. In medieval Europe, the priests deferred to the prince in temporal matters, and the prince deferred to the priests in spiritual ones. (The exact line of demarcation between the two was at times the issue of a savage struggle.) Kings have done penance before popes and clerics, have even offered their naked body to the whip before the assembled people without thereby losing face and forfeiting any of their (merely temporal) authority.

Assumption of spiritual authority by the Roman Church was an important step in the development of Western liberties. The Church took spiritual power away from the political authorities ("Caesar") to whom it did not return when the power of the

[2] There are subtle exceptions to this rule and borderline cases, particularly in situations of grave danger, but the principle stands and the practice approximates it fairly well.

Church declined and her hands, grown weaker, could no longer hold on to it. In our society, the Roman Church still wields spiritual authority over faithful Catholics. Others find it in their respective religious organizations or in leaders of their own choosing. Psychoanalytic patients tend to project their superego onto their analysts and to incorporate them as their superego. People who have undergone analysis sometimes seek their former analyst's judgment in critical situations so that analysts occasionally retain this authority after the analysis. But a large number of people do not recognize any outside authority to decide for them what is right or wrong; they search only in themselves for answers to the riddle of human existence and the questions of morality.

We will call *totalitarianism a system in which power is not subject to* any of the *limitations* or restrictions which are characteristic for Western civilization, and in which *temporal and spiritual authority are united in one hand.*[3] The government is not only the lawmaker, law administrator, and judge, but also the keeper of the individual's conscience.

This concentration of power has been set up in Communism in the name of a socialist ideal; in German National Socialism, in the name of a nationalistic ideal. Past history is full of totalitarian societies.

Authoritarianism, on the other hand, is characterized by a *considerable*, though not necessarily complete, *concentration of temporal power*, but makes no claim of spiritual authority.

Once an authoritarian system has been established in a country that has hitherto been free, it will enforce obedience but not try to reshape the superego of its subjects through reeducation; but totalitarianism invariably starts on a program of reeducation.

The forcible attempt to remold the superego has severe

---

[3] The term "totalitarianism" has been used in this sense by various authors, among them Arnold Toynbee. E.g., in discussing the struggle between the Eastern Orthodox Church and the Byzantine Empire, Toynbee (1948) states: "The battle . . . ended in the Church's becoming virtually a department of the medieval East-Roman state; and a state that has reduced the Church to this position has hereby made itself 'totalitarian'—if our latter-day term 'totalitarian state' means a state that has established its control over every side of the life of its subjects" (p. 179).

consequences for its victims. Morale in times of tribulation depends on whether or not men feel loved by parental powers, by God, by their group and their superego; as long as they do, they may suffer severely but their morale is likely to remain intact. Efforts at undermining a person's superego are therefore for his morale what the cutting off of supply lines is for fighting armies. "By forcing men to abjure their consciences, usurpation deprives them of the last solace of the oppressed" (Constant, *loc. cit.*).

Ethical Monism and Ethical Pluralism

Every political ideology has a moral and a theoretical part—an ideal to strive for and a theory of sociopolitical reality. The theory suggests the ways of how the ideal can be realized. In the case of "Marxist" Communism, the moral impulse is provided by a vision of general material welfare, social justice, and equality. The theory proposes that these goals can be accomplished, and can be accomplished only, in a socialist society and, furthermore, that the ruthless methods applied by Lenin show the correct way to a socialist society.

The moral element in this doctrine, viz., the vision of general welfare and social justice, is in Judaeo-Christian civilization shared by most people, liberal and conservative alike, though they may not share the fervor for equalitarianism nor have the same concept of what constitutes social justice. The (theoretical) assumption that this ideal can be realized through socialism is shared by some (i.e., by Socialists and by some Liberals) and rejected by others. The concept of establishing socialism through dictatorship is rejected by all non-Communists.

The conflict between the Communist ideology and the Western sociopolitical creed lies therefore not in the ultimate ideal of universal social welfare which is deemed desirable by almost all Western men. It lies to a considerable extent in the theory of society; whether socialism would add to, or detract from, welfare and justice; and whether the methods of Lenin would promote socialism or something different. But this is not all; the conflict is also of a moral nature. The Communist ideology knows no values outside of the socioeconomic and political aspirations, whereas for Western man these goals, important though they may be, are only part of a more complex and more diversified set of aspirations. Western man believes not only in the desirability of material welfare for the many but in a great many other things too. Among them are free access to information, freedom of speech, the principle of a rational law with a high degree of predictability, and of a formalistic morality, applicable to friend and foe alike; he believes in the desirability of peaceful development brought about by consent rather than by violence, and of avoiding pain and suffering to others.

Furthermore, Western man feels that strivings of the individual for himself and his family—the pursuit of happiness—are legitimate aspirations; he confesses to them without embarrassment and readily concedes the same to others.

That these goals are at times conflicting, and that some of the moral principles as well as the pursuit of private happiness may interfere with the realization of any social program, is obvious, but Western man is not embarrassed by these contradictions. He feels that the world of human aspirations is highly complex, no less so than the visible world of things, and that nothing can be gained but much can be lost by trying to simplify it.

In short, Western man is a *pluralist* who believes in a polyphonic system of values,[4] both moral and hedonistic, which are often in conflict with each other. The Communist, on the other hand, upholds a *monistic* doctrine according to which one goal alone is worthy of his, or any man's, devotion.[5]

The moral impulse in the Nazi system of thought was provided by the idea of German greatness; the theory supplied the policies by means of which this goal should be achieved. The nationalistic goal was probably shared by most Germans; greater or lesser parts of the theories of Nazism were accepted by some and rejected by others. The distinction between German Nazis and non-Nazi Germans lies partly in these theoretical differences and partly in a moral issue. For Nazis, the greatness

[4] Cf. McIver (1947) for the concept of a "multi-group society."

[5] A Communist I knew often spoke with enthusiasm of the "singleness of purpose" of Lenin and the Communist party.

of the German nation, as they saw it, was the only ideal that any decent German could have; any other aspiration or desire could only be mean and contemptible. With non-Nazi Germans, on the other hand, the nationalistic ideal was qualified and limited, sometimes outbalanced, by other values such as, e.g., Christianity or humanitarianism, the values of family and friendship bonds, or simply the wish for peace and for a chance to work out one's private destiny. The average German was a pluralist, while the Nazis proclaimed a monistic doctrine, the exclusive devotion to their tribal god.

Monism always tends toward *concentrated power* and toward *ruthlessness* in its use. Dahlberg-Acton wrote in 1862: "Whenever a single definite object is made the supreme end of the State, be it the advantage of a class, the safety or the power of the country, the greatest happiness of the greatest number, or the support of a speculative idea, the State becomes for the time inevitably absolute" (p. 184).

We can thus understand why virtually any system can become despotic when it feels vitally threatened. In extreme danger, human purposes can easily be reduced to one: survival.

Monism and pluralism determine whether or not we believe that the *end justifies the means*. The real monists feel no doubt about it; his eyes are fixed on one goal and whoever would refrain from using suitable means of achieving it is for him clearly an enemy, or a traitor, or insane. The pluralist, on the other hand, who has many aspirations will weigh the means against the ends.

The real monists and the pluralists do not understand each other. The pluralist feels that the monist's exclusive occupation with one goal betrays a one-track mind. The monist, on the other hand, sees that the pluralist confesses to share his basic ideals without drawing the same conclusions from them, and considers him, if not an outright traitor, at least a weak character or a neurotic. Liberals look upon Communists as fanatics, while Communists are wont to speak of "confused Liberals" or "Liberal weaklings." A similar mutual appraisal prevailed in Germany between Nazis and Conservative Nationalists.

This does not mean, however, that all believers in a totalitarian creed are actually monists in the defined sense. The totalitarian *ideology* is monistic and so is the *hard core* of the movement, but most followers are not. They are pluralists like most of their contemporaries who cherish their own and their families' well-being and are not deaf to the call of traditional morality. But they do not recognize the contradictions between a rigid monism of goals and their own extrasystematic interests and allegiances. It is one of the main tasks of totalitarian propaganda to prevent them from realizing it.

Monism of values always tends toward totalitarianism; but that does not mean that a totalitarian system cannot permit freedom of thought with regard to ways and means of achieving its ends if there is no inflexible theory of sociopolitical reality and if the rulers proceed by trial and error. But if, in addition to the monism of purpose, the rulers believe that these questions have already been settled by their theory, they will try to extend their spiritual authority beyond the issue of ultimate goals to the questions of means and of theory.[6]

The Impact of Totalitarianism upon the Individual

The impact of a power structure, integrated toward one goal and insisting on allegiance rather than mere obedience, upon an individual within the scope of its power differs according to whether the individual *shares* the same creed, is totally *opposed* to it, or has *divided allegiances.*

1. The individual shares the same creed, i.e., the values of the creed are the standards of his superego. In this case, no pressure is experienced by the individual except pressure of which he basically approves. In his estimation, he lives in a *free* society. If he happens to get in conflict with the power structure and suffers the consequences, he can only feel that: "Wrong hath but wrong and blame the due of blame."

2. The individual does not feel any allegiance to the ideal

---

[6] In every totalitarianism there are questions which the doctrine has not settled and free thought is permitted with regard to them. These areas are few and peripheral and there is no security that the doctrine may not enter them at any time.

proclaimed by the totalitarian ideology and considers it entirely evil. In this case, the individual feels that he is in the hands of a tyrannical power, somewhat like a civilized man who was captured by a savage tribe and is forced to participate in rites which are repulsive to him. In his estimation, the society is *despotic* and he will react to pressures according to his individual patterns, with fear, hatred, submission (which may, or may not, be masochistically sexualized), resistance or apathy.

3. The individual believes to some degree in the values which the totalitarian creed proclaims but feels allegiance to other values as well. In this case, an *inner conflict* is produced in which one part of the superego—the part that agrees with the basic ideals of the ruling creed—together with the ego that fears the punishment is set up against the rest of the superego which embodies all other allegiances, and against all other ego and id tendencies. Rebellion against the totalitarian power is inhibited not only by its overwhelming might but also by the fact that part of the superego sides with the totalitarian demands. Once rebellion is impossible, inner peace can be won only by destroying, or surrendering, the nonconforming parts of the superego. The impact of totalitarianism upon the mind of the pluralist within its power is likely to be his demoralization.[7] Totalitarianism operates in the encounter with the pluralist like a scientifically devised breakup of the personality.

The coercion of the mind is also experienced as a *rape*.[8] One might say that the leader in an authoritarian system is conceived as a father—a severe or a benign father, as the case may be—while people tend to experience the totalitarian leader as an overpowering male conqueror.

The pluralist, beset by inner conflicts, is a poor prospect for

[7] For a similar but not identical analysis of demoralization under totalitarianism, see Röpke (1945, p. 56).

[8] An anti-Nazi Austrian, in personal jeopardy after the *Anschluss*, because of his well-known liberal-socialist leanings, and in agonizing inner conflict over the temptation of avoiding danger by joining Nazism, once had the fantasy that Hitler, wearing heavy boots, physically entered his head and sat down there. The conflict in this case was intensified by strong sadomasochistic trends. For the relation between totalitarian propaganda and hypnotism see E. Kris (1943). Conversations with E. Kris in years past have contributed to the formation of various concepts of this article.

individual resistance against totalitarianism. The believers in democracy—the prototype of pluralism—have not gone to the bitter end in opposing a victorious totalitarianism. Determined resistance against Nazism, e.g., has not come from German Democrats but from people whose ideals were totally different from, and clearly opposed to, the nationalistic ideals such as, e.g., devout religious believers. Similar conditions seem to prevail in countries in which Communism has recently gained power and resistance to the Communist regime seems to come mainly from nondemocratic quarters.

This analysis also helps to understand the different reactions toward terror under traditional despotism and under totalitarianism. In the former, terror increases both the motive for, and the danger of, resistance. Increased terror will lead to more or less resistance according to whether or not hatred grows faster than fear. With some individuals at least, indignation will mount so high as to overrule caution; despots have often learned that there is a point of diminishing returns in terrorism. But in totalitarianism, increased terror leads to increased conformity; it aggravates the conflict; and if rebellion is not possible, the only way out is to try to persuade oneself that the regime is right after all.

Resistance movements eventually rose in Nazi-occupied Europe, but not in Germany.[9] For the French, e.g., Nazi rule was tyranny in the service of an idea which they hated—an alien despotism rather than totalitarianism—while for the non-Nazi Germans the worst brutality of the regime was still committed in the service of an idea in which they believed; although non-Nazi Germans, left to themselves, would not have gone to anything like the same length on its behalf.

The Sense of Freedom

The fact that the same system can be conceived by different people as free, as despotic, or as totalitarian, raises the question

---

[9] The German underground acted only after the invasion of the Normandy when Germany's defeat had become unavoidable and the removal of Hitler appeared to be a patriotic deed—perhaps the only remaining means of mitigating the consequences of defeat for Germany. But even at this late time many leaders of the German underground were still inhibited in their actions by their concern for the military situation of the moment.

as to the conditions for a sense of oppression or a sense of freedom. These feelings are apparently determined by the degree or the nature of the restrictions to which we are subject. Ortéga y Gasset (1946) looks upon freedom as a relative concept and has formulated his views in these provocative words:

Even in times of the most unmitigated tyranny European man was free to move through the street as he pleased, at least before curfew. Modern city administration has deprived him of this freedom. An official with a magic whistle and hieratic gestures now controls his movements at street corners. . . .

The fact that State means pressure must be taken into account before we can begin to look for distinguishing factors between free and unfree public life. Political freedom cannot be defined as absence of pressure; for that situation does not exist. The decisive point lies in the fashion in which pressure is brought to bear. Are we not at any moment subject to the pressure of the atmosphere? Yet, when this pressure affects us in a certain way, it imparts a glorious feeling of free movement [pp. 28, 34].

Psychoanalytic concepts make it possible to define more precisely the "fashion," the "certain ways," in which pressure must be applied to produce either a feeling of freedom or a feeling of oppression. If a visitor from a Pacific island or from a past era would call us slaves because we are not permitted to cross busy streets at our pleasure—and risk—we would reply that we do not consider traffic regulations as relevant restrictions of our freedom. These regulations are set up in the interest of everybody and we see no value in the right of the individual to endanger his and other people's safety by jaywalking on the streets. There may occasionally be a superfluous traffic light or an arbitrary police officer but that seems to be of minor importance.

Western man believes in the freedom of thought and the freedom of scientific inquiry and considers it intolerable that the authorities should define the principles to which scientific theories have to conform, and that qualified scientists who hold different views should have no chance of expressing them or of working along the lines which they think proper. Yet, a subject of the Caliph Omar who thought the library of Alexandria was superfluous if the content of the books could be found in the Koran, and dangerous if it could not; or a faithful Catholic in the times of the Inquisition, a Puritan in the days of the Mathers, or a Communist of our own day, may look upon such restrictions in much the same light in which we regard traffic regulations. The restrictions, in their view, do not curtail any freedom which is worth preserving; they are set up to protect everybody against reckless intellectual jaywalkers.

The example reveals the conditions for the sense of freedom and the feeling of oppression. Whenever the ideal which a restriction is intended to serve is *internalized* and forms part and parcel of our superego, the restriction does not seem to interfere with our freedom. But if this purpose or ideal is not part of our superego and the pressure is merely external, it is felt as oppressive and, beyond a certain intensity, as tyrannical.

This result could have been derived directly from the psychoanalytic theory of superego formation. According to this theory, there is an economic gain in the internalization of external commands and prohibitions. By making them his own, the child escapes the fear of punishment and recaptures, as it were, a sense of freedom.

CHAPTER 29

Psychiatry and the Problem of Criminal Responsibility

(1952)

The Present State of Affairs

Our present penal system provides for punishment of law-breakers, but defines a category of offenders as exempt from punishment: those who are irresponsible. The question of responsibility is decided, in each case, according to the M'Naghten rule;[1] in practice, it is in the hands of the psychiatric expert who has to answer the M'Naghten questions.

Reprinted from *University of Pennsylvania Law Review*, 101:378-390, 1952.

This article has grown out of work done in the Committee on Forensic Psychiatry of the Group for the Advancement of Psychiatry (G.A.P.) to which the author served as a consultant. The ideas of the article are the outgrowth of the give-and-take of the discussions in the Committee, and it no longer is possible for me to disentangle my own part from contributions by the members of the Committee (Drs. Frank C. Curran, Lawrence Z. Freedman, Manfred O. Guttmacher, Philip Q. Roche) and its juridical consultants during the period in question (Professors George Dession, Arthur R. Pearce, Louis Schwartz, and Herbert Wechsler) and former members and others who have contributed to the discussions. While thus recognizing my obligations, I hasten to add that the responsibility for opinion is mine only.

[1] The so-called M'Naghten rule says: (1) To establish a defense on the ground of insanity it must be clearly proved that at the time of committing the act the party accused was laboring under such a defect of reason from disease of the mind as not to know the nature and quality of the act he was doing or if he did know it that he did not know he was doing what was wrong. (2) If a

473

The rationale for this system is simple. It is the purpose of the law to define "minimum standards of behavior which men can disregard only at their peril" (Oliver Wendell Holmes). The penal law is therefore the extreme example of the principle of regulating human behavior by means of reward and punishment—a principle which permeates all spheres of life. We educate our children, by and large, by rewarding certain types of behavior with approval and love, and by punishing others with some kind of sanction. Students in schools, from the elementary to the postgraduate level, have to live up to the standards of the institutions or else they will be punished by low grades or by nonpromotion. Employees have to live up to the requirements of their jobs, or they will not be promoted or may lose their jobs altogether. Business men must meet the requirements of the market and must foresee its fluctuations or face financial loss. Professional people must live up to expectations or lose their clientele. Our life is regulated by this principle from the beginning to the end. There is no reason to doubt that the method, on the whole, is successful and delivers the goods.

But unless it is implemented in the case of any actual infringement of the law, the threat of punishment will soon lose its deterring power. While this principle is accepted in general, we feel that there are certain types of cases in which the failure to punish would not diminish the deterring potential of the threat of punishment for others. This is the case with people who are either unable to grasp or unable to anticipate the threatened punishment and who therefore are not influenced by this threat; or those whose motivation is of such a nature that anticipated punishment makes no difference in their behavior. Punishment, in such instances, is not useful as a means of dissuading the offender from repeating his unlawful act, nor is it necessary for general determent since the man on the street senses well enough that these people are different from himself and cannot be measured by the same yardstick. Punishment of offenders in this

person is laboring under partial delusions only and is not in other respects insane and commits an offense in consequence thereof he must be considered in the same situation as to responsibility as if the act in respect to which the delusions exist were real. M'Naghten's Case, 10 Cl. & Fin. 200, 8 Eng. Rep. 718 (1843).

group is therefore unnecessary from the point of view of upholding the deterring function of the law. Moreover, it seems to us to be morally wrong because we feel that offenders of this group are not "guilty" in the usual sense. Since anticipation of legal consequences formed no part of their motivation, we feel that they have not had an adequate chance of guiding their actions according to the standards of the community.

Once the principle of singling out the nondeterrable group had been recognized, there arose the question of defining simple, easily applicable criteria to determine whether or not a particular offender belonged to this group. The M'Naghten rule offers such criteria, and, whatever else may be felt about it in the light of the experience of a century, it must be admitted that the rule is at least simple. The M'Naghten rule reflects what may be called a *minimalistic policy* regarding the members of this class of irresponsibles. When strictly applied, it exempts from punishment the feebleminded and organic and functional psychotics with impaired perception or blurred consciousness; it exempts some but by no means all paranoiacs and paranoid schizophrenics.[2] It leaves many psychotics and all psychopaths and cases of so-called primary behavior disorder within the reach of punishment.

For some time attempts have been made to enlarge the class

[2] Some of the psychiatric terms used in this article need an approximate definition. Schizophrenia does *not* mean what the word has come to mean in newspaper editorials: an inner conflict, a dilemma. A schizophrenic person has broken with reality over a considerable area of life, i.e., broken both in the sense of a major impairment of perception or judgment of reality, inaccessible to the corrective influence of experience, and of emotional estrangement from people, sometimes to the degree of complete withdrawal and inaccessibility. Angular mannerisms of bodily movement or rigid bodily immobility are often part of it. The illness proceeds usually in episodes after each of which there may be a fargoing, though not quite complete, restoration of the preceding state. The more schizophrenic episodes a patient has incurred, the greater the likelihood of an outcome in intellectual deterioration (demence).

Manic-depressive psychosis is characterized by either severe melancholic depressions with suicidal trends or by excessive elations, or both. The illness usually moves in periods and after each period there is a practically complete restoration of the prepsychotic personality.

Psychopathy is not a uniformly used term. Mostly, it refers to impulse-ridden personalities, to people whose actions are determined by short-term goals of gaining pleasure or avoiding frustration or anxiety, and who are incapable of modifying their behavior by long-term anticipations.

of irresponsibles by adding a criterion of volistic impairment ("irresistible impulse") to the perceptual and conceptual criteria of the M'Naghten rule. Also, there have been attempts at reinterpreting the M'Naghten rule in such a way that it could be applied to cases of "irresistible impulse"—through the reasoning that "knowledge" implies the possibility of acting upon it and, where such possibility is lacking, memory rather than knowledge is involved.

Psychiatric Discontent with the Present State of Affairs

These modern trends seem to indicate dissatisfaction with the operation of the M'Naghten rule. Many psychiatrists and law-yers do not approve of the minimalistic definition of irresponsi-bility and wish to enlarge the class of offenders who can use the defense of insanity because there are many more undeterrable people than are caught by the M'Naghten test.

In addition to such criticism raised by psychiatrists and lawyers alike, there are specific factors that make for psychiatric discontent:

1. Many psychiatrists seem to resent a situation in which they are compelled to speak a language not their own, which they either feel to be prescientific or which they, rightly or wrongly, suspect to be loaded with metaphysical implications not easily perceived.

Clinical psychiatrists are used to thinking in terms of syn-dromes (such as delusions, hallucinations, depressions, elations, etc.) or of disease entities (such as schizophrenia, manic-depres-sive psychosis, etc.). Those who have absorbed psychoanalytic concepts are also accustomed to think in dynamic and genetic terms such as inner conflicts and their attempted solutions, and the conditioning by childhood experience. But in neither case do the terms "right" or "wrong," essential in applying the M'Naghten rule, or the concept of "knowing" the difference between right and wrong, carry a precise psychological or psychiatric meaning. It would be different if these terms merely referred to what is, and what is not, prohibited by law; in that case, the second M'Naghten question would come down to this question: did the offender know that his action was unlawful? But this is not the meaning of the crucial question.[3] As a result, the psychiatrist is prevented from using the language in which he has been trained to organize his thoughts and in which the meaning, the fringes of meaning, and the implications of each term are familiar to him. Instead, he is forced to testify in a language not his own, and he cannot be sure of the implications which his words may seem to carry to the judge or to the jury.

Jurists sometimes do not seem to realize that this is a real problem. Since the words of the M'Naghten rule do not seem problematic to them, they are inclined to conclude that the reluctant psychiatrists are slow in fulfilling their civic duties or are actually trying to obstruct the administration of the law because they disapprove of it. Such obstruction may occur, but it is not the object of the considerable number of psychiatrists who have a sense of futility and even of humiliation comparable to what a physicist might feel were he required to testify in matters of radioactivity but prevented from using the vocabulary of his science and forced to dress his ideas in the language of Aristotle; or what a surgeon might feel were he asked to testify on the consequences of an accident in the language of Galen.

2. Somewhat related to this issue of semantic ambiguity and coercion in matters of semantics is a feeling among psychiatrists that the words of their testimony carry implications for the judge and the jury which these words do not have for them, and that slight differences in the wording of their testimony, equally

---

[3] In the case of the defendant Schmidt who had confessed homicide and claimed that he had been ordered to kill by the voice of God, the New York Court of Appeal held that, had this been the case, the defendant would not have known that what he did was wrong and, hence, would not have been responsible. *People* v. *Schmidt,* 216 N.Y. 324, 110 N.E. 945 (1915).

Once knowledge of what is wrong is not simply interpreted as knowledge of the fact that an act is forbidden by law, we are headed for difficulties. The killer who received the order to kill by a voice which he thought was the voice of God was ruled irresponsible. Another offender may fancy himself under such divine order but without acoustic sensations; he may, or may not, be considered irresponsible. But let us go one step further from the concrete to the abstract: a man who felt he received the order to kill by a less personalized power and who acted on the command of his conscience, persuaded by what he thinks is his duty toward his ideology, his nation, his party, etc., is certainly considered responsible. Yet, from a psychological point of view, the difference between these cases seems hardly fundamental.

justifiable from a psychiatric point of view, may make all the difference in the world for the jury, and may provide either the prosecution or the defense with effective arguments for their causes. The psychiatrist feels maneuvered into a pivotal position. While remaining entirely within the limits of correctly discharging his professional responsibilities, he has actually leeway to decide, in fact though not in theory, the fate of the defendant. Such a situation can be a source of serious inner conflicts.

3. Finally, there is a third factor operative in psychiatric discontent; it may seem less valid than the former ones. Scientists and professional people are often tempted to apply their particular aproach to problems beyond the area in which the approach has developed, and such extensions may, or may not, be fruitful. In this sense, some psychiatrists feel that their professional way of handling things may yet be the answer to many social ills.

In his normal professional life, the psychiatrist meets people as patients whom he is supposed to treat. Thus, when called upon to see a criminal, he may approach him in the same spirit, i.e., as a patient to be given medical treatment. It may happen that the psychiatrist is not sufficiently aware of the fact that the law means to treat the offender not only with a view to his salvation but also with the view of upholding minimum standards of behavior in the society at large. Moreover, a very small but articulate number of psychiatrists have claimed that the threat of punishment does not deter at all—a radical contention in view of everybody's daily experience in office and shop, in the parlor and in the market, on the playfields and on the public highways.

Actually, there is as yet not much to substantiate even the claim that psychiatric treatment could rehabilitate the individual offender in a significant number of cases. Penetrating treatment with a view to a reorientation of the personality—psychoanalysis—is time-consuming and takes a sizable part of the total working life of a highly skilled practitioner; nonetheless, the desired therapeutic result cannot be guaranteed even for psychoneurosis, the subject *par excellence* for psychoanalytic treatment, and the outlook for delinquency is certainly less bright. Whether short-term psychotherapy—the only treatment that could at this point be made available on a relatively large scale—can "cure" the more severe forms of delinquency remains to be seen.

Those psychiatrists who would base their claims on the preventive rather than the therapeutic potentialities of psychiatry encounter another difficulty. It is quite true that psychiatry could well pick out individuals who *might* become delinquent. But psychiatry could hardly say: this person will *certainly* commit, say, homicide. It may say that he might do so, i.e., that he has a 100 times greater chance of doing so than the next person. But so have a number of other, equally tempted and equally labile, people who never actually commit a crime. For one dangerous psychopath who eventually becomes homicidal, there are scores of psychopaths, apparently equally dangerous, who do not make the fatal step from temptation to action. Our system would not countenance the permanent imprisonment of fifty people who have so far broken no law because we know statistically that one of them will commit homicide if given the opportunity.

Two Possible Modifications of the M'Naghten Rule

There are, above all, two modifications of, or additions to, the M'Naghten rule which have been advocated and which are practiced in some legal systems.

1. *The Irresistible Impulse.* It has been suggested that the question as to the offender's knowledge of right and wrong should be supplemented by a question as to his ability to act upon his insight. In this way, allowance may be made for an "irresistible impulse."

Whatever advantages this suggestion may hold from the point of view of our sense of justice, it is unlikely to improve the position of the psychiatrist. The concept of an irresistible impulse is well defined only in a central area where certain impulses are irresistible to all people. We may say, for example, that the need to sleep becomes irresistible after a certain time. Some people may be able to stay awake longer than others, but a point is reached after some hours when the need to sleep cannot be conquered by anyone. The same applies to many other physical needs such as, for example, the need to urinate.

But when we enter the territory of impulses that are resisted by some and not by others, and we should decide whether an urge that Tom could safely check was unconquerable for Dick, we are on shaky ground. There are no criteria for this decision.[4]

2. *The Question of Insanity*. Another possibility is to ask the psychiatrist whether the offender was suffering from a mental disease, and if so, whether or how his act was related to this condition.

However, this method also does not remove the difficulty. The concept of mental disease is well defined and beyond controversial interpretation only in a central core of the concept, i.e., with regard to such conditions in which the sense of reality is crudely impaired, and inaccessible to the corrective influence of experience—for example, when people are confused or disoriented or suffer from hallucinations or delusions. That is the case in organic psychoses, in schizophrenia, in manic-depressive psychosis. Their characterization as diseases of the mind is not open to reasonable doubt.

But outside of this inner core, there is a vast fringe area of conditions which may, or may not, be considered to be diseases of the mind. Are psychopathies, psychoneuroses (like kleptomania) or perversions (like exhibitionism) diseases of the mind? The definition of the term becomes arbitrary, and the above questions will be answered differently by different psychiatrists. Whether or not a psychiatrist is willing to classify any one of these conditions as diseases of the mind depends more on his philosophy than on any factual question that can be settled by observation and reasoning.

One could conceive of a system in which the psychiatrist is asked only such questions about which it is clearly within his professional competence to testify. This would be the case if he

---

[4] In the course of a psychoanalytic treatment, an analyst sometimes is confronted with the problem of finding out whether an impulse is, or is not, irresistible. E.g., an agoraphobic who has long since ceased going out alone may have progressed in his treatment to a point where the analyst may wonder whether the patient's anxiety may not have abated to a degree so as to be tolerable. But there is no way of deciding this question unless the patient puts his anxiety to a test, i.e., actually ventures to go out alone so that it can be determined by trial and error whether his anxiety is still beyond tolerance.

were asked about the offender's mental condition, not in general terms but in concrete terms of specified diagnostic entities. Is this offender a moron? Does he suffer from an organic psychosis? Is he a schizophrenic, a manic-depressive? Is he a "borderline" schizoid, a psychopath, a psychoneurotic, etc.? (Allowance would have to be made for a considerable number of categories.) And if so, to what extent is his act related to this condition?

Psychiatrists can answer these questions without misgivings. While there is no complete standardization of terminology among different schools of psychiatry, the establishment of a uniform terminology is not beyond possibility. But in such a system the answer of the psychiatrist would not suggest that a person was, or was not, responsible. It would (and should) be up to the psychiatrically informed legislator to decide which of these psychiatric categories should, and which should not, substantiate the defense of insanity.

The Center of the Difficulty

This carries us to the core of the problem. The seemingly factual question of whether or not a person *is* (or *was*) mentally ill, or *was* acting under an irresistible impulse, covers a question of morality and public policy: whether he *should* be punished or subjected to some other disposition or be allowed to leave the courtroom a free man. It would not be too difficult to agree that the "normal" offender (e.g., the racketeer who miscalculated his risks) should face the penalty and that the manifestly insane should be committed to a mental institution.[5] But what should be done with a large group of offenders who do not fit into either of these two extreme categories? How should we deal with psychopaths, borderline schizoids, or perverts? They have not made calculations of gain and risk like the racketeer; nor are they insane. They do not seem to be deterrable, but the man on the street does not feel them to be too different from himself and would look askance at their remaining unpunished.

The exhibitionist is a case in point. He has been in and out of jail for the better part of his life. Or perhaps he has not been

[5] At present hallucinating psychotics may pass the M'Naghten test.

apprehended as yet, but jeopardizes a respectable position in life and puts himself at the mercy of a stranger each time he exhibits himself. He has made good resolutions many times over and tried to fight against his temptations; time and again the flesh has proved weak. As a matter of experience one can call him undeterrable. It may well be that he would not exhibit himself were the policeman present at the right moment, but short of this he cannot be deterred by the threat of any punishment that morally can be applied and that will not be so brutal as to be worse than the offense it is meant to forestall. He is certainly not psychotic. The man on the street does not feel this type of offender to be sufficiently different from himself so that he can let him off without danger to his own morale—except after such an offender has been in trouble many times and has continued his perverse practices nonetheless.

Behind the apparent problem of defining criteria of criminal responsibility, there is the real problem of how to deal with the large group of offenders who do not fit into the marginal categories of "normality" and insanity—the group of psychopathies, primary behavior disorders and perversions. This is not a factual question, to be decided on the basis of expert testimony—e.g., whether or not the offender "knew" that what he did was "wrong," or whether or not his particular mental makeup should be properly termed a "disease of the mind," or whether or not his impulse was "irresistible." Rather it is a question of legal policy to be decided by all of us as citizens, guided by prevailing standards of morality and by the social interests at stake. In trying to arrive at a policy in this matter, we have to take advice from experts—psychiatrists among them—as to the facts and as to the probable consequences of any policy on which we may embark. But the decision—and the responsibility—is ours as citizens. We cannot pass it on to the expert witness by asking him questions which appear to be questions of fact but are actually questions of what we ought to do.

Possibilities of a Fresh Approach

Whenever the existing line of approach does not seem to lead to a satisfactory solution, a fresh beginning may be tried. I am a layman in jurisprudence—a shortcoming which must necessarily detract from the validity of my reasoning but may hold some compensation. I may venture into speculation about a desirable solution without regard for the realities of existing law, leaving it to lawyers to decide how much, if any, of such speculation can be used either within the existing legal framework or after such changes of statutory law as reasonably can be attempted.

When we try to make a fresh approach to the problem of dealing with crime and to the role which psychiatry, the science of human maladjustment, could fulfill in a reformed system, we may well start by remembering the various purposes, sometimes contradictory with one another, which society pursues in dealing with offenders. The penal law and its administration seem to serve these purposes: (1) retribution; (2) individual prevention; (3) rehabilitation of the offender; (4) general deterrence.

Whenever somebody has broken a law which we uphold we seem to feel that retribution is his just desert. It is as though his offense had disturbed an equilibrium which can be restored only by his punishment. This demand, operative to some extent in all of us, that the sinner should be punished is more than an expression of the utilitarian principle of enforcing minimum standards of conduct; we seem to feel that is is not "right" for the offender to "get away with it"—though we may differ widely with regard to the harshness of retribution which some think is necessary or the leniency which others are confident is adequate.

Many people have taken a stand against the principle of retribution altogether and have denounced it as a relic of barbarian times. This fact may suggest that the request for punishment of the offender is not a universal need of the human mind. But it turns out upon closer examination that the opponents of retribution are actually not what they claim to be; they are not free of the wish that "evil" men should be punished but have merely changed the object of their retribution strivings. While they do not feel that the criminal is guilty and should be punished, they are in a fully retributive mood towards "society," "the ruling class," the judges, etc. They are no exceptions from the rule that punishment appears to us as a postulate of justice; they have merely turned the tables and substituted the "respectable" citizen for the lawbreaker in their penitentiary.

Why we should all feel the need of retribution for the

violation of a moral principle which we uphold is an important psychological problem which is beyond the scope of this study. For our purpose, it is sufficient to realize that this need, for whatever reason, actually exists.

In view of this sentiment, the complete elimination of the concept of retribution from the legal system may not be without danger. It would tend to dissociate the law entirely from moral sentiment. If the law no longer must conform, by and large, to moral standards, utilitarianism or expediency becomes its only guide. The emancipation from traditional moral sentiments, begun at first for humanitarian purposes, may eventually have consequences not so humanitarian. Once everything can be done that appears to be socially useful, i.e., that is so considered by those who have authority to define social usefulness, a course has been charted that may well end in depotism. Liberal positivism, in its humanitarian distaste for the harsher aspects of traditional morality, may, by undermining the authority of traditional morality, become the pathbreaker of more ruthless successors. The humanitarian goal with which I am in full sympathy seems to me to be better served by the progressive mitigation of the severity of retribution rather than by an attempt to eliminate the retributive aspect altogether.

The other goals of penal regulations, viz., individual prevention, rehabilitation, and general deterrence, are generally recognized. These four goals, however, are often in conflict with one another.

Retribution v. Individual Prevention. The requirements of retribution and of individual prevention interfere with each other whenever retribution seems to require a degree of punishment which may drive a delinquent further along the road of crime ("prisons are the universities of crime") or, vice versa, whenever individual prevention would require a form or a degree of punishment which does not seem warranted in terms of retribution.

Retribution v. Rehabilitation. These goals interfere with each other whenever retribution is such as to make rehabilitation impossible (e.g., capital punishment) or more difficult (deteriorating influence of long prison sentences) and rehabilitation could be advanced only at a sacrifice in terms of retribution.

Retribution v. General Deterrence. Retribution and general deterrence interfere with each other whenever retribution does not operate as a deterrent but as a bait. This may be the case, for example, of homeless destitutes to whom prison sentences may be actually attractive. Any kind of punishment, including capital punishment, may be attractive to masochistic perverts or to people suffering from an unconscious sense of guilt; their number may be small, but they exist. There are also those who wish to be martyrized to serve their cause. No doubt the punishment meted out by the Romans against the Christians was not much of a deterrent. And finally, perhaps most important, there may be the general brutalizing influence of retribution among the people at large.

Individual Prevention v. Rehabilitation. These goals interfere with each other whenever individual prevention would require lengthy, or permanent, custody of the criminal while rehabilitation could be tried only if society was willing to take a chance with him.

Individual Prevention v. General Deterrence. These goals interfere with each other in those cases in which individual prevention could be achieved with little or no punishment while general deterrence seems to require it. Beatrice Cenci, immortalized by Shelley, killed her father, who had forced an incestuous relationship on her; there was no need of punishment from the point of view of individual prevention, but general deterrence seemed to require punishment for parricide.

Rehabilitation v. General Deterrence. Finally, rehabilitation can be achieved often, and sometimes only, if there is no, or no severe, punishment, while punishment may be required from the point of view of general deterrence.

As these goals interfere with each other, the disposition of a case cannot always be equally satisfactory from all angles. Whenever our goals conflict, we have to weigh how much of each of these purposes can be achieved and how much sacrifice in terms of one goal is necessary for the partial realization of another one.[6]

---

[6] Related aspects were discussed in 1936.

On the Possibility of a Trifocal Formulation of the Law

At the present time, the general public is inclined to regard punishment as the only normal and adequate answer to a crime. Other dispositions of the offender such as, for example, a psychiatric commitment, are seen only in a negative light. In the eyes of the public the defendant who was found irresponsible got away with it—although commitment to a ward for the criminally insane is harder on the criminal than any except the extreme punishment.

It seems advisable, first of all, to reformulate our laws in such a way that they are no longer focused on punishment as the normal consequence of crime, with other dispositions taking their place as exceptions from the rule; and to allow for three alternate dispositions of the criminal, principally of equal penological rank, viz., punishment, custody, and therapy (medical or educational). In such a system the court, after determining the facts of the case, would proceed to the consideration of the way in which the offender should best be dealt with from the point of view of the merits of the case, the requirements of public morality and public safety, and the chances of the offender's rehabilitation; and would dispose of each case by punishment, custody, or treatment, or by a combination of these, or by release, as seems best fitted to the total situation.

In this system, the psychiatrist could make a major contribution to the court's decision. He would not be forced to relinquish what insight psychiatry actually has gained into human behavior in favor of a testimony on issues of doubtful meaning and questionable relevance but could bring the resources of his knowledge to an evaluation of the consequences of the various rival dispositions in the case. Instead of the M'Naghten questions, the psychiatrist could be asked three questions which are equally meaningful to him and to an appropriate disposition of the case and which he frequently will be able to answer with reasonable estimates: *is the lawbreaker dangerous,* i.e., how likely is he to commit the same or another crime again: *is he deterrable,* is the motivation of his unlawful behavior such that anticipation of consequences can decisively influence his behavior; and *is he treatable* by medical or educational methods?

The psychiatrist could try to answer these questions without *sacrificium intellectus* and without fear that the implications of his words may carry a jury of laymen in a direction which does not seem warranted in terms of the actual scientific meaning of his words. His answers could substantially assist the court in arriving at a reasonable decision about the disposition of the case through punishment, custody, or treatment, as illustrated in the following scale:

Symbol	Diagnostic Characterization	Disposition
1, 1, 1	Dangerous Deterrable Treatable	Punishment and Treatment
1, 1, 2	Dangerous Deterrable Not treatable	Punishment
1, 2, 1	Dangerous Not deterrable Treatable	Preventive Custody and Treatment
1, 2, 2	Dangerous Not deterrable Not treatable	Preventive Custody
2, 1, 1	Not dangerous Deterrable Treatable	Punishment with Probationary Period and Treatment
2, 1, 2	Not dangerous Deterrable Not treatable	Punishment, perhaps with Probationary Period
2, 2, 1	Not dangerous Not deterrable Treatable	Treatment
2, 2, 2	Not dangerous Not deterrable Not treatable	Release

CHAPTER 30

Freud and the History of Science

(1956)

Freud's work —psychoanalysis—is an aggregate of data, investigative methods, theories, and treatment methods dealing with personality—including illness—and the relation between personality and destiny; or, as Hartmann (1958, 1959) has put it, it is a *scientific* approach to the *nucleus* of the personality.

These simple formulations indicate a break with an ancient, deeply rooted tradition, viz., the traditional separation between science, on the one hand, and the humanities, on the other: philosophy, history, politics, which deal incidentally with man, too. This separation had long been institutionalized in the departmental boundaries of academies and universities.

The distinction was part of the prescientific analysis of reality which underlies our thinking and which we are wont to take for granted like the air which we breathe or the language which we speak. As is the case with many of these categories of thought in the Western world, its basic outlines are apparent in 5th-century Athens; they were then personified in the figures of Anaxagoras and Socrates. Anaxagoras, Ionian immigrant to Athens, friend of Pericles, belonged to the school of the Ionian philosophers of nature. Their thinking can hardly be called scientific by any modern standard, but they deserve to be called ancestors of science, or protoscientists, because they sought to explain the visible world in terms of natural causes; and they had some

Presented at the Freud Centenary Celebration of the American Psychoanalytic Association in Chicago, May, 1956. First published in *Journal of the American Psychoanalytic Association*, 4:602-613, 1956. Also as "Freud und die Geschichte der Wissenschaft," *Psyche*, 11:210-219, 1957.

actual scientific results like the method, discovered by Thales, of measuring the distance of a ship from the harbor.

On the other hand, there was the somewhat younger Athenian, Socrates, whose only concern was what constituted the proper life. The study of the planetary orbits or of the causes of their movements appeared to him, according to Xenophon, as a "waste of time": "He dwelt on the contradictions and conflicting opinions of the physical philosophers...[and] held that those who speculated on the Universe and the laws of the heavenly bodies were no better than madmen." The interest in human conduct, for Socrates, was closely connected with ethics, metaphysics, and politics.

There have been cases of remarkable psychological insight long before Freud, including insight into unconscious motivation and self-deception, but it is found almost exclusively in poets, prophets, and philosophers, not in protoscientists or scientists, i.e., in the intellectual descendants of Socrates, not those of Anaxagoras.

The cleavage between science and the humanities became even wider with the onset of the so-called "scientific revolution" in the 17th century, i.e., the emergence of systematic, self-perpetuating research based on the constant interplay, or crossfertilization, between observations guided by theory and theory derived from observations. If we study that intellectual movement in which Galileo played the decisive role and which was brought to its final triumph by Newton—from then on to continue with ever accelerated speed, to change, for better and worse, the face of the earth—we feel that the new outlook came about through a shift in human ambitions: more and more of the leading intellects of the time ceased to ask the questions which had occupied the mind for centuries, such as: what is the essence of things? Why is the world the way it is and not otherwise as it might be conceived of being? What is the purpose of the world?—questions that had remained unanswered despite all the ingenuity that had been expended on them. Instead, men were content to ask the more modest, answerable questions about what actually happens, with a view to finding some sort of order in it. It was a renunciation of more ambitious goals, a kind of resignation. It is in line with what psychoanalytic theory lets us expect that the renunciation found a princely reward. Man who no longer asked for the purpose of the creation, but merely inquired what happened and how it happened, was rewarded with an ever-increasing body of knowledge of unforeseen predictive and manipulative potentialities.

But little wonder that this very success of self-limitation instilled in the scientists a new ethos that made it the moral obligation, and the glory, of the scientific mind to limit itself to the questions that appear to be answerable through finite efforts of a foreseeable kind, and has made suspect all speculation, all interpretations of highly complex phenomena, and all statements that are not "objectively" verifiable, banishing them either forever to the scientific hell reserved for religion, metaphysics, and mysticism or, at least temporarily, to the scientific purgatory reserved for things not yet ripe to be approached scientifically. Character and destiny, no doubt, belonged to one of these nether regions. No self-respecting scientist would deal with them as they seemed incomparably too complex for a scientific approach at this point, though they would surely become approachable in due course at a future date. Meanwhile, scientific minds would devote their time and resources to what appeared to be more elementary phenomena. In this way, the ethos of science, which was the cause of its success and which became ever more deeply ingrained by this very success, was apt to discourage any approach to the complexities of human personality and destiny, leaving them once more in the domain of poets.

When Freud was in his youth, a philosophy had gained ascendancy in the German universities which formalized the dichotomy between the sciences and the humanities—the *Naturwissenschaften* and the *Geisteswissenschaften*. The former were thought to deal with the repetitive, physical, the latter with the unique, historical, phenomena. The former could be studied in the laboratory, with a view to distilling them into general laws; the latter, nonrepetitive, could be understood on something like their own merits, through what has been called intuition, or empathy, or understanding. Dilthey (1924) coined the famous phrase: "We explain nature, but we understand the life of the mind."

From then on, there were to be two psychologies, a *naturwissenschaftliche* and a *geisteswissenschaftliche Psychologie*, one belonging to science, the other to the humanities, one explanatory, formulative of general laws, the other "understanding," interpretative. One would give a fairly accurate account of peripheral phenomena, the other would deal with fundamental aspects of human existence in a less than objective manner. In short, there were to be nonverifiable intuitions, on the one hand, and well-established irrelevancies, on the other.

While we feel that this dichotomy lost its edge through the work of Freud, it must be said that there was an element of truth in these formulations. Fullness of life and scientific exactitude are indeed what in economics are called complementary goods; the more we have of the one, the less we are to have of the other. The treatment of a subject can be the more exact the fewer the variables are; in the fullness of life there are more variables than the eye can foresee, still less the hand can control. To make a statement about an actual life situation so exact that every informed and sane individual must accept it, is exceedingly difficult. It would be very cumbersome, perhaps practically impossible, to make even such simple facts of life as the interpretation of facial expressions fully exact and objectively verifiable. Yet, even the infant seems to "understand" them, in the sense of reacting adequately to them. A prominent student of animal behavior, Konrad Lorenz (1954), pointed out that dog owners are familiar with forms of canine behavior which it would be extremely difficult to reproduce under controlled laboratory conditions.

The cleavage between science and the humanities was further sharpened because it overlapped, to some degree, with the close isolation or "segregation" required by Victorian and Edwardian morality, between the "higher" and the "lower" manifestations of human existence. No doubt, there was an "animal side" to human nature, but it existed in a sort of enclosure; and the higher activities of man, his civilized behavior, had no relation with it. How deep the need for this separation was may be illustrated by an example. More than half a century ago, William James (1907) suggested that the "history of philosophy is to a great extent that of a certain clash of human temperaments." That seems to us to be an innocuous idea, quite probably true but not too exciting. James adds that such treatment might be considered "undignified"—it was apparently undignified to suggest that anything as lofty as the history of philosophy should have to do with anything as vulgar as human temperament.

There was another separation, rigidly upheld by what we now understand was anxiety. Mental illness or neurosis had to be something *toto genere* different from the functioning of a normal mind. There was no bridge that led from one to the other.

Freud has to a large degree bridged the gap between science and the humanities, as he has also cut down the wall that isolated in human thought the higher from the lower manifestations of human nature, and the wall that separated the doctor from the patient. Perhaps he could do the former because he was also prepared to carry out the latter acts of desegregation.

Science and the humanities have come together mainly in these two disciplines, in the history of science and in psychoanalysis. The latter might be called the science of history, viz., of the only kind of history—the history of individual lives—that has so far occurred in a sufficiently large number of cases to make scientific treatment promising. It is surely not accidental that this was done by a physician because the clinical physician has always been closer to real life with all its complexities than the scientist. The physician was never able to dismiss or shelve a subject as too complex; he was forced to treat the sick as best he could and to make decisions no matter how incomplete his information, proceeding on what seemed to be the most probable assumptions.

Freud could build the bridge, or tunnel, because he combined a powerful imagination with the no less powerful restraints of a scientific conscience. It is characteristic that Ernest Jones (1953-57) felt that had Freud not been a psychiatrist he might have been a writer. There were these two streams in the makeup of Freud's mind. It is also significant that he was stimulated to the study of medicine by listening to a public reading of Goethe's essay on Nature, i.e., by the reflections of a poet.

The difference between Freud's way of thinking and the kind

of approach that was usual among 19th-century scientists became obvious at the first road junction where Freud's ways parted with Breuer's. Both men were confronted with the fact that their patients could remember under hypnosis what they had not remembered otherwise; and each formed his own idea of how this came about. Breuer, presumably influenced by the spectacular cases of fugue (*double conscience*) that had appeared in the literature, thought that there were different states of consciousness, and that the elements of consciousness communicated only within each state but not between them. What the patients had failed to remember but could recall in hypnosis had presumably occurred in a "hypnoid" state of mind which communicated with the condition of the mind under hypnosis but not with normal states. This was a quite sophisticated theory; Breuer assumed that the mind under hypnosis was a specific state of mind, he postulated the continuity of the mind and inferred that contents recalled only under hypnosis must have been experienced in states contiguous with it. But the theory was conceived in utter remoteness from the patients.

When Freud told the story of these years in his autobiography (1925b) he referred to Breuer's theory as "what might be called a physiological theory" (*"eine sozusagen physiologische Theorie"*). But Breuer's theory was not really physiological. It was apparently the absence of any attempt at psychological understanding, the fact that the human mind was approached with the detachment with which the physiologist sees the nerve endings, that made Freud feel that it was "so to say" (*"sozusagen"*) physiological. Freud said of himself that he was "inclined to suspect the existence of an interplay of forces and the operation of intentions and purposes such as are to be observed in normal life" (p. 23); he thought that his patients did not remember the traumatic events because they did not care to remember them; and that memories came back under hypnosis because the force of the hypnotist's pressure had overwhelmed the force of repression.

But when Freud tried to understand his patients he did not thereby become an exponent of a *geisteswissenschaftliche Psychologie* in the sense of Dilthey. For one, while he "was inclined to *suspect* the interplay of forces," he did not accept his suspicion as valid until he had checked and cross-checked his interpretation the way one does with a scientific hypothesis, by confronting its implications with clinical data systematically collected and, as much as conditions permitted, with results of experiments. Then, he did not limit himself to the interpretation of individual cases but developed theories, and there was in his work the same interplay of observation and conceptualization that prevails in science.

It happens often in the development of science, and perhaps of human experience in general, that apparently irreconcilable positions appear as aspects of the same thing on a higher plateau of understanding and are easily integrated. Thus, the juxtaposition of a psychology that follows the laboratory method and one relying on intuition or empathy lost much of its meaning in psychoanalysis. Psychoanalysis combines understanding with methodical scientific cross-checking. There is a constant oscillation between the two attitudes in psychoanalysis. Each time the analyst feels that he has "understood" a process, he tries to investigate in the way of the laboratory whether things always happen this way under the same conditions, or under what conditions they happen this way; and each time he has made a factual observation, he tries to "understand" its meaning. The analyst may swing back and forth between these attitudes many times in any analytic session.

Whenever it is necessary to strike a delicate balance, there are possibilities of deviating in one direction or another. On the one hand are those who strive so much for exactitude that they are willing to pay a high price for it in terms of profundity; their version of psychoanalysis may be more exact, but it is also more shallow and may in extreme cases approach the well-documented trivia of pre-Freudian academic psychology. On the other hand are those whose desire for greater depth is so great that it carries them beyond the point where they can establish at least the probability of their propositions.

Psychoanalysis is still to a large degree a one-man science; to study psychoanalysis means, on the whole, to study Freud. Contributions have been made by others, but they have been amplifications, applications, and minor revisions rather than essential additions. This is a rare, though not a unique situation in the history of science. The most outstanding example of a discipline dominated by the work of one man over long periods of time, indeed over thousands of years, is elementary geometry. Euclid's *Elements* was written about 300 B.C., and has remained the essence of elementary geometry ever since, and textbooks are only a rewording of Euclid's classical treatise; until fairly recently, schoolboys in England used to say they were studying Euclid when they referred to their studying geometry. Another case, less well founded, is the domination of medicine by Galen over almost a millenium and a half.

But such a situation, while not without precedent, still remains remarkable, particularly in the last half century which was a period of tremendous activity in all branches of science. Why, in the midst of this jungle growth, did psychoanalysts alone limit themselves to cultivating the plants which had been put in the soil by the master?

Many people have been wondering whether the revolution in psychological outlook which was started by Freud may not also have been brought to its conclusion by him so that fundamental discoveries can no longer be expected along this line of approach. According to this view, Freud has not only discovered a new continent but has also mapped it out in broad outlines so that only the filling in of details was left to his successors. There are others who hold that great discoveries have not been made by Freud's successors because there was no outstanding creative talent among them.

Neither of these views is convincing and one should look in other directions for an explanation of the relative stagnation of post-Freudian psychoanalysis. There are several factors which seem to me to slow down the development of psychoanalysis, viz., the long time required by every analysis as compared with the time necessary for an individual experiment in most sciences; as consequence of this, the fact that it is not possible for any analyst to acquire within his own experience a comprehensive view of a particular subject; the difficulty of pooling the resources of several observers; and the difficulty of transferring knowledge from one person to another.

Since every analysis takes years, it takes very long to collect adequate clinical material to corroborate or refute a hypothesis.

The number of cases that any individual analyst can study in a lifetime is small, and he cannot hope to gather, in his own work, a complete sampling of the variety of human experience. If he has made an observation in one case, it may take years until he meets another case of the same type, and he may never see enough cases of this type to be able to arrive at conclusive results.

It is difficult to pool the resources of several workers because the contributions which would be pooled are likely to be unequal. When analysts differ in their opinions, it is not certain whether the difference is due to differences in the material or to differences of interpretation of the same material, and for the same reason, agreement does not necessarily indicate identity of material.

Psychoanalysts spend a great part of their professional lives—not only their official training period, long though it is—merely trying to learn what Freud or other, older, workers already knew. An unknown but certainly large part of such insight is not handed down at all but is completely lost when an experienced analyst dies. It may, or may not, be rediscovered by the independent efforts of others.

A new discovery or a new theory in, say, physics will be discussed all over the globe within a few weeks, and as the publication will most probably convey the ideas adequately, the discussion will probably be to the point. New discoveries are thus discussed, evaluated, and digested at record speed, to be followed quickly by new developments that grow out of them.

But the ideas of psychoanalysts are not so easily transferable. While in physics or chemistry or physiology, almost everything is quickly and widely disseminated—at least today, as it has not always been this way—only a small fraction of psychoanalytic observations or ideas becomes fertile in the minds of others, by being a point of departure for their work. An enormous amount of stimulation is necessary if a small fraction of it is to bear fruit.

Some of this is, of course, due to resistances and scotomas, and to that extent it cannot be helped; there are no shortcuts for personality changes. But another part of it may be due to remediable difficulties of communications. Other sciences have been slowed down in their development or have even been stagnating for long periods of time for similar reasons. I should like to discuss an example from the history of the exact sciences in classical antiquity.

The 4th and 3rd centuries B.C. were a period of great intellectual activity in Greek mathematics; in this time, a small number of outstanding men created most of what we now call elementary mathematics. One of them—Archimedes—came within a hair's breadth of the discovery of the calculus. The later discovery of the calculus by Newton and Leibnitz in the 17th century made scientific mechanics, the first chapter of scientific physics, possible, and one may wonder what might have happened had the calculus been discovered in Hellenistic times.

The brilliant phase of Greek mathematics came to an abrupt end at about 200 B.C. After Appollonius, there is no more creative figure in Greek mathematics for centuries and it is only in the declining years of Greco-Roman civilization that two more outstanding mathematicians appear, separated from each other by a century. What might have broken the line of continuous succession between 400 and 200 B.C.?

The historian of science, van der Waerden (1954) suggests that a seemingly secondary matter, the lack of a symbolic notation, was responsible for the decline:

Reading a proof in Appollonius requires extended and concentrated study. Instead of a concise algebraic formula, one finds a long sentence in which each line segment is indicated by two letters which have to be located in the figure. To understand the line of thought, one is compelled to transcribe these sentences in modern concise formulas. The ancients did not have this tool; instead they had the oral tradition.

An oral explanation makes it possible to indicate the line segments with the fingers; one can emphasize essentials and point out how the proof was found. All of this disappears in the written formulation of the strictly classical style. The proofs are logically sound but they are not suggestive. One feels caught like in a logical mousetrap, but one fails to see the guiding line of thought.

As long as there was no interruption, as long as

each generation could hand over its method to the next, everything went well and the science flourished. But as soon as some external cause brought about an interruption in the oral tradition and only books remained, it became extremely difficult to assimilate the work of the great precursors and next to impossible to pass beyond it [p. 266].

In short, the lack of an exact notation made tradition dependent on personal contact, and tradition that depends on personal contact is very precarious. Who is not reminded of the situation in psychoanalysis today, with training mostly built on personal contact? Once again, that is unavoidable in everything pertaining to personal analysis, but it may be capable of considerable improvement in the didactic aspects of psychoanalytic instruction. Furthermore, there is a great amount of valuable knowledge that is not available in monographs and lives only in oral tradition.

Another historian of mathematics, Dantzig (1955), made points similar to van der Waerden's. Like many others, he wondered what circumstances made the scientific revolution of the 17th century possible; he is inclined to see the difference between this era and earlier periods of great secular intellectual activity which had not given birth to science in the modern sense in the breaking of a bottleneck. He emphasizes the importance of the introduction of symbolic notation in mathematics by Vieta (1592): "Greek mathematics had to depend on common speech, a medium replete with ambiguities, yet inflexible; where an interchange of words could jeopardize meaning. . . ." Vieta's discovery, on the other hand, "turned a tongued-tied thinker into a fluent and convincing speaker and, at the same time, immensely enriched the thinker's creative and critical faculties" (p. 184f.).

It seems to me that the development of psychoanalysis would probably be greatly accelerated through the development of a language or a system of concepts that would make it possible to describe personality structure with a high degree of specificity so that it could be correctly and quickly understood by all.

The present situation in psychoanalysis also bears some similarity with the condition of medicine during the long centuries before the introduction of laboratory methods, when observations at the sickbed were the only source of knowledge. Great clinicians seem to have appeared from time to time, but their diagnostic art died with them without having become public property.

But whatever the difficulties of handing knowledge down to the next generation, whatever the losses encountered in the process, we may yet rest assured that as long as men are free to think, to read, and to write, the basic insights of Freud will not perish from the earth.

CHAPTER 31

A Hypothesis about the Nature
of an Archaic Society

(1959)

Since the early days of recorded history, European man has come into contact with peoples to whom he was greatly superior in his ability to control his environment. Such contacts led to conquests or other forms of overlordship, temporary or lasting. Relations between the strong and the weak, be it individuals or groups, always have two aspects—that of leadership, fundamentally protective, and that of dominance, fundamentally abusive and exploitative. The two aspects appear in different ratios in individual cases, ranging from the extreme of a purely protective leadership relationship as in the normal case of parenthood, to the opposite extreme in which the weak one is used merely as a means to the ends of his master. There is often a considerable difference of opinion as to where a specific case is located in the spectrum, and the very same hierarchical order is described as a leadership relationship by some and as exploitative dominance by others.

European colonialism in non-European continents was for a long time seen by most Europeans as legitimate by virtue of an all-embracing superiority which they took for granted, and as ultimately beneficial for the conquered, too. But around the turn of the last century, a new climate developed gradually

This book review essay is reprinted from *World Politics*, 12:92-102, 1959. Princeton University Press.

among European and American intellectuals and colonialism came to be seen in a new light. On the one hand, a new relativism saw European nations and their colonial dependents no longer as occupying different stages of development but rather as representative of different cultures, different solutions to the problems of living, fundamentally of equal value or, as Ranke might have put it, equidistant to God. On the other hand, the relationship between the dominant European and the dependent Asian and African peoples was seen as exploitation and the "backwardness" of the colonial lands was attributed to European domination.

A more radical version of anticolonialism, propagated by the political left, went further and attributed to exploitation by European imperialism not only Asian, African, and Latin American poverty but also European and North American opulence. When the facts in Western Europe and North America all too obviously contradicted the "iron wage law" of Marx, according to which wages were bound to equal the production cost of labor—i.e., the cost of subsistence—the glaring disparity between fact and theory was attributed to the exploitation of colonial labor, in the fruits of which the working classes of Europe and North America had been permitted a share—an international application of the exploitation theory of capitalism.

These ideas were soon eagerly adopted by the new Asian and African intelligentsia. Non-European cultures, so the various Asian and African nationalisms claim, must be looked upon as the equals, if not the spiritual superiors, of European civilization; at the same time, the Western nations must be held responsible for the economic backwardness of Asian and African lands and owe it to them to provide them with the means for rapid economic development. Asian and African nationalists do not seem greatly disturbed by the contradiction between their claim of equality or superiority and their impatience to emulate the European and American pattern in science, technology, and industry, a desire which can hardly be fulfilled without laying themselves open to the influence of other aspects of European and American civilization as well.

In all of this the new nationalisms have been vigorously

supported—and sometimes manipulated—by a revolutionary force within European civilization—communism—which found in the resentment of Asia and Africa a powerful instrument to be used to weaken the Western world.

In recent years, the climate of opinion in the West has been slowly but perceptibly changing. A few things have not gone according to expectations. European nations have lost large colonial empires; according to the exploitation theory of colonialism these imperialist nations should have suffered a marked decline in their prosperity, while the liberated colonial countries should have experienced a corresponding rise in their fortunes. What has happened is almost the exact opposite: the European nations have continued to prosper, while the newly independent areas have progressed but little economically and many of them face serious economic crises. Furthermore, the domestic political development of the new nations has often taken a turn toward authoritarianism or totalitarianism. Experience of this kind provides the background for the new consideration that is now being given to the possibility that the backwardness of much of the non-European world may have more to do with conditions characteristic of these societies than with the actions of the West.

Banfield's book on *The Moral Basis of a Backward Society* (1958) is a symptom of the change in the climate of opinion, and a serious contribution to the understanding of backward societies. His field work was not done in Asia or Africa but in one of the backward areas of Europe, the Italian *mezzogiorno*, in a Calabrian village which he calls Montegrano. The study of a backward area in Europe offers some advantages over the study of, e.g., an Arab, Indian, or African village, because it is much closer to the West and therefore more easily comprehensible to a Western observer. The features of backwardness in a European community can be studied in the absence of many factors that are operative in Asian or African societies. On the other hand, the results of the study cannot be automatically applied to the different conditions of Asia or Africa.

Banfield and his family spent nine months in Montegrano. His material consists of interviews with about 70 persons, official documents and statistics, some autobiographies, and the results of a thematic apperception test applied to 18 persons (peasant and farm hands), using as controls the results of the test applied to similar groups in northern Italy and in Kansas. No attempt was made to employ "sophisticated techniques of interviewing" or, one might add, other techniques of gathering and evaluating material which have been designed with a view to eliminating, or at least substantially reducing, the need for interpretation but which, in this reviewer's opinion, have more often succeeded in hiding than in actually eliminating the subjective aspects of such investigations.

The author informs us at the outset of the final result of his inquiry: the backwardness of the area is due, mainly, to the inability of the people to cooperate for a common purpose. "Most of the people of the world live and die without ever achieving membership in a community larger than the family or tribe. Except in Europe and America, the concerting of behavior in political associations and corporate organizations is a rare and recent thing" (p. 7). ". . . the extreme poverty and backwardness [of Montegrano] is to be explained largely (but not entirely) by the *inability* of the villagers *to act together* for their common good, or, indeed, *for any end transcending the immediate material interests of the nuclear family*" (p. 10; italics added).

There are, e.g., no organized private charities in Montegrano; the Church maintains an orphanage but receives no local help of any kind for it. Meetings of the (advisory) municipal council are poorly attended and often fail to reach a quorum. There are no active political party organizations; an attempt made by a popular physician immediately after the last war to organize a Socialist party unit was at first eagerly welcomed by many villagers, but enthusiasm faded away immediately as soon as they realized that they had to contribute a few lire as dues. "There is no spirit," said the doctor who had taken this initiative; "there is no feeling of working together."

Among the issues which might be approached by concerted action Banfield mentions that there is no secondary school in the community and no hospital. No child can attend school beyond the fifth grade unless he goes out of town to boarding school— for most villagers a financial impossibility. The nearest hospital can be reached in five hours by automobile. In addition to the educational opportunities that it would open to the village

children, a secondary school or a trade school in Montegrano
would have an even more direct importance for the welfare of
the community since it would facilitate the settlement of prosperous people in Montegrano. Schools and hospitals are, in Italy,
public responsibilities, but the villagers could, by concerted
action, bring effective pressure to bear on the authorities. Also,
several communities might join together for private actions that
would provide some improvement of the situation—e.g., the
equipment of an ambulance. Nothing of this kind, we hear, has
ever been done or contemplated.[1]

Banfield discusses the explanations commonly offered for this
lethargy: poverty, ignorance, greed on the part of the upper
class and resentment on that of the lower, a form of land tenure
which allegedly conditions small owners to a stand-pat conser-
vatism and landless peasants to communism, the peasant's
alleged distrust of the state, and the fatalism allegedly characteristic of the people of southern Italy. While allowing some
weight to these factors, the author points out that they cannot
explain the whole picture. Poverty, however dire, need not
prevent people from giving some of their spare time, of which
they have a large surplus, to some common endeavor. Ignorance
in terms of school learning is great, but the peasants are
politically not uninformed and have a remarkably sound political judgment, by no means inferior to that of Americans of low
educational status. Class antagonism cannot explain why the
peasants do not unite to translate this antagonism into action,
i.e., against the upper class. The attitude toward the state
appears to be reasonable, not distorted by ingrained prejudice.
Fatalism fails to show up in many of their actions as individuals.

The main cause for the backwardness of Montegrano can be
found, according to the author, in certain behavioral characteristics which were mentioned at the beginning of the book and
which are summed up again in these words: "...the Montegran-
esi act as if they were following the rule: *Maximize the material,
short-run advantage of the nuclear family; assume that all others
will do likewise"* (p. 85). Banfield calls this state of affairs

---

[1] Regrettably, the author has not quite succeeded in eliminating signs of
moral condescension and impatience with the people for failing to act as they
should for their own good.

"amoral familism." An impressive case is made out to show that this formula effectively covers the behavior of the villagers, and that they fail to cooperate either because the goal transcends the interests of the nuclear family; or because the individual engaging in such activities would have to be willing to accept as reward for his activities not financial gain but honor, prestige, or the mere satisfaction of enjoyable activity or of a contribution made; or because he would have no chance of immediate compensation in any form and would have to be willing to wait for whatever reward might be in store for him.

"Amoral familism," according to the author, is due to the poverty of the region and to the people's ever-present fear of dying prematurely before they can raise their children to adulthood. This fear appears to be well justified, as the mortality rate is high—or, rather, was so until recently[2]—and the lot of orphans, in the absence of the institution of the extended family, is pathetic. The fact that the extended family, which over so large a part of the globe has provided security under conditions of great poverty, did not develop in these regions is attributed to the system of land tenure, in which "the peasant had neither incentive nor opportunity to organize a family to provide labor and management for the enterprise" (p. 154). The point, however, is not worked out in sufficient detail.

Finally, "selfishness in all relations except that of parents to children and [the] tendency to think of the individual as moved principally by forces outside of himself" (p. 154)—the latter somewhat at variance with the statement, made in another

[2] At the present, we hear, the mortality rate is very low, a change which the author attributes, as a matter of course, to antibiotics (p. 167). The validity of this interpretation could be judged only if one knew whether the killers which are now taking a diminished toll are diseases responsive to antibiotics and whether antibiotics have actually been administered to the survivors. But even if that were proved, it would still not be conclusive that credit for the lowered death rate belongs to the new drugs. There are other possibilities; their introduction could, e.g., have coincided with a decline in the toxicity of some invading organisms or the increased adaptation of the human population to them both on the ground of evolutionary changes (Dubos, 1959). Also, the lowering of the death rate in general does not necessarily indicate that the life expectancy of the parents of young children has increased. These are minor points in the context of the study, but they suggest that Banfield's conclusions cannot always be taken at face value.

context, that fatalism is not apparent "where individualistic action is called for" (p. 40)—are attributed to childhood experiences which are said to be typical for this area: selfishness is ascribed to overindulgence by the parents, who applaud selfish and irresponsible behavior on the part of their children even though they may punish it as part of the game; and fatalism to the fact that punishment is meted out erratically, without any recognizable relationship to a moral code, and without regard for the principle *nulla poena sine lege* so that the child is unable to foresee it and to plan accordingly.

"Amoral familism" cannot maintain a working society; without an outside agency—the state—performing some of the functions which the people do not perform themselves, it would collapse in anarchy.

Future possibilities are weighed. A change for the better would presuppose change in the ethos, leadership, and a willingness on the part of the people to tolerate organization. Banfield considers the possibilities for "planners" either so to manipulate the conditions that a different ethos will emerge, or to influence the people through education. The ethos might change through prosperity. Manipulation of the conditions, Banfield realizes, could misfire. Among educational possibilities, the author speculates that a Protestant mission (*sic!*) or Catholic missions from Northern Europe or the United States might bring about the desired effect, but he dismisses the idea as impractical (p. 171).

Finally, the author considers administrative decentralization to encourage local self-government, the improvement of schools, the establishment of weekly newspapers, and the encouragement of the upper classes to take leadership in community affairs, but he is not overly optimistic about the efficacy of such measures.

Banfield's analysis invites psychological considerations which may help to articulate the substance of his findings while throwing a slightly different light on some points.

Talcott Parsons (1950) has suggested that the application of psychoanalysis or other psychological theories to sociological problems is likely to be most fruitful if the psychological categories are not brought to bear directly on the social material, but if the latter has first been subjected to thorough analysis in terms of the appropriate social science, and if the psychoanalytic categories are applied, in a further step of abstraction, to the end product of this analysis. Banfield has carried the analysis of his data to a point where further reduction to psychological formulations requires no great effort.

The three characteristics of "amoral familism"—exclusive emphasis on the interests of the nuclear family, to the disregard of the interests of others; on material advantage, to the disregard of nonmaterial gratifications; and on short-run returns, to the disregard of long-term advantages—amount to an *absorption* of the people *by basic needs*—basic with regard to the persons to be benefited, the nature of the benefits sought, and the waiting time allowed.

1. *The nuclear family.* We begin our lives with an exclusive concern for ourselves, our own personal needs. The infant seeks nourishment and relief from pain and discomfort; soon, very soon, it also seeks love. The objects that supply satisfaction of these needs—primarily the mother or her substitute—are, and for a long time remain, for the child a means to a selfish end. They are suppliers. The child learns to love his mother, but this love is, for a long time, a direct function of the satisfaction received; she is appreciated as the source of the gratifications of the child's self-preservative needs—such as nutrition and bodily care—and of his need to be loved and caressed. It takes years for the child to learn to look upon his mother as a person in her own right; every mother knows how self-centered children usually are and how difficult it is even for a child of beginning school age to realize that his mother may be tired or sick and that the denial of a wish need not indicate lack of love. It takes a long time until the child's relations to others go beyond the need-fulfilling stage and the child is able to love not only because he receives and while he receives. Some people never reach this stage and live their days out without having ever truly loved anybody but themselves, with their relations to others determined by their intake from them. Psychoanalysts suspect that one must have received a great deal of love—which does not mean indulgence—in early childhood to be capable of genuine love for others later. The ability to love seems to be related to a surplus in an early developmental stage.

Furthermore, we know that even those who have reached the full ability of object love may regress to former conditions of exclusive selfishness in situations of great frustration or danger. We are not surprised if people who are severely sick, or in intense pain, or very old, appear to be exclusively interested in themselves.

Nobody can say that the people described in Banfield's book have not reached the stage of object love. They are all intensely interested in, and devoted to, the welfare of their families. But while they have reached the stage of genuine object love, they have limited themselves to the small biological group—the "nuclear" family. They do not take much interest in the welfare of their neighbors, or of the other members of their community—not to mention still larger groups; or, rather, their interest in the welfare of their neighbors or of the community at large, while not entirely absent, is not strong enough to command any sacrifice from them.

2. *Insistence on material rewards* does not in itself indicate that we have to do with basic needs. There are material benefits that do not, and nonmaterial benefits that do, command a high priority for most people. In order to evaluate what "material advantage" means psychologically, it is necessary to know for what purpose income would be used: whether, e.g., for more luxurious living, or for more leisure, or for treasures to be hoarded and enjoyed in loneliness, or for conspicuous consumption, or for masses to be read after one's death, and so forth.

We are informed on what the income of the people is being spent and to what use additional income presumably would be put. The existence of most of the people is marginal; they spend their income for food, household goods, and clothing, all of a very simple kind, for some farm necessities, and a small amount for the doctor and for medicine. The doctor hesitates to prescribe expensive drugs because the patient will probably not be able to have the prescription filled. Beyond these "nuclear" needs, the peasants are hounded by the pressure to save some money for a dowry for their daughters, as without it they have no hope of ever finding a husband. They also wish to be able to send a boy out of town for schooling, which is his only chance of escaping the misery of the peasant's existence. These are elementary needs which would command high priority among most men in our own society. What Banfield calls insistence on material rewards appears as concentration on high-priority needs.

3. *The short-run gratification.* Immediate gratification is demanded whenever the needs are imperative or the tolerance for frustration is low. The latter is true of childhood; only gradually do we learn to stand frustration and to comfort ourselves in the meantime with the anticipation of future gratifications; once again, the final level of frustration tolerance that we achieve varies with persons and circumstances. Equally we insist on immediate gratification if the urge is very strong; sometimes it may well be beyond the tolerance of anyone, as is shown, e.g., by the fact that a wanderer in the desert, exhausted by thirst, may drink water which he knows to contain salt or to be polluted, thus disregarding the virtual certainty of an even more tormenting thirst, or of pestilence, a little later.

In the light of these considerations, the three characteristics of "amoral familism" seem to stem from the fact that the existence of the people is marginal and that they are dominated by the most elementary urges as regards the persons for whom they care, the goals of their desires, and the time they can wait for fulfillment. A vicious circle is thereby established. In order to raise themselves out of their condition, the people would have to make concentrated efforts which will not necessarily benefit each one or his immmediate family directly, will not necessarily bring him monetary reward or, perhaps, any short-term returns at all. The people would have to be more at ease, live a less marginal existence—in short, be less pressed by frustration—to be able to do these things.

Are Banfield's results characteristic only of the *mezzogiorno* or do they have a more general significance? The psychoanalytic reading of his results suggests that they are of wider significance, because emancipation from backwardness is seen as a question of the conditions that allow man to go beyond the struggle for gratification of his most elementary needs. Circumstances, no doubt, vary from society to society, but absorption in fulfilling basic needs and lack of the surplus energy or impulses necessary to transcend them may be factors which many archaic societies have in common.

Perhaps these considerations can throw some light on Max Weber's theory of the origins of capitalism. The idea that the Calvinist search for earthly success as a sign of a place among the elect provided the main motive for the Puritan dedication to the business enterprise was psychologically plausible, and in the light of it many facts, particularly of the development of New England, seemed to fall into place; but, on the other hand, there was the hard fact that capitalism did not emerge only in Calvinist lands and that countries of, e.g., Lutheran and Catholic faith have contributed to it.

Perhaps Weber's hypothesis shows *one*, but only one, way of breaking through the vicious circle of a backward society. The vicious circle, apparently, can be broken at more than one point. A windfall of wealth may come to a people accidentally and raise them from a marginal level of existence, thereby providing some with the leisure and the means for adventure, for study, or for education, and making it possible for others to set their aspirations higher or to wait longer for a return from their efforts. Or, a determined ruler, with a well-organized and loyal elite to carry out his orders, wielding a monopoly of the tools of coercion, may force the people, however marginal their existence, to accept great sacrifices for the building of a modern production machine. Or, in times of supranaturalism, a religion or secular asceticism may achieve the same result through fear of hellfire; the latter was, after all, the motive force in Max Weber's theory.

There is no doubt that, judged on the basis of its record over several generations, modern European and American society is better adjusted to its environment than other societies and greatly superior to them in its ability to provide the people with the things which they—whether Europeans, Asians, or Africans—seem to desire most. But that does not mean that modern society is without grave dangers or that its difficulties may not, in the very long run, turn out to be even more serious than those of archaic societies; a few generations or even centuries are too short a time for a final assessment. It may be that modern societies will yet turn out, *sub specie aeternitatis*, to have been even less well adjusted than archaic societies.

But the frustrations and dangers of modern societies are radically different from those of archaic societies; they are not the difficulties of stagnation but those of rapid change. The problems which will plague modern societies will probably be, first, the need for periodical readjustment between the various parts of the productive apparatus (particularly between those producing consumer's goods and those producing producer's goods), which cannot all expand at equal speed for a prolonged time— the essence of the business cycle and of cyclic unemployment. Then, there must be constant change, at an ever-accelerating pace, if an economy a large and growing part of which is devoted to investment is not to collapse, and this necessity presents an enormous task, which we are just beginning to see, of constant human adjustment to a perpetually changing environment; we will increasingly be confronted with the difference between the speed of technological change, to which no limit is apparent at the moment, and the limited speed of biological processes. Then, man is now doing on an immensely increased scale what he has been doing since the dawn of civilization— that is, destroying the balance of nature—and it is questionable whether he will always be able to find a workable substitute for it. Finally, modern societies with their ever-growing consumption may some day face the limits of the resources within their reach.

But these are worries that belong to a later station in man's pilgrimage through time than do the difficulties of transition from an archaic to a modern society, to the understanding of which Banfield's book, despite some weaknesses, has made an important contribution.

CHAPTER 32

Characteristics of
Totalitarianism

(1960)

In 1951 I described the characteristics of totalitarianism, the
conditions for its emergence and its impact upon men, both
those reared under a different system and "reeducated" under
totalitarianism, and those who grew up under a totalitarian
system and accepted its doctrines as their natural spiritual and
philosophical habitat (see Ch. 28). The basic propositions were
not new; they had been clearly seen by 19th-century authors
whom later writers on the subject had often overlooked. I tried
to carry their analysis one step further, from the level of political
analysis to that of an analysis of the psychological processes
which underlie the political attitudes.

The Nature of Totalitarianism

The first subject was the distinction between authoritarianism and totalitarianism; the term, authoritarianism, should refer
to a system exemplified, among others, by the Poland of
Pilsudski and Rydz-Smigly, the Hungary of Horthy, the Austria
of Dollfuss and Schuschnigg, the Spain of Franco, the Portugal
of Salazar. Totalitarianism, on the other hand, was meant to

Reprinted from *The Psychoanalytic Study of Society*, ed. W. Muensterberger & S. Axelrad. New York: International Universities Press, 1960;
Volume I, pp. 11-25.

refer to Soviet Russia and Communist China, to Nazi Germany, and, in weaker examples, to Fascist Italy or, more recently, nationalist Egypt. The difference between the two types is measured neither in the number nor the severity of restrictions imposed upon the people nor in the extent of the private sphere allowed to them. As a rule, the private sphere is wider in the authoritarian than in the totalitarian system, but this is not necessarily so, because genuine totalitarianism may at times choose to leave relatively wide areas free of interference (as was, e.g., the case in Fascist Italy, at least until the last years before Italy became a German satellite); it may do so because of personal allegiances of the rulers or for reasons of expediency or out of sheer weakness.

It is not the extent of the unregulated sector that makes the difference. The difference is more fundamental than this; it consists of the different impact of the system upon its victims, i.e., upon those who are opposed to its policies or not convinced of their value. One can say that authoritarianism is oppressive for its victims, sometimes very oppressive, but not degrading or demoralizing, while totalitarianism is just that.

This difference was brought out, implicitly, by Constant de Rebècque in a treatise published in 1813: the two systems which he compared are the old-fashioned despotism of the *ancien régime* and the "usurpation" of the Bonapartist Empire. The latter, said Constant, had deprived the people even of the "right of silence."

In an authoritarian system the subjects are compelled to obey the orders of the authorities: to pay their taxes, confiscatory though they may be (without representation); to surrender their property when so required; to render military service at whatever terms are imposed; and, in general, to carry out loyally what they are asked to do; and they have to abstain from revolutionary activities and sometimes also from criticism of the government. But they are *not* required to say that they love the hand that beats them; *they may be whipped, but they do not have to kiss the rod.* This latter requirement, however, is added under totalitarianism.

Totalitarianism denies to its subjects the last refuge of human dignity; the whole coercive power of the rulers is used, mercilessly, not only to ensure obedience to orders (as in authori-

tarianism) but also, in addition to it, to extract continuous
expressions of enthusiastic approval from them. The public
spectacle of persons accused of treason or sabotage in the purge
trials in Soviet Russia in the 1930s, or of exploitation and similar
sins committed in the past, in the numerable orchestrated
lynchings of landlords and other persons in Communist China,
with the humble confessions of the accused and their suppli-
cation for a lenient punishment are cases in point. They are only
the extreme manifestations of pressures that in a less ferocious
degree permeate daily life; the people must not merely passively
obey but actively approve. A Communist paper in Poland was
recently reported to have referred to nonconformist writers who
had taken more advantage of the liberalization in cultural
matters—the "thaw"—than the Polish Communist Party thought
either permissible from their own point of view or wise in view
of Russian supervision: we will judge them not only by what
they say but also *by what they do not say.*

Shakespeare's Henry V, visiting the camp on the eve of the
battle of Agincourt, says to a group of soldiers: Every subject's
duty is his king's; every subject's soul is his own. Authoritarianism is the system that is adamant in demanding *every subject's
duty* but is willing to let the subject's soul be his own; totalitarianism, on the other hand, insists on every subject's *duty and
soul.*

The Essence of Brainwashing

The request for the soul, i.e., the attempt to change the
allegiance of a person whose allegiances have already been
formed, has recently been called brainwashing and there has
been much speculation how it is brought about. Everybody is, of
course, familiar with techniques of propaganda and advertising,
but despite the alarms recently sounded by some authors about
the power of unrecognized propaganda (the "hidden persuad-
ers"), it is doubtful whether the ordinary means of persuasion,
without a monopoly of propaganda and without the power of
physical coercion—both enjoyed by totalitarian governments
but quite out of the reach of manufacturers trying to promote a

product, or of political parties in pluralist democracies—can ever gain any great and lasting power over men's minds. The limits of skulduggery in a competitive market of ideas, without the help of the executioner, have probably been properly defined in the famous saying of Lincoln. Even the influence of the hypnotist over his object—considerably greater than that of any ad-man over the public—has not been considered to be great enough to force a person to a behavior inconsistent with his previous character; in the long discussion, about half a century ago, of the question whether a hypnotist could make a criminal out of an average law-abiding person, students of hypnotism seemed to discount this possibility.

The question remains how one can influence the thinking of adults radically and lastingly. Sheer physical force can, of course, induce most people to behave in the desired way; many, though not all, people have under torture confessed to crimes they did not commit, and have denounced their kith and kin as supposedly guilty of the same crimes. But what force produced in these cases was behavior—speech or signature—not belief; the person who made such confessions and denunciations did not, as far as we know, actually believe that, e.g., she was a witch and her husband a sorcerer. How can thinking be changed against the evidence of the senses and how can the most basic allegiances be changed?

The answer to this question is latent in the quoted lines by Constant. It is true that one cannot really force another person's thought but merely his hand or his tongue; and that he may submit to coercion and yet think his own thoughts. But one can force him to repeat required statements over and over again, and while this does not alter the *theoretical* freedom of his thought, it does create a situation which is *psychologically* very difficult for most people to bear because it involves constant tensions; one must all the time be careful lest one may give oneself away to the watchful eyes of the inquisitor—through a slip of the tongue, a lack of enthusiasm in one's facial expression, or the forgetting of a required formula or ritual. Professional revolutionaries are used to the perpetual need for high-tension self-control, and they may even enjoy it, and diplomats are expected to practice it; but both are specially selected and highly trained individuals, and both can relax from time to time in the company of their own group. Not much opportunity for relaxation is available to the average person in a totalitarian state where neighbors cannot be trusted, children may have taken to the idea of watching over their parents' loyalty, and where even confidences between husband and wife may become a source of disaster if the relationship should ever deteriorate.

The average person finds this constant tension hardly bearable and will eagerly seize the way out that is offered to him, viz., to embrace the ruling philosophy and to learn to believe in it. There are many rationalizations to make the step more palatable and to disguise before oneself and one's *amour-propre* the true nature of the surrender; after all, friends have embraced the new philosophy and prominent people in the land have aligned themselves behind it; why should one be different from all the others? Is it not just being stubborn and uncooperative to say "no" when everybody else says "yes"? What right does one have to think differently where all the others seem to agree?

Once one has accepted the ruling creed, one can perform the required rituals with full conviction. There is no more danger of giving oneself away; life is easy once again. One will all the more readily take this way out the less firm one's previous convictions have been. The skeptic, the opportunist, the relativist, the liberal are therefore an easier prey to totalitarian "brainwashing" than the devout religious believer, the totalitarian of another persuasion or, for that matter, the psychotic.

Thus, brainwashing, in the main, consists simply in forcing people to perpetual professions of belief in certain doctrines. Force is usually sufficient to have them go through these motions, and what people are forced to say over and over again they will very often end up believing.

One is reminded of the James-Lange theory of affects according to which expression *causes* the sentiment: we do not laugh because we are amused, but we are amused because we are laughing. One is also reminded of Alfred North Whitehead's four stages of religious development: ritual, stories, belief, and systematization. In general, the observance of certain rituals— e.g., the folding of the hands in prayer—is often the first step in the religious instruction of a child; belief comes later and is often the more firmly entrenched the more there was of an early conditioning in ritual.

The available data seem to support our conclusion that brainwashing operates through enforced professions of belief.

In a recent presentation of the results of an Army study on the defection of American prisoners in the hand of the Chinese Communists during the Korean war, Eugene Kinkead (1959) describes the political instruction of prisoners; they were taught Marxism: "Repetition was used both in classes and in individual instruction. Prisoners were required to memorize certain material, such as the contents of a pamphlet on Communist ideology, and they were examined on this material day in and day out, week in and week out. While they are being crammed with this literature and questioned on it over and again, the prisoners were . . . allowed to read nothing else" (p. 106).

Kinkead reports the following incident: the Communist instructor had told the class how the "South Koreans had treacherously attacked the peaceful North Koreans" as a consequence of the plan of "Wall Street" capitalists to start a war in order to raise stock market prices. A prisoner raised the question how it happened, if South Korea was the aggressor, that the North Koreans had penetrated forty miles deep into South Korean territory at the end of the first day of fighting. The instructor ordered him to recant; as the soldier refused, the instructor had the whole group stand until this man would give in. After a few hours, with pressure from his comrades mounting, the soldier yielded and recanted. He had then, for several days, to write every day a long piece of self-criticism and to apologize for his conduct (p. 108).

Kinkead's report also illustrates another aspect of the process of brainwashing, which distinguishes it from propaganda in nontotalitarian countries; in brainwashing, the object is treated *like a child* who, in traditionalist education, has to accept explanations and to abide by rules without questioning. This kind of treatment is, of course, profoundly humiliating for those being subjected to it. In any kind of propaganda other than brainwashing, on the other hand, the approach is essentially on an adult level, appealing to existing allegiances and moral principles, and to reason, spurious though the appeal may be (see also Ch. 34).

The Conditions of Totalitarianism

The conditions for the adoption of totalitarian attitudes follow from their nature. Totalitarianism appears whenever there is a "monism of value," i.e., a concentration of human will upon the achievement of *one* goal. Whenever there is a "pluralism of value," ie., whenever people are given too many, often conflicting, pursuits, the resulting political system cannot be totalitarian. Dahlberg-Acton had expressed this principle in 1862: "Whenever a single definite object is made the supreme end of the State, be it the advantage of a class, the safety or the power of the country, the greatest happiness of the greatest number or the support of a speculative idea, the State becomes for the time inevitably absolute" (p. 184).

There is no reason why, if complete power is in our hands, we should refrain from using it for the achievement of our purposes unless we feel some doubt about the worthiness of our purposes—in which case we are not fully committed to them—or feel allegiance not only to these goals but also to some other principles or ideas, e.g., to the idea that violence should not be used because it is felt to be morally condemnable and a source of evil even if used for right ends, or self-defeating in the long run; or if we believe that respect for human dignity is as important as the goal that we might pursue at its expense. In these latter instances we are not pursuing one goal *exclusively* but are trying to steer our way in the midst of different, partially conflicting, values. Even the difference between authoritarianism and totalitarianism must be seen in this light. True monism of values, *undivided allegiance* to one goal only, will always find its expression in totalitarianism.[1]

[1] A readiness to "liberalize" controls under the Soviet system, e.g., by permitting free, or relatively free, discussion in so-called cultural matters—literature, painting, music—if advocated not merely as an expedient of smoother political control must therefore appear from a Bolshevist viewpoint as the introduction of an extraneous value, hence as treason.

Authoritarianism indicates a condition short of complete monism; for a political system to stop at the authoritarian level without going all the way toward totalitarianism there must be, in addition to dedication to the goals of the State, some respect of individual human dignity, or some feeling that there should be a private sphere which the State should not enter; in short, some reason why those who wield full coercive power should be content with their subjects' duty and not demand their subjects' soul, too.[2]

Totalitarianism is probably older than pluralist systems and perhaps also older than authoritarianism, which has a slight touch of pluralism, as it were. One wonders to what degree the idea of liberty in Western civilization may be an end product of the separation of secular and spiritual authority that was inaugurated by the word of Jesus: Render therefore unto Caesar the things that are Caesar's; and unto God the things that are God's. This separation has permeated the life of Europe under the Latin Church and has permitted a degree of liberty to develop in the shadow of the long struggle between Crown and Papacy; and with the decline of the influence of the churches, the spiritual authority which they had wielded became a stray good, for everybody to pick up and keep it if he could.

In the Eastern Church, on the other hand, spiritual and secular authority have remained in one hand, according to the famous word of a Byzantine emperor: *imperator sum et sacerdos.*[3] We still see today in the greater part of what was the domain of Eastern Christendom that unlimited physical coercive power and the authority to define proper beliefs rest in the same hands, viz., the ruling men of the Communist party.

The dedication to one, and only one, goal, to the exclusion of all other considerations, can be brought about in two ways: one is, of course, the conviction of men that only one thing matters,

[2] Sometimes, of course, the comparative restraint of authoritarian rulers may merely be a consequence of their limited strength; they do not dare to go any further. But there are cases of self-restraint, too.

[3] I am aware of the fact that the statement is apocryphal and that Byzantine scholars would question whether this state really fully applied except perhaps under the iconoclast emperors, and again, toward the end of Byzantine history, under the Palaeologi. But if not exactly true, the formula is a good enough approximation to the truth.

at least for the time being, and that everything else must be postponed or subordinated to it; in our age, the idea of socialism and the idea of nationalism have played this role, and totalitarianism has been practiced in the name of one or the other. We may call this the *ideological* case of totalitarianism. It is well enough known today, through the experience of the last four decades. But there seems to be less awareness of another case of totalitarianism, or potential totalitarianism. Domination of the mind by one goal can come about not only as a consequence of an ideology but also through extreme circumstances which tend to reduce the leeway of human actions so that it may all come down to concern for one thing without which nothing else is possible, i.e., to the question of coping with extreme danger, the issue of survival. If shipwrecks are stranded on a deserted island, if a mountain-climbing party is faced with an avalanche, or a nation sees destruction or slavery stare in its face, many issues of property, income, status, convenience, or individual rights may be brushed aside if they stand in the way, or seem to stand in the way, of survival. Extreme dangers have always called forth the temporary suspension of individual rights. Roman constitutional practice had it regularized; the Senate voted emergency powers to the consuls with the standing formula: *Caveant consules ne quid detrimenti capiat res publica.* Beyond that Rome had the institution of temporary dictatorship.

Resort to Potentially Totalitarian Measures in the Struggle against Totalitarianism

This may throw some light upon a discussion that has been going on in the United States for some years. In a fight against totalitarianism, we are told, we must beware lest we become totalitarian in the process of fighting it: "The defeat of totalitarianism . . . must come about by due process of law and not by destroying freedom and the ways of freedom through adopting the methods of totalitarianism" (Kallen, 1954). This is an appeal that is certain to win the favor of an audience, like proclamations in favor of peace, democracy, or economy in government, because like those it implies that what one desires can be had without a price; one can oppose such declarations only at the penalty of unpopularity. Every reduction of freedom, in the face of enemy threat, every measure of political control, however mild in itself, is immediately denounced from many quarters as a step toward totalitarianism and *therefore* automatically disqualified in a fight against totalitarianism; in fact, it is denounced as indication that we are losing the fight in the very act of waging it.

The policies so denounced may, or may not, be effective remedies which fight off the disease without causing evils greater than those they cure. That depends on the respective policy and on the situation in which it is applied. But the *general* assumption, implicit in the criticism, that we *must* be able to counter the threat without ourselves curtailing any liberties, and that any curtailment of liberties necessarily means defeat in the ultimate sense because we would already have succumbed to totalitarianism of the domestic variety, and that delivery from the external threat of totalitarianism, if so purchased, would therefore be necessarily worthless—this assumption shows a fundamental misunderstanding of the nature of emergencies and the prerequisites of coping with them. One cannot take it for granted that it will *always* be possible to defend oneself successfully against a totalitarian threat without concentrating command and imposing discipline. Whenever possible, it is certainly desirable, for the kind of people that we are, to defend ourselves while maintaining the whole fabric of individual liberties. It was possible in the last war because the United States was then not immediately threatened, i.e., because the emergency was not critical enough. But even then the guarantees of liberties and due process broke down in cases in which an immediate and serious threat was felt; the deportation of the West Coast Japanese is the most significant example.[4]

The insistence that in the defense against totalitarianism we must never make any step, however small, toward totalitarian

---

[4] That such situations are used, or abused, by private interests, prejudices, and hatreds or by sheer hysteria, and that such factors may extend the action, in scope, severity or time, beyond the limits of self-preservative necessity is of course also true, but it does not alter the fact that there is a core due to self-preservation.

Robert Waelder

organization ourselves, by exercising pressures on individuals, is obviously based on one of two assumptions; either it is taken for granted that we do not face, and never will face, an emergency serious enough to require enforced discipline to deal with it; or that there is nothing to choose between the permanent loss of all our rights to our enemies and the temporary curtailment of some of our liberties at the hand of our fellow citizens, and that we may therefore just as well risk the former if we can avoid it only at the price of the latter. In short, the critics either do not believe in any great danger or they hate or fear other Americans at least as much as they fear the enemy. Better the crescent of the Turk than the tiara of the Pope, the Eastern Christians used to say in the last days of the Byzantine Empire; their descendants who lived under Turkish rule would probably have taken a different view of the matter if they had still any decisions to make.

Totalitarianism and Paranoia

We have distinguished between totalitarianism as the product of an ideology and totalitarianism as the result of extreme danger. Psychologically, the two types are essentially one because in the mind of the ideologist the condition against which he fights or which might recur if he relaxed his vigilance—e.g., so-called capitalism for the Communists—is so profoundly evil that its prevalence would mean moral or spiritual death for him. The monistic ideologist therefore feels himself always in an emergency; but as different from the threat that is felt by the shipwrecks, the stranded mountain climbers, or the nation under actual threat of subjugation or extinction—say, the Romans at the time of Cincinnatus—the emergency of the ideologist exists only in his interpretation and in most instances does not appear as emergency to outsiders. Perhaps the best *objective* criterion for this difference is the fact that these other emergencies are all temporary and once they have passed, the people will again pursue variegated goals, while the *emergency of the ideologist never ends.*

But the permanent concentration on one goal with the elimination or subordination of all others is the sign of a *distortion of the human form;* popular speech indicates this impression by attributing to such people a "one-track mind." The corresponding scientific expression would be "overvalued idea"; i.e., we have to do with *paranoid* types.[5]

I do not mean to suggest that individuals in question are paranoid schizophrenics or that they suffer from Kraepelinian paranoia in the sense of delusions of grandeur, or delusions of persecution or delusional jealousy. But they may be called paranoid for the following reasons:

They make one ideal or aspiration absolute, to the neglect of all others, like the paranoid querulist who sacrifices his position and his career, the future of his family and the lives of innocent people to his fight for his right and for the redress of grievances which in themselves may well be real. In such cases, a man fights for a goal which we may consider worthy in itself, but he lacks a *sense of proportion.*[6] The old saying, *fiat justicia, pereat mundus,* is a questionable principle at best and must in any case not be applied to minor issues. Justice is a noble value, but so are respect for life, peace, humility, the protection of the innocent, and the preservation of the legal order. Only in extreme circumstances will we feel that everything else can and must be disregarded for the sake of the one: e.g., if the injustice was monstrous, or if peace is not obtainable, and in similar contingencies. But short of extreme conditions it is in some kind of *balance* that a sane mind seeks the solution of a conflict; he will

[5] The paranoid element in millenarian movements throughout history has recently been pointed to by Norman Cohn (1957), who considers the following characteristics as pathognomic: "The megalomanic view of oneself as the Elect, wholly good, abominably persecuted yet assured of ultimate triumph; the attribution of gigantic and demonic powers to the adversary; the refusal to accept the ineluctable limitations and imperfections of human existence, such as transience, dissension, conflict, fallibility, whether intellectual or moral; the obsession with inerrable prophesies . . ." (p. 309).

[6] See Edward Shils (1958): "It has not been the substantive values sought by ideological politics which have done such damage. Rather it has been the rigidity, the exclusiveness, and the extremity with which particular values have been sought. There is nothing evil about loyalty to one's community, national or ethnic or cultural, nor is there anything wicked in the appreciation of equality or the devotion to any particular ideal. What is so malign is the elevation of one value, such as equality or national or ethnic solidarity, to supremacy over all others, and the insistence on its exclusive dominion in every sphere of life."

not pursue any one goal beyond all limits because he is aware of the fact that there are many mutually contradictory values in the world, that the realization is achieved at the expense of another, and that there is a point where the price paid for the realization of one value is too great; e.g., where justice could be bought only at too high a price in human suffering.

The lack of proportion, in the monistic ideologist, goes hand in hand with an unawareness of complexity; it is justified by beliefs which are not accessible to correction by experience. When such people are confronted with facts at variance with their theories, they do not change their theories but find ways to explain away the facts;[7] their attitude runs the gamut from strong bias due to chance experience, indoctrination, and emotional preference to complete inaccessibility to influence by reason (see Ch. 27). More transient advocates of the doctrine may be found at the former, but the enduring protagonists are likely to be found at the latter, end of the spectrum. With them, the basic tenets of the ideology are *a priori* true and no event that would contradict any part of them is even theoretically thinkable.

Thus, when an American group headed by Herbert Hoover distributed food in Russia during the famine of 1921, with the U.S. government contributing to the expense of the operation,

---

[7] The way the mind of the believer operates can easily be observed in analysis. During the Second World War, e.g., a large company decided, apparently under political pressure, to open to Negroes some job categories that had heretofore been reserved to whites; thereupon the white union went on strike. These developments were deeply disturbing to a convinced Marxist who was then in analysis with me. Racial tensions, according to his convictions, were a product of capitalism; the natural condition of men was brotherhood. Racial tensions between workers were an artifact, manufactured, or, at the very least, worked up out of proportion by the capitalists who acted according to the principle: divide and conquer. How could it be that a capitalist company was ready to give job equality to Negroes and that workers opposed it?

For days he walked around in a state of bewilderment. He then strolled around near the factories in the evenings and started conversations with striking workers. In this way, he learned about a few trivial incidents which he interpreted as indicating sympathy with the strike on the part of the company. From this he inferred that the strike had actually been engineered, behind the scenes, by the company, and with this idea which immediately hardened into conviction his mind came to rest.

the Communists did not conclude that humanitarian sentiment existed in the United States and influenced the actions of private groups and of the government; this was theoretically impossible because government actions are determined by class interest and a humanitarian act from a "capitalist" state to a "workers' state" is a double impossibility. Hence, the food distribution must have been caused by other motives, presumably by a desire to plant spies in the Soviet Union and by the need of the capitalists to get rid of surplus goods.

Or, when it became difficult to deny that the living standards of American workers had risen substantially over the subsistence level, this was not taken to indicate that a market economy can provide for the economic betterment of the masses. Marx had proved that all value comes from labor and equals the amount of labor expended; hence, the value of a man's labor is equal to the cost of keeping him alive and in working condition. Wages, under capitalism, must therefore remain on the level of the costs of subsistence (the iron law of wages) and the visible rise of living conditions among American workers must be due to the operation of extrasystemic factors—presumably, enormous war profits made by the capitalists during the two World Wars which enabled them to let the workers share in some of their loot.

Or, finally, if businessmen do not behave the way they should according to the theory of class warfare but devote themselves, not to building a united front against the "proletariat" and against the "workers' state," the Soviet Union, but to their own competitive enterprises, it indicates not that the Marxist theory of classes is wrong, at least as far as the businesmen are concerned, but merely that the capitalist class is so decadent a class that it no longer shows the characteristics of a real class. It is all like in an old Jewish story: two men from different Jewish communities in old Russia competed with each other in praising the merits of their respective rabbis; sometimes one, sometimes the other, had the better of the argument. Finally, one man has an unbeatable trump card: his rabbi is a man of such high virtue that God Himself had talked to him. Nothing is left to the other man than to question the accuracy of the story; perhaps it is not true? "The rabbi told it to me himself," says the first man. "Perhaps he did not tell the truth," counters the other. "You are a fool," says the first man contemptuously, "do you think God would talk to a liar?"

A believer in Communism might be asked whether he can conceive, theoretically, of any event that would invalidate Marxist-Leninist theory. Convinced Communists do not understand the question; Marxist "teachings" are "scientific" Truth, so how could they ever be invalidated?[8]

It is for these reasons that the protagonists of ideological monism, as a rule, impress us as being of the paranoid type; those ideologists who are not of this bent of mind shrink back, sooner or later, from the costs of realizing their ideas—the sacrifices, the injustices, the distortions of truth.

The rank and file followers, on the other hand, are average people, of many kinds of psychological makeup, who have felt the appeal of the ideal, who are pleased to hear that their aspirations can be fully fulfilled, without cost or without serious cost, who are impressed by the determination and self-confidence of the leader and have subordinated themselves to him, putting him in place of their consciences, as was described by Freud (1921).

Totalitarianism may thus be said to be *either the consequence of the imperatives of survival or the outgrowth of a paranoid system.*

Paranoid thinking is a source both of strength and of weakness. It gives strength through the polarization of all tendencies in one direction and the complete intellectual conviction which eliminates doubts and ambiguities; here, clearly, the

---

[8] The Communist's attitude to his doctrine cannot be compared to the attitude of others, who have not accepted a monistic ideology, to their respective political or economic ideas, nor, in general, to the attitude of average people to their views in any empirical matter. It is only comparable to the attitude we all have to *mathematical* theorems. Here we behave in the same way. We think that two and two make four, and if we should ever have the experience that after having put two objects and again two objects in a place, we find afterwards five of them are there, we would think that the fifth was put there by another person or by ourselves in inadvertence, or has somehow been produced from other matter, or, if need be, may even have been dropped from outer space, but we will not consider the possibility that the arithmetic is wrong. The Communist feels this way about Marxist-Leninist doctrine.

native hue of resolution is not sicklied over with the pale cast of thought. But it is a source of weakness, too, because of the failure properly to appraise those aspects of reality that run counter to basic theoretical tenets.

In the real paranoiacs and the paranoid schizophrenics, seen in our psychiatric hospitals, there is no doubt that the liabilities far outweigh the assets. But this is not always the case with the paranoid personalities under discussion; with them, paranoid thought may be limited to one, or a few, propositions, and some such persons combined paranoid thought in a few fundamental tenets on matters outside the experience of average people with an ice-cold realism in other matters, particularly in matters of power and strategy; Lenin is a perfect example of this combination.[9] In such instances, the simple paranoid ideology gives to its devotees the unfaltering conviction of the eternal righteousness of their cause, and thereby a ruthlessness undisturbed by pangs of conscience, a determination to stop short of nothing in the pursuit of their goals. The very impossibility of reaching the totalitarian by any kind of argument is a further source of strength because it drives those in his power into despair and, finally, except in the case of those who are morally supported by firm beliefs of their own, to inner capitulation.

"Strong ideas" that carry everything before them and become a tornado of history are often paranoid ideas. Once the paranoia has gone out of them and the idea is based only on ordinary considerations of expediency and reasoning, strength has left them, too, and the end of the power of the idea over the minds of men is in sight. The last decades of the czarist autocracy provide an example of the latter condition. The system was no longer able to prevent opposition from forming itself and growing rapidly until it finally encompassed practically the entire educated middle class. The czarist government wavered between relative tolerance of and retreat from the popular demands and sudden outbursts of oppression. But either the determination or the power to annihilate the opposition was

[9] Cohn (1957, p. 309f.) comments: "National-Socialist and Communist leaders, despite the hard-headed realism which has characterized their tactics, have also exhibited and imparted to their followers a truly psychotic irrationality wherever the eschatological phantasy itself has been involved."

lacking. Power, presumably, was lacking because determination was lacking or, rather, was held only by very few. With very few exceptions, the supporters of the autocracy no longer believed in the divine ordination of kings which had been its ideological basis and justification; they stood for the czar not for transcendent but for purely practical reasons, above all because they feared the consequences of revolution or reform. The lack of faith in the ultimate right of the system encouraged opposition and weakened the hand of its defenders.

But there was a time when the divine right of kings was an immensely strong idea against which nobody dared to take a stand. In the peasant revolt in England in 1381, under the reign of Richard II, the peasants forced their prisoners to swear an oath of allegiance to the king and to the common people of England. We can hardly judge whether they actually believed, or merely pretended to believe, that the Crown was on their side; but in any case, revolution against the royal principle or against the person of the monarch was apparently out of the question. At most there could be revolution against the lords in the name of the king. Today, the idea of socialism seems to hold a similar power over the minds of men in a large part of the earth. Opposition against the leadership in the Soviet world appears therefore to be possible, at the present time, only in the name of socialism, not as opposition against socialism.

It is difficult to believe that men who are fully convinced that the basic propositions of Marxism-Leninism are absolute truth should ever voluntarily grant a substantial degree of freedom of expression to those who hold views fundamentally different from their own, because such freedom must mean, from their point of view, that dangerous errors have a chance to work mischief. The enormous tolerance of our society in political, religious, philosophical, and social matters is partly due to doubt[10]—to the very wise distrust in our own judgment and to the suspicion that our convictions, no matter how well founded they may seem to us, may yet be mistaken and are indeed likely to appear as at least partly mistaken to a later age—and partly to the multiplicity of

[10] See Freud (1921, p. 98f.) on religious intolerance. See also Ch. 27, where Freud's words are quoted in full.

our values,[11] which lets us cherish not only different and partly contradictory substantive goals but also the very freedom of choice itself. These two characteristics—doubt and pluralism of values—seem to be interconnected, as the cognitive and the emotive aspect of our approach to the world, just as the opposites, intellectual dogmatism and devotion to one aspiration to the exclusion of all others, appear in their more extreme manifestations as the interconnected characteristics of the paranoid attitude.

[11] The Communist conviction that "capitalism" is "decadent" contains a nucleus of truth. If we take capitalism to mean a pluralist society, and decadence to mean the existence of intrinsic weaknesses, the statement comes down to this: pluralist societies have intrinsic weaknesses, and this is correct. Totalitarian societies, of course, are not free of weaknesses of their own which are best visible in the very long run.

CHAPTER 33

Protest and Revolution
Against Western Societies

(1962)

Since [the French Revolution] has made the impression of
striving more for a renovation of mankind than merely for a
reform in France, it has kindled a passion such as even the
most violent political revolutions have heretofore not been
able to produce. It started a proselytizing campaign and
brought propaganda into the world. In this way, it eventually assumed a religious character which astonished contemporaries. Even more, it became itself a kind of religion,
an imperfect religion, to be sure . . . but one which nonetheless has flooded the world with its fighters, its apostles and its
martyrs. . . .

—ALEXIS DE TOCQUEVILLE (1856)

At a time . . . when, with the spread of education and communications, the realisation and impatience of suffering [are]
visibly and rapidly growing. . . .

—JACOB BURCKHARDT (1868)

Congenitally ordained to prey upon his fellows, interminably tempted and interminably deceived, man . . . is

Reprinted from *The Revolution in World Politics*, ed. Morton A. Kaplan.
New York: John Wiley & Sons, 1962, pp. 3-27.

not, at any rate, fitted for happiness by his natural estate: to this day, the whole creation groaneth and travaileth still. There have been times in which this state of affairs was taken more or less for granted. When it appeared that nothing but a conspiracy between privilege and superstition was blocking the way to the infinite perfectibility of the human race, and when the advance of science and the accumulation of wealth promised an endless progress of material welfare, the torrential forces of *temporal* hope broke out. But Time is an infernal ironist; and the invariable rebuffs inflicted upon the appetites, the ambitions and the aspirations of man could not fail to call out in desperate response the full resources of his natural ferocity; for man was not made to stand indefinitely on his hind feet.   —ETIENNE MANTOUX (1946)

We are living in the fifth act of the French Revolution.

—FELIX SOMARY (1959)

The modern movements of protest and revolution against traditional Western society can be seen as part of a worldwide revolutionary process that has gone on for almost 200 years exploding first in one place and then in another, interrupted at times by periods of quiet and restoration, gaining momentum, at first slowly and then rapidly, and now encompassing the entire globe. Its main characteristics are a passionate desire for *change,* with little regard for the needs of conservation and consolidation, and impatience with slow, gradual change; a kind of *evangelical* moral *fervor* for the poor, in earthly goods or in spirit; the twin phenomena of protest against the existing intranational and international stratification, in the form of *socialism* and *nationalism,* respectively, with both movements occasionally hostile and occasionally cooperative. *Hatred for* private *property* and for the frankly acquisitive pursuits of men is characteristic of socialism and often of nationalism, too. Everything receives a particular flavor through the *alienation of the intellectuals,* from whose ranks the political leaders of modern times usually come, from their societies.

The Western Movements

The Progressive Bias

Modern bias is strongly in favor of change, and it often favors quick and violent change over slow and nonviolent evolution. "Progress" always is, and "revolution" usually is, a laudatory term. Even changes that involve no physical violence are called revolutions to give them added prestige; we speak of the urban, the scientific, the industrial revolution, of revolutions in style or taste.

This bias is a relatively new phenomenon. Throughout most of human history, heavy opprobrium was attached to any deviation from the traditional order of things. To be *cupidus rerum novarum* was a serious accusation in ancient Rome. The middle ages held to the concept of a closed world. As late as in the mid-15th century, the humanist Lorenzo Valla still considered "the physician who tries out new and experimental medicines on the sick rather than the time-tested ones to be contemptible," like "the sailor who prefers to hold an uncharted course to one upon which others safely sail their ships and cargoes." Only forty years later, Columbus began his voyage to uncharted seas.

With some interludes of consolidation and restoration, the world has been changing with increasing velocity since, and public opinion has come to identify change with life, conservation with stagnation and death.

But the question of conservation versus innovation need not be a matter of *Weltanschauung*, of principle and ideology. Civilization needs conservation, just as the cultivated soil needs it, as a protection against the return of the jungle and against corrosion; there are many historical examples of regression, of the loss of achievements already gained. But in quiet times and, in particular, in times in which living conditions have been steadily improving, people take for granted what they have and do not consider the possibility that it could be in jeopardy.

Equally, civilization needs innovation if it is to fulfill human aspirations. And in modern, industrialized societies, the end, or the mere slowing down, of economic progress would mean a major calamity because a large part of the people depend, directly or indirectly, on the investment sector of the economy. Whether, in any particular case, we should, or should not, embark on innovation, could be decided on an appraisal of the merits of the case, that is, on the chances and probable costs, material and otherwise, of the innovation. There is no basis for any generalized statement about the optimal relation of conservation and innovation and no likelihood that the same formula will apply in all places and at all times.

There is also the question, not of great immediate importance but possibly crucial in the long run, of how long this constant change at a necessarily accelerating pace can be maintained without progressive interference with the balance of nature and without reaching the limits of natural resources or the possibilities of human adjustment to perpetually changing conditions. Previous speculations about the limits of technology, or the limits of mankind, have proved highly premature, but that does not mean that such limits will not eventually make themselves felt.

However that may be, it is interesting to note that the attitude toward "progress," which is a question of ideology in political and social matters, has been thoroughly de-ideologized in areas in which great advances toward rationality have been made, as in medicine. There was a time when the application, or nonapplication, of surgery was a matter of principle. Physicians foreswore the use of the knife in the Hippocratic Oath; surgery was practiced by another, not always fully respected, profession. Today the determination of medical treatment is no longer a matter of ideology; physicians are not divided into conservatives, always advocating conservative treatment, and liberals, always in favor of radical treatment. It is universally recognized that surgery is indicated in some cases and contraindicated in others. There is still a place for temperamental differences between doctors, but it is a marginal one. Perhaps there will be a day when the question of conservation and innovation in public affairs will be equally free from ideology, or prejudice, and nobody will profess himself in favor or against innovation just as a matter of principle.

The Evangelist Fervor

The Western world has, in the last 200 years, been the scene of a kind of messianic, albeit secular, fervor. It has found expression in may documents and manifestos, as in the American Declaration of Independence, the French Declaration of the Rights of Man, and others down to the Atlantic Charter and more recent documents. The moral climate that these declarations indicate has led to an improvement in the living conditions of countless common people beyond the boldest hopes of the reformers of earlier generations. But it has also had some other consequences: "Moral fervor," as Michael Polanyi (1960) put it, "in our lifetime has outreached itself by its inordinate aspirations and has heaped on mankind the disasters that have befallen us" (p. 1).

The moral demands "outreached" themselves and became "inordinate" when self-criticism, or criticism of one's own government and society, and the attempt at a sympathetic understanding of an opponent's point of view were carried to the point where people could see only the mote in the eye of their own society and never the beam in the eye of its enemies. It is the kind of attitude which Bernard Shaw must have had in mind when he let the tailor Androcles, just about to be thrown into the circus, express his compassion for the poor lions. But although such attitudes make sense in the faithful Christian who is confidently looking forward to eternal life, they are more difficult to understand in their contemporary, secularized version.

The overreaching of moral demands is shown by the fact that no allowance is made by the moralist critics for the pursuit of national interest, including mere self-preservation. The United States is requested, in her dealings with other nations, to follow what is said to be "the right." She is requested to have complete disregard for the consequences which such a course would have for American interest in a world where not everybody is motivated by such exclusive dedication. Yet, self-preservation and the pursuit of one's interest are common to all living creatures who can neglect them only at their peril. Morality sets definite limits to the degree to which, and to the ways in which, interests may be pursued, and it sets up obligations to others. But a morality which plainly condemns the consideration of interest as such is not compatible with survival.[1]

How moral aspirations can outreach themselves can be seen, for example, in the attitude of extreme liberalism to crime and the criminal. The lawbreaker has from time immemorial been fair game for human sadism; people openly and unashamedly enjoyed watching wilfully produced human agony at public executions. The fact that the victims were criminals, hence, supposedly "got their just deserts," quieted whatever stirrings of conscience the spectators might otherwise have felt. In the last two centuries, the more conspicuous expressions of sadism have gradually been taken out of law and law enforcement—a development for which every humane person will feel grateful.

But the process has been carried further to the point where the lawbreaker appears to be fully exonerated as a victim of circumstance—"more sinned against than sinning"—and

[1] American leaders have often encouraged such unreasonable demands by claiming that the United States is guided in crucial decisions by high moral purpose only; e.g., that we resent Castro's attempt to revolutionize Latin America not as a threat to us but because it threatens our Latin neighbors; or that we engage in aid to underdeveloped countries only because we recognize it as a duty. Such claims are believed by no one and resented by all, as moralizing always is. And it seems to produce in people the irresistible urge to debunk these claims by subjecting them to ever more exacting tests until the breaking point has been reached at which the United States can go no further in jeopardizing its vital interests.

The United States should instead assume a more realistic attitude and make more modest moral claims which can be, and have been, lived up to: that, like everybody else, we defend our vital interests but that, in so doing, we always keep a decent respect for the vital interests of others and seek for a formula that combines them both.

It should be added, however, that the neglect of considerations of national interest, characteristic of liberal attitudes to international problems in the United States is not always due to exaggerated moral demands but sometimes merely to the fact that the possibility of a national catastrophe is not realized. The long period of unearned security which the American people have enjoyed because of their geographical remoteness from other centers of power, the balance of power in Eurasia, and the role of sea power—facts which have either disappeared or been downgraded in recent years—have made the people take security for granted; this feeling, together with anti-European resentment and the complacency produced by American successes, had created an atmosphere in which "power politics" was looked upon as something wicked, and the concept of national interest as a fraud.

society is seen as responsible. The judges, the government, the upper classes, and even the victim himself[2] appear as the real culprits, and the plea of conditioning by circumstance is never entered on their behalf.

The position is logically untenable. If all behavior is determined to the exclusion of all culpability and responsibility, neither the lawbreaker nor society can be called to account; neither exhortation nor condemnation makes any sense whatever. If, on the other hand, there is sense in attaching blame to society for its acts of commission or ommission, the same ought to apply to the lawbreaker. The fact that, in this modern view, the lawbreaker is treated on the assumption of complete determinism, while society is treated on the assumption of freedom of choice, merely reflects the will to condemn society.

The basis for this paradoxical moral attitude is the belief, first made popular by Rousseau—and quite fundamental to one branch of liberal thought—that man is good by nature, considerate and kindly to his fellowmen. If he behaves toward others in a selfish, callous, brutal, or even deliberately cruel manner, such behavior must be due, in its entirety, to environmental influences, perhaps to grave provocation and unbearable pressures to which he was subjected. He would assume, therefore, the kind attitude germane to this nature if these pressures were removed. Hence, if, for example, a man has slain another man, the *cause* must be sought in the environment, in society. As cause is, in human affairs, invariably equated with *guilt*,[3] no matter how much men may fancy themselves to be determinists.

In a social and international context this means that if groups or nations resort to violence, it *must* be due to grievances that all would consider legitimate; and such behavior could be remedied, and could only be remedied, by redressing these grievances. Thus, when the Germans embraced a rabid nationalism thirty years ago, it must have been due, entirely, to injustices from the peace of Versailles. "We must give justice to

[2] Shortly after the First World War, a novel by the Austrian writer Franz Werfel was published under the title: *Not the Slayer But the Slain One Is Guilty.*

[3] The Greek *aitia*, e.g., that lives in our word, etiology, has the original meaning of guilt; the negative form *anaitios* means "innocent."

Germany," exclaimed Ramsay Macdonald in the League of Nations Assembly immediately after Hitler's seizure of power. Even the late Adolf Hitler himself, we hear in a recent reinterpretation of history (Taylor, 1961), never aimed at the domination of Europe by force. He had, in fact, no long-term goals at all but was merely pushed to what he did, step by step, by Western unreasonableness.

Or, if the leaders of the Soviet Union face the West with uncompromising hostility, it *cannot* be due to tenets of Bolshevism which antedate any contact with the West; it *must* be a response to Western unfriendliness. Perhaps it is a response to the brief and half-hearted intervention in the Russian Civil War; perhaps it is due to the more recent American demand (in 1945) to have Argentina included in the United Nations; or perhaps it is a response to suspicions aroused by the appointment, by the British government, of a diplomat of not sufficiently high standing for negotiations in Moscow. Similarly, Castro's relentless hostility to the United States, shown from the day of his ascension to power, *must* be due to a lack of understanding on the part of the United States for the aspirations of the Cuban people for a better life. And if the facts glaringly contradict these assumptions, the facts must be selected and rearranged until they seem to fit—because the basic assumptions *must* be true.

As Polanyi has suggested, the evangelical fervor of Western Liberalism should also be seen as a new edition of the ethics of the Gospel (and of prophetic Judaism). The moral prescriptions of the Gospel, the demand to offer the other cheek, with total self-abnegation, can hardly be practiced for any length of time except by people who live under at least partially sheltered conditions—as in monastic orders—so that the harsher necessities of life are performed by others less burdened by scruples or subject to a different code.

It has therefore been suggested that the prescriptions of the Gospels were never meant to govern the daily lives of continuing communities but that they constituted an *Interimsethik*, a set of moral rules for the waiting time, before the final consummation of history and the coming of the Kingdom of God which was then thought to be imminent.

However that may be, the Church interposed herself between man and the text of the Gospels. It was the function of the Roman Church to direct the messianic expectation away from the daily life into an afterlife or a very distant future so to preserve a realistic attitude to the world around us. In this way the Church arrived at a synthesis of hope and realism, of the Don Quixote and the Sancho Panza in us—albeit a synthesis heavily weighted toward immobilism. The compromise became untenable once the possibility of secular improvement had been demonstrated.

The decline of the Churches and of any kind of supra-naturalism seems to have led to a revival of messianism in its original form: the expectation of a consummation of history, in the immediate future, that will establish the realm of justice and happiness for all men of "goodwill."[4]

While this, presumably, is the origin of the immense moral fervor for the "disinherited of the earth" in our time, it is an open question in each individual case to what degree fervor is due to genuine moral passions that have been carried to extreme, even suicidal, conclusions, and to what degree it is due to envy of, or spite for, the establishment in one's own society. Both motivations may, in fact, operate in the same person, although only the first, idealistic one is likely to appear in a man's conscious self-interpretation. The fact that moral fervor for the oppressed may sometimes be fed by unconscious hatred of the establishment may explain the frequent indifference of the moral critic toward oppression and injustice, however severe, when it is practiced by the enemies of his society.

But despite their self-damaging implications, these attitudes, whatever their origin, would not yet constitute any real danger to the vital interests of Western societies were it not for the peculiar present constellation of forces. One school of thought in the messianic tradition, of particular determination and ruth-lessness, has in our time succeeded in establishing complete power over the Eurasian heartland (to use Sir Halford Mackin-der's excellent expression). Its leaders believe dogmatically in a modern version of Manichaeism, according to which their own side represents both the morally good and the wave of the

[4] For the messianic social beliefs see Talmon (1952, 1957, 1960) and Norman Cohn (1957).

future, while our way of life is both irredeemably evil and irreversibly decaying. They not only believe that our downfall is preordained by inexorable laws of history, but so far have held it to be their task to carry out, or at least to help along, the "verdict of history." It is for this reason that the moral passions of Western liberals have often become, in effect, though probably not in conscious intent, an aid to an adversary who frankly rejects the very values for the minor infractions of which they are daily castigating Western society.

At the same time when Nebuchadnezzar threatened the existence of the Jewish kingdom, the prophet Jeremiah urged the people not to resist but to accept servitude to Babylon as a divine punishment for their sins. Like him, and other ancient prophets, many contemporary doctrinaire-liberals profess to believe that our peril is due to our sins and would disappear if we would practice strict morality in all our actions. But although the assumption of a relation between sin and misfortune makes sense for the ancient Hebrews, who believed that God punishes His people for their misconduct, it is less understandable in modern liberal atheists or agnostics who do not think that the moral law determines the course of events. But beliefs can endure long after the rationale for holding them has withered away.

In one important point, however, there is a striking difference between Jeremiah and his contemporary successors: Jeremiah was fully aware of what was in store for the people at the hand of their Babylonian masters; many of his contemporary followers tell us that Nebuchadnezzar does not really exist but that he is merely a hallucination of the State Department.

The Struggle Against the "Establishment"—Domestic and International

The protest against the *status quo* appears as protest against the pecking order of our society and the promotion of the demands of the lower strata at the expense of the higher ones. As has been emphasized before, protest that does not come from the lower orders themselves may be due either to identification with and compassion for them, or to hatred of the higher ones.

The demands for justice for all men have grown ever stronger in the Western world since the 18th century. Justice, at first interpreted as equality of opportunity, is more and more becoming to mean equality of station; and, as Alexis de Tocqueville (1835-40, Vol. 2) foresaw, "the hatred that men bear to privilege increases in proportion as privileges become fewer and less considerable, so that democratic passions would seem to burn more fiercely just when they have least fuel . . ." because in a world in which there are no great differences, the still existing inequalities are all the more unacceptable. Thus, the anti-colonial passions in Asia and Africa have become more inflamed at the very time that more than nine tenths of the Western colonial empires have become emancipated.

Nationalism, on the other hand, creates a feeling of solidarity along ethnic rather than class lines. It was, at times, welded to the political and social revolt as in the French Revolution, whereas at other times the two movements have been bitterly opposed to each other. Nationalism has been universalist as well as parochial, integrative as well as divisive. It was the former when it strove toward the unity of groups conceived as "nations" that had hitherto been divided into smaller traditional, mostly dynastic, political units as the unification of Italy and Germany. It was disintegrative and divisive then it broke up traditional multinational structures such as the Hapsburg monarchy, or pursued its national aspirations without regard for the aspirations, or indeed the very existence, of other nations. In the latter aspect of nationalism, naïve egotism, an attitude which in individuals or groups precedes moral development, has been elevated to a sacred duty, and the innocent selfishness of the primitive has thus been transformed into an evil of civilization, namely, the use of morality for immoral ends.

Not infrequently, nationalism has begun as an integrative force and has shown the latter characteristics only after it had realized some of its fundamental aspirations; this was the case of the German development from the nationalism of the Liberals of 1848 over the militaristic nationalism of the Treitschke generation (which still paid at least lip service to Christianity), to the paroxysmal nationalism of a Hitler who knew no law except "the interest of the German people."[5]

[5] It is unmistakable, however, that the germs of the later barbarism existed from the beginning. Sir Lewis Namier (1952), e.g., said about Mazzini, whom he called "a man outstanding for spiritual integrity" and "a sincere lover of

Nationalism has, therefore, been called a demonic force. There are examples of a nation turning away from nationalism in disillusionment after it has led the nation into disaster (as happened in France and, more recently, in Germany); but there are no examples of a successful appeasement of undefeated nationalism.

Nationalism sometimes sponsors the aspirations of groups at the lower level of the pyramid of power or wealth, and sometimes the aspirations of groups which are relatively high up on an international scale. In the latter case, it has a double face: it is a rebellion against those who occupy the top positions, but it is at the same time oppressive toward the lower echelons. That was the case of nationalism in industrially advanced countries like modern Germany and Japan; they struggled against the "have" nations—above all England and the United States—who, they claimed, had appropriated the best things on earth at a time when the "younger" nations had not yet appeared on the scene. There was either a demand for colonies, as in Germany and Italy, or an attempt to conquer adjacent territories populated by less advanced peoples—the Ukraine, parts of China—with a view to colonizing them and enslaving the inhabitants. This aspect gives nationalism its peculiar and ambiguous character, at once "revolutionary" and "counterrevolutionary."

But where nationalism takes hold of a poor and under-developed people, as in Latin America at the present time, the national and the social revolution may run parallel for some time as is demonstrated by the Cuban revolution, or by some of Mao Tse-tung's revisions of orthodox Marxist doctrine, allowing for a temporary coalition with the "national bourgeoisie." This places the "struggle against imperialism," that is, the international revolution, ahead of the domestic class struggle.

---

liberty," ". . . the moral fervor, purity of purpose and religious sincerity which pervade his writings—words of faith and action rather than of thought—were apt to conceal from contemporaries how deficient his teachings were in substance correlated to every-day reality, and what dangerous germs they contained. National self-glorification and claims to moral superiority were at their core: which entails a measure of depreciation of other peoples, and is not conducive to international comity" (p. 29).

The Austrian poet Franz Grillparzer, a somewhat older contemporary of Mazzini, said around 1848 that the development went "from humanitarianism over nationalism into bestialism."

Whether an individual is more attracted by Socialism (which, under present conditions, means Marxist Socialism and, most probably, Communism) or by nationalism, seems to depend on many circumstances—historical, situational, personal. Among them is also the response of the personality to Marxism's and nationalism's basic attitudes toward life, their implicit *Weltanschauung*. The latter is expressed most clearly in their respective doctrines regarding determinism and freedom.

Marxism is strongly determinist and sees the world moving along inexorable laws of history. Men may accelerate or smooth the course of events by correct action or delay it and make it harsher by error and futile resistance, but they cannot change necessity. *Fata volentem ducunt, nolentem trahunt.*

Nationalism, on the other hand, is indeterminist; the future belongs to him who seizes it. Different temperaments are attracted or repelled by these two philosophies.

The Anticapitalist Bias

The impact of the socialist idea has been cataclysmic. Its strength is probably due, in the main, to a combination of an egalitarian moral fervor with a particular, superficially persuasive interpretation of the nonegalitarian realities, namely, the doctrine that the businessman acting under the profit motive is a social parasite who fulfills no social function but who has, through the possession of the means of production, interposed himself between the worker and his tools. He has thus been able to extract a heavy tribute from the "toilers"—not unlike the medieval robber barons who extracted river tolls from traveling merchants. This interpretation seems convincing to all but the very few who have either personal experience or theoretical training in economic matters.

This means that the problem of economic rationality, that is, the problem of an optimal employment of scarce resources, is little understood. The problem is difficult enough if only one goal is pursued, in which case we usually speak of a question of strategy rather than of economics. However, it receives a new dimension of complexity if there is a multiplicity of goals, each of which can be pursued only at the expense of some others, as in the promotion of general welfare.

It is the justification of a market, or capitalist, economy that it creates a field in which all players are constantly rewarded by an extension, or punished by a contraction, of their operating range, according to the results of their management in terms of consumers' preferences.

It cannot be taken for granted that consumers' preferences should always be the ultimate determinant of action; in fact, virtually everybody agrees that there must be at least some exceptions from the sovereign and irresponsible rule of the consumer (as in the control of the traffic of narcotics or in building and zoning regulations). Furthermore, even if consumers' preferences are accepted as the ultimate frame of reference, it cannot be taken for granted that a market economy is necessarily the only possible, or the best, solution of the problem of economic rationality. The capitalist system can, therefore, become subject to legitimate criticism on either of these two grounds: because it caters to desires which, in the view of the critic, are not worth indulging in, or because its function of selecting the most economic among the possible alternatives of action might possibly be achieved better by some other mechanism.

But capitalism has only extremely rarely been attacked on any such ground. It has been attacked for more than a century not by people who wished to substitute their solution of the problem of economic rationality for the solution of the market, but by people who are unaware of the very existence of the problem. For them the only economic problems are technological; one produces what is needed, it is as simple as that, and except for the engineer's task, the job of management, as Lenin (1917) put it, "can be reduced ... to simple operations of registration, filing and checking."

Unaware of the problem of economic rationality, the Marxists did not understand what hit them (and everyone else) when socialized industries, supposedly freed from the burden of having to produce "surplus value" for the capitalists, did not have that surplus value available for distribution among the wage earners as one had to expect according to the theory. Nor did they later understand how the "exploited" worker in privately owned industry can receive higher wages than his "liberated" opposite number in socialist countries. Even today observers report that leading men in Eastern Germany, looking at the prosperity of Western Germany and West Berlin, do not consider the possibility that something might be wrong with their economic system. The system, they are satisfied, is superior to capitalism, and it must be due to accidental factors such as bottlenecks if the people have not yet reaped the benefits of socialism.[6] Just the same, they are eager to get rid of capitalist Berlin and thereby of the case that visibly contradicts their theories.

It is this inability on the part of most people, including most intellectuals, in particular, to understand the nature of the economic problem that gives the socialist ideology its virtually irresistible appeal. The arguments which the defender of a market economy can put forward are simply beyond the understanding of those who have neither theoretical instruction nor practical experience in economic matters. They are, in any case, suspect of being self-serving if they are advanced by people with vested interests in the preservation of capitalism; and if advanced by others who are conspicuously lacking in such interests, they can be equally discounted as coming from "lackeys" of capitalism.

The problem of economic rationality is often not understood even by men of very high intelligence. We are accustomed to speak of intelligence as though it were a unitary quality which, as much or as little as there is, can be applied with equal success to all areas of reality. Psychometrics, with its IQ measurements, has contributed to this conception.

Yet there is much evidence that an individual can operate on a high intellectual level in one area of reality and on a very low one in another. Theoretical intelligence capable of understanding how things are—in itself but a name for a whole group of abilities, each related to a particular area or aspect of reality—is

---

[6] There is evidence, however, that some economists in Communist countries have become aware of the problem in recent years. Their insight has been acted upon in Yugoslavia through decentralization and the establishment of a market of sorts. There have also been stirrings in this direction among economists in the Soviet Union and particularly in Poland. But they are still viewed with suspicion by the Communist party which fears the impact of any undermining of the labor theory of value (Grossman, 1960).

different from economic intelligence that is quick in realizing how available things could be put to best advantage; from political or military intelligence that grasps the value of everything for a struggle for power; from social intelligence that knows how to make friends and influence people; or from the erotic intelligence of a Casanova.

Several types of higher intelligence are rarely found together in the same person. Lenin was one of the greatest, perhaps the greatest, revolutionary strategists of all times. He sensed like nobody else the points of weakness in existing societies and invented strategies for establishing footholds of power, for enlarging them, and for winning and keeping total power. Even his closest collaborators did not fully understand him for a long time. But the same Lenin was unable to grasp the problem of an optimal allocation of resources to competing goals and the dependence of human welfare on a solution of this problem; he thought economic management was a matter of accounting and statistics.

Andrew Carnegie, an economic genius of the first magnitude, had no understanding for matters of power or ideology. When he set up the Carnegie Endowment for International Peace, he wondered what role the Foundation could play once it would have succeeded in abolishing wars. He told his trustees that it would then be their task to decide on what ills the Foundation should focus next.

In the mid-1930s when civilized men were appalled at the prospect of another war, and one that would involve the bombing of civilians, to boot, a prominent English mathematician is reported to have pointed out that, of course, one would not actually drop any bombs, but in dealing with Hitler it might be necessary to behave for a while as though one would. It does not seem to have occurred to this outstanding man that one cannot bluff a determined adversary while putting one's cards on the table.

The failure to understand the problem of rational allocation of resources and its crucial importance for human welfare may also be seen in another light, namely, as the consequence of *utopian* thinking. Human values are in some degree contradictory, that is one can often realize one value only at the expense of another; liberty and equality or, more generally, individual expression and social order, economic progress and security, income and leisure, are examples of such dichotomies. Decision involves a choice in favor of one value against another or, rather, the determination of an optimal point beyond which any further approach toward the realization of one value would cost too dearly in terms of the other. Because of these contradictions among the things which men hold dear, complete human fulfillment is not possible.

The utopian mind, however, does not accept this kind of reasoning. The utopian refuses to believe that there could be any inherent limits to human fulfillment; the very suggestion, he suspects, is a ruse to protect special privilege. In the good society, all men can be completely fulfilled in their individual aspirations, and society can yet be harmonious, without conflict; as Marx had put it: The free development of each is the prerequisite of the free development of all.

It is a kind of preordained harmony; the skeptics, of course, think that this is merely another way of saying that one can have one's cake and eat it, too.

If one believes that all human aspirations are in natural harmony with each other and with the interests of society, and of the whole of mankind—a harmony only so far disturbed and impeded by the "class structure"—one will, of course, not believe that decisions involve choices between irreconcilable values; for if one believed the latter, one would not have accepted the former.

But if the problem of rational allocation is not understood, the system of *private enterprise appears to have no raison d'etre* but to be *merely* a form of *privilege,* at once immoral and inexpedient.

This belief, somewhat weakened in the West but holding full sway everywhere else, that government operation of the economy is both morally indicated and practically sensible, while business management is both evil and stupid, appears to be the main reason for the fundamental goodwill enjoyed by the Soviet Union and the widespread distrust of the United States. It is for this reason, I submit, that over so large a part of the world, a light view is taken of Communist aggressive moves, while the

West is severely castigated for even moderate acts of self-assertion: Communism stands in the minds of countless people for something fundamentally "progressive," while the West stands for an obsolete system of privilege. Without such fundamental aversion, it would be difficult to understand why a large section of world opinion condemns as aggressiveness in the West what it hails as strength in the East and ridicules as weakness in the West what it applauds as manifestation of peaceful intentions in the East.

To the enormous amount of goodwill which the Soviet Union has enjoyed as the land of Socialism must also be attributed the paralysis of American foreign policy at the end of the Second World War. The Soviet Union established her stranglehold over Eastern Central Europe then, at a time when the balance of physical strength greatly favored the United States and effective resistance would have been possible at small risk. But a vigorous policy toward the Soviet Union would have been vetoed by a substantial part of Western public opinion.

The Alienation of the Intellectuals

The intellectuals of the West, as a rule, are not fully identified with their societies. They stand aloof, and while they may feel enthusiastic about some "ideal" society, they are often indifferent or hostile to their society as it actually is.[7]

To some degree, this has been so in all societies in which intellectuals have enjoyed the freedom of expression. Since the

[7] A characteristic example for the attitude of many Western intellectuals appears in a psychological study of scientists; the author, a noted psychologist, points out that "scientists are very good citizens" and declares: "The scientists involved in espionage have been very few, indeed, and misguided as they may have been, they have acted on principle and not for personal gain" (Roe, 1952, p. 240). Thus, the author is not sure whether she condemns espionage against the United States at all ("misguided as they *may* have been") and, in any case, does not take a grave view of the matter as long as it was done for ideological reasons and not for monetary gain. It would be rash to conclude, however, that intellectuals of liberal persuasion advocate a *general* tolerance for all ideologies, as was done by John Stuart Mill; as a rule, they make no allowances for ideologies of the Right. But the ideologies of the Left are regarded as "idealistic," and action based on them is excused, or only mildly rebuked, whatever its consequences. No question is asked whether these ideologies may not also be fed by emotional sources not necessarily praiseworthy such as, e.g., lust for power or intellectual conceit.

days of the Sophists, they have been in the habit of questioning
and challenging the values and the assumptions that were taken
for granted in their societies. Some intellectuals, on the other
hand, have followed the example of that dissident Sophist,
Socrates, who used his intellectual powers not only to challenge
current beliefs, but also to give the essential values of his
civilization a new, presumably better foundation.

Intellect tends to question and thereby to undermine dogma
and tradition.[8] The act of understanding, said the historian of
science Charles Coulston Gillispie (1960), is an act of alienation.
Psychoanalytic theory suggests a kind of primary antagonism of
the ego against the id, that is, of the rational, goal-directed part
in us against the impulsive and automatic parts. Alienation is an
aspect of emancipation. It is the hostility of *Geist* to life of which
there has been so much talk in German philosophy.

In principle this is unavoidable. It is rooted in the very
nature of freedom because freedom is destructive as well as
creative; the very viability of a free society depends on whether
or not it can take advantage of the creative energies unleashed
by freedom while keeping its destructive aspects within limits.

But this does not explain the degree of the estrangement or
the bitterness with which many Western intellectuals look upon
the society which has provided them with a degree of personal
security and with opportunities of development not enjoyed at
any other time or place. Is this a reaction to freedom which, for
the inner-directed, vital like air, is deeply frustrating to the
other-directed who need guidance? Is it the very consequence of
the emancipation from drudgery and of the newly won leisure
which makes people ask beyond life's necessities or luxuries for a
meaning in life while they are not able to find it in themselves? Is
it the constant increase in possible fulfillments and the simple
fact that in such situations aspirations always grow a little faster
than fulfillments? Or is it the attitude of those who have been
conditioned in their childhood to expect immediate fulfillment

[8] See Frank H. Knight (1960): "the 'liberation of the mind' seems to have
released a tendency to acute discontent, criticism, fault-finding that was
there all along but held in check by the harsh discipline of pre-liberal
culture—or possibly new conditions have caused it to develop with astonishing
speed as a culture trait" (p. 144).

of every wish, who have accordingly failed to acquire any tolerance toward frustration, and who go to pieces, bundles of despair and fury, whenever they meet with even the slightest frustration, as is, after all, not forever avoidable? Somewhere along these lines an explanation must be sought for a phenomenon like the "angry young men," for the bitter hatred of their society by members of a generation who, perhaps as the first in history, "never ate their bread with tears."

It must be added, however, that the destructive criticism of Western societies comes only rarely from those intellectuals who have special training or experience in the areas which are particularly relevant for sociopolitical problems; they come rarely from historians, economists, political scientists, professional diplomats, etc.

This, obviously, does not mean that historians, economists, or political scientists are miraculously free from the disintegrative potentialities of the intellect; but it suggests that in the field in which one has sound knowledge and with which one is in constant contact, such potentialities are likely to manifest themselves mostly in the form of *creative* destruction, as a restructuring of the field[9] with creative value. But without such knowledge, the destructiveness of the intellect has full sway.

What then appears as antagonism of the intellectual to his society must, therefore, be attributed not only to the alienation inherent in the life of the intellect, but also to the naïve and arrogant confidence of individuals with higher education. They feel competent not only in matters within the areas of their training and experience, but on any subject of public interest—a pretension to which taxi drivers or plumbers are far less prone.

The fact that the intellectuals of the type of Protagoras are the perpetual debunkers of their society would not change the balance of forces in the world if all societies were equally exposed to such pressures. But if this is not the case, if some societies are shielded against the consequences of intellectual skepticism and debunking as is largely the case in present totalitarian societies, the pressures which intellectuals exert where they are in a position to do so may have the effect of

[9] The expression is taken from M. Wertheimer (1945).

influencing the balance of power in favor of those societies in which they are not in such a position—in favor of monolithic Sparta, against free Athens.

The Anticolonial Revolution

The Setting of the Stage

"Western culture," said C.C. Gillispie (1960), "is set off from those of Asia, Africa and the world of Antiquity by two fundamental factors. From one of these it emerged: its religious chrysalis was Christianity, investing history with the promise of fulfillment of a sort. The other it produced: the most dynamic, distinctive and influential creation of the Western world is a progressive science of nature. Only there, in the technical realm, indeed, does the favorite Western idea hold any demonstrable meaning" (p. 8).

These two characteristics contain the germ of the history of contact between Western culture and other cultures. The achievements in the *rational* analysis and control of man's environment gave Western culture an easy superiority over other people's, provoking them, at first, to futile resistance or to surrender—both exemplified in Caesar's story of the two Aedui brothers, Diviticus and Dumnorix—and later stimulating identification, envy, and emulation. The *moral and metaphysical* beliefs of the West in an ultimate historical consummation, seen in modern times in the picture of continuous progress, on the other hand, manifested itself at first in missionary activities, both by religious and nonreligious bodies, to bring the message of Western creeds to alien cultures; soon there were also men who espoused the cause of the natives against Western rulers. To the leaders of non-Western peoples, finally, Western moral beliefs gave the spiritual weapons with which to ask for a redress of their grievances.

Two Types of Group Antagonism

Group antagonisms take different forms according to whether they are directed against more advanced, or against less advanced, groups. "Advancement," in this context, should be understood as advancement in terms of *alloplastic adjustment*, that is, in terms of man's ability to control his environment and to find suitable means for advancing his ends in relation to his environment. It does *not* mean a higher degree of *autoplastic* adjustment (as the ability to bear frustration and suffering with equanimity or the wisdom of an Epicurus, a Buddha, or a Confucius); nor does it mean *moral* superiority. Least of all, of course, can it be taken as superiority in ultimate human values, or superiority before God—matters about which this writer has no knowledge.

Advancement, in the preceding sense, of greater control of the environment implies a lengthening of the road from impulse to action, that is, a larger measure of self-control in significant areas of human behavior. Under conditions of relatively fair competition, it is reflected by a person's place in the social hierarchies of power, wealth, income, and status. The relative advancement of a group in social interaction with other groups is manifested by the proportional participation of the group in the occupational hierarchy, inasmuch as occupations are open to them. A group is more advanced if fewer of its members are engaged in unskilled or semiskilled labor than would correspond to their number, and if it has more than its proportional share in leading occupations—administration, spiritual leadership, science, education, arts. The Jews, for example, were a more advanced group in medieval Europe or, in modern times, in Central and Eastern Europe and in Arab lands; so were the Greeks and the Armenians in the Turkish Empire; the Jainas in India; the French in Algeria; so are whites in general as compared to Negroes in Africa, America, or Arabia; so is, on the whole, the West in the global community of men.

The antagonism which the more advanced group feels toward the less advanced one, such as the feelings of American Southerners toward the Negro, is quite different from the antagonism of a less advanced group toward a more advanced one, as in the case of the attitude of African Negroes toward the white settler or Algerian Moslems toward European settlers.

The less advanced group is not resented as such by their more advanced neighbors; rather, it is welcome to perform menial labor and, in some cases, has been imported for that very purpose. As long as their members "know their place," there is no opposition to them in the more advanced group; many people of the latter group may even have a personal affection of sorts for them. It is only if the members of the less advanced group step beyond the limits either of the general rules of conduct prevailing in the society, or of the social conventions regulating their social position, that they arouse resentment. In the cases in which the less advanced group is also believed to be closer to savagery and to an unbridled expression of sexuality, they arouse fear and horror as well.

A group that is more advanced than its environment provokes a different kind of antagonism. Its members usually behave with arrogance, and even if they should not do so, the simple fact of their superiority, difficult to hide, is felt as an insult. One then watches them carefully for any signs of weakness, for flaws; once these flaws are found, as needs they will, they are seized upon by the less advanced group and exploited to the full. Anti-American sentiment, and anti-Western sentiment in general, belong to this category; it is remarkable how closely current accusations against the West resemble the accusations against the Jews that run through the history of anti-semitism.

While outbreaks of violence against backward groups rarely go beyond actions that should "teach them a lesson," so that they may assume again the humble station to which the more advanced group would like to confine them, the hostility to a more advanced group has no built-in limitations and may go all the way to effect their physical elimination.

These easily observable differences have been obfuscated by catch phrases such as "minority groups" (as though the relative place of groups in the pecking order were determined by their quantitative strength) or by pseudoscientific investigations of prejudice in which the outcome of the research was implicit in the design of the experiments. For example, anti-semitism and antinegro sentiment in the United States have been grouped together as sentiments or prejudices against "minority groups," although they differ radically in motivation and goal. Anti-Semitism has never been willing to tolerate the Jews, even if they were to behave deferentially toward Gentiles and take their meals in the kitchen; and antinegro sentiment has never aimed at eliminating the Negroes from the land through expulsion or harsher measures. The analogy to anti-semitism can be found not in the antinegro sentiment of whites but rather in the violent forms of antiwhite sentiment among Black Muslims.

Both responses to the phenomenon of difference in development are natural and therefore, in some measure, unavoidable. They represent a conflict of interest which only time can heal through elimination of the developmental difference and which, in the meantime, charity can do much to mitigate. To ideologize this conflict by seeing it in Manichean terms as a struggle between good and evil can only inflame it and may make it insoluble except for the solutions unmitigated violence provides.

Conditions of Revolution

Thus, in the contact between groups at different levels of development, the more advanced group is motivated by a fear of being pulled down from levels already reached, while the less advanced group reacts to a blow to their pride.

But it does not react on any large scale unless and until the gap between the two groups is narrowed sufficiently so that a comparison between them is possible.

There is still a further step from resentment to action. For a long time the enormous superiority of Western power discouraged any thought of resistance until, in the Second World War, Western prestige was severely damaged through the defeats suffered at the hands of Germany and Japan. A revolutionary situation existed once the sense of grievance was ignited by the hope of success.

Revolutions do not seem to break out where men are most downtrodden, but rather where conditions have begun to improve.[10] As long as the prevailing conditions, no matter how bad, are stable, they are taken for granted. Men *adjust* to them

[10] For example, see the following statements by contemporary scholars: "it is not the backward countries which need revolutions. Being backward, Spain had not yet developed those internal strains which made France, with all its enlightenment, a social volcano" (Trevor-Roper, 1957, p. 271). "Paradoxically as it may seem, colonial nationalism is far less the response to oppression than to the widening horizons opened up by progressive colonial governments" (Emerson, 1960, p. 45).

as one adjusts to the climate, to incurable disease, or to death. But once the possibility of improvement has been realized, conditions never improve fast enough to keep pace with rising aspirations.

This is closely analogous to a well-known psychiatric phenomenon and may be a manifestation of the same *biological truth:* The danger of suicide in severe depressions is great not at the height of the depression but rather at the time *when the depression has begun to lift.*

But the tremendous momentum which the anticolonial revolution has gained in recent years is due, above all, to extraneous circumstances: namely, the Soviet Union, with all her might, has been backing up and encouraging the most radical anti-Western groups anywhere on earth. Under these conditions, a premium has been placed on the most radical revolutionary action.

So far this refers to events in Asia, Africa, and Latin America. But the revolution may yet spill over United States boundaries; revolutions of American Negroes, Chinese in Hawaii, or Mexicans in the Southwest will not be out of the question if the Western position further disintegrates.

In a recent article on the social life of baboons, Washburn and De Vore (1961), two biologists, stated: "In troops where the rank order is clearly defined, fighting is rare" and "fighting [*sc.* over a female] may take place if the dominance order is not clearly established among the males" (p. 70). One may say that fighting between humans, individuals and groups, may break out *if power relationships are unclear,* or liable to different interpretations. As long as power relationships are unambiguous, and so interpreted by all, there is likely to be peace. The existing power distribution is the basis for the legal order; when the pecking order is not universally recognized, either because power relationships have changed and human thinking has not kept up with the change, or because different people interpret them differently, fighting may break out until a new pecking order has been established and recognized. This will result in a new legal order.

The Predicament of the West

The American Response

The anticolonial revolution has assumed, or tends to assume, an anti-American stance, except in those countries or groups that feel themselves under pressure from the Soviet bloc or from a country or group that enjoys Communist support.

This development should have surprised no one. The United States has been on top of the world politically and economically for quite some time; with only about 7 percent of the world's population, the United States has close to one half of the world's capital. Its situation among the nations is comparable to that of the wealthiest landowner in a district where most people are destitute, at a time when the social order is no longer taken for granted.[11]

The new development came as a surprise to many, however, partly because revolutions were thought of as strictly national affairs and were not considered a part of a concerted international action, and partly because it was widely assumed that revolutions were reactions to oppression and injustice. The record of the United States as a neighbor and as a member of the international community, although not entirely spotless, compared very favorably with that of any other nation. Many a nation owes much to American generosity. It was overlooked, however, that there are reasons other than oppression and injustice, in the ordinary sense, as these words are understood in the West, why people may feel bitter against those more fortunately placed, and that they will feel little difficulty in interpreting their resentment and their aspirations, whatever they may be, as manifestations of a demand for justice.

There is tragic irony in the present situation in which the American people find themselves at the receiving end of a worldwide populist revolution, as Americans have seen themselves for generations as the *avant garde* of such movements against oligarchy-ridden Europe. For a long time this country has been a leader of populist and nationalist revolutions all over the world, busily undermining the traditional political structures and the balance of power all over the earth in the name of the

[11] Despite its wealth, the United States could maintain its role as the leader of populism in the world as long as American borders were wide open to immigration and everybody was invited to share in the advantages of the American situation. But once the immigration laws had set up "no trespassing" signs around the American real estate, the American people became a privileged nation. No amount of public relations artistry can erase this fact from world consciousness.

principle of self-determination until quite recently.[12] All this was with the expectation that the emancipation would appease rather than appetize the colonial peoples, and that they would behave with the moderation shown by the American colonists in the late 18th century with an emphasis on prosperity rather than on military power—assumptions for which there was no basis whatsoever.

There are many Americans even today who believe that the anti-American turn of the nationalist and populist revolutions in the "underdeveloped" countries was not a necessary phenomenon but merely the consequence of political mistakes which might have been avoided; perhaps the United States had "supported" dictators who were later overthrown, or failed to put pressure on friendly governments in favor of land reform, or failed to help one-crop countries out of their precarious situation by using American financial strength for a stabilization of world market prices of this commodity, etc. We had permitted ourselves, so it has been said, to be lined up on the wrong side, against the "aspirations of the common people," in the role of the Holy Alliance. If, so the arguments runs, Americans only could fearlessly take up again the banner of the populist revolution, all would be well. One wise observer (Somary, 1950) commented on this some years ago: "A people with the highest standard of living in the world tries desperately to remain the leader of the Left." The unsolved contradictions between the needs of self-preservation which urged the greatest possible conservation of the essentials of the old international order of Western dominance, on the one hand, and the ideological bias in favor of

[12] One fairly recent example: when the Central Powers, Germany and Austria-Hungary, recognized their defeat in October 1918 and appealed to President Wilson to mediate an armistice and peace on the basis of his fourteen points, the President requested, as a prerequisite of his mediation, from Germany that "the power of the king of Prussia" be curtailed, and in the case of Austria-Hungary he took the position that it was up to the various national groups of the Monarchy to decide what concessions to their aspirations by the central government would be satisfactory to them. He thus gave *carte blanche* to the nationalist movements in the Monarchy. In this way, Wilson enforced the overthrow of the Hohenzollern monarchy and the dismemberment of the Austro-Hungarian State. This led, in the first case, to the establishment of the unpopular Weimar republic, soon to be overthrown by the disastrous Hitler movement; and, in the second case, to the creation of a power vacuum in Central Europe, soon to suck in, at first, German, and then, Russian, power.

revolution, on the other, was, and I submit still is, at the bottom of the ineffectiveness of American foreign policy.[13]

There are four possible reactions to revolution on the part of those who feel threatened by it. It is the *conservative* response to try to stem the revolutionary tide. The *Bonapartist* (or fascist) solution consists in the setting up of a counterrevolutionary totalitarianism which steals some of the revolutionary thunder and uses the same terror methods as the revolution. There is the *me-too* policy of trying to join the revolution and march with its legions, preferably in its spearhead. Finally, one may attempt to placate the revolutionary forces by inaugurating *reforms*, in the hope of thus weakening the revolutionary élan. These are, of course, marginal types (*Idealtypen*) of political behavior and, in practice, a policy may lie somewhere in between these sharply defined categories and show characteristics of more than one.

The conservative answer is historically represented most brilliantly by Clemens von Metternich; in our days, Winston Churchill tried it within the narrow limits of his power. It is widely asserted today, particularly in this country and in Britain, that such a policy would, in the present world, be doomed to failure. This may well be so, but it is questionable to what degree this assessment is based on a dispassionate analysis of the forces involved and to what degree on the progressive bias, which is part of the protest attitude itself. There are antirevolutionary forces everywhere in the world, and the current revolution, like every other revolution, cannot go on forever; a point must be reached where people can no longer adjust sufficiently fast to the constantly accelerating pace of events. One can hardly state *a priori* that a policy of digging in, defending crucial positions, and waiting for the next swing of the pendulum to occur is necessarily doomed to failure. But it runs strongly against the progressive stream of Western thinking.

[13] I can see no chance of the United States regaining its former international position except, *perhaps*, if the American people were willing to repeal the immigration laws and to open the country to countless millions of immigrants from Latin America, Asia, and Africa—a move that would play havoc with American standards of living and with the free institutions and the Western character of the nation. If, however, the American people wish to defend these goals, as every nation would, it would be better to acknowledge the realities of the situation.

The Bonapartist solution is quite alien to American traditions. But a policy of trying to stay ahead of the revolution has been repeatedly followed by the United States, although the pressures of national interest have made its *consistent* application impossible. The advocates of this policy believe that if the United States sides with Arabs against England, France, and Israel; with Algerian Moslems against France; with Indonesia against the Netherlands; or with African nationalists against Portugal, and African and Asian nationalists will appreciate these American attitudes and will in some way show their appreciation; to the very least, according to this theory, they will be less hostile than they would otherwise have been. Others, however, believe that this is an unwarranted extrapolation of political experience in a democracy from the domestic to the international scene. Only under conditions in which physical violence is effectively excluded, as is the case within a well-established legal order, so these critics think, is the accumulation of goodwill the royal road to power and influence. In international relations, however, particularly in the present conditions of extreme lawlessness in which nearly every nation faces grave perils, goodwill is of limited value. They believe, furthermore, that for Asian, African, and Latin American intellectuals, the United States is the arch imperialist power, not because of what it does but because of what it *is*, namely, it *is* the world's richest capitalist nation. It is believed, too, that manifestations of benevolence are not likely to alter the course of unfriendly nations, except adversely, by convincing them that the United States is already in such desperate straits that it can be abused with impunity; but that unfriendly nations may, nevertheless, at any moment, change over to the Western side if they feel threatened by Communist powers and *if* they believe that the United States can render them effective assistance.

The last answer to the challenge of revolution, finally, that of reformism, has been the main United States policy all during the crisis; support for a liberal policy of reform everywhere has been further emphasized by the present administration.

It is the basic idea of this American policy to try to convince the world that the American "Revolution," rather than the French and Russian Revolutions, holds the message for their present aspirations. It aspires to win a major part of the people of "underdeveloped" countries for a program of meliorism, financed by the United States, in preference over revolution—a repetition of the Roosevelt New Deal on a world scale. Success or failure of this policy is still hidden in the future, but it is clear that it is undertaken under conditions far less auspicious than those under which the New Deal was launched. A rich man of moderate temperament like Franklin Roosevelt was acceptable to the lower income groups of America as their leader, but that does not mean that rich and moderately tempered America will be acceptable as leader to the *descamisados* and African hut dwellers or to the students in Bogota and Rangoon, particularly while the Soviet world offers its full support for more radical alternatives. The United States can only offer help toward an improvement of living conditions, which must needs be slow, at the price of domestic tranquillity. At the same time, the more radical alternative promises, in addition to the immediate confiscation and distribution of accumulated consumers' goods (including durable goods such as luxurious homes or beaches), the excitement of revolution, with ample opportunities for the squaring of old accounts and for sadistic gratifications. While the embourgeoisement of the poor is more satisfactory in the long run, the expropriation of the rich suggests itself to human impatience as so much quicker and easier. It is the ancient cry: *panem et circenses.*

Strength and Weakness in the Western Position

The weaknesses of the Western position are patently obvious; they appear to be rooted in the following facts:

1. The contact of the poor with the rich, together with the progressive breakdown of caste barriers, has brought about constant comparison by the poor of their condition with that of the rich, and with it a sense of suffering, resentment, and envy. These sentiments can hardly be appeased by the prospect of slow improvement because, for a great part of the road at least, impatience *increases* as actual differences diminish and the goal is closer in sight.

2. Under these circumstances, utopian ideas seem entirely plausible to all but a few. Their plausibility rests in the failure of

most people to understand the economic problem of rational choice, and in the naïve belief that all problems can be easily solved once the authorities have set themselves to them. Furthermore, a democratic party is in a poor position to compete with a totalitarian movement because the democratic party cannot make utopian promises with impunity; a totalitarian movement is under no such restraint; it does not have to worry about redeeming its promises, because on the day of their maturing it has long achieved unchallengeable power.

3. Finally, there is, for Americans, an inner difficulty: the current revolutions strive for goals that Americans have traditionally upheld such as the right of self-determination of all nations, large or small, of all groups whose leaders declare them to be nations. Many of the declarations of nationalist leaders today might have been bodily lifted from speeches of American leaders in the past.

In particular, the following beliefs, widely held in this country, tend to weaken it in the present struggle:

(a) The egalitarian illusion: the assumption that all branches of the human family have been equipped with equal genetic endowment, and that actual differences of performance can, therefore, be due only to differences in opportunity; lack of achievement of some is therefore the responsibility of the more successful ones.

(b) The democratic illusion: the belief that self-government is always workable and indeed the best possible government, regardless of the level of education and information, and that there is something sacred about the principle, "one man, one vote," or its present international application: "one sovereign unit, one vote."

(c) The materialist prejudice: the belief that people are always motivated by economic interest and by a correct evaluation of their economic interest, to boot. A revolution in, say, Asia, must therefore be due to a clamor for land reform denied by the American-supported government, or similar conditions; facts at variance with this theory simply cannot be true.

(d) The sentimentalist illusion: the belief that relations between nations are governed not by the demands of self-interest as interpreted by them but by emotions such as likes or dislikes for another people or admiration or disparagement for its domestic achievement.

(e) The rationalist and moralist illusions: the belief that the establishment of law need not have a basis in a community existing in the minds of men and in physical power, but that law can be based on an appeal to conscience alone, and that the social contract can create an effective community.

(f) The distorted view of revolution: the belief that revolution always is made by those at the bottom of the social pyramid and is caused by oppression and injustice of the regime in power. The very fact of the revolution appears then as *prima facie* evidence for the injustice of the regime;[14] and it is felt that unjust rule must eventually lead to revolution.

The fact that a substantial part of articulate public opinion holds some, or all, of these propositions to be true greatly interferes with a realistic evaluation of the situation.

But there is also one point of strength for the West in its competition with Communism for the allegiance of the remainder of mankind: while the West, in the present climate of opinion, appears to be outclassed in the propaganda battle—as was the Hapsburg Monarchy in its final struggle for survival in the midst of revolutionary forces, and for similar reasons—there is also one strong card in the Western hand, and much will depend on whether it will be played with skill (as it has hardly been so far). The strength of the Soviets consists in the fact that the Socialist *idea*, which they incarnate, has an enormous appeal to the intellectuals and, to a lesser degree, to the poor; but it is their weakness that the Socialist *reality* is quite unattractive. No amount of argument and of good deeds is likely to convince liberal opinion in this country or abroad, or the masses in backward lands who have become aware of the possibility of a better life, that a capitalist country could do any right except by retreating and surrendering; but neither persuasion nor good deeds are necessary to convince, say, the East Germans.

---

[14] How unreal this assumption is will be seen when we translate it from the vertical, intranational, to the horizontal context, i.e., from the civil to international war: Who would entertain the notion that the fact that one nation has taken up arms against another is sufficient evidence for the justice of its cause?

Among men, as well as in animal and plant life, favorable living conditions bring about a proliferation of life, and whatever people may think ideologically, the direction of their migrations indicates the differences of living conditions. Where migration has been possible at all, as in Berlin and Hong Kong, it has been going from socialism to "capitalism."

It is the Western system, not the Soviet and the various other government-operated systems, that has actually worked better for the satisfaction of human needs and of the aspirations of people in their private lives. The strength of Socialism lies in the plausibility of its *arguments* and *promises;* the strength of the West lies in its *actual deliveries.* But the latter take a long time before they tell their story—long, not only because much experience must have accumulated before much inference can be drawn from it, but also because few people will revise satisfactory theories on account of inconvenient facts; most people will not notice such facts or will explain them away in some fashion. Also, governments unfriendly to the West can easily suppress such facts. It therefore takes at least the coming of age of another generation before there is any chance that widely accepted theories might be revised.

The Crucial Problem in the Struggle

The fundamental fact in the struggle between a pluralist society and a totalitarian system is the permanent *reversibility* of every victory of the former and the *irreversibility* of a victory of the latter. Whenever an attempt by totalitarians at seizing power has failed, the totalitarian movement, or the totalitarian countries that back it up, remains in a position to repeat that attempt tomorrow, the day after tomorrow, and forever after. Whenever totalitarians have seized power in a country, the result is irreversible (except for outside intervention such as overthrew Mussolini and Hitler), because totalitarians destroy every focus of possible resistance after a seizure of power. They must set up, as Lenin put it, a government that nobody will ever overthrow. This has been greatly facilitated in more recent times by modern technology, which has made possible an effective monopoly of the tools of coercion and communications such as has not existed for a long time and perhaps has never existed to quite the same degree.[15]

These ground rules put Western societies at a grave disadvantage. Nevertheless, they need not necessarily lead to catastrophe as long as the likelihood of a totalitarian take-over is as small as one chance in twenty, because the time that would have to pass until a totalitarian take-over became probable is sufficiently long that unforeseen events may upset all calculations. But, if the totalitarian chance is fairly good, perhaps one chance out of three, totalitarian victory becomes very probable within a relatively brief period of time. Eventual victory, by Communism or totalitarian movements allied to it, over most of the "underdeveloped" world appears, therefore, likely, unless the West can effect a change in the ground rules and make a Communist take-over a reversible event.

It may be that Communism, though with its prestige greatly increased, may yet have less easy sailing in many countries than it had in Russia, China, and Cuba, because the middle classes, the peasants, and unionized labor may be less naïve as to what is going to happen. But within the reach of Soviet power, effective resistance against a Communist regime already established is nevertheless an inauspicious enterprise, as events in Eastern Germany and Hungary have shown.

It may be different in countries which are not within easy reach of the Red Army and its air transport and which lie in the shadow of Western sea power. The latter has recently been shown to be of little effectiveness in the case of a left-handed support for a small force of invading exiles, but it may yet be

---

[15] In the 18th and 19th centuries, the main weapon of regular armies was the rifle; and rifles could be owned and operated by civilians, too. They could be hidden in backyards or smuggled across frontiers. Hence, the advantage of a governmental force over rebellious citizens was narrowed down to the advantages of superior training and discipline; these were real, but not necessarily decisive advantages, and men of courage had a chance against regular security forces. This was, therefore, the age of minutemen, barricades, and expanding democracy; it was in this period that the word was coined that one could do everything with bayonets except sit on them. But tanks and bombing planes can neither be hidden under the floor nor operated without a large visible organization. *Present technology* therefore *favors absolute State power.*

effective in enforcing a hands-off policy against a foreign, Hungary-style intervention to crush a local uprising. In this way, perhaps, Alfred Thayer Mahan's concept of the influence of sea power upon history may not yet be entirely obsolete. It may be one of the present-day possibilities of sea power and, therefore, one of the chances of the "world island" (Mackinder), which so largely depends on sea power for its survival, to keep revolutionary results reversible within a certain radius from its power center and thereby give trial and error a chance to work itself out.

From this point of view, the establishment of Communist states distant from the Soviet center of power contains, in addition to all too obvious dangers for the West, some possibilities for it as well. If conditions are reversible, Communist propaganda might be defeated in a certain area by the only effective argument there is—by a demonstration of Communism in action.

We therefore may question whether it is in the best interest of the United States to continue the policy of containment and to try its utmost to deny Communism access to Latin America and Africa. This policy is straining American resources to the utmost; it greatly antagonizes many people in these countries, as people do not like being told by others what they should do in their own best interest, which they prefer to judge for themselves; and it has not been conspicuous for its success of late. One may wonder whether it would not be preferable for the United States to take more of a backseat and, with the exception of the strategically most sensitive spots, to allow events to take their course. Under such circumstances, one must assume that Communist governments will be set up in some countries in these continents (as they probably will be anyhow); but it is also likely that some other countries will pursue a vigorous anti-Communist course and look to the United States for help. The United States would then not be in the thankless role of a proponent of an unpopular policy and an easy prey for blackmail but would be in the strong position of a power whose help is eagerly sought. In this way, a kind of equilibrium may be established in these continents which, though fraught with dangers for the West, may yet be one that can be lived with and upheld with less strain than is incumbent upon the present attempt of holding an umbrella over these continents and all their people—the willing, the disinterested, and the hostile alike. As time passes, Communism may find itself in these transoceanic outposts confronted with difficulties similar to those it faces in Eastern Europe, albeit without the possibility of easy military intervention.

The obstacle against the adoption of such a policy may lie not only in its undeniable perils, but also in the reluctance of the American people to part with universalist moral schemes and to have recourse to the despised strategies of "power politics."[16]

[16] Many of the thoughts expressed here were taken further in the author's *Progress and Revolution* (1967a).

CHAPTER 34

Demoralization and Reeducation

(1962)

It was a great shock to the American public to learn that during the Korean War some American prisoners had cooperated with their captors. It was obvious that they had acted under pressure, and it came as a surprise both that helpless prisoners had been subjected to such pressures and that Americans had yielded to them. It had long been taken for granted that prisoners of war would be treated according to the gentleman's code (except, possibly, for isolated outrages). It was overlooked that modern totalitarianism had never recognized the gentleman's code but had denounced it as a fraud, meant to facilitate the exploitation of the masses.

But the shock was greatly intensified when it turned out that some prisoners had not merely cooperated with the enemy but had actually been converted to his creed. While it had always been clear that, from all but a very few, virtually any statement could be obtained under torture—as shown by the history of witch trials—it had been taken for granted that only the hand or the tongue but not the mind could be coerced. "Compulsion by society," as a prominent scientist recently put it, "is powerless to change my private attitudes. A realization of this is part of the armory of self-respect of the individual" (Bridgman, 1959b, p. 261). That it could be otherwise, that man's thoughts can indeed be coerced within wide limits, was felt as a threat to that armory

This book review essay is reprinted from *World Politics*, 14:375-385, 1962. Princeton University Press.

and as a violation of the inner sanctum of the personality and it conjured up memories of horror stories about hypnotism.

Yet there need have been no surprise. The essence of the matter had not been unknown; Alexis de Tocqueville (1864-66) formulated it in the terse statement: "nothing comes more naturally to man than to recognize superior wisdom in those who oppress him." More recently, the impact of totalitarianism upon the mind of its subjects had been observed and adequately described. George Orwell (1949), for example, gave a detailed account of it in his novel *1984*, albeit with some artistic exaggeration. His main character, Winston Smith, who had been tortured, ended up by *loving* Big Brother. Orwell showed the main psychic mechanism through which this—to Western minds,[1] paradoxical—result was brought about: in a most extreme situation, facing horrible torture, Smith betrayed the woman whom he loved, by shouting—and shouting with relish, to boot—that she rather than he should be subjected to this ordeal. Thereupon the torturer stopped the procedure, as his purpose—the subject's utter demoralization—had been achieved. Smith had now been completely stripped of any self-respect: he could have only contempt for himself. He could however recuperate, to a degree, if he accepted the tenets of the regime: for then his moral fall became not a betrayal but a necessary, albeit painful, step on the road to salvation.

I

The authors of three recent works on this subject come from different quarters of the scholarly universe. Theodore H. E. Chen is head of a Department of Asiatic Studies; Robert Jay Lifton and Edgar H. Schein have their roots in academic psychiatry and psychology respectively. Chen deals with the thought reform of Chinese intellectuals, Schein with the indoctrination of American civilian prisoners, Lifton with all groups —Western military and civilian prisoners and Chinese literati. Chen treats his subject as a historian, and describes the history of

---

[1] I.e., to the minds of those who have never had to face extreme situations.

thought reform of scientists and scholars on the basis of available sources, particularly the confessions published in the Chinese press. Lifton and Schein proceed as behavioral scientists; their material is intensive interviews with persons who had been subjected to this reeducation.

In the thought reform of educated Chinese, as described by Chen (1961), nobody suffered, or was threatened with, physical harm. Pressure was limited to social pressure: if one wanted to live in China and continue with one's work, one had to make one's peace with the regime.

Though reform took place in so-called "revolutionary colleges" where the disciples assembled, more or less voluntarily, for the purpose of political "studies." There was constant pressure through criticism and demand for honest self-criticism, not only for specific misdeeds but for one's total cultural makeup—pressures to purge oneself of one's former self by making comprehensive and humiliating public confessions. Induced to cooperate by their manifest interest, the intellectuals made concessions and, once started on this road, they found it increasingly difficult to turn back. Chen believes that "many intellectuals signed the confessions without complete surrender of their inner selves" and he emphasizes that "the confessions neither broke the spirit nor warped the mind of the intellectuals" (p. 71). His picture is more one of behavioral compliance than of genuine conversion.

With Westerners, as studied by Lifton (1961) and Schein (1961), the same demands were buttressed by more or less severe physical pressure. To begin with, the subjects were prisoners unaware of the length of their confinement; they lived under the threat that they might be held indefinitely if they did not cooperate. Then, the continuous pressure of the cellmates, themselves prisoners but in a more advanced stage of Communist rehabilitation, urging the prisoner to struggle against his bourgeois self, to cleanse himself completely of his crimes by comprehensive confessions without mental reservation, leaving him no moment of peace, no time to collect himself, assumed the quality of physical pressure by its physically exhausting persistence.

Finally, a man who showed himself uncooperative might

have his legs and hands painfully shackled for weeks, the hands upward in a most uncomfortable position; his cellmates would take care of his elementary physical needs and clean him after defecation. One prisoner was severely injured.

Thought reform, says Lifton, derives "its emotional scope and power" from "the combination of external force or coercion with an appeal to inner enthusiasm through evangelical exhortation" (p. 13). In the process "an adult human being was placed in the position of an infant or a sub-human animal, helplessly being manipulated by larger and stronger 'adults' or 'trainers.' Placed in this regressive stance, each felt himself deprived of the power, mastery and selfhood of adult experience" (p. 67). The subjects are driven to guilt feelings, forced to betray others and themselves: "some degree of self-betrayal is quickly seen as a way to survival. But the more of one's self one is led to betray, the greater is one's involvement with the captors, for by those means they make contact with whatever similar tendencies already exist within the prisoner himself—with the doubts, antagonisms and ambivalences which each of us carries beneath the surface of his loyalties. This bond of betrayal between prisoner and environment may develop to the point where it seems to him to be all he has to grasp; turning back becomes ever more difficult" (p. 69).

There is an excellent description of "ideological totalism"— that is, of the Communist way of thinking and operating (Chapter 22)—and many an epigrammatic statement like these: "The Communists. . . did everything to make men fit the image" (p. 236); "The will to orthodoxy requires that men be modified in order to reaffirm the myth" (p. 432); or, the doctrine is called a "blend of counterfeit science and back-door religion" (p. 429).

Schein emphasizes that the development of thought reform by the Chinese Communists represented a much milder way of dealing with the bourgeois intelligentsia than had been employed by the Russian Communists, because it was a policy of salvage and rehabilitation—from the Communist point of view—rather than physical liquidation. This is an important historical insight.

He also points out that reindoctrination includes three stages: unfreezing (of old beliefs and attitudes), changing, and refreez-

ing. This concept is derived from the treatment in psychoanalytic writing of superego changes in hypnosis and in mass
situations, though Schein does not seem aware of this origin. He
pays particular attention to the stimulation of social guilt
feelings in the process of unfreezing.

Schein finds a person's accessibility to thought reform dependent on a variety of factors, among which are his liability to
guilt feelings on account of a privileged social position, the
degree of his attachment to a set of values and of his inner-
directedness, his acquaintance with Communist operations, his
age, and the moral support, or lack of it, provided by the local
population. As far as the events during the imprisonment are
concerned, he finds that the lenient, slow-moving interrogator
was more effective than the harsh one who, while arousing fear,
aroused hatred even more.

His data strongly suggest that the constant "struggling" of the
cellmates for the prisoner's soul was the most effective weapon of
thought reform. He has also some interesting things to say about
the released prisoner's attitude toward American society, and his
constant checking of Communist predictions against his own
subsequent experience.

Schein explains the Communist insistence on general acceptance of Marxism-Leninism in all walks of life by assuming that a
"passion for unanimity" is characteristic of totalitarianism, and
he proceeds to explain it in terms of demands of the ideology,
interests of the leaders, and characteristics of leaders and
followers, all subdivided into many categories. But it seems
doubtful whether Communist intolerance of deviation is due to a
passion for unanimity *per se.* The various branches of the
Christian Chruch tried to stamp out heresy, not because they
saw any special virtue in unanimity as such but, at least as far as
conscious motivation is concerned, because they were convinced
that they were in possession of absolute truth, and because they
believed that heresy was a mortal threat to the Church and to
the spiritual health of the community.[2]

We, too, insist on unanimity whenever we are convinced of

---

[2] Consideration of unconscious factors will add to, or alter, the picture,
but it is hardly likely that a passion for unanimity would be added from this
point of view.

the correctness of our proposition, and of the perils of disregarding it. We insist that surgery be carried out under aseptic conditions and we would not tolerate doctors or nurses disregarding this rule or encouraging students to disregard it. If the Communists insist on unanimity in many subjects in which we do not, it seems to be due to the fact that they believe they are in possession of absolute truth in these matters—truth that can be disregarded only at grave public peril—while we do not.

It seems regrettable to me that, with Lifton and with Schein, pertinent insight is often embedded in the fashionable theories, or at least the language, of the "struggle for identity." Thus, for example, when a prisoner had to submit repeated confessions until the authorities were satisfied, Lifton speaks of various "confession identities" (p. 80); or, the fact that a successfully resisting clergyman interprets his ordeal to himself in Christian theological terms is called "identity re-enforcement" (Lifton, p. 147); or, people who carry their norms within themselves and are therefore not dependent on approval by others are said to have a "strong sense of identity" (Schein, p. 161). I would see in the first case a series of successive adaptations (more or less deep, more or less superficial); in the second, an attempt to understand the situation, which is a first step toward mastery; in the third, a high degree of internalization of norms. Examples such as these abound in both books. The term "identity" has just the right combination of vagueness and suggestion of profundity to recommend it for wide application.

Lifton and Schein look for situations in our society that contain, in however small doses, the ingredients of brainwashing. Schein deals with reeducation in prisons, reformatories, hospitals, religious orders, and the like. Lifton goes further and looks for analogies in psychotherapy or in the training of psychiatrists in psychoanalytic institutes, situations in which the coercive aspect, if any, is infinitesimal.

There is merit in treating all manifestations of coercive persuasion together, from the severest to the mildest form of pressure, as they may have common denominators. But it also seems necessary to treat the more severe cases of pressure separately. After all, almost all persuasion has *some* element of coercion, as there is usually one opinion more popular than others and thus some pressure toward adopting it; every persuasion may thus be looked upon as coercive persuasion. Furthermore, response to pressure is not simply proportional to the degree of pressure applied; there is a breaking point for an individual where his response changes in kind, where, as a Marxist might put it, quantity turns into quality. Under a very great pressure, men may do things that are alien to them otherwise—for example, betraying their closest friends. In Orwell's novel, the high party official points out that a special study is made in each individual case to determine the one thing that, for that individual, is entirely unbearable.

All in all, the three books are tightly packed with valuable information, and the theoretical perspectives, often illuminating, are always stimulating.

II

It seems to me that in any comprehensive theory of reeducation, special consideration should be given to four points:

1. The relation of coercive persuasion to *moral education.* Childrearing not only consists of support and protection during the years of maturation and instruction in knowledge and skills, but also requires the implantation of rules of conduct and moral principles. We have in recent times considerably reduced the extent or the articulateness of the rules of conduct that we lay down for our children, and we encourage them to make up their own minds on many more subjects that former generations did. But there remains an irreducible core of implantation and indoctrination. We do not tell a four-year-old child who tries to throw his infant brother out of his crib that he should decide for himself what to do about the new arrival; we stop him and enforce our prohibition. And where we want to guide our children toward an autonomous decision of their own, we have to implant the very idea of the desirability of autonomy.

All these rules make up the superego, or conscience; its main building materials are identifications—that is, internalizations of parental commands and prohibitions. What makes this implantation possible is the long period of dependence, physical as well as psychological, of the child on his elders. Thus, the condition of coercive persuasion—that is, the combination of psychological influence with overwhelming physical power—exists, naturally and unavoidably, in childhood.

The superego implanted in childhood is subject to revision in later life in the light of growing criticism but, except for extraordinary conditions such as mass situations, such revisions rarely touch its most basic principles.

Moral education of children is therefore *necessarily* similar to coercive persuasion; it is the *prototype*, and coercive persuasion is the *copy*. Coercive persuasion is a reeducation of an adult, an attempt to introduce a new set of moral standards in a person in the place of a superego already formed.

From this it can easily be seen that, in brainwashing, the existing structure must first be "unfrozen" before it can be shaped anew. But it also follows that the unfreezing is done by encouraging a partial regression of an individual to attitudes of a child—a process already initiated by the helplessness of an individual in the hands of overwhelming power unrestrained by law and custom, and helped along further by countless humiliating experiences, from being treated as a sinner and urged to repent, down to the inability of the shackled prisoner to take care of his fundamental bodily needs, which, as with an infant, are attended to by others.

This enforced regression to the psychological condition of a child makes it possible for the already internalized parental authority—which, incidentally, is now shown as unable to protect the prisoner and is therefore partially devalued—to lose its power to the external authorities of the moment, who are subsequently incorporated and become the new inner authority.

If the fundamental relation between moral education in childhood and "brainwashing" is not realized, some pseudoproblems may present themselves. Lifton reports on a seminar attended by the faculty of a girls' college in which the similarities between educational practices and thought reform caused the faculty members some anguished soulsearching. One professor accused the college of being engaged in brainwashing; another protested and claimed innocence; while a third, "facing the continuities [of education] with thought reform . . . as an unavoidable paradox," suggested as a way out a measure of relativism, recommending that educators hold their beliefs "with a certain amount of tension" (p. 443).

But the whole problem is unreal. College education is education of human beings who have not yet matured and it *must* have elements of indoctrination; even the most liberal and the most skeptical education must at least request the acceptance of the liberal faith. There are many who think that there should be more, rather than less, indoctrination of youth with the fundamental values of our civilization if this civilization is to survive. The issue is not that, in our civilization as well as in any other, children are being treated like children; the issue is that in totalitarianism *adults are being treated like children*.

2. The second point has to do with what to this reviewer seems an overvaluation of the specific techniques employed by the Chinese for the process of thought reform. This reform, I submit, is brought about, to a large extent, by the *impact of the totalitarian climate*, with its combination of mass enthusiasm and all-pervasive terror, with or without special programs and techniques such as those introduced by the Chinese Communists.

The evidence for this contention seems to me to lie in the experience of the Nazi era in Germany. The Nazis had no special reeducation program—no revolutionary college, no ritual of public confessions—but after a very few years the great majority of Germans were nonetheless effectively *gleichgeschaltet*—that is, had accepted, in the main, the Nazi ideology. There is no reason to believe that the Chinese have achieved more, or indeed as much.

The thought reform of German civil servants who had stayed on under Hitler was described in 1945 in simple words by the German economist, Wilhelm Röpke:

> One persuaded oneself and others that by staying on one's job one could "prevent worse things from happening," that one could not permit oneself to be "passed over," that "perseverance" demanded greater sacrifice than withdrawal, that one could not "desert the fatherland in this grave hour," and more of the same. But he who had given his little finger to the Nazis soon came to the

point of keeping silent where conscience would have required him to speak out, of remaining inactive where an honest man should have acted, of lying and being a hypocrite and doing things that made one a partner in the conspiracy. Then there remained only three possibilities: one could still make up one's mind to break with the regime; or one had to hold oneself in contempt, day in, day out; or one had to try to convince oneself that one had after all been somewhat off the beam in one's original judgment of national socialism. For the first course one had no longer the courage; the second would have been against human nature. So there remained only the third way out and one began to talk of the "good sides of the regime, which after all were real, too," of the possibility of a progressive normalization of the regime, or of the so-called necessity of supporting the "decent ones" among the Nazis against the worse elements [p. 55f., my tr.].[3]

This is the process of yielding under pressure and rationalizing one's concessions in moral terms. The result is a gradual corrosion of one's former moral principles and their gradual replacement by new ones—similar to, though less dramatic than, the story of Orwell's hero.

Under relentless pressure from an overwhelming power which is not content with securing the silent obedience of its subjects but requests genuine faith, those for whom the ruling creed carries no appeal whatever are in the position of travelers from Western civilization who have fallen into the hands of a cruel savage tribe bent on the conversion of its captives. Those for whom some aspects of the creed have at least a partial appeal are in an even more difficult position, as the external enemy has an ally within their own minds. If they render lip service to the regime, they must constantly take care lest they be found out, and if they collaborate with the regime to the point of acting against their consciences—e.g., by betraying their friends—they must live with guilt and shame. But there is a way out of this

[3] See also Chs. 28 and 32 in this volume.

predicament by identification with the regime and acceptance of its tenets as correct and just.

3. The main questions asked by the authors about the conditions of thought reform are perhaps not the only ones that need asking; we should also ask by what means we, in *our* dealing with defendants, succeed in *avoiding* brainwashing.

We are always inclined to accept what is pleasing to us as "normal" and thus not in need of explanation, and to ask for "causes" only in regard to what frustrates us. "Cause" is still largely what it originally was: *aitia*, guilt. Thus, man has asked for a long time about the causes of illness, assuming that health needs no explanation, and we have only recently come to realize that the success of an organism in functioning adequately and in maintaining a sense of well-being under the constant onslaught of life is perhaps more wondrous than its occasional, and at last its final, failure. One has studied time and again the causes of war, yet the reasons for strife are not difficult to understand; it would perhaps have been more rewarding to study by what means men have sometimes succeeded in keeping peace over a considerable time. In the same way, we ask for the causes of "brainwashing" because it shocks and frightens us. Yet is is probably the *original* condition between victor and vanquished, and part of the surrender of the latter. *Cuius regio, eius religio* has probably been true over most of history. Only through a long moral and legal development have Western societies arrived at an effective protection of the weak against spiritual as well as bodily violence. Among these innovations are laws that limit the power of the state and make its actions predictable within large limits, thereby removing the terror of the unknown; laws, furthermore, that provide the accused with a counsel to whom he can open his heart without fear of betrayal and who will stand at his side, extracting every ounce of advantage from a law heavily weighted in favor of the accused.

4. Finally, there is the question why we have no information of a prisoner having tried to indoctrinate his captor. The odds, of course, are heavily against the success of such an endeavor and its risks are obvious. Yet, some early Christians are said to have converted their jailors. Perhaps these accounts are legends; but there are well documented reports of this kind in a more recent case—the revolutionary movement in czarist Russia.

For example, Sergei Gennadovich Nechaev (1847-82) was imprisoned in the Peter-Paul Fortress for his participation in the murder of the student Ivanov. He was considered a particularly dangerous prisoner and was held in isolation, his legs and arms shackled part of the time. Nevertheless, in the course of a checkup after the assassination of Czar Alexander II (1881), the authorities found that Nechaev, the isolated prisoner, had slowly won over the soldiers of the Guards—sixty-nine of them were arrested—and with their help had established contact with the revolutionary committee outside. Plans for Nechaev's escape from the fortress had been made and might have been carried out had Nechaev not given priority to the assassination of the Czar (Venturi, 1960).

We see here the unshakable conviction of a fanatical revolutionary as to the rightness of his cause—coupled with complete disregard for life and limb, unimpaired by personal attachments, ever ready to be a "witness" (martyr) for his cause—encountering the feeble beliefs of the defenders of the czarist order, beliefs that once had been as powerful as the revolutionary creed was then (or is now) but that had long since lost the power to move the hearts of men.

In Chinese thought reform, however, fanatical belief was on the side of the captors, while the Western beliefs of the prisoners were, in most cases, corroded by ambivalence and doubt. There arises the crucial question whether the ideological softness shown by most Western prisoners was only a characteristic of those individuals or an ominous cultural symptom. Perhaps the Western creed—empiricism and pragmatism—skeptical by its very nature, does not lend itself to fanatical devotion. But this is not conclusive; there have been men utterly devoted to the ideal of an autonomous conscience, or to its secular offspring, the ideal of liberty—men for whom these were not negotiable issues. But in our day their number seems to be small. Perhaps liberal empiricism has overreached itself by extending the test of empiricism from questions of fact to the very question of whether there is merit in the dispassionate pursuit of truth; by extending the right, or the need, to question and to doubt from concrete issues to the very desirability of questioning and doubting; by keeping an open mind even to the proposition that there is no need for openness. In one of those logical paradoxes that fascinated Greek thinkers, empiricism and pragmatism may have done away with themselves as the last consequence of their own principles.

Be that as it may: thought reform or coercive persuasion, deriving, as Lifton put it, "its emotional scope and power" from a "combination of external force...with an appeal to inner enthusiasm" (p. 13), is a function of both the kind and degree of physical pressures and the individual's reactions to them, and the relation of the existing superego structure to the usurping ideology. It can be effectively resisted only by those who are equipped with the full measure of moral strength and physical fortitude.

CHAPTER 35

The Concept of Justice
and the Quest for a
Perfectly Just Society

(1966)

I

The demand for justice, for more and more justice, for absolute justice, is in the center of the sentiments of our time. We read every day in our papers what injustices are committed here and there in every part of the globe and that it is our responsibility to set things right, or else there will be the most dire consequences. This is a rather novel attitude.

Of course, it has been held since ancient times that *justitia fundamentum regnorum,* justice is the foundation of kingdoms. But that meant essentially justice in the conflicts between individuals or small groups *within* the established social order. It did not mean to challenge the existing social stratification *as such.*

Part I is based on a speech delivered on September 9, 1965 at the Twenty-Eighth Annual Judicial Conference of the Third Judicial Circuit of the United States. First printed in: *Federal Rules Decisions,* 39:413-423, 1966; also in: *Proceedings of the Twenty-Eighth Annual Judicial Conference Third Judicial Circuit of the United States.* St. Paul, Minn.: West Publishing Co., 1966, pp. 413-423; and in: *Journal of Criminal Law, Criminology and Police Science,* 57:1-6, 1966. The modified version of this speech is reprinted from *University of Pennsylvania Law Review,* 115:1-11, 1966.

Part II is reprinted from *University of Pennsylvania Law Review,* 115:17-21, 1966.

The idea that the social stratification itself has to be just, i.e., has to comply with an abstract concept of justice, is fairly new, probably not more than 200 years old.

During the recent student rebellion in Berkeley, one of the students was reported to have said that what the students wanted was a society of justice and brotherhood. His formulation was essentially identical to one given by Maximilien Robespierre in his speech on June 7, 1794. It was the goal of the regime, said Robespierre, *"de fonder sur la terre l'empire de la sagesse, de la justice et de la vertu,"* to establish on earth the empire of wisdom, justice, and virtue.

The two statements differ slightly in the style of expression; Robespierre uses some words which sound dated to us. The word "wisdom" is not fashionable today and we prefer to speak of "reason" or "sanity," and "virtue" is altogether antiquated; we would rather say "brotherhood." But the ideas are substantially identical.

What really is justice? This is something about which people have always agreed as long as one remained on a highly abstract level, and have always disagreed as soon as one got down to concrete details. *Suum cuique*—to each his due—is the Roman formation of justice. The digest of Roman law prepared on order of the Emperor Justinian in the middle of the sixth century A.D., the so-called *Institutiones*, begins with the words: "Justice is the constant and perpetual disposition to render to every man his due."

So far it is easy to agree. But what is every man's due? If we turn, for instance, to the greatest thinker of antiquity, Aristotle, we see the following:

> It is thought that justice is equality, and so it is, though not for everybody but only for those who are equals; and it is thought that inequality is just, for so indeed it is, though not for everybody, but for those who are unequal [*Politics*, 211].

Justice thus means for Aristotle to treat unequal things unequally.

This concept can serve to justify practically everything. One can justify slavery in these terms and that is in fact what Aristotle has done.

In later times, a different view of the matter was taken. Justice was no longer considered to be the unequal treatment of things which were unequal by nature (or social conditions) but the equal treatment of all men regardless of how unequal they might be in terms of nature or social conditions. Justitia, the Goddess of Justice, was depicted as blindfolded; she would give her verdict without regard of person, equal for the mighty and the weak, for the rich and the poor.

In modern times, a still different view has more and more taken hold, viz., that the Goddess of Justice should not be blindfolded at all, but should be made to see again so that she may differentiate between the people in a way opposite to that envisaged by Aristotle, compensate for the inequalities of nature and social situation, and give preferential treatment to the weak, the sick, the poor—to the "disinherited of the earth" as they have sometimes been called.

Social justice is often viewed as equal opportunity for all. But here, too, we face a variety of possible interpretations. We may perhaps hold that it means equal opportunity for human beings as they are now; all should have equal access to the good things of life—for instance, all should receive equal consideration for employment or promotion—regardless of family origin, race, ethnic extraction, religion, sex and the like. This is one interpretation.

A second interpretation may hold that this is not justice at all because there are vast differences in previous education; in order to make things just, all would have to have equal education first.

A third interpretation goes still further. It is pointed out that equal schooling is not sufficient to make conditions really fair and equal, because there are vast differences in the home situation of people. Formal education is received by youths who are differently equipped, depending on whether or not they had received stimulation in their homes, had a good home atmosphere, adequate objects of identification and so forth.

And finally, there is a fourth view that would argue that even if this were equal, there still would be no equality of opportunity because people have been equipped differently by nature: some, for instance, are in sturdy health, others are sickly; some have been endowed with high intelligence, others with low; some are attractive, winning immediately the good-

will of people, others are not, etc. Not until all natural endowment is equal, or its inequalities properly compensated for, can
we speak of real equality of opportunity.

One can readily see that as we proceed in this sequence of
interpretations, the ideal of equality of opportunity gradually
turns into an ideal of equality of station.

It seems to me that the concept of social justice is today
oscillating between the poles of equality of opportunity and
equality of station, between the ideal that all people should
participate in the race of life on equal terms, and the ideal that
they should all arrive at the same spot at the same time. If the
latter is to be achieved, if all are to arrive at the finish line
together, it must be a race of differential handicaps.

One can also see that this question of equality of opportunity
versus equality of station is related to the question of liberty and
equality.

Liberty and equality have been coupled together in the
slogan of the French Revolution and have remained so in the
consciousness of countless people ever since. Nevertheless, it is
easy to see that there are instances in which liberty and equality
interfere with each other. If, for instance, people are free to
engage in acquisitive activities, it will soon turn out that some
will be more prosperous than others; if we want them to be
equal in income and possessions, we must prevent them from
engaging in such activities, or determine the rewards they are
permitted to receive or to keep.

If people are free to choose the neighborhood in which they
live, and the circles in which they move, there will soon be a
social differentiation of residential neighborhoods and social
circles; if we want to prevent this from happening, we must
reduce, or cancel out, the freedom of choosing one's neighborhood or one's circle.

How did it happen that liberty and equality have so long
been considered as brothers when they are actually often
antagonists? The answer to this question should not be too
difficult.

There is an area of life in which liberty and equality actually
go together, and an area of life in which they do not go together.

For a group of oppressed—say, for slaves who want to be

emancipated from slavery—liberty and equality mean actually the same. They want to be *free from* their masters and *equal to* their masters; that means the same to them.

But as soon as one extends the concept of liberty from the relations of the lower to the higher echelons into the relations *within the peer group;* as soon as liberty means not only freedom from domination by the master but also freedom in the inter-relations within one's group, liberty and equality become ir-reconcilable because freedom within the peer group will imme-diately lead to social differentiations. If this is to be prevented, liberty must be curtailed.

A simple example from daily life may serve to illustrate the point. There may be a group of children at a birthday party. If they are left free, without adult supervision, there will soon be some who will dominate and others who will follow, some who will determine what games are to be played and who will allocate the more desirable roles in these games to themselves and to their friends, and others who will have to take what remains. If we want them to be equal, all to have the same influence in the choice of the games, and all the same chance of occupying the desirable places in them, an adult must be there to supervise the proceedings and to lay down the law and restrict the freedom of some of the children. Equality inevitably de-mands authority which constantly interferes whenever, in the free play of forces, social differentiation appears. It is note-worthy that the situation, simple though it is, has rarely been faced. Thomas Jefferson was well aware of it. Goethe wrote shortly after the French Revolution: "Legislators and revolu-tionaries who promise equality and freedom at the same time are either dreamers or charlatans."

In the beginning of our century George Santayana (1953) said: "The only free man in a social democracy [social demo-cracy is Santayana's term for an egalitarian society] would be one whose ideal was to be an average man."

But such voices are rare and the confusion persists in the public conscience.

It is possible to inculcate through education the kind of conscience that demands sharing. In that case, the authority necessary to counteract the emergence of stratification becomes internal, within the person, rather than external; outside pressure would be needed only in the beginning during the childhood years, while this education and indoctrination is taking place, and might relax later. But this kind of conditioning, while effective with some people all the time, and with most people some of the time, does not work with all the people all the time; external authority ready to interfere must remain as *ultima ratio* to insure compliance. Moreover, an internalized demand to love others like oneself, if effective, is hardly equally effective with regard to *all* objects; its effectiveness is likely to diminish the more we move away from an inner circle like the family, party, nation, etc.

Pertinent to this problem is the so-called pecking order of animals, a universal phenomenon of nature. In groups of animals, a social order or hierarchy establishes itself. The zoologist, Schjelderup-Ebbe, discovered nearly half a century ago (1922a, b, 1923) that a kind of social hierarchy exists among chickens: there is a top animal that pecks everybody else in the flock with impunity; the victim does not resist but suffers it to happen, although it must often be very painful and may on occasions be fatal. Then, there is another hen who is being pecked by the top bird but pecks everybody else, and so forth down the line to the "buck private" who is pecked by everybody and does not peck anybody else. Schjelderup-Ebbe saw in these conditions the prototype of social stratification and called it a "pecking order."

It is not always as simple as with chickens. Chickens have one of the more tyrannical and more rigidly stratified societies. In other instances things are more complex and the hierarchy is a matter of relative statistical frequency, of a quotient of pecking versus being pecked, rather than a strict line of command and obedience. Sometimes there are circular orders: *A* pecks *B*, *B* pecks *C* and *C* pecks *A* (Allee, 1942). There are all kinds of complications just as there are among humans.

In general, one may sum up the essential points of this research in approximately these terms: there are several criteria of social hierarchy; some have to do with preferred access to desirable things, others with the possibility of using another ruthlessly as a means to one's ends.

The superior animal has, first of all, preferred access to food. It feeds first; others do not touch the food before the dominant animals are fully satisfied. If supplies are scarce, they may get nothing.

Second, there is preferred access to the sexual object. If the big male is around in a group of baboons, the bachelor males are practically condemned to celibacy; they do not dare to come close. If the big male is not there, they may take a chance (Zuckerman, 1932).

Third, there is preferred access to safety. In danger, the dominant animal can escape first. It was about this way in the "Titanic" disaster when more men were saved in first class than children in third.

Finally, there is the possibility of abusing others with impunity; this is the case of pecking, which was discovered first and gave the whole system its name.

By and large, all these criteria coincide; i.e., those who are dominant according to one criterion are so according to the others too. But there is one important exception: one of the criteria of hierarchy, the preferential access to safety, is in contradiction with another feature also found in the hierarchy—that of leadership. A leading animal does not escape first in danger; rather, it goes ahead of the flock, exposing its body to danger first and permitting the rest to take cover behind it. This point marks the difference between genuine leadership and mere dominance.

Dominance in the animal kingdom depends on a variety of factors; among them are health, physical strength, age, and sex. In most mammals the male is dominant except for the time of oestrus in which dominance may shift to the female. Pugnacity and courage also are important factors. A smaller animal who is an excellent fighter may be dominant over a physically stronger one. The ability to bluff also has something to do with it. And so has closeness to home territory.

Hierarchy among humans seems to manifest itself in fundamentally similar terms, though, of course, with many more variations and complications.

After this cursory glance at phenomena of the animal kingdom, we may return to our question: where does justice lie?

Does it lie in *sanctioning* the order established in the free play of forces, as it is rooted in nature or in individual or collective history? Or does it lie in *correcting* and changing the natural order, either *wholly or partially*? Should we allow more to those who have occupied the top places than to others, or the same, or less?

There are various answers to these questions and the views change with time, place, and circumstance.

In any case, we must realize that if we feel that justice demands compensating for the inequalities of the natural order, authority is needed to carry out this compensation and to maintain it against the constant pressures of the natural order to reassert itself; and the further we wish to go in correcting the natural order, the more authoritarian the regime has to be.

Once again, where does justice lie? A few examples may help to show how difficult it is to answer the question in concrete cases, and how impossible to give a general answer which would be satisfactory to all.

Should one, for instance, educate highly gifted children in the same classes with less gifted ones, or should one place them in separate classes? If we do the latter, we give them opportunity to progress faster, at their own speed, and to realize their abilities better. On the other hand, such a setup is humiliating for the other children who know quite well that they do not belong to the elite. They are stigmatized. If all are put together in the same classes, the stigma is avoided at the price of handicapping the development of the more gifted ones. Where does justice lie?

Let us assume that a couple has three normal children and one retarded one. Perhaps, by denying their three normal children a college education, they may be able to provide for their retarded child such special remedial training as will make the difference between permanent institutionalization and a restricted life outside of institutions. Which course is just? Different people will take different views of this matter.

In the simplest possible form the question appears in the family between two brothers of different, but not too different, ages—perhaps two or three years apart. It often happens that the younger brother wants to go along with the older brother, to join in the games the latter is playing with his group; he thinks he is old enough. But the older brother takes a different view of the matter; he thinks the kid brother does not belong in his crowd and would merely disturb the fun. In a certain sense one can say that every older brother is naturally a segregationist, every younger brother an integrationist.

Where exactly does justice lie?

The simple fact is that every solution involves sacrifices for some. *Who shall sacrifice what for the sake of whom* is a question for which I see no clear, unambiguous, moral answer.

For this reason, it would appear as the first result of our considerations that an absolutely just order cannot exist, in fact *cannot be devised;* not only because people are morally imperfect—or sinful, if you like—but simply for the reason that there is no agreement as to what justice is and no likelihood of there ever being complete agreement. There will always be situations in which one man's justice is another man's outrage.

Second, the demand for absolute justice which is so strong in this day and age adds to the difficulties of the situation rather than diminishing them. As long as we look upon such conflicts—as between older and younger brother, or between the gifted and the average, or the average the retarded, child—as conflicts of interests only, they can be adjusted with charity. But once we ideologize and moralize them and see them as conflicts between Good and Evil, they become inaccessible to compromise and thus insoluble, with nothing but violence left.

It seems to me that the demand for absolute justice, the very *evangelical fervor* of our time, *makes all problems insoluble,* with violence the only possible outcome, noble though the idea is in the abstract.

The French poet Paul Valéry (1943) once said "every doctrine, every sentiment, if carried pedantically to its ultimate conclusion, must lead to the destruction of man."

Let me now offer some suggestions regarding the historical significance of the modern movement. It seems to me that what we are witnessing today is a change in moral concepts.

All morality is a restriction and modification of inborn strivings. If man were only good by nature, no morality would be needed; he would always want to do what he should do—a state of affairs which ancient writers like Ovid attributed to a mythical golden age of the past but which has not existed in historical times.

The morality of the Christian ages has put the emphasis on the restriction of sexuality. Complete "purity," i.e., actual abstinence, was the goal of an elite, while to the masses the ideal of a "clean life," in which sexuality was severely restricted, was held up.

At the same time, these ages took a lenient view of the manifestations of selfishness; callousness and cruelty in the pursuit of one's interests or whims were readily condoned. The rule "thou shalt love thy neighbor like thyself" was part of the religious teaching, but few took it even half seriously. Social stratification with enormous distance between the highest and the lowest was unquestioningly accepted; punishment in the home, the army or the law courts was savage and war was accepted as a fact of life.

In our days, things have completely turned around. Sexuality is now considered as needing practically no restrictions whatsoever. Selfishness has become the main target of moral censure; men are expected to be concerned only about the good of all and not about their own personal interests. Aggression in the service of self-assertion or self-aggrandizement including the mitigated expression of aggressiveness in the form of status differentiation—one man considering himself as better than another man and looking down on him—is completely condemned. The change is from a form of morality which puts the main emphasis on the restriction of sexuality while making generous allowances for the pursuit of self-interest and for aggression, to a form of morality which is permissive toward sexuality but outlaws self-concern. The demand for chastity has been replaced by a demand for universal brotherhood. This difference is perhaps due to the fact that Christianity looked for the main virtue in man's relation to God, while the modern age, with its humanistic rather than supernaturalist orientation, seeks the main virtue in man's relations to his fellowmen.

Only those whose youth was still cast in the Victorian or Edwardian age can fully realize the magnitude of the change. Just half a century ago, at the beginning of the First World War in 1914, the British Minister of War, Field Marshall Lord

Kitchener, said in his order to the British Expeditionary Force which every soldier had to carry in his pay book on his body and which formulated the rules of conduct for the soldier:

> In this new experience you may find temptations both in wine and women. You must entirely resist both temptations, and, while treating all women with perfect courtesy, you should avoid any intimacy [Arthur, 1920].

Thus, the head of the British Army asked soldiers in wartime in all earnestness never to touch any woman. Anything of the kind would seem absurd today.

On the other hand, I may cite a recent newspaper article which dealt with topless bathing suits. The author found it preposterous that anybody should take objection to them on the ground of public morals. Breasts are an organ of the body; why should any organ be obscene? What is really obscene, he argued, is for one man to call another man a nigger.

We can see here the change in the meaning of "obscenity" from a term of opprobrium for certain sexual expressions to a term of opprobrium for an expression of status differentiation. It is a radical shift of emphasis.

The recent revolt of students at the Berkeley campus of the University of California broke out when the Board of Regents refused the students the use of college grounds for the preparation of sit-ins in the community of Berkeley. These sit-ins were obviously related to the current civil rights movement. The last act in the series of events, on the other hand, was an episode in which a group of students shouted Anglo-Saxon four-letter words for some time.[1]

It seems to me that these two events, the first and the last act, are closely interrelated; they are the two sides of the same coin, viz., of the newly emerging morality that has no objection to any kind of sexual expression at all but objects strenuously to social inequality or status differentiation.

I submit that in both cases, the Christian and the modern, radical "idealists" have gone too far in their demands, beyond the capabilities of the flesh. The moralists of yesterday tried to

[1] See also Waelder (1964, 1967b).

purge man of sexual lust; they refused to believe that, with most people, sexuality cannot be suppressed except at enormous cost in terms of other human values. The moralists of today try to purge man of all selfishness and personal aggressiveness; they refuse to believe that, in most cases, self-concern and a measure of aggressiveness cannot be completely suppressed except at enormous cost in terms of other human values. The attempt to make all people chaste has failed; the attempt to establish complete equality will eventually fail as well.

In the ages now past, the attack against sexuality did not really obliterate or totally subdue the sexual aspect of man. It came out in other ways: in hypocritical behavior, in actions in which the right hand did not know what the left hand was doing, in perversions—including, in particular, sadistic attitudes whose sexual implications were not seen, in hysterical symptoms so frequent at the time, and in other forms as well.

The attempt at wiping out selfishness and aggressive self-assertion including the moderated and mitigated expression in the form of status differentiation will not succeed any better because these strivings, too, turn up somewhere through the backdoor.

As had been mentioned before, an egalitarian society needs an authority which has the power to enforce equality and which sees to it that nobody gets out of line. In this indirect way, the attempt to wipe out the power of man over man and to achieve complete equality, when carried to its logical conclusion, actually leads to the setting up of an authoritarian rule; with it, the power of man over man has returned. Those who started out to eliminate every differentiation between the people end up, inevitably, by creating greater differentiations than have existed before. We may remember the words of Horace: *Naturam expellas furca, tamen usque recurret"*—you may drive nature out with a pitchfork, she will always return.

Some day, of course, the present exaggerated demands will exhaust themselves, as the exaggerated demands for the restriction of sexuality have exhausted themselves. But if previous history is any guide, I doubt whether this will happen until men have embraced another fanaticism because, as the late Sir Richard Livingstone, Vice Chancellor of Oxford, once said (1959, p. 43):

Men can rarely walk in the middle of the road. They reel drunkenly from the ditch on the one side to the ditch on the other.

II

A Reply to Professor Morris's
Statement of Dissent

(1967)

I am grateful to Professor Morris for his challenge because it forces me to spell out implicit assumptions and to try to improve on my formulations.

There are essentially two issues at stake between Professor Morris and myself, one a matter of (moral) *ideal*, the other a matter of (psychological) *fact*.

The *first issue* is the question whether the concept of justice, or morality in general, is the same for all people and all times—an eternal essence in the Platonic heaven of ideas—or varies with time and place.

Without trying to formulate any moral philosophy of my own, I have merely noted, as an observer of human events, that very different kinds of order have been considered as just by different people, at different times; and furthermore, that the norms of Western civilization provide a basis for different and often contradictory claims.

That does not mean that every kind of action can be presented as just. Genocide, for instance, cannot be defended in

---

In his dissent to Dr. Waelder's theory of justice, Clarence Morris (1966) argued that the lack of a definition of absolute justice did not warrant the toleration of injustices. While he agrees that aggressiveness is rooted in human nature, he does not believe "that willingness to be the butt of such aggression is also inborn and therefore bound to persist." He asks: "Shall we believe that since some are made so that we cannot down their aggressiveness in the form of status differentiation, others must inevitably be second class members of the human race?"

terms of Western values or, for that matter, in terms of the values of any of the great historical civilizations; there is no moral tenet in any of them that would give one branch of the human race the right to exterminate another branch according to its pleasure.

But there is a large area within which more than one position can be argued in terms of traditional Western norms. A few examples may illustrate this point.

It is arguable that, in justice, all men should have a chance to realize their potential and to reach a place in society proportionate to their abilities and achievements. It is equally arguable that no man should derive any privileges from the fact that he was born with better health, greater endurance, higher intelligence or more creative ability, or had better opportunities for realizing his potential, than another man. It is even arguable that those more niggardly endowed by nature should be compensated for their privations.

It is arguable that in the name of justice, in a family or in an alliance of nations, all members, old or young, large or small, should participate equally in decisionmaking. It is also arguable that the kind of equality which is just in such situations is not equality between members but is equality between power and responsibility in each member so that the voice of each has weight commensurate with the responsibility he carries for the consequences. According to the latter view, it would be unjust for the breadwinning father of a family to be outvoted by his minor children on a question of budgeting.

It is arguable that all members of a community have the right to be welcomed by other members with whom they wish to associate, and to live in the environment of their choice. It is also arguable that people have the right to associate or not to associate with others according to their pleasure or whim, and to congregate with those like-minded if they so desire.

In these and similar instances we do not have a clear division of right and wrong (as in the case of genocide) but a set of *conflicting rights*. It seems to me that in such cases the *moral harvest is greatest* if one approaches them "with charity toward all, with malice toward none" rather than by trying to impose one right at the expense of others.

This is essentially the view that Judge Learned Hand (1916) once expressed in his definition of justice as "a passable accomodation between the vital and self-conscious interests of society."

The *second issue* is a question of fact, viz., to what degree can nature be remolded so as to make her conform to moral requirements, and what price is to be paid in terms of other human values.

There are two extreme views on this issue: on the one hand the view of the Right which sees "human nature" as forever unchangeable, and on the other hand the Left view which holds that "society" can be so constructed as to make one's moral ideal a reality, at no appreciable costs to anything worth preserving.

I believe that both views are mistaken. There is no *unchangeable* human nature. It is "the nature of man to transcend nature," as Denis de Rougemont (1963) put it. All human history is the story of the transcendence of nature.

On the other hand, nature is *not infinitely malleable*. This is particularly true of living matter and more particularly of human beings. Moreover, interference with the natural course of things often has consequences beyond those intended; for instance, in medicine, the noxious "side" effects of remedial drugs, radiation damage to healthy tissue, mutations of microorganisms attacked by antibiotics or iatrogenic diseases in general. These unintended consequences are not always easy to deal with. There is a point of diminishing returns beyond which further intervention is likely to be counterproductive, at least for the time being, or to exact a high price in terms of other human values.

A simple example of the limits with which egalitarian ideals meet in reality is provided by the history of the Soviet Union. Lenin started out to establish complete equality; all incomes were to be exactly equal and state power over the individual was to evaporate by itself. The results after fifty years are these: millionaire incomes have indeed been abolished but, apart from them, the spread of income is about as wide in the Soviet Union as it is in the West (Kuznets, 1963) and is probably less flexible. In order to achieve this modest degree of egalitarianism, a far greater power of the state over the individual had to be established and maintained than had ever existed in the time of the Czars. In order to avoid the reemergence of a prosperous merchant class, the Soviets recently found it necessary to decree the *death penalty* for "economic crimes," i.e., for private trading.[1]

That should also answer Professor Morris's question: "Shall we believe that since some are made so that we cannot down their aggressiveness in the form of status differentiation, others must inevitably be second class members of the human race?"

Stratification is a universal phenomenon of nature, both subhuman and human. It exists in every family, every nursery, every school class, every office or club. There is a hierarchy among monks, among martyrs and, of course, among fighters for egalitarianism. The great majority of people have to take not second but nth place.

Hierarchies can be reshuffled, the rules of competition can be conventionalized, and the prize of victory can be reduced; but they cannot be abolished altogether. Mitigation has been going on for a long time; the stakes—originally life and death—have been replaced by milder, or symbolic ones. The wages of defeat are no longer death but a lesser share in the amenities of life. Further mitigation is no doubt possible. But it is not certain that the frustrations of the losers have lessened in proportion to the amount by which the stakes have become less deadly.

Full equality cannot be achieved by voluntary cooperation alone; it needs a new hierarchy of supervisors. Being human, they too will come to use their powers for their own aggrandizement.

Moreover, it may be questioned whether complete abolition of the struggle leading to status differentiation, if possible, would be entirely desirable. Educators have often criticized the "overprotectiveness" of some parents who wish to spare their children the encounter with more aggressive youngsters. They think that this kind of protectiveness is not in the children's own long-term interest; short of protection against extreme abuse, children should be allowed to develop their own maximum strength under challenge, thus finding and eventually accepting a place in the group commensurate with their capabilities.

[1] *Soviet Criminal Law and Procedure*, tr. Berman & Spindler, 1966, pp. 61f., 188.

Professor Morris sees moral progress toward equality in developments in which I can see only a growth of abundance which removes inequalities on one level only to have them reappear on another level. "In some ancient societies," Professor Morris states, "only a tycoon-father could afford to send daily letters by a private messenger to his distant son. Today our postal system has equalized (or almost so) that opportunity....In this petty sphere we have equalized both opportunity and station. This insignificant example can be multiplied many times; we now enjoy many equalities of opportunity *and* station undreamed of a few generations ago" (p. 15).

To my mind, this is merely a consequence of progress in technology and wealth. A few centuries ago, postal transportation was so expensive that it could not be available to more than a few; today, we have become technologically so efficient that we can handle hundreds of millions of pieces of mail every day at modest expense.

But the very technological progress which removes scarcity in some areas, and with it the need for differential allocation and the question of its justice, opens new, previously undreamed-of possibilities which are, for some time at any rate, just as scarce. What was the case with postal services at the time of Lord Chesterfield is now the case with, say, fine suburban homes in an attractive countryside or with elegant new automobiles. Inequalities in these matters are now bitterly resented. There are also the advances of modern medicine—marvelous but enormously expensive—which cannot, or cannot quickly, be made equally available to all; there is not a sufficient number of highly trained and experienced specialists to give everybody the care which is currently available in only a few outstanding centers. This is a cause of the great indignation of social critics who call it "the shame of American medicine" (Langer, 1966, p.6).

It seems safe to predict that when there is a sufficient number of highly skilled professionals and a sufficient supply of modern gadgetry, there will be new inventions requiring even greater skill and more sophisticated machinery which, for some time at least, will be available only to a minority; and that will probably be considered an even greater shame. The issue continuously recurs on a higher level; technological progress and growing wealth create new inequalities as fast as they remove old ones.

The question of just distribution becomes an issue only where goods or benefits are scarce. But scarcity is an unpleasant predicament; thus Professor Morris refers to my example of the parents who can either send three normal children to college *or* provide for one retarded child such remedial training as may keep it out of institutions, and comments that "these agonized parents cannot act justly." Just distribution, for Professor Morris, is apparently possible only where the supply is sufficiently plentiful so that everyone can get what we would like him to have. To my mind, the question of justice does not even arise in these happy circumstances.

Professor Morris finds me "more than just negatively complacent." This interpretation of my motivation and attitude is based on an insufficient familiarity with the facts. As an immigrant from Europe and, in particular, a refugee, I have looked more closely into the abyss of human privation and degradation than have most native Americans. It is precisely *because* I know what human destiny can be like, and *because* I know how fragile is the modicum of civilization that we enjoy, that I am alarmed by the present tidal wave of militant utopianism which is daily weakening, and may well destroy, a society which, while certainly far from perfect in terms of the Sermon from the Mount, is yet the most humane the world has so far known. Once people expect from the institutional setup not merely a guarantee of life, liberty, and the pursuit of happiness and "a *passable* accomodation between the vital and self-conscious interests of society" but the creation of a "just society," things seem to me to be headed for disaster, because a state of affairs which is acknowledged as just by all is not possible and the constant stimulation of hopes which must remain unfulfilled can only be explosive.

CHAPTER 36

Conflict and Violence

(1966)

Wars—external and internal—have been fought as a means to an end or as an end in themselves—for bringing about or maintaining a favorable order or things or for the sake of fighting. In practice we should expect both ingredients to be mixed in varying proportions.

The second attitude can be found, for instance, in India before the Moslem conquest. Fighting was the professional duty—the *dharma*—of a warrior caste, and only by properly fulfilling the duty of his caste could the Hindu hope for a more favorable reincarnation.

This kind of motivation seems to have little importance in modern times. There may still be professional officers who look upon war as an opportunity to enjoy the thrills of command and adventure and as a chance of extraordinary advancement, but this does not seem to have been a significant factor in the causation of wars in this century.

Large-scale group violence in modern times has essentially been the outgrowth of conflicts over *issues*. As Thomas Hobbes (1651) said:

> If any two men desire the same thing which nevertheless they cannot both enjoy, they become enemies; and on the way to their end (which is principally their own conservation and sometimes their delectation only) endeavor to destroy or subdue one another.

Reprinted from *Bulletin of the Menninger Clinic*, 30:267-274, 1966.

The recognition that human conflict is rooted in the diversity of human purposes and in the fact that these purposes are sometimes difficult to reconcile and at times outright irreconcilable, does not mean that all conflicts must inevitably lead to violence. In fact, only a small minority does.

This is due to the fact that action depends not only on impulse but on the relation between impulse and inhibitory forces. While it is true that the pursuit of one's purposes tends to lead to violence wherever it meets with opposition, it is equally true that there are also effective restraints. They can be classified under the headings of *Love, Fear,* and *Morality.*

We may refrain from violence because, divergent interests notwithstanding, we have some *positive feelings* toward our adversary and do not wish to hurt him, or to hurt him too much. This is of great importance in the relations within the family and between friends but of lesser importance in group relations.

Or, we may refrain from violence because we are *afraid* of undesirable consequences for ourselves through retaliation or third-part intervention or, on the most sophisticated level, because we believe that there are undesirable long-term consequences of violence even where it is immediately successful.

Finally, we may refrain from violence because we consider it as *evil.*

The probability of conflict leading to violence depends both on the intensity of the desires and the strength of the inhibitions. That in turn depends, *inter alia,* on the *nature of the issue* at stake.

Before entering into this discussion, however, a brief view may be taken of the theories which have been popular in modern times.

Popular Modern Beliefs

During the 18th century, the theory had gained wide ascendency that wars were due to dynastic rivalries over matters in which the people had no stake. Wars, therefore, would disappear once the monarchic system had been abolished. Thus, Immanuel Kant proposed in his treatise "On Perpetual Peace"

(1796) that the first Article of an international Covenant should stipulate that "the constitution in every nation is to be republican." The underlying assumption was that republics would be peaceful by nature.

This theory lost prestige when the decline of monarchical power was not accompanied by a simultaneous decline of war; wars fought by democracies seem to grow even more fierce. But the theory still had enough hold on political thinking at the end of World War I to make President Wilson demand, as a prerequisite for mediating an armistice which the Central Powers had requested, that the power over war and peace be transferred from the German Kaiser to the German people.

The theory was gradually replaced by a theory according to which the causes of wars were "economic."[1] This theory reigned for some time almost without challenge. In the 1930s, for instance, it was widely believed in America and England that wars could be avoided by "taking the profits out of war," i.e., by nationalizing the munitions industry.

Historical scholarship has supplied little evidence to support the economic doctrine of war. The report on the results of a fifteen-year study of war by a group headed by Quincy Wright (1942) contained little about economic causes of war. In a subsequent political science meeting, Wright replied to a questioner that his group had found little evidence of them and such economics as there were, were bad economics, i.e., that they were not real economic interests but misconceptions about economic interest and thus, in effect, noneconomic factors causing a distorted view of economic interest.

Part of this study was an investigation of the role of foreign investment in the causation of war by Eugene Staley (1935). Contrary to the views advanced by C. K. Hobson and V. I. Lenin who saw imperialist expansion as the outgrowth of the capitalist search for profits abroad, made necessary by the decline of domestic profits presumed by Marxist theory, Staley

---

[1] "Economic determinism" means something entirely different on the starvation level from what it means on levels of higher prosperity. On the starvation level, it merely means that those who do not survive do not make history; on higher levels, it means that greed has always precedence over all other human motives—a highly questionable proposition.

arrived at the conclusion that foreign investments "have been considerably more useful as an aid to navies than navies have been as an aid and protection to foreign investment." And: "Private investments seeking purely business advantages have rarely of themselves brought great Powers into serious political clashes."

Thus, in cases like the Russo-Japanese War (1905) or the Italian conquest of Libya (1912), it was not that capitalists had been attracted by prospects of high returns from investments abroad and that military force was called in to support them, but rather that politicians had embarked on projects of conquest **for strategic reasons or for reasons of prestige, and had used** business as a cover. In some instances, as in the Libyan case, they had to overcome considerable business reluctance by offering substantial inducements for business cooperation.

It was all reminiscent of what the last German Kaiser once said to a group of German business school graduates about to go to the German colonies: "The German merchant should everywhere drive a nail into the wall on which we can hang our good German sword."

Many later studies have led to similar conclusions. In a recent study of U.S. intervention in the Caribbean, Dana G. Munro (1964) finds no evidence to support the generally accepted view that interventions in Cuba, Panama, San Domingo, Nicaragua, and Haiti had been motivated by private economic interest and ample evidence that they had been dictated by considerations of security.

This result is only what we should have expected. Economic prizes, as Raymond Aron (1962) has pointed out, can be divided while some others cannot. Moreover, it is characteristic for economics that everything has its price; and the most critical conflicts concern goods which men deem priceless.

The Critical Issues

It seems to me that historical experience as well as psychological considerations suggest that there are crucial issues which have a particularly high potential of violence. These are the issues which defy calculations of risks and costs, issues which by their very nature tend to be *nonnegotiable*, goods which escape the calculation of costs because they are considered to be *priceless*. They are the issues involving *self-preservation, narcissism,* and *moral principles.*

(a) *Self-preservation,* with most people, has priority among all needs and aspirations. Hardly any price is too high when life is in jeopardy. For the sake of life men will consent to the amputation of limbs or forego their earthly possessions. As a rule, object relations are withdrawn and superego structures abandoned in extreme danger and men regress to an exclusively self-centered existence. There are some individuals, though, who maintain their object relations and their moral allegiances throughout all dangers and tribulations; but their number is small. We worship them as heroes or saints.

The term self-preservation is often used in a larger, or figurative sense referring to a threat not to physical existence but to the continuous enjoyment of the amenities of life to which one has grown accustomed. Properly speaking, this is not a matter of self-preservation; but is often so conceived psychologically because, as civilization advances, the level of what is taken for granted as minimum necessities of life rises, and men guide their actions by an ever wider anticipation of the future so that remote threats elicit the same response as immediate threats do under more primitive conditions.

(b) *Collective narcissism.* Next to life itself and the necessities of physical survival, status or prestige loom large among human aspirations. To some people and in some cultures they appear even more important than life itself as is expressed in the often quoted words of Juvenal:

> Deem it the worst of sins to prefer mere breathing to honor
> And for the sake of life to lose the reasons for living.
>
> [*Satires,* VIII, 83]

Prestige plays an even greater role in group conflict than in individual conflict since collective narcissism is one of the factors that makes for group cohesion so that a narcissistic blow may lead to group disintegration.

Diplomats have always known that prestige is a highly

sensitive point in international relations. Disraeli, as British Prime Minister, brought back from the Berlin Congress (1878) "peace with honor"; the obvious implication was that had there been no honor, there would have been no peace.

After the defeat of the Hungarian Revolution (1849) the Hungarian leaders, Lajos Kossuth and General Bem, fled into Turkey; Austria and Russia demanded their extradition. The Sultan, though of course out of sympathy with revolutionaries, felt that his honor did not permit him to deliver to the hangman unarmed fugitives who had placed themselves under his protection. He was supported by England and France.

The situation was critical: the Russian army demanded the head of Bem who was a Russian subject. Alexis de Tocqueville (1893), then French Foreign Minister, instructed the French Ambassadors in Vienna and St. Petersburg in these words: "Take up your business gently, be *careful not to set our adversary's self-esteem against us*" (italics added). Similarly, the Sultan's special emissary to the Czar was careful not to call on the representatives of England and France and "refused to see anybody before his audience with the Tsar to whose free will alone, he said, he looked for the success of his mission."

Conversely, when Bismarck wanted war with France (1870), he edited a news item in such a way as to make it appear that the Ambassador of France had been insulted by the King of Prussia.

In our time, President Kennedy showed himself well aware of the perils of this issue during the Cuban missile crisis. While insisting on what he considered necessary for American security, he was careful to avoid, as far as possible, any appearance of Russian humiliation; when Khrushchev announced the withdrawal of the missiles from Cuba, Kennedy congratulated him on an act of "statesmanship."

A sharp contrast to this can be found in the attitude of contemporary Chinese leaders. If repeated reports can be trusted, the Chinese have rebuked Russian advice to let the Americans "off the hook" in Vietnam; in any case, they have publicly *accused* the Russians of trying to find a dignified way out for the United States.

Loss of face is a symbolic castration and exposure in this condition to public ridicule. At the same time, there is a close relationship in many animal societies between phallic strength and the position in the order of dominance. The previously dominant stag who has lost his antler sinks to the bottom of the hierarchy. Conversely, subjection to another's will is conceived as emasculation. "Half a man's manhood takes the far seeing Zeus away when the day of servitude dawns," says Homer (*Odyssey*, 17, 322ff.), and similar views have been expressed in modern times with regard to colonialism. "I am no man and you are the man instead if you can score this victory unpunished," says Creon to the defiant Antigone in Sophocles' drama.

Prestige is the reputation for victory. Loss of prestige may therefore embolden all enemies and dishearten and demoralize all friends and so bring about a radical change in the power relations. Eventually it may lead to a situation in which a nation ceases to be master of its own destiny, becomes dependent on the goodwill of others, and may even fall under foreign domination altogether.

The latter may in some instances mean a direct threat to physical survival as was the case with the people of Poland and Russia under Nazi occupation. Where this is not the case, where the victor behaves with forebearance or even with benevolence it is still subjection to an alien will.

What we see in later history may only be a modification and symbolic representation of what was actually practiced in primeval times. Perhaps the original fate of the vanquished was death or emasculation for men, rape for women. Emasculation may have been carried out literally through castration, or symbolically by blinding or enforced celibacy—both widely practiced in Byzantium—or, milder still, through enslavement.

In the English-speaking countries, and more particularly in the United States, concern for honor is much weaker than in countries with feudal and military traditions. This attitude has roots in the traditions of both the Right and the Left. The ideology of the Right is business and the salesman can have no pride; the ideology of the Left is evangelical and the evangelist recommends offering the other cheek. Two world wars and the fear of a third, far more destructive one, have reinforced these native tendencies.

But while the American people are thus inclined to disregard

insults, they can no more than other people be indifferent to the
threat to freedom and self-determination which may be at the
end of the road if its international position disintegrates. The
disregarding of minor insults may therefore make it more likely
that one will have to face major challenges.

(c) *Moral issues.* The demand of the superego is—not always, to be sure, but often—a "categorical imperative." Conflicts due to divergent moral principles are therefore not subject
to genuine compromise. This fact has given the Wars of Religion
and their contemporary analogue, the wars of conflicting ideologies, their particular intractability and viciousness: it used to be
said that there is no hatred like *odium theologicum.* We may not
be able to make Right prevail at a particular moment, but as
long as we consider it the Right, we cannot look upon compromises as more than temporary expedients.

Superego demands are a major factor of war not only in the
direct sense of a clash of conflicting moral concepts but also
indirectly by making otherwise viable solutions impossible.

From the point of view of military security, the United States
may have had reason to welcome a certain amount of Japanese
expansion at the expense of China in the 1930s. Japan was an
island empire off the Continent of Asia much as England was an
island empire off the Continent of Europe. Just as England had
effectively sealed off the Continent of Europe for a century, to
the benefit of American security, so Japan might have done with
the Continent of Asia; and Japan did not have sufficient power
of her own to become herself a serious threat to the American
Hemisphere. American interest, purely militarily conceived,
might thus have been best served by an alliance with Japan and
war might have been avoided. But a policy of condoning the
subjugation of parts of China was morally unacceptable for the
American people; the United States was forced by moral sentiment to oppose Japanese expansion and war resulted.

Similarly, from the point of view of mere *Realpolitik*, an
accomodation and even an alliance with the United States would
probably be in the interest of the Soviet Union today, in view of
the growing menace of Chinese expansionism. But, for the time
being at least, this road is blocked for the Soviet leaders by their
moral principles. They cannot align themselves with the arch
"capitalist" power against a "socialist" nation.

The historian, Elie Halévy, said once: "Idealism makes wars and revolutions." At the least, the dedication to ideals not universally shared stands in the way of otherwise possible peaceful accommodations of conflicting interests.

In summary: The most critical issues seem to be those which imply threats of death, of castration, or of moral death—or their latter day modifications and symbolic representations.

CHAPTER 37

Adaptational View
Ignores "Drive"

(1966)

Adaptational psychodynamics is a doctrine of radical rationalism and environmentalism, that eliminates the inner frontier.

Kardiner et al. aimed at examining psychoanalytic methodology and appraising "the reasoning and the operational devices used by Freud to explain his clinical observations." They attempt "to make clear which of Freud's concepts are acceptable to us today." Unfortunately, it is *not* clear what is meant by "us": Do the authors include only themselves and like-minded persons, or do they claim to be the spokesmen of some alleged consensus of the scientific community?

Psychoanalytic theories and propositions are not all equally important for the system; some are central, others are peripheral. I have previously (Ch. 15) distinguished several levels: clinical data, clinical interpretations, clinical generalizations, clinical theory, and metapsychology. The latter is a more or less speculative superstructure—the Witch Metapsychology, as Freud (1937a) once called it.

This paper is an invited discussion of a paper on "A Methodological Study of Freudian Theory" by Abram Kardiner, Aaron Karush, and Lionel Ovesey (1966), which the authors summarize: "The usefulness of Freud's constructions is impaired by placing them within an instinctual and energic frame of reference. Psychoanalysis must be purged of assumptions which are not founded upon recognizable data. This leaves an imposing body of creative theory that has demonstrated its vitality and usefulness over and over again." Reprinted from *International Journal of Psychiatry*, 2:569-575, 1966.

606

Some of the current criticism is directed against central positions of psychoanalysis, some at peripheral points. The latter is the case, for instance, in the attack against the concept of psychic energy. There must be many so-called "orthodox" analysts in whose writings one will search for the term in vain. I am among them.

As I see it, there is clearly an economic aspect to psychic phenomena. Men cannot love more than a few objects—"he who claims to love all things has no notion of what is involved in loving just one," as Jean Rostand (1962) put it. Men absorbed by inner conflict or the work of mourning may have little interest in, or ability to deal with, other matters; there is displacement from one object or aim to another, etc. But it does not follow that these and similar phenomena should best be seen in terms of the distribution of one quantity called psychic energy. We cannot measure it, we have no reliable criteria to estimate it, and we do not know the factors that would determine its total amount. Above all, as there is no evidence for it beyond the very phenomena which necessitated its invention, its explanatory value is questionable. It is somewhat like explaining a fact by postulating a faculty, and is in this sense tautological. This will remain so unless or until independent ways for corroborating the hypothesis have been found. In the meantime, there is a limited role for it as a prop for the imagination.

But this is peripheral to the cause of psychoanalysis; all important psychoanalytic propositions can be formulated without committing oneself to any particular theory about the economic aspect.[1] It is a question on the frontier of psychoanalytic theory. When Freud, in a letter to Otto Rank (1924), reiterated his well-known position that people must have a common basis if they are to work together but need not agree on all points, he listed among the nonessential propositions the division of the mind into an ego and an id (see Taft, 1958). How much more this would apply to the concept of psychic energy.

I shall now concentrate on the main positions of the authors and try to follow these ideas down to what seem to me to be their ideological roots. These, I fear, are what make their main positions inaccessible to argument.

[1] I have tried to do so in my *Basic Theory of Psychoanalysis* (1960a).

The Crucial Issue

Kardiner et al. claim that "Freudian theory . . . attributes all social behavior to instinctual forces." Thus, in their eyes, psychoanalysis assumes that "cultural differences would have little impact on the development of the human personality." The authors go on to state that their observations "will be derived from an adaptational frame of reference rather than the Freudian instinctual one."

But the authors' image of Freudian theory is grossly distorted, and their dichotomy—instinctual versus adaptational framework—is a false dichotomy. Instinctual drives may be juxtaposed with habit, purposive action, or moral demand; adaptation may be juxtaposed with maladaptation or nonadaptation. But "adaptational" is not a genuine alternative to "drive-propelled."

In assuming this juxtaposition, the writers seem to imply that a psychological theory can *either* mirror the fact of adaptation, *or* the working of instinctual drives, but cannot do both. It is like saying that actions of a government must be explained either in terms of foreign policy or in terms of domestic policy, and that these perspectives are irreconcilable. To my mind, they are complementary. This is the very essence of psychoanalytic theory.

I described this situation in Ch. 5. I explained psychoanalytic theory in a kind of model in which the "ego" (purposive action guided by a hierarchy of interests) confronts the "id" (diffuse appetites), the "superego" (various "oughts" rooted in the reflective attitude characteristic of man), and the demands of the outside world operating through reward and punishment. In this complex situation, man tries to serve all masters as far as possible while at the same time trying to gain control of each of them.

What is called "adaptation" has to do with the relation of the organism to the outside world; the phenomena dealt with by theories of instincts and defenses have to do with an internal frontier. Freud, incidentally ascribed *"psychosis"* to a *break in the relations to the outside world*—a failure to adapt, if you will—and ascribed *"neurosis"* to an *inner break:* "Neurosis is the result of a conflict between the ego and its id, whereas psychosis is the analogous outcome of a similar disturbance in the relations between the ego and the external world" (1924a, p. 149).

Adaptational psychodynamics proposes that everything *hinges on the relation of man to the outside world, its challenges and his responses.* Thus, differences of behavior between males and females "can be explained as adaptational responses to environment without recourse to inherited dispositions." (*Does that also apply to the different tractability of boys and girls from earliest infancy on, of which mothers of both can tell a story?*) Castration fear of boys is solely due to intimidation. (*But why do boys in the phallic stage react to the observation of the female genitals or to trivial dangers as though they were castration threats?*) Penis envy of little girls is due to "the privileges of greater freedom in play and assertion given to the boy in our society." (*But what about the reaction of very small girls who have not yet learned of these privileges at their first observation of difference in sex?*)

Furthermore, sadism "is an adaptive response to a danger situation." (*But where does the sexual pleasure come from? And why does the pleasure tend to get stale with many repetitions so that ever stronger stimuli are required?*) The obsolescence of gratifications through repetition and the need for ever new stimulants are not characteristic of security. Masochism is due either to an indoctrination which stresses that "sex is dirty, shameful and degrading," or to the self-infliction of a token amount of the dreaded punishment, or to the denial of one's own aggression. (*But once again, in any one of these alleged three types, whence comes the sexual pleasure? And why do these pleasures get stale so that more refined stimuli are required?*)

In a similar vein, all opposition to sexuality is due to cultural prohibitions; "sexual impulses are not inherently dangerous." (*But how did sexually oppressive cultures come into being in the first place?*) All aggression and destructiveness are adaptive; its "ultimate aim is to achieve security. It is never destructiveness alone, as an end in itself." (*How can the authors be so sure that even such extreme acts as the denucleization of the eyes by a psychotic or self-immolation as a means of political pressure will fall under this formula?*)

Thus, the vast variety of life is explained exclusively in terms of adaptation to the environment, i.e., "responses of an organism which enhance its chances for health and survival." It is a doctrine of *radical rationalism and environmentalism*.

The situation is exactly the opposite from that prevailing in my youth. Then, psychoanalysis was under heavy attack in medical quarters for allegedly explaining everything "unscientifically," in terms of environmental influences, instead of "scientifically," in terms of organic heredity. We always emphasized that Freud had not neglected the constitutional factor, but we met with the same kind of skepticism we encounter today when we state that psychoanalysis deals constantly, *in every hour*, with the impact of the environment.

The doctrine of adaptational psychodynamics can be derived from the composite Freudian schema of the personality as hovering between inner and outer challenges, by way of reduction, i.e., by *eliminating the inner frontier*.

This becomes explicit when the authors intimate that the current versions of psychoanalytic theory would be acceptable to them *provided* the theory of instincts is discarded: "We advocate that [the instinctual and energic aspects of Freudian theory] be dropped."

It is interesting to note that exactly the opposite deduction has been made by the school of Melanie Klein. There, life appears to be fully explicable in terms of an inner drama, with little or no reference made to external environment. To my mind, both theories are fragmentations of a more complex reality.

The issue may thus be described as follows:

1. According to adaptational psychodynamics, human behavior can be *completely* explained in terms of responses to external challenges; according to Freudian theory, it must be explained in terms of responses both to external and internal stimuli.

2. According to adaptational psychodynamics, the organism faces the outside world as a unit; in terms of Freudian theory, it faces external reality as a house divided against itself.

3. For adaptational psychodynamics, disease and disturbances of all kinds are due to inappropriate or anachronistic

adaptations. The world is fundamentally *rational*, so that disturbances are due to misfired rationality. According to Freudian theory, this is just one aspect of reality; there is also genuine irrationality.

In a speech reviewing her career Anna Freud (1964) remarked:

> I was never concerned one-sidedly with either id, ego, or superego, but always with the interactions between them . . . the attempts of the rational personality to deal with the irrational [p. 514f.].

Psychoanalysis offers neither a purely rational nor a purely irrational view of life, but sees it as a complex of interactions between drives and purposes.

In another field and another frame of reference, the historian Friedrich Meinecke (1962) expressed a similar idea: "The history of the world is . . . a continuous struggle between sense and senselessness, always waged and never finally decided. . . ."[2]

The viewpoint represented by the school of adaptational psychodynamics is also an *evolutionist*, Darwinian, viewpoint; for in the perspective of evolutionist theory, genuine irrationality in behavior would be eliminated in short order by the pressures of selection.[3]

I am inclined to think this viewpoint correct for the animal kingdom, at least as far as wild animals are concerned. For them, evolutionist pressures are relentless and organisms equipped with characteristics unfavorable to survival are likely to be eliminated. Expressed in psychoanalytic terms, the reality principle reigns supreme.

Man, however, has a far greater margin of survival and he can afford the luxury of teleologically unfavorable characteristics. He can afford unadjusted and unadjustable drives, and prolonged parental care for the young permits the pleasure principle to become firmly entrenched.

Without the theory of evolution, theorists of adaptation

[2] Letter to Siegfried A. Kaehler, August 17, 1934.

[3] Thus, a prominent student of animal behavior explains aggression in terms of its survival value (Lorenz, 1964).

would have to face the argument that their concept is teleological, like Aristotle's *entelechy* or the medieval *vis medicatrix naturae*. Kardiner et al. give Freud credit for having "laid the basis for an adaptational theory of ego functions" but castigate him for what they deem his insistence "that the ultimate explanation be energic." They apparently do not realize that Freud's reluctance to admit adaptation as an ultimate explanatory frame of reference was due to the teleological character of the concept and his feeling that teleological concepts have no place in ultimate theory. The following words of Dr. William Welch in his Presidential Address before the Congress of American Physicians and Surgeons (1897) are characteristic of the scientific ethos of the age: "The teleological concept of a useful purpose in no case affords an explanation of the mechanism of an adaptive process."

The climate of opinion has meanwhile changed in some quarters, but the argument cannot be dismissed out of hand.

Ideological Implications

The truth is that medicine, professedly founded on observations, is as sensitive to outside influences, political, religious, philosophical, imaginative, as the barometer to the changes of atmospheric density.

— OLIVER WENDELL HOLMES

Adaptational psychodynamics appears as a doctrine of extreme environmentalism, which implies the native equality and virtually unlimited environmental malleability of man.

This doctrine is advanced ostensibly on the ground that other assumptions such as sexual constitution or inherent destructiveness are "unprovable." This is true if the criterion of proof is taken to be the classical experiment in which all relevant factors can be altered at will. But given this criterion, the doctrine of integral environmentalism is equally unprovable.

It is a standing feature of ideological debate that proponents of a thesis try to establish their case in an area of ambiguity (and which area in human and social affairs is free of ambiguity?) by shifting the burden of proof to the other side: unless you can exactly prove your thesis, you must accept mine. The argument could, of course, be turned around with equal justification (or lack of it).

The appearance of this kind of reasoning is a pretty good indication that we are walking on ideological ground.

We are living in an age of great ideological passions; they have taken the place of the religious passions of old. While religious emotions were attached to supernatural concepts, i.e., matters of Eternity, the modern ideological passions are dedicated to secular propositions. The former dealt with the Kingdom of God in Heaven, the latter deal with the coming Kingdom of Man here on earth. But these differences notwithstanding, they are both dedicated to propositions which have no adequate basis in experience but which are firmly rooted in fantasy and in what William James called the "will to believe."

The most powerful ideology of modern times is based on two assumptions which are rarely verbalized because they are taken for granted: (1) All human ills are due to the frustration of desires (or so-called "needs") which could be cured through the satisfaction of these desires; (2) universal satisfaction is possible in an appropriately organized society.

The first assumption is a half-truth, derived from the profound truth that "lack of fulfillment is at the root of much organic as well as of mental disease" (Dubos, 1965b, p. 425), and of many other ills as well.

But fulfillment is not the same as satisfaction of desires, since it contains ego and superego satisfactions predicated on the frustrations of some id desires.

The second assumption stems from the 18th-century doctrine of the providential harmony of all nature (though few of its contemporary believers are aware of this ancestry).

Both assumptions together amount to a belief in the infinite perfectability of the estate of man through appropriate environmental manipulation.

All those parts of psychoanalytic theory which run against one or the other of these assumptions as do concepts of sexual constitution, inborn bisexuality, conflicting drives in general; inherent antagonism of the ego toward id drives regardless of possible external consequences, genuine aggressiveness not reducible to concern for security, great constitutional differences between individuals—in short, all propositions which would *set limits to the environmental malleability of man*—must be odious to all who are engulfed by this all-pervasive modern philosophy.

It so happens that they are the very propositions which Kardiner, Karush, and Ovesey find unacceptable.

The prominent prehistorian Piggot (1965) stated:

There seems to be a prevalent reluctance to admit that many characteristics of man which conflict with our current views of good and bad behavior may well be as indelible a part of his natural make-up as those we regard as desirable. The myth of the Noble Savage as restated in different terms—violence and hatred, aggression and brutality . . . are often regarded as unfortunate deviations from the assumed norm of socially . . . acceptable behavior, natural to man when not exposed to corrupting forces . . . some have found it necessary to assume a Fall from original goodness, while others depend on optimistic views of the natural nobility of man as a basis for doctrines of ultimate perfectibility within an appropriate political system [p. 14].

"Man," said Bertrand de Jouvenel (1957), "is no great inventor of ideas. The good ones are far from new and the bad ones are no less antiquated" (p. 199). Thus, it should surprise none that this debate was already waged, with basically similar arguments, in ancient Greece. One Phaleas advanced the environmentalist theory: he thought that crime could be forestalled by equal distribution of property. Against this proposition, Aristotle argued:

Men do wrong not only for the sake of bare necessities . . . but also in order to enjoy the things which they desire.

. . . The greatest wrongs are done for the sake of superfluities, not of necessities. . . .

The depravity of men is inexhaustible. At first one wants two obols only. But one that has an established custom, people always want more and so they go on without limit. For it is in the nature of desire to have no limits, and it is for the satisfaction of desire that most people live [*Politics*, 1267, a,b,].

What, according to Aristotle, stands in the way of a purely environmental explanation and a purely environmental cure of crime is *hē tēs epithymias physis*—the nature of desire. Or, as we may also translate it, the nature of drive.

In a nutshell, this is also the point that distinguishes Freudian psychoanalysis from adaptational psychodynamics.

CHAPTER 38

Conflicts of Values
and Moral Dilemmas

(1967)

The German philosopher Arthur Schopenhauer said once that "truth is a brief holiday between two long and dreary seasons during the first of which it was condemned as sophistry and during the second ignored as commonplace."

Schopenhauer has the reputation of having been a pessimist, but in this statement at least I cannot find much pessimism because he does think that every truth has its day in the light—even though it be short—a day in which it is recognized as at once novel and important.

But there seem to be truths which do not get this chance; they are considered as sophistry and as platitudinous at the same time and often enough by the same people.

That may seem impossible; for how could a statement be too obvious to merit saying and yet be inacceptable at the same time?

The paradox is more apparent than real. What happens is that a statement is considered to be platitudinous as long as it is formulated in abstract terms and appears as outrageous once it is applied to concrete cases. Men view *practical situations* according to their needs as *living beings*, and view *general propositions* according to their needs as *thinking beings;* and they keep these areas separate as long as possible.

Based on an address before the Assembly, Pennsylvania Bar Association, delivered on January 20, 1967 at Philadelphia. Reprinted from *Pennsylvania Bar Association Quarterly,* 38:410-426, 1967.

The thesis of this article belongs in this class. It is rather obvious when formulated in general terms, but its application to concrete situations may seem offensive to many. The proposition, in short, is this: Men value a variety of things which are not always mutually reconcilable. Sometimes, one aspiration conflicts with another one so that it can be fulfilled only at a price in terms of the other. Total human fulfillment is therefore impossible not only on account of obstacles due to nature or to the intersection of human wills but also on account of inherent contradictions in man's aspirations.

Among human aspirations are, for instance, liberty, equality, justice, quality of achievement, progress, security, and peace. Any two of them may at times interfere with each other so that the advance of one goes at the expense of the other.

Justice and Peace

Justice is itself not a clearly defined goal because justice refers to the adjustment of various interests to which different people may give different weight so that one man's justice may be another man's outrage.

But in whatever terms justice may be conceived, it may conflict with the ideal of peace. There is hardly any definition of justice according to which the existing world would appear as perfectly just all the time; there is always injustice. Hence, if we "stand for the Right as God gives us to see the Right," we have to take action against injustice; and that may give offense to the unjust. The promotion of justice may thus imperil peace and the promotion of peace may require the toleration of injustice and sometimes even active cooperation with it.

In this issue as in many others, each one of the competing political camps applies different moral principles according to the case at issue. In the dilemma between the enforcement of justice and the preservation of peace, the political Right is inclined to give priority to the former in foreign affairs, and to the latter in domestic ones; thus, it may advocate taking an unequivocal stand in the defense of the rights of nations conquered by Communist powers (like Hungary or Eastern Germany), regardless of the perils to peace that such a course may entail, but it cautions against, say, civil rights legislation at home which may alienate certain regions and a substantial body of white citizens in other parts of the country and so imperil domestic peace.

The Left, on the other hand, does just the opposite. It advocates the pursuit of what it conceives as justice in domestic affairs, regardless of consequences, but it is opposed to the application of such principles in foreign affairs in areas in which this may embroil the country in conflict with Communist Powers and gives priority in these cases to the preservation of peace.

Liberty and Equality

In Tocqueville's days, equality merely meant that there should be no legal privileges of birth, that all occupations should be open to everybody, and that social mobility should permit the rise of individuals from the lower to the higher echelons. Equality so conceived does not conflict with liberty; it is an aspect of it. But once equality is meant to apply not only to accessibility—which is often theoretical since the concrete chances are unequal and extremely difficult to equalize—but to actual station in life, a conflict with liberty is about to make itself felt. For men differ in their natural endowment—a fact too obvious for denial in organic characteristics such as longevity and congenital illnesses but stubbornly denied in matters of the mind—and the different environmental influences in the early, most impressionable years of life may create further differences; and wherever men are left to themselves, a pecking order, a hierarchy, quickly emerges. Equality can then be established and maintained only by outside interference which prevents the stronger ones from taking advantage of their possibilities.

After the defeat of Nazi Germany, the wretched survivors of the concentration camp of Bergen-Belsen were given permission to stay in the barracks until they could find a place to go. Thus, the liberated concentration camp was for some time peopled by former inmates turned into unemployed roomers. Some of them began trading in the surrounding communities. After a few months, some of the survivors who were alert and resourceful had become relatively rich; what had only recently been a mass of helpless victims, nearly equalized in misery, became an economically highly stratified group. This result could have been prevented or corrected only by outside interference which would have curtailed the liberty of an enterprising minority.

The clash between liberty and equality can be seen daily. A college newspaper which recently came to my attention carried a letter from the mother of a freshman student who had not been pledged by any fraternity. She protested against fraternities as creating a privileged group of insiders and an underprivileged group of outsiders, and thus offensive to the ideal of equality. A member from the interfraternities council replied that fraternities were voluntary associations of students who wished to live together, and that students should be free to choose their associates. One spoke for equality, the other for liberty, and the two goals are sometimes irreconcilable.

The attempt to institute economic and social equality on the largest scale in Russia or China has involved vast interference with individual liberty.

Liberty and Peace

The requirements of individual liberty may also conflict with the pursuit of peace.

When Stalin's daughter appeared at the American Embassy in New Delhi and asked for asylum in the United States, opinion on this matter was divided. Some people thought that she should be discouraged from coming to this country because they feared that her presence and activities, magnified by the inevitable publicity adhering to her name, might adversely affect current efforts to improve the climate between the United States and the Soviet Union—efforts recently reinforced by the hope that the Soviet Union might exercise a moderating influence in North Vietnam. Others felt that the only policy consistent with the traditions of a free country was to allow her to come here if she so wished and to enjoy such public attention as she may desire and be able to secure.

The Indian government, apparently, had taken the first view

as far as their country was concerned and had advised Svetlana Alleluyeva to move on.

Conflicts of this kind appear whenever the activities of an individual may give offense to a foreign government, or when public utterances of an individual may involve the prestige of a foreign power or otherwise jeopardize delicate international negotiations, and in other similar cases.

We see here on the one hand those who would give free reign to liberty even though this might jeopardize the quest for peace; and on the other hand those who will pursue the cause of peace even though this may mean a curtailment of some individuals' liberty of expression.

Equality and Quality

The quality of performance varies greatly between people; there is the usual distribution curve, with a broad area of mediocre performance and minorities on both ends. The striving for higher quality may conflict with the promotion of equality.

This is clearly the case when equality is conceived as equality of actual conditions because it is easier to stunt the growth of some than greatly to raise the level of achievement of the many. It is easier to level downward than upward, easier to thwart and inhibit than to uplift and create.

But it is also the case if equality is interpreted not as actual equality of performance but merely as a state of affairs in which everybody is provided with whatever he may need for the optimal realization of his potential; the conditions which are apt to insure a better average, or to stimulate the development of those on the lower levels, are not the same as would provide the best chance of development for the minority of the most gifted.

After the setting up of the comprehensive high school in this country at the beginning of this century, the level of achievement of American high school graduates was distinctly lower than the level of achievement of the graduates of a German or Austrian gymnasium or a French lycée which educated only a small minority. In the 1920s a diploma from a gymnasium or lycée was generally considered as the equivalent of two years of American college.

In the last few years, since Sputnik, things have changed in many places in this country and standards have been raised spectacularly. The price is new inequalities. Advanced placement classes have been set up within the "comprehensive" high school. College admissions have become extremely discriminatory and the graduating high school students are distributed among colleges of vastly different educational standing and prestige, thus establishing among the youths a hierarchy, as stratified as the bureaucracy of ancient China.

We are, of course, in this as in many other instances pursuing contradictory goals at the same time; driving relentlessly toward equality with one hand while creating new inequalities with the other.

Furthermore, the democratic insistence that one man is as good as any other man may easily lead—not logically but psychologically—to an attitude that deems one man's thought as good as any other man's thought, and so to extend equality from the metaphysical or moral worth of a person to the actual validity of his intellectual output. Such an attitude is not conducive to the development of clear criteria of quality which is prerequisite to the cultivation of higher quality.

In general it seems that cultures which have emphasized equality have been more successful in the promotion of a good average than in the production of intellectual or cultural elites.

Progress and Security

Progress as it has been understood in modern times, i.e., progress in the mastery of man's environment, is in conflict with security for progress means change while security implies predictability and thus elements of stability.

It is trivial that technological change renders the work of some people expendable; they stand to suffer in their income, their social status, their sense of achievement, and their feeling of being needed. Legislation may conceivably protect them against the loss of income, but it is difficult to see what could protect them against the loss of status in the eyes of others and in their own.

It has been pointed out that technological progress, in the

end, creates more jobs than it abolishes. This is probably true, but it does not mean that those who have lost the latter will be the ones to fill the former. Those whose jobs have become expendable are not always able to acquire the new skills which are now demanded, and if they are, it often involves a change of environment, a loss of status, and at least a temporary impairment of the sense of achievement.

Change, in short, requires new adjustments and the human ability to adjust to new conditions, great though it is, is not unlimited; it markedly declines in advanced age.

Progress and Equality

Progress and equality must interfere with each other because progress is bound to create inequalities. It brings innovations which cannot immediately be made accessible to all.

The automobile is an example of such an innovation. It was, at first, the luxury of a few. In the United States, the most prosperous country, it took a generation until the automobile had become fairly widespread; it took three generations in Europe and it is an open question when—or even whether—it will become equally common in Asia and Africa.

This is not a question of the "socio-economic system." The latter will determine who belongs to the privileged minority but not that there is a privileged minority. We cannot conceive of any socioeconomic system that could have given to every man a motor car right away. That would have required the immediate creation of an enormous industry (including all subsidiary industries and installments such as oil drills and refineries, repair facilities, filling stations, car shelters) and for this there were neither the funds nor the trained manpower available. Even if all that had been available, no responsible government could have allocated it for this purpose since the role which the automobile could play in our lives was still a matter for speculation.

A country may embark on a large program of home building. It is impossible to proceed in such a way that all people will get their homes at the same time; some will get the first ones, others will follow in a year, in two, and so forth for at least a generation.

A new open heart operation is developed. There are hundreds of thousands of Americans for whom such an operation would be advantageous, but they cannot all have it. The inventor cannot operate on more than a limited number of patients; and the number of others skilled in the new technique will grow only slowly. Not everybody can be trained in it—only surgeons are suitable candidates—and the number of those who can do the instructing is very limited and can increase only gradually. For some time, the lifesaving operation remains the privilege of a minority.

Moreover, as the experience of disciples will at first not equal that of the pioneers, their results may, for some time at least, not be equal either so that even the patients who actually receive this treatment may not all be equally well served.

There is no reason to doubt that after a time, the operation will become standard performance, available in every community hospital. But by the time that this will have happened, there will probably be new medical inventions which, for the time being, will be available only to a minority.

The Ambiguity of Justice

As has been mentioned before, the ideal of justice is not without ambiguities of its own. Justice has to do with the adjudication of conflicting claims according to their merits, and these merits may be and more often than not are controversial. A few examples may suffice:

Individual Rights versus the Rights of the Community

The "right" of an individual, i.e., those of his interests which are considered worth supporting, may conflict with the rights of the community, the state.

The terms "community" or "state" are not meant to refer to a kind of superindividual entity as has been maintained by etatists and organicists in political theory but merely as a shortcut

expression for the rights of others including the rights of those
who are not yet able to speak for themselves, and the rights of
the as yet unborn.

There are instances in which the actions of individuals in
exercising their "rights"—i.e., in the pursuit of interests considered as legitimate—do not interfere with "rights" of others.
That is the case whenever the consequences of our actions do not
reach beyond a "private sphere": for instance, the worship of
Deity after one's own fashion in the privacy of one's home as
long as it does not entail unacceptable practices like human
sacrifice. But once the consequences of one's actions extend
beyond this private sphere, the exercise of his right by one person
implies the obligation of other persons to put up with the
mischief that may result for them.

An example that was mentioned earlier in the context of the
possible contradictions between liberty and peace falls in this
category. If we uphold the "right" of a refugee to speak freely
and to seek such publicity as he or she may be able to get, the rest
of the people must needs accept the untoward consequences that
may accrue to them from a worsening of their country's
international relations.

As is usually the case, each side in the political arena applies
different standards in different cases, upholding the rights of the
individual in some instances and the rights of the collective in
others.

In general, the political Right stands for the rights of the
community in matters of foreign policy; the citizen has to submit
to military service and has to accept the personal sacrifices which
the promotion of the national interest (as interpreted by the
government) requires; "politics" has to stop at the waterfront
and people have to close ranks in the case of war or national
emergency.

At the same time, the Right upholds in economic matters the
rights of the individual. He may manage his property and
conduct his business as he sees fit; the community should not
interfere with him.

The political Left does just the opposite. It maintains that in
economic matters individual interests have to be disregarded
when the interests of the community are believed to be at stake;

at the same time, it gives absolute priority to individual rights over collective interests in matters such as foreign policy and war, and it insists that, in these matters, the citizen's right of "dissent" must be absolute, including the right of active sabotage of government policy.

One case of collision between individual rights and the rights of the community that is now much in the public eye has to do with the role of the police in crime detection.

All political communities define minimum standards of behavior to which individuals are expected to live up. Violations of these standards are called crimes. It is a function of the state to enforce these standards, i.e., to minimize the incidence of crime.

This goal can be pursued in one of two ways: one can either try to establish conditions in which people will never be tempted to commit a crime; or one can set up deterrents which might discourage criminal action.

The first of these approches is based on theories about the causes of crime—usually on the theory that crime is caused by frustrations, in particular by poverty. But these theories are rather tenuous; crimes have been committed by rich people and there are communities of extreme poverty in which crime has been almost nonexistent. This issue was first discussed in ancient Greece; one Phaleas had advanced the theory that crime was caused by poverty; Aristotle criticized the theory and suggested that "the greatest crimes are committed not for the sake of basic necessities but for the sake of superfluities."

Be that as it may—any approach of this kind could yield results, if at all, only over a long period of time; it holds no comfort for those who feel threatened today. In the short run in any case, only deterrence has so far been found workable. That means a criminal law and law enforcement agencies.

But lawbreakers cannot be brought to trial unless they are first apprehended, and since it is extremely rare that culprits turn themselves in voluntarily, it means the need for crime detection.

But that inevitably implies that some people will be inconvenienced in the process, in particular those who have become suspect for one reason or another.

This is especially the case if pressure is being brought to bear to induce suspects to confess. Over vast periods of history the most intense pressures were applied for this purpose in the form of extreme physical and mental tortures; that has still been the case in some parts during our life time. There is no doubt under such pressures countless people confessed to crimes which they never committed. Such procedures are now universally condemned in our climates.

But it is questionable whether entirely without coercion confessions will be forthcoming in more than a few isolated cases; in most instances, some degree of pressure—such as a cross-examination in which the subject becomes entangled in contradictions—may be necessary.

Evidence of a crime can come from three sources—confessions, the testimony of witnesses, and circumstantial evidence— and the elimination of confessions would diminish the number of offenders who can be brought to trial, and so lower the risks of punishment for the lawbreaker and weaken the deterrent capacity of the criminal law.

Every citizen is a potential victim of crime and every citizen is a potential suspect of a crime he has not committed. The interest of the citizen *qua* potential victim requires that crime detection be made as effective as possible; his interest *qua* potential suspect requires that the utmost safeguards be taken against the entrapment of the innocent. Either of these interests can be safeguarded only at a price in terms of the other.

Throughout a great part of history, exclusive emphasis was put on maximum effectiveness of deterrence. The suffering of innocents was accepted as an unavoidable price. Today, we seem to place exclusive emphasis on protecting the interests of the citizen *qua* potential suspect, with little regard for the requirements of effective protection against crime.

It is not my purpose to argue in favor of any particular course of action; I merely want to emphasize that there is a conflict between two human interests which both seem worthy of support. Only if we recognize the existence of a *genuine antinomy* which makes a fully satisfactory solution impossible, can the situation be fruitfully discussed and an arrangement be sought which would minimize human damage without ever eliminating it.[1]

[1] All this is obvious enough, but such is the power of passion that the

To call one set of these conflicting interests "civil rights" and so to give them the character of a categorical imperative and with it the aura of ultimate sanctity is not helpful in the search *for such an optimal solution.* The interests of citizens *qua* potential victims, though not sanctified by a term which currently carries unchallengeable prestige, are just as deserving of protection.

Conflicting Claims

Conflicting claims which are presented with respectable argument are the daily experience of lawyers. I should like to mention a particularly clear example from international life.

Jews have striven for a "national home" in Palestine, the land of the ancient Hebrews. They have legitimized their claims by pointing at the singularly tragic destiny of the Jewish people over a thousand years of European history. Throughout this time Jews have not found more than a temporary haven in other lands; after periods of toleration and, sometimes, prosperity they have time and again encountered relentless hostility on the part of the people in whose midst they were living, leading to dis-

---

discussion of such issues rarely proceeds by a judicious weighing of assets and liabilities of various possible compromises; rather each side emphasizes the requirements of the interest with which it is concerned, without paying much attention to the other interest.

As usual, the side that is pressed against the wall is more ready to concede some right on the part of their opponents while the party which is in triumphant advance—which at the present time means the "liberal" side—is carried along by complete selfrighteousness.

Thus, Mr. Ramsey Clark, United States Attorney General, stated: "Court rules to not cause crimes.... In the long run only the elimination of the cause of crime can make a significant and lasting difference in the incidence of crime." Such a statement is not helpful in the search for an optimal solution; it simply denies the existence of the problem.

The "causation" of crime, as of all human action, has two aspects—impulse and restraint; the outcome depends on the relative strength of impulse and inhibitory factors. Court decisions which make detection more difficult *do not "cause" impulse but diminish the risk* and, with it, the inhibitions.

The last part of the quoted statement could well be used as an argument for altogether abolishing criminal law as essentially irrelevant to the elimination of crime "in the long run."

franchisement, expropriation, exclusion from economic life, massacre, expulsion, and, in our time, even wholesale liquidation. Neither ethnocultural separateness nor assimilation seemed to guarantee security.

Zionists have pointed out that Palestine has never ceased to live in Jewish tradition as the land of hope. They have maintained that the people of the Bible have the right to a place of their own in which they can be themselves, without having to worry whether the kind of people that they are may arouse the disaffection of their neighbors—a right enjoyed by any tribe of cannibals.

Against this claim, the spokesmen of the Palestinian Arabs have simply pointed out that Palestine was populated by Arabs who had lived there all their lives as had their parents and grandparents; they have held to the proposition that all peoples have the right to live in the land of their ancestors, and to live there according to the laws and institutions of their traditions or of their liking. From this point of view, Jewish immigrants were invaders who arrived under the protection of a foreign power and who later maintained themselves by their own military might. Whatever misfortune the Jews had encountered in other lands was not an Arab responsibility.

Chaim Weizmann, the Zionist leader who was instrumental in securing the Balfour Declaration and who became the first President of Israel, stated the issue in these terms: It was true that injustice was done to the Arabs, but there was only a choice between two kinds of injustice; one could either altogether deny a homeland to the Jewish people and leave them to the continuation of their Diaspora existence, to manage as best they could, or force the Arabs who live and enjoy political independence in an area of two million square miles extending from the Atlantic Ocean to the Persian Gulf to relinquish control over 8,000 square miles for the Jewish state; and that between these two injustices the latter was the lesser by far.

Weizmann's conclusion may have embodied the wisdom of a Solomon—it was not inspiring to an age like ours. Social justice is the dominant idea of our time and countless people are prepared to go to any length in promoting it. But it has to be "justice"—or something that can be so presented; the lesser injustice does not move their hearts. Thus, it happened that many people who have been giving the Jewish cause abundant verbal support have turned their eyes in embarrassed silence from the realities and the needs of the state of Israel. They prefer to ease their consciences by periodically castigating the Bonn Republic for still harboring Nazis; that, in any case, is easier and does not involve the necessity of facing the untidiness and the moral complexities of the real world.

Another case of conflicting rights are the rights of the old versus the rights of the young—the right of the *beati possidentes* versus the rights of the have-nots desirous for a place in the sun.

Throughout the 19th century, so-called acquired rights were considered sacrosanct as the following example may illustrate. After a few decades of liberal sentiment, anti-Semitism became rampant again in Austria in the 1880s. To be sure, it was as yet not the paroxysmal anti-Semitism of Hitler, but it was far more than a mere social anti-Semitism manifested in social exclusiveness which had been endemic all along. It was an open hate campaign against the Jews who were held responsible for all and sundry ills and frustration of the people.

The leader of the new movement, Karl Lueger, became Mayor of Vienna in 1897. During his campaign, he had promised that, if elected, he would dismiss all Jewish city employees. This promise he carried out, but he made it his business to find for all discharged employees equivalent employment in private industry. This respect for acquired rights has disappeared in this century. The new attitude began rather spottily with the expropriation of enemy nationals during the First World War, to be consummated to the full in the expropriations and disfranchisements carried out by the Bolshevik Revolution, the Nazi regime, and other revolutionary or counterrevolutionary powers.

As always happens when one set of values is replaced by another set of values, language changed and new words supplanted old ones. Instead of "acquired rights," an expression suggestive of legitimacy and even of sanctity, one began to speak of "vested interests," an expression suggestive of selfishness obstructing the promotion of the common good. The different words refer to the same facts, but they stimulate different sentiments.

Conclusion

Whenever people strive simultaneously toward several goals which interfere with each other so that one can be advanced only at a sacrifice of the other, full satisfaction is impossible. One can only seek an optimal point beyond which the further advance toward either of the two goals would mean an unacceptable price in terms of the other. But that involves some moderation and restraint in the pursuit of any partial goal, no matter how worthy it may appear when viewed in isolation.

Moderation does not carry much prestige in this time. It is looked upon as an ideological device by means of which the privileged try to block, or to slow down, reforms long overdue: or as the counsel of those who lack courage or have grown tired in the struggle with obstacles—as old age impotence masquerading as wisdom.

So of course it *may* be. But moderation may also be the attitude of those who have come to realize that the cosmos of values is necessarily antinomic, that the pursuit of one ideal exacts a price in terms of another so that there is a point of diminishing returns in terms of total human fulfillment. This kind of moderation is not the result of disillusionment but rather the consequence of an appreciation of the complexities of reality.

To my mind, *all* the political and social philosophies of our age—progressivism and traditionalism, individualism and collectivism, populism and elitism, capitalism and socialism, nationalism and internationalism—have a core of defensible interest and respectable doctrine; and all become destructive of life once moderation is discarded and one doctrine is carried to its ultimate conclusion, without regard for interfering values and considerations. As one observer has recently put it: Our age is too rational[2] for sanity.

[2] Perhaps one should better say "rationalistic" because true rationality would take account of these complexities.

It was the essence of classical thinking that tragedy does not stem from any particular interest but from *hubris*—from the *self-righteousness* and the *moral solipsism* to which all people, all classes, all nations, are prone—particularly when opportunity seems favorable.

CHAPTER 39

Psychoanalysis and
Moral Values

(1967)

The question of the relations of psychoanalysis to moral values has three layers or aspects, according to whether we mean by "psychoanalysis" a scientific study of the human mind, a method of therapy, or a philosophy of life, akin to Socratic humanism which many psychoanalysts hold but which does not necessarily follow from psychoanalytic tenets or therapeutic attitudes.

The Scientific Aspect

1. As a science, psychoanalysis is an attempt to find out how things *are*. Of course, as human beings we all have feelings—sometimes passionate feelings—about how things *ought* to be. But as long as we are searching for truth, we should not permit these feelings to influence our judgment of what is.

Transcending our desires in the study of reality is both possible and desirable for a better chance of influencing the course of events, as has long been recognized in medicine.

This paper, dated September 12, 1967, was to have been Dr. Waelder's Position Statement as a panelist on Psychoanalysis and Moral Values at the Fall Meeting of the American Psychoanalytic Association. It was read on March 22, 1968, by Dr. Paul G. Ecker, at the scientific meeting of the Philadelphia Association for Psychoanalysis, to honor the memory of Dr. Waelder, who died on September 28, 1967. Reprinted from *Bulletin of the Philadelphia Association for Psychoanalysis*, 18:25-26, 1968.

Physicians can arrive at a proper assessment of whether a tumor is benign or malignant regardless of whether they like or dislike the patient.

The same separation between "is" and "ought" does not exist in the so-called social sciences which are still largely in the grip of wishful thinking or deliberate manipulation of people. For instance, those who feel that men *should* be equal almost invariably deny or underestimate their actual native inequality; those who feel that men *should* be unequal do just the opposite.

2. The need for transcending our wishes in the study of realities has many aspects; not the least important among them is the postulate that our concepts should be derived from characteristics inherent in the object rather than merely reflecting our preferences. Primitive man, like children, classify the objects around them according to subjective criteria, viz., the relationship these objects have to their wishes. Primitive man may divide animals according to whether they are useful, harmless, or noxious to man. A more sophisticated outlook divided them into protozoa, porifera, coelenterata, etc. This emancipation from egocentricity is part of the reality principle.

Psychoanalysis, particularly psychoanalytic ego psychology, still has concepts loaded with cultural variations (like the "mature" ego). The purge of psychoanalytic theory from such ideological remnants has not yet begun.

3. While the assessment of facts should be independent of our wishes, the choice of the subject to be studied is invariably dependent on our aspirations.

The Therapeutic Aspect

As a therapist, the psychoanalyst will apply his method of treatment through an enlargement of consciousness whenever this seems to offer a good chance of cure or improvement, and will refrain from applying it when it may imperil the patient's welfare. He is not a mere researcher but his actions must be responsible in terms of a desired outcome. The system of values under which he operates is essentially *medical*. It should be kept in mind, however, that this principle gives only a bare outline.

There are cases in medicine in which the morals are controversial (e.g., how much organismic damage can be accepted as a fair price of the cure of a specific condition). Moreover, psychoanalysis itself leads in this respect to questions which would not present themselves in a less exacting study of a patient.

The Philosophical Aspect

Many psychoanalysts, and some patients, hold that the enlargement of consciousness represents a value in itself, regardless of whether or not it is therapeutic. This view is implicit in Freud's famous dictum: Where id was, there ego shall be.

A psychoanalyst so motivated acts neither as a pure scientist nor as a therapist but as a prophet of humanism. This is a function which psychoanalysts may, or may not, find to their taste. In any case, they should be aware of the role they are playing.

CHAPTER 40

Observation, Historical
Reconstruction, and Experiment

An Epistemological Study
(1970)

Clinical and historical disciplines and disciplines engaged in field studies have often been confronted with the request to validate their claims by experiments or by statistically fortified mass studies, and they have been criticized for failing to do so. Compliance with such requests has sometimes been seen as indispensable before the claims of these disciplines can be taken seriously. At times it has even been seen as prerequisite for their continued toleration.[1]

Requests and criticisms of this kind have come from both outside and inside these disciplines. The criticism may at times be justified, but often the critics seem to have given insufficient weight to the following considerations:

　　1. That the application of laboratory methods is limited by

Reprinted from *Psychoanalysis and Philosophy*, ed. Charles Hanly & Morris Lazerowitz. New York: International Universities Press, 1970, pp. 280-326. This paper was published posthumously.

[1] For example, the philosopher Michael Scriven said, with reference to psychoanalysis: "As a set of hypotheses [psychoanalysis] was a great achievement fifty years ago; as no more than a set of hypotheses it is a great disgrace today. The logical reason is that experimental design in this area is difficult. It is far from being impossible, however, and we have the resources, the need, and the absolute moral obligation to execute such experiments before encouraging or *condoning* the future practice of psychoanalysis" (see Hook, 1959, p. 226).

the nature of both the questions asked and the subject studied.

2. That attempts at applying laboratory methods to areas in which the conditions for their proper applications are lacking may lead to erroneous results.

3. That for certain types of questions there are other approaches available; these, if carefully executed, can in many cases lead to answers which are secure, if not beyond all possible doubt, at least beyond what lawyers call reasonable doubt; and that no rational life would be possible, and with it no laboratory science, if this kind of reasoning were denied all validity.

An attempt will be made in the following to distinguish between different types of questions that we may ask of reality, and to formulate the ways of validation appropriate for each.

Problems Related to Types of Questions Asked

Men may ask different questions about the world accessible to our senses. There are, accordingly, different ways of proceeding in trying to answer them, of testing the validity of answers, and of demonstrating them to others so that one man's knowledge may become part of a common body of knowledge.

First of all there are questions regarding *contemporary* phenomena. Among these are such questions as: What is the shape of the surface of the earth? How high are its mountains, how deep its seas? How are minerals distributed in the shell of the earth? What is the condition of the coronary arteries of a particular person? How much arithmetic does he know? Does this man love his wife?

Answers to such questions are found by observation. They are demonstrated to others by pointing to the respective objects and by encouraging others to observe them, too. It may be observation of *spontaneous* phenomena (unaltered except for whatever change may be effected by our looking at them), or it may be observation of the response of the system to *probing stimuli* (measurement, testing).

Then there are questions about the *past*, involving reconstruction and explanation of past events. We here have to do with questions such as: When did our planet come into being? When did life first appear on earth? What was the condition of the earth (or solar system) at that particular time? When did *homo sapiens* appear on earth? Did he appear in one place or in several places independently? If the latter, did it happen at different times and in different forms? What was the average lifespan of man at a particular time and place? From what diseases did he suffer? What is the core of historical truth in the Gospel story of the ministry and execution of Jesus? Who killed John F. Kennedy?

Again, there are questions such as: How did life come into being? How the human mind? What were the causes for the decline and fall of the Roman Empire? Through what conditions did modern civilization, characterized by a self-perpetuating science and its regular application to medicine, technology, and industry, come into being? Why did it happen in Europe at a particular time and not, for instance, in Hellenistic antiquity or in China? Why did the American Civil War or the First World War break out? Why does a person acquire a particular psychoneurosis, or by what circumstances or forces has his character been shaped? What motivated a particular person to commit suicide? How did a traffic accident come about? What started the fight in the nursery?

At stake in all these instances is a *reconstruction of the past.* In the first group of examples, emphasis is on the various *elements* in a time sequence, while in the second group, emphasis is on the *connection* between these elements, i.e., in the way things follow from their antecedents.

Reconstructions are based on *memories* of human beings, including those that have been entrusted to records (written, pictorial, or other), and on *circumstantial evidence,* evaluating clues in the light of our knowledge of, or opinion about, regularities and probabilities in events of nature or human affairs. This, in essence, is the *historical method.* It follows, by and large, what lawyers call the *rules of evidence.*

Finally, there are questions regarding *repetitive patterns:* Such patterns may be purely *empirical regularities,* like the movements of the sun, the moon, and the planets; the life cycle of plants and animals; or the typical stages of maturation and decay in the ages of man. Or they may be what are thought to be *universal laws,* manifestations of a necessity inherent in the nature of things, like the law of gravitation, the law of the preservation of energy, or Gresham's law of bad money driving good money out of circulation.

Regularities and laws are tested and demonstrated by prolonged *observation* and, in particular, by the *possibility of predictions*. Sometimes it can only be the prediction of phenomena that will occur spontaneously in the natural course of events, as the prediction of an eclipse of the sun; or the prediction, on the basis of Newton's law of gravitation, of the appearance of an as yet unknown planet at a particular time and place. But sometimes the situation is sufficiently subject to our control so that we not only can check on the prediction of events under ordinary conditions, but can vary the conditions at will and so check on predictions for a whole spectrum of conditions. This is the case of the *experiment*. Obviously, testing and demonstrating in the latter way, corroborating a whole spectrum of predictions, carries greater conviction than corroborating one, or a few, predictions in the natural course of events. Hence, testing of general propositions by experiment is clearly preferable, *provided* experiments are possible, i.e., provided that all factors of the situation are actually under control and can be varied independently.

Problems Related to Observational Science

The reality testing of images is a constant occupation of the mind, and the demonstration to others of observations accepted as real is a constant part of social interaction. It works well enough in a myriad of ways in daily life.

But there are two pitfalls in observation and hence in science built upon it. One has to do with inadequacy of perception and errors of observation; the other, with the impact which observation, and, in particular, probing, has upon the facts observed.

There are, first, the inadequacies of the sense organs. Some people are totally blind; many more have visual impediments such as myopia, or a greater or lesser degree of color blindness. There are illusions to which all men are prone, such as the fata morgana of the desert or hallucinations under toxic influence; there are also the hallucinations of the psychotic. We can easily deal with sense deceptions of the fata morgana type or of the toxic type by showing that they depend on certain conditions—atmospheric, in the first case; physiological, in the second—and that they do not fit in with an otherwise coherent body of perceptions. In the case of inadequacies of sensual perception and in the case of psychotic hallucinations, we accept a coherent world picture of a majority as standard against a number of dissident individual perceptions which are mutually irreconcilable.

But in practice, things are not always as smooth as the theoretical formulation suggests, and it often comes down to this: those perceptions are held to be correct which are so considered by the *scientific community* in a particular field (and, often enough, by something less than unanimous consent, at that). Because the scientific community is, for all practical purposes, a self-perpetuating body, we come uncomfortably close to accepting *power* as the criterion of truth.

But these difficulties are not overwhelming so long as we confine ourselves to physical data. They become very serious once we deal with the data of an *inner life*—such as love, fear, anguish, hope, desire; or, more particularly, when we deal with an inner life not subject to self-observation, i.e., with *unconscious* psychic phenomena.

The data of psychic life have often been called subjective, or private, data, accessible only to the subject himself, to distinguish them from physical data, which are public and, "in principle," accessible to all. Psychic data, in this viewpoint, are therefore not demonstrable to others and so cannot be part of a common body of knowledge.

This raises the question: how do we come by our knowledge of the psychic life of others? For no matter how subjective or private psychic life may be, there is no doubt that it does exist and that it greatly influences physical behavior. The husband reacts to what he senses about his wife's feelings; the diplomat or labor negotiator, to what he feels to be his opponent's intentions; even the infant reacts—and, it seems, reacts strongly—to his mother's moods.

With the exception of those of us who believe in extrasensory perception, we are all agreed that the psychic life becomes known to others through physical manifestations. But how this comes about is another question.

There are theories according to which man *infers* the inner state of another person, on the basis of the physical manifestations, by processes of association, intuition, or reasoning. Scheler (1954) was perhaps the first who suggested that we do not infer the existence of another mind and its contents but *perceive* them immediately, i.e., that we actually *see* that someone is elated, enraged, suspicious, or afraid.

We may stand on the speaker's platform and see a man in the audience yawning. Can we say that we see he is bored, or have we merely concluded it on the basis of experience with ourselves or others, experience which has taught us that whenever we have made this facial grimace, we have been bored, or whenever we have seen it in others, we have had independent reason for believing them to be bored? Or can we say that we see they are bored? This is a relatively simple case, inasmuch as most people will probably agree that yawning indicates boredom; thus, the question is, in this case, practically not very relevant. But there may be another man who does not yawn, and we may feel we "see" that he, too, is bored. More than that, we may perhaps be sure, not only that he is bored, but also that he tries hard to hide his boredom and to give the impression of concentration.

The development of concepts pertaining to our understanding of psychic activity in others parallels the development of views dealing with perceptual theory in the visual field. Here, too, there is an older theory according to which a raw material of sense impressions is organized and integrated into perceptions by mental operations; and a more recent school of thought which considers this distinction artificial, holding that gestalt is part and parcel of the process of perception from the very beginning. Do we see a field of colored dots and *conclude* that here is a chair, a desk, a davenport? Or do we actually *see* a furnished room with a chair, a desk, a davenport?

Modern theory of perception (Gibson, 1950) has gone in the direction of the second possibility, a position strongly supported by observation of patients suffering from severe visual impediments due to cerebral lesions (Goldstein, 1942). Some of these patients have a syndrome called *agnosia*, viz., the failure to see gestalts. A patient suffering from this condition may actually see only a field of color dots. With time he will probably learn to adjust to living with his defect and even make up for it, to some degree, through the development of substitute activities which are carried out without conscious awareness. The eye will perhaps trace with very rapid movements the contours of objects, and the patient will then *conclude* that here is a chair, a desk, a davenport. Thus, what older concepts had supposed to be the *normal* process of perception turned out to be a *substitute performance* in *pathological* cases in which the ability of normal perception had been impaired. Psychological research militates, therefore, in favor of the proposition that gestalt perception is an integral part of the process of perception itself and not a mental process superimposed upon it.

The ethologist, Konrad Lorenz, pleaded recently (1959) for the admission of gestalt perception as a source of scientific knowledge. His thesis is summed up in these words:

> ...among the functions participating in the total performance of the human organism, none, not even that of quantification, possess a primateship over some other, with regard to being the source of scientific cognition; and...in the sum total of all cognitive performances, the perception of complex gestalt plays a part which is not only scientifically legitimate but completely indispensable.

But there are *epistemological* difficulties which stand in the way of this proposition.

People vary enormously in their gestalt perceptions (and in what they "perceive" of the inner life of others). Many people are more or less "gestalt blind" (or "psychologically blind") just as many people are in some degree color blind. Hence, gestalt perception and the perception of the inner life of others are not directly *intrasubjektiv verifizierbar* (objectively verifiable).

This is a source of difficulty when one wants to demonstrate one's observations to others in order to make them a part of a common heritage of knowledge. The difficulty looms particularly great in matters involving the *perception of the inner life of others*.

Thus, if we admit, as a source of knowledge, gestalt perception and, in particular, perception of the inner life of others, we must accept that people who are equal before the law are not equal before the doors of knowledge, i.e., *admission of gestalt perception implies an aristocratic rather than a democratic theory of knowledge.*

It was readily accepted in the past that people differ vastly in their abilities and that some can see more of the truth than others. The German poet, Stefan George (1868-1933), formulated it defiantly. "Ein Wissen gleich fur alle ist Betrug" ("A knowledge equal for all is a fraud"). Constitutional endowment, learning, and inspiration or genius, define for him the steps of knowledge which "only the deluded fancy can leap over."

Such a theory is distasteful and unacceptable to moderns, not, it would seem, because it has been proved to be incorrect, but rather because it is inconvenient, and because it goes against the grain of our moral sentiments. It is inconvenient to base a theory of knowledge on authority, and it seems immoral that knowledge should be accessible to some and inaccessible to others. Democratic ideology demands that all good things be equally accessible to all. In the confusion of the moral with the factual, of the "ought" and the "is," which is common to all ideological thinking, it appears that what is not moral cannot be true; i.e., what is not accessible to all cannot be knowledge.

However, we are not quite consistent in this. From the fact that some people are blind or deaf and that most people are to some degree color-blind, we do not conclude that colors do not exist; rather, we think that they exist to the full score of the color discrimination of the perfect eye of a tiny minority and that the rest of us must accept the fact that our vision is in some degree defective.

It is also not literally true that the results of the exact science can be demonstrated to all. One cannot really demonstrate the validity of, say, the theory of relativity or the quantum theory, to all people; the great majority is not sufficiently adept in abstract thinking to be able to really understand these doctrines. The universal consent boils down, in practice, to the consent of the academic community in the respective discipline—in other words, to the consent of a self-perpetuating group; hence, the ultimate court of appeal is authority, power. Moreover, the agreement of the academic community is not always total; there are, in even the most exact disciplines—i.e., in the measuring disciplines—some heretics who hold views which are considered false by the bulk of their colleagues. *Universal* consensus is almost always a fiction.

It is nevertheless true that there is a *higher degree* of agreement about elementary sensations than there is about gestalts. More people can agree that somewhere red exists than can agree that anxiety or hatred exist. *The democratic philosophy demands the reduction of data to those over which there is least controversy;* hence, the elimination of gestalt perception.

This trend appears first in the 17th century, when the sense of touch was given preference over the perception of the eye. As the historian, Wolfram von den Steinen (1949), put it:

> The pioneering scientists of the 17th century and the enlightened thinkers of the 18th, fully conscious of what they were doing, gave preference, in accordance with Condillac, to the sense of touch over the eye. The divine, sun-like, sense was subordinated to the one that man has in common with the jelly fish [p. 49].

The modern attempt, in science, to exclude "subjective impressions" and replace them entirely with objective dial readings is actually a move in this direction. *For the dial readings, in the last analysis, do not need the eye at all.* Apparatus could easily be so constructed that all "readings" can be done by the *touch of the fingers.* Elimination of gestalt perception thus amounts to reducing perceptions to the sense of touch which, in von den Steinen's words, "man shares with the jelly fish."

The roots of this approach are largely *ideological:* the postulate of equality of all men, which is a moral aspiration rather than an established fact of nature.

A *second difficulty* in admitting gestalt perception as a legitimate source of knowledge lies in the fact that gestalt perception may be faulty, i.e., that people may see gestalts which are not there. That is typically the case with the paranoiac; he *sees* clearly the hand of a conspiracy behind the daily events—events which, for the most part, seem trivial to others—and he cannot understand how others can be so "blind" as not to see it. Adolf Hitler "saw" clearly the hand of "World Jewry" behind capitalism, labor unions, the peacemakers of Versailles and bolshevism. Yet his vision was faulty. The percentage of Jews among capitalist enterpreneurs, labor leaders, and revolutionaries was relatively high, but so has the share of Jews been, for centuries, in all innovations, and in the emancipation from tradition, and the rationalization of life. But neither in capitalist development nor in the socialist movement was their participation decisive, as later events showed. Above all, the participation of Jews in various heterogeneous movements, such as capitalism and socialism, was a spontaneous expression of individual inclinations, a centrifugal phenomenon, and not a concerted, centrally directed activity. An integrated, homogeneous "World Jewry" never existed, except perhaps in moments of grave common danger.

I have suggested the term *hypergnosia* to signify the trend of seeing more gestalt in reality than there is justification for; the word was constructed in analogy with "agnosia," the established term for the inability to see gestalt in the visual world (see Ch. 15).

The demand for universal demonstrability has led to a concentration on subjects that do not require gestalt perceptions but can be easily reduced to dial readings, with other questions being neglected. Karl Mannheim (1929) charged that social scientists "instead of attempting to discover what is the most significant, with the highest degree of precision possible under the existing circumstances... [tend] to attribute importance to what is measurable merely because it is measurable" (p. 46).

For a long time psychology remained limited to questions which permitted reduction to dial readings or their equivalent, as, for instance, questions concerning perception or memory. Questions regarding character formation, life conduct, and psychopathology remained outside, presumably to be approached later, when, hopefully, one would have learned to reduce them to dial readings as well. When Freud appeared and attacked just these questions by way of prolonged observation in depth in an appropriate setup, his efforts were widely rejected as unscientific. Today, clinical psychology, which to a great extent developed in response to the impetus provided by Freud, has grown immensely in the number of practitioners, and so in voting power. But there is still (or again) a wide gap between experimental and clinical psychology, a gap which even threatens to split the psychologists' professional organization.

Together with the trend of limiting study to subjects reducible to dial readings, there has also been a trend toward quantifying phenomena which do not easily lend themselves to quantification. Out of this trend have come public opinion polls, taxonomic studies, such as the Kinsey report on sexual practices, or sociological studies, such as Middletown and Yankee City. Some of the results may well be examples of what one critic (Tresolini, 1961) called "the bogus quantification of the obvious."

More recently, there have also been voices from within the natural sciences, expressing regret that their disciplines insisted on the requirements of reduction to dial readings, and demanding that entrance requirements into the sacred precincts of Science be changed so as to make allowance for observation of psychic conteñt and for gestalt perception. Among them is the voice of Konrad Lorenz, whose views were mentioned earlier. The microbiologist René Dubos (1965a) put forth a similar argument:

> It is a moral obligation for the scientific establishment to devote itself in earnest to the study of ecosystems, both those of nature and those of men. But ecosystems cannot be studied by the use of over-simplified models which constitutes the stock-in-trade of orthodox experimental science.... The study of natural and man-made ecosystems, as well as of man's response to environmental forces, has as much intellectual dignity and deserves as much academic support as the study of isolated particles and elementary reactions [p. 241].

But these voices have been few, and their influence on the Powers in Being has been small.

Problems Related to the Nature of the Observer

Different people find different kinds of evidence convincing; some trust their eyes, others trust only the dials.

Two examples may illustrate the situation:

Example 1. Edward E. Jones (1965), an experimental psychologist, studies conformity as a tactic in ingratiation. His theses amount to approximately this: It is common for people to try to ingratiate themselves with others by playing up to them and agreeing with them. Jones considers this fairly general, but he also notes that "in this particular area" he has "learned through research experience that people are extremely likely to deceive themselves," and that therefore "only by comparing appropriate experimental and control treatments can we begin to specify the variables essential to construction of a theory concerning it" (p. 145).

There exists what the author calls "the dilemma of the ingratiator": The more dependent a person is upon another's goodwill, the more interested he is in using this kind of tactic—but the more will the other be on his guard. And if the ingratiator makes himself too obvious, the whole thing may boomerang. Experiments were devised which showed that people find a way out of this dilemma through a more sophisticated form of ingratiating behavior—mixing agreement with disagreement, i.e., hiding the substance of the former under a pretense of the latter.

The conclusion will seem obvious to many. Instances of it abound in the world's literature, are narrated in novels, enacted in plays, commented on in works of worldly wisdom and satire, and described in treatises on diplomacy and salesmanship; they are even reflected in idioms of the language: "laying it on too thick."

The behavior in question is very much like flattery. Many a young man knows that flattery, skillfully dosed so as to be credible, is a way of "making" a girl. Some young men even conduct a preliminary study of where the weak spots of their prospective prey lie—girls who have heard time and again that they are beautiful may be hungry for reassurance about their intelligence, others who have been assured on the latter score, may be grateful for appreciation of their bodies. All this is so obvious, it could well be used in a psychological test. Beyond a certain age, those who do not know these things are either not very bright or emotionally blocked.

But for Jones and for many people with him, all this is apparently not "scientific"—i.e., it is not trustworthy and needs to be shown in the laboratory before it can be accepted as true.[2]

Example 2. The historian, Jacques Freymond (1960), published a study on the Saar conflict during the first decade after the Second World War. He proceeded in the way common to historians (or criminologists), assessing motives and consequences of human actions according to experience and common sense psychology. He supplemented this traditional historical approach with quantifying methods more recently developed in the systematic social sciences, such as observation of the frequency with which an issue turns up in parliamentary debates or in the press. But Freymond treated these data with a certain amount of caution and used them only as supplementary evidence: "These few quantitative analyses have no value as proof, but the information they supply reinforces what we already obtained from a careful survey of the newspapers" (p. 277). "These polls are unfortunately so few as to make all generalisations open to question and, moreover, they provide only vague indications as to motives" (p. 280).

Thus, one side takes it as rather obvious that in an age of nationalism the destiny of the Saar would be important to Germans and that the persecution of national leaders would, under ordinary circumstances at any rate, enhance their prestige

---

[2] It may be worth noting that the author of the above-mentioned paper does, in fact, make some judgments that do not stem from laboratory experiments but from observations with the naked eye. These judgments manifest a credulity such as would hardly be found in those who openly accept natural observations as a valid source of insight and are accustomed to subject their impressions to critical scrutiny. Jones assumes that the ingratiator has to be circumspect about the way he goes about his business, not only because his purpose may become too transparent and so incur sales resistance, but also because of a "natural reluctance" to see himself as deceitful or manipulative."

That seems to me an unwarranted generalization. Many people have no compunction whatever about "manipulating" others; in fact, they enjoy it. Boys sometimes boast about the "line" they hand the girls. (Guilt feelings may come later, but then, as a rule, not simply because of manipulation as such.) Perhaps, if the mind is absorbed by laboratory studies, it is less open to experience of daily life.

among their followers. It takes these propositions for granted on the basis of historical experience and psychological plausibility. At the same time, it is cautious about drawing conclusions from, say, the frequency with which an item appears in the news- papers, because these appearances are only counted, not weighed, and because their appearance or nonappearance may be due to a variety of motives, not all of which are historically significant.

The other side, however, considers assumptions about hu- man reactions like those made by Freymond as extravagant, wild conclusions based on a view of the statistical elaboration of data without evaluative judgment of their significance.[3]

As has been suggested earlier, neither side seems to me to be entirely right. Both hold fragmented views, reflecting the fact that some people are stronger in synthetic intuition than in critical analysis, while others are stronger in analysis than in intuition.

The situation appears to be this: *If we do not admit gestalt perceptions and limit ourselves to dial readings*, we are in danger of losing a great part of reality; *we have purchased demonstra- bility at a price*—sometimes an enormous price—*in terms of content and depth. If we admit gestalt perception, we are defenseless against hypergnosia* and may fall prey to paranoid systems. In order to avoid the latter, we would have to establish an *authority* to decide whose gestalt perceptions are trustworthy and whose are not; and that creates a problem which cannot be

---

[3] The following is an extreme example of the latter from my personal experience. I recently received a circular letter from a research group in one of the country's most prestigious institutions; it contained a long list of state- ments, and recipients were invited to indicate with regard to each statement whether they approved or disapproved, strongly, moderately or mildly.

I replied that however much I wished to cooperate, I could not fill out the questionnaire because my opinion could not usually be compressed into a simple "yes" or "no"; I would have to add qualifying comments. I demon- strated this in connection with one of the statements and showed that, without amplifying comments, my answer was bound to be misconstrued.

I thereupon received a letter from the head of the research unit, admitting that "it is certainly difficult to respond with a 'yes' or 'no' answer to complex statements," but adding that "nevertheless, for the purpose of research, such a task must be imposed and your discomfort in it can be readily understood."

Thus, the research leader apparently believed that I had been complaining about personal discomfort and did not see, or pretended not to see, the point, that the data he was about to collect "for the purpose of research" were meaningless.

decided by immanent criteria. It would, once again, make truth a question of power.

We must try to minimize both dangers. While *admitting gestalt* perceptions, we must constantly *check* them against *elementary* experience, i.e., experience reducible to dial readings.

There is no foolproof road to Truth, and the belief that such a road exists in something called "The Scientific Method" is an illusion, a modern analogy to ancient fantasies like the philosopher's stone or the fountain of youth. But the best approach in matters of mind and society still seems to be to try (in the words of Justice Oliver Wendell Holmes to a 50th Reunion of the Harvard Class of 1861) "to see as far as one may," i.e., to have the results of prolonged observation by those most perceptive checked wherever possible by dial readings.

Problems Related to the Influence of the Observer

Another set of problems arises if observation is not limited to the passive reception of sensual impressions, but if the observer is *probing* nature in order to elicit responses. We must then ask whether the probing is sufficiently thorough so that the responses can be taken as characteristic; and if it is, to what degree it has itself changed, or even produced, the phenomena it was meant to test.

The first question must be considered whenever the probing is applied to a relatively small sample of reality: How representative of the whole subject was the sample selected for study? Was for instance, the piece of liver sucked up in a liver biopsy characteristic of the composition of the entire organ? Are the people interviewed by the Kinsey group representative of the American population as a whole as far as sex practices are concerned?

The second question presents itself whenever the forces involved in the probing are of an order of magnitude comparable to that of the phenomena themselves. In such cases, our study teaches us only about the *response of nature to the probing stimuli*. The question remains of how to infer from these data the behavior of nature not so irritated.

This question of the influence of the measuring device has

been particularly important in the physics of the very small. One might think that the influence of measuring devices can itself be investigated by means of finer instruments and so gradually corrected. But it was found in this century that, in the range of the very small, the atomistic structure of the universe makes such asymptotic elimination of errors impossible and sets insurmountable finite limits to the accuracy of measurement. This realization, while setting limits to man's aspirations, has itself been the source of a deepened understanding of the phenomenal world.

In the field of psychology and behavior, animal or human, the attempt to consider and to diminish or, if possible, to eliminate the error due to the fact of probing has led to various devices. The anthropologist may live for a considerable time in the midst of the people whose culture he studies, hoping to be accepted as part of the landscape; or he may camouflage his research interests by other pursuits so that the people, he hopes, are not aware of being observed. The psychoanalyst makes the analytic situation itself an object of observation and probing, trying to understand it himself and then making his analysand aware of it and its implications, with a view to thus weakening or eliminating it.

Problems Related to Historical Reconstruction and Explanation

The following are typical examples of reconstructions of the past:

Example 1. Objects found at the site of a crime may show fingerprints which are then traced to a particular person. The conclusion is then drawn that the person has had his hand on the object in question. This reconstruction of the past is based on the wide experience that the pattern of the fingerprints is not duplicated but is a unique personal characteristic.

General biological experience has taught us that the ratio between radioactive and nonradioactive isotopes of carbon can determine the time when a once living organism died. The age of a particular level in excavations is thus determined by a reasoning based on certain regularities known from accumulated experience.

Example 2. An elderly lady is found shot dead in her home; the location of the wound and the absence of any weapon seem to rule out suicide. Suspicion turns to her impecunious nephew, a spendthrift continually in need of funds. Suspicion is intensified through evidence that the nephew was actually in a financial squeeze, that he had appealed to his aunt for help and had been turned down. It gets a further boost when a man appears who testifies to having seen the nephew in the vicinity of the old lady's home in what appeared to him an excited condition. When evidence is supplied that the fatal bullet fits a gun that was in the nephew's possession, the case for the state is sufficiently strong for prosecution. At the time when the matching of bullets to weapons was exclusively a matter for the judgment of experts, with the possibility of disagreements, the efforts of the lawyer for the defense may have been concentrated on forcing the expert witness to qualify his statements and to admit the possibility of error, or to undermine his authority before the jury. Today, this approach would probably not be tried, and the attorney for the defense may concentrate on suggesting a missing link in the chain of causality. Perhaps the gun has been purloined by unknown hands for the purpose of framing the nephew.

There is a point at which circumstantial evidence seems so conclusive that the attorney for the defense does not challenge it at all but prefers to enter a plea of "not guilty by reason of insanity" or pleads for mercy on account of mitigating circumstances.

The reconstruction of the crime or the explanation of observed facts (an old lady shot dead) is based on the consideration of all possibilities, both as they appear in the beginning and as they suggest themselves in the course of the progressing investigation, ruling out those which, in the light of all circumstances, are impossible or highly improbable. If the range of alternatives under consideration is complete (in terms of our knowledge of nature and human events), if one reconstruction is possible and psychologically plausible and covers all data, and if all others are ruled out as impossible or extremely improbable, the case of the reconstruction and explanation is well established. It is, as lawyers say, proved *beyond reasonable doubt.*

Example 3. One of the most famous Corinthian vases, the so-called Francois vase, was reassembled from some 2,000 potsherds found over a wide area, presumably scattered by tomb robbers. A few fragments are still missing. As described by Pfuhl (1955), the vase is richly decorated with paintings which illustrate mythological stories, "the details of incredible finish, even to the almost microscopic friezes in the decorated bands of certain garments" (p. 25). It is universally accepted among archaeologists that the object assembled from these shards and now exhibited in Florence is, but for minor imperfections due to the ravages of time, identical with an object manufactured in the 6th century B.C. by human hands and meant to be a vase. This is a statement about events of the past.

It is conceivable that the shards actually did not belong together but came from many different vases, fitting together only by accident, as it were—conceivable, but so unlikely as to be hardly worth considering. There are cases in which reconstructions seem dubious, but when things fit together completely, down to "the almost microscopic friezes," archaeologists do not doubt the substantial correctness of the reconstruction. It is similar with jigsaw and crossword puzzles; perhaps there is a solution completely different from the one we have worked out, but we discount this possibility.

The reconstruction of the past is accepted in such cases on the strength of the consideration that *any other explanation is extremely improbable.*

Example 4. Several cases of typhoid fever have turned up in a major city, and the Health Department searches for the origin of the epidemic. The Department holds a list of persons known as carriers. All persons who have fallen ill are interviewed with a view to reconstructing all their movements and contacts at the time they contracted the disease. It turns out that all patients but one have been customers in a produce store located in a building complex in which one known carrier has his apartment. A follow-up on this clue reveals that the sewage pipe from the carrier's apartment leads over the ceiling of the produce store, and that the pipe is defective at that point, with moisture accumulating in the ceiling.

This seems to explain all cases but one: a patient who lives in an entirely different section of town and who has claimed never to have been in the district in which the produce store is located. This patient is interviewed again and encouraged to retrace all **his movements during the critical time.** He suddenly remembers that he once drove through this part of town on his way to a suburb and, suffering from the heat, stopped at a fruit store and bought a bunch of grapes. It turns out that this was the store in question.

The ring is now closed. All produce found in the store is destroyed, the defective pipe is repaired, and no new cases are reported. Afterward we feel justified in assuming that the events have been adequately reconstructed and the outbreak of the epidemic adequately explained.

Example 5. The deciphering of hieroglyphs is another example of reconstruction of the past. The Rosetta stone carried three inscriptions: one in Greek, one in hieroglyphs, and a third one in still different characters. Deciphering started with the hypothesis that all told the same story, i.e., that it was a trilingual announcement—a plausible enough hypothesis, yet one that could not be taken for granted. Then came another hypothesis to the effect that a number of hieroglyphs framed by a cartouche were the Egyptian equivalent of the name of the king found in the Greek version. In proceeding further, hypothesis was piled upon hypothesis. All of them found their justification in the fact that they eventually permitted the reading of the text; and that they permitted the deciphering of numerous other inscriptions as well. Today, ancient Egyptian, like ancient Greek or Sanskrit, can be learned from textbooks, and, but for possible occasional errors and inaccuracies, no scholar doubts that the reconstruction is not just a concatenation of speculations and delusions, but is substantially correct.

All reconstructions of the past contain an *implicit prediction:* if the past has been correctly reconstructed, one can predict that no evidence will turn up in the future that will invalidate the reconstruction. That means, in the case of example 1, that no evidence will ever turn up to suggest that the person to whom the fingerprints have been traced could not have touched the object in question, perhaps because he was dead before it had been manufactured. It means, in example 2, that no evidence will turn up to show that the nephew could not possibly have killed the old lady. It means, in the case of example 3, that no evidence will ever turn up to indicate that the Francois vase did not exist in antiquity in the form of, and with the decorations shown by, the object exhibited in Florence.

These predictions are purely negative, and because they have been borne out over a considerable period of time add little to the persuasiveness of the reconstruction.

But not so in the last two examples. We can predict, in example 4, that no new cases of typhoid will appear, once what we believe to be the source of the infection has been dried up. We can predict, in the case of example 5, that other Egyptian inscriptions, including those not yet excavated, will be understandable on the basis of the reconstructed script, requiring, at most, minor additions or modifications.

That these predictions have been borne out by subsequent events adds substantially to the persuasiveness of the reconstruction; in the case of the deciphering of the hieroglyphs, it virtually makes any other explanation seem absurd.

The reason for this difference between the implicit predictions in the first three and in the last two cases seems to lie in the fact that the reconstruction, in the earlier cases, refers to purely *individual* events (a person touched an object, a person killed another one, a potter made a vase), while in examples 4 and 5 reconstruction refers to *typical* events—situations likely to be repeated in other instances (people getting sick in an epidemic, people using language and script). From the fact that John has touched a piece of furniture, or that a young man has shot his aunt, nothing follows for the behavior of others. But if there is a source of infection in a populated city, it is reasonable to expect that others will come down with the disease, and that this no longer happens once some measures have been taken, supports the hypothesis on which these measures had been passed. So too, script and language are collective rather than individual phenomena, and if one person has used a semantic system, others also must have done so.

At the time of the deciphering of cuneiform script, the Royal Asiatic Society sent a newly discovered Assyrian inscription to four scholars then working in the field, asking them to decipher it, independently of each other. The translations made by these four scholars were remarkably similar, encouraging the scientific community to accept the claims of the assyriologists. The fact that a number of scholars understand a text in the same way does not in itself prove that their translations are correct; they may all be guilty of a common error. But it is unlikely that a delusional system could be applied to a *text as yet unknown.*

The deciphering appears to be fully proved as more and more texts are read with results which are consistent with each other and with data from other sources. The more such interconnected results accumulate, the less likely is it that it could all be the play of coincidence; eventually, the chances of coincidence become infinitesimal.

The situation in intelligence work is similar. If counterintelligence "breaks" the enemy code, his coded messages yield a meaning that makes sense. If further intercepted messages can be read according to the same system, and if the conclusions drawn from these translations are borne out by facts, the decoding will be considered correct.

In all these instances, a course of events has been reconstructed from available clues which can completely explain what happened, while possible alternative explanations are highly improbable.

The great historian of science, Charles Singer (1941), once said about the theory of evolution: "Evolution is perhaps unique among major scientific theories in that the appeal for its acceptance is not that there is any evidence for it but that any other proposed interpretation of the data is wholly incredible" (p. 487).

But in this lies the appeal for the acceptance of all *historical*[4] *interpretations;* and the theory of evolution *is* a historical interpretation. Singer's astonishment was probably due to the fact that he had not often to deal with historical reconstructions and explanations.

It should be added, however, that historical interpretations

---

[4] The term "historical" is used here, and in what follows, in the broad philosophical sense of a reconstruction of the past by any means, not in the specific sense of the academic discipline "history," which is limited to the reconstruction of the past of literate peoples from written records.

can rarely, if ever, be proved *beyond all possible doubt*. The gun of the old lady's nephew and heir could have been taken from the drawer by an unknown intruder and returned to it without leaving discoverable traces. The corroboration, by fact, of the predictions implicit in historical interpretations adds weight to the interpretation, particularly in those cases in which the interpretation refers to typical rather than to unique events. The theory of evolution, for instance, finds support in the daily experience of micromutations of organisms in response to the introduction of antibiotics and pesticides. But even then, reconstruction is rarely beyond possible doubt; the epidemic of our example may have had a different, undetected source, and its termination could have been a matter of coincidence. Even the deciphering of hieroglyphs and cuneiform may yet be shot through with fundamental errors, although, in this case, it seems absurd to maintain that the deciphering is entirely invalid—a mere delusional system.

Thus, a reconstruction can be highly probable, sometimes overwhelmingly probable. But very improbable things do occur occasionally. The Law takes account of these limits of certainty and requires only that a case be proved *beyond reasonable doubt*, thus making allowance for a residual uncertainty in all things human.

On this area of uncertainty rests the view that historical and clinical disciplines are inexact and therefore not scientific at all or are, at best, "protosciences," i.e., collections of experiences and more or less clever guesses out of which a science may some day be developed. But, as we have seen, historical reconstruction can often be proved beyond reasonable doubt, with a very high degree of probability. The reconstruction of ancient Egyptian language and script is perhaps, on the whole, more convincing than some experimental verifications of theories even in the natural sciences.

The high degree of probability that can often be achieved in historical studies is quite sufficient for human purposes; and in any case, whether sufficient or not, it is all that *can* be had in some circumstances. No rational life would be possible if we considered all these conclusions untrustworthy.

It should be added, however, that there are some historical problems for which an answer is close to impossible. One may, for instance, inquire into the motives of Abraham Lincoln's policies prior to the Civil War. Was Lincoln motivated (a) by a distaste for the institution of slavery; or (b) by a determination to preserve the Union; or (c) by the interest of the bourgeois class in industrialization; or (d) by personal characteristics due, perhaps, in varying proportions, to genetic endowment, early childhood experiences, or later indoctrination, religious or otherwise? Or was he moved by several, or by all of these factors, and if so, to what degree did each contribute to the final result?

These questions are unanswerable, and the historian's fantasy and bias have free sway.

Situations of this kind and the fact that the same events are continuously interpreted differently by different writers, with agreement never in sight, has probably contributed to the widespread belief that history—whether the history of nations, groups, institutions, or cultures which we commonly have in mind when we speak of "history" or the reconstruction of the history of an individual, as in psychoanalysis—is not a science but an "art." But it should not be forgotten that while some historical questions—both of the group and the individual—are fairly unanswerable, there are many others which can be answered beyond reasonable doubt. To discard the latter because of the intractability of the former would be pouring the baby out with the bath water.

On the other hand, because it is often possible to demonstrate facts of the past and explanations of unique events beyond reasonable doubt, it does not follow that all historians—those studying the history of groups and those studying the history of individuals—have always been proceeding painstakingly, with proper regard for pitfalls. There are also what Carl Becker called historian *sans peur et sans recherche*—without fear and without research—who present historical explanations as fiat, so to speak, without adequate attention to the rules of evidence.

There is yet another pitfall in historical studies both of groups and of individuals: the inclination to project later events back into the past, to see the past in the light of events that crystallized later. The Austrian poet, Grillparzer (1791-1872) once said: "It is difficult to know the future, but it is impossible to know the past because we can never emancipate ourselves from the knowledge of what came out of it in the meantime."

Thus, it is extremely difficult to realize what Rousseau, Marx, or Nietzsche actually meant. When Rousseau speaks of the General Will and the need to "bring all particular wills in conformity with [it]," we cannot help thinking of Robespierre and the *Terreur;* when reading in Marx about the dictatorship of the proletariat, we see Lenin and Stalin; when reading in Nietzsche about *Herren-Moral* and *Sklaven-Moral* and the coming of the superman, we see Auschwitz. Yet, Rousseau, Marx, and Nietzsche almost certainly meant nothing of the kind, and it had probably never occurred to them that their words, uttered against the background of a fairly stable culture in which much could be taken for granted, might be so translated into practice by their followers.

To sum up: historical investigations, guided by the rules of evidence, will often lead to results that are secure beyond reasonable doubt; but they will do so only *if* they are actually guided by these rules.

It is unfortunately true that the most absurd propositions have been advanced by some historians. Thus, A. J. P. Taylor (1961), the prominent Oxford historian, argues that the Austrian crisis of March 1938, which led to the *Anschluss*, was brought about not by Hitler but by—Schuschnigg. David Hogan, an American historian, argues that World War II was not brought about by Hitler's aggressiveness but was "forced upon" mankind by, of all people, Lord Halifax.

The existence of this kind of literature, written by professionals, goes a long way toward discrediting the historical method in the eyes of the public. Yet, this conclusion is not justified. These absurd results are reached by leaving relevant facts out of consideration, and neglecting chronology. If a laboratory technician were to do similar things with his samples, he could produce equally absurd "results," but this would be no argument against the reliability of chemical analysis, properly conducted.

Problems Relating to the Role of the Experiment
in Historical Investigations

We cannot find the causes of a past event by experiment, for we cannot put the clock back and have things played over again with conditions varied at will. If we want to experiment with unique situations, past or present, we can do it only by *constructing a model* which we think is like the real system in question or approximates it sufficiently, and experimenting with this model. But that involves the question of how similar the model actually is to reality. Sometimes the similarity is sufficiently established beyond reasonable doubt, as, for instance, when an illness is attributed to some hitherto unknown or unsuspected agent—say, a chemical used as food preservative—and experiments are made to determine whether this agent actually produces these consequences. If this turns out to be the case, we will probably be satisfied that the previously observed cases had the same etiology, i.e., we assume that the model closely parallels reality.

But conditions cannot always be so simply reproduced in the laboratory, and the correspondence between reality and the model may be more tenuous. This is particularly the case in the social sciences. Once it had become known that Chinese intellectuals and Western prisoners had been subjected to "coercive persuasion" (Schein et al., 1961)—more vulgarly called "brainwashing"—Western scientists experimented by studying the suggestibility of individuals under various artificially produced stresses.

Such studies are valuable for what they tell, but claims that they throw light on the process of coercive persuasion in Chinese prison camps are based on the assumption of a fundamental similarity between the real situation and the laboratory situation, i.e., between the predicament of the person subjected to the real procedure and the predicament of those who participated in the experiments. This assumption is highly questionable because the terror of an individual who finds himself helpless in the hands of ruthless fanatics, without any material or moral support from his own people, is different by many orders of magnitude from any stresses that can be artificially produced in an American laboratory.

The question of whether or not, or to what degree, the model constructed for an experiment is analogous to the reality under study cannot be decided by experiment. It rests on operations of reasoning, commonly called judgment; and judgment, in its more explicit activities, involves the very kind of reasoning we have discussed as criteria of historical interpretations.

If, then, the experiment was brought in so as not to have to rely on judgment believed to be subjective and inexact, it must be noted that, however clear the outcome of the experiment, the undertaking has not been entirely successful. For judgment, that unreliable, subjective agent that was to be ousted in favor of an exact procedure, actually still remained indispensable in the original choice of the model with which experiment was to be made. This fact was clearly understood by Kant (1790-96):

> It is obvious that there needs to be an intermediary link between theory and practice regardless of how comprehensive the theory may be; for the theoretical intelligence [*Verstand*] which has conceived a rule must be supplemented by a judgment, so that the practitioner can decide whether or not a certain thing falls under sway of this rule. It is not possible to formulate any rules according to which that could be judged, as this could go on *ad infinitum*. Hence, there may be theorists who can never become practical because they lack judgment, e.g., physicians or lawyers who have done well in school and don't know what to do when called in for consultation [p. 127].

This is true with but one qualification. Sometimes it may be possible to check experimentally on the accuracy or the probable accuracy of a model by so constructing it that it can *make predictions about facts which are already known but which had not been built into the model itself*. A case of this kind was described by Dennis Gabor (1962). The model, in that case, was not constructed with a view to explaining events that had already taken place but with a view to predicting the future; nevertheless, the principle is the same.

A large silt bar about seven miles wide had accumulated across the entrance of the Rangoon River in Burma. By 1931 the depth had decreased to about 12 feet and was still decreasing. The authorities, concerned about the situation, called in a civil engineer, Sir Alexander Gibbs, as consultant. Gibbs constructed a model of the harbor in the proportion of 1:200. The tides of the sea were mechanically reproduced, alternating at great speed, so that 15 hours in the model were equivalent to one year in nature, or about one week in the model equivalent to 11 years in nature. The model was constructed so as to reproduce the conditions of the harbor, not at the time of its construction (1932), but rather the conditions that had existed 57 years earlier, in 1875. The model was then put into operation. The first five weeks should have brought things up to 1932. That was actually the case; after five weeks the silt bar in the model had reached the size corresponding to nature in 1932. This was taken as indication that the model did actually reproduce reality correctly. It was then operated for one more month to bring things up to 1982. It turned out that the silt bar would grow until 1937 and then shrink, a conclusion that was borne out by later events.

There are also occasions in which experiments are made as an auxiliary of a historical investigation. In the investigation of an airplane accident, it may seem that the plane disintegrated in the air. Suspicion is voiced that the building material may have disintegrated under stress, and experiments are made by subjecting the same kind of material to similar stresses. An affirmative outcome of these experiments does not necessarily prove that this is what actually happened in the accident. The plane, even though earmarked for destruction by structural weaknesses of the material, may have come to ruin by, for example, a bomb explosion, before it reached its destined doom. But the experiment proves that structural weakness could have been responsible and was, in fact, bound to cause the plane to disintegrate at some time, and, in the absence of any clues pointing to other sources of destruction, we will accept it as actual cause.

This is only a special case of the general condition that all historical reconstructions are made *on the basis of known regularities or laws*. When the police identify a particular person from fingerprints, they do so on the basis of the general experience that fingerprints are a personal characteristic, not duplicated in others. When the archaeologist determines the age of an object through carbon dating, he applies his knowledge of the speed of radioactive carbon decay. The only difference between these cases and the case of the plane which disintegrated in the air is that, in the former cases the respective regularities of nature had already been known prior to the study of the individual case, while in the latter case the existence of the respective regularities had been suggested only in the course of the investigation of the particular case and ascertained thereafter. Hence, what we have before us in the latter type of case is not really an application of experiments to historical investigations, but rather an *experimental study of regularities of nature which are relevant for the historical case under study*.

When experiments were most effectively applied to psychoanalytic problems, it was in the same way in which experiments appear in historical investigations in general, viz., as an *auxiliary*, demonstrating the possibility rather than the reality of a reconstruction. The classic examples are the experiments regarding sexual symbols. Schrötter (1911) and Roffenstein (1923) showed their existence by producing them artificially through posthypnotic suggestion; Betlheim and Hartmann (1924) by provoking them in a patient suffering from Korsakoff's psychosis, a condition characterized by loss of memory and confabulations. These experiments proved that sexual symbols exist; they did not prove that a particular image which might be a sexual symbol was in fact one in a specific case.

Problems Relating to Regularities in Nature and in General Laws

We can make two types of statements regarding repetitive phenomenological patterns. First are the purely empirical statements with respect to repetitive events: Kepler's planetary laws, for example, or the life cycle of animals. The second type are general laws establishing such repetitiveness as the consequence of the inherent nature of things: Newton's derivation of the planetary movements from his law of gravitation, for example, or the laws of thermodynamics, electrodynamics, relativity, and quantum mechanics.

Since, in the statement of regularities of the first type, no claim is made with regard to their causes, and thus no implied claim that those causes are inherent in the objects, the discovery of discordant facts does not invalidate the statement; it merely restricts its range. But a discordant fact disproves a presumed *law*.

There are children whose development does not quite conform to the maturational scheme, or who do not reach this or that stage of development at all, or reach it much earlier or later than is typical. Such findings restrict and qualify the schemes of typical development described in medicine and psychology but do not make them useless. The schemes are still valid for the majority of individuals. Rational large-scale planning can still be based on them.

Essential hypertension was discovered around the turn of the century, and its clinical manifestations and possible development were described. It was later found that essential hypertension has a more sinister prognosis among American Negroes than among Caucasians. This discovery did not invalidate the clinical researches that had been done with Caucasians; it merely defined their limits and added new knowledge to the old. New knowledge can easily be assimilated in the tolerant, "pluralistic," atmosphere of purely empirical patterns.

But things are different once the existence of a law has been proclaimed. A law is a jealous authority that does not tolerate rival authorities. A single refractory fact that cannot somehow be subsumed under it, destroys its validity.

Prolonged observation discovers regularities. Laws are never definitely proved, because their claims, implying inner necessity, go beyond what can ever be observed. But if *predictions* made on the assumption of these laws are borne out by observation, the laws become widely or generally accepted.

In some instances we cannot manipulate reality at will and have to wait until nature offers the occasion to observe the predicted phenomena, as in the case of eclipses of the sun or the moon, or in the case of the bending of light passing close to the gravitation field of the sun. In such cases, the persuasive power of an observation bearing out a prediction largely depends on the *precision* of the prediction which has been so borne out. The fact that Leverrier could locate the planet Neptune precisely on the spot predicted was decisive for the general acceptance of Newton's law of gravitation. But the fact that "capitalism"—in itself an imprecise concept—has disappeared over vast parts of the world has not proved the validity of Marx's theory of history, except in the eyes of those already unalterably convinced, and it will not be proved if market economies should disappear in the remainder of the world as well; for the prediction that would have been borne out was not very specific. Every past political or economic system has been superseded by others, and every present one will probably be superseded at some future time.

In other cases, phenomena are so completely under our control that we can corroborate, not only a few predictions of isolated events, but a whole continuum; i.e., we can predict what will happen under any combination of parameters. Such is the case of the experiment, which makes the experiment the incomparable tool in the search for general laws, the *via regia* toward the discovery of what is inherent in nature. But the experiment, all but indispensable for the formulation of general laws, is not universally applicable. It does require a subject matter which in all relevant aspects, i.e., in all aspects known to have an influence on the phenomena under study, can be manipulated at will. It must be possible to vary individual parameters independent of each other. As the mathematician Warten Weaver (1955) put it, the parameters must be "loosely coupled" (p. 1256). When this is not the case, when the change of one parameter is bound to be accompanied by changes in a number of others, experiment, in the strict sense of the word, is not possible. The more intimate the coupling, the more will the efforts at *disentangling* the various factors *depend on reasoning of a different kind.* And there is no basis for an *a priori* assumption that under such conditions the data of the so-called experiment will always permit more exact inferences than could be drawn by historical reconstruction. In fact, it seems to me that outside the realm of its proper applicability, i.e., outside the area in which parameters are loosely coupled and can be varied independently, the evaluation of "experimental" data requires the apparatus of the historical method and may be altogether misleading without it.

The Ideological Roots of Scientism

Modern Western civilization, which may be said to have had its earliest infancy in the age of humanism, which grew and gained momentum with the so-called "scientific revolution" in the 17th century, and gathered momentum with the industrial and political revolutions in the 18th century, and which is now encompassing the entire globe, storming ahead in the rapidly expanding movements of science and technology, and political and social reform, seems to be propelled by two powerful impulses: the one an impulse toward mastery, by man, of his habitat, viz., a *manipulative* impulse; the other a *moral* impulse toward social justice, usually seen in terms of equality.

There is little doubt that these movements have bestowed immense benefits on the great majority of men. The first of these impulses has, in the most advanced countries, added many years of life, and of productive and enjoyable life to boot, to the human life span, and it has all but emancipated man from the ancient curse of a constant struggle against hunger and of backbreaking toil. The second impulse has meant that the anonymous masses of mankind, who all through history had to serve the purposes of their masters and could pursue their own only after their masters' had been satisfied, had come into their own.

But while it would be ridiculous to underestimate the magnitude of the achievement, it would be equally erroneous to overlook the fact that achievements are bought at a price. Whatever does not serve either the manipulative or the egalitarian drive has been neglected and has withered.

In the field of human knowledge with which we are here concerned, the *first* of the two modern orientations has meant that all attention has been focused on what can be manipulated. Subjects which cannot be manipulated but can be approached only in a receptive attitude—contemplation, philosophy—either have shriveled into insignificance, or vain attempts have been made to emulate the triumphant manipulative disciplines in these matters, too. Hence, the nearly exclusive interest in the formulation of general laws that would permit the manipulation of things and that require for their proof the experiment, which requires that its subject can be manipulated at will. Hence, the loss of interest in historical fact. "The depreciation of historical fact," said Thomas S. Kuhn (1962), "is deeply, and probably functionally, ingrained in the ideology of the scientific profession, the same profession that places the highest of all values upon factual details of other sorts" (p. 137).

The *second* orientation has meant that knowledge has to be justified in egalitarian terms, and that knowledge which is not accessible to all—or cannot be made to appear accessible to all, with the benefit of some maneuvering—is not knowledge at all.

No branch of human life can avoid being touched by the prevailing attitudes of men, by what F. M. Cornford (1950) called their "unwritten philosophy." Disciplines which approach the world in a nonmanipulative fashion and which make allowance for the possibility of a knowledge not equal to all are pressed against the wall. The best they can hope for is to somehow survive until a day when the present imbalance of outlook will be corrected and the pendulum of alternating human extremisms will swing back again. One may hope, without too much confidence, that it will not be toward another extremism, for human beings, as Sir Richard Livingstone (1959) said, "rarely walk in the center of the road; they reel drunkenly from the ditch on one side to the ditch on the other" (p. 43).

The Epistemology of Psychoanalysis

The empirical basis of psychoanalytic claims is exclusively the prolonged observation of individuals. These individuals are studied both dynamically and historically (Hartmann and Kris, 1945). An attempt is made to find: (a) what "makes a person tick," that is, in what way his inner life and his behavior grow out of varying and, as a rule, conflicting motivations both conscious and unconscious, i.e., both accessible or inaccessible to self-observation; and (b) how, out of the raw material of constitutional endowment and environmental influences, he has become the kind of person that he is.

For the purpose of this investigation, the individual under study is instructed to follow the so-called analytic rule, i.e., during the sessions of study, to permit every idea to enter his mind, regardless of whether or not it seems relevant to the purposes pursued at the moment, and to communicate to the observer the total content of the mind rather than only a selection made from one point of view or another. This setting permits the observer to acquire a more complete knowledge of a person's mental life than could be had otherwise. It also opens to view aspects of life and feeling which are ordinarily withheld from one's own and, even more, from anybody else's attention. These communications form the raw material in which the observer searches for a dynamic and historic understanding of his object.

The analyst sets himself three tasks: (a) to discover the way the mind of his analysand works; (b) to find in it gestalts, such as repetitive patterns; (c) to reconstruct their development in the past.

In the *first* of these activities, he proceeds largely by trying to see what is going on. Anybody who denies the possibility of perceiving mental content in others and believes that perception is limited to physical data only, while everything else is a matter of inference, will look upon psychoanalysis as a matter of speculation.

What has been said before in general terms about different people putting their trust in different kinds of evidence, can be applied here. For some, the evidence of what they feel they "see" is immediately convincing. Little is added to their conviction by corroborative "objective" data—i.e., data which in the last resort could be reduced to dial readings. In fact, there are some who approach corroborative objective data with distrust, wondering whether the result was not brought about by some hidden *petitio principii* or by faulty reasoning. Others, on the other hand, look upon the perceptions of the former group as subjective impressions and accept the indirect proof by objective reasoning as convincing.

The different approaches, which have previously been described in relation to investigations involving psychic life or gestalt perception, should now be brought to bear on psychoanalytic propositions in particular. There is, for instance, the psychoanalytic doctrine of the relations between paranoia and (unconscious) homosexuality: in the delusion of persecution the paranoid person is seen as desperately denying and disclaiming a sexual attachment to the persecutor who is (or stands for) a person of the same sex. In some cases at least, direct observation puts this contention beyond reasonable doubt for some people (including the present writer).

On the other hand, psychologists have tried to check this thesis by objective methods: by investigating the frequency of overt homosexual behavior or of obvious homosexual symbolism in paranoids or by their rating on a masculinity-femininity test scale. The results showed a significant correlation between paranoia and homosexuality (Gardner, 1931; Strahosch, 1934; Page and Warkentin, 1938).

Some people who are unimpressed by gestalt perception will accept such studies as a convincing proof of a relationship. Others will be unconvinced, feeling that the correlation may be due to unknown causes.

The same is the case with the psychoanalytic interpretation of what Freud called the psychopathology of everyday life. For instance, Freud (1916-17) reports the following story:

> I was once the guest of a young married couple and heard the young woman laughingly describe her latest experience. The day after her return from the honeymoon she had called for her unmarried sister to go shopping with her as she used to do, while her husband went to his business. Suddenly she noticed a gentleman on the other side of the street, and nudging her sister had cried: 'Look, there goes Herr L.' She had forgotten that this gentleman had been her husband for some weeks. I shuddered as I heard the story, but I did not dare to draw the inference. The little incident only occurred to my mind some years later when the marriage had come to a most unhappy end [p. 57f.].

For some people, forgetting the fact that one is married to a person and reacting to him as a stranger will be a rather convincing indication of a less than complete acceptance of the relationship, or of an estrangement; but how could this be proved by objective data? One might follow up a number of such cases with a view to establishing whether their divorce rate is significantly different from that prevailing at their time and place. But since the slip can indicate only alienation at the particular moment, i.e., it may be only temporary, while divorce, presumably, is the consequence of a more lasting alienation, one would need a sizable number of cases before conclusions would have any significance. And it may be difficult to find a sufficient number of comparable, well-documented incidents of this kind. Yet, even if these were found, and if the investigation showed no statistically significant difference in the subsequent divorce rate of these cases, there would still be some who would continue to believe that the slip did indicate a lack of involvement, and that the fact that it did not show up in the divorce rate was probably due to undetected minor causes.[5]

There are many instances of this kind. In practical life situations many people respond to slips as though they understood the meaning which Freud (1901) attributed to them, even though they may not be willing to endorse the Freudian view in its abstract formulation. If a young man does not turn up for a date, his girl will hardly accept it as a valid excuse that he has "just" forgotten about it; rather, she will probably feel that this explanation adds insult to injury.

During the Italian campaign of World War II twenty-three villagers of Caiazzo in Southern Italy were machine-gunned at the order of a German officer. He had asked the villagers in which direction "the enemy" had gone and they, inadvertently, did not point in the direction of Allied troop movements but in that of the Germans. The barbarism of a mass execution of people for an inadvertent show of sympathy needs no emphasis; but who will question that the slip of the villagers did, in fact, betray where their sympathies lay?

[5] Considerations of this kind are not limited to psychological matters. In the physical sciences too, a theory can seem so well established that the scientific community disregards incongruous data, satisfied that they are due to secondary, if undetected, causes. Half a century ago physicists disregarded F. Ehrenhaft's reports of having measured electric charges smaller than the elementary quantum of electricity. They did so, even though Ehrenhaft's observations had never been satisfactorily explained.

However, it must be emphasized that in a properly conduct-ed psychoanalysis, the psychoanalyst should not rely exclusively on his impressions, no matter how strong. While believing that the psychic life of others is accessible to observation, he must be aware of the fact that this kind of observation is subject to many errors and illusions. Even in the story of the newlywed quoted above, Freud (1916-17) emphasized that "Our interpretation is...no more than a suspicion to which we ourselves do not attach too much importance. Later, however, something hap-pens which shows us how well-justified our interpretation had been" (p. 57).

This later event, in the case of the story, is the unhappy ending of the marriage. Freud, as we see, operated by *combin-ing psychic insight with objective corroborations.*

In a similar way, the psychoanalyst checks his "perceptions" by means of external data which do not require the same "looking into" the mind (Waelder, 1960a). He is therefore constantly *oscillating between gestalt perceptions and checking by way of nongestalt operations.*

The *second* part of the psychoanalytic procedure, the search for repetitive patterns, is a matter of (logical) reasoning.

The *third*, or historical, part of the psychoanalyst's job is pure reconstruction of the kind that is practiced by historians, archaeologists, criminal investigators, accident investigators, supervisors who conduct surveys, and many others. It is subject to the same criteria that these activities are: i.e., the fact that a reconstruction is plausible does not prove it to be correct. We may have a plausible explanation of a person's character in terms of the family constellation in his childhood—father, mother, siblings, their characteristics and interrelations—but that does not mean it is necessarily the correct one. In order to accept it as such, it must also be shown that it can account for all pheno-mena, that all its implications can be found in reality, and that all alterantive explanations can be ruled out.

In some instances, a psychoanalytic reconstruction can also acquire the same predictive and manipulative aspect that we have noticed in some historical reconstructions (e.g., in the case of the typhoid epidemic). If a psychoanalyst has succeeded in "solving" a neurotic symptom, i.e., in understanding it as a manifestation of an inner conflict, the reappearance of the symptom in a given constellation of circumstances becomes predictable. So does its disappearance, once its emergence under the circumstances has been understood and the underlying conflict, of which it appears to be a manifestation, has found a different solution. There are cases in which a person who has satisfactorily understood his neurosis can, on the basis of this understanding, virtually make and unmake his symptoms at will.

Thus, psychoanalytic interpretations properly arrived at can, in my opinion, reach a very high degree of probability—beyond all reasonable doubt. This does not mean, however, that such near-certainty can be claimed for all explanation suggested by psychoanalysts, anymore than all interpretations of the past advanced by historians, or all measurements made in a laboratory, are necessarily correct. There is little doubt that the quantitative measurement required in some fields serves as a useful restraint on the flight of the imagination in those whose restraints are otherwise not too strong. But that, in turn, does not mean that the responsible application of a subtle procedure should be discredited because some people fall short of its stringent requirements.

But psychoanalysis is not only a collection of individual case histories; it has a doctrine, and that doctrine serves in the study of individual cases by suggesting directions for the search.

The doctrine consists of *generalizations from individual case studies* and formulates regularities rather than universal laws. Among these are developmental and maturational patterns: the phases of psychosexual development, for example, including concepts such as latency, or the stages of ego and superego development. They describe typical patterns and are tolerant to qualifications and exceptions. The anal-sadistic phase of infantile development may be all pervasive in some cases and barely hinted at in others. Latency may be all but lacking, with infantile sexuality continuing virtually uninterrupted into puberty. "Postambivalent" genital attitudes may never be reached at all, etc. The conditions, biological or environmental, for this spectrum of variations is a subject for study.

A particularly interesting case of this kind is the theory of the oedipus complex which, according to Freud, is the culmination of infantile sexuality. It represents a kind of anticipation of adolescence, and, because of the child's physiological immaturity, is doomed to failure. Under conditions of family life, the oedipus complex ordinarily assumes the form of a desire reaching out toward the parent of the opposite sex and competition with the parent of the same sex. There are, however, variations according to circumstances, and the oedipus complex of the institutionalized orphan, whose parents live only in fantasy, or of the child of a prostitute who receives different men every night, necessarily shows deviations from the typical form. There is also the "inverted oedipus complex" (Freud, 1923b) wherein the child takes the parent of the same sex as object, in competition with the parent of the opposite sex.

In recent decades, anthropologists have described societies which are not assemblages of monogamous families, but in which children live with the maternal clan, and the mother's brother is the dominant male figure in their early life. Clearly, a variation of the pattern typical in partrilinear structures must be expected under these circumstances; but there is no reason why this should invalidate the basic assumption of a premature flowering of genital sexuality, with adults as important objects.

Once the data about these societies had become known, many anthropologists proclaimed that the psychoanalytic theory of the oedipus complex had been exploded; they acted on the assumption that psychoanalysis had claimed that the oedipus complex is a manifestation of a universal law of nature rather than a regular maturational stage, and that the form which the oedipus complex tends to take in children growing up in "normal," monogamous, families is its only possible form. Neither of these claims had in fact been made; and even if they had been made, the new material would require only qualification, not abandonment, of the theory.

We have an outside observer's report of Freud's reaction to Malinowski's description of societies in which children are brought up by their mothers and their maternal uncles. From the anthropological writings referred to, one should expect Freud to have felt that a decisive shot had been fired at one of his doctrines. But that had apparently not occurred to him at all.

Victor von Weizsaecker (1954) reports a conversation with Freud in 1926:

> When the extent of the application of psychoanalysis came up, Freud implied that psychoanalysis would have interesting material for about another fifty years. He mentioned, for example, the psychology of the African matrilinear tribes where the Oedipus complex is directed, not against the father, but against the brother of the mother, since he represented the authority of the family [p. 66].

Thus Freud saw in these anthropological findings material for a refinement of psychoanalytic knowledge; it had not occurred to him that others might look upon them as evidence against fundamental propositions of psychoanalysis.

Perhaps the most important piece of psychoanalytic doctrine is the theory of neurosis. According to Freud, psychoneurosis is due to an unresolved inner conflict which involves libidinal strivings. The conflict has been evaded by repression which has succeeded only in making the strivings unconscious but not in incapacitating them. The neurotic manifestations represent a return of the repressed, distorted so as not to be recognizable.

This concept, too, must be considered an empirical finding rather than a universal law. Perhaps the *return of the repressed* may turn out to be the essential factor in neurosis, if we define neurosis as a condition in which men are forced to behave against their better judgment, to think what they do not want to think, to do what they do not want to do. But the fact that a *sexual* impulse is involved is purely *empirical*. In fact, Freud himself (1936) once ascribed a feeling of unreality, a phenomenon akin to neurosis, to a guilt feeling that had not been recognized as such and that had forced its way into consciousness in this distorted form ("it is not true" instead of "it should not be true"). There seem to be other such cases (Waelder, 1960a) in the realm of psychoneurosis proper. But such findings are refinements of, rather than contradictions to, the original theory. They will be important if and when the ultimate principles or laws are some day distilled from the wealth of experience. But that day is not yet. We are not yet at the point where we can safely proceed to the highest level of abstraction and formulate all-embracing laws.

Which leads to the final point. Psychoanalysis consists of individual case studies and generalizations drawn from them. But what about universal laws in psychoanalysis?

Laws that define the *necessary and sufficient conditions* of phenomena do not, to my knowledge, exist. There are many rules that formulate *necessary though not sufficient* conditions of an event; and many more that formulate probable ones. These rules are a matter of experience, and intrinsic necessity can hardly be claimed for them. They are more like Kepler's laws than like Newton's. Their verification must therefore be sought through observation rather than through experiment. The role which the genuine *experiment, the via regia to the validation of general laws,* can play in the verification and refutation of psychoanalytic propositions is correspondingly small.

The day may come—will come, I hope—when a few grains of intrinsic necessity can be extracted from a ton of known and well-studied patterns of phenomena, so that the latter can be derived from the former. When this day dawns, experiments will be called for to prove or disprove these propositions.

Summary and Conclusion

There seem to me to be three basic approaches to the study of the empirical world: the observation of contemporary events; the reconstruction of the past; and experimentation to establish universally valid cause-effect relations.

Observational science struggles with the question of the admissibility of gestalt perceptions and the question of observer bias. In the first of these questions we have to do with genuine differences in the ways men perceive and think, and universal agreement cannot be expected.

The rationale of *reconstruction* of the past is fundamentally the same, whether an astrophysicist studies the origin of the solar system, an archaeologist reconstructs the living conditions of a prehistoric people, a historian evaluates the reliability of written records, or a psychoanalyst tries to uncover the formation of a neurotic symptom. It is always a reconstruction of the past on the basis of clues available at present, in the light of assured regularities, whether physical, biological, or psychological.

Reconstruction has to steer its course between a naïve confidence in the plausible, and a radical skepticism which, if taken seriously, would make all life, and with it also all laboratory science, impossible.

Experimentation is the royal road toward the formulation and demonstration of universal laws. Its applicability is limited to conditions that can be manipulated in relevant aspects. Outside of this area, the ambiguities of experimental research multiply rapidly. Application of laboratory results to life situations requires, in any case, an act of *judgment* which in itself can only rarely be tested experimentally.

The various doctrines advanced by philosophers of science or of history, from positivism to historicism, contain (greater or lesser) elements of truth and have therefore their areas of applicability. But their claims have often been extended beyond this area of legitimate application; this is partly because generalizations from experience, natural to the intellect, are likely to go beyond what is justified—experience is almost always more contingent than we appreciate at the time—and partly because of a "will to believe." In particular, the currently prevailing scientistic and positivistic assumptions appear to be largely ideological, i.e., rooted in attitudes and aspirations rather than in facts.

Bibliography

Abraham, K. (1924), A Short Study of the Development of the Libido. *Selected Papers on Psycho-Analysis.* London: Hogarth Press, 1949, pp. 418-501.

———— (1927), The Psycho-sexual Differences between Hysteria and Dementia Praecox. *Selected Papers of Karl Abraham,* London: Hogarth Press, 1949, pp. 64-79.

Aichhorn, A. (1936), On the Technique of Child Guidance: The Process of Transference. In: *Delinquency and Child Guidance,* ed. O. Fleischmann, P. Kramer, & H. Ross. New York: International Universities Press, 1964, pp. 101-192.

Alexander, F. (1925), Einige unkritische Gedanken zu Ferenczis Genitaltheorie. *Int. Z. Psychoanal.,* 11:444-456.

———— (1929), The Need for Punishment and the Death Instinct. *Int. J. Psycho-Anal.,* 10:256-269.

Allee, W. C. (1942), Social Dominance and Subordination among Vertebrates. In: *Levels of Integration in Biological and Social Systems,* ed. R. Redfield. Lancaster, Pa.: Jacques Cattell Press.

Arlow, J. A. (1959), Psychoanalysis as Scientific Method. In: *Psychoanalysis, Scientific Method, and Philosophy,* ed. S. Hook. New York: New York University Press, pp. 201-211.

Aron, R. (1962), *Peace and War: A Theory of International Relations,* tr. R. Howard & A. B. Fox. Garden City: Doubleday, 1966.

Arthur, G. (1920), *The Life of Lord Kitchener.* London: Macmillan.

Asch, S. (1945), *One Destiny.* New York: G. P. Putnam's Sons.

Bak, R. C. (1951), Discussion of Dr. Wexler's Paper. In: *Psychotherapy with Schizophrenics,* ed. E. B. Brody & F. C. Redlich. New York: International Universities Press, pp. 202-215.

———— (1954), The Schizophrenic Defence against Aggression. *Int. J. Psycho-Anal.,* 34:129-134.

Bally, G. (1933), Die frühkindliche Motorik im Vergleich mit der Motorik der Tiere. *Imago,* 19:339-366.

Banfield, E. C. (1958), *The Moral Basis of a Backward Society.* Glencoe, Ill.: Free Press.

Becker, B. (1957), Pioneers of the Atom. *N.Y. Times Mag.,* October 30.

Berlin, I. (1954), *Historical Inevitability.* New York: Oxford University Press.

Bernfeld, S. (1932), Der Begriff der Deutung in der Psychoanalyse. *Z. angew. Psychol.,* 42:448-497.

———— (1935), Über die Einteilung der Triebe. *Imago,* 21:125-142.

Betlheim, S. & Hartmann, H. (1924), On Parapraxes in the Korsakoff Psychosis. In: *Essays on Ego Psychology*. New York: International Universities Press, 1964, pp. 353-368.

Bibring, E. (1937), Contribution to: Symposium on the Theory of the Therapeutic Results of Psycho-Analysis. *Int. J. Psycho-Anal.*, 18:170-189.

———— (1941), The Development and Problems of the Theory of Instincts. *Int. J. Psycho-Anal.*, 22:102-131.

Binswanger, L. (1956), *Sigmund Freud: Reminiscences of a Friendship*. New York: Grune & Stratton, 1957.

Bleuler, E. (1911a), *Dementia Praecox or the Group of Schizophrenias*. New York: International Universities Press, 1950.

———— (1911b), *Die Psychoanalyse Freuds: Verteidigung und kritische Bemerkungen*. Vienna: Deuticke.

Brenner, C. (1955), *An Elementary Textbook of Psychoanalysis*. New York: International Universities Press.

Bridgman, P. W. (1959a), Comments to: Psychoanalysis: Protoscience and Metapsychology, by G. Kennedy. In: *Psychoanalysis, Scientific Method, and Philosophy*, ed. S. Hook. New York: New York University Press, p. 282.

———— (1959b), *The Way Things Are*. Cambridge, Mass.: Harvard University Press.

Brierley, M. (1947), Notes on Psycho-Analysis and Integrative Living. *Trends in Psycho-Analysis*. London: Hogarth Press, 1951, pp. 180-293.

Brosin, H. W. (1955), Report on Panel: Validation of Psychoanalytic Theory. *J. Amer. Psychoanal. Assn.*, 3:489-495.

Bühler, K. (1927), *Die Krise der Psychologie*. Jena: Fischer.

———— (1934), *Sprachtheorie*. Jena: Fischer.

Burckhardt, J. C. (1868), *Force and Freedom: Reflections on History*, ed. J. H. Nichols. New York: Pantheon Books, 1943.

Burlingham, D. (1934), The Urge to Tell and the Compulsion to Confess. *Psychoanalytic Studies of the Sighted and the Blind*. New York: International Universities Press, 1972, pp. 33-51.

Burnet, M. (1962), *Natural History of Infectious Disease*. Cambridge: Cambridge University Press.

Butterfield, H. (1949), *Christianity and History*. New York: Scribner.

Carr. E. H. (1961), *What Is History?* London: Macmillan.

Chen, T. H. E. (1961), *Thought Reform of the Chinese Intellectuals*. Hong Kong: Hong Kong University Press.

Cohn, N. (1957), *The Pursuit of the Millennium*. London: Seeker & Warburg.

Constant de Rebècque, H. B. (1813), *De l'esprit de conquête et de l'usurpation, dans leur rapports avec la civilisation européene*. Paris: Nicolle et Le Normant, 1814.

Cornford, F. M. (1950), *The Unwritten Philosophy*. Cambridge: Cambridge University Press.

Dahlberg-Acton, J. E. E. (1862), Nationality. *Essays on Freedom and Power*. Glencoe, Ill.: Free Press, 1948, pp. 166-195.

Dantzig, T. (1955), *The Bequest of the Greeks*. New York: Scribner.

Deutsch, H. (1922), Über die pathologische Lüge. *Int Z. Psychoanal.*, 8:153-167.

Dilthey, W. (1924), Ideen über eine beschreibende und zergliedernde Psychologie. *Gesammelte Schriften*, 5. Leipzig: Teubner.

Dollard, J. & Miller, N. (1939), *Aggression and Frustration*. New Haven: Yale University Press.

Dubos, R. (1959), *The Mirage of Health*. New York: Doubleday.

―――― (1965a), Science and Man's Nature. *Daedalus*, 94:223-244.

―――― (1965b), *Man Adapting*. New Haven: Yale University Press.

Emerson, R. (1960), *From Empire to Nation*. Cambridge: Harvard University Press.

Federn, P. (1952), *Ego Psychology and the Psychoses*. New York: Basic Books.

Feldman, S. (1951), Anxiety and Orgasm. *Psychoanal. Quart.*, 20:528-549.

Fenichel, O. (1926), Identification. *The Collected Papers of Otto Fenichel*, 1:97-112. New York: Norton, 1953.

―――― (1932), *Outline of Clinical Psychoanalysis*. New York: Norton.

Ferenczi, S. & Rank, O. (1924), *The Development of Psychoanalysis*. New York: Nervous and Mental Disease Monographs, 1925.

Finley, J. H. (1955), *Pindar and Aeschylus*. Cambridge: Harvard University Press.

Frank, P. (1959), Psychoanalysis and Logical Positivism. In: *Psychoanalysis, Scientific Method and Philosophy*, ed. S. Hook. New York: New York University Press, pp. 308-313.

Frankel, C. (1959), The Status of Freud's Ideas. In: *Psychoanalysis, Scientific Method and Philosophy*, ed. S. Hook. New York: New York University Press, pp. 324-328.

Freud, A. (1926-27), Four Lectures on Child Analysis. *The Writings of Anna Freud*, 1:3-72.*

―――― (1927), The Theory of Child Analysis. *The Writings of Anna Freud*, 1:162-174.

―――― (1930), Four Lectures on Psychoanalysis for Teachers and Parents. *The Writings of Anna Freud*, 1:73-136.

―――― (1932), Neurotic Mechanisms under the Influence of Education. Paper read at 12th Congress of the International Psycho-Analytical Association, Wiesbaden.

―――― (1934), Psychoanalysis and the Upbringing of the Young Child. *The Writings of Anna Freud*, 1:176-188.

―――― (1936), *The Ego and the Mechanisms of Defense*, rev. ed. *The Writings of Anna Freud*, 2.

―――― (1952), The Mutual Influences in the Development of Ego and Id: Introduction to the Discussion. *The Writings of Anna Freud*, 4:230-244.

―――― (1958), Child Observation and Prediction of Development. *The Writings of Anna Freud*, 5:102-135.

―――― (1963), Regression as a Principle in Mental Development. *The Writings of Anna Freud*, 6:93-107.

―――― (1964), Doctoral Award Address. *The Writings of Anna Freud*, 5:507-516.

Freud, E. L., ed. (1960), *Letters of Sigmund Freud (1873-1939)*. New York: Basic Books.

* *The Writings of Anna Freud*, 7 Volumes. New York: International Universities Press, 1968-1974.

† *The Standard Edition of the Complete Psychological Works of Sigmund Freud*, 24 Volumes. London: Hogarth Press and the Institute of Psycho-Analysis, 1953-1974.

Freud, S. (1896), Further Remarks on the Neuro-Psychoses of Defence. *Standard Edition*, 3:159-185.†

_____ (1900), The Interpretation of Dreams. *Standard Edition*, 4 & 5.

_____ (1901), The Psychopathology of Everyday Life. *Standard Edition*, 6.

_____ (1905 [1901]), Fragment of an Analysis of a Case of Hysteria. *Standard Edition*, 7:3-122.

_____ (1907 [1906]), Delusions and Dreams in Jensen's *Gradiva*. *Standard Edition*, 9:3-95.

_____ (1908), Creative Writers and Day-Dreaming. *Standard Edition*, 9:141-153.

_____ (1909a), Analysis of a Phobia in a Five-year-old Boy. *Standard Edition*, 10:3-149.

_____ (1909b), Notes upon a Case of Obsessional Neurosis. *Standard Edition*, 10:153-320.

_____ (1910a [1909]), Five Lectures on Psycho-Analysis. *Standard Edition*, 11:3-56.

_____ (1910b), Leonardo da Vinci and a Memory of His Childhood. *Standard Edition*, 11:59-137.

_____ (1911a), Psycho-Analytic Notes on an Autobiographical Account of a Case of Paranoia (Dementia Paranoides). *Standard Edition*, 12:3-82.

_____ (1911b), Formulations on the Two Principles of Mental Functioning. *Standard Edition*, 12:213-226.

_____ (1912), Recommendations to Physicians Practising Psycho-Analysis. *Standard Edition*, 12:109-120.

_____ (1913 [1912-1913]), Totem and Taboo. *Standard Edition*, 13:1-161.

_____ (1914a), On Narcissism: An Introduction. *Standard Edition*, 14:67-102.

_____ (1914b), On the History of the Psycho-Analytic Movement. *Standard Edition*, 14:7-66.

_____ (1915a), Instincts and Their Vicissitudes. *Standard Edition*, 14:111-140.

_____ (1915b), Thoughts for the Times on War and Death. *Standard Edition*, 14:273-302.

_____ (1916), On Transience. *Standard Edition*, 14:303-307.

_____ (1916-17 [1915-17]), Introductory Lectures on Psycho-Analysis. *Standard Edition*, 15 & 16.

_____ (1917), Mourning and Melancholia. *Standard Edition*, 14:237-260.

_____ (1918 [1914]), From the History of an Infantile Neurosis. *Standard Edition*, 17:3-123.

_____ (1920a), Beyond the Pleasure Principle. *Standard Edition*, 18:7-64.

_____ (1920b), The Psychogenesis of a Case of Homosexuality in a Woman. *Standard Edition*, 18:145-172.

_____ (1921), Group Psychology and the Analysis of the Ego. *Standard Edition*, 18:67-143.

_____ (1922), Some Neurotic Mechanisms in Jealousy, Paranoia and Homosexuality. *Standard Edition*, 18:221-232.

_____ (1923a [1922]), Psycho-Analysis. *Standard Edition*, 18:235-254.

_____ (1923b), The Ego and the Id. *Standard Edition*, 19:3-66.

_____ (1924a [1923]), Neurosis and Psychosis. *Standard Edition*, 19:149-158.

_____ (1924b [1923]), A Short Account of Psycho-Analysis. *Standard Edition*, 19:191-209.
_____ (1924c), The Loss of Reality in Neurosis and Psychosis. *Standard Edition*, 19:183-187.
_____ (1924d), The Economic Problem of Masochism. *Standard Edition*, 19:157-170.
_____ (1925a), Some Additional Notes on Dream-Interpretation as a Whole. (B) Moral Responsibility for the Content of Dreams. *Standard Edition*, 19:131-134.
_____ (1925b), An Autobiographical Study. *Standard Edition*, 20:3-74.
_____ (1926a), Inhibitions, Symptoms and Anxiety. *Standard Edition*, 20:77-175.
_____ (1926b), The Question of Lay Analysis. *Standard Edition*, 20:179-258.
_____ (1927a), The Future of an Illusion. *Standard Edition*, 21:3-56.
_____ (1927b), Humour. *Standard Edition*, 21:159-166.
_____ (1930 [1929]), Civilization and Its Discontents. *Standard Edition*, 21:59-145.
_____ (1931a), Libidinal Types. *Standard Edition*, 21:215-220.
_____ (1931b), Female Sexuality. *Standard Edition*, 21:225-243.
_____ (1933a [1932]), Why War? *Standard Edition*, 22:197-215.
_____ (1933b [1932]), New Introductory Lectures on Psycho-Analysis. *Standard Edition*, 22:3-182.
_____ (1933c), Sándor Ferenczi. *Standard Edition*, 22:227-229.
_____ (1935), To Thomas Mann on His Sixtieth Birthday. *Standard Edition*, 22:255.
_____ (1936), A Disturbance of Memory on the Acropolis. *Standard Edition*, 22:239-248.
_____ (1937a), Analysis Terminable and Interminable. *Standard Edition*, 23:209-253.
_____ (1937b), Constructions in Analysis. *Standard Edition*, 23:255-269.
_____ (1939 [1934-1938]), Moses and Monotheism. *Standard Edition*, 23:3-137.
_____ (1940 [1938]), An Outline of Psycho-Analysis. *Standard Edition*, 23:141-207.
Freymond, J. (1960), *The Saar Conflict 1945-1955*. New York: Praeger.
Fromm, E. (1959), *Sigmund Freud's Mission*. New York: Harper.
Fuller, J. F. C. (1954), *The Decisive Battles of the Western World*, Vol. 1. London: Spottingwood & Eyre.
Gabor, D. (1962), Predicting Machines. *Scientia*, 47:113-117.
Gardner, G. E. (1931), Evidences of Homosexuality in 120 Unanalyzed Cases with Paranoid Content. *Psychoanal. Rev.*, 18:57-62.
Gibbon, E. (1788), *The History of the Decline and Fall of the Roman Empire*, Vol. 7. London: Methuen, 1909-1914.
Gibson, J. J. (1950), *The Perception of the Visual World*. Boston: Houghton Mifflin.
Gillispie, C. C. (1960), *The Edge of Objectivity*. Princeton: Princeton University Press.
Giovacchini, P. L. (1960), On Scientific Creativity. *J. Amer. Psychoanal. Assn.*, 8:407-426.

Gitelson, M. (1952), The Emotional Position of the Analyst in the Psycho-analytic Situation. In: *Psychoanalysis: Science and Profession*. New York: International Universities Press, 1973, pp. 173-200.

Glover, E. (1931), The Therapeutic Effect of Inexact Interpretation: A Contribution to the Theory of Suggestion. *Int J. Psycho-Anal.*, 12:397-411.

―――― (1934), Medical Psychology or Academic (Normal) Psychology: A Problem in Orientation. *Brit. J. Med. Psychol.*, 14:31-49.

―――― (1935), A Developmental Study of the Obsessional Neuroses. *Int. J. Psycho-Anal.*, 16:131-144.

―――― (1937), Contribution to: Symposium on the Theory of the Therapeutic Results of Psycho-Analysis. *Int. J. Psycho-Anal.*, 18:125-132.

―――― (1956), *On the Early Development of Mind*. New York: International Universities Press.

―――― & Ginsberg, M. (1934), A Symposium on the Psychology of Peace and War. *Brit. J. Med. Psychol.*, 14:274-293.

Goethe, J. W., *Faust*, tr. W. Kaufmann. New York: Anchor Books, 1961.

Goldstein, K. (1939), *The Organism*. New York: American Book.

―――― (1942), *After Effects of Brain Injuries in War*. New York: Grune & Stratton.

―――― & Gelb, A. (1920), Psychologische Analysen hirnpathologischer Fälle. Leipzig: Barth.

Greenacre, P. (1967), The Influence of Infantile Trauma on Genetic Patterns. In: *Psychic Trauma*, ed. S. S. Furst. New York: Basic Books, pp. 108-153.

Groos, K. (1896), *Die Spiele der Tiere*. Jena: Fischer, 1930.

―――― (1922), *Das Spiel*. Jena: Fischer.

Grossman, G. (1960), *Value and Plan*. Berkeley & Los Angeles: University of California Press.

Haag, E. van den (1959), Psychoanalysis and Its Discontents. In: *Psychoanalysis, Scientific Method, and Philosophy*, ed. S. Hook. New York: New York University Press, pp. 104-116.

Hand, L. (1916), The Speech of Justice. *Harvard Law Rev.*, 29:617,619.

Hartmann, H. (1927), *Die Grundlagen der Psychoanalyse*. Leipzig: Thieme.

―――― (1928), Psychoanalyse und Wertproblem. *Imago*, 14:421-440.

―――― (1933), Psychoanalyse und Weltanschauung. *Psychoanal. Bewegung*, 5:416-429.

―――― (1934-1935), Psychiatric Studies of Twins. *Essays on Ego Psychology*. New York: International Universities Press, 1964, pp. 419-445.

―――― (1948), Comments on the Psychoanalytic Theory of Instinctual Drives. *Ibid.*, pp. 69-89.

―――― (1952), The Mutual Influences in the Development of Ego and Id. *Ibid.*, pp. 155-181.

―――― (1953), Contribution to the Metapsychology of Schizophrenia. *Ibid.*, pp. 182-206.

―――― (1958), Comments on the Scientific Aspects of Psychoanalysis. *Ibid.*, pp. 297-317.

―――― (1959), Psychoanalysis as a Scientific Theory. *Ibid.*, pp. 318-350.

―――― & Kris, E. (1945), The Genetic Approach in Psychoanalysis. *The Psychoanalytic Study of the Child*, 1:11-30. New York: International Universities Press.

————, Kris, E., & Loewenstein, R. M. (1949), Notes on the Theory of Aggression. *The Psychoanalytic Study of the Child*, 3/4:9-36. New York: International Universities Press.

Head, H. (1920), *Studies in Neurology*. London: Frowde.

Heiden, K. (1936), *Adolf Hitler*. Zurich: Europa Verlag.

Hobbes, T. (1651), *Leviathan*. London: Printed for A. Crooke. New York: Dutton, 1950.

Homer, *Iliad*, 1:260f.

———— *Odyssey*, 17, 322ff.

Hook, S., ed. (1959), *Psychoanalysis, Scientific Method, and Philosophy: A Symposium*. New York: New York University Press.

Hospers, J. (1959), Philosophy and Psychoanalysis. In: *Psychoanalysis, Scientific Method, and Philosophy*, ed. S. Hook. New York: New York University Press, pp. 336-357.

Hume, D. (1739-1740), *A Treatise of Human Nature*, 189.

James, W. (1907), *Pragmatism*. New York: Longmans, Green.

Jekels, L. (1952), *Selected Papers*. New York: International Universities Press.

Jones, Edward E. (1965), Conformity as a Tactic of Integration. *Science*, 149:144-150.

Jones, Ernest (1928), *Psycho-Analysis*. London: Ernest Benn, 1942.

———— (1927), The Early Development of Female Sexuality. In: *Papers on Psycho-Analysis*. London: Baillière, Tindall and Cox, 1948, pp. 438-451.

———— (1929), Fear, Guilt and Hate. *Ibid.*, pp. 304-319.

———— (1932), The Phallic Phase. *Ibid.*, pp. 451-484.

———— (1935), Early Female Sexuality. *Ibid.*, pp. 485-495.

———— (1953-57), *The Life and Work of Sigmund Freud*, 3 Vols. New York: Basic Books.

Jouvenel, B. de (1957), *Sovereignty*. Cambridge: Cambridge University Press.

Juvenal, *Satires*, VIII, 83.

Kallen, H. (1954), In: Considerations Regarding the Loyalty Oath as a Manifestation of Current Tensions and Anxiety. *Group for the Advancement of Psychiatry*, Report 1.

Kant, I. (1790-96), Über den Gemeinspruch: Das mag in der Theorie richtig sein, taught aber nicht für die Praxis. *Werke in sechs Banden*. Darmstadt: Wissenschaftliche Buchgesellschaft.

———— (1796), *On Perpetual Peace*. New York: Liberal Arts Press, 1957.

Kardiner, A. (1959), Social and Cultural Implications of Psychoanalysis. In: *Psychoanalysis, Scientific Method, and Philosophy*, ed. S. Hook. New York: New York University Press, pp. 81-103.

————, Karush, A., & Ovesey, L. (1959), A Methodological Study of Freudian Theory: IV. The Structural Hypothesis, the Problem of Anxiety, and Post-Freudian Ego Psychology. *J. Nerv. Ment. Dis.*, 129:341-356.

———— ———— ———— (1966), A Methodological Study of Freudian Theory. *Int. J. Psychiat.*, 2:489-544, 1966.

Katan, M. (1934), The Spontaneous Attempt at Recovery in Schizophrenia: A Contribution. *Int. J. Psycho-Anal.*, 15:494-495.

———— (1936), Points of Resemblance in the Delusional Mechanisms of Schizophrenia and Melancholia. *Int. J. Psycho-Anal.*, 18:91, 1937.

———— (1946), *De Grondbeginselen van de waanvorming*. Leiden: Proefschrift.

———— (1949), Schreber's Delusion of the End of the World. *Psychoanal. Quart.*, 18:60-66.

————(1950a), Schreber's Hallucinations about the "Little Men." *Int. J. Psycho-Anal.*, 31:32-35.

———— (1950b), Structural Aspects of a Case of Schizophrenia. *The Psychoanalytic Study of the Child*, 5:175-211. New York: International Universities Press.

Keynes, J. M. (1926), *The General Theory of Employment, Interest and Money*. New York: Harcourt, Brace.

Kinkead, E. (1959), *In All Wars But One*. New York: Norton.

Klein, M. (1932), *The Psycho-Analysis of Children*. London: Hogarth Press.

———— (1948), *Contributions to Psycho-Analysis*. London: Hogarth Press.

Knight, F. H. (1960), *Intelligence and Democratic Action*. Cambridge: Harvard University Press.

Köhler, W. (1929), *Gestalt Psychology*. New York: Liveright.

Kraepelin, E. (1901-1905), *Clinical Psychiatry*. New York: London: Macmillan, 1907.

Krehl, L. von (1929), *Krankheitsform und Persönlichkeit*. Leipzig: Thieme.

Kris, E. (1934), The Psychology of Caricature. *Psychoanalytic Explorations in Art*. New York: International Universities Press, 1952, pp. 173-188.

———— (1943), Some Problems of War Propaganda. *Psychoanal. Quart.*, 12:381-399.

———— (1955), Neutralization and Sublimation. *The Psychoanalytic Study of the Child*, 10:30-46. New York: International Universities Press.

———— (1956), The Recovery of Childhood Memories in Psychoanalysis. *The Psychoanalytic Study of the Child*, 11:31-54. New York: International Universities Press.

Kubie, L. (1959), Psychoanalysis and Scientific Method. In: *Psychoanalysis, Scientific Method, and Philosophy*, ed. S. Hook. New York: New York University Press, pp. 57-77.

Kuhn, T. S. (1962), *The Structure of Scientific Revolutions*. Chicago: University of Chicago Press.

Kuznets, S. (1963), Quantitative Aspects of the Economic Growth of Nations: VIII. Distribution of Income by Size. In: *Economic Development and Cultural Change*, 11:22.

Laforgue, R. (1930), On the Erotization of Anxiety. *Int. J. Psycho-Anal.*, 11:312-321.

Langer, E. (1966), The Shame of American Medicine. *N.Y. Rev. Books*, 6(9):6-12.

LaPiere, R. (1959), *The Freudian Ethic*. New York: Duell, Sloan & Pearce.

Lazerowitz, M. (1959), The Relevance of Psychoanalysis to Philosophy. In: *Psychoanalysis, Scientific Method, and Philosophy*, ed. S. Hook. New York: New York University Press, pp. 133-156.

Leavy, S., ed. & tr. (1964), *The Freud Journal of Lou Andreas-Salomé*. New York: Basic Books.

Lenin, N. (1917), *The State and Revolution*. London: G. Allen & Unwin, 1919.

———— *Collected Works*, 4th ed. Moscow: Foreign Languages Publishing House; Progress, 1960.

Lifton, R. J. (1961), *Thought Reform and the Psychology of Totalism: A Study of "Brainwashing" in China*. New York: Norton.

Livingstone, R. W. (1959), *The Rainbow Bridge*. London: Pall Mall Press.

Loewenstein, R. M. (1947), The Historical and Cultural Roots of Anti-Semitism. In: *Psychoanalysis and the Social Sciences*, 1:313-356. New York: International Universities Press.

Lorenz, K. Z. (1952), *King Solomon's Ring*. New York: Crowell.

———— (1954), *Man Meets Dog*. London: Methuen, 1955.

———— (1959), Gestaltwahrnehmung als Quelle wissenschaftlicher Erkenntnis. *exper. angew. Psychol.*, 6:118-165.

———— (1964), *On Aggression*. New York: Harcourt, Brace & World, 1966.

———— (1965), *Man and Aggression*, ed. M. F. Ashley Montagu. New York: Oxford University Press, 1968.

McIver, R. M. (1947), *The Web of Government*. New York: Macmillan.

M'Naghten's Case (1843), 10 Cl. & Fin. 200, 8 Eng. Rep. 718.

Mann, T. (1911), Death in Venice. *Stories of a Lifetime*, 2:7-71. London: Mercury Books, 1961.

———— (1926), Mein Verhaltnis zur Psychoalse. *Almanach der Psa.*, 32-33.

Mannheim, K. (1929), *Ideology and Utopia*. London: Routledge & Kegan Paul, 1936.

Mantoux, E. (1946), *The Carthaginian Peace*; or, *The Economic Consequences of Mr. Keynes*. London, New York: G. Cumberledge, Oxford University Press.

Meinecke, F. (1962), *Ausgewählter Briefwechsel*. Stuttgart: K. F. Koehler.

Mill, J. S. (1859), *Utilitarianism, Liberty, and Representative Government*, 99. London: Everyman's Library, 1910.

Morris, C. (1966), A Dissent to Dr. Waelder's Theory of Justice. *Univ. Penn. Law Rev.*, 115:12-16.

Munro, D. G. (1964), *Intervention and Dollar Diplomacy in the Caribbean, 1900-1921*. Princeton, N.J.: Princeton University Press.

Nagel, E. (1959), Methodological Issues in Psychoanalytic Theory. In: *Psychoanalysis, Scientific Method, and Philosophy*, ed. S. Hook. New York: New York University Press, pp. 38-56.

Namier, L. (1952), *Avenues of History*. London: Hamish Hamilton.

Nunberg, H. (1925), The Will to Recovery. *Practice and Theory of Psychoanalysis*, 1:75-88. New York: International Universities Press, 1965.

———— (1951), Transference and Reality. *Int. J. Psycho-Anal.*, 32:1-9.

———— (1926), The Sense of Guilt and the Need for Punishment, *Int. J. Psycho-Anal.*, 7:420-433.

———— (1932), *Allgemeine Neurosenlehre*. Bern, Berlin: H. Huber.

Onians, R. B. (1951), *The Origins of European Thought about the Body, the Mind, the Soul, the World, Time, and Fate*. Cambridge: Cambridge University Press, 1954.

Ophuijsen, J. H. W. Van (1927), Remarks on the anal complex in persecution Mania. *Nederl. T. Geneesk.*, 1490.

Ortéga y Gasset, J. (1930), *The Revolt of the Masses*. New York: Norton, 1932.

———— (1946), *Concord and Liberty*. New York: Norton.

Orwell, G. (1949), *Nineteen Eighty-four*. New York: Harcourt, Brace.

Page, J. & Warkentin, J. (1938), Masculinity and Paranoia. *J. Abnorm. Soc. Psychol.*, 33:527-531.

Parsons, T. (1950), Psychoanalysis and the Social Structure. *Psychoanal. Quart.*, 19:371-384.

Peisker, T. (1911), The Asiatic Background. In: *Cambridge Medieval History*, Vol. 1: *The Christian Roman Empire and the Foundation of the Teutonic Kingdoms*. New York: Macmillan, 1924, pp. 323-359.

People v. Schmidt (1915), 216 N.Y. 324, 110 N.E. 945.

Pfuhl, E. (1955), *Masterpieces of Greek Drawing and Painting*. New York: Macmillan.

Piggot, S. (1965), *Ancient Europe*. Edinburgh: Edinburgh University Press.

Polanyi, M. (1960), *Beyond Nihilism*. London: Cambridge University Press.

Portmann, A. (1953), *Das Tier als soziales Wesen*. Zurich: Rhein Verlag.

Rado, S. (1922), The Course of Natural Science in the Light of Psychoanalysis. *Psychoanal. Quart.*, 1:683-700, 1932.

———— (1925), The Economic Principle in Psycho-Analytic Technique. *Int. J. Psycho-Anal.*, 6:35-44.

Rangell, L. (1955), On the Psychoanalytic Theory of Anxiety: A Statement of a Unitary Theory. *J. Amer. Psychoanal. Assn.*, 3:389-414.

Rank, O. (1924), *Trauma of Birth*. New York: Harcourt Brace, 1929.

Rauschning, H. (1940), *Hitler Speaks*. London: Eyre & Spottiswoode.

Reik, T. (1925), *Geständniszwang und Strafbedürfnis*. Leipzig, Vienna, Zurich: Internationaler psychoanalytischen Verlag.

Rickman, John (1936), *On the Bringing Up of Children*. London: Kegan Paul.

Riviere, J. (1936), On the Genesis of Psychical Conflict in Earliest Infancy. *Int. J. Psycho-Anal.*, 17:395-422.

Roe, A. (1952), *The Making of a Scientist*. New York: Dodd, Mead.

Roffenstein, G. (1923), Experiments on Symbolization in Dreams. In: *Organization and Pathology of Thought*, ed. D. Rapaport. New York: Columbia University Press, 1951, pp. 249-256.

Röpke, W. (1945), *Die deutsche Frage*. Erlenbach-Zurich: E. Rentsch.

Rostand, J. (1962), *The Substance of Man*. New York: Doubleday.

Rougemont, D. de (1963), *The Christian Opportunity*. New York: Holt, Rinehart, & Winston.

Santayana, G. (1925), *Dialogues in Limbo*. New York: Scribner, 1928.

———— (1953), *The Life of Reason*. New York: Scribner, p. 146.

Schein, E. H. (with I. Schneier & C. H. Barker) (1961), *Coercive Persuasion: A Socio-Psychological Analysis of the "Brainwashing" of American Civilian Prisoners by the Chinese Communists*. New York: Norton.

Scheler, M. (1927), *Die Stellung des Menschen im Kosmos*. Darmstadt: O. Reichl, 1928.

———— (1954), *The Nature of Sympathy*. New Haven: Yale University Press.

Schilder, P. (1924), *Medical Psychology*. New York: International Universities Press, 1953.

Schjelderup-Ebbe, T. (1922a), Beiträge zur Sozialpsychologie des Haushuhns. *Z. Psychol.*, 88:225.

———— (1922b), Soziale Verhältnisse bei Vögeln. *Z. Psychol.*, 90:106.

———— (1923), Weitere Beitrage zur Sozial- und Individualpsychologie des Haushuhns. *Z. Psychol.*, 92:60.

Schrötter, K. (1911), Experimental Dreams. In: *Organization and Pathology of Thought*, ed. D. Rapaport New York: Columbia University Press, 1951, pp. 234-248.

Seidel, Fritz (1910), *Intellektualismus und Voluntarismus in der platonischen Ethik.* Weida: Thomas & Hubert.

Shils, E. (1958), Ideology and Civility: On the Politics of the Intellectual. *Sewanee Rev.*, 66:450-480.

Simmel, G. (1918), *Lebensanschauung.* Munich: Duncker & Humblot.

Singer, C. (1941), *A Short History of Science to the Nineteenth Century.* Oxford: Clarendon Press.

Somary, F. (1950), From Portsmouth to Korea: The Balance Sheet of American Foreign Policy (unpublished memorandum). German translation: *Neue Schweizer Rundschau*, Dec. 29, 1950.

_____ (1959), *Erinnerungen aus meinem Leben.* Zurich: Manesse-Verl.

Staley, E. (1935), *War and the Private Investor.* Chicago: University of Chicago Press.

Stärcke, A. (1921), Psychoanalysis and Psychiatry. *Int. J. Psycho-Anal.*, 2:361-415.

_____ (1935), The role of anal and oral quantities in delusions of persecution and in analogous systematizing. *Int. Z. Psychoanal.*, 5-22.

Steinen, W. von den (1949), *Das Zeitalter Goethes.* Bern: Francke Verlag.

Sterba, R. (1934), The Fate of the Ego in Analytic Therapy. *Int. J. Psycho-Anal.*, 15:117-126.

Strachey, J. (1934), The Nature of the Therapeutic Action of Psycho-analysis. *Int. J. Psycho-Anal.*, 15:127-159.

Strahosch, F. M. (1934), *Factors in the Sex Life of Seven Hundred Psychopathic Women.* Utica: New York State Hospital Press.

Taft, J. (1958), *Otto Rank.* New York: Julian Press.

Talmon, J. L. (1952), *The Origins of Totalitarian Democracy.* New York: Praeger, 1960.

_____ (1957), *Utopianism and Politics.* London: Conservative Political Center.

_____ (1960), *Political Messianism: The Romantic Phase.* New York: Praeger.

Tausk, V. (1913), Compensation As a Means of Discounting the Motive of Repression. *Int. J. Psycho-Anal.*, 5:130-140, 1924.

_____ (1934), Ibsen the Druggist. *Psychoanal. Quart.*, 3:137-141.

Taylor, A. J. P. (1961), *The Origins of the Second World War.* London: Hamish Hamilton.

Tocqueville, A. de (1835-40), *Democracy in America*, 2 Vols. New York: Knopf, 1945.

_____ (1856), *The Old Regime and the French Revolution.* Garden City: Doubleday, 1955.

_____ (1864-66), *Oeuvres Complètes.* Paris: Michel Lévy.

_____ (1893), *Recollections.* New York: Meridian, 1959.

Toynbee, A. J. (1947), Russia's Byzantine Heritage. *Horizon: Review of Literature and Art*, 16:82-96.

_____ (1948), *Civilisation on Trial.* New York: Oxford University Press.

Tresolini, R. J. (1961), Letter to the Editor. *Amer. Political Sci. Rev.*, 55:885.

Trevor-Roper, H. R. (1957), The Spanish Enlightenment. *Historical Essays.* London: Macmillan, pp. 260-272.

Valéry, P. (1943), *Tel Quel.* Paris: Gallimard.

Venturi, F. (1960), *Roots of Revolution: A History of the Populist and Social-*

ist Movements in Nineteenth Century Russia, tr. F. Haskell. New York: Knopf, 1964.

Waelder, J. (1935), The Analysis of a Case of Night Terror. *The Psychoanalytic Study of the Child*, 2:189-227. New York: International Universities Press, 1946.

––––– (1936), Communication to the Vienna Psychoanalytic Society, June 17.

Waelder, R. (1928), [Review of] R. Allers, Glück und Ende der Psychoanalyse. *Int. Z. Psychoanal.*, 14:410-411.

––––– (1929), [Review of] *Zeno Cosini* von Italo Svevo. *Psychoanal. Bewegung*, 3:170-173.

––––– (1930), Die latenten metaphysicischen Grundlagen der psychologischen Schulen. *Sitzungsber. I. Int. Kongr. ang. Psychopathol. Psychol.*, 178-194.

––––– (1932), [Review of] H. Deutsch, *Psychoanalyse der Neurosen. Int. Z. Psychoanal.*, 18:125-129.

––––– (1934), [Review of] H. Egyedi, *Die Irrtumer der Psychoanalyse. Imago*, 20:253-254.

––––– (1935), Referat über den heutigen Stand der Ich-Psychologie. *Int. Z. Psychoanal.*, 21:459-460.

––––– (1936), Die Bedeutung des Werkes Sigmund Freuds für die Sozial- und Rechtswissenschaften. *Rev. Int. Theorie du Droit*, 10:83-99.

––––– (1938), Kampmotive und Friedensmotive. *Almanach Psychoanal.*, 103-115.

––––– (1939a), [Review of] O. Kraus, *Die Werttheorien. Int. Z. Psychoanal.*, 24:181-182.

––––– (1939b), *Psychological Aspects of War and Peace*. Geneva: Geneva Research Center.

––––– (1940), Symposium on the Areas of Agreement in Psychotherapy. *Amer. J. Orthopsychiat.*, 10:704-708.

––––– ed. (1941), *The Living Thoughts of Sigmund Freud*. New York: Longmans, Green.

––––– (1948), Report on Panel Discussion: Mechanisms of Prejudice. *Bull. Amer. Psychoanal. Assn.*, 4(3):7-9.

––––– (1949), Report on Panel Discussion: Dream Theory and Interpretation. *Bull. Amer. Psychoanal. Assn.*, 5(2):36-40.

––––– (1950), Report on Panel Discussion: Problems of Transference and Countertransference. *Bull. Amer. Psychoanal. Assn.*, 6(2):24-27.

––––– (1954a), Discussion in: Problems of Infantile Neurosis: A Discussion. *The Psychoanalytic Study of the Child*, 9:55-57. New York: International Universities Press.

––––– (1954b), Discussion in: Problems of Technique in Adult Analysis. *Bull. Phila. Assn. Psychoanal.*, 4:44-69.

––––– (1954c), Discussion of "Considerations Regarding the Loyalty Oath as a Manifestation of Current Social Tension and Anxiety." *G. A. P. Symposium*, 1:19-21.

––––– (1954d), Sydney Geoffrey Biddle. *Bull. Phila. Assn. Psychoanal.*, 4:102-103.

––––– (1956), Critical Discussion of the Concept of an Instinct of Destruction. *Bull. Phila. Assn. Psychoanal.*, 6:97-109.

_____ (1957), Discussion of: Paul Sloane, Resistance as a Narcissistic Defense. *Bull. Phila. Assn. Psychoanal.*, 7:28-30, 36.

_____ (1958), Discussion Remarks to: Freud, A., Child Observation and Prediction of Development. *The Psychoanalytic Study of the Child*, 13:123-124. New York: International Universities Press.

_____ (1960a), *Basic Theory of Psychoanalysis*. New York: International Universities Press.

_____ (1960b), The Psychoanalytic Theory of the Neuroses: An Outline. In: *Current Approaches to Psychoanalysis*, ed. P. H. Hoch & J. Zubin. New York: Grune & Stratton.

_____ (1960c), In Memoriam: Edward Bibring. *J. Amer. Psychoanal. Assn.*, 8:377-378.

_____ (1964), Civil Disobedience. *Jewish Exponent*, July.

_____ (1965a), *Psychoanalytic Avenues to Art* [Freud Anniversary Lecture]. New York: International Universities Press.

_____ (1965b), Neurosis and Malaise. *Friends-Jefferson Newsletter*, 1(2): 3-4.

_____ (1965c), [Contribution to Panel] Psychodiagnosis and Psychotherapy as a Professional and Disciplinary Entity. Quoted by S. Guttman in: Some Aspects of Robert Waelder. *Bull. Phila. Assn. Psychoanal.*, 18:35-37.

_____ (1967a), *Progress and Revolution: A Study of the Issues of Our Age*. New York: International Universities Press.

_____ (1967b), Anna Freud Doctoral Award Addresses. *J. Amer. Psychoanal. Assn.*, 15:831-833.

_____ (1967c), Guaranteed Annual Income: Its Effect On Human Motivations and Values. Columbia School of Social Work, Annual Alumni Conference, April 22 (mimeographed).

_____ (1967-68), The Philosophy of the New Left. *The Activist*, Winter, pp. 5-6, 32.

_____ (1968), The Intellectuals. *Bull. Phila. Assn. Psychoanal.*, 18:14-24.

Waerden, B. L. van der (1950), *Science Awakening*. Groningen: P. Noordhoff, 1954.

Washburn, S. L. & De Vore, I. (1961), The Social Life of Baboons. *Sci. Amer.*, 204 (June):62-71.

Weaver, W. (1955), Science and People. *Science*, 122:1255-1259.

Weizsaecker, V. von (1954), Reminiscences of Freud and Jung. In: *Freud and the 20th Century*, ed. B. Nelson. New York: Meridian Books, 1957, pp. 59-75.

Welch, W. H. (1897), *Adaptation in Pathological Processes*. Baltimore: Johns Hopkins University Press, 1937.

Wertheimer, M. (1945), *Productive Thinking*. New York: Harper Brothers.

Williams, D. C. (1959), Philosophy and Psychoanalysis. In: *Psychoanalysis, Scientific Method, and Philosophy*, ed. S. Hook. New York: New York University Press, pp. 157-179.

Winthuis, J. (1928), *Das Zweigeschlechterwesen bei den Zentralaustraliern und anderen Völkern*. Leipzig: Hirschfeld.

Wright, Q. (1942), *A Study of Wars*, 2 vols. Chicago: University of Chicago Press.

Zuckerman, S. (1932), *The Social Life of Monkeys and Apes*. London: Kegan Paul Trench Trubner.

INDEX